THE INSIDERS' GUIDE® TO NORTH CAROLINA'S Outer Banks

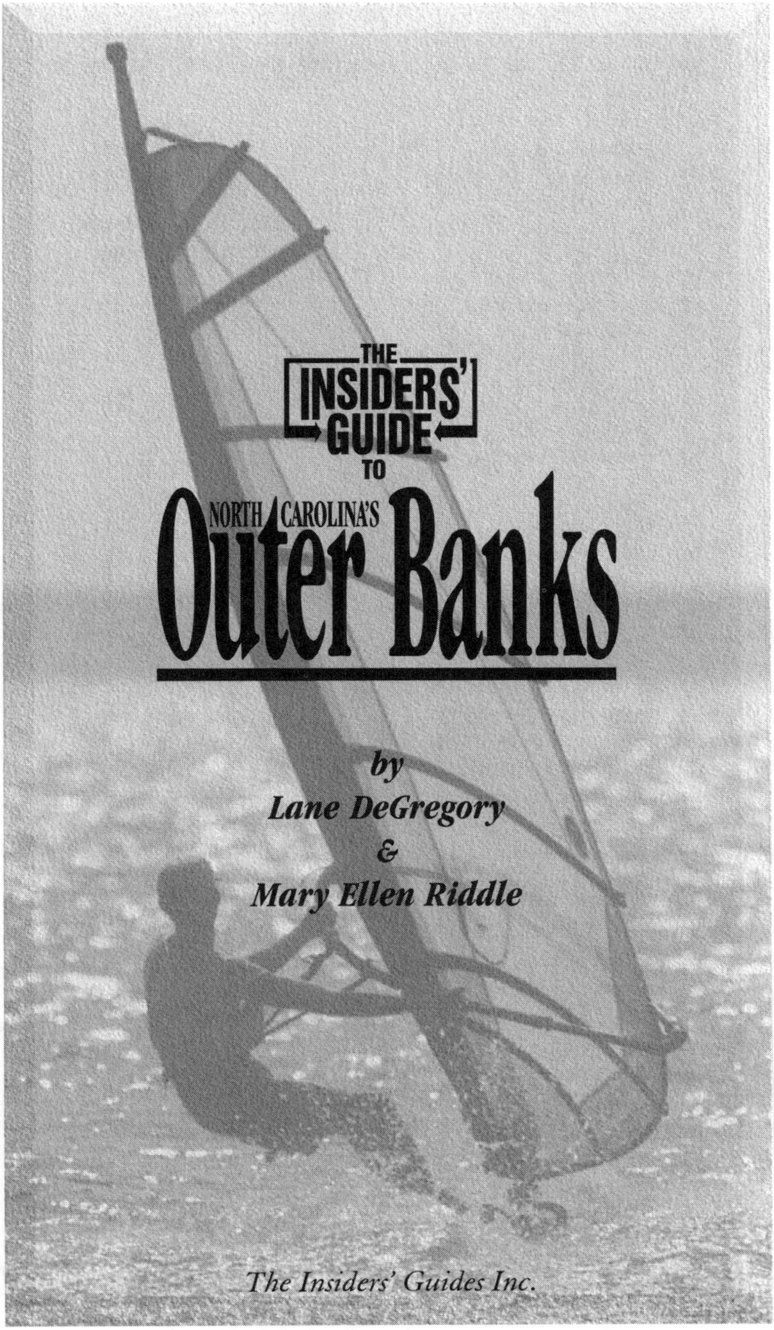

THE INSIDERS' GUIDE TO NORTH CAROLINA'S Outer Banks

by

Lane DeGregory

&

Mary Ellen Riddle

The Insiders' Guides Inc.

Published and distributed by:
The Insiders' Guides Inc.
The Waterfront • Suites 12 &13
P.O. Box 2057
Manteo, NC 27954
(919) 473-6100

•

SEVENTEENTH EDITION
1st printing

•

•

Printed in the United States
of America

•

Publications from The Insiders' Guides® series are available at special discounts for bulk purchases for sales promotions, premiums or fundraising. Special editions, including personalized covers, can be created in large quantities for special needs. For more information, please write to The Insiders' Guides Inc., P.O. Box 2057, Manteo, NC 27954 or call (919) 473-6100 x 233.

ISBN 0-912367-97-0

The Insiders' Guides Inc.

Preface

Wide beaches, rolling dunes fringed with sea oats and Carolina blue skies that seem to stretch forever . . . welcome to the Outer Banks.

Here, the first English colonists set up camp on sandy shores. Blackbeard and his band of pirates anchored sloops along the shallow sounds. And Wilbur and Orville Wright soared the world's first airplane atop blustery winds.

From remote national wildlife refuges and protected maritime forests to upscale resort communities — complete with indoor tennis, health clubs and, of course, golf courses — these thin strips of shifting sand provide peace and tranquility, adventure and excitement, for newcomers and natives alike.

Wild horses roam the northern beach villages, descendants of Spanish mustangs who swam ashore from shipwrecks more than three centuries ago. Waterfowl abound throughout these islands and peninsula, attracting bird watchers, hunters and long-lens photographers. And the East Coast's best fishing awaits anglers on the decks of offshore charter boats, the planks of long, wooden piers and atop numerous bridges.

Four lighthouses dot these storm-swept shores, sentinels for sailors traversing the shipwreck-strewn Graveyard of the Atlantic: Currituck's red brick beacon, the inland light at Bodie Island, Cape Hatteras's candy-striped tower and a squat, whitewashed structure on Ocracoke Island. Painters, sculptors and other artisans open their galleries to browsers in almost every local village. And musicians, comedians and poets provide evening entertainment in a variety of cafes and nightclubs.

Athletic individuals enjoy surfing some of the seaboard's best breaks along 70 miles of shoreline, trying their wings in flight after leaping off the tallest sand dune on the Atlantic or skimming across whitecaps on rainbow-sailed windsurfers. There are plenty of biking and in-line skating paths along flat roadways — miles of new ones opened over the past two summers. Water-skiers, Jet Ski enthusiasts, even stunt-plane passengers all will find perfect outlets for their passions in this paradisiacal place.

You don't have to dress up on the Outer Banks — ever. Even the finest dining restaurants accept patrons in casual attire, sandals and shorts. Seafood is our speciality, much of it locally caught by fifth-generation watermen. And if you're tired of laboring to pick the meat out of blue crabs, be sure to bite into a softshell crab sandwich while you're here: Go ahead, eat the spidery legs and all.

Since this book's first edition 17 years ago, these Banks have changed immensely. Miles of open beach have become populated areas; the islands themselves have moved slightly closer to the mainland; northern beaches have become covered with upscale resorts, restaurants and shopping strips; recreation outlets and eco-tour enterprises have set up shop along the sounds; even Ocracoke has a few condominiums and is becoming immersed in tourism — although you still can only access this isolated island on a free state ferry.

Some things, however, have stayed the same since Sir Walter Raleigh's settlers first set foot on Roanoke Island more than 400 years ago. These barrier beaches still startle visitors as well as longtime residents with their pristine beauty and constantly changing topography. The fragile islands remain at the mercy of the sea, tumultuous with storm one season — placid and glittering the next.

With their unusual environment and laid-back lifestyle, the Outer Banks continue to attract wildlife and vacationers, families and retirees — and creative people from all walks of art.

Summer isn't the only time to enjoy the Outer Banks — although the season from Memorial Day through Labor Day is by far the most packed with people and things to do. But fall offers fabulous fishing and windsurfing; spring brings bird-watching and bicycling. And winter is deliciously devoid of almost everyone.

So pack your bags and binoculars, grab your swimsuit or surf rod, and be sure to bring an appetite for adventure as well as fresh steamed shrimp.

Telephone Information

- Unless otherwise noted, all telephone numbers listed in this guide have a 919 area code.
- All phone calls made within Dare County, including the Outer Banks and mainland, are local calls. Calls to Corolla, which is in Currituck County, do not require an area code but do charge tolls. Calls to Ocracoke Island, in Hyde County, are long-distance and require a 919 area code when dialing.

About the Authors

Lane DeGregory . . .

When she first visited the Outer Banks in 1982, Lane DeGregory was a teenager riding in the back of her parents' station wagon. Her family fell in love with the barren barrier island beaches and began vacationing here each August. The wind-swept dunes and tangled maritime forests were a welcome relief from their real lives in Rockville, Maryland.

Lane moved to Charlottesville in 1985 to attend the University of Virginia. By the time she graduated, she had worked her way through the ranks of the college paper, becoming editor-in-chief of *The Cavalier Daily* in 1988. The next summer was the best one of her life.

In 1989 Lane moved to Nags Head to become an intern reporter for *The Virginian-Pilot* newspaper's Outer Banks bureau. Her three-month stay amidst the sparkling sea, sweltering sun and laid-back lifestyle convinced her that she had to keep coming back. After finishing classes for her master's degree in Rhetoric and Communication Studies while working for U.Va.'s public relations department, Lane worked for two years as a journalist with *The Daily Progress* newspaper in Charlottesville.

She returned to the Outer Banks in 1992 — this time, as a full-time reporter for *The Virginian-Pilot*.

During her four-year stint as one of two writers at the daily newspaper's Nags Head bureau, Lane has covered everything from unsolved murders to East Coast surfing contests for *The Virginian-Pilot* and its free weekly tabloid, *The Carolina Coast*. Her articles have appeared across the country on the Associated Press wire service, in fishing magazines along the East Coast and on refrigerators of various vacationers. In April 1996, a national writing coach awarded Lane second-place in *The Virginian-Pilot's* news reporting competition.

She has climbed the nation's tallest lighthouse as its 208-foot tower reopened for tours. She has watched wranglers corral Corolla's wild ponies behind a new fence, onto a wilderness refuge. She has hiked through the only ghost town east of the Mississipppi River. She has flown over the site of the world's first flight in an antique, open-cockpit biplane. And she's watched with wide-eyed wonder as dump truck drivers struggled to hold back shifting sands of the Atlantic coast's largest sand dune.

All on a 60-mile stretch of beaches known as the Outer Banks.

Lane lives in a wooded, swampy section of Colington Island with her husband, Dan, a book editor and musician, and their two crazy dingo dogs, Chelsea and Dakota. When she is not chasing stories or dingos, Lane enjoys camping, hiking, beading jewelry, in-line skating and cooking. Her favorite escapes are dancing to Dan's band, swimming with the dogs and sunbathing with Ken Kesey novels in South Nags Head.

Mary Ellen Riddle . . .

Mary Ellen Riddle has been living on the Outer Banks consistently since 1986. She vacationed here while attending East Carolina University as an art student in the mid-'70s and loved the area so much she eventually made it her permanent home. She tells her family that they will have to bury her in the backyard of her Manteo home because she has no intention of ever leaving Wingina Street. What she loves about the Outer Banks is obvious: the land, wind, lack of crime and pollution, and the people who have graciously accepted her presence. Riddle covers art for *The Virginian-Pilot's Carolina Coast*, and she's a feature writer for the *Sportfishing Report*. Along with producing freelance work for several national and local publications, Riddle is also a practicing and exhibiting photographer. She's created public information programs for radio that have won national and state awards. Her work has allowed her to meet and interview a multitude of personalities in all walks of life. From holding an infant red wolf in her hands to soaring 1,500 feet in the air on a glider, Riddle has had her share of exciting experiences. This is why she stays in the news business.

Riddle loves to read and collect books and play Ping-Pong (she brags she's only been beaten a few times. This is probably an exaggeration but she loves to get her opponent's dander up for a good match!). She loves Mozart and Mahler and Caruso. She loves going down to the Full Moon Cafe to visit with friends and has an on-going love affair with the Ye Olde Pioneer Theatre. Riddle says she is an uncomplicated person who just wants to wiggle her toes in the mud while smelling the roses. If she catches a glimpse of a shooting star, all the better. Parenthood is her biggest challenge and greatest joy.

Acknowledgments

Lane DeGregory

Since the longest article I've ever written only filled three broadsheet pages, this book is undoubtedly the biggest project I've ever undertaken. There's so much to know — and learn — about this area I've called home for the past four years that it just kept growing. Thanks to everyone who's helped me understand and better appreciate these beautiful barrier islands.

Primarily, thanks, Beth, for giving me the opportunity to author the 17th edition of this guide. Much thanks and admiration to Eileen, my understanding editor, for her infinite patience, wisdom and willingness to work with me. Thanks, Mary Ellen, for all the long talks, lunches and nights of lending your ear and unfaltering encouragement.

Thanks also to: Drew, Hellen, Sarah and Wynne at the Outer Banks History Center, for helping me fill in the past; my co-horts at *The Virginian-Pilot*, Paul and Cate, who have heard about this book since its infancy, thanks, mostly, for listening; and Ron, for letting me tackle this long-term assignment — and giving me the time and support to finish it. You're truly the coolest coach and friend I could ever hope to have. Thanks to Jewel — who's been one — and taken more phone messages than the AT&T operator, in addition to her full-time role as confidant; Elizabeth, Alan, Jeff and John for their constant friendship and daily words of wisdom; and my parents, Lissie and Neill, who helped me fill in the blanks everywhere I needed aid and always have backed me in every endeavor.

Special thanks go to my shadow dog, Dakota, who kept her furry brown chin on my left foot and her goofy grin smiling up at me through more than 200 hours of typing at my terminal. And, most of all, thanks to Dan — my best friend and heroic husband — who has explained, edited, formatted, re-configured and printed every portion of this text and cooked for, consoled and comforted me through each word I've written; for driving me from Ocracoke to Corolla more times than I can count and for pulling all-nighters with me for the first time since college. This book — and my life — would be incomplete without you.

Mary Ellen Riddle

Writing a book as diverse as *The Insiders' Guide® to the Outer Banks* takes a lot of cooperation. The subjects covered are so diverse that I depended on the help of the experts in several fields. I want to thank Richard Hess for making sense of Real Estate, and Skip Saunders of Outer Banks Homes who is always a warehouse of knowledge. Thanks goes to Terry Kirby at the NC Aquarium for her willingness to take time during a very busy schedule and talk with me. Thanks also to Rhett White and Joe Malat at the aquarium. Thanks to my bird experts, Pam Rasmussen and Mike Tove, for supplying exacting information for the Natural Wonders Chapter. Thanks to Tom Hocking at the Morehead Planetarium for sharing his "celestial" knowledge. Special thanks to nature lovers Jeff Smith with Nags Head Woods, Marcia Lyons with the National Park Service and Don Perry with Fish and Wildlife. Thanks to Shannon Twiddy for Manteo information. Wynne Dough at the Outer Banks History Center is always a great help. Thanks to David Stick for chatting with me and to Marjalene Thomas for our interesting session on *The Lost Colony*. Didi Tupper was a delight to talk about art with. Special thanks to Vanessa for the use of her darkroom, to Phillip Howard on Ocracoke Island, who happily supplied me with Inside information. Thanks to my son Chris, who gave me great tips for several chapters and helped me record businesses from Corolla to Hatteras. My daughter Zoe behaved well during this intense project and thanks for sneaking in and telling me you love me! Thanks to Scott for his Golf expertise, for help with the Manteo to Corolla drive, for dinners and fielding phone calls. Thanks to Eileen, my editor, a dear dear woman, who is a true diplomat. Special thanks goes to my sister Elizabeth who knows what it's like to work on a deadline. If it had not been for her on a certain day in March, well, let's just say her words of wisdom and encouragement still ring in my ears, plus her tip to go buy some quality chocolate to get me through was a good one! Thanks to Beth and Michael for this opportunity. And lastly, thanks to my wonderful co-author, Lane. She was a ray of sunshine from beginning to end!

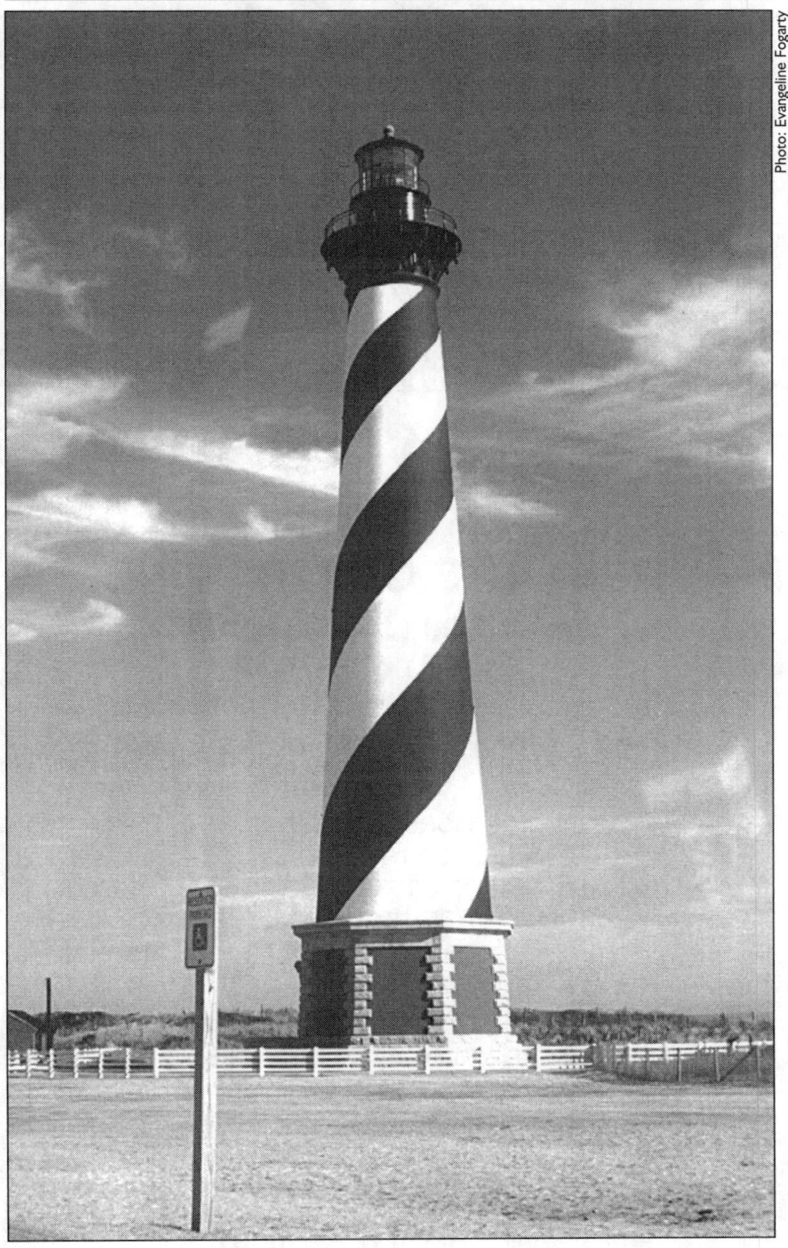

Photo: Evangeline Fogarty

Count the steps as you make your way to the top of Cape Hatteras Lighthouse.

Table of Contents

Directory of Maps

Distances To The Outer Banks

Distances From Major Cities To Kitty Hawk (miles)	
Atlanta	625
Baltimore	319
Buffalo	714
Boston	642
Charleston SC	380
Chicago	956
Cleveland	627
Cincinnati	745
Montreal	776
New York	417
Norfolk	90
Philadelphia	320
Pittsburgh	530
Richmond	175
Toronto	776
Washington	278

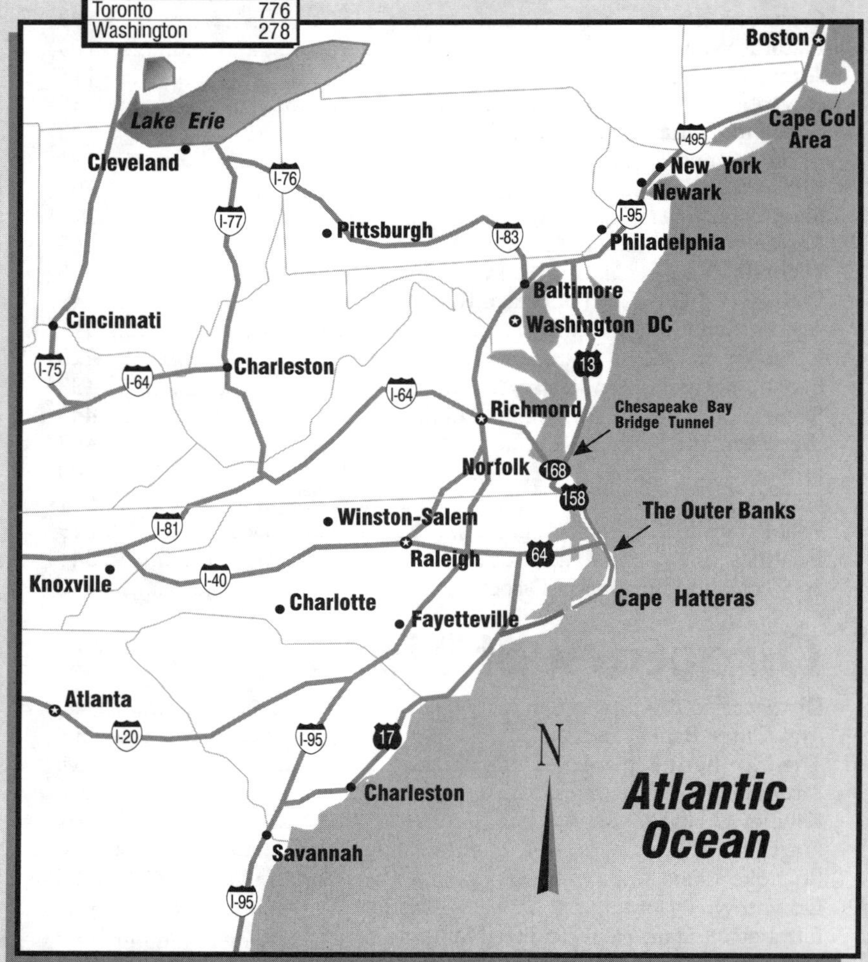

The Outer Banks

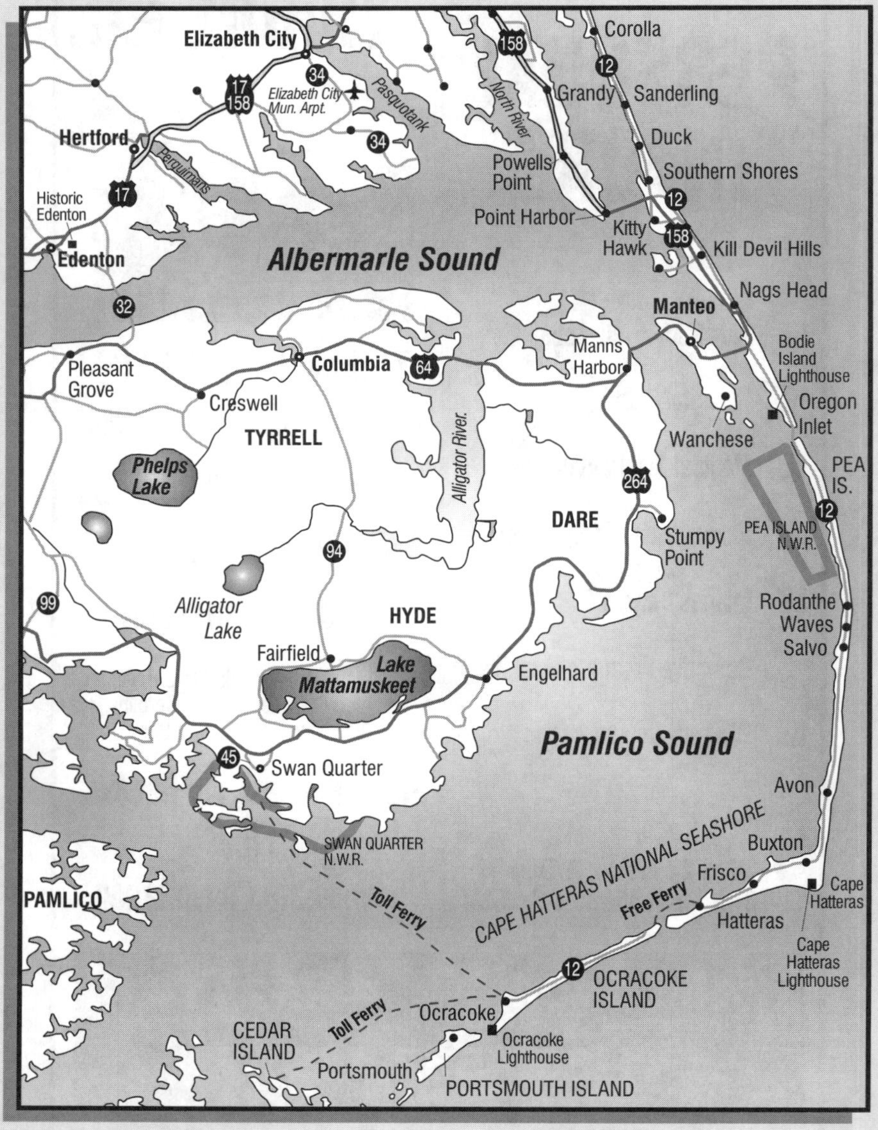

Northern Banks

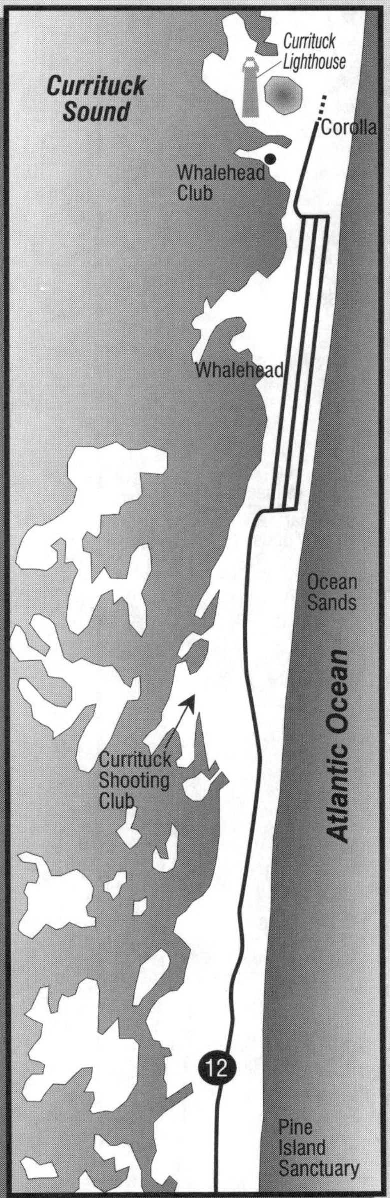

Currituck Sound
Currituck Lighthouse
Corolla
Whalehead Club
Whalehead
Ocean Sands
Atlantic Ocean
Currituck Shooting Club
12
Pine Island Sanctuary

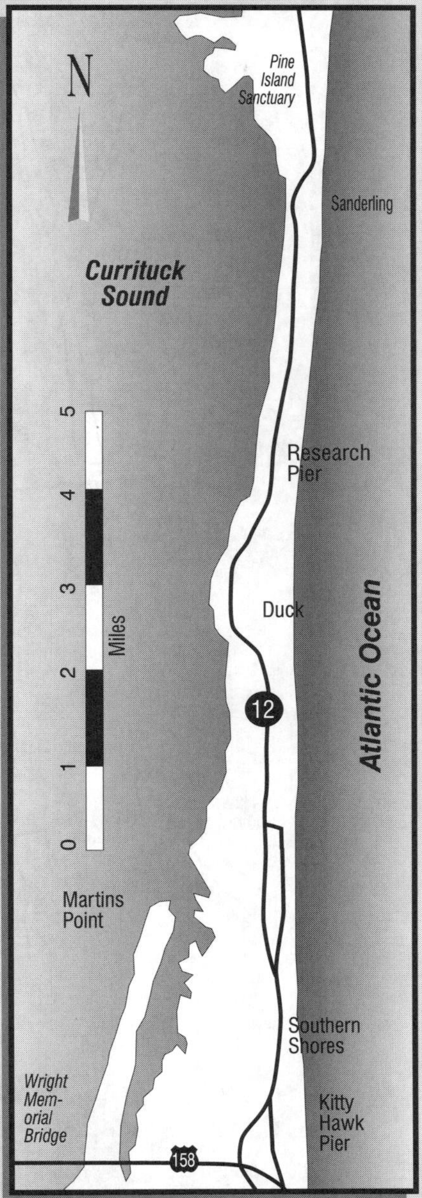

N
Pine Island Sanctuary
Sanderling
Currituck Sound
5
4
3
2
1
0
Miles
Research Pier
Duck
Atlantic Ocean
12
Martins Point
Southern Shores
Kitty Hawk Pier
Wright Memorial Bridge
158

Kitty Hawk

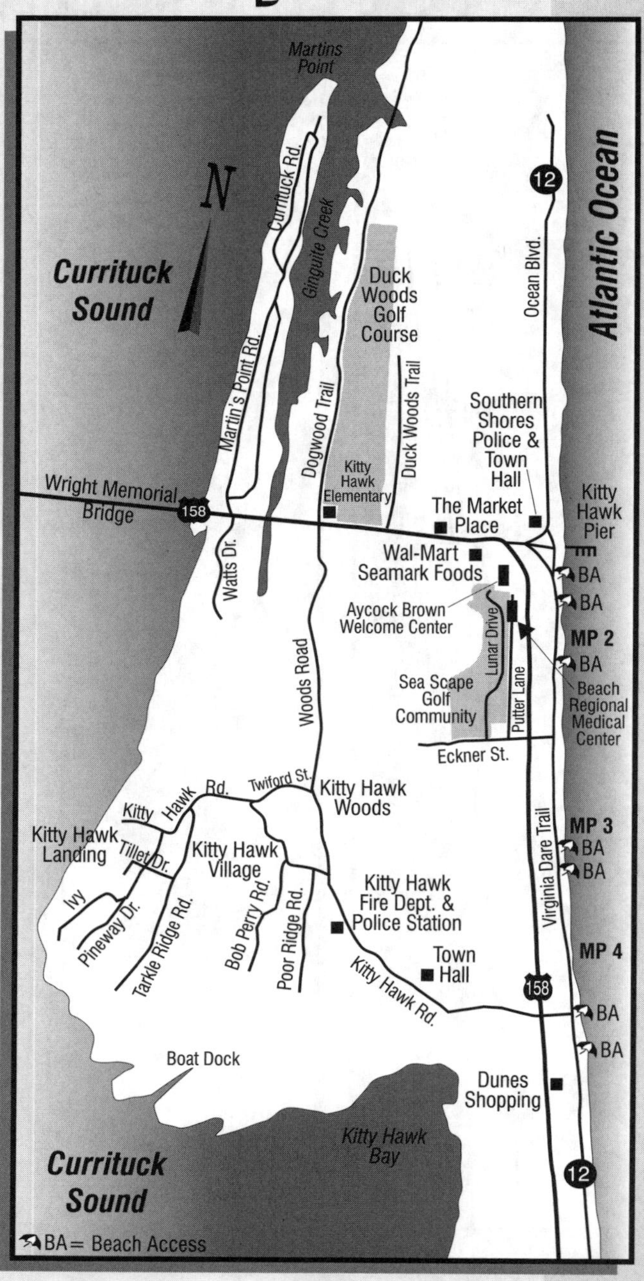

Martins Point
Currituck Rd.
Ginguite Creek
N
Currituck Sound
Duck Woods Golf Course
Ocean Blvd.
12
Atlantic Ocean
Martin's Point Rd.
Dogwood Trail
Duck Woods Trail
Southern Shores Police & Town Hall
Wright Memorial Bridge
158
Kitty Hawk Elementary
The Market Place
Kitty Hawk Pier
Watts Dr.
Wal-Mart
Seamark Foods
BA
BA
Aycock Brown Welcome Center
Lunar Drive
MP 2
BA
Woods Road
Sea Scape Golf Community
Putter Lane
Beach Regional Medical Center
Eckner St.
Kitty Hawk Rd.
Twiford St.
Kitty Hawk Woods
Kitty Hawk Landing
Tillet Dr.
Kitty Hawk Village
MP 3
BA
BA
Virginia Dare Trail
Ivy
Pineway Dr.
Tarkle Ridge Rd.
Bob Perry Rd.
Poor Ridge Rd.
Kitty Hawk Fire Dept. & Police Station
MP 4
Town Hall
Kitty Hawk Rd.
158
BA
BA
Boat Dock
Dunes Shopping
Kitty Hawk Bay
Currituck Sound
12
BA = Beach Access

Kill Devil Hills

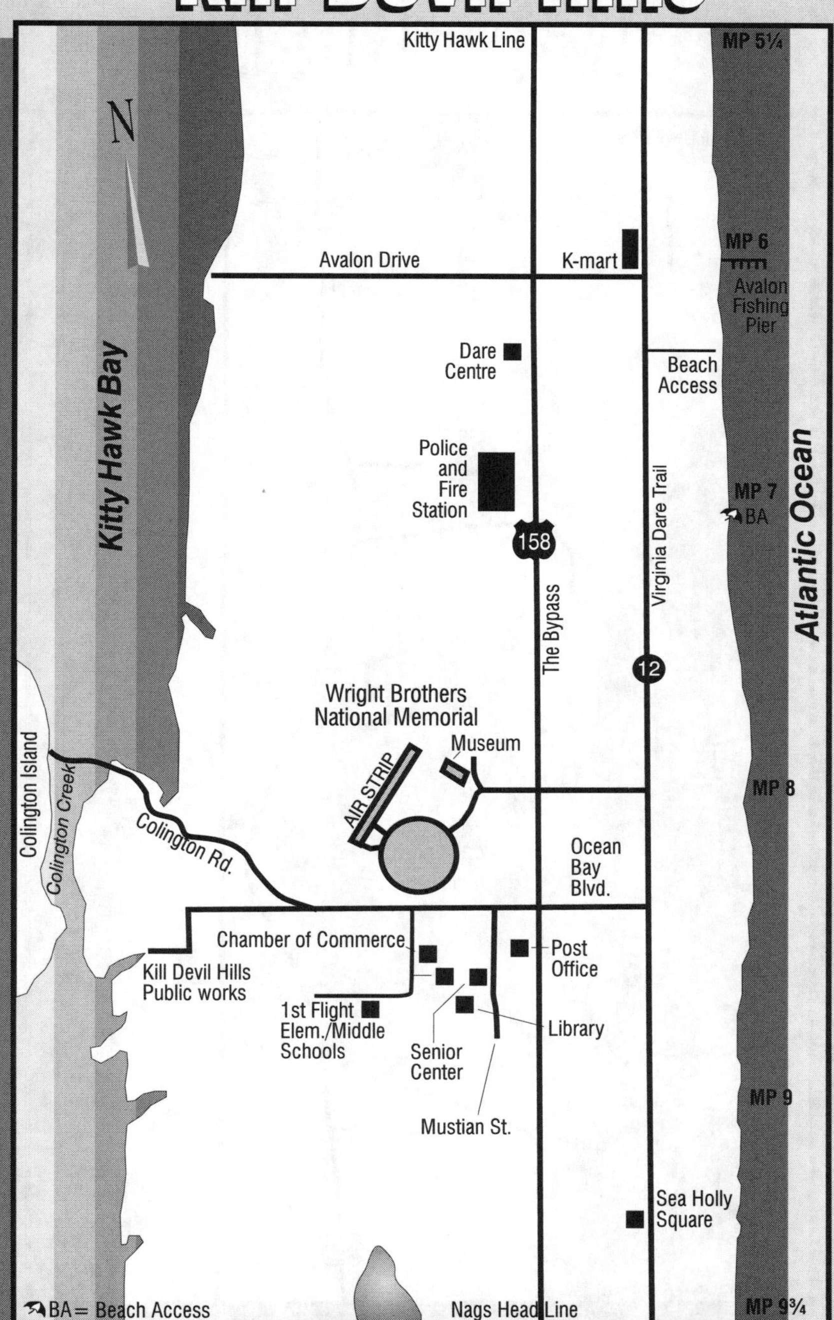

Kitty Hawk Line
MP 5¼
N
MP 6
Avalon Drive
K-mart
Avalon
Fishing
Pier
Dare
Centre
Beach
Access
Kitty Hawk Bay
Police
and
Fire
Station
MP 7
BA
Atlantic Ocean
Virginia Dare Trail
158
The Bypass
12
Wright Brothers
National Memorial
Museum
AIR STRIP
Colington Island
Colington Creek
Colington Rd.
MP 8
Ocean
Bay
Blvd.
Chamber of Commerce
Post
Office
Kill Devil Hills
Public works
1st Flight
Elem./Middle
Schools
Library
Senior
Center
MP 9
Mustian St.
Sea Holly
Square
BA = Beach Access
Nags Head Line
MP 9¾

Nags Head

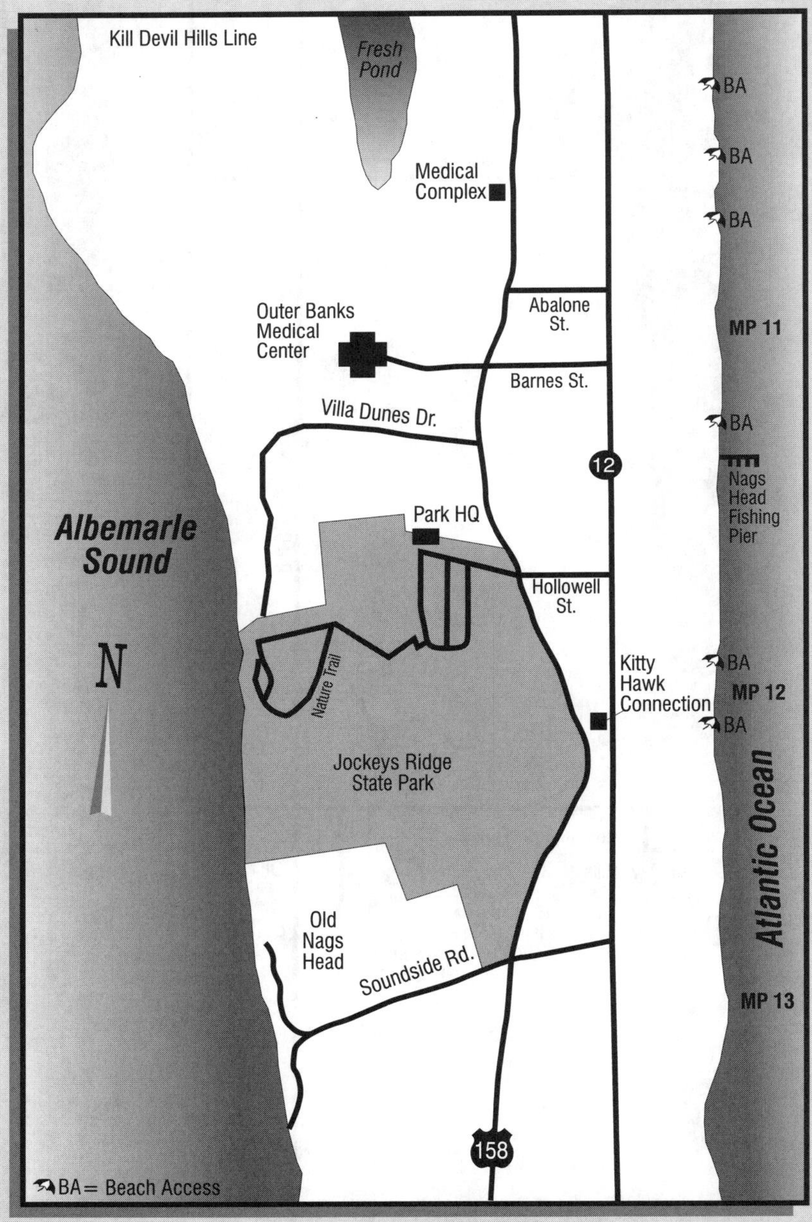

Kill Devil Hills Line
Fresh Pond
BA
BA
Medical Complex
BA
Abalone St.
Outer Banks Medical Center
MP 11
Barnes St.
Villa Dunes Dr.
BA
12
Nags Head Fishing Pier
Park HQ
Albemarle Sound
Hollowell St.
N
Kitty Hawk Connection
BA
MP 12
Nature Trail
BA
Jockeys Ridge State Park
Atlantic Ocean
Old Nags Head
Soundside Rd.
MP 13
158
BA = Beach Access

Nags Head (Cont.)

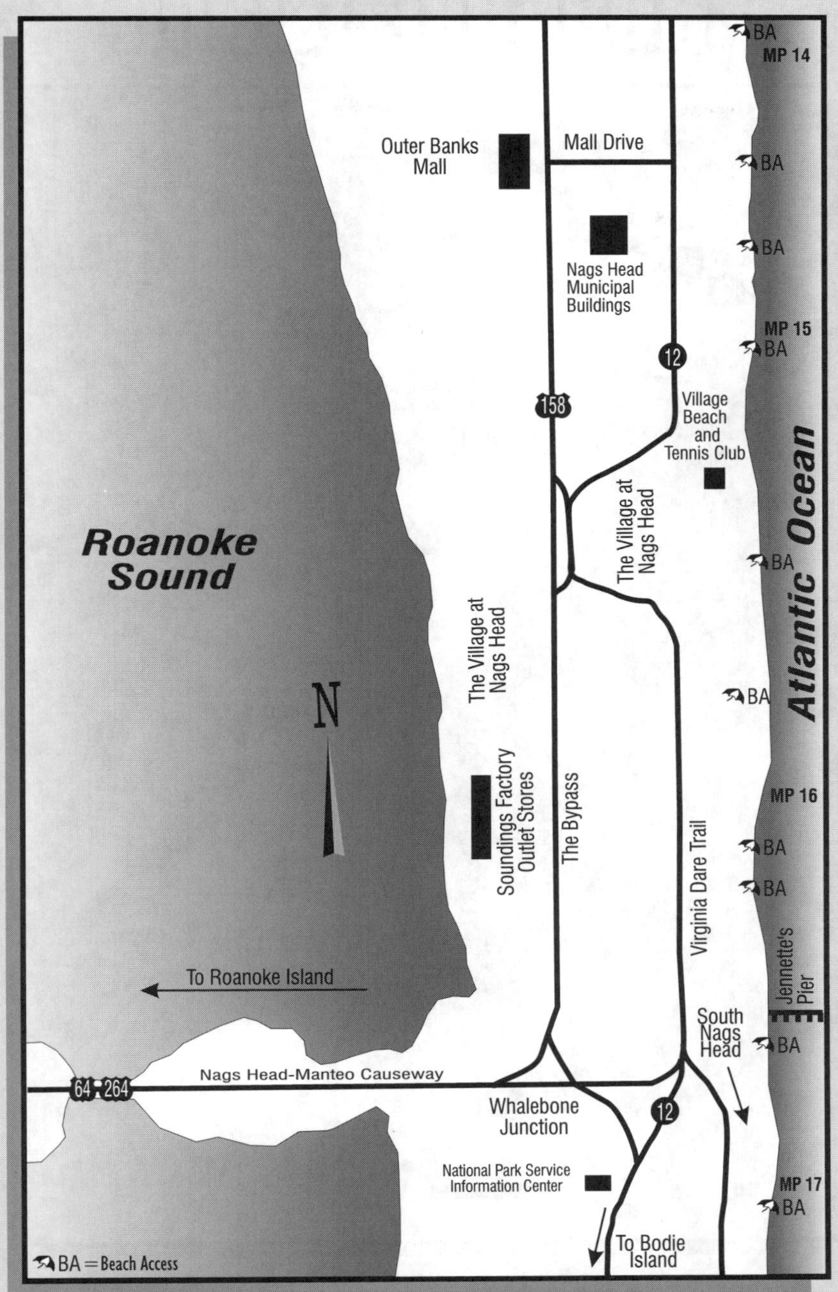

BA
MP 14
Outer Banks Mall
Mall Drive
BA
BA
Nags Head Municipal Buildings
MP 15
BA
12
158
Village Beach and Tennis Club
Roanoke Sound
The Village at Nags Head
The Village at Nags Head
BA
Atlantic Ocean
N
BA
Soundings Factory Outlet Stores
The Bypass
MP 16
BA
BA
Virginia Dare Trail
Jennette's Pier
To Roanoke Island
South Nags Head
BA
Nags Head-Manteo Causeway
64
264
Whalebone Junction
12
National Park Service Information Center
MP 17
BA
To Bodie Island
BA = Beach Access

Roanoke Island

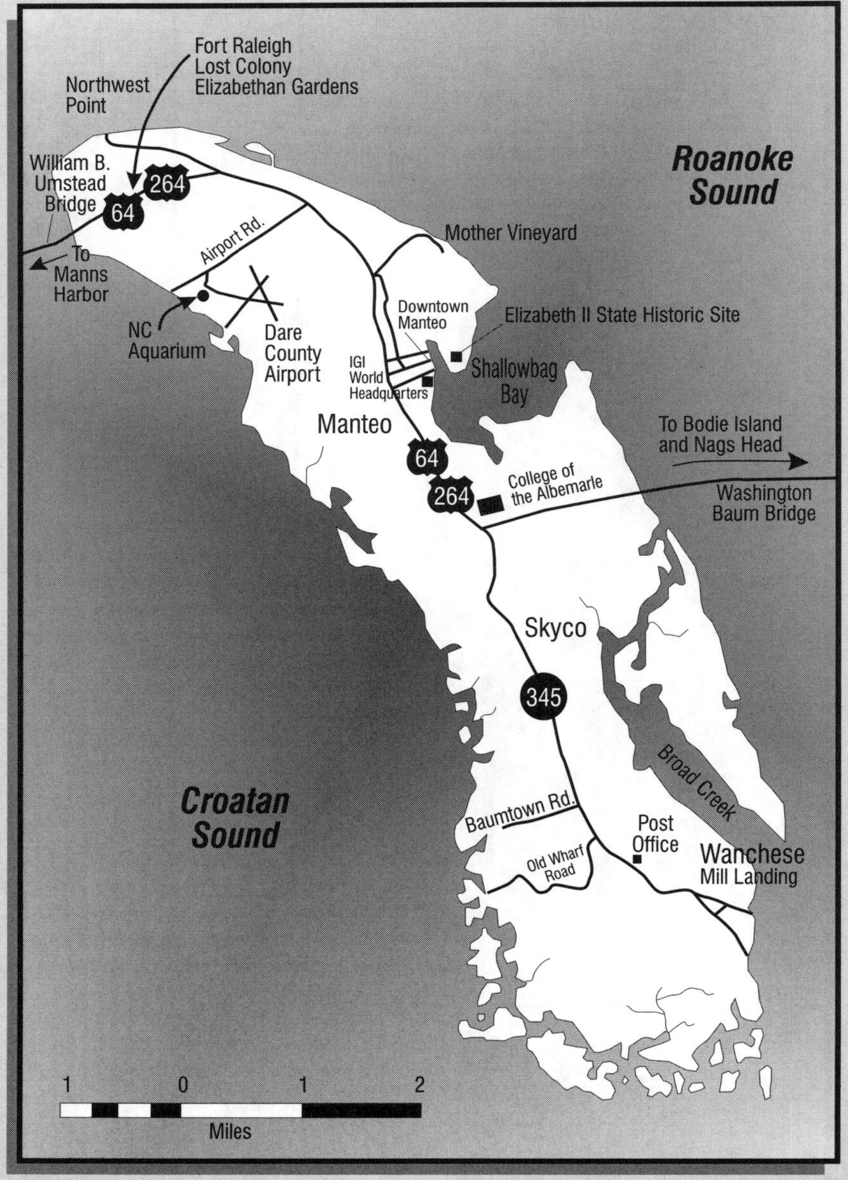

Fort Raleigh
Lost Colony
Elizabethan Gardens
Northwest Point
William B. Umstead Bridge
264
64
Roanoke Sound
Airport Rd.
Mother Vineyard
To Manns Harbor
NC Aquarium
Dare County Airport
Downtown Manteo
Elizabeth II State Historic Site
Shallowbag Bay
IGI World Headquarters
Manteo
To Bodie Island and Nags Head
64
264
College of the Albemarle
Washington Baum Bridge
Skyco
345
Broad Creek
Croatan Sound
Baumtown Rd.
Post Office
Old Wharf Road
Wanchese
Mill Landing
1 0 1 2
Miles

Downtown Manteo

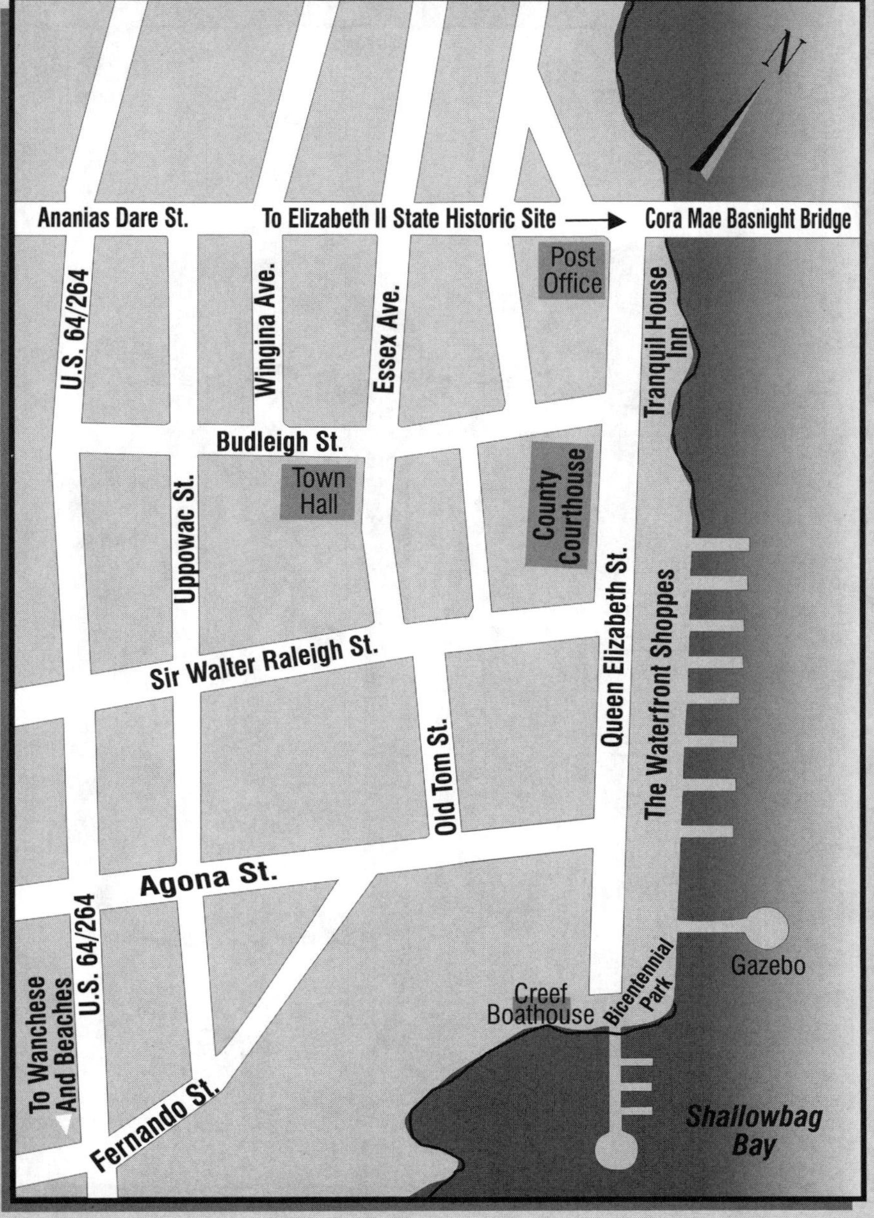
N
Ananias Dare St.
To Elizabeth II State Historic Site
Cora Mae Basnight Bridge
Post Office
U.S. 64/264
Wingina Ave.
Essex Ave.
Tranquil House Inn
Budleigh St.
Town Hall
County Courthouse
Uppowac St.
Queen Elizabeth St.
The Waterfront Shoppes
Sir Walter Raleigh St.
Old Tom St.
Agona St.
Gazebo
To Wanchese And Beaches
U.S. 64/264
Creef Boathouse
Bicentennial Park
Fernando St.
Shallowbag Bay

Elizabeth II State Historic Site, Manteo

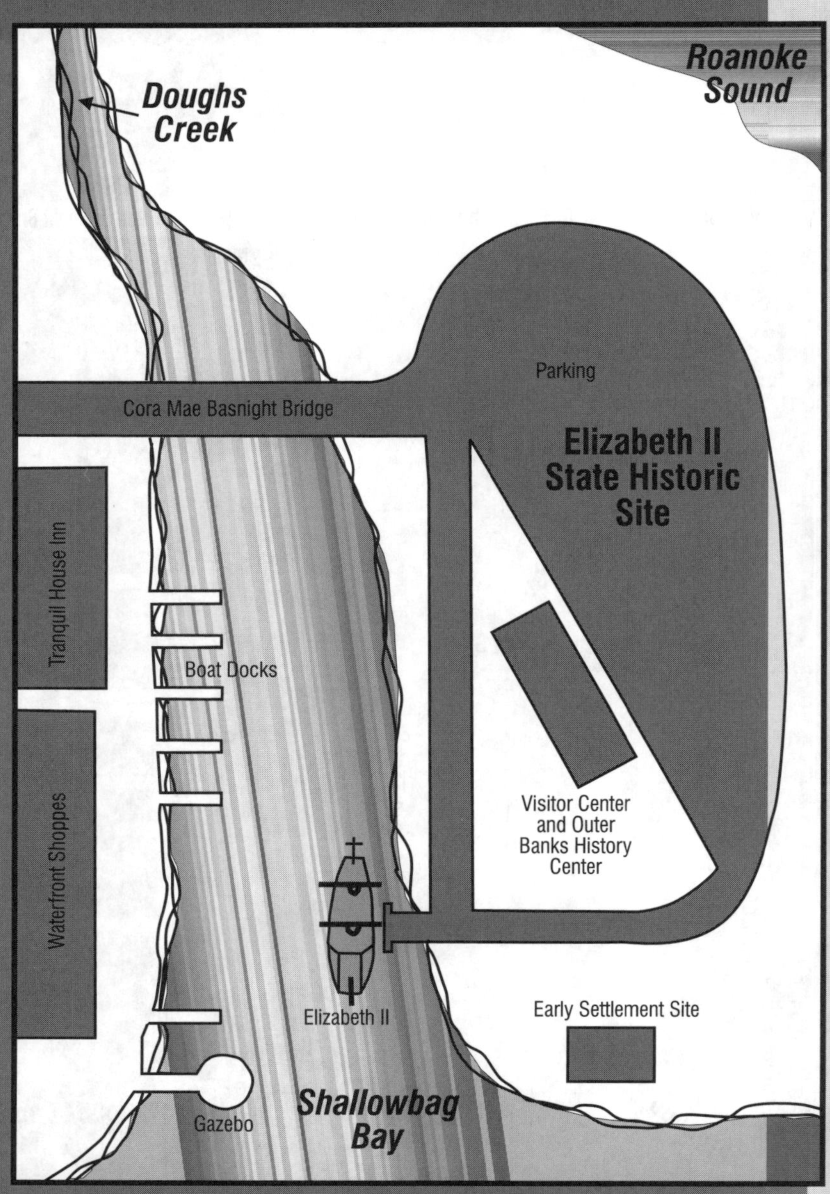

How To Use This Book

Continuing the 17-year tradition of *The Insiders' Guide® to the Outer Banks*, we've updated, reorganized, revised and added to our extensive collection of favorite restaurants, shops, attractions, events, getaways and much more. Besides introducing you to the area's fascinating history and hidden treasures, we provide practical information on medical services, camping, real estate, vacation rentals, ferry schedules, fishing sites and other areas of interest. We've designed *The Insiders' Guide® to North Carolina's Outer Banks* as a handy reference for all aspects of life. Don't let it gather dust on a shelf. Keep it in hand and let us accompany and guide you along every step of your Outer Banks journey.

After beginning with a chapter on getting to and around the Banks, we provide colorful overviews about each area along these barrier islands: From the sand-trail villages of Carova to the windswept shores of Ocracoke Island. Comprehensive chapters tailored to meet your personal needs follow about each area. You'll find Accommodations, Real Estate, Arts and Culture, Annual Events, Kidstuff, Recreation and more — in total there are 31 information-packed chapters. If you're looking for a cozy dinner spot, browse through our Restaurants chapter. If you want to spend the afternoon in search of a special souvenir, turn to Shopping. If you've always wanted to try scuba diving, all the information you'll need is waiting in Watersports.

We've arranged this book so you can read it bit by bit, turning to those particular pages that pique your interest while breezing by those that don't. But please go back and thumb through any parts you may have skipped at first. We bet you'll learn something — and maybe even discover some new favorite spots or pastimes along the way.

Finally, feel free to mark up this guide. Jot down your own discoveries, observations and experiences — and let us know about them. We'd love to hear any suggestions or comments you have that will help us improve our effort to make the most of your time on the Outer Banks. Drop us a line and let us know how we're doing — there's a self-addressed comment form in the back of this book. Or drop by our headquarters on the waterfront in Manteo and tell us in person. We'll be around — we all enjoy the Outer Banks so much that we've decided to stay.

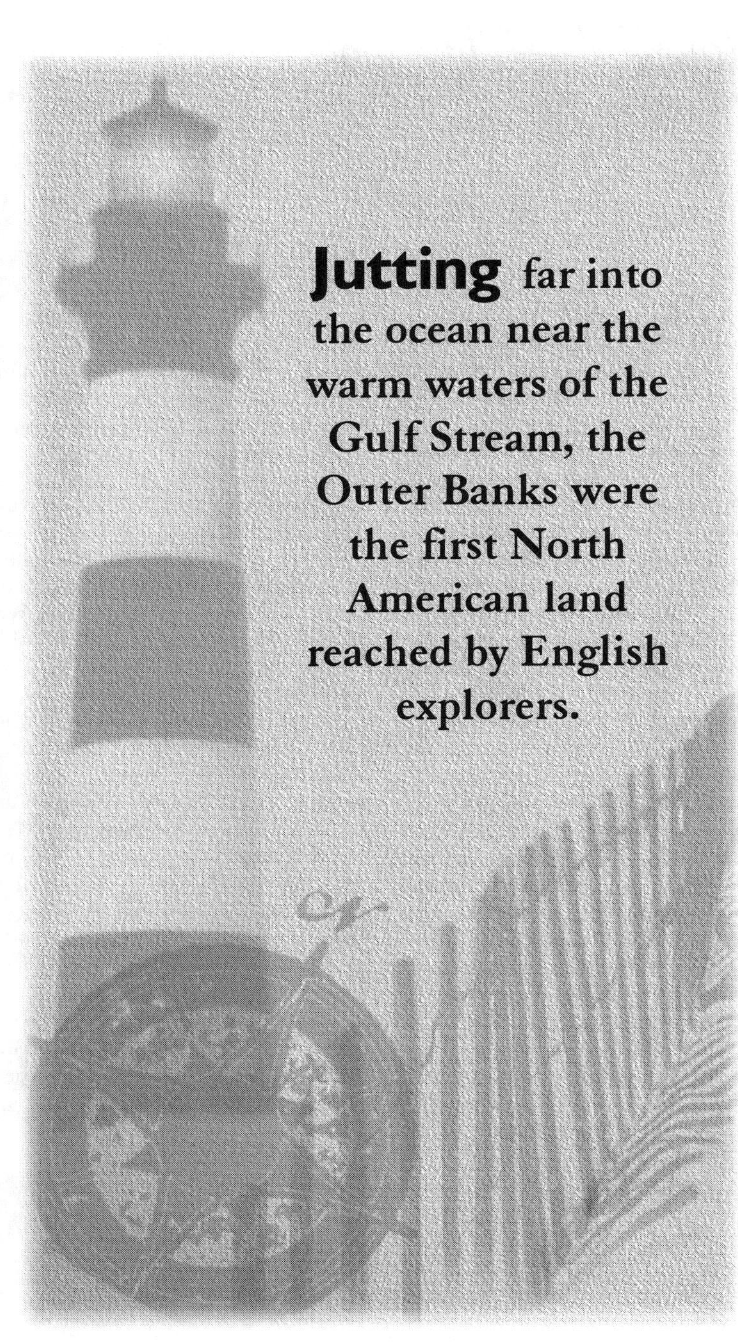
Jutting far into the ocean near the warm waters of the Gulf Stream, the Outer Banks were the first North American land reached by English explorers.

Inside
Outer Banks History

Slender strips of sand that sit less than 50 miles inside the Gulf Stream and more than 20 miles in places from the North Carolina mainland, the Outer Banks are a geological phenomenon. These beautiful barrier islands are accessible only by bridges, boats and planes. Their remoteness, fragility and exposure to sea and storms give the islands and inlets a constantly changing appearance.

In the Beginning...

About 18,000 years ago, when continental glaciers trapped much of the world's ocean water, sea levels were almost 400 feet lower than they are today. North Carolina's coastline was 50 to 75 miles east of its present-day location. And the principle rivers of the region — the Neuse, the Tar, the Currituck and the Chowan — flowed across the continental shelf and cascaded over its front slope into the Atlantic Ocean.

When the sinking sea reached its lowest level and winds began carrying sediment from the west, a high ridge of sand dunes formed on the easternmost edge of the mainland. Glaciers began to melt. The sea level began to rise. And the land's vast forests and marshes began a slow retreat away from the rising waters. In their wake, they left huge river deltas rich in materials. Those materials ultimately formed the Outer Banks.

Sea levels continued to rise over the next few thousand years. But the newly formed barrier islands that paralleled Carolina's coast weren't covered by the higher tides. Instead, an unusual combination of winds, waves and weather enabled the Outer Banks to maintain their elevation above the ocean and to migrate as a unit.

Today, the islands' eastern edges still move backward in response to rising waters. On the west side, they build up, narrowing the wide series of brackish bodies of water called sounds that separate the barrier islands from the mainland.

Ocean levels rise about one foot every 100 years. The shoreline moves westerly at a rate of 50 to 200 feet per century along most of North Carolina's coast. On parts of Hatteras Island, the Atlantic eats 14 feet of beach each year.

Sand to Salt Marshes: An Overview

Geologists refer to the Outer Banks and similar land forms as "barrier islands" because they block the high-energy ocean waves and storm surges, protecting the coastal mainland. Barrier islands are common to many parts of the world, and many have similar features — yet no two of them are alike. Winds, weather and waves give each its own personality. Inlets from the sounds to sea are ever shifting, opening new channels to the ocean one century, closing off primary passageways the next. And folks who venture from one area of the Outer Banks to another soon will realize that even along this small stretch of sand, there is a vast variety of topography, flora and temperature (see our Natural Wonders chapter).

Tidal zones, for example, shelter multitudes of small fish, crabs and shellfish in their shallow swash areas along the seaside. Sandpipers skitter to the surf line, searching for mole crabs and coquina clams — then retreat in the face of cresting waves. Terns, skimmers and pelicans wheel across the water as osprey scout out fish in the deeper channels of ocean that separate series of sand bars from the beach.

Above the high tide line, a progression of vegetation including sea oats, sea rocket and Spartina climb the sloping dunes. Windblown sand collects behind these pioneer plants, which often grow in otherwise barren soil. With the right combination of currents and breezes, these dunes grow to protect areas that lie behind them, sheltering wax myrtle and silvering, less hearty yaupon, live oak, red cedar and pine. When conditions are ideal and the dunes form tall barriers against the salty sea spray, maritime forests form along the Outer Banks' more western regions. In Nags Head Woods, on Colington Island and even in areas of Roanoke Island, deep tangles of trees and vines twist around huge hardwoods cloaked in lacy, shadow-striped Spanish moss.

The maritime forests abound with freshwater marshes, vast tracts of cattail-filled wetlands that attract songbirds and heron. Rainwater collects in shallow saucer-shaped aquifers, called "lenses," that lie just below the ground's surface. Wild horses once roaming the entire Outer Banks exposed this cool, fresh water by digging with their hoofs. The marshes also are home to redwings and grackles, egrets and herons, rails and bitterns. Arrowheads, black needle rushes and marsh mallows grow in quiet places where few visitors ever venture.

Beyond the forests, salt marshes shelter these barrier islands from the sounds. Cordgrass and other vegetation break much of the wave action — and act as safe havens for crabs, birds and fish. Biologists estimate that 65 percent of the fish and shellfish harvested along North Carolina's coast depend on the saltwater marsh at some point in their short life cycles.

With more than 2.2 million acres of sounds and bays between its barrier islands and mainland, North Carolina ranks behind only Alaska and Louisiana in the amount of estuarine acreage. And with 2 million acres covered by the vast Currituck-Albemarle-Pamlico sound system, the Outer Banks region ranks second in size only to the Chesapeake Bay in terms of water surface area. Each day, more than 15 billion gallons of water pass into the barrier islands' estuaries. The bulk of it flows into Pamlico Sound, then on into the Atlantic through four major Outer Banks inlets.

Early Explorers

Jutting far into the ocean near the warm waters of the Gulf Stream, the Outer Banks were the first North American land reached by English explorers. A group of colonists dispatched by Sir Walter Raleigh set up the first English settlement on North American soil in 1587. But Native Americans inhabited these barrier islands long before white men and women arrived.

Historians say humans have been living in North Carolina for more than 10,000 years. Three thousand years ago, people traveled throughout the Outer Banks hunting, fishing and feeding off the forest. The Carolina Algonkian culture, a confederation of 75,000 people divided into distinct tribes, spread across 6,000 square miles of northeastern North Carolina.

About 1,000 years ago, Croatan tribes

Photo: Mary Ellen Riddle

This old dugout canoe was salvaged from the Gulf Stream by a charter boat captain. If it could talk, just imagine the tales it would tell.

settled along the southern shores of the Outer Banks, at present-day Buxton, on Hatteras Island. Numbering as many as 7,000 at their height, these Native Americans formed the only island kingdom of the Algonkians. Isolation afforded these people protection and the sole use of the island's seemingly limitless resources. The Croatan lived comfortably for more than 800 years in the protection of the Buxton Woods Maritime Forest at Cape Hatteras. Contact with Europeans proved fateful, however. Disease, famine and cultural demise had eliminated all traces of the Carolina Algonkians by the 1770s.

Early ventures to America's Atlantic seaboard proved difficult for European explorers because of the high winds, seething surf and shifting sandbars. In 1524, Giovanni de Verrazzano, an Italian in the service of France, plied the waters off the Outer Banks in an unsuccessful search for the Northwest Passage. Verrazzano thought the barrier islands looked like an isthmus — the sounds behind them, an endless sea. According to historian David Stick, the explorer reported to the French king that these silvery salt waters must certainly be the "Oriental sea . . . which is the one without doubt which goes about the extremity of India, China and Cathay." This explorer's misconception — that the Atlantic and Pacific oceans were separated by only the skinny strip of sand we now call the Outer Banks — was held by some Europeans for more than 150 years.

About 60 years after Verrazzano's visit, two English boats arrived along the Outer Banks, searching for a navigable inlet and a place to anchor away from the ocean. The captains, Philip Amadas and Arthur Barlowe, had been dispatched by Sir Walter Raleigh to explore the American coast. They were hoping to find a suitable site for an English settlement.

The explorers finally found an entrance through the islands above Cape Hatteras — probably at the present-day Jeanguite Creek north of Kitty Hawk. They sailed south through the sounds until arriving at Roanoke Island. There, they disembarked, met the natives and marvelled at the abundant wildlife and cedar trees. Their expedition had been successful, and they reported to Raleigh on the riches they had found and kindness with which the Native Americans had received them.

During the next three years, at least 40 English ships visited the Outer Banks, more than 100 English soldiers spent almost a year on Roanoke Island, and Great Britain began to gain a foothold on the continent — much to the dismay of Spanish sailors and fortune-seekers.

Lost Colonists

In May of 1587, three English ships commanded by naturalist John White set sail for the Outer Banks with Sir Walter Raleigh's blessing and backing. Earlier explorers had dubbed the land "Virginia," in honor of the virgin queen Elizabeth. The expedition, which included women and children for the first time, arrived at Roanoke Island on July 22. Colonists worked quickly to repair the cottages and military quarters left by the earlier British inhabitants. They fixed up a fort the soldiers had abandoned on the north end of the island and made plans for a permanent settlement. Less than a month later, the first English child was born on American soil. Virginia Dare, granddaughter of Gov. John White, was born August 18 — a date still celebrated with Outer Banks feasts and festivities.

One week after his granddaughter was baptized, John White left her and 110 other colonists on the Outer Banks while he returned to England for food, supplies and additional recruits for the Roanoke Island colony. A war with Spain, meanwhile, had broken out. So when White was again ready to set sail for the Outer Banks the following spring, his queen refused to let any large ships leave England — except to engage in battles. White did not get back to the American settlement until 1590. By then, it had disappeared.

The houses were gone, destroyed and deserted. White's own sea chests had been dug from their shallow hiding places in the sand, broken open, their contents raided. His daughter, granddaughter and all the other English colonists had vanished — leaving no trace except for two cryptic carvings in the bark of Roanoke Island trees. "CRO" was scratched into the trunk of one tree near the bank of the Roanoke Sound. "CROATOAN" was etched into another, near the deteriorating fort. White thought these mysterious messages meant the settlers had fled south to live with the friendly Croatan Indians on Hatteras Island.

The abandoned settlement site showed no signs of a struggle — no blood or bodies or even bones. Some say the colonists were killed by natives or carried away in a skirmish. Others think they were lost at sea, trying to sail home to England. Still others believe they skirted west across the sounds and began to explore the Carolina mainland. Or perhaps they headed to other areas of the Outer Banks, their footsteps scattered in the blowing sands. . . .

Historians have debated the "Lost Colony's" fate for more than 400 years. Archaeologists continue to dig on Roanoke Island's eastern edges. Scholars from across the country gather to discuss the strange disappearance — and even have established a special research office on the subject at East Carolina University in Greenville.

And each summer, for more than half a century, actors have recreated the unsolved mystery in America's longest running outdoor drama, *The Lost Colony* — held at the settlement site in Waterside Theatre (see our Attractions chapter).

Shipping and Settlement into the 1700s

A century passed before English explorers again attempted to establish settlements along the Outer Banks.

Origins of Outer Banks Place Names

Bodie Island

Pronounced to rhyme with toddy — not toady — this stretch of sand is bordered on the north by South Nags Head, on the south by Oregon Inlet. It was really an island until 1819 when Roanoke Inlet closed on the north, linking it with the other northern barrier island beaches. The name first appears in the 1720s in a land grant for the area. Legend has it that "bodie" was a misspelling of "body," and the island was so named because of the many bodies washing up on the beaches from shipwrecks. The first Bodie Island lighthouse was built to save sailors from the dangerous shoals in 1847.

Hatteras Island

Probably from an Algonkian term for sparse vegetation, this name has been used for the southern Outer Banks island, inlet and village since the first English settlers set up camp on Roanoke Island more than 400 years ago.

Jockey's Ridge

The tallest sand dune on the East Coast, this mini-mountain may have earned its name because it afforded such a grand view of a horse race track set up on the adjacent flatlands. "Jockey's Hill" was listed on a 1753 land grant for the area. And "Jockey Ridge" first appeared in an 1851 newspaper article about Nags Head as a summer resort destination.

Kill Devil Hills

The single Kill Devil Hill is the large sand dune in front of which Wilbur and Orville Wright launched the world's first airplane in 1903. The plural form, Kill Devil Hills, refers to the first incorporated town on the beach, established in 1953. Kill-devil was a 17th-century English term (derived from Dutch) that referred to rum. The liquor may have been distilled locally, washed up in barrels from shipwrecks or sold at a nearby tavern. "Killdevil Hills" first appears on a map in 1808.

Kitty Hawk

Eighteenth-century records show the name of this northern beach community as "Chickahauk." Theories say the name came from local Indians' references to goose hunting season as "killy honker" or "killy honk." Through the years, people say, the name evolved to "killy hawk" and, finally, Kitty Hawk. Another legend says the beach town got its name from the area's large number of mosquito hawks, which people called "Skeeter Hawks." Kitty also was the name of a type of local wren, so Kitty Hawk may have been an osprey or other type of raptor that preyed on the smaller birds.

Nags Head

The primary resort destination on the Outer Banks for more than a century, Nags Head has been the official name of the area since at least 1738 when it first appears on maps. Historians say the beach town got its name from the free-range horses that once roamed throughout the barrier islands. Legend has it, however, that Nags Head is so-called because the local beach residents used to tie a lantern around a horse's neck and walk the animal up and down the beach after dark. The swing of the light resembled that of a lantern hung on the deck of a sailboat. Other vessels would steer toward the beacon, lured by the light, and wreck on the shores. Then the local residents could salvage what was left of the ship.

Ocracoke Island

The southernmost accessible island on the Outer Banks, this area has carried versions of its present name for more than four centuries. John White drew a map of the barrier islands in 1585, labeling what is now Ocracoke "Wokokon," after a nearby tribe of Woccon Indians. In 1657, a survey map showed the island as "Wococock." Tall tales say Ocracoke was a bastardizing of "Oh, cock crow," a cry foes of Blackbeard were said to have uttered in an attempt to bring daybreak to the dark seas — and with it a chance to escape the fierce pirate who frequently plundered other ships throughout the area.

Oregon Inlet

Formed by a hurricane in September 1846, this wide waterway separating South Nags Head and Bodie Island from Hatteras Island didn't have an official name for the first two years it was open. But in 1848, the side-wheel steamer *Oregon* from Washington, North Carolina, cruised through the channel — marking the first successful crossing by a large ocean-going vessel.

Roanoke Island

The site of the first English settlement in North America, this Outer Banks island gets its name from an Algonkian term for either "shell beads" or "northern people." English colonists used the name for the area as early as 1580. It also refers to the nearby sound and a now-nonexistent inlet.

Wanchese and Manteo

Of these two historic villages on Roanoke Island, Wanchese is primarily inhabited by commercial fishing families, while Manteo is the county seat and the area's governmental hub. The two towns effectively took on characteristics of their namesakes, two Algonkian Indians who befriended Sir Walter Raleigh's colonists and returned with them to England to meet the queen in 1584.

Throughout this time, however, European ships continued to explore the Atlantic seaboard, searching for gold and conquerable land. Scores of these sailing vessels wrecked in storms and on dangerous shoals east of the barrier islands. Spanish mustangs, some say, swam ashore from the sinking ships on which they were being transported overseas. Descendants of these wild stallions continue to roam freely around the northern beaches of Corolla today. Others are corralled in a National Park Service pen on Ocracoke Island.

Although the Outer Banks beaches had few permanent people until the early 1700s, small colonies sprouted up across the Virginia and what is now the Carolina coast during the late 1600s. The barrier islands blocked deep-draft ships from sailing into safe harbors, where they needed to anchor and unload supplies for mainland settlers. So smaller vessels, fit for navigating the shallow sounds, transported goods from the Outer Banks to the mainland. People passed through these strips of sand long before they settled here.

Ocracoke Inlet, between Ocracoke and Portsmouth islands, was the busiest North Carolina waterway during much of the Colonial period. The inlet was a vital yet delicate link in the trade network — and deeper than most other area egresses. Navigational improvements to the inlet began as early as 1715 when the British government made it an official port of entry. Pilot houses were set up at Ocracoke to dock the small transport boats and temporarily house goods headed inland. Commercial traffic increased along this Outer Banks waterway for many years.

Countless inlets from the sea to sound have formed and closed since the barrier islands first formed. More than two dozen inlets appear in the historical record and on maps dating from 1585. Yet only six inlets currently are open between Morehead City and the Virginia border. Studies of geographic formations and soil deposits indicate that, at some point in time, inlets have covered nearly 50 percent of the Outer Banks. Attempts to harness the inlets have proven costly and, for the most part, been doomed to failure. Even today, recreational and commercial watermen continue to fight environmentalists for the rights — and federal funding — to build $97 million jetties in an effort to stabilize Oregon Inlet, which separates Nags Head from Hatteras Island.

The first land the British government granted in North Carolina was what is now Colington Island — a small spit of earth surrounded by the Currituck, Albemarle and Roanoke sounds, between Kill Devil Hills and the mainland. Sir John Colleton, for whom the island is named, set up a plantation on the island's sloping sand hills. His agents planted corn, built barns and houses and carried cattle across by boat to graze on the scrubby marsh grasses. According to historians, this was the beginning of the barrier islands' first permanent English settlement.

Over the next several decades, stockmen and farmers set up small grazing stocks and gardens on the sheltered sound side of the Outer Banks. Run-

Insiders' Tips

To get a gull's-eye view of these fragile ribbons of sand, charter a small airplane over the islands. Reasonably priced one-hour flights are available daily from airstrips on Roanoke Island and behind the Wright Brothers Memorial.

aways, outlaws and entrepreneurs also arrived in small numbers — stealing away in the isolated forests, living off the fresh fish and abundant waterfowl, running high-priced hunting parties through the intricate bogs and creeks. All of these inhabitants also engaged in salvaging: When a shipwrecked vessel floated onto the shore, local residents made quick work of wielding the wood off the boat, loosening sails from the masts and scavenging anything of value that was left on board. If victims were still struggling ashore, the locals helped them — even setting up makeshift hospitals in their humble homes.

The inaccessibility of the barrier islands — and wealth of goods that passed through the ports — made the Outer Banks a prime target for plundering pirates. The most infamous of all these high seas henchmen was Edward Teach, better known as Blackbeard, a rum-drinking Englishman whose raucous crew set up shop on the south end of Ocracoke Island. After waylaying countless ships and stealing valuable cargo for more than two years, Blackbeard finally was beheaded by a British naval captain in 1718, in a slough off his beloved Ocracoke (see the Blackbeard sidebar in our Ocracoke chapter).

Settlement and sparse development continued through the early 1700s, and by 1722 almost all of the Outer Banks were secured in private ownership. Large tracts of land — often in parcels with 2,000 acres or more — were deeded to noblemen, investors and cattle ranchers. Some New England whalers also relocated to the barrier islands after British noblemen encouraged such industry. Whales were sliced open and their blubber, oil and bones sold and shipped overseas. The huge marine mammals were harpooned offshore from boats or merely harvested on the sand after dying and drifting into the shallow surf.

Although small settlements and scores of fish camps were scattered from Hatteras Village almost to the Virginia line, Ocracoke and the next island south, Portsmouth, continued to be the most bustling areas of the Outer Banks through the middle of the 18th century. British officials enlisted government-paid pilots to operate transfer stations at Ocracoke Inlet, between the two islands, and carry goods across the sounds to the mainland. A small town of sorts sprang up, as the people finally had found some steady occupation and were assured of regular wages.

In 1757, the barrier islands' first tavern opened amidst a sparse string of wooden warehouses and cottages on Portsmouth Island. About 11 years later, a minister made the first recorded religious visit to the Outer Banks when he baptized 27 children in the sea just south of the tavern. Today, a Methodist church and a few National Park Service-supervised cottages are all that remain on Portsmouth Island — the only ghost town east of the Mississippi River (see the Portsmouth Island sidebar in the Daytrippin' chapter).

War and Statehood

As much of a hindrance as the string of barrier islands and their surrounding shoals and sounds had been to shipping, the Outer Banks proved equally invaluable as a strategic outpost during the Revolutionary War.

Only local pilots in small sailing sloops could successfully navigate the shifting sands and often unruly inlets that provided the sole passageway between the Atlantic Ocean and North Carolina mainland. So big British warships could not anchor close enough to sabotage most Carolina ports. Colonial crafts, instead, ferried much needed supplies through Ocracoke Inlet, up inland rivers and small waterways, to the new American strongholds in New England.

JAMES B. GASKILL
JULY 2, 1919
MAR. 11, 1942
Lost at sea,
But sush a tide as moving
seems asleep,
Too full for sound and foam,
When that which drew from

Photo: Mary Ellen Riddle

This grave marks the resting place of an Ocracoke native lost at sea.

By the spring of 1776, however, British troops began threatening the pilots at Ocracoke, even boarding some of their small sloops and demanding to be taken inland, where they could better wage war. Colonial leaders then hired independent armed companies to defend the inlets. They abandoned these small forces by autumn of the following year.

British boats, however, continued to beleaguer the Outer Banks. Ships landed along Currituck's islands so sailors could steal cattle and sheep. The Red Coats anchored off Nags Head, going inland for fresh water and whatever supplies they could abscond. They raided fishing villages, plundered small sailboats and came ashore beneath the cloak of darkness. Ocracoke Inlet, especially, suffered under their persistent attacks.

In November 1779, North Carolina legislators formed an Ocracoke Militia Company, hiring 25 local men as soldiers to defend their island's independence. This newly armed force was issued regular pay and rations. Its members successfully saved the inlet and American supplies until fighting finally stopped in 1783 — six years after the United States declared its independence.

About 1,000 permanent residents made their homes on the Outer Banks by the time North Carolina became a sovereign state under the 1789 Constitution. Most of these people sailed down from Tidewater, Virginia, or across from the Carolina mainland. These hearty folk lived in two-story wooden structures with an outdoor kitchen and privy. They dug gardens in the maritime forests, built crude fish camps on the ocean and erected rough-hewn hunting blinds along the waterfowl-rich marshlands. After frequent storms crashed along their coasts, the residents continued to find profit in the shipwrecks strewn along nearby shoals and shores.

Lighthouses along the Graveyard of the Atlantic

More than a dozen ships a day were carrying cargo and crew along Outer Banks waterways by the dawn of the 19th century. Schooners and sloops, sailboats and new steamers all journeyed around the sounds and across the oceans, often dangerously close to the coast in search of the ever-shifting and shoaling inlets. At that time, waterways were the country's primary highways, and North Carolina's barrier islands were the Grand Central Station of most eastern routes.

Hurricanes and northeasters —

which still scare Outer Banks locals — took many boats by surprise, ending their voyages and hundreds of lives. Statesman Alexander Hamilton dubbed the ocean off the barrier islands "The Graveyard of the Atlantic" because its shoals became the burying grounds for so many ships. More than 650 vessels have been lost along North Carolina's craggy coast.

In an attempt to help seamen navigate the treacherous shoals, the federal government authorized the Banks' first lighthouses in 1794: one at Cape Hatteras in the fishing village of Buxton and the other in Ocracoke harbor, on a half-mile-long, 60-mile-wide pile of oyster shells dubbed "Shell Castle Island." Shell Castle Lighthouse first illuminated the Atlantic in 1798. The Cape Hatteras beacon took a little longer to erect. It was finally finished in 1802. Two subsequent structures have sat on the same spot, but the Shell Castle beacon has long since succumbed to the sea.

Ship captains complained that the early lighthouses were unreliable and too dim. Vessels continued to smash into the shoals. So in 1823, the federal government financed a 65-foot-high lighthouse on Ocracoke Island. The squat structure was whitewashed, with a glass tower set slightly askew on its top. It is the oldest lighthouse still standing in North Carolina.

Officials raised the Cape Hatteras tower to 150 feet in 1854. Five years later, they built two new Outer Banks beacons, at Cape Lookout and on Bodie Island. Both of those lighthouses were improved and rebuilt in later years. The Bodie Island beacon opened its new visitor center in summer 1995.

On December 16, 1870, the third lighthouse at Cape Hatteras was illuminated. Standing 180 feet tall and using a multifaceted lens to refract its whale-oil beam across miles of sea, this spiral-striped structure is the tallest brick lighthouse in the world. It's open for tours about six months of the year, but tides and hurricanes are threatening to erode its foundation and send this tall tower tumbling into the sea (see the Cape Hatteras Lighthouse sidebar in our Hatteras Island chapter).

Currituck Beach's red-brick beacon was the last major lighthouse to be built on the barrier island beaches. A 150-foot tower that also is open for tours, this lighthouse was completed in 1875. It watches over the Whalehead Club, near the western shores of Corolla. It is the only unpainted lighthouse on the Outer Banks — and the only one held in private ownership. All other Banks beacons are owned by the National Park Service and operated by the U.S. Coast Guard.

Summer Settlements

In the early 1800s, mainland farmers and wealthy families along Carolina's coast suffered each summer from the malady of malaria. They thought this feverous condition was caused by poisonous vapors escaping from the swamps on hot, humid afternoons. Physicians recommended escaping to the seaside for brisk breezes and salt air.

Nags Head was established as a resort destination primarily by a Perquimans County planter who bought 200 acres of ocean-to-sound land for 50¢ an acre in the early 1830s. Eight years later, the Outer Banks' first hotel sprang from the sand near the sound, near what is now Jockey's Ridge State Park. Guests arrived at "Nags Head Hotel" from across the sounds on steamships, disembarked at a long, low boardwalk behind the 200-room hotel, and spent weeks enjoying the beaches and the hotel's formal dining room, ballroom, tavern, bowling alleys and casino.

In 1851 workers enlarged the hotel and added a mile-long track of rails so mule-pulled carts could ease vacationers' journeys to the ocean. The hotel burned down and was rebuilt; later, it was buried by sand. Jockey's Ridge dune, the East Coast's tallest, swallowed the two-story structure bit by bit. Hotel clerks offered discounts during the final years for fellows who didn't mind digging their way into their rooms. But some bachelors complained that chickens rather than chicks were following them home at night through the dark tunnels of sand (see our sidebar on Jockey's Ridge in the Attractions chapter).

Wealthier visitors who wanted to stay the whole summer built their own vacation cottages on the barrier islands' central plains and eventually on the ocean. Some fathers carried their entire households — cows, pigs, sheep and all — across the sounds on small sailing sloops to spend the season at Nags Head. By 1849 a local visitor remarked that between 500 and 600 visitors were bathing daily at the barrier island beach.

Meanwhile, locals lived in small wooden houses in the woods, selling fresh fish and vegetables to the new tourists — thereby earning unexpected extra income each summer.

Civil War Skirmishes

Outer Banks inlets again proved important military targets after the War Between the States erupted in 1861. Union and Confederate troops stationed armed ships at Hatteras and Ocracoke inlets and set up early encampments. North Carolina crews, who joined their Southern neighbors and seceded from the United States, captured boats filled with fruit, mahogany, salt, molasses and coffee along the enigmatic inlets.

Forts, too, were built along the barrier islands, although erosion and storms have long since erased all traces of such structures. Fort Oregon was constructed on the south side of Oregon Inlet; Fort Ocracoke on Beacon Island, inside Ocracoke Inlet. Fort Hatteras and Fort Clark were across from each other at Hatteras Inlet — by then, the primary passageway between the ocean and sounds. Approximately 580 men defended those two forts. Seven cannons were mounted inside, aimed across the inlet from one fort to the other in a cross-fire position so that the entire waterway could be covered from within the high walls.

By the fall of 1861, however, federal forces had overtaken Hatteras Inlet and controlled most of the Outer Banks and lower sounds. Confederate troops still ruled Roanoke Island and the upper sounds. They built three small fortresses on the north end of their stronghold to reinforce their position and to block all access through Croatan Sound.

Union troops also were amassing. In January 1862, Gen. Ambrose Burnside led an 80-boat flotilla from Newport News to North Carolina's Outer Banks. Water was so scarce on this trip that some soldiers resorted to drinking vinegar out of sheer thirst. Others died of typhoid before the battle even began. But on February 7, more than 11,500 members of the federal army amassed for a Roanoke Island attack (an overlook at Northwest Point on the northern end of the island commemorates this site today). At least 7,500 men raided the shores at Ashby's Harbor that night — near present-day Skyco. About 1,050 Confederate soldiers fought to maintain their foothold.

After hours of battle around what is now the Nags Head-Manteo Causeway, the rebel troops finally were forced to surrender. Union troops captured an estimated 2,675 of these Southerners. Federal forces held Roanoke Island — and most of the Outer Banks — for the rest of the Civil War.

A Settlement for Freed Slaves

Only a few hundred slaves lived along the Outer Banks at the outbreak of the

Photo: Mary Ellen Riddle

Corolla's Whalehead Club was originally built as a gift to a lady who was an avid outdoors woman. There was a time when women were excluded as members from "all men" hunt clubs.

Civil War. But two months after falling to Union troops, Roanoke Island was filled with more than 1,000 runaway and recently freed slaves. The federal government offered these African-American men $8 per month and a "ration of clothes" to build a fort, Fort Burnside, on the north end of Roanoke Island.

By June of 1863, officials had established an official Freed Man's Colony on Roanoke Island, west of where the Elizabethan Inn now stands. The government granted all unclaimed lands to the former slaves and outfitted them with a steam mill, sawmill, grist mill, circular saws and other necessary tools. About 3,000 African-Americans lived here in a village with more than 600 houses, a school, store, small church and hospital.

Union forces, however, began accepting African-American troops soon after they established the settlement. By the end of July, more than 100 members of the Freed Man's Colony formed the nation's first African-American army regiment. The new colony would have survived were it not for the government's decision to return all lands to the original landowners after the war was over.

The Freed Man's Colony was abandoned in 1866. Federal officials quickly transported many of the former slaves off the Outer Banks. Others remained on Roanoke Island to work the waters and the land.

Brave Men and Britches Buoys

After the war, normal life resumed on the barrier islands. Commerce commenced again along the ocean, increasing quickly with steamers now outnumbering sailboats — and onetime warships joining private shipping companies. Storms, too, continued to wrack the shores and seamen, with even iron battleships sinking into oblivion.

Seven U.S. Lifesaving Stations were established on the Outer Banks in 1874 in an attempt to help save sailors lives, if not salvage some of the ships. The stations included: Jones's Hill near the Currituck Beach lighthouse; Caffrey's Inlet north of Duck; Kitty Hawk Beach south of the present pier; Nag's (sic) Head within current town boundaries; Bodie's (sic) Island was south of Oregon Inlet; Chicamacomico, which is still open to visitors in Rodanthe and conducts simulated rescue drills each summer (see our Attractions and Hatteras Island chapters); and Little Kinnakeet, on the west side of N.C. 12 in Avon, which is being renovated by the National Park Service as part of a historic preservation project.

During their first season of employment, lifesaving station keepers were paid $200 per year to supervise six surfmen from December through March. Lifesavers lived in the sparse wooden stations, often sleeping six to a room, and kept constant watch over the Atlantic from inside elevated towers that poked out of the stations' roofs. At night, the men walked the beach. Two from each station would leave after dark, one heading north, the other south. After three to six miles, they'd meet a surfman from the neighboring station — also walking either north or south — and exchange tokens to prove they had completed their patrol.

Stations were operated mostly by longtime Outer Bankers. Good swimmers and sea captains who knew the wild waters, these men risked their lives — and many perished — trying to pull others from the ocean. During the winter of 1877-78, more than 188 shipwreck victims and surfmen died within a 30-mile stretch of beach on the northern Outer Banks. That summer, Congress authorized 11 additional lifesaving stations, including ones for Wash Woods and Penny's Hill in Carova, Kill Devil Hills, Hatteras and Pea Island (which had an all-African-American crew). The Lifesaving Service also added a seventh surfman to each station. Crews were then employed from September through April. Rescue techniques advanced with new equipment and the surfmen's experience in ocean survival.

Before motorized rescue craft were available, lifesaving teams had to row deep-hulled wooden boats, often through overhead waves. If they made it through the seething seas to shipwrecks, they sometimes couldn't carry all of the sailors back to shore in one trip. As a result, they devised a pulley system to haul men off the sinking vessels. Dubbed a "Britches Buoy," the device consisted of a pair of short pants sewn around a life preserver ring and hung on a thick rope by wide suspenders; the rope was wound around a handle crank mounted to a wooden cart on shore. Shipwreck victims struggled into the britches — usually with the assistance of surfmen in the rescue boat — and gave an "all-clear" tug on the rope. With the buoy sewn into the seams around their waists, these sailors didn't sink. Even in the highest seas, they could keep their heads above water while lifesaving crews back on shore reeled them safely onto the sand.

Surfmen at Outer Banks lifesaving stations saved thousands of lives during hurricanes and hellacious northeast blows. In 1915, the Lifesaving Service became part of the U.S. Coast Guard. Coast Guardsmen continue to aid barrier is-

Insiders' Tips

More than 650 ships have been lost along the Outer Banks. Some were smashed on sandbars, others hurled onto the beach in hurricanes. A group of Hatteras Island residents is collecting private and state funds to build a Graveyard of the Atlantic museum to chronicle these shipwrecks. Plans call for construction to be near the Hatteras Village ferry docks.

Net-mending is a practical art that's been handed down generation after generation on Hatteras Island.

land boaters with a variety of state-of-the-art rescue craft stationed at modern Oregon Inlet and Hatteras Island stations.

Historic Happenings, Modern Influences

Government jobs as lifesavers, lighthouse keepers and postmasters employed increasing numbers of Outer Banks residents at the dawn of the 20th century. Other locals continued to profit from summer tourists. But most remained poor fishermen, farmers, stockmen, store clerks, hunters and hunting guides.

In 1902, however, the barrier islands recorded another first when Thomas Edison's former chief chemist began experimenting with wireless telegraphy. Radio pioneer Reginald Fessenden transmitted the first musical notes to be received by signal from near Buxton on Hatteras Island to Roanoke Island. He wrote to his patent attorney that the resulting sounds were "very loud and plain, i.e., as loud as in an ordinary telephone."

In 1900, Ohio bicycle shop owners Wilbur and Orville Wright arrived by boat at Kitty Hawk, looking for reliable winds. Three years later, on December 17, 1903, the Wright brothers soared over Kill Devil Hills sand dunes in the world's first airplane. Only a handful of local Bankers looked on in amazement as the flyer stayed aloft for 59 seconds, flying 852 feet. The site is now marked with a stone monument in a National Park set along the original runway. A replica of the historic airplane, hangar and brothers' shack are on display (see our sidebar in the Kill Devil Hills chapter).

In the 1930s, bridges linking the Outer Banks to the mainland brought thousands more tourists — and profound changes — to the islands. Visitors now could drive to popular summer resorts at Nags Head rather than relying on steamships. Hotels, rental cottages and restaurants sprang up to accommodate the influx.

Post-Depression era politics promulgated the Civilian Conservation Corps (CCC), which set up six camps along the barrier islands. Throughout the '30s, these government workers performed millions of dollars worth of dune construction and shoreline stabilization. Dunes along the east side of N.C. 12 did not grow that tall naturally. CCC workers planted much of the grass and scrubby shrubbery to help stave off erosion along the ocean.

Although it was mostly waged continents away, World War II spread all the way across the ocean to the Outer Banks' doorstep. German U-boats lurked in near-shore shipping lanes, exacting heavy losses to Allied vessels. At least 60 boats fell victim to the submarines, though the Germans experienced losses of their own: The first U-boat sunk by Americans lies in an Atlantic grave off the coast of Bodie

Island. Longtime barrier island residents recount having to pull their shades and extinguish all lights each night throughout the war so that ships and submarines could not easily discern the shoreline.

Talk of the country's first national seashore began in the 1930s. By 1953, when the Cape Hatteras National Seashore finally was established under the auspices of the National Park Service, it stretched from Nags Head through Ocracoke Island. Today, the Outer Banks are some of the most popular — yet pristine — beach resorts on the Atlantic coast. Fewer than 30,000 people make the barrier islands their permanent home. But more than 300,000 visit our sandy shores each summer weekend.

Population Figures

Locality	*1980*	*1990*	*Growth rate:*
Kill Devil Hills	1,796	4,238	+126%
Nags Head	1,020	1,838	+80%
Dare County	3,377	22,746	+70%

Source: 1990 U.S. Census of Population and Housing

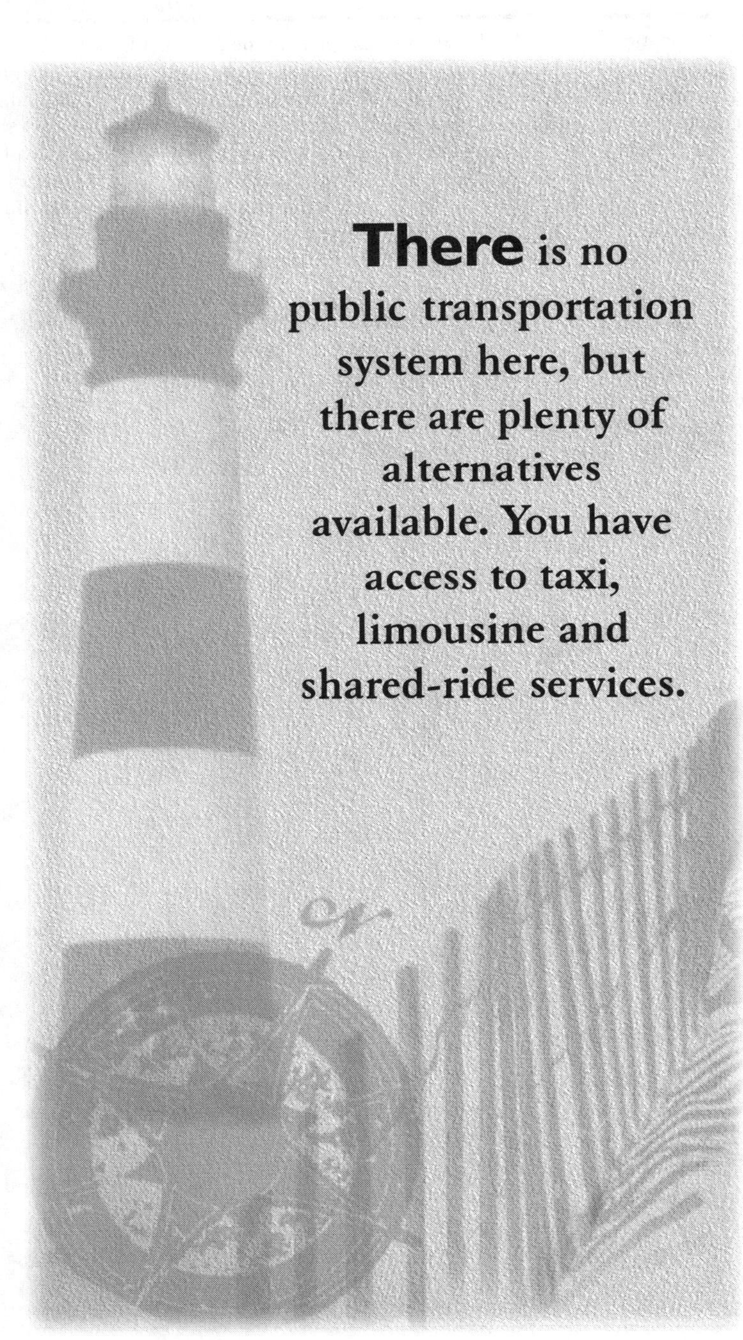
There is no public transportation system here, but there are plenty of alternatives available. You have access to taxi, limousine and shared-ride services.

Inside Getting Here, Getting Around

If you're not already here in body, you may be here in spirit. Many of the folks who etch out days or weeks of their years to vacation on the Outer Banks never really leave. As they return to Ohio, Virginia, Washington, D.C., and other destinations, they carry with them the memory of a barrier island existence that few vacation spots in the United States can match. So let's go from a dreaming state to a more concrete one and get you here posthaste. Then you can make your own memories by the sea.

Getting Here By Land

Most folk come to the Outer Banks on four wheels and usually have no problem arriving, having their vehicles serviced if necessary (see our Service and Information Directory), finding their way around and returning home. Traffic can get congested during a hurricane evacuation and on holidays, but apart from those instances, it's really not too hectic. For locals, summer traffic offers a great contrast to the less-traveled highways of fall and winter, but we know that visitors enrich our economy, and we welcome you, traffic and all. If you're used to big-city traffic, you'll find the summer traffic tolerable, especially after reading this guide and learning what's out there waiting for you.

Special note: The northern route up N.C. Highway 12 toward Duck and Corolla can get a bit bogged down on summer weekends — especially during lunch and dinner hours. Waiting isn't so bad with the views, roadside swaying grasses and incredible sunsets (beware of the gorgeous cloud formations; they are very distracting to the driver), and if passengers have some snacks the wait is fairly painless. (There are also plenty of places to stop for snacks, drinks and shopping along this route.) Just remember to allow an extra half-hour or more when traveling to the northern Outer Banks on summer weekends. You may want to call the various municipalities or radio stations to see when traffic is heaviest during holidays. Folks answering phones at local information and sightseeing spots will be happy to guide you.

If you travel from western North Carolina or from the southern United States along interstates 85 or 95 you'll move along U.S. Highway 64 E. to Roanoke Island. Along this journey keep a look out for deer, black bears, red wolves and a wide variety of birds — there are usually blue herons wading in the roadside creeks. The state plants an abundance of colorful poppies and wildflowers along the roadside of this highway. It's very tempting to pick these flowers with their brilliant multicolored petals, but please leave them in place for the next traveler to enjoy. (Besides, there's a fine if you're caught on the roadside with a bouquet.)

This stretch of Highway 64 is lined with canals and creeks, and the reflection of trees and the sun sparkling on the water make this route particularly refreshing. It is a sparse area with few stops

Photo: Mary Ellen Riddle

Colington's newly installed bike path makes getting around more enjoyable — and healthier too!

after Columbia, so fuel up before you leave Williamston. If you have to pull off the road, do so carefully and choose a wide shoulder, if possible. Canals alternate sides of the road, and it's safer to pull off on the side without the canal.

Highway 64 will take you through Williamston, Jamesville, Plymouth (hold your nose through here — the paper factory smell is bad some days!) Creswell, Columbia (home of Pocosin Arts on Water and Main streets, nice art and museum!), over the Alligator River, through East Lake, Manns Harbor and Roanoke Island. You'll cross several bridges with spectacular views before you arrive at the home of the Lost Colony. If you continue to travel east on Highway 64, you'll pass through quaint Manteo (where you must stop and see the historic sights. See our Roanoke Island Chapter.) After Manteo you can turn right to go to the fishing village of Wanchese or veer left to head toward Nags Head and the beaches. The signs are clear, and you can navigate like a local by using the ocean and sound to guide you.

Traveling from the same direction on Highway 64, you may choose to turn in Williamston at the U.S. Highway 17 junction that will take you to Elizabeth City. If you follow signs to Nags Head and Manteo from there, you'll arrive on the beach from the north. Highway 17 is also the route most Virginians follow.

Folks traveling from points north can pick up Highway 64 E. in Virginia Beach or Norfolk. From Richmond and points northwest, follow Highway 64 E. to Highway 664 E. and take the Monitor-Merrimac Bridge-Tunnel across the James River. Highway 64 continues near Suffolk.

From Highway 64, Exit 83 B takes you down Battlefield Boulevard in Chesapeake to Va. Highway 168. Follow Highway 168 E. to U.S. Highway 158 E. At this junction you will be about an hour from the Wright Memorial Bridge that crosses the Currituck Sound to the Outer Banks. Travel at your leisure on Highway 158, for the road from Chesapeake to the Wright Memorial Bridge is dotted with antiques shops, thrift stores and vegetable and fruit stands. A Thai restaurant and shiny new diner aren't too far from the bridge.

Northern travelers can choose to take Highway 17 S. to Deep Creek instead of taking Highway 64. Highway 17 follows the Intracoastal Waterway through the Great Dismal Swamp before intersecting N.C. Highway 343 near South Mills. Follow Highway 343 to Camden and then pick up Highway158 E. to the Outer Banks. It doesn't matter which way you arrive — those who love our home here believe that eventually, "All roads lead to the Outer Banks."

When approaching the Wright Memorial Bridge, bear in mind that peak travel times are from noon through 6 PM on Saturday and Sunday in the summer season (Memorial Day to Labor Day). Delays can occur as a result. Travel advisories are posted for your convenience. The addition of the new bridge span in the summer of 1995 has helped the traffic flow to and from the Outer Banks.

After crossing the Wright Memorial Bridge, you will be in Kitty Hawk. Well-marked signs will lead you to your destination. Turn left on Highway 12 to head to Southern Shores, Duck, Corolla and Carova, or turn right onto Highway 158 to go to Kitty Hawk, Kill Devil Hills, Nags Head, Roanoke Island and Hatteras Island. At this junction, the Aycock Brown Welcome Center is on the right. Stop here for a wealth of vacation information. Eventually the road, headed south, will fork. To the right is Manteo, and to the left is the Cape Hatteras National Seashore and Ocracoke Island. Just remember that the ocean is always to your left when you are headed south, and you'll make out just fine.

By Air

If you own your own plane and would like to fly to the Outer Banks, contact the **Dare County Regional Airport** on Roanoke Island, 473-2600, or the **First**

Flight Airstrip at the Wright Brothers National Memorial in Kill Devil Hills, 441-7430. At the First Flight Airstrip your stay is limited to 24 hours, and you need to land and take off in daylight since there are no lights there. No reservations are necessary at First Flight, and there is a sign-in book on the premises.

Most major airlines offer passenger service to Norfolk International Airport. From there, **Outer Banks Airways**, 441-7677, offers charter service to Kill Devil Hills, Roanoke Island and Pine Island in Duck. The **Kitty Hawk Aero Tours** component of this company also offers sightseeing air tours. Advance reservations are required. (See our Attractions chapter for details.) **Southeast Airlines**, 473-3222, also offers charter service from the Norfolk airport, as well as air tours and biplane acrobatic rides. If you're looking to take a short trip from Hatteras Island to Ocracoke or want to fly around that area, contact **Burrus Flying Service**, 995-6671, in Frisco or **Pelican Airways**, 928-1661 or 986-2679, in Ocracoke. Please call for reservations and additional information.

By Water

A great way to recapture some of the excitement early settlers must have felt as they approached the Outer Banks by water is to do it yourself! Talk the journey over with a local sailor or captain first. This is a good rule of thumb to follow when navigating foreign waters. And pick up a copy of the *Mid-Atlantic Waterway Guide* that provides the most detailed information available about the area's waterways.

From points north, you'll begin at the Intracoastal Waterway in the Hampton Roads, Virginia, area. If the weather is fair, it takes a full day to travel down the ICW to the Outer Banks, and the open waters of the Albemarle Sound can be quite choppy, even dangerous, so beware.

There are two ICW routes to the Outer Banks. One is from Great Bridge, Virginia, across the Currituck Sound to Coinjock, North Carolina, the North River and the Albemarle Sound. An alternate route from Hampton Roads takes you to Deep Creek, Virginia, through the Great Dismal Swamp to Lake Drummond in North Carolina, through South Mills to the Pasquotank River where "the ditch" joins the Albemarle Sound. Follow charts across Albemarle Sound to the Alligator River, then choose either Croatan Sound or Roanoke Sound to the town of Manteo.

The **Waterfront Marina** in Manteo, 473-3320, provides public docking facilities. The marina supplies power and water at each slip and charges rates on a per-foot basis. Here, you'll find a lovely boardwalk and a small town full of friendly locals and interesting sights. Shops, restaurants and entertainment are all within easy walking distance, as are several lovely inns if you want a break from your berth. (See the Roanoke Island and Attractions chapters for details.) Another docking option is **Pirate's Cove Marina** on the Roanoke Sound between Manteo and Nags Head, 473-3906. Open year-round, Pirate's Cove accommodates pleasure craft as long as 75 feet. Showers and laundry facilities are included with slip rental. The on-site ship store and restaurant are open to the public (great food and view upstairs), and tennis and pool facilities are available for a nominal fee. Personalized service is this marina's specialty. Offshore and inshore fishing charters are the most popular form of recreation here. From Pirate's Cove, Oregon Inlet and the Atlantic Ocean are just a short ride away. Yet another option — and a good one — is **Salty Dawg Marina** in Manteo, 473-3405. This top-notch facility sports 55 slips, all with power and water and a modern, air-conditioned bathhouse. Just minutes from downtown Manteo, the Salty Dawg provides a cour-

Driving Along the Outer Banks

These barrier islands have only three major roadways.

• **U.S. Highway 158** crosses the Wright Memorial Bridge into Kitty Hawk and winds through the center of the Banks to Whalebone Junction in Nags Head. This five-lane highway (the center lane is for turning vehicles only) also is called the Bypass or Croatan Highway. In this book, we will refer to it as the Bypass.

• **N.C. Highway 12** runs parallel to Highway 158 along the beach. A two-lane road, it stretches from the southern border of the Currituck National Wildlife Refuge in Corolla to the ferry docks at the southern tip of Hatteras Island. Highway 12 picks up again in Ocracoke, spanning the length of the tiny island, ending in its picturesque village. N.C. 12 also is called Ocean Trail in Corolla, Duck Road in Duck, Ocean Boulevard in Southern Shores and Virginia Dare Trail or the Beach Road from Kitty Hawk through Nags Head. In this book, we will refer to it as N.C. 12.

• On Roanoke Island, **U.S. Highway 64/264** also is called Highway 64 or Main Highway. This stoplight-filled road begins at the Nags Head-Manteo Causeway, runs across the Washington Baum Bridge, through Manteo, across the William B. Umstead Bridge and through Manns Harbor on the mainland.

It's not as confusing as it sounds. The main roads all run primarily north and south. Smaller connector streets link seaside rental cottages to year-round neighborhoods west of the Bypass. And most locals are friendly, patient, helpful folk who will be glad to point you in the right direction.

tesy car. The marina is open year round, seven days a week. It's a good idea to call for reservations on holidays. For information other marinas, please see the "Boating" section of our Watersports chapter.

Arrival by boat from the south begins by crossing the Core Sound to pick up the ICW near Beaufort, North Carolina. Cross the Pamlico Sound to the mouth of the Neuse River. Cross the Neuse to Belhaven, where the canal resumes to the northeast.

Ferries

Landlubbers can also enjoy an Outer Banks arrival by boat thanks to the North Carolina Ferry System. If coming from North Carolina, follow Highway 70 E. from New Bern to Havelock and pick up N.C. Highway 101; follow to N.C. Highway 306, then take the ferry to Bayview near historic Bath. Follow N.C. Highway 99 to Belhaven, where you pick up Highway 264 to Swan Quarter. Choose an overland course along N.C. Highway 94 across Lake Mattamuskeet, then Highway 64 to Manteo — or select another ferry from Swan Quarter to Ocracoke Island. It sounds complicated, but signs will guide you.

An alternative route follows Highway 70 E. through Havelock to Beaufort. Highway 70 continues from Beaufort to Harkers Island, following the Core Sound to Highway 12, where you pick up the Cedar Island Ferry to Ocracoke Island. The voyage across the Pamlico Sound is well worth the 2½ hours it takes to arrive in Ocracoke. Cross Ocracoke Island from south to north and pick up the Hatteras Island Ferry to the upper Outer Banks.

Ferry passage is a good way of reducing your driving time if you're heading to the southern portion of the Outer Banks. And unless you have your own boat or plane, it's the only way of reaching picturesque Ocracoke Island. The ferries transport cars to the island, although we suggest biking or walking as the best ways to get around Ocracoke.

Information on the ferry services available on the Outer Banks follows. You can get more information by writing to Director, Ferry Division, Morehead City 28557, or by calling 726-6446 or 726-6413.

For more information about ferry schedules, call (800) BYFERRY (293-3779).

Hatteras Inlet (Ocracoke) Ferry

This free state-run service links the islands of Hatteras and Ocracoke. The 40-minute crossing carries you from Hatteras Village past Hatteras Inlet across the Pamlico Sound. The ferries accommodate cars and even large camping vehicles and are run frequently in the summer to avoid excessive delays. The Hatteras Ferry does not require reservations, as do the Cedar Island and Swan Quarter ferries to and from Ocracoke Village. There are public restrooms at the Hatteras Island dock, and heads are on board. The information number is 986-2353.

Summer Schedule

May 26 through October 16

Leave Hatteras	Leave Ocracoke
5 AM	5 AM
6 AM	6 AM
7 AM	7 AM
8 AM	8 AM

Then every 30 minutes until

6:30 PM	7:30 PM
8 PM	9 PM
10 PM	11 PM
Midnight	

Winter Schedule

October 17 through May 25

Leave Hatteras every hour on the hour from 5 AM to 6 PM, and at 8 PM, 10 PM and midnight.

Leave Ocracoke every hour on the hour from 5 AM to 7 PM, then at 9 and 11 PM.

Swan Quarter and Cedar Island ferries

To avoid possible delay in boarding the Cedar Island-Ocracoke Toll Ferry and the Swan Quarter-Ocracoke Toll Ferry, reservations are recommended. These may be made in person at the departure terminal or by telephone. To make reservations for departures from Ocracoke, call 928-3841; from Cedar Island, call 225-3551; and from Swan Quarter, call 926-1111. Office hours are usually 6 AM to 6 PM, but the office stays open later during the summer.

Reservations may be made up to 30 days in advance of departure date and are not transferable. These reservations must be claimed at least 30 minutes prior to departure time. The name of the driver and the vehicle license number are required when making reservations.

Information on tolls and vehicle weight limits follows the ferry information.

Ocracoke-Swan Quarter Toll Ferry

This 2½-hour ferry ride, which can accommodate 28 cars, connects Ocracoke with Swan Quarter in Hyde County on the mainland. You'll go through Swan Quarter National Wildlife Refuge and connect with Highway 264 with its gracious old cedars lining the way.

Year-round Schedule

Leave Ocracoke	Leave Swan Quarter
6:30 AM	9:30 AM
12:30 PM	4 PM

One-way fares and rates are listed at the end of this section.

Ocracoke-Cedar Island Toll Ferry

Though it takes 2½ hours, this is a popular path for those going south from Ocracoke. (The alternative is to drive back to Nags Head and get on Highway 264 E. or to take the ferry to Swan Quarter.) This ferry, which can carry 50 cars, leaves Ocracoke Village and takes you across the Pamlico Sound to Cedar Island. From Cedar Island, those going south can take Highway 70 to Morehead City. Take a good book and a basket of snacks. Relax and enjoy the view from the ferry.

Summer Schedule

May 26 through October 2

Leave Cedar Is.	Leave Ocracoke
7 AM	7 AM
8:15 AM	9:30 AM
9:30 AM	10:45 AM
Noon	Noon
1:15 PM	3 PM
3 PM	4:15 PM
6 PM	6 PM
8:30 PM	8:30 PM

Spring and Fall Schedules

May 11 through May 25
October 3 through October 30

Leave Cedar Is.	Leave Ocracoke
7 AM	7 AM
9:30 AM	9:30 AM
Noon	Noon
3 PM	3 PM
6 PM	6 PM
8:30 PM	8:30 PM

Winter Schedule

October 31 through May 10

7 AM	7 AM
10 AM	10 AM
1 PM	1 PM
4 PM	4 PM

Fares and Rates (One Way)

Pedestrian — $1
Bicycle and Rider — $2

Single vehicle or combination 20 feet or less in length and motorcycles (minimum fare for licensed vehicle) — $10

Vehicles or combinations from 20 to 40 feet in length — $20

All vehicles or combinations 40 to 55 feet in length having a maximum width of 8 feet and height of 13 feet 6 inches — $30

Vehicle Gross Load Limits

The following weight limits apply for all crossings.

Any axle — 13,000 pounds

Two axles (single vehicle) — 24,000 pounds

Three or more axles — 36,000 pounds (single or combination vehicle)

Getting Around

We've gotten you here, now let's get you around.

If you truly want to relax and spend your vacation days island-style, kick off your shoes and travel on foot. You can

Insiders' Tips

Locals avoid grocery shopping on crowded summer weekends and shop for several weeks worth of food at a time.

Photo: Philip S. Ruckle Jr.

A beautiful sunset over Roanoke Sound is a common sight.

walk for miles down the beaches, collecting shells and wading, stopping at various beach accesses to turn onto the Beach Road (N.C. Highway 12). When crossing the Beach Road, watch out for the vans with the mirrors that stick out, the road is narrow. There are plenty of restaurants and fishing piers that run the length of the Outer Banks, so you're usually not far from food and drink. Most spots welcome casual diners.

If walking is not your style, biking may be just the ticket. The Outer Banks boasts several bike paths. Running the length of Roanoke Island is an asphalt path dotted with benches. The path has awakened the athlete in many locals, young and old, who are now seen walking, riding bikes and in-line skating regularly. It's a wide, safe path that we are grateful to have. In South Nags Head a wide concrete path runs the length of Old Oregon Inlet Road down to Highway 12, accommodating those headed toward the Cape Hatteras National Seashore. In 1996, the town of Kill Devil Hills established a scenic asphalt route off the Colington Road, running down National Park Service property past the rear of the Wright Memorial. A new path is proposed for Duck, but the length and location have not been decided. Construction was scheduled to begin at the end of April 1996, with a projected completion date of Memorial Day. The path will begin about a mile south of Duck Village. Officials at the NCDOT are not sure where the path will end or where phase two will pick up, but work on the second stage will not start until after Labor Day 1996, so summer traffic should not be hindered.

If you're going to enjoy these paths or bike anywhere else on the Outer Banks, please wear a helmet. You can rent bikes at several rental services, and many accommodations also offer them as a courtesy (see our Recreation chapter). Watch out for the sand that blows on the road. This can be slippery when applying brakes and get in your eyes as you pass the dunes. Follow the normal rules of the road that apply to cars, stopping at lights and stop signs and yielding to pedestrians. There is a lot of foot traffic near the beach, so whether you're on a bike or in a car, watch out for that rolling beach ball usually followed by a child.

Taxis, Limos and Tours

There is no public transportation system here, but there are plenty of alternatives available. You have access to taxi and limousine service, and the Beach Bus is a fun ride that will spice up any journey.

If it's a stretch limousine you want, **Island Limo** has a selection to suit your every need. (Ask your driver to take you to Jennette's Pier for a glimpse of the ocean while you dine from a picnic from Petrozza's Deli!) They provide a daily shuttle to and from Norfolk International Airport, (call for more information) and you can also take advantage of their four-wheel drive off-road excursions to Hatteras Island, Oregon Inlet and Carova Beach. Call 441-LIMO. For limousine service only, call (800) 828 LIMO. **Outer Banks Limousine Service**, 261-3133 offers limo service to points all along the Outer Banks and **Island Taxi**, 441-8803, run by the same folks, provides 24-hour cab service. **Outer Banks Transit**, 441-7090, provides scheduled trips to Norfolk International Airport and other Norfolk destinations. Package delivery and pickup are also accommodated. **Beach Cab**, 441-2500, offers 24-hour service and airport pickups. **Bayside Cab**, 480-1300, is on U.S. 158, MP 6, and offers point-to-point service 24 hours a day.

New to the Outer Banks is **The Connection**, a local shared-ride service. This passenger van service operates under a flat rate from an air-conditioned vehicle fully equipped with child safety seats. The Connection offers Norfolk Shuttle service, and group rates and discounts are available. Call (919) 473-2777 or write: The Connection, P.O. Box 175, Manteo 27954 for more information.

For more taxi service call **Atlantic Cab**, 453-4108 in Corolla or 261-3074 in Duck; **Bayside Cab**, 480, 1300; **Beach Cab**, 441-2500; and **Buxton Under the Sun**, 995-6047. (See our Service and Information Directory for details on shuttle services to Norfolk International Airport.)

You may have seen those great big red double-decker buses around. They're a great way to see the sights. See our Attractions chapter for more information.

Historically Speaking offers step-on tour guiding and receptive tours for motor coach travelers, complete with historical commentary on Roanoke Island and the Outer Banks. Call 473-5783 for your personalized tour reservation.

Car Rentals

Car rentals are available at the Dare County Regional Airport in Manteo and at a few other places on the Outer Banks.

B & R Rent-A-Car, U.S. 64, Manteo, 473-2141; Airport Road (Dare County Regional Airport), Manteo, 473-2600

R.D. Sawyer Ford, U.S. 64, south of Manteo, 473-2141

Outer Banks Chrysler/Plymouth/Dodge/Jeep, U.S. 158, MP 6, Kill Devil Hills, 441-1146

Atlantic Auto Rental, Nags Head, 441-7256, (800) 441-7256

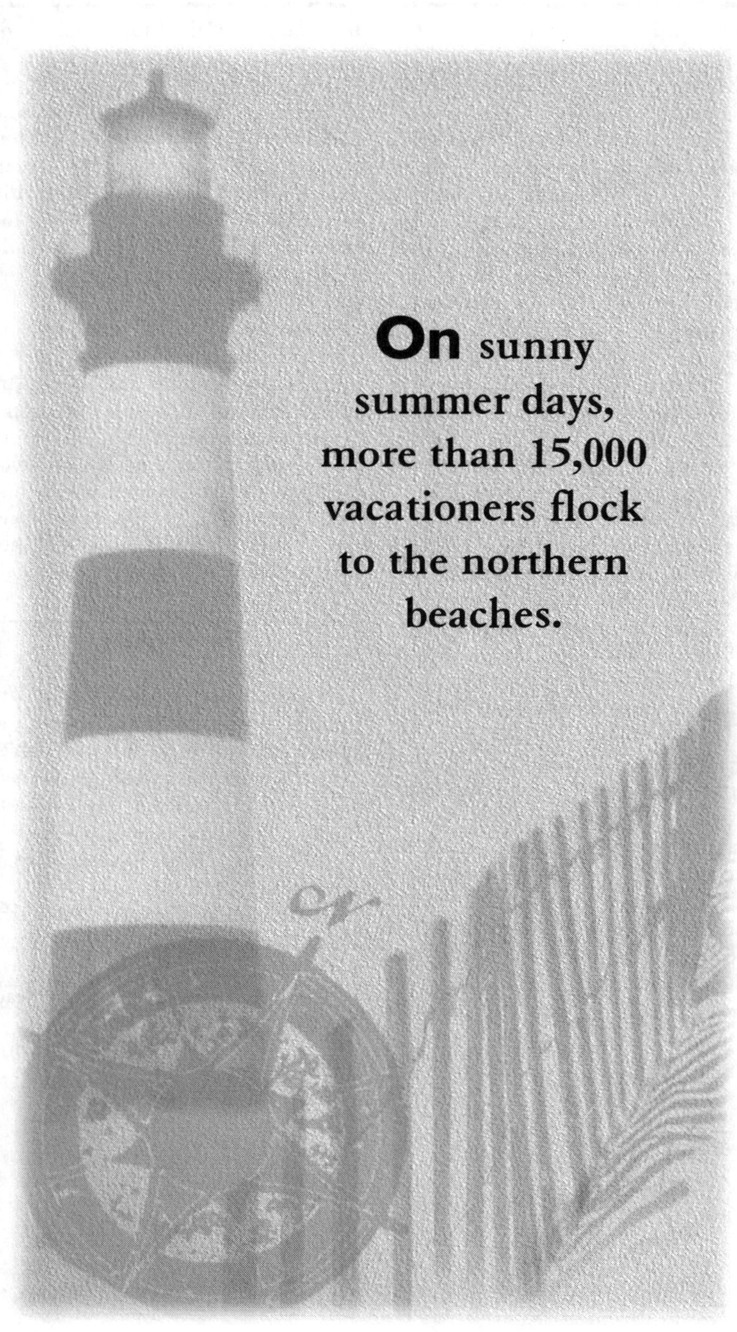

On sunny summer days, more than 15,000 vacationers flock to the northern beaches.

Inside Corolla and Currituck's Beaches

Fewer than 12 years ago, Currituck County's Outer Banks beaches were wide, windswept expanses of sand that seemed to stretch indefinitely from north of Duck to the Virginia border.

A few fishing shacks and a handful of private homes broke up the barren barrier-island landscape, but wild horses and great blue heron were more prevalent than people. A family-owned convenience store supplied the only local goods for fewer than 100 permanent residents. A lighthouse, post office and abandoned lifesaving station were the only other noticeable structures. And armed guards prevented visitors from traveling north of the Dare County line.

Today, racquet clubs, resort-wear retailers and 5,000-square-foot mansions line 13 miles of recently paved subdivision roads. Two dozen restaurants, a Food Lion grocery store and a four-screen movie theater offer a variety of cuisine and evening entertainment. On sunny summer days, more than 15,000 vacationers flock to the northern beaches.

What a difference a decade makes.

"Everything has changed," said Mary Bichner, who became Corolla's 17th year-round resident when she moved to the remote village in 1971. "We used to exchange Christmas gifts with everyone in the village. Now, I don't even know all the permanent people, much less the property owners. We've really grown all of a sudden."

From Fishing Village to Vacation Destination

After the Civil War, Currituck Beach was the largest community on the Outer Banks between Kitty Hawk and Virginia. Fishing families lived in small wooden houses near the sound. The only visitors were hunters who came to bag geese, duck and swan in what Currituck officials still call "Sportsman's Paradise."

In 1874, the U.S. government put Currituck's beaches on the map by building a lifesaving station and lighthouse near the center of the skinny strip of sand. The lifesaving station, one of the Outer Banks' original seven outposts, was first named Jones Hill, then Whales Head and, finally, Currituck

Insiders' Tips

If you want to see wild horses roaming through the sand dunes and you have a four-wheel-drive vehicle, travel through the gate at the end of N.C. Highway 12, north of Corolla, onto the sand, into the Currituck National Wildlife Refuge. You also can park your car at the blacktop's end and walk into the refuge.

The view from Corolla's Currituck Beach Lighthouse is spectacular, and the climb's not too bad either.

Beach. The Currituck Beach Lighthouse was the last major lighthouse built on North Carolina's barrier islands. A 150-foot tall, red-brick beacon, it cost $178,000 to construct.

A post office opened at Currituck Beach on March 6, 1895, adopting the official name of Corolla, which the village still uses today. Situated now in a shopping plaza beside a pizza place and convenience mart, the Corolla post office remains the only one on the Outer Banks operating north of Kitty Hawk. It's longtime postmaster, Norris Austin, retired several years ago but continues to keep his home above the small, square office.

Throughout the early 1900s, Currituck County's barrier islands were a popular retreat for recreational hunters who flocked to the sea oat-strewn marshlands each fall for the annual waterfowl migration. You can still spot crudely built duck blinds along the swampy shores. And the elaborate hunt clubs erected by Northerners in the 1910s and 1920s have been turned into resort community clubhouses, real-estate offices and county-owned estates. The Whalehead Club (see the sidebar in this chapter), the largest and most elaborate of all the Outer Banks hunting lodges, is being restored with tourism tax profits. This Currituck County facility is open for tours daily throughout the summer season and will someday house a wildlife museum.

Hunting and fishing remained Corolla's only attractions until the early 1970s. Marshall Cherry, whose ancestors have lived in Currituck since the late 1600s, said when his family purchased property near Aydlett, on the mainland, last century, they "got the barrier island beach directly east of the property line too. Except for duck hunting, it was all useless sand," Cherry said. "Nobody even wanted to pay taxes on it, so the county just gave it away with mainland tracts."

Dare County's beaches became a resort area early in the 1880s. In 1930, when the Wright Memorial Bridge across the Currituck Sound was completed, tourism boomed from Kitty Hawk through Oregon Inlet. But the remoteness of the Currituck Outer Banks — and the lack of a permanent population and services — kept that area isolated long after the southern beaches had grown into travel destinations.

Getting to Currituck County's Outer Banks

In the 1950s, Virginia and North Carolina officials began talking about building a road from Sandbridge, in Virginia Beach, to Corolla — traversing a long spit of solid sand and the state line. That route, however, was never started. Today, only property owners with special permits can get through a metal gate at the North Carolina border and arrive in Corolla from the north.

The rest of the populace must drive up N.C. Highway 12 from the south to get to Currituck's beaches. Turn onto N.C. 12 at its junction with U.S. Highway 158 in Kitty Hawk, 1.5 miles east of the Wright Memorial Bridge's eastern terminus. Then travel through Southern Shores, Duck and Sanderling and you'll hit the county line. The trip takes approximately 45 minutes in moderate traffic; but keep in mind that it could take an hour or more on certain days during the peak season.

In 1972, coastal officials called Currituck County's 23 miles of beaches "the longest undeveloped strip of coastal land on the Eastern Seaboard." One telephone, which only allowed outgoing calls, served the entire area. Families placed weekly food orders with the postmaster, who ran a tiny general store in his house.

"You had to get there as soon as the food was delivered or you were out of luck," said Lori Bowden Quidley, who grew up in Corolla. "He only ordered about five loaves of bread and six cases of six-ounce Cokes every week — maybe some orange Nab crackers if you were really lucky. But that was it. If you didn't get it right when it got here, you didn't get it at all."

In 1973, Winston-Salem developer Earl Slick set his sights on Currituck County's sandy beaches and changed the face of the northern Outer Banks. For $2 million, he and his Coastland Corporation purchased 636 acres on the barrier islands from Texas oil tycoon Walter B. Davis. The sound-to-sea tract sat just north of the Dare County line.

Currituck County commissioners approved the first planned unit development for their Outer Banks later that year: 800 single-family homes, 2,800 condominiums and a 1,250-room hotel. The development was dubbed Ocean Sands. It has its own sewage system now, but the condos and hotel have not yet been built.

To keep gawkers and daytrippers out of his exclusive community, Slick erected a wooden guardhouse at the southern tip of his property in 1975. He paved a clay road from the county line through Ocean Sands. But only people who lived or owned property north of the Dare border were allowed to travel the road into Currituck. Two armed guards working around the clock kept everyone else out.

"There were a lot of fights at that gate," recalled Austin, the postmaster. "They wanted trucks delivering supplies to our little store to pay a fee. We wouldn't do it. So they blocked our deliveries. We had to go down there in our own pickups with our property owners passes to get fuel, food and other goods ourselves."

Northern Outer Banks residents protested such privatization of the only thoroughfare and took their case to the state Supreme Court. Finally, on November 1, 1984, the North Carolina Department of Transportation took over the road that stretched from the Dare County line north. As security officers watched, bulldozers toppled their guard post — opening passage all the way to Corolla and clearing a path for widespread development.

Corolla Today

The village post office, once only a room filled with small postal boxes, began offering home delivery to Corolla residents in 1986. Three years later, the community got its first bank. By the early 1990s, an upscale strip shopping center had unfurled its colorful window displays on the west side of N.C. 12.

In the past decade, developers and individuals have built more than 1,500 homes between the Dare County line and the Virginia border. At least 100 businesses have opened their doors. Planning officials have approved development of another 6,700 structures.

For an area considered a wasteland less than 30 years ago, the northern Outer Banks have come a long way in a very short time.

In 1995 alone, the county issued more than 100 building permits for new stores and houses. Corolla's first hotel, **Inn at Corolla Light**, opened that year, offering kitchenettes, video cassette recorders and cable television in every room. Many accommodations at this inn also include fireplaces, whirlpool tubs and sleep sofas.

Most visitors to Currituck's beaches, however, tend to rent the huge homes that straddle the undulating sand dunes. The average Corolla house sleeps 10 to 15 people, includes 3,332 square feet of living space, and is available for weekly rentals. Many of the contained communities also offer exercise facilities, racquet or golf clubs, indoor and outdoor swimming pools, boardwalk beach accesses and hot tubs for their guests.

Corolla Light, in the heart of "downtown" Corolla, even has its own trolley to transport families from their doorsteps to the beach, sound, shopping, restaurants or any of the myriad of exclusive amenities. This community also includes a game room, tennis courts, shuffleboard, boccie ball, basketball, swings, sliding boards, seesaws, a snack bar and meticulously landscaped footpaths offering shortcuts through the sand to waterfront gazebos and ocean accesses.

Other Currituck beach communities, from south to north, include: **Pine Island**, which adjoins a 5,000-acre Audubon sanctuary and includes an indoor tennis club; **Ocean Sands**, the oldest community, with 450 single-family homes; **Buck Island**, a Victorian seaside enclave near the TimBuck II shopping plaza that has 78 single-family homesites and 41 lots for townhouses; **Monteray Shores**, featuring mango-colored villas with arched verandas and red tile roofs near the Food Lion shopping plaza and new Ace Hardware; **Whalehead**, which has an eclectic mix of home styles from the traditional to the sublime; and, north of Corolla Light, **Ocean Hill**, where 300 single-family homesites cover 153 acres of wide, white sand reaching to the end of N.C. 12.

Retail stores scattered throughout this uppercrust area sell items ranging from handmade hammocks to custom-designed jewelry. Restaurants appeal to all tastes from raw or steamed seafood to elegant European dining. And watersports — Jet Skis, windsurfing, sailing and more — across the silvery sound are available from early spring through fall (see our Shopping, Restaurants and Watersports chapters for details).

Although the streets and sidewalks often overflow during the summer tourism season, the permanent population of Currituck County's Outer Banks is still fairly small, estimated at fewer than 500 people. A county satellite office keeps them connected with Currituck's services. But children who live in Corolla year round travel more than two hours by bus to attend Dare County schools — the closest ones to their resort community.

Reining in the Wild Horses

A few miles north of the Currituck Beach Lighthouse, the multistory mansions become more sparse and the paved two-lane highway dead ends at a sand hill. Here, the Currituck National Wildlife Refuge provides a safe haven for endangered piping plover, feral boar and Corolla's well-known herd of wild horses. A 4-foot-tall fence, stretching a mile from sound to sea, marks the southern barrier of this 1,800-acre sanctuary. People can walk through the fence, however, and four-wheel drive vehicles can cross through a cattle gate.

The Whalehead Club: Corolla's Crown Jewel

When Outer Banks huntsmen refused to let Amanda LeBel Knight join their all-male Lighthouse Club during the early 1920s, her husband shot back by building the most expensive, extravagant retreat on North Carolina's barrier islands.

The Whalehead Club sits in the shadow of Corolla's Currituck Beach Lighthouse, facing the Currituck Sound. It was completed in 1925 after three years of continual work and cost $383,000. The magnificent 20,000-square-foot mansion, which defies its humble "hunting lodge" moniker, has 6 chimneys, 15 bedrooms and bathrooms with customized ceramic-tile tubs of varying sizes.

Today, the Whalehead Club is owned by Currituck County, and is open daily from 10 AM to 3:30 PM from June through September. Admission is $3 for adults, $1 for children ages 6 to 12 and free for children 5 and younger. For more information, call 453-9040.

Officials are planning a $3 to $5 million renovation for the house, to be funded with tourism tax revenues. Tour proceeds also will help finance a wildlife museum slated to be housed on the Whalehead Club's ground floor.

Edward Collins Knight, who commissioned the huge home, invented the Pullman coach and was president of the Pennsylvania Railroad. He and his French-born wife, Amanda, lived in Newport, Rhode Island, in a 104-room house dubbed Clarendon Court. But the couple frequently traveled to the Outer Banks for hunting expeditions because waterfowl were so abundant along the marshy sounds.

Photo: Mary Ellen Riddle

Built by Rhode Island railroad industrialist Edward Collings Knight in 1925 for $383,000, Corolla's Whalehead Club was a hunting retreat with 15 bedrooms and six fireplaces and staffed by 15 servants.

In 1922, the Knights purchased 3,000 acres of waterfront property, extending from the lighthouse south to Crown Point. Their opulent estate boasted the area's first in-ground swimming pool, a full basement, wine cellar and hand-dug moat. It was the first building in the county to have electric lights. A gilt elevator carried guests through the three stories. Indoor plumbing — a rarity during that time — pumped hot and cold fresh and salt water throughout the luxurious lodge.

Cork tiles covered the ballroom floor, where a custom-made Steinway grand piano provided music for Gatsby-like galas. The Knights loved to entertain and often brought full orchestras in by boat for week-long soirees. Two kitchens, a gun room, coat room, butler's station and dining room with 24-seat table and solid mahogany walls also occupy the first floor.

Second story walls are white cypress — hand-routed to resemble corduroy. Three main bedrooms fill this level: those of Mr. Knight, Mrs. Knight and his longtime friend, Dr. Brown. Three additional smaller guest rooms also are on this floor. Upstairs, on the third story, seven bedrooms once housed 12 full-time servants.

The Knights enjoyed their "Currituck Castle" for 11 falls and winters. But when the couple died in 1936, they left no heirs. A caretaker oversaw the club for the next four years. In 1940, Ray Adams of Washington, D.C., and his wife purchased the Whalehead Club to entertain friends and business associates.

Adams leased the property to the U.S. Coast Guard during World War II. George T. McLean and W.I. Witt of Virginia Beach and Portsmouth, Virginia, respectively, bought the club a few years later. They ran the Corolla Academy for Boys at the Whalehead Club from 1959 to 1963.

The mansion was abandoned for the next seven years. Then, in 1970, Atlantic Research purchased it. Scientists tested the first aeronautic nose cones for rockets on the lodge's sprawling, slightly sloping grounds.

No one has inhabited the home since the mid-1970s. Vandals removed many of its lavish furnishings and fixtures. Gaping holes now spread across ceilings where crystal chandeliers once hung.

In 1992, Currituck County commissioners bought the club, its boathouse, boat basin, foot bridge and 27.5 acres of land for $2.4 million. They added another 10.4-acre, $1.26 million tract to the estate two years later. Using private donations and tour proceeds, local officials hope to renovate the club and restore some of its interior.

Already, the owner of two Tiffany lamp globes that once hung in the dining room has donated the $500,000 antiques to the county — and the club. Private contributions for the Whalehead Club's restoration have topped $40,000. And tour revenues are growing each summer as July 4 fireworks celebrations draw thousands of families to the grassy grounds for a day-long annual festival (see our Annual Events chapter).

Osprey now nest in three of the mansion's tall brick chimneys. A half-century of salt spray has coated the club's once-gleaming copper roof with a dull, moss green sheen. Mango-colored paint peels from paneled walls.

But decades of disuse have not stripped the Whalehead Club of her former grandeur. Visitors today still marvel at illustrious antiques crouching in corners of the long-abandoned rooms. Tourists traverse the pockmarked dance floor and admire the customized slate fireplace hearths.

By taking tours of the vanilla-colored club, people can help restore the most pretentious, expensive and extravagant hunting lodge ever built on the Outer Banks.

The horses, who some say are descendants of Spanish mustangs that swam to Outer Banks shores from shipwrecks 300 years ago, roamed freely throughout Corolla until March 1995. Then, a group of volunteers erected the fence and herded a dozen wild horses behind it to keep them out of harm's way. Traffic has killed at least 15 members of the herd since 1989. The Corolla Wild Horse Fund hopes to keep the animals away from vehicles. But the group's members want the horses to remain free to explore the northern expanses of the barrier islands that have been their home long before people permanently settled here.

An estimated 35 to 150 additional wild horses already lived north of the fence, on the wildlife refuge.

Despite untold efforts to corral the rest of the horses north of the barrier, the animals have found ways to swim and wade around the fence — and even to roll under it. They seem to prefer the landscaped lawns of Corolla's gardener-tended subdivisions to the scrubby pines and dune plants of the wildlife refuge. Visitors often still see the equines nibbling grasses around tennis courts after the animals escape from their human-mandated habitat.

Isolated Outposts North of the Road's End

There is no real route from Corolla to the Virginia border. Still, a few hundred homes line this expanse of sand. On summer afternoons, more than a thousand four-wheel-drive vehicles create their own paths on the beach as they drive into and around a community called **Carova** — where North Carolina meets Virginia.

People don't need passes to drive along this sparsely populated stretch. But some permanent residents and property owners have protested the giant influx of weekend warriors who cruise through Carova from May through October. Soon, a special permit may be required for vehicles to venture north of the highway's end.

For now, however, the area is wide open. If you don't have a four-wheel-drive automobile, local guides will be glad to show you around in theirs. And Corolla Outback Adventures rents open-air, low-to-the-ground four-wheelers for

Although Corolla's students travel up to two hours by bus to attend Dare County classrooms, children in this northern Outer Banks seaside village once had their own school. The former one-room school house is now a private residence west of the U.S. Post Office.

Insiders' Tips

Photo: Philip S. Ruckle

The Northern Banks' wild ponies are fun to watch, but don't get too close.

breathtaking sunset soirees. Watch out for tree stumps, though. An ancient forest that historians say grew along the sound more than 800 years ago still thrusts its sea-withered trunks through the waves at an area known as Wash Woods.

If you travel off-road in this area, you'll soon see a giant sand dune near the sound. Lewark's Hill, which some people call Penny's Hill, is the tallest dune on Currituck's beaches. From the top, hikers can spot a string of marsh islands in the sound, including Monkey Island, which contains a dilapidated hunting lodge and is accessible via a Corolla sailboat cruise.

State officials have dropped all plans to build a road through this portion of the Outer Banks, preferring, instead, to keep the Currituck and Back Bay wildlife refuges free from as much traffic as possible. But North Carolina transportation workers plan to build a bridge connecting Corolla to the Currituck mainland near the turn of the century. The termini of this span have not yet been determined. The eastern end probably will be somewhere near the Food Lion, in the most densely developed area. Legislators are considering imposing a toll of up to $10 on this Mid-County Bridge, which would make it the first toll bridge in North Carolina.

For now, however, the Currituck beaches can only be reached by driving the two-lane state highway north of Kitty Hawk. Corolla is fast becoming the most exclusive and upscale destination on the Outer Banks. And the villages north of the road's end — including **Swan Beach** — remain the most remote of all barrier island resorts.

Whether you're staying in one of Currituck Beach's ritzy rental homes or camping somewhere on the southern Outer Banks, Corolla is well worth exploring. If you have a four-wheel-drive vehicle, Carova is probably the most wide-open area around for driving on the sand. Once that new bridge is built, the still isolated northern barrier island beaches are bound to boom even more.

Inside Duck and Sanderling

A sleepy seaside village spanning the Outer Banks' skinniest strip of sand, Duck woke up to tourism in the early 1980s. Since then, it's burgeoned into a week-long — and daytrip — destination all its own. Some people insist they won't stay anywhere else.

The two-lane highway through the center of town teems with tourists throughout the summer. More year-round locals are moving here every month. And restaurants and retail shops are opening by the dozens each May.

Duck has a quaintness and an air of "yuppiness" about it, with its waterfront boutiques, art galleries and eclectic eateries. Vacationers who choose to stay here are generally a bit more affluent than those who select the central beaches or Hatteras Island. Most stay in rental cottages that are nicely tucked into shady, tree-lined niches. A bed and breakfast inn accommodates nightly guests. But no hotels or fast food joints have sprung from these sandy shores.

Along the sound, Duck resembles a historic New England port town. The brilliant white spire of the Duck Methodist Church rises above the gnarled live oaks and wind-bent hickory groves. Weathered clapboard buildings of simple, single-gable construction are linked by wide wooden boardwalks spanning swampy wetlands. These shops, which look like clusters of quaint, colorful cottages, carry everything from kaleidoscopes to locally designed kids' clothing.

And there's no place better to watch the tangerine sun sink into the sound than from the sea oat-lined decks of Duck's soundfront stores and restaurants.

Photo: Mike Booher

Even at the height of the season, a visitor can enjoy the solitude of a sunrise over the Atlantic Ocean.

Eel Pots and a Growing Economy

Like most barrier island beach communities, Duck was a small fishing village during its early existence. Families lived in rough-hewn wooden houses set atop two-foot blocks that kept the floors above the level to which the sea or sound had been known to rise during storms. With more trees and thicker underbrush here than in other areas of the Outer Banks, some Duck residents successfully farmed small garden plots to supplement their seafood diets.

Watermen worked from dawn until dark, netting fish from the beach with long-haul seines, taking dorries out in the sound to set pound nets and trapping crabs with wooden crates. Eel pots also were prevalent along the shallow shores and shoals. Made of thin wood and more rounded than the crab pots, these contraptions' contents gave local fishermen an item to export. They packed the long, snakelike creatures in salt, stored them in barrels and trucked them along the sand trails to Hampton Roads markets, where eel were once eaten in abundance.

The first post office opened in Duck in 1909 but was abandoned by 1950. Year-round residents have to travel to Kitty Hawk for their mail. Children go there to attend school as well.

Little changed in Duck until the late 1970s. Single family homes were sparsely scattered throughout the thick shrubbery, and small wooden boats bobbed from tree trunks turned into pilings.

Tourism took over about 1980, when small shops began lining up along the two-lane road through town and larger houses sprang from the beach areas. Barrier Island Station, among the biggest and most popular time-share resorts on the Outer Banks, opened one of Duck's first full-service restaurants and now includes an indoor and outdoor pool, tennis courts, a communal hot tub and live evening entertainment on a covered waterfront deck.

In 1990, you had your choice of five restaurants between Kitty Hawk and Corolla. Today, more than 25 locally owned establishments offer breakfast, lunch and dinner. These include a coffeehouse that offers a variety of flavors you can drink in or take out; a pizza parlor; an upscale deli with unusual homemade salads; scads of sandwich shops; a marvelous bistro called Blue Point with spicy soups and wild combinations of seafood; and an unsurpassed dining experience for wine lovers at Elizabeth's Cafe.

Shopping runs the gamut of galleries, boutiques and other colorful shops spread along N.C. 12 through the village in single- and double-level marketplaces: Scarborough Faire, Scarborough Lane, Osprey Landing, Loblolly Pines, Duck Waterfront Shops, Wee Winks Square and Duck Village Square. Their wares include intimate apparel and body lotions, tie-dyed candles, unique jewelry, coffeetable books, Christmas decorations, clothing from discount catalog outlets, Western wear, outdoor gear and local artists' sculpture, paintings and wire works.

Recreational offerings abound here too and are being added to every season. You can learn to windsurf, or you can

Insiders' Tips

Sailing lessons are offered daily in the summer at Barrier Island Station on the sound in Duck.

rent a sailboat or let a captain take you on a sunset cruise. Speed across the sound on a Jet Ski, paddle around a marsh island in a canoe or kayak, or bounce about the waves on a blow-up banana boat.

No matter what your tastes in food, fashion or fun, you will find something to enjoy in the now-bustling village of Duck.

Getting to Duck

To get to Duck, turn left onto N.C. 12 at its junction with U.S. Route 158 in Kitty Hawk, 1.5 miles east of the Wright Memorial Bridge's eastern terminus. Travel through the flat-top homes of Southern Shores and wind around the dunes on the two-lane highway. On good days, Duck is a 10-minute drive from Kitty Hawk. In heavy summer traffic, bottlenecks form in the village, causing backups that last for miles and, sometimes, more than 30 minutes.

N.C. 12 curves through the center of Duck, and all the commercial development is along this road, confined to the highway by zoning ordinances, landscaped with lovely local foliage.

The sea is quite close to Duck, as is the sound, so many rental homes provide the rare opportunity for viewing both bodies of water from upstairs open-air decks. Wild beans, peas and cattails cover the marshy yards, most of which are at least partially wooded, with the houses tucked between the trees.

True to its name, Duck is home and passageway for a variety of nesting and migrating shore birds and waterfowl. Streets are named after these feathered creatures, which often come to call. Loons, cormorants, gannet and flocks of terns and gulls soak up the sun's warmth

Photo: Philip S. Ruckle Jr.

A great blue heron in the sound.

near the water's edge. You can sometimes see swan and mallards swimming in the sound at sunrise.

On the northern edge of Duck, a U.S. Army Corps of Engineers research facility stretches across the isthmus on the site of a former Navy bombing range. Military weapons recovery crews have dug up thousands of unexploded ordinances around here. And an 1,800-foot-long pier now provides scientists an important opportunity to track subsurface currents, study the effects of jetties and beach nourishment projects and chart the movements of the slender strips of sand. Other equipment includes an amphibious craft and stilt-like camera contraption that wades into the waves, advanced computer data collecting devices that are linked to the World Wide Web network, and machines that measure the ocean's temperature, wave height and erosion activities. The research pier is not open to the public, but officials offer occasional tours for interested visitors. This world-renowned facility often hosts international conferences.

Beyond the pier, heading north toward Corolla, the Duck Volunteer Fire Department, the Dare County Sheriff's Office northern beach station and the Duck Recycling Center offer free local services; **see the Service Directory for contact numbers.**

Sanderling

Situated about 5 miles north of Duck, through an open wilderness area, Sanderling is the northernmost community on Dare County's beaches — an isolated, exclusive, upscale enclave with 300 acres stretching from sound to sea.

The community itself was initiated in 1978, setting a precedent for excellence among vacation destinations. These neighborhoods, barely visible from the road, approach land planning sensitively, preserving as much natural vegetation as possible and always aiming for architectural excellence. They are well worth searching out.

In 1985, the **Sanderling Inn and Restaurant** opened in the restored Caffey's Inlet Lifesaving Station, built in 1874. With cedar shake siding, natural wood interiors and English country antiques, it has the appearance of turn-of-the-century Nags Head resorts and the ambiance of a European escape. It's large and airy, with wide porches that provide plenty of room for conversation, drinks and soaking in the sunrise in wooden rocking chairs.

Rooms at the Sanderling are among the most luxurious on the Outer Banks. Some feature central sound systems and outdoor, oceanside Jacuzzi spas. This posh place includes conference and reception facilities and a health club; it is a favored site for catered events. It is extremely popular for weddings and serves the beach's best gourmet Sunday brunch. From welcome baskets in every room to high tea served each afternoon, no details are overlooked at this pampering, ritzy resort.

Sanderling shares its amenities with the inn's overnight guests and property owners. A soundside racquet and swim club, 3 miles of groomed nature trails and soundfront piers are paid for with dues collected by the Sanderling Property Owners Association.

North of Sanderling, **Palmer's Island Club** is a 35-acre development with 15 oceanfront 1-acre lots and at least eight estates ranging from 6,000 to 10,000 square feet each. The homes are engineered to withstand 120 mph winds. Signature architectural embellishments are scaled to match the grandeur of the natural environment.

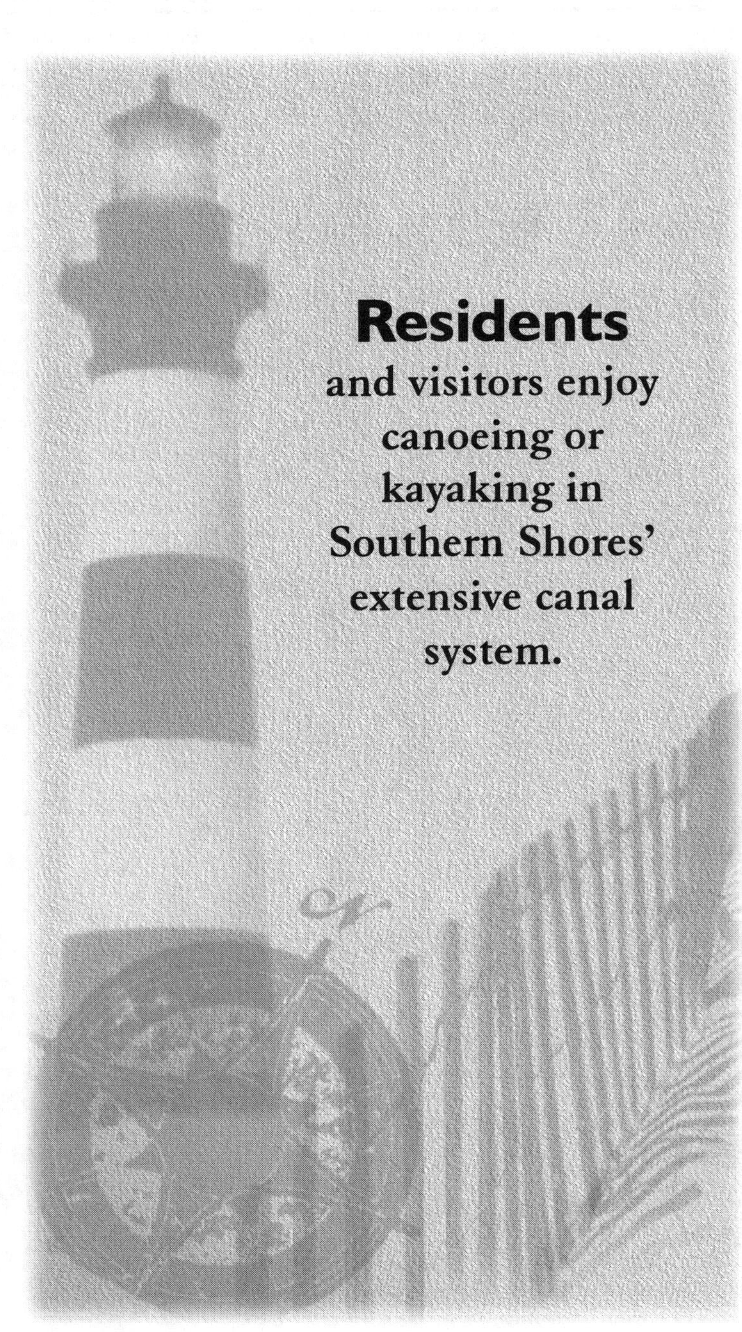
Residents
and visitors enjoy
canoeing or
kayaking in
Southern Shores'
extensive canal
system.

Inside Southern Shores

Stretching from sound to sea between Duck and Kitty Hawk, Southern Shores is interwoven with canals, maritime hardwood forests, dunes and private beaches. The small oceanside community consists of approximately 4 square miles and lies alongside N.C. 12 as it stretches along the northern Outer Banks. As you drive through the town along this winding, two-lane road, you'll see open skies, dunes with low scrub vegetation and vacation homes — old-style cottages intermittent with large, expensive beach homes. If you turn off the highway away from the ocean onto one of the side roads, the landscape changes dramatically. Here you'll find neighborhoods and subdivisions of year-round homes, green lawns, hardwood trees draped with Spanish moss, dogwoods and a sprawling golf course.

Southern Shores was the first planned community on the northern Outer Banks. The visionary Frank Stick, artist, developer, outdoorsman and self-trained ichthyologist, bought the land comprising Southern Shores back in 1947 for $30,000. Today it is worth more than $150 million.

Stick touched the Outer Banks like few have and was instrumental in protecting some of the area's most treasured lands. Stick helped secure much of Hatteras Island to become the first national seashore and proposed the establishment of a wildfowl refuge (now Pea Island National Wildlife Refuge). He worked for eight years developing the northern Outer Banks community of Southern Shores, and his careful development is evident throughout the town today. Stick had his hands full designing and building cottages and homes, supervising the platting of lots and the installation of roads. A master illustrator, who studied under the distinguished Howard Pyle, Stick later shared the task of developing the virgin land with his son, David. Much like a watercolor from the era in which Stick thrived, Southern Shores was developed to resemble a *Wind in the Willows* paradise.

Home to cardinals, finches, mocking birds, Canadian grosbeaks, woodpeckers, quails, raccoons, deer and squirrels, this idyllic place with seas of white dogwoods blooming in spring speaks to the Sticks' love and dedication for preserving the natural habitat. Perhaps no where else on the Outer Banks better illustrates the harmonious coexistence of human development and nature.

The 40 original families who inhabited Southern Shores formed the town's first civic association. Nearly 50 years later, the population has expanded to nearly 1,450 year-round residents. But the development still maintains its beauty. Residents enjoy canoeing or kayaking in the canal system designed by the younger Stick, a local historian and published author. Though not the painter his father was, David's artistic talent was in full swing when he created these panoramic lagoons that connect interior properties to Jean Guite Bay and

David Stick on Southern Shores

David Stick, Outer Banks historian, author and developer, and his father, Frank, were the driving forces in the development of Southern Shores. Consisting of 4 miles from ocean to sound, the land cost $30,000 back in 1947. The community today can be described as well thought out and environmentally gorgeous, threaded with canals and filled with wildlife and woods. Stick actually played in the wooded areas as a boy and later grew up to walk through every square inch of them to plot where canals would be placed.

Photo: Mary Ellen Riddle

David Stick

His father, a well-known artist and illustrator, developed the beach side of Southern Shores.

Stick had many challenges. He describes how he developed the wooded, swampy environment. It began with the sale of two lots, for a total of $5,000. Stick convinced the powers that be, including his father, to give him the money to experiment with developing the sound side and wooded area.

"That's the area I love most because of this experience as a kid, going up there so much. And the first thing that I did was to put in what is now the marina. And I came in and cut across the road and put in a little bridge, then came into a swamp and dug that out and ended up with an area that had eight lots in it. And I set the price at $1,500, a lot that would bring in $12,000. And that was the beginning of the sound side.

"The next thing I did was to move north and improve the lots that still had swamp. At that time you could dig out swamp and marsh. And I guess within not much more than a year, I had paved the road to the beach and paved the road north through where I established the sound side bathing beach.

"And so it was going, and we had dug the first of these lagoons — I called them, actually, canals, but lagoons seemed to be more appealing. They're all handmade; I mean, we dug them with drag lines.

"I came up with the idea of leaving an island out there in the middle, making this real pond out of it, this natural island, so I could dispose of a lot of the fill there. And it worked, and the next year I extended that," said Stick.

When the developers were getting ready to begin the initial stages of the overall development, Stick's father came up with the name Southern Shores, but not before seeking his son's opinion. Stick asked his father why he wanted to call a development on the northern Outer Banks "Southern Shores." His father said that the area would attract people from the North, and as the northern regions of the Outer Banks developed, Southern Shores would become the headquarters for the whole area.

"Well, he's about right when you consider what's happening in Duck and Corolla," Stick said.

Photo: Mike Booher

Come and find your place in the sand.

Currituck Sound. (See David Stick's oral history sidebar in this chapter.)

Comprised of mostly single-family homes, Southern Shores dwellings dot the land from the oceanfront to the sound. Oceanside structures include large modern houses, classic beach cottages and vintage flat-top cottages. The predominantly residential town is uncluttered by the commercial aspects of other Outer Banks areas, making it the perfect place for a relaxing vacation. The town's only retail establishment, a shopping center including a movie theater, a grocery store and shops, sits at the edge of Southern Shores, just east of the base of the Wright Memorial Bridge. However, the shops, restaurants and services of Kitty Hawk and Duck are only minutes away.

Many recreational opportunities enhance the Southern Shores experience. All of the town's beach accesses are private, available only to residents and vacationers staying in the area, affording every beachgoer enough elbow room to comfortably spread a blanket or throw a Frisbee. A soundside swimming and windsurfing area, Soundside Bathing Beach on N. Dogwood Trail, is a favorite spot for families because the shallow sound water is a safer place for children to swim than the ocean. There is a picnic area, and in summer, there are toilet facilities on site. Paved and unpaved bike trails meander through the town, and a private marina is available to residents and visitors staying in the area. The golf course at Duck Woods Country Club winds its way through a residential neighborhood of Southern Shores, offering outstanding play in a pristine setting among tall pines, dogwoods and other foliage. The 18-hole course is the oldest on the Outer Banks and accepts public play year round.

The town continues to be environmentally conscious as the first Outer Banks community to offer curbside recycling. The Southern Shores recycling center is behind the Volunteer Fire Department on S. Dogwood Trail.

Incorporated in 1979, Southern Shores is but a rock's skip from celebrating its 20th anniversary. While growth has occurred in the development over the last 49 years, the developers' spirit of conservation is felt with every bike ride, every sunset and every tour of the waterways that weave together flora and fauna.

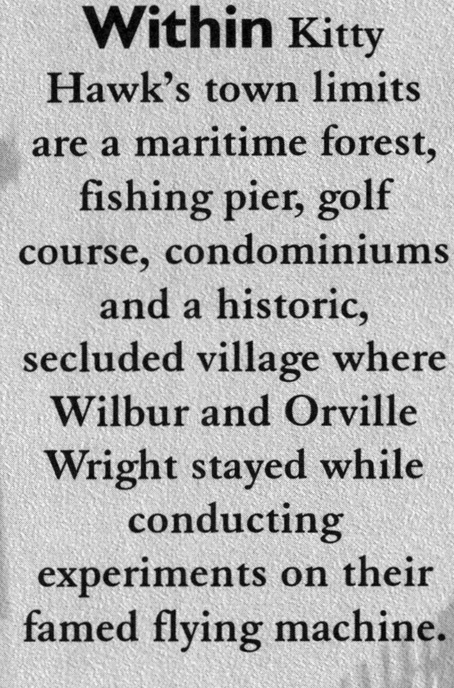

Within Kitty Hawk's town limits are a maritime forest, fishing pier, golf course, condominiums and a historic, secluded village where Wilbur and Orville Wright stayed while conducting experiments on their famed flying machine.

Inside
Kitty Hawk

If you're coming to the Outer Banks from Virginia, the first town you'll reach is Kitty Hawk. This beach municipality begins at the eastern end of the Wright Memorial Bridge over the Currituck Sound and stretches sound-to-sea for about 4 miles. Within its town limits are a maritime forest, fishing pier, golf course, condominiums and a historic, secluded village where Wilbur and Orville Wright stayed while conducting experiments on their famed flying machine.

Southern Shores forms the northern boundary of Kitty Hawk; Kill Devil Hills is to the south. Throughout all three towns, milepost markers give travelers hints about where they are. Most rental cottages, shops, restaurants, attractions and resorts in this area can be located by green milepost markers along U.S. 158 (locals call this the Bypass) and N.C. 12 (locals call this the Beach Road). The first milepost marker is in Kitty Hawk where the highway splits near the **Aycock Brown Welcome Center**.

Primarily a fishing and farming community from the late 18th through early 20th centuries, **Kitty Hawk Village** grew up along the wide bay that juts into the barrier islands along Albemarle Sound. By 1790, a builder, merchant, shoemaker, minister, planter and mariner all owned deeds to the sandy, sloping marshlands that now comprise Kitty Hawk. The community received additional goods from ships and ferries arriving from Elizabeth City and Norfolk.

In 1874, one of the Outer Banks' seven original Lifesaving Stations was built on the beach at Kitty Hawk. A U.S. Weather Bureau opened there the following year and remained in service until 1904. This weather station provided the Wright brothers with information about local wind patterns, which was the impetus for the Ohio bicycle shop owners to test their wings at Kill Devil Hill.

The first families of Kitty Hawk were named Twiford, Baum, Etheridge, Perry and Hill. These hearty folk were self-sufficient, building their own boats, fishing, farming and raising livestock on the open range. Many descendants of these early inhabitants still live on the west side of Kitty Hawk. A drive along winding Kitty Hawk Road, which begins just north of the 7-Eleven, will lead you to other streets with such names as Elijah Baum Road, Herbert Perry Road and Moore Shore Road. Along the latter is a monument that designates the spot where Orville and Wilbur Wright assembled their plane before successfully completing their historic flight a few miles away in 1903.

"I assure you, you will find a hospitable people when you come among us," Kitty Hawk Lifesaving Station Captain Billy Tate wrote to Wilbur Wright in 1900. Tate described the local terrain as "nearly any type of ground you could wish . . . a stretch of sandy land 1 mile by 5 with a bare hill in the center 80 feet high, not a tree or a bush anywhere to break the wind current." The winds, he wrote, were "always steady, generally from 10 to 20 miles velocity per hour. If you decide to try your machine here and come, I will take pleasure in doing all I can for your convenience and success and pleasure."

Wilbur arrived at Kitty Hawk in September of that year. He traveled by rail from Dayton, Ohio, to Elizabeth City, where he boarded *The Curlicue* bound for the Outer Banks. The boat trip took two days in hurricane winds. Wilbur stayed with the Tates until Orville arrived, then the two set up camp in Kitty Hawk Village.

Members of the Kitty Hawk Beach Lifesaving Station crew assisted the brothers with their early experiments. Even though many of the first flights were conducted near Kill Devil Hills, the Wright's first Outer Banks visit — and their letters carrying a Kitty Hawk postmark — etched this town's name in the annals of history around the world. Even today, many visitors think the Wright Brothers National Monument is in Kitty Hawk, instead of 3 miles south atop Kill Devil Hill.

The first post office in Kitty Hawk opened November 11, 1878. A second one was established in 1905 to serve the western section of the community. In 1993, the biggest post office facility on the Outer Banks was built on the eastern side of U.S. 158 in Kitty Hawk.

Residents of this town floated their own $7,000 bond in 1924 to build a school. Housed in a single building, the grammar and high school served fewer than 100 students until a Dare County high school consolidated Outer Banks children at a single facility in Manteo. Today, Kitty Hawk still has its own elementary school. Middle school students travel by bus to Kill Devil Hills to attend First Flight Middle School. And high school students still ride to Manteo, almost an hour's commute each way for some.

Unlike Nags Head, which has been a thriving summer resort since the before the Civil War, Kitty Hawk didn't become a vacation destination until about 65 years ago. A group of Elizabeth City businessmen bought 7 miles of beach north of **Kitty Hawk Village** in the late 1920s and formed the Wright Memorial Bridge Company. By 1930, they had built a 3-mile wooden span across the Currituck Sound from Point Harbor to the Outer Banks.

Now, travelers could finally arrive at the barrier island beaches by car from the mainland. Kitty Hawk land became popular — and a lot more pricey. Summer visitors streamed across the new bridge, paying $1 per car for the privilege.

With the advent of tourism, Kitty Hawk's development shifted from the protected soundside hammocks to the open, wind-swept beaches. Small wooden cottages sprung from behind dunes on the oceanfront. A general store offered locals and visitors almost everything they needed.

Some of the original beach houses still cling to the shifting sands of Kitty Hawk, but many others have long since succumbed to the waves, winds and weather. Since 1993, at least a half-dozen houses have been swept away by the tides in hurricanes and nor'easters. The Atlantic eats away the foundation first, then slurps up

Insiders' Tips

The old Kitty Hawk Village is at the western end of Kitty Hawk Road near the sound.

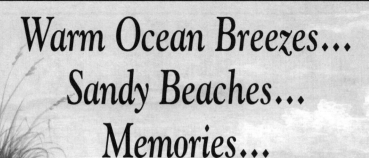

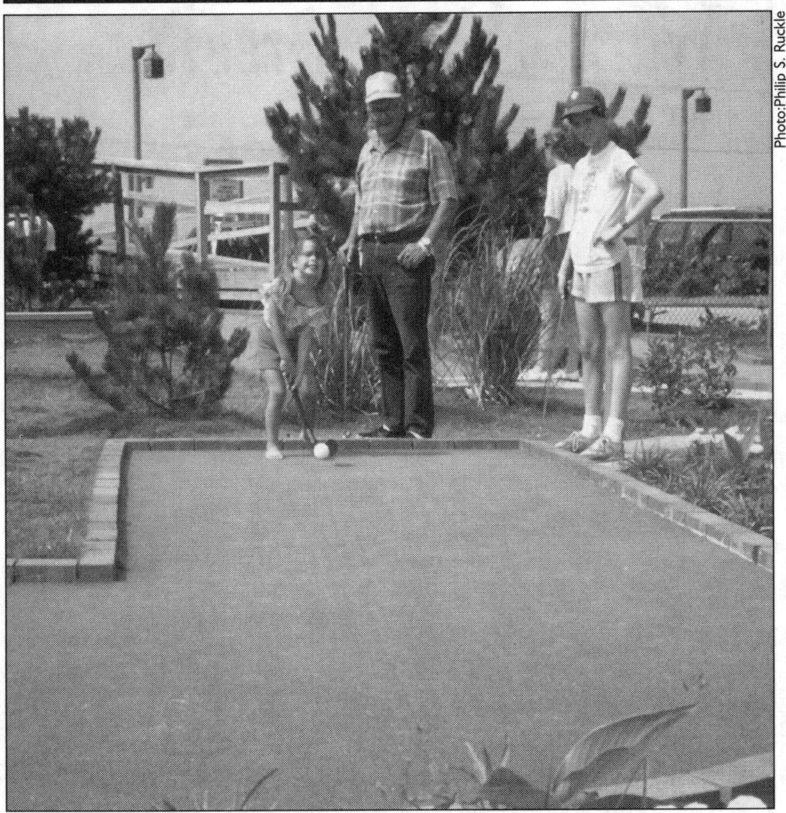

Putt-Putt golf is a game the whole family can enjoy.

the stairs, decks and porches. Finally, the entire structure just groans, collapses and floats out to sea.

The beaches of Kitty Hawk are among the narrowest on all of the barrier islands because of the severe erosion. In some places, houses on the west side of the Beach Road actually can boast ocean frontage because the building across the street recently washed away.

Even the original Kitty Hawk Lifesaving Station had to be jacked up and moved to a more protected site on the west side of the Beach Road to prevent tides from carrying it to a watery grave as well. The station is now a private residence, but travelers can still recognize the original Outer Banks gabled architecture of this historic structure.

In the western reaches of this community, the maritime forest of Kitty Hawk Woods winds for miles over tall ridges and black-water swamps. Here, primarily year-round residents make their homes on private plots and in newly subdivided developments. Some lots are a lot larger here than in other central beach communities. The twisting vines, dripping Spanish moss and abundant tall trees also offer a seclusion and shelter from the storms not found in the expansive, open oceanfront areas. On summer days, locals often ride horses around the shady lanes of old Kitty Hawk Village, reminiscent of days before bridges.

Although you'll find some businesses tucked back in the trees of Kitty Hawk Village, most of this town's commercial outposts are along the Bypass. The Beach Road boasts several restaurants, **Kitty Hawk Fishing Pier** — which has its own restaurant and tackle shop — some souvenir shops and lots of little motels and rental homes. At about milepost 4, **John's Drive-In** sells fresh dolphin, shrimp and trout boats — and the best milk shakes in the Western Hemisphere.

Regional Medical Center offers a full range of emergency and outpatient services on U.S. 158, next to the **Aycock Brown Welcome Center** at MP 1½. The Outer Banks' only **Wal-Mart** opened a couple of years ago in Shoreside Centre near the end of the Wright Memorial Bridge. There's also a **McDonald's, Subway** sandwich shop, **Seamark Foods** grocery store, **Radio Shack** and movie rental outlet at this new strip mall.

Tourism and related occupations employ nearly 2,000 year-round residents in Kitty Hawk. If you're headed for the beach, you'll find a public bathhouse at milepost 4½. The public is also welcome to use the Dare County boat launch at the end of Bob Perry Road, where locals and visitors can set sail after a hot summer day and watch the dolphins frolic in Kitty Hawk Bay.

From water-skiing to big bluefish blitzes, Kitty Hawk has history, recreation, fine dining, shopping, medical services, and natural beauty beyond compare.

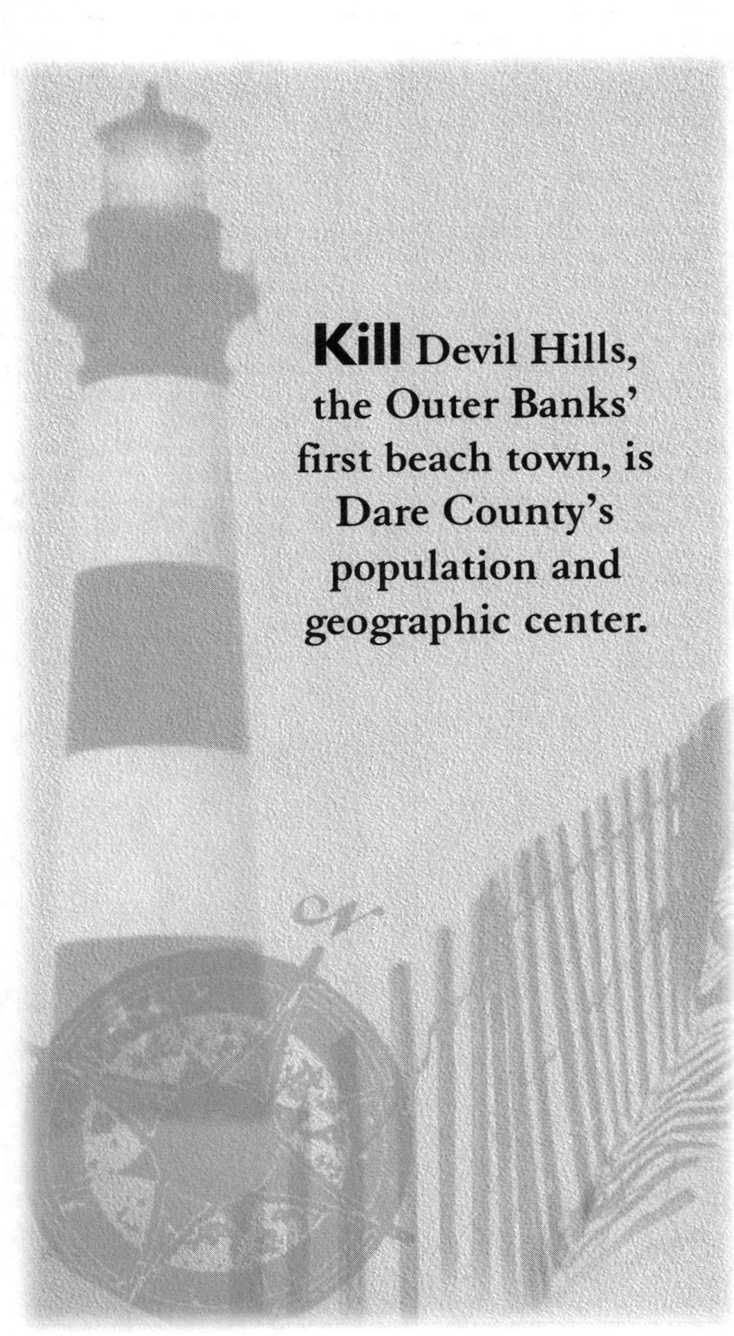

Kill Devil Hills, the Outer Banks' first beach town, is Dare County's population and geographic center.

Inside Kill Devil Hills

In the summer of 1952, U.S. Rep. Lindsay C. Warren, D-N.C., was vacationing at the Croatan Inn on the Outer Banks. One night, historians say, Warren met Kill Devil Hills Coast Guard Capt. William Lewark on the hotel's sprawling deck.

The men looked around them at the four dozen wooden beach boxes that had sprung from the sand over the past 20 years. And Warren warned of over-expansion. He told Lewark that his seaside village ought to be zoned.

He told the captain to create a town.

So Lewark drafted a petition, called on his neighbors and convinced 90 of the area's 93 voters to support incorporation. On March 6, 1953, the General Assembly officially recognized Kill Devil Hills as the first town on Outer Banks beaches.

But the new town almost died in infancy.

On May 4, 1955, the day that Emily Long Mustian, the town's first elected mayor, was scheduled to take office, the new town ceased to be a town. Fed up with taxes that had jumped to 30¢ from 10¢ per $100 of property value since incorporation, 37 citizens — more than 25 percent of the registered voters — had signed a petition to hold a referendum to "repeal the town charter." The referendum later passed by a vote of 76 to 70.

But Kill Devil Hills was reborn. On February 29, 1956, the North Carolina Supreme Court ruled that the petition by which the referendum had been conducted was invalid and reversed the repeal vote.

Today, the Outer Banks' first beach

Photo: Mary Ellen Riddle

Popular local artist Susan Vaughan immortalized her version of Kill Devil Hills on canvas.

The Wright Stuff

From in front of a tall, sandy hill that is now marked by a tall, trapezoidal national monument, Wilbur and Orville Wright completed the world's first powered airplane flight on December 17, 1903.

The brothers bunked in Kitty Hawk, at a merchant's home, when they arrived at the Outer Banks by steamship. But they set up a hangar and makeshift camp in the central portion of the barrier islands at what is now Kill Devil Hills. The National Park Service commemorates the site with a popular visitors center, tours, and a replica of the famed flying machine.

Bicycle shop owners from Dayton, Ohio, the Wright brothers first built bikes, then winged gliders and finally airplanes. When they began to track weather conditions to determine the best place to test their heavier-than-air machine, they found ideal conditions in Kitty Hawk. Constant winds and soft hills of sand met their requirements.

Responding to their inquisitive letters, Capt. Bill Tate of the Kitty Hawk Weather Station wrote to the Wrights encouraging them to come to the Outer Banks and try their machine. Tate promised to do everything possible to assure a successful venture in a convenient location among friendly people. He even offered his home as the brothers' temporary lodging.

Wilbur Wright arrived on the barren beaches September 13, 1900, after a dismal schooner trip from Elizabeth City. He set up camp near Capt. Tate's home in Kitty Hawk Village, about 4 miles north of Kill Devil Hills. Orville Wright arrived two weeks later, and the brothers began assembling their first glider.

First, they experimented with tie-lines on the contraption, as though they were flying a kite. Later, they carried the glider 4 miles to a 90-foot-high sand hill and made about a dozen glides off the summit, taking turns piloting the powerless plane. Their total time aloft was about 15 seconds.

By the fall of 1900, gliding season was over. Although their time in the air had been short, the Wrights had made some important observations. The lifting power of the wings was less than they had expected. But the wing warping system they had invented to enable them to turn the machine worked well. They left for Dayton, Ohio, resolving to return the following year.

In the summer of 1901, Wilbur and Orville completed their second glider. This model had 22-foot-wide wings and a 7-foot chord, with increased curvature to conform to Otto Lilienthal's advanced aerodynamic theories. The brothers arrived at Kill Devil Hill with their new glider on July 10 and put in a few days building a large shed to house it and drilling a well nearby.

Between July 27 and August 20, the Wrights made several dozen flights in the glider from atop the tall dune. These flights proved Lilienthal's figures inaccurate. And, after watching shore birds soar for several more days, the brothers decided their glider needed a vertical surface at the tail.

Climb the hill at the Wright Brothers Memorial to honor the dedication of Wilbur and Orville Wright.

They returned to Dayton that winter and continued in the bicycle business. They also built the first scientifically accurate wind tunnel to carry out their own calculations of wing curvature and lift. By September 19, 1902, the Wright brothers were back on the Outer Banks.

They brought a new glider with a tail and designed it with their added knowledge of aerodynamic principles and theories. During September and October, tests proved they were very near to unlocking the secret of flying. The glider soared, remaining aloft for more than a minute and going more than 600 feet.

When they added a movable rudder to the vertical tail, the basic idea of the airplane was finally complete.

Back in Dayton that winter, the Wrights built their own engine. A four-cylinder, aluminum-block gasoline motor that delivered between nine and 12 horsepower was completed according to specific calculation. Then they built a complete new plane.

No one had ever built propellers before, so the ingenious, industrious brothers designed and crafted a model for their new flying machine. The final result produced all the elements of today's aircraft: A 40-foot span of double wings with aileron control interacting with a movable rudder, the plane also had a gasoline-powered engine placed alongside the prone pilot on the lower wing. This pilot drove two counter-rotating pusher props. The launching system consisted of a rail down which the plane could roll before dropping off about ground level.

The brothers' fourth trip to Kill Devil Hills came in September 1903. They stayed busy building another shed, repaired a number of breakdowns and finally ground-tested their machine. By December 14, they were ready to fly.

Men from the local lifesaving station were called to come and help. The launch rail was set up near the top of the hill. Wilbur won a coin toss. The engine began to buzz. Then, with a couple dozen curious onlookers watching in amazement, the fabulous flying-machine slid down the rail. Wilbur enthusiastically brought the nose up too fast, stalled the plane and dropped it into the sand at the foot of the hill.

The brothers worked quickly to repair their aircraft. And on December 17, with cold winds blowing 21 miles per hour, the Wrights again pulled out their machine. The breezes were so strong, they decided to fly from a level track and set up the launching apparatus near their sheds.

At 10:35 AM, Orville climbed aboard and started the engine. The propellers began to turn. The machine started very slowly when Orville released the hold-down wire. Wilbur ran alongside the moving aircraft. The flier, in Orville's words, "lifted from the track just as it was entering on the fourth rail. Mr. Daniels took a picture just as it left the tracks. I found the control of the front rudder quite difficult on account of its being balanced too near the center and thus had a tendency to turn itself when started so that the rudder was turned too far on one side and then too far on the other. As a result, the machine would rise suddenly to about 10 feet and then as suddenly, on turning the rudder, tip towards the ground. A sudden drop, when out about 100 feet from the end of the tracks, ended the flight."

Orville had been in the air only 12 seconds.

At 11:20 AM that day, Wilbur piloted a second flight. The wind dropped for a time and the machine flew faster, going 175 feet in 12 seconds. Twenty minutes later, Orville piloted the plane for a distance of 200 feet in 15 seconds. A fourth flight began at noon, with Wilbur flying, and continued over 852 feet for 59 seconds.

The brothers planned to go for distance on the next flight, perhaps as far as the lifesaving station in Kitty Hawk. But a few minutes later, as the flier was sitting on the sand, a gust of wind struck. The machine rolled over and over. It was destroyed. The 1903 flying season was at an end.

That afternoon, after eating lunch and washing their dishes, the Wright brothers walked to the Kitty Hawk weather station, which had a telegraph connection. Orville sent this now famous message, announcing the first successful heavier-than-air flight — an accomplishment which would change the world: "Success Four Flights Thursday Morning. All Against Twenty-One Mile Wind. Started From Level With Engine Power Alone. Average Speed Through Air Thirty-One Miles. Longest 59 Seconds. Inform Press. Home Christmas. Orville Wright."

The next year, the Wright brothers shifted their experiments to a field near Dayton, extending their flights to 24 miles in 38 minutes by the end of 1905. Incredibly, these attempts attracted very little attention, even in Ohio. In 1908, Wilbur and Orville returned to Kill Devil Hills to test new aircraft, engines and control arrangements.

This re-enactment of the Wright brothers' historic flight was staged at Jockey's Ridge.

The press discovered the unprecedented experiments around this time, and history was recorded, marking a place for Kill Devil Hills as the birthplace of aviation.

town is Dare County's population and geographic center. And Kill Devil Hills continues to carry the highest property tax rate of all Dare County municipalities.

Located between Kitty Hawk and Nags Head, spanning the barrier island from sound to sea, Kill Devil Hills is the home of the world's first powered airplane flight — and the permanent residence of more than 4,500 people. Hundreds of thousands of tourists also visit this bustling beach town each summer. And activities from fishing on **Avalon Pier** to surfing at the First Street beach access abound.

Condominiums and franchise hotels dot the 5 miles of once-barren dunes. More than 41 miles of paved roads have replaced sandy pathways. Fast food signs have sprung up along the five-lane U.S. Highway 158, forming the Outer Banks' commercial hub.

Kill Devil Hills is the only town on the beach that has streetlights along the Bypass. And it's the only place on the Outer Banks where you can get just about everything you need within the municipal limits. The town has something for everyone, from thrift shops and a liquor store to loads of public beach and sound accesses. And it has more traffic lights than in any other area of the beach.

The newest schools on the Outer Banks — First Flight Elementary and First Flight Middle — are in Kill Devil Hills, off Colington Road, near the town hall and Outer Banks Chamber of Commerce. The Dare County Reverse Osmosis Water Treatment Plant produces most of the centrally supplied water for northern beach residents. A public library and the Thomas A. Baum Center for senior adult activities are in this midbeach town. Dare County satellite offices are here too, offering services from building permits to zoning information. And this town boasts the barrier islands' only **Kmart**.

Despite the trend toward bigger and better resort homes and amenities elsewhere on the Outer Banks, Kill Devil Hills remains attached to its place in history as a family-oriented beach for visitors and a centrally located town of moderately priced housing for the permanent population. Kite flying, sea kayaking, windsurfing, sunbathing, air flight tours, shopping, restaurants, motels, churches and schools continue to make this town a top choice for many — as it has been for more than half a century.

Unlike Nags Head, which has been a resort destination since the mid-1800s, Kill Devil Hills' population did not really begin to grow until new bridges were constructed from the mainland across the sounds in the early 1930s. Kitty Hawk and Nags Head both had docks for steamer ships bringing passengers from Elizabeth City and Norfolk. But Kill Devil Hills visitors primarily drove in over the bridges to the north or south after cars could more easily reach the Outer Banks.

The federal government built a lifesaving station in Kill Devil Hills in 1879. At the time Wilbur and Orville Wright arrived from Ohio to test their famed flying machine at the turn-of-the-century, the few permanent residents living along the barren central beaches were mainly lifesavers, fishermen and salvagers. Even on December 17, 1903, when the Wrights made their first historic flight above Kill Devil Hill, only a handful of local people watched in awe as the airplane finally soared under its own power (see the sidebar in this chapter).

Legends about how Kill Devil Hills got its name are as numerous as the sandy dunes that line this Outer Banks beach town. The name "Killdevil Hills" first appears on a map in 1808. "Kill Devil Hills" begins showing up on maps of the northern Outer Banks around 1814.

One popular account says the town was named after a Jamaican rum called Kill Devil that was described in historical accounts as "hot, hellish, terrible liquor." William Byrd, returning to Virginia after a 1728 trip to the barrier islands, reported drinking rum that was strong enough to kill the devil.

A far-fetched variation on the tale says a ship carrying a cargo of the caustic liquor wrecked offshore. A resident nicknamed Devil Ike volunteered to guard the rum. Not wanting to snitch on neighbors who stole the coveted cargo by tying ropes around crates and dragging them off with horses, Devil Ike explained that the devil had stolen the goods, but he had caught and killed the devil by the sand hills.

Other stories say sailors navigating the sound reported that the area's shallow waters were enough "to kill the devil to navigate." Even today, sailing around the shallow shoals is difficult for first-time visitors who don't know the waters. Local tackle shops and boat rental outfits supply good maps of Outer Banks waterways.

Kill Devil Hills got its own post office in 1938. In the mid-1950s, when Kill Devil Hills' founders began planning their incorporated community, they worked from a town hall on a site that now houses **Four Flags Restaurant** on the Beach Road. Newly elected officials struggled to provide fire and police protection while residents balked at climbing taxes.

Residents of neighboring communities began looking for similar services but worried that the municipality might expand to encompass them. A 1955 newspaper report said that Kill Devil Hills commissioners refused to let their "new" 1925 fire truck respond to a call in neighboring Nags Head because the blaze was outside town limits. Nags Head was incorporated six years later.

Developers, meanwhile, aimed at selling prime properties in the newly incorporated town of Kill Devil Hills. "The guys who developed Avalon — which probably was the Outer Banks's first subdivision — used to sit down at the end of

Colington: An Island of Contrasts

When Lewis Beasley was a boy, he could "lay on the day bed and tell you who went by from the sound of their car without even raisin' up."

Today, more than 11,000 motorists per day cruise the crooked, dead-end street in front of the fisherman's home.

Some are crabbers, their pickup trucks brimming with peeler pots. Others are retirees driving Cadillacs to an upscale cafe. Natives and newcomers, they are preserving the past of this eclectic Outer Banks island while paving the twisting road toward its future.

"It's a beautiful area. But it's all changing fast," said crabber Irvin Midgett, who moved to Colington from Hatteras Island 12 years ago. "It's still a great place to be a waterman, though."

In 1663, Colington Island became the first land in Carolina deeded to an individual. Exactly three centuries later, the county's first community with a guard gate sprang from its wooded waterfront. Despite recent development, the butterfly-shaped isle remains one of the last Outer Banks areas to evolve.

The east end of Colington Island lies a mile west of the Wright Brothers memorial, linked by a brand-new bridge over Colington Creek, which separates the island from Kill Devil Hills and the Dare County beaches. Colington's other three sides are surrounded by open water. Kitty Hawk Bay is to the north, Buzzard Bay to the south. And the mouths of four sounds — Currituck, Albemarle, Croatan and Roanoke — converge on the west side of this quiet community.

Two miles long and 2.5 miles wide, Colington is an island of contrasts. High, irregular dunes dip into deep, brackish swamplands. Thick groves of pine, dogwood, live oak, beech and holly drip Spanish moss over expanses of sandy shoreline. Thin creeks widen to unexpected harbors and bays.

Soft-shell crab holding pens line much of the shoreline, their bare light bulbs swinging above hand-hewn boards, looking like a Christmas display in July. Nearby, professionally stenciled placards hawk waterfront property in pricey new subdivisions. Trailers and campgrounds squat along reclaimed marshlands. Melon-colored mansions peer from steep, sandy cliffs. And a pawn shop offers "Cash in a Flash" a mile east of the Colington Harbour Yacht and Racquet Club.

"Most of the subdivisions began showing up on Colington in the late 1980s. But they're really only beginning to develop now," former Dare County Tax Administrator Jim Kelly said.

The most heavily traveled secondary road in North Carolina, Colington Road twists over two bridges, winds past family seafood shops and leads straight into the sunset. Transportation officials replaced both bridges and widened and repaired the road in 1995, so access is abundantly easier now.

Late 16th-century maps drawn by Capt. John White show but a bulge on Bodie Island's western shoulder where Colington Island ought to be. By the early 1600s, however, Colington was shown separately, a narrow stream between the bulge and the beach. Cartographers called the land Carlyle — or Carlile Island — after the stepson of a sailor who accompanied Sir Francis Drake to the Outer Banks in 1586. Seventy-seven years later, Colleton Island appeared on paper for the first time.

English Lords Proprietors granted Sir John Colleton (who happened to be one of the Proprietors) a tract of land "lyeing near the mouth of Chowane now Albemarle river (present Albemarle Sound) contayneing in lenkth 5 or 6 myles, in bredth about 2 or 3 myles."

Historian David Stick, a former resident of the island, said Colleton "made arrangements with Captain John Whittie to proceed to Carolina and establish a plantation there. Whittie arrived late in 1664 and entered at old Roanoke Inlet. . . . Land was cleared and what was undoubtedly the first Banks settlement was founded."

For the next three years, settlers struggled hard to make their American colony pay. They planted grapes to start a winery; sowed rows of tobacco between the arbors; harvested corn, vegetables and fruit; even raised cattle and horses in the island's lush maritime forest. Storms, however, plagued the plantation. In August of 1667, a hurricane destroyed the crops. Another hurricane swept buildings away two years later. A third followed in 1670.

Lancaster's 1679 "Map of the Albemarle Area" shows at least one identifiable house on Colington Island. Court documents recorded several years later include requests to restrain a man from killing cattle on Colington and a 1698 announcement of a cattle sale there. By 1750, Thomas Pendleton of Pasquotank County had acquired the entire island.

"About that time, a meandering creek which ran about halfway through the island was extended from Kitty Hawk Bay on the north to Roanoke Sound to the south," Stick wrote in his *Outer Banks of North Carolina*. "This combination creek and canal was known as the Dividing Creek, and by 1769 the two islands thus formed were known as Great Colenton and Little Colenton."

By the early 1800s, an extensive fishing community had sprung up on both halves of Colington's tree-lined shores. A post office was established in 1889. A one-room school opened shortly thereafter. A general store provided cloth, dry goods and canned food to about 80 residents. A weekly steamer delivered supplies from the mainland.

The 20th century brought tourists to Nags Head. But west of the Outer Banks, Colington remained isolated. Thick woods harbored deer, rabbit, squirrel, fox and raccoon. Muskrat, nutria and snakes roamed black water swamps. Flocks of waterfowl flew overhead. And most menfolk earned their living on the water — raking oysters, potting eels and netting at least a dozen species of fish and shellfish.

"We never had much money to spend. But always had somethin' to eat," said James L. "Junnie" Beasley Jr., whose sons, Lewis and Carson, help run the family fish company, **A & B Seafood** at the bend before the second bridge.

Views of the water from Colington offer a peaceful respite from everyday hustle and bustle.

These brothers sell fresh crabs almost all year, and they import some of the saltiest, most succulent oysters to be found on the Outer Banks.

Junnie Beasley was born in Colington and has worked on the water all his life. The island has altered around him. But he still fishes from the docks, which have been in his family for at least four generations. Seafood provided most of Beasley's meals growing up. For meat, his "daddy'd kill a couple hogs and salt 'em down or the guy'd come 'round in a horse cart takin' orders to kill a cow." Beasley's mother tended a vegetable garden.

In the fall, he and his brothers rowed across the Albemarle Sound to "dig 'taters" — extract the potatoes Currituck County farmers didn't find in their fields.

In winter months, Beasley remembers, New York fur buyers found their way to Colington Island's pristine habitat. Muskrat pelts brought $5 each. Sometimes the buyer would purchase snapping turtles too. Two community stores, one on each section of the island, provided whatever groceries couldn't be caught or grown.

One teacher served as janitor, bus driver and instructor in the four-grade school during the '40s.

"I pumped water for the pitcher we drank out of, cut wood for the stove. One year I even made all the kids' sandwiches every morning. But that was too much," said former Colington School mistress Irene Midgett.

Because the same families populated Colington over the centuries, many island natives are related. Fisherman Barney Midgett and his uncle shared the same name. So when the nephew started his own family, he added an "e" on the end to help the postmaster with mail sorting. Barney's wife, Zenora "Nornie," and their children still use the new spelling. Zenora Midgette married at 15. She said her husband crafted the Outer Banks' first wooden surfboard and occasionally took "outside" men on bass fishing trips around the island.

A "more than 70-year-old" Colington native, Zenora Midgette enjoyed "roasting sweet potatoes on the heater" as a child and said some of her fondest memories revolve around the old Methodist church, which is nestled in the road's most crooked curve.

Like many of her neighbors, Zenora Midgette didn't get electricity or running water until 1963. The island's 4-mile-long road had been completely paved by then. Sturdy bridges traversed Colington Creek and the mid-island canal. With easy transportation to the growing beach resort communities, there was no need for a separate school or post office. Those facilities had long since closed.

Outside developers were beginning to eye the untouched, overgrown forests of Colington and the island's easy access to the Outer Banks. In the early 1960s, a Washington, D.C., businessman bought 550 untouched acres on the northern edge of Colington Island. He outlined plans to build a single-family home community at the end of the road and called the project "The Lord Proprietors' Colony."

Financial troubles besieged the development, however, and by 1965 American Central Corporation of New York had purchased the property at a courthouse auction. The new developers renamed the island's first subdivision **Colington Harbour**.

To offer as many waterfront lots as possible, builders bulldozed much of the maritime forest. They dug canals throughout the new development to give boat owners direct deep-water access to Oregon Inlet and the Atlantic. They filled wetlands with the excess sand. They added a boat basin, marina and clubhouse to their plans.

While village homes are sprawled across Colington's hammocks in spacious disarray, Harbour homes were drawn in neat 50-foot by 150-foot grids. Homes in the gated community are close together, with common areas for a playground, Olympic-size swimming pools and tennis courts, the houses are of diverse architectural styles and sizes. Nearly 2,000 people live in Colington Harbour today — more than reside on the rest of the island — making it the largest private community in unincorporated Dare County. Hundreds of lots remain to be sold.

Other planned communities are springing up along the winding road.

"The prices back here are about a third of what they'd be between the highways at the beach and less than half of what they'd be west of the Bypass," said Colington Realty Agent Cristina Garey, who also lives in the Harbour. "Plus, you get away from the hustle and bustle of the strip back here. But you're right on the water."

In 1990, developers purchased Cozy Cove campground on the south end of Colington and drove hundreds of trailer owners out of the area.

Now, **Water's Edge** subdivision occupies the space. Restrictive covenants prevent property owners from building homes smaller than 1,200 square feet in that neighborhood. Architectural guidelines limit floor plans and designs.

Bay Cliff, **Swan View Shores** and the **Cliffs of Colington** are other new subdivisions with similar charters. Lots range from $20,000 to almost $100,000 each. Some contain spectacular acres of untouched cypress swamp. Dozens are beginning to host houses.

Hundreds of years ago, sand trails were etched along the island in haphazard paths to each family's homestead. So when the roadway was paved, it traced those trails. State Road 1217 follows the same route. Along its twisting curves and culverts, the island's past rides shot gun to its future.

The two-lane highway begins between classy **Colington Cafe** and classic **Blue Crab Tavern**. On the south side, a manicured lawn surrounds Range Rovers and sedans. On the north side, pool tables are the main drawing card at the island's only beer joint.

Farther west on the road are a fondue restaurant, **Zanzibar**, and a gourmet seafood eatery, **Bridges** — owned by the daughter of one of the area's biggest crab producers and specializing in fresh fish.

About 200 of the island's estimated 3,500 permanent inhabitants live in mobile homes. Others stay year round in campgrounds. But most own single family houses valued at $40,000 to $400,000.

The island has two convenience stores now, both run by the same family. **Billy's Seafood** at the foot of the first bridge sells fresh fish, beer and groceries. **TJ's Market** just outside Colington Harbour's guarded gate offers gasoline, propane, a deli, groceries and automotive supplies.

Five seafood dealers on the island buy crabs and commercial catches from local watermen.

A resident of the island for more than 60 years, Edith Beasley has watched most of the newcomers move into her once-isolated Colington community. She and her husband, Junnie, agree that the place isn't what it used to be. But they don't plan on ever leaving their island paradise.

"I liked it before a little better, mostly because there weren't a lot of traffic on the road," said Edith Beasley, whose trailer is on the north shoulder of the highway, next to her sons' A & B Seafood docks.

"I used to play hopscotch and jump rope out there with my young 'uns in the middle of that road. Now, I'm fixin' to get me a stoplight just so's I can back out my driveway."

(As appeared in The Virginian-Pilot)

the pier with card tables and beach umbrellas selling lots for $250 each," said former town commissioner Richard Baer, whose father bought the **Trading Post** store and the Kill Devil Hills post office in 1961. "They were affordable starter lots, and they sold pretty well."

Most of the property purchasers had their permanent homes in Hampton Roads. Today, those lots list at more than $25,000. But they're still some of the cheapest land in Dare County.

By the 1970s, business was booming in Kill Devil Hills — both with summer cottage rentals, motel traffic and year-round residents. The Outer Banks' first fast food restaurant, **McDonald's**, opened in 1978. The next year, **Pizza Hut** set up shop on a nearby Bypass lot. The rest of what locals call "French Fry Alley" developed in '79 and '80, said Raymond Sturza III, the town's planning director from 1982 to 1987.

"The '80s were a real explosive period for Kill Devil Hills," said Sturza, now head of planning for Dare County. "Condo-mania was sweeping the beaches. Developers were stacking modular high-rises along the ocean. And though they were trying to stimulate growth, commissioners had enacted a 35-foot building height moratorium because they were worried about looking like Virginia Beach."

To help handle the barrier islands' increasing water needs, Kill Devil Hills became home to the county's reverse-osmosis water-desalting plant in 1986.

The next year, commissioners financed streetlights for the town's 5 miles of highway, giving their municipality a special glow at night. By the end of the '80s, Kill Devil Hills workers had moved into a new complex on Veterans Drive, and the town had gotten its first large-scale shopping center. Complete with a full-size **Food Lion**, The Dare Centre completed the town's self-sufficiency in late 1989.

By the time the town turned 40 four years later, about 98 percent of Kill Devil Hills' private property already had been platted. Some residents began looking for ways to retain their small-town feeling while becoming increasingly citified. Others expressed amazement at the ways in which their community was developing: adding a new soccer field for children, creating adult recreation programs and welcoming new retail shops each summer.

"In 20 years, I think Kill Devil Hills will be close to the size of Elizabeth City," Baer said. "We're more developed than any other town down here. That's because we're the only town that seems to want to grow."

Inside Nags Head

Home of the Outer Banks' first resort, the community of Nags Head is south of Kill Devil Hills and north of Oregon Inlet. It stretches from the Atlantic Ocean to the Roanoke Sound and has remained a popular vacation destination for more than 150 years.

The booming summer scene was once anchored by cottages towering over the shallow sound, elaborate hotels facing the mainland and calm-water canoeing, crabbing and conversation. This relaxed style of soundside vacationing has long since been overrun with shifting sands and varying values.

People seem to prefer the powerful ocean to the tranquil tides today, and most visitors only see the sound when they're crossing it by bridge, or if they're boating or windsurfing. But for nearly a century, the sound was the place to see and be seen. The beach was merely a midday diversion, and Nags Head was the center of Outer Banks tourism.

In the early 1830s, a Perquimans County planter explored the then-deserted Outer Banks "with the view of finding a suitable place to build a summer residence where he and his family could escape the poisonous miasma vapors and the attendant fevers," wrote author and historian David Stick in *The Outer Banks of North Carolina*. "He explored the beach and the sound shore and picked his house site overlooking the latter, near the tallest of the sand hills."

The planter paid $100 for the 200 acres and built the first summer house on the Outer Banks in Nags Head.

In 1838, the Outer Banks' first hotel was built in Nags Head midway between the sound and the sea. A two-story structure, the grand guesthouse had accommodations for 200 travelers, an elaborate ballroom, a bowling alley, covered porches and a 5-foot-wide pier that extended from the hotel's front a half-mile into the sound.

The 1850 census showed that 576 people — including 30 slaves — lived year round in Nags Head, but hundreds more came each summer. By that time the soundside community had become a well-known watering hole for the families of mainland farmers, bankers and lawyers.

Elizabeth City doctor William Gaskins Pool was the first person to build a home on the seaside in 1866, according to a 19th-century journal kept by Outer Banks resident Edward R. Outlaw Jr. On September 14, 1866, Pool purchased 50 acres "at or near Nags Head, bordering

Insiders' Tips

To arrange a hiking or canoe tour of the Nags Head Woods Nature Conservancy Ecological Preserve, call 441-2525.

Photo: Mary Ellen Riddle

Nags Head beaches are just the spot for a "dig to China."

on the ocean, for $30" and constructed his one-story cottage 300 feet from the breakers.

"But over there by themselves, his family was very lonely," Outlaw writes in his book, *Old Nag's Head*.

Seeing that the Pools could survive beside the sea, more people began building their houses on the eastern edges of Nags Head. By the early 1900s, homeowners were erecting their cottages on logs so they could roll them back from encroaching tides. Some of the houses moved three or four times during residents' lifetimes. Along skinny strips of sand, after big storms, you can still see house movers jacking up rental homes and sliding them away from the sea.

Today, hotels, restaurants, piers, go-carts and rambling residences line Nags Head's oceanfront. Primarily private cottages remain secluded on the sound and along the quiet, exclusively residential community of South Nags Head. A Scottish links-style golf course beckons travelers to tee off on some of the area's most challenging fairways.

Nags Head became an incorporated town in 1961. As it did more than a century ago, this beach area continues to attract anglers and surfers, nature lovers and shoppers, families and fun-seeking adventurers.

A half-century ago, Newman's Shell Shop opened as the first store on the beach. Charter boat captains Sam and Omie Tillett opened a restaurant at Whalebone Junction more than 50 years ago to serve breakfast to their fishing parties. The one-story wooden eatery across from Jennette's Pier still bears their names — and still serves some of the best she-crab soup around.

Hang-gliding enthusiasts, both aspiring and experienced, come here from across the East Coast to soar from atop the Atlantic's tallest inland sand dune, Jockey's Ridge, and over dolphins leaping in the sound. Artists from all around display their work in a variety of mediums in shops and studios along Gallery Row. The Carolinian, one of the Outer Banks' oldest still-operating hotels, offers nightly comedy shows in a large downstairs nightclub throughout the summer.

The barrier islands' only amusement park, Dowdy's, has a Ferris wheel, bumper cars and merry-go-round near MP 11. The Outer Banks' only enclosed mall is on the Bypass at MP 17. A year-old bike path winds along the Beach Road from Whalebone Junction through South Nags Head.

And although the old Casino has long-since closed across from Jockey's Ridge, nightspots including Kelly's Tavern, George's Junction and others continue to offer live entertainment most summer nights.

Hotels and good restaurants abound in Nags Head. Rental cottages range from seedy to spectacular — in corre sponding price ranges. Nags Head has tennis courts, personal watercraft rental outfits, surf shops, movie theaters, miniature golf courses, in-line skate rental stores and even the area's only bowling alley.

Since it's centrally located on the Outer Banks, Nags Head is a favorite destination of people who want to take daytrips to Hatteras Island and Corolla. If you don't want to get in the car again once you've arrived at your vacation destination, you can get everything you want within walking distance of most Nags Head hotels and cottages.

Whether you're looking to escape the bustle of the beach by taking a quiet stroll through the Nature Conservancy's Nags Head Woods Ecological Preserve or dance the night away at a tropical tavern, this Outer Banks beach town remains one of the area's most popular resorts.

Buried in the waters on Roanoke Island are artifacts that hold hidden, centuries-old secrets. Many locals, archaeologists and scientists have combed the island for relics from the earliest English settlements, Native American culture and Civil War times.

Inside Roanoke Island

Despite its role as one of the most historic places in America, Roanoke Island — sandwiched between the Outer Banks and the North Carolina mainland as well as the Roanoke and Croatan sounds — is still not a household word. But just say the magic words "Lost Colony," and a memory stirs that was established, more than likely, from a meager paragraph in a grade-school history book. It's a scant description of one of the most profound New World adventures. But it's verbose in comparison to the single word "CROATOAN" that a member from the first colony of the New World carved in a Roanoke Island tree as a final gesture before the colony vanished without a trace from this treasured land.

Folks sometimes confuse our history with that of Jamestown, Virginia, where the first "successful" English colony thrived. The fact remains, however, that this island is the very place to which Sir Walter Raleigh dispatched an expedition of Englishmen who first stepped foot in the New World in 1584. Later, in 1587, John White led 120 men, women and children from Plymouth, England, to establish a colony here. On August 18, 1587, Virginia Dare was the first English child born in the New World. John White returned to England that year, and when he revisited the New World in 1590, the colonists had disappeared in a cloud of mystery.

Before the English first arrived on Roanoke Island in 1584, it was inhabited solely by Native Americans and flora and fauna. The waters of the nearby sounds, rivers and inlets were teeming with sea life. Thomas Hariot, an early naturalist, documented more than 111 species of birds in the late-16th century, which probably included the now-extinct Carolina paraquet and passenger pigeon.

Just gaze from the grand bridges that connect this tiny island to the rest of the world across sound to shore, and the history of the island comes alive. It's easy to imagine what it must have been like hundreds of years ago. Visions appear of Roanoke Island's early inhabitants paddling canoes through sounds and waterways. Colonists striking down reeds to forge a path seem to step through the marsh and trees. Listen as the rustling leaves call Croatan!

Buried in the waters on Roanoke Island are artifacts that hold hidden, cen-

Insiders' Tips

Two of the best desserts on Roanoke Island: cheesecake with chocolate or raspberry sauce at the Full Moon Cafe on the waterfront and the fresh chocolate-chip cannolis at Garden Pizzeria on U.S. Highway 64.

Photo: Mary Ellen Riddle

Roanoke Island is famous for its boat-building trade.

turies-old secrets. Many locals, archaeologists and scientists have combed the island for relics from the earliest English settlements, Native American culture and Civil War times. Old English coins, a powder horn, a vial of quicksilver, weapons, bottles, iron fragments, Native American pottery and arrowheads have been discovered here. Some of these remnants can be seen at Fort Raleigh National Historic Site on the north end of the island (see our Attractions chapter), while others found their way into personal collections. Even today, archaeologists search for clues to the bygone era.

Manteo, Wanchese and California

By the mid-19th century, islanders had established three main settlements on Roanoke Island, naming the town of Manteo and the village of Wanchese after two Native Americans who befriended the early English explorers. These settlements were once simply called the Upper End and the Lower End respectively. Former slaves formed a third settlement on the island and called it California.

Between Shallowbag Bay and Croatan Sound, south of the Dare County Regional Airport, California referred to land that stretched from Bowserstown Road to Burnside. At the turn of the century, the tract was bought by 11 black men and divided among them. Nobody is sure why the area was named California, but its history includes an account of children tacking a hand-painted sign to a tree in a fig orchard on the west side of the community, christening it such.

Today, California is home to most of Roanoke Island's African-American population, although the number of residents has dwindled since its inception. More than 75 years ago, almost 100 children attended the Roanoke School, a wooden two-story structure located across from where Cartwright Memorial Park now exists. Today's black population is about a third what it was in the mid-1860s when it rose to more than 3,000.

The isolation of the island may have helped blacks and whites weather the postwar civil rights conflict without mayhem. Skin color did not prevent neighbors from helping one another. Baskets

Dare Day

Every year on the first Saturday in June, Manteo celebrates Dare Day. Originally held as a kickoff to the Bicentennial, Dare Day is celebrating its 21st year in 1996. The festival features entertainment for everyone. National and local performers entertain audiences in front of the courthouse; local artists display art and crafts at booths on the waterfront; children enjoy pony rides, a moon walk and typical fair games; and vendors cook traditional treats and seaside delights for hungry revelers. We really dig the scrumptious soft-shell crab sandwiches, elephant ears and funnel cakes. The celebration ends with a street dance.

People from all walks of life mingle at the day-long event. Dare Day chairperson Linda Midgett reports that in a good year 8,000 to 10,000 people attend the festival. Since it's held before most tourists have arrived, we locals have this event pretty much to ourselves. But we welcome visitors with open arms. Waterfront businesses appreciate the crowd Dare Day draws, and they fling their doors open with spirit.

of fruits and vegetables were delivered to anyone in need — black or white.

Manteo became Dare County's seat in 1873 and was incorporated as a town in 1889. Islanders soon erected the first courthouse and established a post office. The white-columned brick courthouse that stands in downtown Manteo today was built in 1904 to replace the original wooden structure. The first private home was built on the Upper End in 1872. This Colonial-style dwelling became the Tranquil House, whose rooms would later entertain Thomas Edison, Orville and Wilbur Wright and Reginald Fessenden. The Tranquil House also did a tour of duty as a barracks during World War II. Today there's a new Tranquil House Inn, which operates as a bed and breakfast in downtown Manteo on the waterfront.

In the late 1800s Roanoke Island acted as a valuable port. Large boats from Old Dominion Streamline of Norfolk, Virginia, made daily stops on the southern end of the island at Skyco (located between Manteo and Wanchese), while Manteo's Shallowbag Bay was a busy port for smaller boats. In 1906, Shallowbag Bay was dredged, allowing access to larger boats such as the river steamer *Trenton*. For nearly 20 years, mail, freight and passengers arrived daily on this vessel.

As new infrastructure tied the island to other areas, Roanoke Island became less remote and things began to change. In 1928 the Washington Baum Bridge was completed, linking Roanoke Island to the Outer Banks beaches. Two years later the Wright Memorial Bridge was constructed to tie those beaches to Currituck from the north. New roads were built from Elizabeth City and Manteo, and as the automobile became more popular, boat usage declined somewhat.

Fire has ravaged the Manteo waterfront five times since 1920. All that was available to put the early fires out was an old-fashioned bucket brigade, with volunteers forming a line and handing buckets of water from one person to another. When the town was rebuilt in 1940 with bricks, adequate fire-fighting equipment was installed along with a modern water system.

An interesting place to read up on Manteo history is in *The Manteo Walking Tour*. A copy of the book can be picked up at the town hall on Sir Walter Raleigh Street. The town hall was once the site of Roanoke Island Academy where just one or two teachers taught grades 4 through 11 and the auditorium doubled as a movie house.

There are interesting old-time pictures in *The Manteo Walking Tour,* including a great photograph of the old Fearing's Soda Shop. The Fearings were eclectic entrepreneurs and the first to deliver bread and ice cream from Virginia to Roanoke Island. Unfortunately their shop burned down in 1981. But memories of sundaes and Coca-Colas remain ingrained in the minds of the locals.

Despite the passage of time, Roanoke Island's three original settlements still exist today, and it's believed that actual descendants of a Freed Man's Colony still reside on the island.

After Roanoke Island fell to Union troops on February 8, 1862, Union leaders had to decide what to do with the slaves from the former Confederate camp. Gen. Benjamin F. Butler at Fortress Monroe set a precedent by declaring slaves as contraband, successfully using the notion against the rebels. Word spread of this action, and black women and children began flocking to Union camps where they were allowed to settle peacefully. Once word reached the underground network of servants, abolitionists and free blacks, the number of "freedom seeking" folk migrating to Dare and Currituck counties increased.

Inhabitants of the colony worked as porters for the Union officers and soldiers, and as cooks, teamsters and woodcutters. The male refugees who worked as government employees were paid $10 a month plus ra-

Insiders' Tips

Lather up with bug repellent before you attend *The Lost Colony*!

tions and clothing. Women and children — who comprised an estimated 7,500 of the 10,000 free blacks on the island at that time — collected only $4 a month, including clothing and ration benefits.

In May, 1863, army chaplain Horace James was ordered to establish a colony of freed slaves on the island (see our History chapter for more information).

Manteo continues to be the hub for Dare County's business. From 1983 through 1987, major renovations took place in the town as part of America's Quadricentennial. Fifteen-hundred live oaks and crape myrtles were planted on the island's main corridor along Highway 64. Buildings and streets were restored, bringing new glory to the town.

On July 13, 1984, Manteo entertained Princess Anne of England, Gov. James B. Hunt Jr. of North Carolina and newsman Walter Cronkite as part of America's 400th Anniversary Celebration. A memorial stone on the waterfront commemorates this event.

Manteo does a good job reflecting its history. The *Elizabeth II*, which is berthed across the bay on the Manteo waterfront, reminds us of our English ancestors. Many of the town's streets are named after English and Native American figures who played a major role in the history of our island.

In Manteo proper on Budleigh Street, you'll find the 62-year-old Ye Olde Pioneer Theatre, the oldest family-operated movie theater in the United States (see our Attractions chapter). You can actually get a bag of popcorn here for 50¢, and that's after paying only $3 to get in. The owners greet you cheerfully every evening regardless of the crowd size or the weather. Some nights there are only about six people in the old relic. Owner and operator H.A. Creef only shows family films, so it's not unusual to see mom, dad and the kids out together on Friday nights.

Silent films, with Miss Pearl Baum Scharff playing along on the piano, were the first shows held at the Ye Olde Pioneer Theater. Miss Scharff added excitement and romance by tickling the ivories. The carbon-arc projectors in use today were first installed in 1947.

Wanchese, on the southern end of the island, has a more isolated feel than Manteo. For years the village has operated as a fishing port. As many as 50 fishing trawlers from up and down the East Coast use Wanchese Harbor, as do hundreds of smaller commercial and sportfishing boats. The village features several seafood companies that ship fish all over the country. One dealer alone reported packing 2.5 million pounds of a single species caught in a year's time. Boats fish North Carolina's offshore and inshore waters and also depart Wanchese Harbor to fish off New England in the winter. On the east side of the harbor is the state-owned Wanchese Seafood Industrial Park where seafood and marine-related industries exist (see our Attractions chapter). The park features boat-maintenance facilities, packaging plants, boat companies and state fisheries operations.

Many old seagoing vessels fill Wanchese Harbor, living out their last days in a place that decades of men have used as a regular point of departure.

Insiders' Tips

Local head boats offer scenic tours of Roanoke Sound and Wanchese Harbor.

Smelling the roses at the Elizabethan Gardens.

While time will always bring change in the fishing industry — change in species, seafood quantities, boat styles and government regulations — in Wanchese today, you can track living threads that were established long ago when men thrived in the industry and navigated solely by the stars. Still living today are at least three or four generations of fishermen, men and women alike, from families who have at one time or another called Wanchese home. The Tillets, the Baums and the Etheridges are just a few. Some have crossed over from commercial fishing to become sport fishermen, and many work as boat builders.

The village of Wanchese reflects a quieter, simpler life than its northern island neighbor. Drive the streets and you'll see wooden houses, built in some cases 80 to 100 years ago, that have been lovingly maintained. And in many backyards you still find boats in various sizes and states of repair, linking their owners with the ever-important sea.

Boat Building

Boat building is a major part of Roanoke Island living. From the small bateau put together in a backyard shed to the 72-foot yachts constructed at major boat-building operations, Manteo and Wanchese share in this rich heritage. Winters of the past would find many fishermen holed up in shops crafting juniper vessels that would take them farther from home than many had ever imagined. The Sharpie and the Shallowbag Shad Boat were designed and built in Manteo. Near where the Elizabeth II Boathouse is now located on the Manteo waterfront, George and Benjamin Creef operated the Manteo Machine Shop and Railways in the 19th century. The shop was built in 1884, and boats were hauled out of the water and serviced there. It was at this location that "Uncle Wash" Creef built the first shad boat, now documented as one of the most important fishing vessels of its time.

Boats are still built on Roanoke Island today — huge, sleek vessels painted in light hues and buffed to a sun-splintering shine. And each spring, these brand-new 50-foot-plus boats emerge from private building barns and are tugged slowly down the highway to Wanchese to be put in the water for the first time. On board the boat, the happy construction crew carefully lifts power lines as their vessel moves down the road, invariably delaying traffic. Smiles wreath the faces of the crew — after six to eight months of hammering, sanding and painting they are ready to christen the fruit of their labor. It is a tense time, too, for no one really relaxes until they see that the boat sits and moves "just right" in the water. You can hear the admirers exclaim "pretty work" as the vessel begins her maiden voyage. The crowd always includes family members and friends who wouldn't miss the celebration.

Attractions

At the heart of Roanoke Island, people have the desire to preserve a small-town feeling while moving forward into modern ways of making a living. While Roanoke Island's economy is based less on summer tourism than the beach communities', due in part to the year-round nature of the Manteo and Wanchese, many businesses still keep their fingers crossed all winter long that summer will bring a big "pay off." Fortunately we have a history we can market to summer visitors.

Historic hot spots fill Roanoke Island. The peaceful Elizabethan Gardens, built in honor of the colonists' homeplace, offer a splendid respite from hot beach activities. Stop in at Fort Raleigh while you're on the same grounds. This National Historic Site includes a restored colonial fort and visitors center. *The Lost Colony* outdoor drama is performed nearby in Waterside Theatre.

The *Elizabeth II,* docked in Manteo's Shallowbag Bay, is a fun spot for adults and kids alike. The large ship, a reproduction of a 16th-century sailing vessel,

Insiders' Tips

Check out the Elizabethan Gardens in the spring. The tulips are breathtaking!

Virginia Dare Remembered

Much speculation surrounds the disappearance of the Lost Colony, the group of English settlers who arrived in the New World in the 16th century. Before they vanished, documents show, a child was born — Virginia Dare — the first offspring of English parents to take her first breath on Roanoke Island, on August 18, 1587. Despite the fact that historians don't believe the child lived beyond her infancy, her fans haven't let go of her legacy.

Photo: Mary Ellen Riddle

This statue of Virginia Dare, much like its namesake, has a strange history.

In memory of the New World's first babe, the Virginia Dare Memorial Association constructed a "Virginia Dare" desk and chair out of white holly grown on Roanoke Island. The chair, which eventually was lost, was decorated with pine cones and branches. The desk featured five hand-carved panels made by Miss Kate Chesire of Tarboro in 1892. A white doe carved in the center panel represents the missing child. (As Native American legend has it, the infant was turned into a white doe and lived in the vicinity of Fort Raleigh; local bookstores carry accounts of this legend.) Other panels feature Sir Walter Raleigh's coat of arms, the island's native scuppernong grapevines and the pinnace that carried the first colonists to Roanoke Island. The year of Virginia Dare's birth and the year the desk was made are inscribed on it as well. This beautiful memorial to a lost innocence is in the office of the Director of the State Department of Archives and History in Raleigh.

Today, a statue of Virginia Dare as a young woman sits at the end of a path in the Elizabethan Gardens on Roanoke Island. The statue has a strange history. Shipped from Italy in 1860, it was lost when the boat hit sand off the coast of Spain. After two years on the bottom of the Atlantic, it was recovered and shipped to America. The statue eventually was willed to the State of North Carolina in 1926. But its adventures were not over. Evidently, its nudity embarrassed a local secretary who stored it for a time in a shed on Roanoke Island. A storm damaged the shed, and Mother Nature stole the Carrara marble statue again, dumping it into the sound. Following a second rescue, the statue was given a more fitting resting place in the Chapel Hill garden of *Lost Colony* playwright Paul Green. Green later donated the statue to the Elizabethan Gardens where it stands today — home at last.

was built right on the island. Guests get to climb on board and imagine what it was like to journey the high seas in such a ship. Some visitors on board the ship have even had a taste of fresh crab soup, but most declined the moldy biscuits that were traditional seagoing fare.

Preserved at the Outer Banks History Center on Ice Plant Island, also the home of the Elizabeth II Visitors Center, is a tomb of impressive Outer Banks history, maps and memorabilia. Stored in the archives are stacks of photographs that chronicle the island's people, traditions and growth through at least three centuries. The North Carolina Aquarium at Roanoke Island on Airport Road offers a glimpse of the awesome life that exists under sound and sea and in our salt marshes. The shark exhibit is fairly new, and you can also see some good nature flicks here. And next door is Dare County Regional Airport where small craft arrive and depart daily.

Back on Highway 64, you find the main branch of the Dare County Library. You might want to check out their North Carolina Reference Room if you're a history buff. And for overall Outer Banks information — maps, brochures and other local data — stop in at the Dare County Tourist Bureau, situated beside the 7-11 on Highway 64. The staff is friendly and helpful, and there's even a convenient drive-through window if it's too hard to get the kids and paraphernalia out of the car.

These are the obvious spots to visit (and you should see our Attractions chapter for details). To learn some of the more subtle history, we advise you to talk with some of our old-timers.

Living History

H.A. Creef is down at the Ye Olde Pioneer Theatre every night, and he's said to have a head full of information. Inscribed in the minds of our senior citizens is a body of knowledge that would give the Outer Banks History Center a run for its money. Listening to longtime locals, you'll learn of the days when islanders drove horses and buggies through the mud to catch a movie downtown and how it felt to venture offshore to fish for the first time. You'll hear tales of pregnant women who delivered their babies with the help of a midwife at the local doctor's house and spent time recuperating there.

Some of the most exciting tales revolve around *The Lost Colony*, the historic outdoor drama that outlines the story of the first English settlement and its disappearance. Pulitzer Prize-winning playwright Paul Green brought this production to Manteo in 1937, and it has played a major role in the lives of the local folk ever since. Generations of families grew up acting in the annual play. From representing the infant, Virginia Dare, to playing the role of Gov. John White or Chief Manteo, many a Roanoke Island resident nurtured a love of history through the play and a love of theater as a result. And Andy Griffith, who played Sir Walter Raleigh in his first acting stint, is now a Manteo resident.

Weather

Islanders always have great storm stories to tell. And all old-timers remember just how far up the road the water came during the worst of their days.

Storms make up a major part of life on Roanoke Island and the Outer Banks. Manteo and Wanchese have had their share of floods, especially in 1993 when a

March storm caused severe flooding. But all in all the island has been pretty lucky. Hurricane season is stressful whether a hurricane hits land or not, for islanders still have to play the waiting game. As a hurricane moves in, residents board windows, elevate furniture and gather prized possessions. It is always in your best interest to leave the island in the face of a hurricane. But most locals have traditionally stayed put. Fortunately each hurricane, more folks leave, especially after witnessing all the recent film footage of hurricanes past. After all, while in the case of hurricanes you might know which *way* the wind is going to blow, you're never *absolutely* sure how strong.

At times it's been necessary to helicopter remaining radio news folks and emergency personnel off the island when it became too dangerous to drive due to the rising water. Rescues by boat are not uncommon to Roanoke Island residents when a big storm has caused severe flooding. Local newscasters remember wading through waist-deep floods in Wanchese and watching as unfortunate rabbits and other fauna swirled helplessly by during Hurricane Gloria. Residents, with no thought to their own safety, moved the elderly to safer ground.

The spirit of the people is also evident when a lightning strike causes a bad marsh fire in Wanchese. For hours, volunteer fire fighters from all over the Outer Banks work to set up fire walls to stop the flames from spreading. Afterwards, Wanchese marshland, blackened from the fire, sprouts new growth. We mark time by the height of the bright green shoots rising against the charred black remains. It's eerie, yet beautiful.

Roanoke Islanders are nature lovers as a rule. One local newspaper editor wrote of his fondness for the marsh rabbits that line the roadside grasses for miles in the spring and summer. Red-winged black birds adorn the roadside scrub like ornaments. If you look in the marsh, just before entering Roanoke Island from the west, you can see turtles lined like soldiers on fallen logs. Ospreys fly overhead clutching dangling snakes or fish in their claws. And, of course, fish are always jumping in the surrounding waters. Boats of all sorts share the sounds and bays — crabbers, sailors, small fishing boats and big charter vessels pass each other on a daily basis. This is life on Roanoke Island.

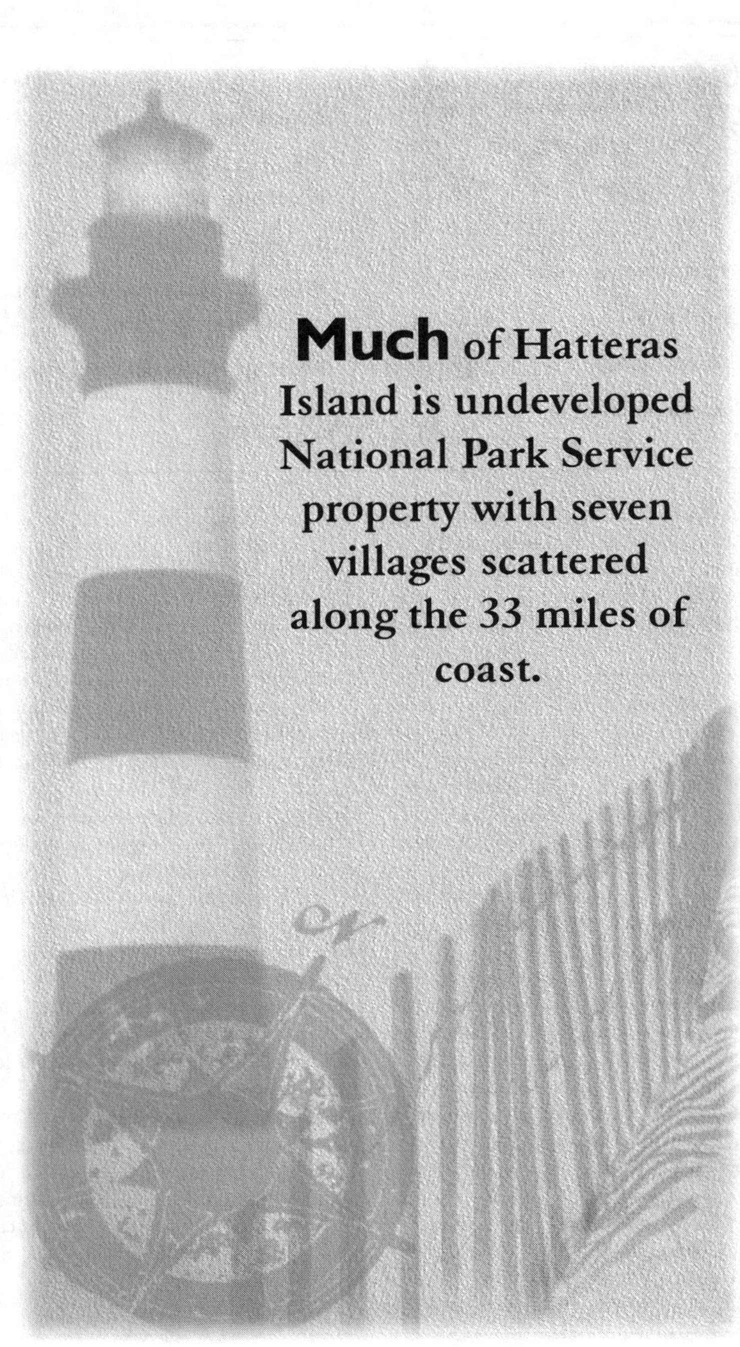
Much of Hatteras
Island is undeveloped
National Park Service
property with seven
villages scattered
along the 33 miles of
coast.

Inside Hatteras Island

The sea is a strong tonic that humans crave at the expense of safety, security and common sense. Nowhere is this desire more obvious than in the spirit of the people who live on the little stretch of sand that juts precariously out into the great Atlantic Ocean just off North Carolina's coast. On Hatteras Island, residents battle wind and sea while carving out lives in the shifting sand. In return they win solitude, beauty and a lot of power outages. Despite the hardships, there are few places in the United States as peaceful as Hatteras Island and few folk as resolute as these residents.

Much of Hatteras Island is undeveloped National Park Service property. But scattered along the 33 miles of coast are seven villages: Rodanthe, Waves, Salvo, Avon, Buxton, Frisco and Hatteras, hugging what is loosely termed "Highway 12," — a thin strip of blacktop often covered with sand and water. Hatteras' residents live and work between sea and sound supported mostly by tourism, fishing, teaching and government employment.

Storms play an ever-present role in the lives of Hatteras residents. While more and more people leave the area every year when hurricane warnings are announced, there are always those tenacious souls who refuse to leave. Like the moss that clings to briny rocks, they remain secured in their homes prepared and waiting for the storm to pass. And pass it does — sometimes it doesn't even strike — but usually there is ocean overwash and in the worst times, structural damage that causes financial hardship to the folks who depend on seasonal income.

It is not unusual for Highway 12, the only main road, to become impassable

Photo: Mary Ellen Riddle

The Cape Hatteras Point is a mecca for surf-casters who really get "into it" waist high!

Cape Hatteras Area

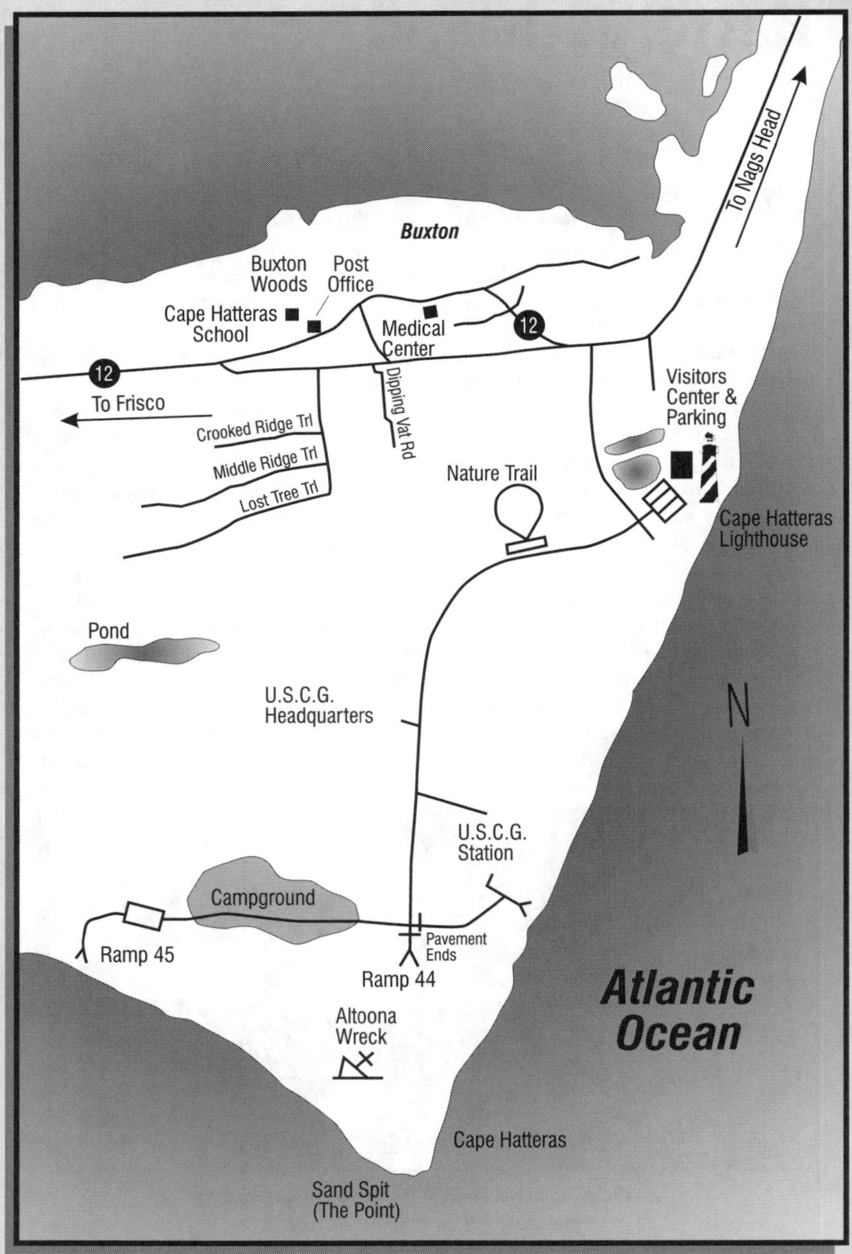

Buxton
Buxton Woods
Post Office
Cape Hatteras School
Medical Center
12
12
To Nags Head
To Frisco
Dipping Vat Rd
Crooked Ridge Trl
Middle Ridge Trl
Lost Tree Trl
Visitors Center & Parking
Nature Trail
Cape Hatteras Lighthouse
Pond
U.S.C.G. Headquarters
N
U.S.C.G. Station
Campground
Ramp 45
Pavement Ends
Ramp 44
Atlantic Ocean
Altoona Wreck
Cape Hatteras
Sand Spit (The Point)

Cape Hatteras Lighthouse

Since 1870, the Cape Hatteras Lighthouse has held its ground.

Hurricanes have devoured hundreds of homes and businesses near the spiral-striped tower. Waves have slashed rivers through storm-battered Buxton. Winds of more than 100 mph have felled forests of thick pine trees.

But throughout the tumultuous tides and battering gales, the lighthouse has clung fast to shifting sands.

Its octagonal brick base has been submerged in surging saltwater dozens of times. Its shoreline has eroded from 2,000 feet to a skinny strip of land less than 150 feet wide. But the floating foundations set just beneath the water table have kept the 208-foot tower erect.

Despite federal geological predictions that the beacon should have tumbled into the ocean by now, the nation's tallest lighthouse still beams hope to mariners attempting to traverse the Graveyard of the Atlantic.

But officials say the next severe storm could topple the tower.

About 14.5 feet of sand wash away from around its base every year. The U.S. Army Corps of Engineers recommended the lighthouse be moved a half-mile inland by 1994. National Park Service officials say there's no money for the $12 million project.

"We requested funds from our regional office. But it's not even currently under consideration at the congressional level," Cape Hatteras National Seashore assistant superintendent Mary Collier said. "It is one of our primary concerns for the park.

"The lighthouse's tenuous situation was really underscored in the fall of 1994 when Hurricane Gordon carved a niche through the sandbags surrounding it," Collier said. "We lost 30 feet of dune in one tide. Workers dumped truckloads of road rubble around the base. But all that was taken away during the next high tide.

"That storm caused the most critical erosion action around the lighthouse since the early '80s. If that hurricane had continued up the coast and come closer to us . . . who knows what might have happened to the lighthouse?"

The National Park Service, Collier said, is determined to move the lighthouse back from the beach to save it. Some historians balk at the plan, saying it would alter the tower's contextual significance. But Collier and hundreds of others believe the national monument is meaningful enough that it should be spared a watery grave.

"I've seen this light many, many times from sea. I was in the Merchant Marine during World War II. And this light marks a pathway around one of the roughest places in the world for ships," said Guy Carter, a retiree from Alabama who was visiting the Buxton beacon.

"Everyone who has traveled the Atlantic between the Panama Canal and Boston knows this light," Carter said, awed at seeing the structure up close for the first time. "It's such a landmark. The Cape Hatteras Lighthouse has been the salvation of many sailors this century.

"I think they should do all they can to save it."

Although it was built almost a quarter-mile from the sea, powerful ocean currents and almost annual storms have eaten away the beach area around the lighthouse's wide base ever since its initial construction.

Photo: Mike Booher

The Cape Hatteras Lighthouse is the tallest brick lighthouse in the country.

Waves washed around the tower by 1935, threatening to claim it with their tugging tides. The lighthouse keeper abandoned the beacon that year, replacing it with a skeleton steel structure a mile northwest. Dune construction work by the Civilian Conservation Corps and natural processes built the beach back up over the next decade.

On January 23, 1950, the Cape Hatteras Lighthouse again blinked its bright beam over the Atlantic.

Officials still struggled to keep the surrounding sand in place.

They pumped 312,000 cubic yards of sand from offshore onto the beach in 1966. Four years later, to stave off erosion, they built three sheetpile groins 650 feet apart in the ocean, stretching perpendicular to the shoreline around the lighthouse. Another 1.5 million cubic yards of sand — at a cost of almost $1 million — was added to the eroding beach by 1972.

Most of it washed away that same year.

"Without those groins," a 1992 federal study committee concluded, "the site of the lighthouse today would be at least 150 feet SEAWARD of the present shoreline."

Along with the added sand and offshore groins, thousands of sandbags were stacked along the lighthouse's base. Workers planted seagrass beneath the ocean, hoping it would hold some of the shoreline steady. But despite millions of tax dollars and dozens of individual projects, the beach continues to deteriorate.

During the early 1980s, erosion narrowed the shore east of the lighthouse so much that only 70 feet of sand remained between the tower and the tides. National Park Service officials and local historians began to worry about how long the black-and-white beacon could continue to cling to the changing coastline. They solicited ideas for long-term solutions to save the historic landmark.

"At that time, the preferred alternative was to build a seawall around the entire lighthouse," National Park Service Ranger Alex Fraser said, offering a sketch of a round, concrete wall obscuring the bottom third of the beacon and its base. "They thought they could allow the beach to erode elsewhere but save the sand around the tower. Waves would just wash out around it."

A 1982 National Park Service report said a seawall would have cost about $5.3 million at that time. "The lighthouse can be preserved," the study said. "But it could become an island in 50 to 100 years as beach erosion continues."

The report also analyzed other options for saving the structure, from sinking ships offshore to slow wave action to installing additional breakwaters or groins. Offshore breakwaters would cost taxpayers about $4.4 million, said the study. Beach nourishment — sand pumping — would total about $3 million initially, with an expense of $60 million for maintenance over the next 50 years.

Moving the lighthouse, the study said, would cost $5.9 million. The recommendation at the time was to slide it 3,000 feet inland on nine-foot-wide rails. That suggestion was not preferred, according to the study, because it would change the historic context of the lighthouse's location.

A separate report by the National Academy of Science, however, said that instead of trying to save the ever-eroding shoreline, the lighthouse should be moved.

In 1989, the National Park Service adopted the relocation proposal. Officials plan to lift the lighthouse on hydraulic jacks and place it on a rail system, similar to the one used in transporting the NASA space shuttles. They want to slide the tower about a half-mile southwest, away from the ocean.

An estimated $1.4 million in federal funds to plan for moving the lighthouse, however, has not been found.

Instead, Congress continues to dole out millions of dollars for Band-Aid solutions. After Hurricane Gordon crumbled one concrete-and-steel groin, burst through a row of sandbags and dunes and surrounded the beacon's base with a 15-foot-deep moat, crews laid 380 sandbags along the beach south and north of the lighthouse. The bags weigh three tons each and are piled more than 8 feet high in some places. The project cost $100,000.

A groin repair effort undertaken at the same time cost taxpayers $356,000. The U.S. Army Corps of Engineers also is building a fourth groin south of the existing ones. Design and construction for the new temporary stopgap measure are estimated at $1.5 million.

"That lighthouse has stood here for more than 125 years. They might as well just pay the money to move it and save it," said Gary Scott, a visitor who was vacationing on Hatteras Island with his teenage son. "You know, $12 million is nothing to the federal government these days."

History of the Cape Hatteras Lighthouse

A major shipping channel since the early 1700s, the ocean just off North Carolina's barrier islands also is extremely dangerous for seamen.

The Gulf Stream comes precariously close to shore near Cape Hatteras, pinching an inshore current about 10 miles off Buxton. That current forces southbound ships into a narrow passage around Diamond Shoals. The shoals are submerged fingers of sand that migrate with storms and tides.

Wreckage of more than 500 ships from many nations is scattered along the Outer Banks' treacherous shores.

In 1794, the U.S. Congress authorized construction of a permanent lighthouse at Cape Hatteras to help boat captains navigate around the sharp shoals. Nearly a decade passed before a single sperm whale oil lamp was illuminated from atop a 90-foot tower in October 1803. Its thin beam barely penetrated the dark nights.

Sea captains complained about the faint light's unreliability. In the mid-1850s, workers raised the tower to 150 feet and installed a more powerful lighting device: a first-order Fresnel lens. With prisms and magnifying glasses, the newly designed lens intensified a small oilwick flame into a powerful beacon.

Civil War soldiers embroiled the lighthouse in many battles, because its beams were necessary guideposts for ships from both sides. Union forces managed to save the tower during an 1861 skirmish. But retreating Confederates stole the Fresnel lens. The lighthouse was left dark — and badly damaged.

Congress appropriated $75,000 to reconstruct the Cape Hatteras structure in 1867. Recognizing the danger of encroaching erosion, a new lighthouse was built 600 feet north of the original tower. Its black and white spiraling bands — reminiscent of old-timey barber poles — helped sailors navigate the treacherous shoals in daylight.

The new beacon beamed forth the evening of December 16, 1870.

Towering 208 feet above the ocean — and still standing in the same spot, for now — it contains 268 spiraling stairs and more than a million bricks. It cost taxpayers more than $150,000. Its two rotating, 1,000-watt lamps reach about 20 miles offshore.

In clear weather, the Cape Hatteras light has been seen from 51 miles at sea. See our Attractions chapter for tour times and information.

Cape Hatteras Lighthouse Facts

- Is the nation's tallest lighthouse, 208 feet tall
- Built in 1870 for $150,000
- Has 268 spiraling stairs
- Stands 150 feet from the Atlantic in Buxton, on Hatteras Island
- Black and white spiral stripes are a daytime navigation aid
- Two 1,000-watt lamps, visible 20 miles offshore, blink every 7.5 seconds
- Each year, more than 150,000 people tour the tower
- The tower contains 1.25 million bricks
- Its base is octagonal, set on two layers of 6-foot by 12-foot yellow pine timbers that were placed crossways below the water table

(*As appeared in* The Virginian-Pilot)

Hatteras Island (South)

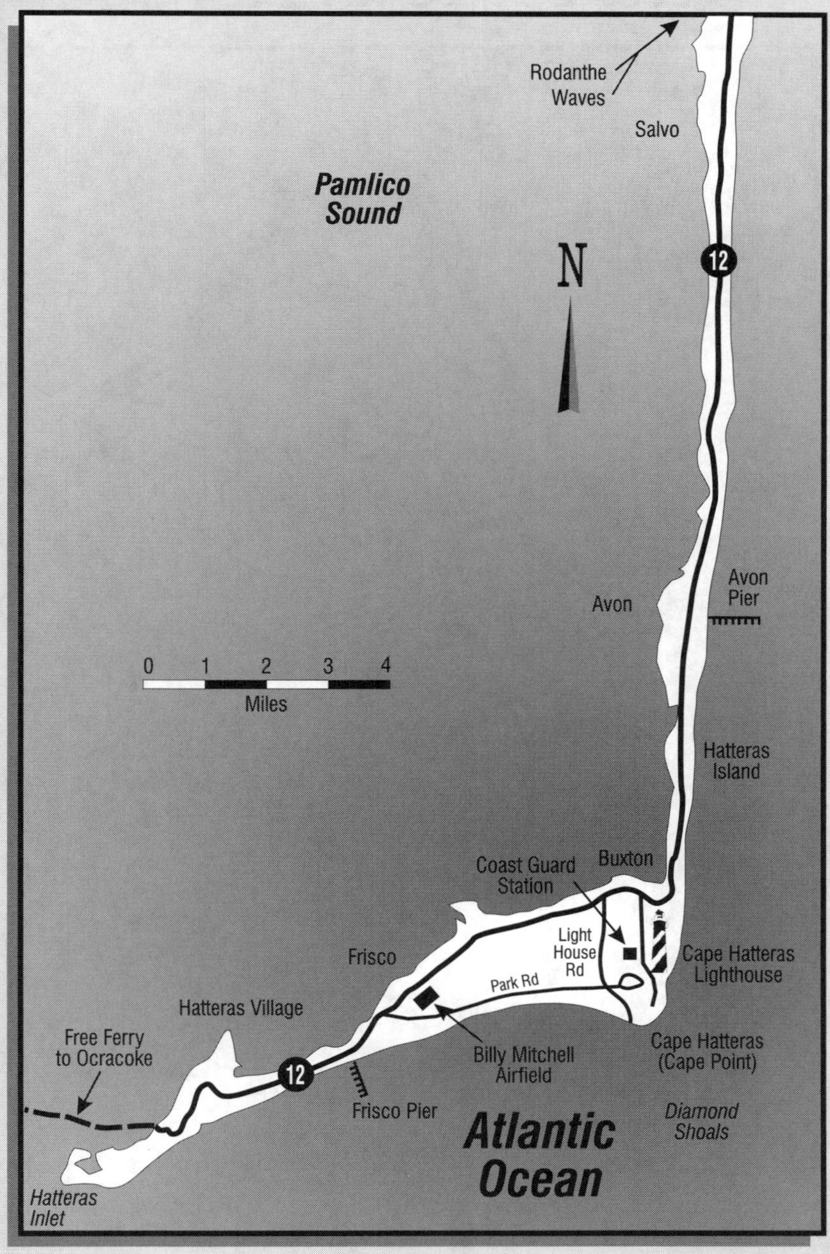

Rodanthe
Waves
Salvo
Pamlico Sound
N
12
Avon
Avon Pier
0 1 2 3 4
Miles
Hatteras Island
Buxton
Coast Guard Station
Light House Rd
Cape Hatteras Lighthouse
Frisco
Park Rd
Hatteras Village
Free Ferry to Ocracoke
12
Billy Mitchell Airfield
Cape Hatteras (Cape Point)
Frisco Pier
Diamond Shoals
Atlantic Ocean
Hatteras Inlet

Hatteras Village

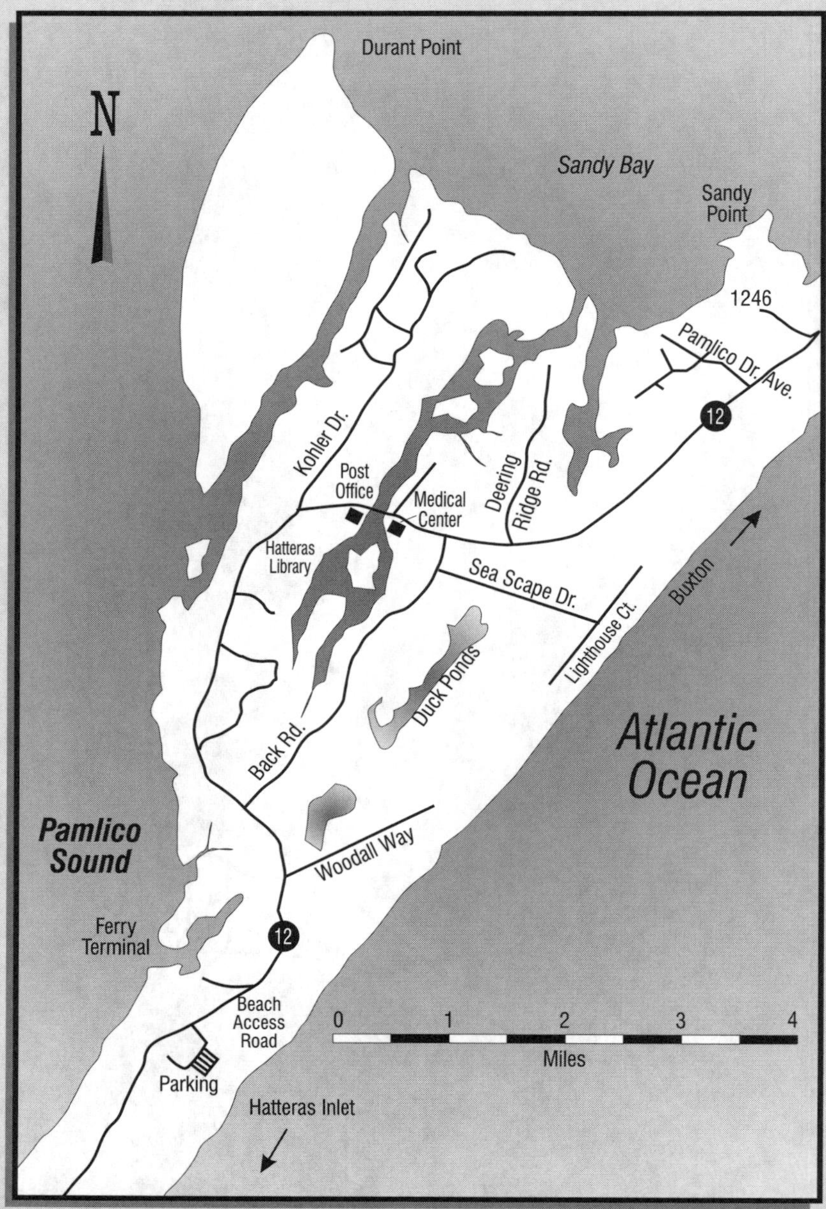

Durant Point
N
Sandy Bay
Sandy Point
1246
Pamlico Dr.
Ave.
12
Kohler Dr.
Post Office
Medical Center
Deering Ridge Rd.
Hatteras Library
Sea Scape Dr.
Buxton
Lighthouse Ct.
Duck Ponds
Back Rd.
Atlantic Ocean
Pamlico Sound
Woodall Way
Ferry Terminal
12
Beach Access Road
0 1 2 3 4
Miles
Parking
Hatteras Inlet

in some spots due to ocean overwash during or following a storm. A shore-hugging section of road near Rodanthe was recently moved inland to prevent further overwash in that area.

When the Herbert C. Bonner Bridge that spans Oregon Inlet was knocked and damaged by a unwieldy dredge during a storm in October 1990, islanders who worked on the mainland or needed to leave had to travel off the island by boat or ferry.

Families have continued to thrive on Hatteras Island despite the inconveniences and the need to rebuild homes, businesses, roads and bridges as high tides, nor'easters, tropical storms and hurricanes go about their usual and accepted business. Nature and earthlings are so entwined, it's hard to tell where the sea mist ends and the foggy breath of life begins.

Originally marked Cape S. John on 16th-century maps, Hatteras Island's history is filled with diverse tales of stalwart people. Thousands of years ago, Native Americans began settling here and called the place Croatan. These people, called the Hatteras Indians or Croatan, were part of the Carolina Algonkian culture, and stayed here nearly 800 years. Archaeologists believe as many as 7,000 Croatan might have lived on Hatteras Island.

Confederate forts were built on the island's tip and Civil War battles were fought at Hatteras Inlet and Chicamacomico in 1861. The island's treacherous shoals have claimed hundreds of vessels, and lifesaving teams, at one time riding horse-drawn carts through the sand, have saved thousands of lives off these shores. Tales are told of island-roving livestock gobbling up protective vegetation, of commercial fishermen harvesting whale oil, turtles, oysters, even seaweed and of pirates lurking in the surrounding waters. (See our History chapter and sidebar on Blackbeard in our Ocracoke chapter.)

Hatteras residents, who could only reach the outside world by boat until the Bonner Bridge was built to span Oregon Inlet in 1963, were a people so isolated that their speech today still maintains the direct flavor of their predecessors. The islanders were a self-sufficient people who appreciated the slow pace and absence of pressure from the modern world, yet they were ready to rush to sound or sea to rescue brethren and strangers alike from the churning waters.

During the early to mid-1800s a series of lighthouses were built to aid sailors. The current Cape Hatteras Lighthouse was completed in December of 1870. Rising 208 feet, it is the tallest brick lighthouse in North America and the tallest lighthouse in the world (see our sidebar in this chapter).

Within reach of the light shed by the tower are the treacherous and ever-changing Diamond Shoals, sandbars so feared that Alexander Hamilton dubbed the waters "The Graveyard of the Atlantic."

Earlier in the century when the original and shorter Cape Hatteras Lighthouse was operating, the light didn't stretch far enough offshore to reach the dangerous shoals. So in 1825 a lightship was anchored off the tip of Diamond Shoals, but it eventually broke loose and wrecked during a hurricane. Another lightship was sunk by a German submarine, and a third lightship remained intact until the late 1960s when it was replaced by a steel structure.

Over time more than a thousand ships have wrecked off the Hatteras Coast. Residents and lifesaving crews on Hatteras Island have saved thousands of sailors and seamen whose ships ran ashore these dangerous shoals. In 1874, the U.S. Life Saving Service was begun here. Seven stations were built at the points of greatest danger for oceangoing vessels. Each station was supervised by a keeper and six strong surfmen. One of these stations, the Chicamacomico Life Saving Station in Rodanthe, has been restored to its original condition. The Pea Island Life Saving Station, the only station to be manned entirely by African Americans, has been reduced to concrete remnants.

Today, modern equipment aids in navigation, and the Cape Hatteras Light still operates, but the power of the sea, shuffling weather patterns and changing inlets still cause captains to traverse the waters with care.

Moving through the ocean about 40 miles offshore are the Gulf Stream, a shelf current and the Deep Western Boundary Current that cross near the Continental Shelf's edge. The influence of this convergence is both positive and negative. These crossing currents spawned Diamond Shoals, creating the groundwork for danger while also supplying a rich habitat for game fish (see our Natural Wonders and Fishing chapters).

While boats fill the watery Graveyard of the Atlantic, a wide variety of species of fish travel up the Gulf Stream giving Hatteras a more positive name to sport: "The Billfish Capitol of the World." World-record fish have been caught both offshore Hatteras and in the surf at Hatteras Point where red drum come to feed.

Sea or land, Hatteras Island is home to incredible natural wonders. North of Rodanthe and just south of Oregon Inlet is the Pea Island National Wildlife Refuge, and a unique maritime forest lies farther south in Buxton. Much of the tip of Hatteras is lined with marinas where recreational charter boats take visitors to the inshore and offshore waters.

Despite the imposing tone Mother

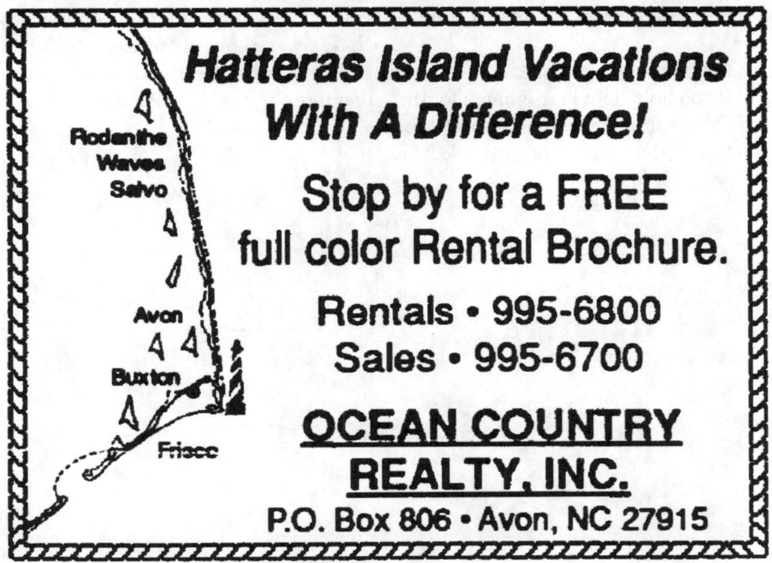

Nature can set on the island, visitors flock here annually to enjoy the beauty and isolation of the barrier island. Today there are enough restaurants and diversions within reach to entertain even the sophisticated vacationer. But more than likely, folks who come here want to relax Hatteras style, to do a little crabbing, clamming, fishing, beach walking, birdwatching or chatting with the old fishermen who relax at the docks.

On the other hand, many people flock here strictly for the recreational opportunities. Some of the best windsurfing and surfing in North America can be done in the waters along Hatteras Island. Windsurfing enthusiasts from all over the world flock to a point called Canadian Hole on the Pamlico Sound between Buxton and Avon. Canadian Hole, named in honor of the number of Canadians who windsurf there, is considered one of the three best spots in the United States to windsurf. Some days when the wind is up, hundreds of colorful sails can be seen zipping across the sound. Surfers from all over the East Coast come to Hatteras Island to surf the breaks off Rodanthe, Frisco and Cape Point, especially during strong nor'easters. Surfers look forward to hurricane season from June through November when big northern swells push the waves to 8 feet, sometimes higher.

There are three National Park Service campgrounds currently operating on Hatteras Island — at Oregon Inlet, Frisco and Cape Point — offering more laid-back and less expensive camping that the rest of the Outer Banks camping facilities. Several private campgrounds are also established in the communities (see our Camping chapter).

More often than not it seems that the children of Hatteras' old-timers return to carry on family traditions. This may be why the flavor of the area has not changed too drastically over the years. And most people who move here are looking for the atmosphere the island presents, the domination of nature coupled with the feel of a small community.

The wind chases some folks away. But if you hold tight long enough for the sand to get in your shoes and the salt in your hair, the sunsets begin to seduce you. The wind roars loud enough to chase away thoughts of city life. Then she'll gently rock you to sleep in the arm that juts out into the great Atlantic.

Inside Ocracoke Island

Between 600 and 700 people live year round on a little strip of land south of Hatteras Inlet called Ocracoke. Many years ago, word got out about just how pretty this little island is, and vacationers have flocked there during the warm months ever since. Tourism and traffic have changed the pace of this traditional fishing village, but the natives have managed to accommodate the influx of visitors and still maintain the integrity of their island.

To pinpoint what makes Ocracoke Island so special is at once easy and difficult. It's beautiful, off the beaten track and much of it is protected as a National Seashore and therefore undeveloped. There's so much mystery and history hidden in this land and soaked in the people that it's hard to find words to express that which is almost vaporous. To understand this idyllic place you must go and breathe the salty air that has filled the lungs of its inhabitants and visitors for centuries.

Access to Ocracoke Island is limited to sea and air. A free 45-minute ferry ride across the waters of Pamlico Sound transports islanders and visitors to the north end of Ocracoke from Hatteras Island. Once you hit land it's a 12-mile drive past undeveloped marshlands and dunes to the village. Two toll ferries connect the island with the mainland. The Cedar Island and Swansboro ferries, each a two-and-a-half-hour ride, arrive and depart from the heart of downtown Ocracoke on the southern end of the island. (See our Getting Around chapter.) A small airfield allows private planes to land near the heart of the island.

Ocracoke is a narrow strip of sand geographically much like the other Outer Banks islands. At its widest the 16-mile-long island is only about 2 miles across, narrowing in some spots to a half-mile where sound and sea are both visible from the two-lane road. After disembarking from the Hatteras ferry, you are released onto N.C. 12 toward the village. Sea oats and dunes line the left side of the road. On the right, marshland grasses, sometimes filled with munching marsh rabbits and other wildlife, and exquisite creeks meander toward the sound. Occasionally you'll see some old fishing skiffs tied up on the creeks, giving you the first hint of human life on Ocracoke Island.

On the oceanside about halfway to the village, you'll see tents and camping trailers dotting the dunes. This popular National Park Service campground is

Insiders' Tips

Bring your binoculars for the ferry ride from Hatteras to Ocracoke.

Ocracoke Village

Ocracoke Island

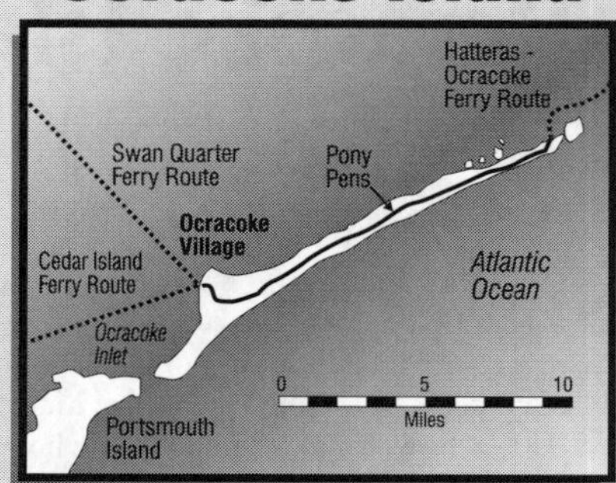

N

Northern Pond

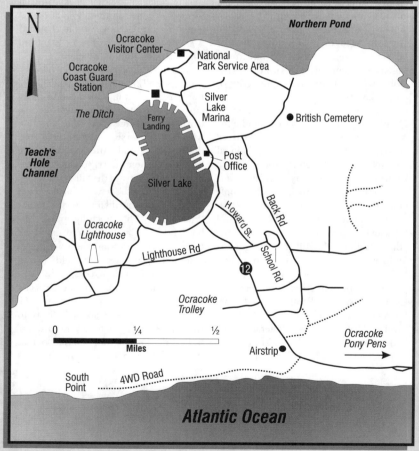

Ocracoke Visitor Center

National Park Service Area

Ocracoke Coast Guard Station

Silver Lake Marina

The Ditch

Ferry Landing

British Cemetery

Teach's Hole Channel

Post Office

Silver Lake

Back Rd

Howard St.

Ocracoke Lighthouse

School Rd

Lighthouse Rd

12

Ocracoke Trolley

0 ¼ ½

Miles

Ocracoke Pony Pens

Airstrip

South Point

4WD Road

Atlantic Ocean

Blackbeard's Booty

On clear nights, locals claim, Blackbeard's body swims slowly around Silver Lake, searching for its skull.

It was off Ocracoke Island, after all, that the 18th century's most infamous pirate finally fell. Five pistol shots and 20 stab wounds ended Blackbeard's short — but profitable — reign over the high seas. English Royal Navy Lt. Robert Maynard brought the pirate's head back to Virginia on a bowsprit.

But no one ever found the pirate's treasure.

Born in 1680 to a wealthy family in Bristol, England, Edward Teach (or Drummond, as some historians assert) was well-educated and of striking stature. He stood more than 6 feet tall — a head above most of his contemporaries — and was extremely muscular. A thick, black beard that often was tied with red ribbons grew from just beneath his eyes to well below his waist.

In the early 1700s, Teach joined a group of Jamaica-bound sailors who were fighting Queen Anne's War against France. He was hired as a privateer — a sailor whom the government sanctioned to rob ships from enemy countries. Back on shore, privateers shared their stolen goods with the monarch.

But Teach embraced the plundering lifestyle as a full-time career. Three years after the war ended, he apprenticed himself to Capt. Benjamin Hornigold — a notorious pirate of the times. Blackbeard soon stole a sloop for himself, however, and began his own empire.

Securing a 70-sailor crew, he mounted six cannon on his single ship. Less than two years later, when he moved operations to North Carolina, Teach had four vessels and 400 pirates in his command. At least 25 ships already had succumbed to his sword and pistol.

"A lot of piracy, at the time, was image," said George Roberson, owner of an Ocracoke pirate gift shop and the island's only Blackbeard museum. "They liked being fierce. But they liked being feared even more."

Teach cultivated his evil image — already, an awe-inspiring sight. Before waging battle on a passing ship, he lit slow-burning cannon wicks beneath his broad-brimmed hat. Smoke billowed around his wizened visage, obscuring fierce features. But captains quickly learned to recognize and fear the long, black beard. He dressed all in black, too: a floor-length cape, tall boots, and, of course, a black hat.

Potential victims weren't the only people who cowered from Blackbeard. His crew often feared for their lives. One night the pirate captain led some of his sailors below deck and locked them in a hold. "Come," he reportedly said. "Let us make a hell of our own and try how long we can bear it." Closing the hatches, Blackbeard lit pots full of sulphur and waited for choking fumes to fill the close, dark space. The sailors soon cried for fresh air. Triumphantly, their captain threw open the hatches. By lasting the longest, Blackbeard had beaten his men.

Another time, according to legend, Teach invited two of his top underlings into his cabin to drink. After several draughts of rum — the pirate's favorite beverage — he blew out the lantern. One crewman crept away in the dark. The other heard a pistol cock.

Blackbeard shot his first mate in the knee cap, leaving the man with a permanent limp. "When other crew members asked the captain why he would intentionally injure a friend," Hugh F. Rankin writes in *Pirates of North Carolina*, "Blackbeard explained that if he didn't shoot one or two of them now and then, they'd forget who he was."

Less than a year after arriving in Carolina waters, Blackbeard decided he had amassed enough loot to retire. He sailed to Ocracoke Inlet, left his schooner anchored in a channel now called Teach's Hole, and took a smaller sloop inland to Bath. There was no permanent settlement on Ocracoke then. Just a few small squatters' shacks dotted the marshy clam flats. But in Bath, a colonial government was growing. Trade ships sailed from overseas, bringing foreign goods. So Blackbeard moved to Bath and lived comfortably on land. There, North Carolina Gov. Charles Eden performed a marriage ceremony for Teach and his 16-year-old bride. Some say she was the pirate captain's 14th wife. She must have had some unusual power over Teach, however, because she convinced her new husband to take an oath to abandon plundering and settle down. Blackbeard did — for six months.

Soon, he began waylaying ships along the Carolina coast again, even raiding some small vessels in the shallow sounds. For victory parties, he and his pirate crew holed up on Ocracoke for week-long drinking binges at the beach. They stole barrels of rum from passing boats when their own supply ran dry.

Gov. Eden caught Blackbeard once and charged him and his crew with piracy. But the pirates were found not guilty for lack of witnesses. So they sailed back to sea.

Blackbeard shared his booty with his governor as he had with his queen, so Eden remained in the pirate's pocket.

Fearful that Teach would take over isolated Ocracoke — and weary of their own leader's liaison with the pirate — North Carolina colonists called Virginia Gov. Alexander Spotswood for help. Spotswood had campaigned to rid the colonies of all hindrances to commerce. The people's plea convinced him to make Blackbeard the focus of those efforts.

Shortly after dark on November 21, 1718, English Navy Lt. Robert Maynard stole into Ocracoke Inlet with two ships Spotswood had commissioned. Blackbeard's sloop, *Adventure*, was anchored in open water. Maynard attacked at daybreak. The two crews exchanged shots. Blackbeard's pirates boarded the British ship. At least 18 men were killed in the ensuing battle.

"Blood gushing from the neck wound and from Maynard's early pistol shot, Blackbeard was struck again and then again, five times in all," historian David Stick writes in *The Outer Banks of North Carolina*. "He was hacked and slit and cut by sword thrusts until his body was covered with gashes. Yet he still stood his ground — and his men with him. He stepped back to cock a pistol, half raised it, then slumped forward and crumpled to the deck. The rest of the pirates, observing the death of their leader, jumped overboard into the shallow water — then quickly surrendered."

Ocracoke's golden age of piracy had ended, but Blackbeard's ghost — like his legend — lives on.

Today, Ocracoke Island is filled with the pirate's fearsome face. Two shops carry almost exclusively pirate goods and souvenirs. A waterfront pub at Silver Lake is dubbed the Jolly Roger. A 57-foot gaff-rigged schooner offers evening cruises under a skull and crossbones flag. A museum has educational Blackbeard displays sought out by more than 15,000 tourists each summer.

Blackbeard's Lodge includes 37 rooms and efficiencies, a bigger-than-life pirate grinning sideways from a sign on the roof, and a front desk shaped like the bow of a ship — and stencilled with the name of Teach's sloop, *Adventure*.

"I think Blackbeard has always been a part of Ocracoke," said lodge owner Barbara Martin, who has hung pistols and pirate flags in most of the guest rooms. "He's definitely part of this place today. People want to learn about Blackbeard. He really brings a lot of people down here to this island."

On summer afternoons, Martin said, her son and his friends play pirates instead of cowboys and Indians. The boys use homemade maps to scour the island for buried treasure. For Although Capt. Maynard carried Blackbeard's head away, he never got the gold.

open from late spring to early fall and requires advance reservations.

On the eastern flyway of migrating land and water birds, Ocracoke is a birder's paradise with brown pelicans flying in formation over the waves, sandpipers leaving thin footprints in the sand with their tenuous steps, herons gracing the salt marsh and warblers, grosbeaks, cardinals and willets dotting the trees.

Famous for its legendary wild ponies, Ocracoke has 180 fenced-in acres set aside for the small herd to roam, and visitors to the island can see a group of them at a special lookout midway down N.C. 12. The National Park Service rotates four ponies at a time from the range to a pen to let folks get a close-up view. Legend says that these wild ponies are descendants of shipwrecked horses that arrived with Spanish explorers on the island in the 16th century. Scientific research has been done to document their Spanish ancestry, but historians continue to debate how they got to the island.

Islanders once used the good-natured beasts for horse patrols along the beach and to haul rescue apparatus. Boy Scout troops mounted the horses in the mid-1950s, and during an annual Fourth of July event the wild ponies were gathered up, branded and released. With the con-

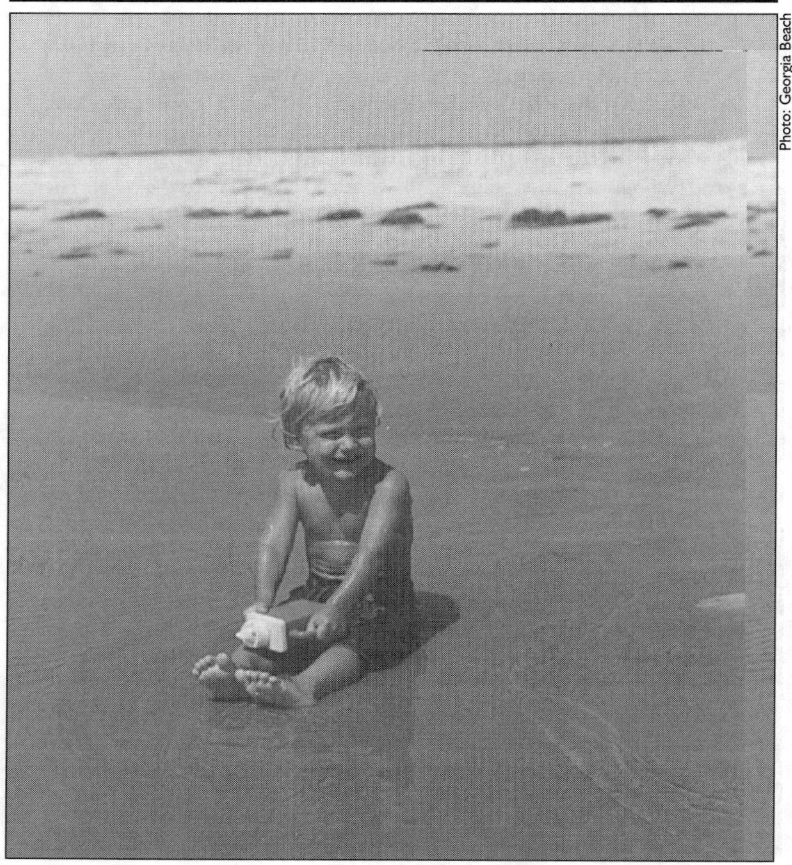

Photo: Georgia Beach

Cooling down on the isolated beach at Portsmouth Island.

struction of N.C. 12 on the island in 1959 and the arrival of more and more visitors, the National Park Service decided to pen the ponies, putting an end to their wild and wandering days. Today the National Park Service tends to the herd, protecting them from traffic behind 3 miles of fence. What was once a herd of hundreds of wild ponies roaming the island is now a modest group of 26.

In stark contrast to the changes on the island is a solid structure that has stood steady in Ocracoke village for 173 years. The Ocracoke Lighthouse, which has guided sailors to safety since it was built in 1823, holds distinction as the oldest lighthouse in operation on the North Carolina coast and the second-oldest in operation in the nation. Emitting 8,000-candlepower electric light, the white brick structure is closed to the public, but is a favorite spot for shutterbugs and lighthouse enthusiasts just the same. Of course, salty sea-lore is woven into the beams that can be seen a full 360 degrees and at a distance of 14 miles.

Change is constant on this island that coexists with the sea. The sea steals lives,

Dictionary of Ocracoke Dialect

The 700 permanent residents of Ocracoke have a distinctive dialect all their own. Here is a sampling:

Call the mail over: Distribute the mail; "Is the mail called over yet?"

Chunk: To throw; "Chunk the rock in the water."

Haint: A ghost; "Some people think they've seen haints."

Poke sack: A bag; "Did you put the duck in the poke sack?"

Russian rat: A large rodent technically known as a nutria; "Look at that Russian rat!"

Wampus cat: A fictitious cat, used to refer to a rascally person; "He's a classic example of an off-island wampus cat."

Winard: Moving into the wind; "We have a better catch going winard."

Dingbatter: An outsider who moved to the island; "He's no better than a dingbatter."

Quamish: Feeling bad, having an upset stomach; "I'm feeling quamish today."

Mommuck: To hassle, irritate, annoy; "I've been mommucked."

(*As appeared in* The Virginian-Pilot.)

coughs up food and actually moves land. It is said that when the first English explorers arrived at Ocracoke, the island was attached to Hatteras Island and jointly bore the name of Croatan. Ancient maps indicate that Ocracoke may once have been connected to its southern neighbor, Portsmouth Island, and together the islands were called Wokokon.

Names are great history trackers, and while folks entertain many stories as to how Ocracoke was named, two theories hold most popular. One is that the name descended from Wokokon — not a far stretch from the island's current moniker. The Wokokons, a tribe of Native Americans, journeyed to Ocracoke to feast on seafood, historians say. A more fanciful story surrounds the legend of Blackbeard the Pirate. It is said that on the morning of his demise, Blackbeard's assassin impatiently awaited the dawn and the coming of his enemy, looking ashore to the island and yelling "O Crow Cock Crow! O Crow Cock!" (See our sidebar on Blackbeard in this chapter.)

During Blackbeard's era of the early 1700s, it became clear to the colonists of North Carolina that there was a need to improve trade and navigation along the coast. The colonial assembly passed an act in 1715 to establish the island as a port and to maintain pilots and their assistants who helped guide ships safely from sea to shore at "Ocacock Inlett."

But it was not until 1730 that they actually came. Their numbers increased over the years, and 33 years later these "squatters" were given 20 acres of land for themselves and their families. By November of 1779 the Ocracoke Militia Company was established to protect the inlet. Comprised of 25 inhabitants, the militia protected their island home until the end of the Revolutionary War.

Ocracoke history is filled with sad stories of shipwrecks and lost lives from torpedoed vessels. The treacherous ocean, however, also offered up bounty that kept the islanders alive. They were well fed on crabs and a wide variety of seafood, and lumber-carrying ships often tossed

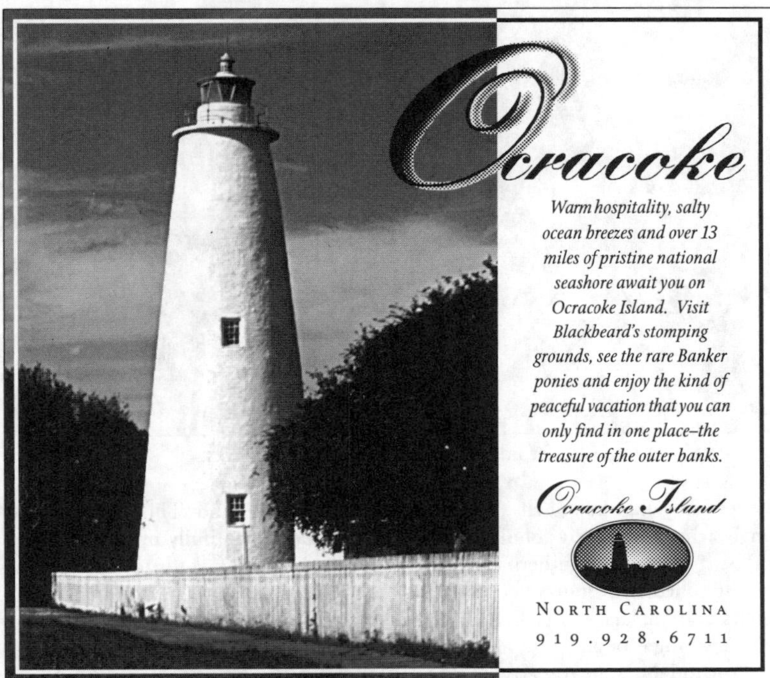

up precious wood for building. Other ships produced floating shoes, produce and clothing. These luxuries were small in contrast to natives having to stand by, helpless at times, as the churning waters swallowed not only sailors, but women and children. Ocracokers are known to be an unselfish lot with roots steeped in the history of lifesaving. They worked to rescue stranded sea travelers and ships and housed and fed those who survived.

Since tourism has become their main source of income now rather than fishing, Ocracokers welcome visitors year round and provide a quaint atmosphere where you can relax and ponder the tales that surround this history of this island.

We've only touched on bits and pieces of the island lore. To truly understand Ocracoke and her people, you must go there. You don't need to bring much with you. You can ride bikes all over the island, and the village is small enough to be seen on foot. Park the car and walk around the heart of the town that surrounds Silver Lake. Wander around on the back roads: Specialty shops and galleries, old island cottages and historic graveyards are just waiting to be discovered. Casually elegant restaurants and come-as-you-are eateries offer several opportunites for a meal, and friendly natives will make recommendations and point you in the right direction. Sailboats moor in the protected cove of Silver Lake, and charter and fishing boats fill the downtown docks. All accommodations — bed and breakfast inns, a few hotels, rental cottages and private campgrounds — are close to the activity of the island. (See our Restaurants, Shopping and Accommodations chapters for more about Ocracoke.)

The island's vast beaches have gentle

A cat naps down by the Ocracoke docks.

slopes that yield whole shells. The northern beaches are sparsely populated, while the surf along the southern beaches is usually lined with four-wheel-drive vehicles and anglers, especially in the fall when fishing is best.

You might want to carry a copy of *Ocracokers* by Alton Ballance when you head for the island. This Ocracoke native speaks beautifully of the history of his home, giving words to the vaporous and salty spirit of the people like no one else has. And to emphasize the above assertion that Ocracokers are a giving folk, all proceeds from this gem of a book go to the Ocracoke School.

Inside
Natural Wonders

It is only through understanding the sea that you come to fully appreciate the Outer Banks. The ocean dominates the islands, influencing their weather, land, flora and fauna and the lifestyle of the people.

Our barrier island system is one of the most physically remarkable areas in the United States. Many people work all their lives spurred on by visions of retiring in a natural paradise such as this one, where areas remain untamed despite an increase in development. While the old timers will rightfully argue that things have changed dramatically here during the last 20 years, one thing remains unchanged: the sea. She rules, period.

Outer Banks' history is steeped in harrowing accounts of lifesaving efforts — the sea is not always a kind mistress — and the economy is heavily based in beach-oriented tourism, the commercial seafood industry and recreational fishing. Newcomers who arrive here to work in these livelihoods and those who come merely to pursue life at the sandy, windswept edge of a continent find their existence immeasurably affected by the sea.

Because the Atlantic Ocean forms the basis for life here, our role as environmental stewards becomes an essential part of that life. This stewardship is manifested in efforts to preserve our maritime forests and protect our waters, marine life and beaches by stopping huge conglomerates from drilling for natural gas off the coast. We have self-imposed restrictions on game fish. We support tag-and-release programs, protect the wild horses and red wolves and actually escort infant loggerhead sea turtles off the sand and into the

Photo:Philip S. Ruckle Jr.

Jockey's Ridge is fun for everyone.

water. Young and old alike participate annually in a nationwide coastal cleanup. Scientists work daily at the Army Corp of Engineers Federal Field Research Facility in Duck studying currents in order to understand erosion.

Outer Bankers have battled for years over Oregon Inlet shoaling. The local access to the sea is in constant need of dredging, and some are calling for the creation of jetties to stabilize the inlet. Environmentalists argue that if we harden the coast to protect the channel, the land will erode in other spots. When a strong nor'easter blows, getting through this vital passage can be a hellish experience.

Speaking of storms, weather is always on our minds whether we're crossing the bar or merely hanging clothes on the line. We become good at reading the wind and the sea. But just when we relax a bit, a storm arises and Mother Nature reminds us that we are temporary visitors living on the fringe of a mercurial power.

We satisfy ourselves by appreciating the gifts the ocean bears. Where there's water, there's wildlife.

The position of Cape Hatteras, jutting into the Atlantic, puts us in close proximity to the the Continental Shelf's edge approximately 37 miles southeast of Oregon Inlet and near the junction of three ocean currents, the Deep Western Boundary Current, Gulf Stream and Shelf Current. These physical combinations create a nutrient-rich habitat for sea life, resulting in a world-renowned offshore fishing hotspot and a wonderland for pelagic birds (see our sidebar in this chapter).

If you were to fly over the Outer Banks, it would become clear that this string of islands is more than a child of the Atlantic. It is rimmed by freshwater wetlands and estuaries. The Albemarle Sound, the mouth of which sits west of Kitty Hawk, is fed by seven major rivers and is the largest freshwater sound on the East Coast. The Currituck Sound, also freshwater, lies northeast of the Albemarle. Due south of these bodies of water are two brackish sounds, the Roanoke and the Croatan. Farther south is the saltwater Pamlico Sound. Nestled in the crook of this sound, where Cape Hatteras indents toward the sea, is the famous Canadian Hole, one of the nation's top windsurfing spots (see our Watersports chapter).

The Outer Banks landscape is also defined by its salt marshes. These wetlands are rich nursery grounds for marine life — including the seafood that we love — and are therefore attractive to waterfowl and other bird species, which find food here. In fact, the Outer Banks is situated on one of the great migratory flyways of America — a wonderful place for fall and winter birding.

Cape Hatteras marks the dividing line between northern and southern species, so the Outer Banks enjoys a rich diversity of animal and plant life. Folks are surprised when they discover we even have alligators in — where else? — the Alligator River. When you include the mainland to the west, where the Alligator River National Wildlife Refuge encompasses 150,000 acres of wetlands and wooded fields, the Outer Banks region is home to black bears, white-tailed deer, gray fox, bobcat, raccoon, mink, beaver, squirrel, possum, river otter and the protected red wolves (see our sidebar in this chapter). Nutria, though not native to North America, have been introduced to our coastal marshes. Alligators feed on them. East Lake and South Lake offer good fishing for striped bass, perch and croaker (see our Fishing chapter).

Even manatee and harbor seals have visited our waters, and we've had rare washups of the dense beaked whale.

Is it any wonder that natural wonders abound on the Outer Banks? Here, where life cycles are woven together, the great common denominator to the incredible diversity of life on the Outer Banks is always the sea. Let us be your

Whale Watching

There are more species of whales passing by the coast of North Carolina than anywhere in Eastern North America. Mostly groups of small- to medium-toothed whales make passage both far offshore and within sight of the beach.

The three largest species are the sperm whale, humpback and fin whale. The sperm whales make their way past our coast in the springtime. In the winter you can see both humpback and fin whales.

The humpbacks are particularly visible from the shore. They can be seen breaching and lunge feeding. In the latter action, the whale blows a bubble net to corral fish, then leaps through it open-mouthed to gulp everything in.

Pilot whales can be seen offshore year round. Even the most endangered species, the Northern right whale, was identified while scratching its head on an Outer Banks sandbar.

Deeper offshore is the migration path for killer and blue whales.

Offshore sightings have been made of the Cuvier's beaked whale and the first live sighting of the True's-beaked whale was made 33 nautical miles southeast of Hatteras Inlet.

Exactly one year later from the date of this sighting, in May of 1994, a type of bottle-nosed whale about 25 to 30 feet long was spotted. Biologists suspect that this particular mammal may be a new species.

Whether you're sitting on the beach with binoculars or viewing the creatures from an offshore charter boat, whale watching is an awe-inspiring pastime. It really makes you feel small, a good feeling for humankind in the steward business.

guide to this world of natural wonders. All we ask is that you treat this fragile ecosystem with care, for it is our home and home to our less vocal friends who thrive on the air, sea and land.

By Land

Cape Hatteras National Seashore

Cape Hatteras was the first seashore in the United States to become a national seashore (1953). The park covers 85 percent of Hatteras Island, which stretches south of Whalebone Junction for 33 miles through Ocracoke Island.

The beaches are marked by cleanliness and an uncrowded atmosphere. Beauty abounds in the park. There's a regal quality to the swaying sea grasses. And while the shifting sands and tenacious vegetation appear monochromatic at first glance, a closer study reveals a richness and diversity. Delicate white-petaled flowers with scarlet centers and lush purple flowers grow entwined in the roadside brambles. In the marshes, sea lavender, morning glories and marsh aster are some of the species of flowers that add color.

If you enter the park from the north in the early morning or late afternoon, you can usually see dozens of brown marsh

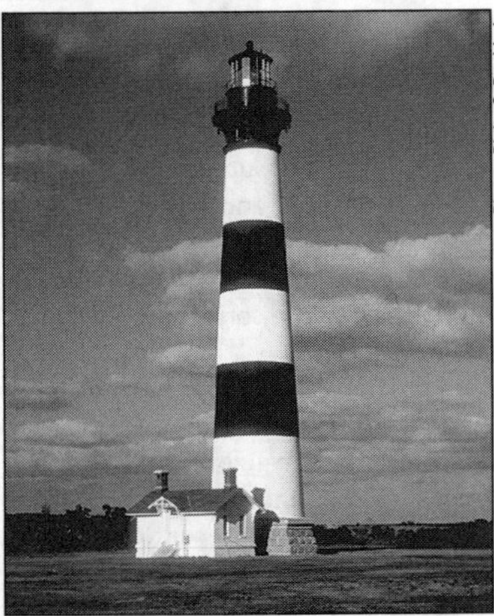

Photo: Philip S. Ruckle Jr.

Bodie Island Lighthouse is one of four lighthouses still standing along the Outer Banks.

rabbits nibbling grasses along the roadside. As you travel south, the Pamlico Sound and salt marshes filled with waterfowl are on your right. Plan to stop and bird-watch at the platform available just off the road.

Birds flock to the marsh for food. In fact, at the Pea Island National Wildlife Refuge just south of the Oregon Inlet bridge, 5,000 acres of mainly wetlands is both a year-round and seasonal home for more than 3,000 species including the snow goose, Canada goose and whistling swan.

During the fall you can watch large flocks of snow geese ascend from their watery resting places. Their flight is breathtaking.

Life teems in the salt marshes, which are the nursery grounds for seafood. Ninety percent of all commercial seafood species must spend at least part of their life cycle in the salt marsh. They spawn offshore then release their eggs into the inlets, where currents carry them into the marsh. Oysters, crabs, shrimp and flounder flourish in the calmer waters of the marsh, which offer places to hide and lots of food.

This section of the park may be one of the most poetic spots on the Outer Banks. The waterfowl are just far enough away to appear untouched by the human element. It's as if we spy on them in their unassuming glory. Photographers enjoy this stretch for the interesting tree lines, sunsets on the salt marsh and, of course, the birds.

The absence of signs and structures through this area coupled with the calming effect of the swaying grasses brings momentary respite from the frenzy of living in a resort community. It's a peaceful ride down N.C. 12 and always a welcome one except when the ocean washes away the dune and claims the road. Not all natural wonders are "wonderful."

Hatteras Island dog-legs to the west, making it one of the farthest points out on the Eastern Seaboard. Its steep beaches cause high-energy wave action, so unbroken shells rarely make it to the shore. But the sea tosses up lovely blue mussels, quahog, jack-knife clams, slipper shells, baby's ears, jingle shells and oysters. A good time to search for shells is at changing tides, after high tide or following a storm. (If you're seeking whole shells, continue south to Ocracoke Island, where the beaches have gentle slopes.)

All along the seashore, ghost crabs burrow in the sand and can be seen scurrying about by day and night — a pure delight for children. One of the more spectacular sights is the occasional glow of phosphorous visible in the waves breaking on shore on a dark night. Sometimes even the crabs glow eerily.

In Buxton at the tip of Cape Hatteras is an area of beach only approachable by four-wheel drive vehicles. Locals call this "The Point," and it serves as a well-used haven for surf-casters. The sea is powerful at this spot, marked by strong currents,

The Red Wolves Return!

On the sprawling, sandy expanse of the Alligator River National Wildlife Refuge — about a half-hour drive west of the Outer Banks — an almost extinct species is starting to reproduce in the overgrown underbrush.

Biologists declared there were only 14 purebred red wolves left roaming throughout North America in the mid-1970s. By 1980, disease, predator control programs and land clearing for human settlement had virtually wiped out the once-prevalent animals. The federal government declared red wolves extinct in the wild that year. And U.S. Fish & Wildlife Service officials caught the remaining red wolves to begin controlled breeding programs. All living red wolves are descendants of those animals.

In 1987, federal wildlife officials released four pairs of red wolves onto the 141,000-acre refuge that covers parts of mainland Dare, Hyde and Tyrrell counties. Another 12 animals were confined to chain-link pens in a secluded section of the thicket-filled forests. There, volunteers and five full-time biologists feed the fenced-in wolves raw meat and dog food, fill their water bowls daily and administer to health and reproductive problems.

More than 50 red wolves have been set free in this area so far. At least 25 pups have been born in the wilds of northeastern North Carolina. And in 1990, a female wolf born on the refuge gave birth to her own litter of pups — proving that the creatures could adapt to their surroundings and reproduce beyond a single generation.

Federal officials say the program marks the first time in the history of wildlife conservation that a species declared extinct in the wilderness has been successfully reintroduced. The entire operation costs taxpayers about $350,000 annually.

Weighing 50 to 60 pounds, with cinnamon-colored coats, wet black noses and thick, bushy tails, red wolves resemble skinny German shepherds with longer legs. These shy, skittish animals generally are not aggressive with people — and tend to stay confined to the perimeter of their 50-foot-square pens or hidden beneath waist-high weeds on the refuge. The only way biologists can find them in the wild is by affixing radio-controlled collars onto the adults and implanting dime-size monitors into the pups.

Red wolves live in family groups, helping one another find shelter and sustenance. Their only natural predator is man. At least a dozen red wolves have died after being struck by cars on U.S. 64 and U.S. 264, which border the Alligator River refuge. Others have been killed by hunters. On January 1, 1995, North Carolina legislators passed a law allowing landowners in Hyde and Washington counties to trap and kill red wolves on private property if the wolves venture off the refuge and appear to be threatening humans or livestock. Fish and Wildlife Service officials, however, say that law flies in the face of the federal Endangered Species Act, which protects the wolves unless they are attacking a person. Local officials say they have no records of red wolves becoming aggressive with people.

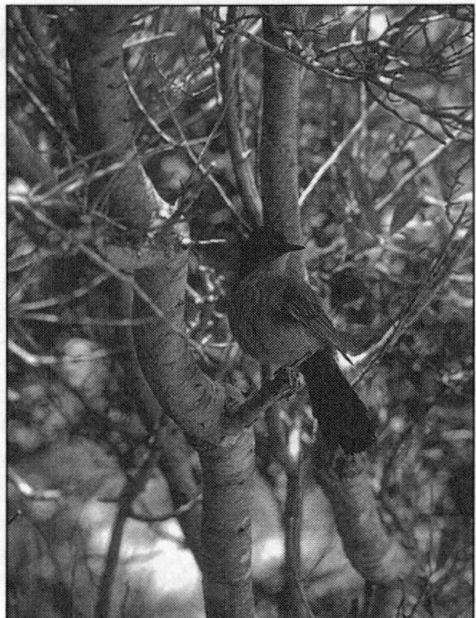

Even this bird is a natural wonder to Outer Banks folks.

deep holes and shoals and opposing waves crashing into each other. Wildlife writers and anglers alike call it heaven. The bottom topography created by strong shoaling and The Point's proximity to the Gulf Stream and its spin-off eddies justify calling this wet and sandy spot a real Outer Banks natural wonder (see our Fishing chapter).

For more information on CHNS, see our Attractions chapter.

Nags Head Woods

A maritime forest flourishing on the Outer Banks seems to defy the rules of nature. Normally, vegetation that is constantly battered by salt and wind is stunted and minimal. In the Nags Head Woods preserve, 1,400 acres of maritime forest contain a diversity of flora and fauna that's nearly unheard of in a harsh barrier island climate. This forest has been able to thrive due to a ridge of ancient sand dunes, some 90 feet high, that has shielded the land from the effects of the sea.

The woods also owe their diversity to the supply of fresh water beneath the forest. The high dunes absorb and slowly release rainwater into the underlying aquifer, swamps and freshwater ponds. The area has three dozen year-round ponds and some seasonal ones that appear in the winter and dry up in the summer.

The most diverse population of reptiles and amphibians on the Outer Banks have found a permanent home in Nags Head Woods. These include five species of salamanders, 14 species of frogs and toads, more than 20 species of snakes and multiple species of lizards and turtles.

This unusual forest is a nesting spot for more than 50 species of birds and home to a wide variety of mammals including raccoons, river otters, gray fox, white-tailed deer and opossums.

Plant life is equally rich here. Botanists have identified more than 300 species in the forest, which is a mixture of maritime deciduous forests and maritime swamp forests. This combination is rare, existing in fewer than five places in the world. Because of its rarity, Nags Head Woods is classified as a globally endangered forest system.

Many hardwoods in the forest are said to be as much as 300 to 400 years old. The oldest tree in Nags Head Woods is thought to be a 500-year-old live oak, but tests indicate that woody plant species were growing in the area more than 1,000 years ago.

After leaving your car in the tree-surrounded lot, you sign in at the registery at the preserve's entrance. You can pick up information here or sit on the connecting veranda that's lined with built-in benches. The scent of cedar is overpowering here. Sit and listen to the sounds of the woods before you venture in. Once inside the preserve, you can follow several trails, which vary in length. The Center Trail is a half-mile long and features a scenic pond overlook. It's fun to watch the turtles climb

Pelagic Bird-watching

As you travel along N.C. 12 south toward Hatteras, you don't have to be a bird lover to realize you have entered a unique bird-watching area. Off in the distance, in the wetlands, a variety of species feed and sun. You can see them easily with a pair of binoculars or even the naked eye. What is not so obvious is the gold mine of pelagic species offshore, where bird-watchers can witness both common and rare birds that never come to our shores.

Local fishing headboats have been taking bird-watchers to the deep water for years. In fact the sightings are so fruitful, a good part of Capt. Allan Foreman's charter boat business involves these trips. Foreman's *Country Girl*, 473-5577, which fishes out of Pirate's Cove Yacht Club on Roanoke Island, is a 57-foot headboat built to carry large parties offshore. Down in Hatteras, Capt. Spurgeon Stowe runs bird-watching excursions aboard the 72-foot *Miss Hatteras*, 986-2365, from Oden's Dock. (See our Fishing chapter for more information.) Bird enthusiasts spend the day searching for more than two dozen species that live on the water.

The petrel and shearwater families are the largest groups of birds available to bird-watchers here. Traveling from the Caribbean and the coast of Africa, these species leave their winter climate to spend summer off the Outer Banks.

Among the petrels, the black-capped petrel is probably one of the most common to North Carolina waters. Twenty-five years ago this species was believed to be on the verge of extinction. No one knew where the birds were. Scientists now say that the world's population hangs out in the Gulf Stream off the Outer Banks area. For comparison's sake, Florida bird-watchers may see one or two black-capped petrels per trip, whereas trips departing from the Outer Banks can yield as many as 100 sightings on a good day.

What's exciting about these trips is you have the chance to view species that only come to land to breed. But when we speak of land, we refer to oceanic islands, not any place you can easily bump into these creatures. These birds are highly adapted for life on the sea. They could be mistaken for gulls or ducks, but as a group they are quite unique. Their tubular nostrils allow them to drink salt water and then expel the salt.

A much rarer bird sighted off North Carolina is the white-faced storm petrel. In a good year, one or two sightings are recorded. This bird shows up in the late summer or early fall and is very difficult to spot anywhere else in the world.

While bird-watching off the Outer Banks, Mike Tove, a biologist from Cary, North Carolina, discovered two species of petrel that were rarely seen near North America. One of them, called the herald petrel, up until 10 years ago was known from only a handful of recordings going back to the 1920s.

"In 1991 boats started venturing offshore farther than usual," Tove said. "We started finding them. It's now a bird we see a half-dozen times a year. People come great distances looking for them."

Tove officially presented to discovery another rare species in May 1991. "I had a bird that was identified as a Cape Verde petrel," he said. Prior to Tove's sighting, resurrected field notes revealed only three other recorded sightings of the bird.

This species was entirely unknown in the United States and is extraordinarily rare anywhere in the world. "And we're seeing them with almost predictable regularity in late spring in very deep offshore waters past the edge of the Continental Shelf," he said. Tove's sightings form the baseline data for research. All the birds have been well-documented with photographs.

You don't have to have a doctorate, as Tove does, to enjoy bird-watching. If you want to get a glimpse of these offshore species here are a few tips from Pamela Rasmussen, who has voyaged off North Carolina in search of birds. She suggests the following:

• Bring fairly low-power, waterproof binoculars (Zeiss or Leitz 7X or 8X are excellent).

• Don't bother to bring your spotting scope; if you're a photographer, bring a telephoto lens to aid in documentation of rarities.

• Constantly scan the horizon and wavetops for birdlife, and call out your sighting with the boat as reference; for example, 6 o'clock is directly off the stern.

"Don't wait to try and identify the bird before calling it out; many eyes on the bird will aid in that," Rasmussen said. "Identification is often very difficult, and to do it accurately you must have a great deal of field experience and ability to interpret flight patterns, molt patterns and the effect of wind and light conditions, often all during heavy seas!"

Expect long periods where no birds are seen, but be prepared for the appearance of a good number and variety. "Always take good notes on any unusual species before consulting your field guide," Rasmussen said. "Describe and sketch exactly what you saw without allowing outside influences to color your recollection."

Offshore bird-watching can be an exciting new adventure for you. If you haven't spent any time on the water, don't allow your fears to get the best of you. Captains won't take you out if the weather is too risky, and you can follow our tips on preventing sea sickness (see our Fishing chapter). Happy bird-watching!

out of the pond and splash back in. The 2-mile-long Sweetgum Swamp Trail takes about an hour to hike. The newest trail, called Blueberry Ridge, is 3.5 miles long, but the hike is worth it for the beautiful views of the woods and water.

(Please note: Dogs, four-wheel-drive vehicles and bikes are tolerated on the road that runs through Nags Head Woods, but they are not allowed in other parts of the preserve.)

The fall is a good time to enter the forest. Cooler weather and fewer mosquitoes make the trek more appealing, and you have plenty of visiting birds and waterfowl to look for. Several species of heron and egrets, including the great blue heron, little blue heron and snowy egret, are common to the woods at this time. Mallards nest in the woods, as do the red-shouldered hawk and the mourning dove.

Several species of songbirds may serenade you as you walk through the forest. In the fall you may hear the music of the Eastern kingbird, barn swallow, house wren, ruby-crowned kinglet or the magnolia warbler.

Plant lovers will appreciate the woods year round. The forest is lush with ferns, pines, cedars, mosses, grasses, cattails, bamboo, seaside morning glory, spotted wintergreen, wild olive, sassafras, black willow, mistflower, sweet gum, swamp rose, blazing star and hundreds more species. Several species rare to North Carolina occur in the forest: the wooly beach heather, water violet, Southern twayblade and mosquito fern.

Historians believe that the first inhabitants of the forest were Algonkian Indians, who were here before the arrival of the English settlers in the late 16th century. Families began settling in the woods by the mid-1700s and formed the foundation for a thriving community in the early 20th century. By 1948 the last resident left.

The Nags Head Woods Preserve, 441-2525, is overseen by The Nature Conservancy, an international nonprofit conservation organization. The North Carolina chapter of The Nature Conservancy manages 47 preserves and natural areas in the state, including Nags Head Woods. Local preservation is a cooperative effort between the Conservancy, the town of Nags Head and the Friends of Nags Head Woods.

If you wish to contribute to the Nature Conservancy, send your donation to The Nature Conservancy, 701 W. Ocean Acres Drive, Kill Devil Hills 27948.

Buxton Woods

Buxton Woods is the largest maritime forest in North Carolina. The 3,000-acre forest sits on the sole source of drinking water for the inhabitants of the area from Avon to Hatteras Village. Measuring 3 miles wide and 50 feet high at the tallest ridge, this land mass has the capacity to act as a storage area for freshwater.

Only 900 of the 3,000 acres are owned by the National Park Service. But recently the state of North Carolina bought an additional 800 acres to protect as the North Carolina Coastal Reserve. The county also designates Buxton Woods as a special environmental district.

Buxton Woods is much simpler ecosystem than Nags Head Woods for it sticks out 30 miles into the ocean and obviously doesn't have the protection that the Nags Head forest has. But compared to the surrounding land at the National Seashore, Buxton Woods holds an incredible diversity.

The woods lie at the meeting place for Northern and Southern species, and have

Insiders' Tips

The best month to watch for migrating whales off the Outer Banks is December. You can usually see humpback whales playing in the waters off the shore.

Anglers flock to the Gulf Stream to try their luck at bluewater fishing.

a viable population of dwarf palmetto and laurel cherry. The woods are a mix of wetlands and forests that are a combination of both Northern deciduous maritime forests and Southern evergreen maritime forests.

A bird's-eye view shows an overall ridge and lowlands throughout the area. Within the woods is Jennette's Sedge, one of the largest, most highly developed and diverse freshwater marsh systems found on a barrier island in North Carolina.

No where else on Hatteras Island will you find the diversity in mammal population as in Buxton Woods. The woods are home to white-tailed deer, gray squirrel, eastern cotton tail rabbit, raccoons and opossum.

The National Park Service maintains a .75-mile trail through Buxton Woods; access is near the Cape Hatteras Lighthouse. It is important to stay on the trail, for cottonmouth snakes live in the woods year-round.

Audubon Wildlife Sanctuary at Pine Island

A 5,000-acre wildlife sanctuary at Pine Island on the northern Outer Banks is protected habitat for deer, birds, rabbits and a huge variety of plant life. There is an unmarked 2½-mile trail you can walk, but the sanctuary is not really a park for people. While you are allowed to wander down the path, there is no planned parking. The land is primarily soundside marshland with lots of pine trees and waterfowl. The sanctuary runs 3 miles long north to south and is approximately 200 yards wide from east to west.

Jockey's Ridge State Park

At Jockey's Ridge State Park in Nags Head, huge migrating dunes heralded as the largest sand hills on the East Coast create one of the most popular attractions on the Outer Banks (see our Attractions chapter). It is an amazing sight to see the sand moving ribbon-like as the wind whips across the dune.

Human forms, insignificant against the towering backdrop, dot the landscape, climbing the dunes like ants to fly kites, hang glide or simply to view the sound and ocean from atop an 85-foot-high ridgetop. At sunset, the visual drama intensifies. The forms coming and going become stark silhouettes. Come nightfall, the dunes are silent.

But there's life on the dune, apparent by animal tracks. Fox roam the area as do deer and opossums, and vegetation thrives in the sand. Wild grapes and bayberry, along with black cherry and Virginia Creeper are found along the park trail.

Jockey's Ridge has been a protected area since it was established as a state park in 1975.

By Sea

The Point

In our section about Cape Hatteras, we mentioned The Point, a fishing mecca for surf-casters at the tip of Cape Hatteras. Here we discuss another area, in the ocean, about 37 miles southeast of Oregon Inlet, that is also called "The Point" by local charter boat captains. It is the primary fishing grounds for more than 70 charter boat captains, and local environmentalists hope to one day preserve this habitat as a marine sanctuary.

Conditions at The Point are unlike any other on the East Coast. The Point is found where three currents — the Gulf Stream, Shelf Current and Deep Western boundary currents — converge just off the edge of the Continental Shelf. This is the last spot where the Gulf Stream appears near the Continental Shelf before it veers off in an east-northeasterly direction. The three currents play a vital role in The Point's success as a fishing paradise. The crossing currents have carved an intricate pattern of canyons and crevices on the ocean floor. This ancient topography provides a nutrient-rich environment for fish. The currents create an upwelling as they cross the ocean floor, which concentrates bait fish and therefore attracts game fish.

The Gulf Stream's proximity to the shelf's edge is very valuable to anglers, for anywhere you have an edge, you have fish. Measuring about 60 miles wide and a half-mile deep, the Gulf Stream rarely gets colder than 65 to 70 degrees. It is a comfortable habitat for many species of sea life. Weather permitting, the Gulf Stream sometimes entirely covers The Point, but prevailing winds can push it farther offshore.

Water depths vary at The Point starting at 50 fathoms, but this site is the last place in the United States where the Gulf Stream consistently touches 100 fathoms.

The list of credentials for The Point is lengthy. Since the Continental Shelf is particularly narrow off the Cape Hatteras coast, it is not far from land. Estuarine waters nourish it, making it a proverbial banquet table for its inhabitants. The Point is called the most productive fishing ground on the East Coast. Yellowfin, bigeye and blackfin tuna are mainstays at the Point year-round. Blue marlin, wahoo and dolphin show up in the spring. The Point provides the chance of a lifetime to glimpse rare seabirds that never come to our shore (see our birdwatching sidebar in this chapter).

Several species of whale — including fin, sperm, humpback and pilot — pass through The Point's blue waters. And you can always enjoy the playful antics of the bottle-nosed dolphin. A large concentration of hammerhead and mako shark also can be spotted at The Point in the winter.

Gulf Stream

A swift flow of water in the Atlantic Ocean passes off the Outer Banks' shores every day. It is called the Gulf Stream, and it is a forceful ribbon of blue sea that has been flowing by since time immemorial. Powered by forces arising from the earth's rotation and the influence of the winds, the energy and warmth it emits has had a profound effect on mankind.

While the Stream's course is influenced

A sunset is reflected on the Scuppernong River at Columbia, North Carolina.

somewhat by gales, barometric pressure and seasonal changes, the general flow remains fairly constant. This constancy creates a dichotomy, for while the Stream is ever-present, its contents are ever-changing. Millions upon millions of tons of water per second are carried along this ancient path. Swept along are fish, microscopic plants and animals and gulf weed that originates in the Sargasso Sea.

Gulf weed lines the edge of the Stream creating a habitat for baitfish. You can easily pull up a handful of vegetation and find it teeming with life. The weed offers protection to infant fish, turtles, crabs, sea horses and the most peculiar sargassumfish. Endangered loggerhead sea turtles less than 2 weeks old, their egg beaks still intact, have been spotted in the weed.

Flying fish are always fun to watch — although what we see as antics is actually the fish's sprint for life as it glides about 200 to 300 yards to escape a predator. You can watch tuna racing underwater, chasing a flying fish, then exploding through the water's surface. The tuna usually win.

The offshore life cycle is fascinating, and no where is it more evident than at the Gulf Stream.

Hiking Trails

Try an Outer Banks hiking trail for a close-up view of nature. Trails are:

- Pine Island Audubon Wildlife Sanctuary
- Nags Head Woods
- Bodie Island Trail
- Pea Island Trail
- Buxton Woods Trail
- Ocracoke Island Hammock Hill Trail
- Thomas Harriot Nature Trail at Fort Raleigh
- North Carolina Aquarium Nature Trail on Roanoke Island.

Inside Attractions

Besides the natural beauty of the Outer Banks, which abounds, a wide range of attractions also await you on North Carolina's barrier islands. The first English colony in America settled upon these shores — you can visit Fort Raleigh's ruins on Roanoke Island. The tallest brick lighthouse in the country towers over Cape Hatteras — you can climb its spiraling staircase throughout the summer. There are wide-open wildlife refuges across the islands and fluorescent-lighted fish tanks at the state aquarium. You can dive into history by boarding a 16th-century representative sailing ship or scuba dive beneath the Atlantic to explore a Civil War shipwreck. Whatever your interests, you'll find outlets for them here. There's never enough time to see everything the Outer Banks have to offer.

A word here about sightseeing: The best vantage point we can think of is on the top deck of one of our British-style tour buses. The **Beach Bus**, 255-0550, offers authentic double-decker buses that provide sightseeing tours from the Wright Brothers Monument to Roanoke Island. Local youngsters have enjoyed birthday party tours complete with ghost tales. Daily and weekly passes are available. The ride is highlighted by commentary from the conductor. On pretty days the buses that feature open-air, second story levels are tops. The kids get a thrill out of climbing the steps to look over the Outer Banks while cruising in a bigger-than-life bright red vehicle. The Pub Crawl is a popular Beach Bus feature in the evenings, and a safe alternative to drinking and driving. The beach bus stops at a number of Outer Banks Restaurants and will also take you to *The Lost Colony* outdoor drama (see the Attractions chapter).

For this chapter, we have highlighted our favorite attractions. There are many others you'll discover on your own, and locals will gladly share their own secret spots. Many of these places have free admission — or request nominal donations. We begin with the northernmost communities and work southward. Each area has its own section, so pick your pleasure.

And don't overlook our chapters on Recreation, Shopping, Arts and Culture, Watersports, Fishing and Nightlife for more exciting, educational and unusual things to do on the Outer Banks.

Insiders' Tips

Don't throw food to the sea gulls if you're riding on the Hatteras-Ocracoke ferry. They'll follow you all the way across the inlet — and leave messy presents on the windshield of your vehicle.

Corolla

Pine Island Audubon Sanctuary

N.C. 12, between Duck and Corolla

Ducks, geese, rabbits, deer, fox and dozens of other animals make this 5,000-acre wildlife refuge on the northern Outer Banks their home. Hundreds of other species fly through the skies during annual migrations. Set between remote villages of sprawling vacation rental cottages, Pine Island Audubon Sanctuary is a secluded outdoor enthusiast's paradise — and a major resting area for birds along the great Atlantic flyway.

Live oaks, bayberry, inkberry, pine, yaupon, holly and several species of sea grass also grow naturally in this wild, remote wetland habitat. The Pine Island Clubhouse and grounds are privately owned. But if you're a member of the Audubon Society, tours are available.

Kill Devil Hills Lifesaving Station

Off N.C. 12, Corolla

Built in 1878, the Kill Devil Hills Lifesaving Station is now the setting for Outer Banks Style — a specialty shop in Corolla. The interior doesn't look anything like the old outpost. But the exterior appearance — peaked roof and crossed timber frame — remains relatively unchanged.

The U.S. Lifesaving Service was established in the late 19th century, and stations were built every 7 miles along the Outer Banks. Crews lived in the wooden structures throughout winter months, patrolling the beaches for shipwrecks and survivors. This station, which was moved almost 30 miles north of its original location, is especially significant because it was frequented by the Wright brothers during their several sojourns to the barrier islands. The Kill Devil Hills Lifesaving Station crew assisted Orville and Wilbur with their early experiments in flight — and some crew members witnessed the world's first powered airplane soar over the sand dunes.

This lifesaving station was brought from Kill Devil Hills to Corolla in 1986, then restored and renovated. History buffs are welcome to visit Outer Banks Style and the lobby of Twiddy & Company Realtors (behind the station) for free, where a collection of memorabilia used by the lifesaving service and the Wrights is on display. This unique, hand-wrought structure is at the foot of the Currituck Lighthouse on the west side of N.C. 12 in historic Corolla village.

The Whalehead Club

Off N.C. 12, Corolla *453-9040*

Overlooking the windswept wetlands of Currituck Sound, this grande dame of days gone by was once the Outer Banks' biggest, most modern structure. It was built in 1925 as a hunt club for a wealthy industrialist's French wife who had been denied admission to the nearby all-male hunt clubs that dotted the barrier island marshes. The Whalehead Club remains one of the area's most charming attractions and affords a romantic trip back in time to an era of lavish accommodations, elaborate ornamentation and Gatsby-like galas that guests once enjoyed in this great house.

The copper-roofed retreat needs restoring. The ballroom's cork floor is crumbling. And the 1902 Louis XIV low-signature Steinway piano that sat in the mansion for more than a half-century has been sent out for repairs. Currituck County officials and a dedicated group of volunteers are trying to raise funds to bring the Whalehead Club back to its former glory. They also want to include a wildlife museum on the first floor. Proceeds from tour fees are earmarked for reconstruction efforts.

Today, visitors can still see the structure's solid mahogany doors and interior walls. The Tiffany chandelier and

The ferry ride to Ocracoke is fun.

wall sconces, custom designed in a waterlily motif, still hang from the ceiling and alongside the dining room fireplace's slate hearth. The 16-room basement still secludes an extensive wine cellar and root cellars for potatoes and onions. The bathrooms, which were the first on the Outer Banks to contain hot and cold indoor plumbing — and pumped fresh and saltwater into the clawfoot tubs — still look inviting to vacationing house guests.

Outside, the area's first in-ground swimming pool, which once flanked the premises, has long since been demolished. The footbridge and boathouse, however, remain. You can walk the grounds of this historic hunt club for free. Tours of the mansion are offered from 10 AM to 3:30 PM daily from Memorial Day through September. Cost is $3 for adults, $1 for children ages 6 to 14. Children younger than 6 and Currituck residents are admitted for free. For more information, see our related sidebar in the Corolla chapter.

Currituck Beach Lighthouse

Off N.C. 12, Corolla Village *453-4939*

The Outer Banks' northernmost lighthouse, this red brick beacon was built in 1875 just north of the Whalehead Club in Corolla. The 214 steps to the top bring you eye to eye with the 50,000-candlepower lamp that still flashes every 20 seconds. This 158-foot-tall lighthouse is open from Easter weekend through Thanksgiving from 10 AM to 5 PM seven days a week, weather permitting. And the $4 entry fee is donated to the Corolla Wild Horse Fund, which maintains headquarters at the base of the tower. There's also a museum shop at the lighthouse.

The Lighthouse Keepers' House, a Victorian stick-style dwelling, was constructed from pre-cut, labeled materials shipped by the U.S. Lighthouse Board on a barge — then assembled on site. In 1876, when the Keepers' House was completed, two keepers and their families shared the duplex in the isolated seaside setting. When the lighthouse became automated, keepers were no longer needed to continually clean the lenses, trim the wicks, fuel the lamp and wind the clockwork mechanism that rotated the bright beacon. So the Keepers' House was abandoned.

Today, the Keepers' House is listed on the National Register of Historic Places. Outer Banks Conservationists Inc. assumed responsibility for its restoration in 1980. Exterior reconstruction already is complete.

The Keepers' House is open daily in-season, permitting the public to recall the lifestyle of another era when faithful keepers kept the light burning to provide safe passage for sailors of the dark seas.

Duck

U.S. Army Corps of Engineers Duck Pier Research Station

N.C. 12, Duck *261-3511*

Set on a former Navy weapons test site, the Waterways Experiment Station of the U.S. Army Corps of Engineers has helped scientists study ocean processes for 16 years. This 173-acre federally owned site north of Duck includes state-of-the-art equipment to monitor sand movement, wave forces and water currents, temperatures and sedimentation. In 1994, its 12 full-time employees hosted more than 100 scientists from around the globe at the world's largest near-shore research experiment — held on the Outer Banks.

The grounds, research station and 1,840-foot-long pier at the Duck experiment station are open weekdays from mid-June through mid-August. Federal researchers conduct free tours of the facility at 10 AM. Access to beach areas and the pier will depend on ongoing research experiments.

Besides the pier itself, the U.S. Army Corps of Engineers' experiment station owns several other unusual pieces of oceanographic equipment. Scientists have full-time use of a 150-foot research vessel, a metal surf sled and a 35-foot-tall Coastal Research Amphibious Buggy — the CRAB — which carries people and equipment from the shore into the sea. Research conducted at the station could eventually alter the way engineers design bridges; help people pick sites for beach nourishment projects; improve projections about where the shoreline might erode; determine how and why sandbars move; and predict what effect rock jetties might have on Oregon Inlet.

Kitty Hawk

The Aycock Brown Welcome Center

U.S. 158, MP 1 *261-4644*

Information is abundant at the Aycock Brown Welcome Center, which appears like a lifesaving station at the end of a long journey to rescue weary travelers and first-time visitors to the Outer Banks. Named for a locally legendary 1950s photographer, this building sits a mile east of the Dare County base of the Wright Memorial Bridge. It is one of two such welcome centers that the Dare County Tourist Bureau operates.

Resources include area maps, tide charts, ferry schedules and brochures. Free community newspapers such as the *Carolina Coast*, published by *The Virgin-*

Insiders' Tips

For a bird's-eye view of the Outer Banks, take a half-hour trip in a small plane from the Dare County airport in Manteo, the Wright Brothers airstrip near the Wright Brothers National Monument in Kill Devil Hills or the Frisco airstrip on Hatteras Island. Most of these tours cost less than $40 per person — and provide an incredible perspective on the fragility of these skinny barrier islands.

ian-Pilot, and the *North Beach Sun* offer feature stories that highlight the local area. The welcome center is staffed with Insiders who can answer all your questions.

The center is open from 9 AM until 5 PM, with extended hours during the spring, summer and fall months. The building is handicapped-accessible. So are the public restrooms. The picnic area is a welcome sight for those who have been riding a long time. Contact the Dare County Tourist Bureau at (800) 446-6262 for more information.

Kitty Hawk Public Beach & Bathhouse

Beach Road, MP 4¼

Across the road from the ocean, a bathhouse and small, free parking area offer visitors a place to go on the beach as soon as they arrive on the Outer Banks at Kitty Hawk. If you get here too early for check-in, you can change into bathing suits here and enjoy a few hours at the ocean until it's time to head to your hotel or beach cottage. Public showers also are available to rinse off after one last stop in the sand on the way home.

Kitty Hawk Village

Along Kitty Hawk Rd., west of U.S. 158

If you want to see where the Wright brothers stayed when they first visited the Outer Banks by ferry — and check out one of the islands' oldest neighborhoods — head west on Kitty Hawk Road, turning just north of the 7-Eleven in Kitty Hawk. This winding, two-lane street dead-ends after about 3 miles at Kitty Hawk Bay. Drivers pass through at least two centuries in the process.

The old post office for this isolated village still stands on the north side of the road. It's been abandoned since the big, new brick building was built on the Bypass three years ago. Several two-story farmhouses still stand along the shady streets and shallow canals. Boats on blocks and fishing nets tied to trees are strewn along back yards. And on warm weekend afternoons, families still ride horses down the live oak-lined lanes, waving to neighbors sitting on their covered porches. You can forget you're at the beach in this quaint, quiet community on the western shores of the Outer Banks.

Kill Devil Hills

Wright Brothers Memorial

U.S. 158, MP 8 *441-7430*

Set atop a steep, grassy sand hill in the center of Kill Devil Hills, the trapezoidal granite monument to Orville and Wilbur Wright is within easy walking distance of the site of the world's first powered airplane flight. From in front of where this lighthouse-style tower now stands, on the blustery afternoon of December 17, 1903, the two bicycle-building brothers from Dayton, Ohio, changed history by soaring over a distance of more than 852 feet and staying airborne for 59 seconds in their homemade flying machine. The monument was erected in Orville and Wilbur Wright's honor in 1932.

In the low, domed building on the right side of the main drive off U.S. 158, the National Park Service operates a visitors center, gift shop and museum. Here, people can view interpretive exhibits of man's first flight and see displays on later aviation advancements. Explanations of the Wright brothers' struggles to fly include parts of their planes, engines and notes. Reproductions of their gliders are displayed in the flight room. And rangers offer free guided historical tours year round.

Outside the exhibit center, four markers set along a sandy runway commemorate the landing sites of each of Orville and Wilbur's December 17 flights. Reconstructed wooden sheds replicating those used at the Wrights' 1903 camp and han-

Shifting Sands of Jockey's Ridge

In the past 20 years, the East Coast's tallest natural sand dune has buried a miniature golf course, swallowed a house and spilled more than 20,000 cubic yards of sand onto a residential road.

State legislators have allocated almost $400,000 to purchase private property that the inland dune is encroaching on — and spent another $40,000 scooping sand off the street.

Officials are determined to put Jockey's Ridge State Park back in its place.

A rare geographical formation, Jockey's Ridge is 87 feet tall, 1.5 miles long and more than 414 acres in area. Scientists say it is the southernmost extremity of a barrier island dune system that extends north to False Cape State Park in Virginia. The half-mile-wide Nags Head dune is one of North Carolina's five most popular state parks, providing a haven for hang-gliders, kite-fliers and sunset hikers.

Each year, more than 790,000 people visit Jockey's Ridge.

The dune itself, however, is constantly moving. Although the state set boundaries for Jockey's Ridge when it formed the park in 1975, the sand hill has migrated southwest at ever changing rates. In the past 25 years, the steepest side of the hill has shifted more than 1,500 feet to the southwest.

Topographic maps show that Jockey's Ridge also is losing height off its tallest peak. At the turn of the century, the dune was estimated to be about 140 feet tall. In 1971, it was about 110 feet tall — 25 feet steeper than the peak stands today.

Besides natural winds, storms and vegetation growth, development has had a profound effect on the migration — and shrinking — of Jockey's Ridge, state officials said. Before buildings came between the dune and the beach, sand could easily blow from the seaside into the more central spaces on the Outer Banks. But now that trees, two-story homes and high-rise hotels block the tall dune from its sand supply, the dynamics have changed considerably.

Nature is no longer able to rebuild the dune. So taxpayers are having to hire men to move the Outer Banks' mountain of sand.

Jockey's Ridge State Park, which includes the East Coast's tallest natural sand dune, is open year round. Admission and parking are free. A visitors center displays photographs and information about the natural phenomenon. Rangers offer frequent hikes, stargazing sessions and talks. Sheltered picnic facilities are available. A handicapped-accessible boardwalk affords grand views of the center of the desert-like dune. Wear shoes when walking through this giant sand box — the surface gets unbearably hot in the summer.

Kitty Hawk Kites conducts private and group hang-gliding lessons on top of the dune all year. Private and group instruction is available (see our Recreation and Attractions chapters).

(*As appeared in* The Virginian-Pilot)

gar also are on the grounds and open to visitors. These sheds are furnished with tools, equipment, even cans of milk like the brothers used.

A short hike takes you from the visitors center to the monument. If you'd rather drive or ride, parking is available closer to the base of the hill. Paved walkways make access easier. But cacti and sand spurs abound in the area. So don't try to brave it barefoot or even in sandals.

In addition to tours, the Exhibit Center at the Wright Brothers National Memorial offers a variety of summer programs. Grounds and buildings are open to vehicles from 9 AM until 5 PM. Hours may be extended during the summer.

Cost for entry at the guard gate is $2 per person or $4 per car.

For more details about humankind's first flight, see our Wright Brothers sidebar in the Kill Devil Hills chapter.

Kitty Hawk Aero Tours

Behind the Wright Memorial *441-4460*

For a bird's-eye view of the Outer Banks — and a unique perspective on how fragile the barrier islands really are — take a 30-minute air tour over the land and ocean in a small plane.

A short runway and parking lot sit behind the Wright Brothers' monument. In front of a tiny ticket booth, blue and yellow airplanes beckon adventurers to fly the same skies that hosted the world's first flight. Pilots will gear tours to passengers' wishes but usually find a few dolphins splashing near the shores or dip over the rare maritime forests on the islands' western reaches. Views are breathtaking, and the experience is one that's not to be missed. Bring your camera for this high-flying cruise.

Rates are $19 per person for parties of three to six; $24 per person for parties of two; and $22 per person for parties of four on larger planes.

Biplane flights in an open-air cockpit late 1800 Waco also are available from the same site starting at $48 per person. These 15-minute trips take you back in time — complete with goggled leather helmets. Pilots fly south to Jockey's Ridge State Park and back to the Wright Brothers' monument.

Air tours are offered year round, weather permitting. Advance reservations are accepted.

Outer Banks Chamber of Commerce Welcome Center

Colington Rd. and Mustian St.
(Off U.S. 158, MP 8) *441-8144*

On the south side of Colington Road, near the corner of U.S. 158, a wooden building with a covered porch houses the Chamber of Commerce's Welcome Center in Kill Devil Hills. This center overflows with free information that's helpful to both visitors and permanent residents. It's a clearinghouse for written and telephone inquiries. And the friendly staff can assist in relaying information about activities, accommodations and annual events.

The chamber's mailing address is P.O. Box 1757, Kill Devil Hills 27948. The center is open year round from 9 AM to 5 PM Monday through Friday. Telephone inquiries are accepted 24 hours a day on an answering service.

Nags Head Woods Ecological Preserve

Ocean Acres Dr. (West of U.S. 158) *441-2525*

If you've had a little too much sun, or if you'd just like to spend time in a secluded forest on a part of the Outer Banks few people get to see, allocate an afternoon for the Nags Head Woods Ecological Preserve.

The Nature Conservancy, a privately funded organization dedicated to preserving pristine ecosystems, oversees this maritime forest. It is private property — not a park. But most areas are open to visitors

Photo: Georgia Beach

The Ocracoke Lighthouse is the shortest of the North Carolina coast's famous beacons.

Tuesday through Saturday from 10 AM until 3 PM during the summer and Monday through Friday from 10 AM until 3 PM during the spring, fall and winter.

More than 4 miles of trails and tiny footbridges wind through forest, dune, swamp and pond habitats. There's an old graveyard near the site of an early 20th-century farming community that once included a school, church and dozens of homes. The maritime forest itself is well-hidden on the west side of the Outer Banks, and many rare plant and animal species abound within this virtually untouched ecosystem.

No camping, loitering, bicycling, firearms, alcoholic beverages, picnicking or pets are allowed in the preserve. There is a small visitors center, gift shop and gazebo near the entrance. The staff offers a variety of free field trips, including guided bird walks and kayaking excursions during warm months.

Write to the Nature Conservancy at 701 W. Ocean Acres Drive, Kill Devil Hills 27948. All donations are welcome, and memberships start at $25. Monies support the preserve's environmental education and research programs.

Dare County Reverse Osmosis Water Production Plant

600 Mustian St. *441-7788*

If you've ever wondered how scientists turn saltwater into drinking water, take the fascinating tour of Dare County's reverse osmosis plant. This water production facility makes water that's pumped through the pipes of homes from Duck through Whalebone Junction. It opened in 1989 and is monitored by a computer 24 hours a day.

At 10 AM and 2 PM Monday through Friday, operators take time out to offer visitors free tours of the water production facility. Here, you'll learn how brackish water pumped from deep wells beneath the barrier islands is filtered through hundreds of synthetic membranes to remove salt, particles and sediment. Then, it's tested and re-filtered until it's ready to drink.

The Dare County facility is the state's biggest reverse osmosis plant and was the second to open in North Carolina. It cost $10.6 million to build and was financed jointly by county officials and town boards in Nags Head and Kill Devil Hills. The plant produces more than 2,000 gallons per minute and can make up to 3 million gallons of water each day.

Nags Head

Jockey's Ridge State Park

U.S. 158, MP 12 *441-7132*

The East Coast's tallest sand dune — and one of the Outer Banks most phenomenal natural attractions — Jockey's Ridge has been a favorite stop for tourists for more than 150 years. In the early 1970s, bulldozers began trying to flatten the top of the dune to make way for a housing subdivision. A Nags Head woman, Carolista, single-handedly stopped the destruction and formed a committee that saved Jockey's Ridge. State officials made the sand hill a protected park in 1975 (see the sidebar in this chapter).

Today, the 87-foot-tall, 1.5-mile-long, 414-acre dune is open to the public year round until sunset. It's a popular spot for hang gliders, summer hikers and small children who like to roll down the steep, sandy slopes. More than 790,000 people visit Jockey's Ridge each year, making it one of North Carolina's most popular parks.

Getting to Jockey's Ridge has been easier since state Department of Transportation workers installed a crosswalk across U.S. 158 a few summers ago. If you park at Kitty Hawk Connection, where the colorful flags are flying on the east side of the highway, you can walk across the road and enter the state park on foot. If you'd rather drive in, park headquarters is near the northern end of a parking lot off the west side of U.S. 158. You'll notice an entrance sign at MP 12, Carolista Drive in Nags Head.

A natural history exhibit in a small display area adjacent to the headquarters office explains how the sand dune was formed and how it moves and migrates. Maps available from the park ranger indicate walking areas and trails. Jockey's Ridge State Park offers natural history programs throughout the summer, including stargazing evening hikes and early-morning wildlife discovery adventures. Sheltered picnic areas also are available for leisurely lunches. Call 441-7132 for program schedules.

It's a long, hot hike to the top of the ridge — but well worth the work. Bring shoes or boots. Don't try it barefoot. You'll burn your feet. And some lower areas around the dune are covered with broken glass. From the top of Jockey's Ridge, you can see both ocean and sound. Cottages along the beach look like tiny huts from a miniature train set. Kite-flying and hang-gliding enthusiasts catch the breezes that flow constantly around the steep summit, shifting the sand in all directions. The desert-like appearance of the sand dunes reveals strange but artistic patterns of those winds and of footprints made by people climbing the hills.

A self-guided mile-long nature trail was dedicated at Jockey's Ridge in 1989. It starts from the southwest corner of the parking lot and proceeds toward Roanoke Sound. The trail is marked by plant identification placards. It takes about an hour to walk the path at a leisurely pace.

If your mobility is impaired, there's a 360-foot boardwalk that affords wheelchairs and baby strollers a slightly sloping incline onto a wooden platform overlooking the center of the dune. For the visually handicapped, audio guides are available at the park office.

Newman's Shell Shop

Beach Rd., MP 13½ *441-5791*

This bright pink establishment on the ocean side of the beach road is an Outer Banks shell shop, tourist attraction and local museum. Newman's was the first store on the beach, opening in 1939. It's remained a family-owned business through the years and stocks shells from all over the world. Owner Susie Stoutenberg displays a labeled collection of shells from as far away as India and Peru. A large variety of gifts, local and imported crafts, and accessories also are arranged in attractive displays.

Wind chimes, shell sculptures and jewelry made from ocean artifacts abound at this charming seaside shop. There's even a display of antique guns, pistols and swords that have been in the family for many years. After being in business for more than a half-century, Newman's has supplied thousands of Outer Banks visitors with reminders of their summer sojourns to the beautiful barrier island beaches.

Besides shells and crafts — many of

which are made on the premises — Newman's is known for its hermit crabs. On the last Saturday in July, the shop hosts a Hermit Crab Race that has become increasingly popular with the younger set (see our Annual Events chapter). So select your crustacean critter early and start training for the big event.

Newman's Shell Shop is open seven days a week in season. See our Shopping chapter for related information.

Old Nags Head

Beach Rd. (MP 12-13) and Soundside Rd.

Most of the villages on the Outer Banks began as small soundside communities. Just south of Jockey's Ridge, there's a narrow road leading toward the sound appropriately dubbed Soundside Road. Here, some of the original, old-style Outer Banks homes still teeter toward the water on stilts. Some of the houses were repaired with timbers that washed ashore from shipwrecks. Others have succumbed to the rising tides or the shifting sands of Jockey's Ridge.

On the ocean end of the street, along the Beach Road in both directions, some of the original seaside cottages still cling to the shore. Called the "unpainted aristocracy" by one Outer Banks author, these sprawling wooden houses reflect their age in the weathered, dark brown cedar-shake siding and shutters. Many grandchildren and great grandchildren of the original landowners who built these first beach homes still inhabit the historic structures each summer.

Gallery Row

Between U.S. 158 and Beach Rd., MP 10½

A green sign off the east side of U.S. 158 indicates the entrance to an artisans' alley known as Gallery Row in northern Nags Head. Here, Glenn Eure's Ghostfleet Gallery, featuring Glenn's eccentric oil paintings on strangely shaped tree limb-mounted canvases, sits across the street from Jewelry by Gail's handmade gem creations. Morales Art Gallery offers an array of works by area and out-of-town artists in its sprawling showroom. Lighthouse Gallery and Gifts has hundreds of bright beacons in every style and size. And Ipso Facto Gallery shows unusual artifacts from all over the globe.

Most of these shops are open year round and are free for people who just want to browse. To learn more, see the Gallery Row listing in our Arts and Culture chapter.

Roanoke Island

The Elizabethan Gardens

Off U.S. 64/264 (North of Manteo) 473-3234

Created by the Garden Club of North Carolina Inc. in 1960 to commemorate the efforts of Raleigh's colonists at establishing an English settlement, these magnificent botanical gardens offer an exquisite, aromatic environment year round. They include 10.5 acres of the state's most colorful, dazzling flora. The flower-filled walkways are the perfect contrast to the windblown, barren Outer Banks beaches.

Six full-time gardeners tend more than 1,000 varieties of immaculately manicured trees, shrubs and flowers in the Elizabethan Gardens. Translucent emerald grass fringes marble fountains. And beauty blooms from every crevice.

Visitors enter at the Great Gate into formal gardens along curving walkways carefully crafted from brick and sand. The bricks were handmade at the Silas Lucas Kiln, in operation during the late 1800s in Wilson, North Carolina. The tree-lined landscape is divided into a dozen gardens.

Although this botanical refuge is breathtakingly beautiful all year, offering different colors and smells depending on the season, it is, perhaps, the most striking in spring. Azalea, dogwood, pansies, wisteria and tulips bloom around every bend. Rhododendron, roses, lacecap and hydrangea appear in May. Summer brings fragrant gardenias, colorful annuals and perennials, magnolia, crepe myrtle, Oriental lilies and herbs. Chrysanthemums and the changing colors of leaves signal the beginning of autumn. And camellias bloom from late fall through winter.

In the center of the paths, six marble steps down from the rest of the greenery, the crowned jewel of the Elizabethan Gardens awaits discovery. A sunken garden, complete with Roman statuary, tiered fountains and low shrubs pruned into geometric flower frames springs from the sandy soil. The famous Virginia Dare statue nearby is based on an Indian legend that says Virginia, the first English child born in America, grew up among Native Americans (see our Roanoke Island chapter).

The Elizabethan Gardens are open daily from 9 AM to dusk except Saturday and Sunday in December, January and February. From June 1 through September 1, the gardens will stay open seven days a week until 8 PM. Admission is $3 for adults, $1 for youths ages 12 through 17 and free for children younger than 12.

Wheelchairs are provided. Most paths are handicapped-accessible. Some plants are for sale in the garden gift shop. The gardens also are available for weddings.

Fort Raleigh National Historic Site

Off U.S. 64/264
(3 mi. north of downtown Manteo) 473-5772

On the north end of Roanoke Island, near the Roanoke Sound's shores, Fort Raleigh marks the beginning of English settlement in North America. Designated as a National Historic Site in 1941, this 500-acre expanse of woods and beach includes the 1585 and 1587 settlement sites of Sir Walter Raleigh's colonists, the National Park Service's Cape Hatteras National Seashore visitors center and headquarters, a restored fort and a nature trail.

The visitors center offers interpretive exhibits in its small museum. A 17-minute video provides an introduction to this historic site. Here, the recreation of a 400-year-old Elizabethan Room from Heronden Hall in Kent, England, is on display. The furnishings, carved mantelpiece, paneling, stone fireplace and blown glass in the leaded windows offer a glimpse of America's origins across the ocean.

Self-guided tours and tours led by Park Service personnel are available at this archaeologically significant site. Programs vary depending on the time of day and year. The Thomas Hariot Nature Trail is a short, self-guided trail with pine-needle paths that lead to the sandy shores of Roanoke Sound. It is thought that Sir Richard Grenville first stepped ashore here on Roanoke Island in the late 16th century.

Fort Raleigh National Historic Site is open year round. From mid-June until late August, hours are from 9 AM until 8 PM Sunday through Friday and Saturday from 9 AM until 6 PM. From September through mid-June, the site is open from 9 AM until 5 PM seven days a week. Fort Raleigh is closed Christmas Day.

The Lost Colony

Of U.S. 64/264, near Fort Raleigh 473-3414
Waterside Theatre (800) 488-5012

The nation's longest running outdoor drama, this historical account of the first

Insiders' Tips

At the Weeping Radish Brewery on Roanoke Island, take a free tour of the microbrewery and see how beer is made from scratch. Then, you can sample some from a frothy mug in the outdoor Oktoberfest gardens.

English settlement in North America is a must-see for Outer Banks visitors. Pulitzer Prize-winning author Paul Green brought the history of English colonization to life through an impressive combination of Elizabethan music, Native American dances, colorful costumes and vivid drama on a soundside stage in 1937. His play continues to enchant audiences today at Waterside Theatre on Roanoke Island.

The Lost Colony is a theatrical account of Sir Walter Raleigh's early explorers who first settled on the shores near the present day theater in 1585. The play is understandable to audiences of all ages. But the wooden seats are not padded, so bring stadium cushions or blankets or rent one of the pillows available at the theater. It can get chilly on evenings when the wind blows off the sound, so we recommend sweaters, even in July and August. Mosquitoes at this outdoor drama also can be vicious, especially after a rain, so bring plenty of bug repellent. The theater is wheelchair-accessible. And the staff is glad to accommodate special customers.

Once you arrive, settle back and enjoy a thoroughly professional, well-rehearsed, technically outstanding show. The leads are played by professional actors. Most of the backstage personnel are pros too — and it shows. Supporting actors are often locals, with some island residents passing from part to part as they grow up. Andy Griffith is among *The Lost Colony's* best-known former cast members who got his start playing Sir Walter Raleigh in the summer show.

All shows start at 8:30 PM and are performed nightly except Saturday. The season runs from mid-June to late August. Tickets are $14 for adults, $7 for children 12 and younger and $13 for senior citizens. Adult-accompanied children 12 and younger are admitted at half price for Sunday night performances. Those 65 and older are admitted for $12 on Fridays. Groups of 15 or more can call for a discount.

This is probably the most popular summertime event on the Outer Banks, and we recommend you make reservations, though you can try your luck at the door if you wish. You can make paid mail reservations by writing The Lost Colony, 1409 Highway 64/264, Manteo 27954; or make phone reservations starting in early June. Reservations will be held at the box office for pickup until 7:30 PM.

North Carolina Aquarium

Airport Rd. *473-3493*

Down a winding road northwest of Manteo near the Dare County airport, the North Carolina Aquarium at Roanoke Island offers an air-conditioned, indoor excursion that's open all year.

Accessibly set up and labelled to provide a detailed glimpse of sea life along North Carolina's barrier islands, this educational attraction includes an 8,400-gallon, wall-size, well-lighted shark tank; a multimedia dolphin display; a video of on-site osprey nesting near the parking lot; state laboratories and a marine reference library; and a touch-me tank where visitors can pet horseshoe crabs and watch saltwater fish scurrying through shallow ponds.

Fluorescent lights glow like jewels along long, darkened corridors where sea turtles float on iridescent driftwood, long-nose gar bump against the glass walls of their world, and octopi and burrfish dive through their tanks, swirling sand. Sea life starts out with fresh water species at the aquarium, shading through brackish to salt water. A wetlands exhibit features freshwater turtles and amphibians, including some small alligators.

Visitors can view films on marine and biological topics. Staff members conduct summer daytime field trips and talks for all age groups. Check at the front desk for a monthly calendar of events, or consult the *Carolina Coast* free weekly newspaper. The aquarium caters to groups of any kind and can supply meeting facilities in

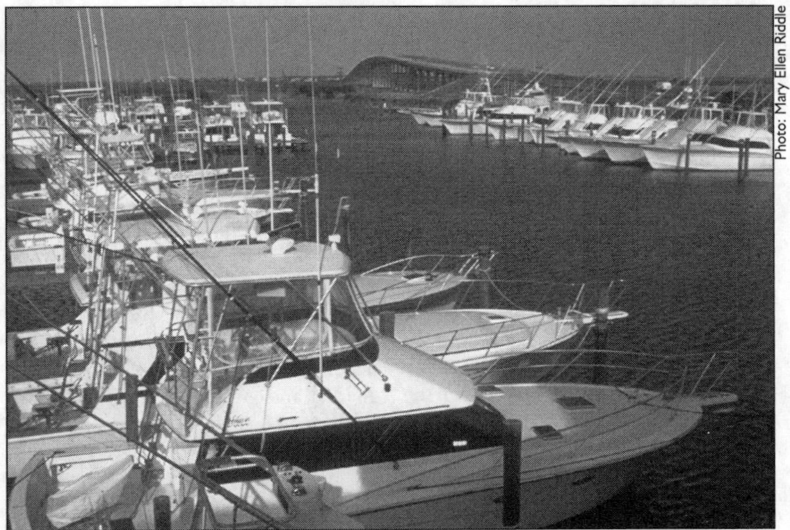

Photo: Mary Ellen Riddle

Pirate's Cove Yacht Club is a hot spot for big catches nearly year round. The boats roll in between 4:30 and 6 PM daily.

its conference room, seminar room or 240-seat auditorium. There's also a great gift shop with marine-related collectibles, books and T-shirts.

To reach the aquarium, drive north from Manteo on U.S. 64/264. Turn left on Airport Road, following signs to the airport. After the big 90-degree turn in the road, the aquarium will be on the right. It's open from 9 AM to 5 PM Monday through Saturday and 1 to 5 PM on Sunday. Admission is $3 for adults, $2 for senior citizens and active military, $1 for children ages 6 to 17 and free for children younger than 6. Aquarium Society members also are admitted free.

Weirs Point and Fort Huger

North end of Roanoke Island, off U.S. 64/264

At the Roanoke Island base of the bridge to Manns Harbor, Weirs Point is an attractive, easily accessible public beach on the Croatan Sound. Free parking is available at the turnoff on Roanoke Island just before the end of the bridge. The brackish water is warm and shallow here. Sandy beaches are wide enough to picnic, sunbathe or throw a Frisbee across.

About 300 yards north of Weirs Point, in 6 feet of water, lay the remains of Fort Huger. This was the largest Confederate fort on the island when Union troops advanced across the Outer Banks during the Civil War battles of 1862. The island has migrated quite a bit in the last 130 years. The fort used to sit securely on the north end on solid land.

In 1901, from a hut on Weirs Point beach, one of the unsung geniuses of the electrical age began investigating what was then called "wireless telegraphy." Reginald Fessenden held hundreds of patents on radiotelephony and electronics but died without credit for many of them. In a letter dated "April 3, 1902, Manteo," Fessenden tells his patent attorney that "I can now telephone as far as I can telegraph. . . . I have sent varying musical notes from Hatteras and received them here with but 3 watts of energy." One of the world's first musical radio broadcasts was completed on this soundside sand of the Outer Banks.

Picnic benches, a Dare County information kiosk and restrooms are provided at Weirs Point. Watch for stumps and broken stakes in the water. The tide also creeps up quickly, so beware of needing to move beach blankets away from its encroaching flow.

Mother Vineyard

Off Mother Vineyard Rd., Manteo

The oldest-known grapevine in the United States grows in Manteo. When the first settlers arrived here, the Outer Banks were covered with wild grapes. Arthur Barlowe wrote to Sir Walter Raleigh in 1584:

". . . Being where we first landed very sandy and low toward the water side, but so full of grapes as the very beating and surge of the sea overflowed them, of which we found such plenty, as well there as in all places else, both on the sand and on the green soil, on the hills as in the plains, as well on every little shrub, as also climbing toward the tops of high cedars, that I think in all the world the like abundance is not to be found."

The Mother Vine is one of those ancient grapevines, so old that it may have been planted even before Europeans arrived in the New World. Certainly it was already old in the 1750s, as records attest, and scuppernong grape vines do not grow swiftly. Another story is that this vine was transplanted to Roanoke Island by some of the Fort Raleigh settlers. Whichever story is true, the Mother Vine is more than 400 years old, and it's still producing fine fat, tasty grapes. In fact, for many years, a small winery owned by the Etheridge family cultivated the vine on Baum's Point, making the original Mother Vineyard wine until the late 1950s.

Mother Vineyard Scuppernong, the Original American Wine, is still produced by a company in Petersburg, Virginia. It is a pink wine, quite sweet, similar to a white port or Mogen David. You can find it at many Outer Banks groceries.

The Mother Vine is on private property and a bit out of the way. To find it, drive north from Manteo on U.S. 64/264. About three-quarters of a mile past the city limits, turn right on Mother Vineyard Road. Go less than a half-mile, where the road makes a sharp turn to the right at the sound. About 300 feet past the turn, on the left, the patient old vine crouches beneath a canopy of leaves, twisted and gnarled, ancient and enduring. Please stay on the road if you're sneaking a peek.

Dare County Tourist Bureau

U.S. 64 — *473-2138*
Manteo — *(800) 446-6262*

With the state's only drive-up information window and a new sprawling headquarters on the main road through Manteo, the Dare County Tourist Bureau is equipped to help visitors and residents find almost any Outer Banks information. The bureau has a large collection of brochures, maps and promotional materials about area offerings. The staff can answer most questions quickly. Data on demographics and business opportunities on the Outer Banks also are available.

Tourist Bureau offices are open year round Monday through Friday from 8:30 AM to 5 PM and Saturdays and holidays as well during the summer season from 10 AM to 3 PM. For specific information and a free detailed vacation guide, write to Dare County Tourist Bureau, P.O. Box 399, Manteo, 27954.

The Christmas Shop and The Island Gallery

U.S. 64, outside Manteo — *473-2838*
(800) 470-2838

The original Outer Banks ornament shop and a perfect excuse for celebrating

Santa year round, the Christmas Shop and Island Gallery offer an exquisite world of fantasy and festive delights. Edward Greene opened this unique boutique on June 1, 1967. It remains the only one of its kind — although others have tried to emulate its wide array of holiday statues, decorations and unusual collectibles.

This shaded shopping complex includes seven rambling, multilevel buildings. Each room is furnished with well restored antique furniture — that's not for sale. The trip will fill visitors with wonder.

The Christmas Shop stocks about 50,000 different items from 200 companies, 150 artists and craftspeople and 35 countries, says Greene, a former New York City actor who decorated Christmas trees for area department stores. Whole walls are filled with toys, pottery and handcrafts. Some rooms feature nothing but porcelain eggs. Others overflow with baskets, carvings, miniatures, handmade jewelry, ornaments, seashells, candles and Christmas cards. The shop's 125 switches control innumerable atmospheric lights that give everything a magical glow. There's even a year-round Halloween room, an old-fashioned candy store, a card and stationery shop, a basket shop, sun-catchers and fun things for kids.

The Christmas Shop is open Memorial Day through mid-October, Monday through Saturday from 9:30 AM to 9:30 PM and Sunday from 9:30 AM to 6 PM. From mid-October through mid-June, hours are Monday through Saturday 9:30 AM to 6 PM and Sunday 9:30 AM to 5:30 PM. It's closed Christmas Day.

The Weeping Radish Brewery

U.S. 64
1 mi. south of downtown Manteo 473-1157

Historians say the first beer made in America was brewed on Roanoke Island. In 1585, they write, English colonists made a batch to befriend the Native Americans — or maybe to calm their own nerves. Roanoke Island today boasts its own brewery at a Bavarian-style eatery called The Weeping Radish.

On the shaded grounds just south of downtown Manteo, a full-time brewmaster makes both light and dark lager beers which can be sipped on-site at the restaurant or taken to go in five-liter pony kegs and one-liter refillable bottles. Weeping Radish beer in 22-ounce bottles also is sold at area retailers. Notice the artistic labels that depict local landmarks.

Free, daily tours of the brewery are offered throughout the year. And, of course, you can sample the frothy mugs afterward in the pub or outdoor patio tables.

An annual OktoberFest is held the weekend after Labor Day. Events and activities include oompah bands and German folk dancers (see our Annual Events chapter). Locals find this a favorite evening spot in the off-season. Visitors will feel at home too. There's even a new, colorful playground for the kids.

Andrew Cartwright Park

Sir Walter Raleigh St., Manteo

A small state park near downtown Manteo, Andrew Cartwright Park commemorates a man who devoted his life to spreading the Gospel. Cartwright organized 12 African Methodist Episcopal

Insiders' Tips

Take a bluefin tuna charter fishing trip from Hatteras Village docks from January through March. Catch, tag and release giant fish weighing 300 pounds and more. Be sure to bring a video camera to watch some of the world's biggest fish jump for bait.

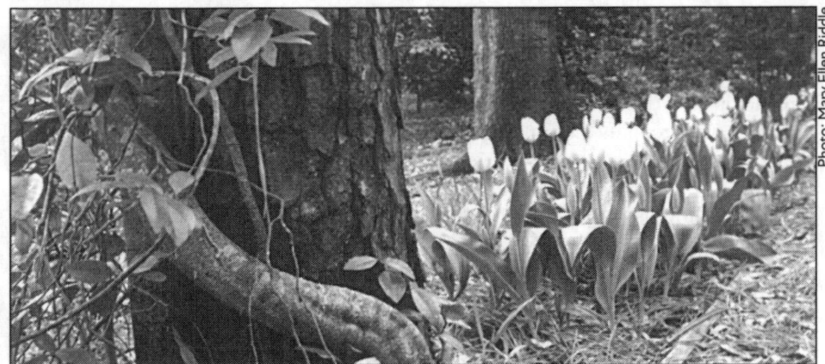

In springtime, tulip beds line this path through the Elizabethan Gardens.

Zion churches on or near Roanoke Island after the Civil War. He founded the first Zion Church in Liberia and worked in Africa until his death in 1903.

Plaques at the park recount the history of the Freedman's Colony on Roanoke Island where emancipated slaves lived after the Civil War; the Pea Island Lifesaving Station Crew, an all-black group of heroes honored for their bravery along the Outer Banks shores; and the AME Zion Church that Cartwright founded.

To reach the park, turn west off U.S. 64/264 at Sir Walter Raleigh Street and go less than a half-mile. The park is on the right. Admission is free.

Mill Landing

N.C. 345, Wanchese

Near the end of a winding 5-mile road, past a long expanse of wide, waving marshlands overflowing with waterfowl, Wanchese is well off the beaten path of most visitors (see our Roanoke Island chapter) and remains one of the most unspoiled areas on the barrier islands. At the very end of N.C. 345, one of the most picturesque and unchanged areas of the Outer Banks is often overlooked: Mill Landing, which embodies the heritage of the Outer Banks. Here, active fishing trawlers anchor at the fish scale-strewn docks, their mesh still dripping seaweed from the wide roller wheels. Watermen in yellow chest waders and white rubber boots — Wanchese wingtips — sling shark, tuna and dolphin onto cutting room carts. And pieces of the island's past float silently in the harbor, mingling with remade boats that are still afloat and sunken ships that have long since disappeared.

The fish houses at Mill Landing include Wanchese Fish Company, Etheridge's, Jaws Seafood, Quality Seafood, Moon Tillett's and others, ship seafood to restaurants in Hampton Roads, Baltimore, New York, Boston and Tokyo. Some also will sell walk-in customers fresh fish off their boats. Scallops, shrimp and crabs also are available here in season.

North Carolina Seafood Industrial Park

615 Harbor Rd., Wanchese 473-5867

A 69-acre industrial park on a deep harbor at Wanchese, this state-supported facility was built in 1980 with $8.1 million in state and federal funds. It was designed to attract large-scale seafood processing companies to set up shop on the secluded Roanoke Island waterfront. But after federal promises about stabilizing Oregon Inlet failed to materialize, few deep-draw fishing trawlers could afford to keep risking the trip through the East Coast's most dangerous inlet.

Oregon Inlet continued to shoal terribly through the 1980s. Unpredictable weather patterns still affect the channel's navigability. So the seafood park remained largely vacant until 1994 when some smaller area businesses and fish processing plants began establishing themselves there.

Today, the 29-lot industrial area is about half full. There's a Marine Maintenance Center, Coastal Engine and Propeller, Harbor Welding, Wanchese Trawl and Supply, the state's oyster planting program offices, Bay Country Industrial Supply that makes fish boxes and Top Fin Seafood Co., which buys fish right off the boat from Wanchese watermen and ships its seafood overnight to Raleigh, North Carolina, New York and Japan.

The seafood park is an educational attraction for anyone interested in how fish are commercially caught, cut, packed, processed and distributed. Visitors are welcome to watch boat builders work or watermen unload their catches at the wide docks. Park Director Rodney Perry also will arrange free tours of the facility for families or groups with advance notice.

The state seafood park hosts the annual Wanchese Seafood Festival the last Saturday in June each summer when businesses open their doors — and kitchens — to the community. See our Annual Events chapter for details.

Pirate's Cove Yacht Club

Manteo-Nags Head Cswy. *473-3906*
(800) 367-4728

This busy 140-slip marina is surrounded by upscale permanent and rental waterfront homes and has a ship's store that can supply almost every maritime need. Reservations are accepted for dock space. A growing number of charter fishing boats run Gulf Stream trips from Pirate's Cove most of the year (see our Fishing chapter). Besides fishing supplies, the Ship's Store at Pirate's Cove sells sportswear, T-shirts, souvenir hats and drink huggies, groceries and ice. A restaurant above the store includes a raw bar and fresh steamed seafood. Boaters can brown bag liquor at this establishment that sells only beer and wine.

The community at Pirate's Cove includes more than 600 acres — much of which is marshland. Plans call for 627 residential homes, townhouses and condominiums to eventually be developed on the site. All residences have deep-water dockage and access to a clubhouse, pool and tennis courts. A boardwalk winds throughout the waterfront at Pirate's Cove where summer sunset festivals are held Wednesday afternoons from 4 to 8 PM all summer. Crafts, food, live bands, *Lost Colony* actors, pirates, puppets and free beer make these lively events a popular area attraction. Proceeds benefit a local cancer support group.

Insiders' Tips

Some of the seafood that might end up on your plate at local restaurants is landed and processed at the North Carolina Seafood Industrial Park in Wanchese. You can take a free tour of tuna cutting houses and see how commercial seafood is hauled in by area watermen, prepared and packaged by local workers and shipped from the Outer Banks to New York, Atlanta and even overseas.

Downtown Manteo

Off U.S. 64/264
Waterfront and Budleigh and Sir Walter Raleigh sts.

Named for a Roanoke Island Native American who accompanied English explorers back to Great Britain in the 16th century, Manteo is one of the oldest Outer Banks communities and has long been a commercial and governmental hub for the area.

When Dare County formed in 1870, and Manteo became the county seat, there were only a few houses lining the sandy lanes along Shallowbag Bay. Today, hundreds of permanent residents make this Roanoke Island town their home. Businesses from a candle-making shop to the Insiders' Guides Inc. corporate headquarters have recently opened in the Waterfront Shops. New restaurants and bed and breakfast inns beckon tourists from other areas. And thousands of visitors arrive each summer to explore this historic waterfront village.

On the wooden wharves of Manteo's Waterfront, 53 modern dockside slips with 110- and 220-volt electrical hookups offer boaters overnight or long-term anchorage. A comfort station with restrooms, showers, washers and dryers also serves vessel crews and captains. And there's plenty of shopping and dining within walking distance in Manteo for people who've left their wheels on the mainland.

Across the street from the Waterfront, in the center of the downtown area, more than 40 small- to medium-size shops, eateries and businesses offer everything from handmade pottery to fresh flowers — all in a four-square-block area. There's plenty of free parking across the street from Manteo Booksellers. But watch time limits on curbside spots: You will be ticketed if you overstay your limit.

Around the southeast point of the Waterfront, the town's American Bicentennial Park is tucked in between the courthouse and a four-story brick building that houses shops and condominiums. There's an emotionally moving inscription under the cross. Picnic benches afford a comfortable place to rest and enjoy the view across the bay — where the state's 16th-century representative sailing ship *Elizabeth II* rocks gently on small sound waves.

If, as most visitors do, you reach the Banks via U.S. 158, you can get to Manteo by continuing south until you reach Whalebone Junction. Bear right onto U.S. 64/264 at the traffic light near RV's restaurant. Continue across the causeway and high-rise bridge past Pirate's Cove, then bear right at the Y-intersection. Turn right at either of the town's first two stoplights to go downtown.

The Waterfront

Manteo Docks 473-2188

Overlooking smooth wooden docks along Shallowbag Bay, the Waterfront is a 34-unit condominium and marketplace at the head of downtown Manteo. This four-story complex is styled in Old World architecture — open around a breezy courtyard, built above a ground-level parking garage. Three-hour free public parking is available in this shaded facility.

The Waterfront's second level contains 20,000 square feet of retail space, including a jewelry shop, nautical gift store, European-style cafe, hair salon and seafood restaurant. The third and fourth levels are entirely residential. Condominium owners keep their boats at the backdoor docks on the Manteo harbor.

The Elizabeth II

Ice Plant Island 473-1144

Designed as the centerpiece for the 400th anniversary of the first English settlement in America, the *Elizabeth II* is a representative sailing ship similar to the one that carried Sir Walter Raleigh's colonists across the Atlantic in 1585.

This state-owned vessel is anchored

Photo: Mary Ellen Riddle

Every March, participants gather at the Nags Head Fishing Pier to get ready for the St. Patrick's Day Parade, reputed to be the largest of its kind in North Carolina.

to wide docks at Ice Plant Island, across a wooden bridge from the Manteo Waterfront. It's two-level decks are open to visitors all year. Throughout the summer, interpreters clad in Elizabethan costumes conduct tours of the colorful ship.

Although it was built in 1983, the *Elizabeth II's* story really began four centuries earlier, when Thomas Cavendish mortgaged his estates to build the *Elizabeth* for England's second expedition to Roanoke Island. With six other vessels, the original ship Elizabeth made the first colonization voyage to the New World and landed on the Outer Banks.

There wasn't enough information available about the original vessels to reconstruct one. So shipbuilders used the design of one of Sir Richard Grenville's vessels from his 1585 voyage to build the state boat. Constructed entirely in a wooden structure on the Manteo waterfront, the completed ship, *Elizabeth II*, slid down hand-greased rails into Shallowbag Bay in front of a crowd of enthusiastic dignitaries and locals in 1983.

Stretching 69 feet long, 17 feet wide and drawing eight feet of water, the *Elizabeth II* cost $750,000 to build and was funded entirely through private donations. Its decks are hand-hewn from juniper timbers. Its frames, keel, planking and decks are fastened with 7,000 locust wood pegs.

Every baulk, spar, block and lift of the state ship are as close to authentic as possible, with only three exceptions: a wider upper-deck hatch for easier visitor access; a vertical hatch in the afterdeck to make steering easier for the helmsman; and a controversial pair of diesel engines that were installed in the *Elizabeth II* in 1993. The 115-horsepower motors help the grand sailing ship move under its own power, instead of relying on expensive tug boats that had to tow it before. Now, the vessel can cruise up to 8 knots per hour with no wind — and travel for up to 40 hours without refilling its two 150-gallon gas tanks. The state ship stays on the Outer Banks most of the year. But during the off-seasons, it sometimes travels to other North Carolina ports, acting as an emissary for its Roanoke Island home — and serving as the state's only moving historic site.

To reach the *Elizabeth II*, drive over the arched wooden bridge past the Manteo post office and park on Ice Plant Island. There's plenty of free parking here. But you can walk from downtown Manteo too, if you prefer. The Elizabeth II State Historic Site will be on your right, past the Outer Banks History Center. The building is in the style of classic Old Nags Head cottages, with cedar shingles and wide porches. Inside, there's an exhibit area, gift shop, auditorium and restrooms. Behind the center, a raked path leads to the ship and to another summer event, the Early Settlement Site. *Elizabeth II* is to the right, and the settlement to the left. The site is locked in time, depicting life on August 17, 1585, with soldier's tents, a general's tent and living history demonstrations of woodworking, ninepins and cooking.

Admission to the ship and settlement is $3 for adults; $2 for senior citizens; $1.50 for students; free for children 5 and younger. Groups of 10 or more who call in advance receive 50¢ off each admission. The price of admission includes a 20-minute presentation held every 30 minutes in the auditorium and a tour of the ship and the settlement site. Costumed sailors and soldiers, employing an Elizabethan dialect, explain how the ships of Elizabethan England were built and sailed. Hours of operation are 10 AM to 4 PM, Tuesday through Sunday from November 1 through March 31; 10 AM to 6 PM daily from April 1 through October 31. The costume presentation is Tuesday through Saturday in the summer only, from early June through August. In order to allow for a complete tour, the last tickets are sold at 3 PM from November 1 through March 31 and at 5 PM from April 1 through October 31.

Outer Banks History Center

Ice Plant Island *473-2655*

Next to the *Elizabeth II*, across from the Manteo Waterfront on Ice Plant Island, the Outer Banks History Center is the most remarkable repository of northeastern North Carolina chronicles collected in any place.

More than 25,000 books, 4,500 official documents of the U.S. Coast Guard and the U.S. Life Saving Service, 25,000 photographs, 1,000 periodicals, 700 maps and hundreds of audio and video recordings are housed in this state-supported cultural site. Special collections include the David Stick Papers, the Frank Stick Collection, the Cape Hatteras National Seashore Library, the Cape Lookout National Seashore Oral History Collection and the Aycock Brown Tourist Bureau Collection of 17,000 photographs. There are maps of the area more than 400 years old here.

Opened in 1988 on the right hand side of the *Elizabeth II* visitors center building, the Outer Banks History Center includes a comfortable reading room with long tables for research and a gallery with rotating exhibits open for free to the public. North Carolina natives will enjoy exploring their own history here. Visitors will find the Outer Banks legacy equally enchanting.

Most of the collections included in this library belonged to Outer Banks historian David Stick, who still serves as a semi-advisor to the history center and lives in Kitty Hawk. The author of many books on the Outer Banks, Stick gathered much of the information during his years of research and writing. Stick's father, David Stick, helped found the Cape Hatteras National Seashore as part of the National Park Service.

Staffers at the history center are knowledgeable and happy to help anyone access the facility's vast resources. Journalists, history buffs, students, archaeologists, writers and even interested tourists will find the stop well worth their time. The reading room is open year round from 9 AM until 5 PM Monday through Friday and 10 AM until 3 PM Saturday. Gallery hours are 10 AM to 4 PM Monday through Friday and 10 AM to 3 PM on Saturday, year round.

Ye Olde Pioneer Theatre

113 Budleigh St., Manteo 473-2216

With an old-timey candy counter that still sells sodas for a quarter and fresh buttered-popcorn smells filling the front lobby, this historic movie house is our favorite place to see films on the Outer Banks. The original Manteo movie theater, built in 1918, burned. The one still showing first-run films today opened in 1934.

It's the oldest theater operated continuously by one family in the United States. George Washington Creef was the founder. Today, his grandson, H.A. Creef, sells tickets from the street-front window. The projector that has been used since 1947 is an open carbonarc — a rare find for old movie buffs. Every once in a while, it breaks down during a screening. But there's still no better place to watch a movie for the feel, history and price of the place: $3 for adult admission.

One movie is shown at 8 PM each night, as long as there are at least three people in the theater. Listings change weekly, on Fridays. Check the billboard on U.S. 64/264 in downtown Manteo — or call the theater for current listings.

Bodie Island

Bodie Island

South of Whalebone Jct., north of Oregon Inlet

On the north shore of Oregon Inlet, Bodie Island hasn't been a real island since 1811. During a storm that year, Roanoke Inlet closed and what had once been Bodie (pronounced "body") island joined the upper Outer Banks at Nags Head. Several inlets have existed near the current Oregon Inlet site since English explorers first discovered the barrier islands.

Hatteras Island Welcome Center

Whalebone Jct.

Operated by the Dare County Tourist Bureau, this wooden welcome center sits just south of the Whalebone Junction intersection on N.C. 12. It's open daily from Memorial Day to October 1 from 9 AM until 5 PM and on weekends in April, May and November. The staff can answer all kinds of questions about southern destinations along the Outer Banks. The restrooms are some of the few you'll find on this remote stretch of N.C. 12. This wooden structure also serves as a hunter contact station.

Bodie Island Lighthouse and Keepers' Quarters

West of N.C. 12
6 miles south of Whalebone Jct. 441-5711

This black-and-white beacon with horizontal bands is one of four lighthouses still standing along the Outer Banks. It sits more than a half-mile from the sea, in a field of incongruously green grass. The site is a perfect place to picnic.

In 1870, the federal government bought 15 acres of land for $150 to build the lighthouse and keepers quarters on. When the project was finished two years later, Bodie Island Lighthouse stood 150 feet tall and was the only lighthouse between Cape Henry, Virginia, and Cape Hatteras — and was very close to the inlet. But the inlet is migrating away from the beacon. And the current lighthouse is the third to stand near Oregon Inlet since

Insiders' Tips

Catch a big blue crab on a chicken neck at the appropriately named Chicken Neck Creek in Colington. In season the graveled platform flanking the second bridge on Colington Road heading west routinely teems with people.

the inlet opened during an 1846 hurricane. The first light developed cracks and had to be removed. Confederate soldiers destroyed the second tower to frustrate Union shipping efforts.

Wanchese resident John Gaskill served as the last civilian lightkeeper of Bodie Island Lighthouse. As late as 1940, he said, the tower was the only structure between Oregon Inlet and Jockey's Ridge. Gaskill helped his father strain kerosene before pouring it into the light. The kerosene prevented particles from clogging the vaporizer that kept the beacon burning.

Today, the lighthouse grounds and keeper's quarters offer a welcome respite during long drives to Hatteras Island. Wide expanses of marshland behind the tower offer enjoyable walks through cattails, yaupon and wax myrtle. You can stick to the short path and overlooks if you prefer to keep your shoes dry.

The National Park Service added new exhibits to the Bodie Island keepers quarters in 1995. The visitors center there is open daily from Memorial Day through Labor Day from 9 AM to 5 PM. Off-season hours vary depending on federal funding and staffing levels. The lighthouse itself is not open, but you can look up the tall tower from below when National Park Service employees are present to open the structure. Even a quick drive around the grounds to see the exterior is worth it.

Coquina Beach

N.C. 12, 6 miles south of Whalebone Jct.

Once one of the widest beaches on the Outer Banks, this stretch of sand was heavily damaged during 1993 and 1994 storms. The National Park Service expanded and repaved parking areas in 1995. But, at presstime, the portable restrooms still haven't been replaced by a permanent building.

This remote area, miles away from any business or rental cottage, is still a superb spot to surf, swim or sunbathe. The sand is almost white. The beach and offshore areas are relatively flat.

Drawing its name from the tiny butterfly-shaped coquina clams that burrow into the beach, at times almost every inch of this portion of the federally protected Cape Hatteras National Seashore harbors hundreds of recently washed up shells and several species of rare shorebirds. Coquinas are edible and can be collected and cleaned from their shells to make a fishy-tasting chowder. Local brick makers also have used them as temper in buildings.

The Laura A. Barnes

Coquina Beach

One of the last coastal schooners built in America, the *Laura A. Barnes* was completed in Camden, Maine, in 1918. This 120-foot ship was under sail on the Atlantic during a trip from New York to South Carolina when a nor'easter drove it onto the Outer Banks in 1921. The *Laura A. Barnes* ran aground just north of where it now rests at Coquina Beach. The entire crew survived. The National Park Service moved the shipwreck to its present location in 1973.

Oregon Inlet Fishing Center

N.C. 12, at the northern terminus of the Bonner Bridge 441-6301, (800) 272-5199

Sportsfishing enthusiasts — or anyone remotely interested in offshore angling — must stop by this bustling charter boat harbor on the north shore of Oregon Inlet. Set beside the U.S. Coast Guard station on land controlled by the National Park Service, Oregon Inlet Fishing Center is a federal concessionaire — so all vessels charge the same rate. A day on the Atlantic with one of these captains almost guarantees anglers a marlin, sailfish, wahoo, tuna or dolphin on the end of the line. See our Fishing chapter for details.

Oregon Inlet Coast Guard Station

N.C. 12, near Oregon Inlet Fishing Center

In the last century, the federal government operated two lifesaving stations at Oregon Inlet. The Bodie Island station was on the north side of the inlet. The Oregon Inlet station was on the south. Both of these original facilities are now closed. The Oregon Inlet station sits perilously close to the migrating inlet, the victim of hurricanes and decades of neglect. The Bodie Island station has been replaced by the current Coast Guard facility behind the Oregon Inlet Fishing Center.

Opened in 1991 with wide boat docks and ample parking area, the Oregon Inlet Coast Guard station includes a 10,000-square-foot building, state-of-the-art communications center, maintenance shops, an administrative center and accommodations for the staff. Coast Guard crews have rescued dozens of watermen off the Outer Banks. They also aid sea turtles and stranded seals by helping the animals get back safely to warmer parts of the ocean.

Oregon Inlet and the Bonner Bridge

N.C. 12, 8 miles south of Whalebone Jct.

Sea captains call this "the most dangerous inlet on the East Coast" — and with good reason. Since 1960, at least 25 lives and an equal number of boats have been lost at Oregon Inlet. During the winter of 1995, watermen were only able to use the channel at high tide, during daylight hours, because its depth shallowed from 12 feet to an average of 10 feet.

The only outlet to the sea in the 140 miles between Cape Henry, in Virginia Beach, and Hatteras Inlet, Oregon Inlet lies between Bodie Island and Pea Island National Wildlife Refuge. It is the primary passage for commercial and recreational fishing boats based along the northern Outer Banks. But in recent years, the channel has shoaled so much that many deep-draw vessels have not been able to get to sea.

Federal officials keep promising to build jetties — rock walls that some scientists say would stabilize the ever shallowing inlet. But environmentalists and other scientists oppose the project, saying it would cause increased erosion on beaches to the south. So the sand keeps building up in the area's only outlet to the Atlantic.

Oregon Inlet was created during a hurricane in September 1846 — the same storm that opened Hatteras Inlet between Hatteras Village and Ocracoke Island. It was named for the side-wheeler Oregon, the first ship to pass through the inlet.

In 1964, the Herbert C. Bonner Bridge was built across the inlet. This two-lane span finally connected Hatteras Island and the Cape Hatteras National Seashore with the northern Outer Banks beaches. Before the bridge was built, travelers relied on ferry boats to carry them across Oregon Inlet.

Hurricane-force winds blew a dredge barge into the bridge in 1990, knocking out a center section of the span. No one was hurt. But the more than 5,000 permanent residents of Hatteras Island were cut off from the rest of the world for four months before workers could completely repair the bridge.

Four-wheel-drive vehicles can exit N.C. 12 on the northeast side of the inlet and drive along the beach, even beneath the Bonner bridge, around the inlet. Fishing is permitted along the catwalks of the bridge and on the beach. Free parking and bathrooms are available at the Oregon Inlet Fishing Center. There are also parking and portable toilets on the southern end of the bridge. A trip across this span at sunset provides postcard-like photographs.

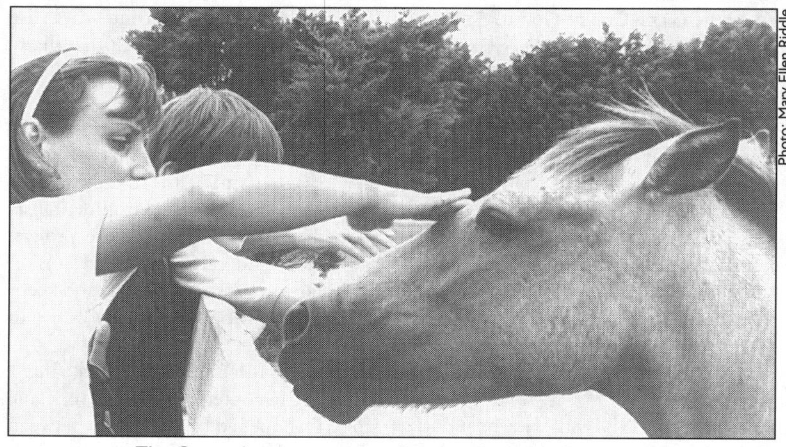

The Ocracoke pony pen is a fun stop for kids of any age.

Hatteras Island

Pea Island National Wildlife Refuge

North end of Hatteras Island
Both sides of N.C. 12 *987-2394*

Pea Island National Wildlife Refuge begins at the southern base of the Herbert C. Bonner Bridge and is the first place you'll come to if you enter Hatteras Island from the north. The beach along this undeveloped stretch of sand is popular with surfers, sunbathers and shell seekers. On the right side of the road, heading south, salt marshes surround Pamlico Sound and birds seem to flutter from every grove of cattails.

Founded on April 12, 1938, Pea Island refuge was federally funded as a winter preserve for snow geese. President Roosevelt put his Civilian Conservation Corps to work stabilizing the slightly sloping dunes, building them up with bulldozers, erecting long expanses of sand fencing and securing the sand with sea oats and grasses. Workers built dikes near the sound to form ponds and freshwater marshes. They planted fields to provide food for the waterfowl.

With 5,915 acres that attract more than 250 observed species of birds, Pea Island is an outdoor aviary well worth venturing off the road — and into the wilderness — to visit. Few tourists visited this refuge when Hatteras Island was cut off from the rest of the Outer Banks, and people arrived at the southern beaches by ferry. But after the Oregon Inlet bridge opened in 1964, motorists began driving through this once isolated outpost.

Today, Pea Island is one of the barrier islands' most popular havens for bird watchers, naturalists and sea turtle savers. Endangered species from the Kemps-Ridley sea turtle to the tiny Piping Plover shorebirds inhabit this enchanted area. Pea Island's name comes from the "dune peas" that grow all along the now grassy sand dunes. The tiny plant with pink and lavender flowers is a favorite food of migrating geese.

If you enter the refuge from the north on N.C. 12, note the new roadbed — completed in December 1995. This three-mile stretch of highway had to be moved more than 300 feet west of its former site to get it further away from the waves. During 1994, state officials had to shut down the two-lane road at least three times because the ocean had washed across it, spilling up to two feet of sand in some spots. The 5,000 residents of Hatteras Island were shut off from the rest of the world.

So to keep the road clear and provide a more permanent pathway through the Outer Banks, transportation engineers decided to re-route the most threatened portion of the pavement closer to the sound. The project cost taxpayers about $3 million. Since 1990, state transportation officials have spent more than $31 million trying to keep N.C. 12 open. They invested another $18 million in routine maintenance on the road. Special efforts have included a $1.8 million beach nourishment project to pump sand back on the beach and $920,000 worth of sandbags stacked along the shore.

Four miles south of the Bonner Bridge's southern base, at the entrance to the new portion of N.C. 12, the Pea Island Visitors Center offers free parking and easy access to the beach. If you walk directly across the highway to the top of the dunes, you'll see the remains of the more than century-old federal transport *Oriental*. Her steel boiler is the black mass, all that remains since the ship sank in May 1862.

On the sound side of the highway, in the marshes, ponds and endless wetlands, whistling swans, snow geese, Canada geese and 25 species of ducks make winter sojourns through the refuge. Savannah sparrows, migrant warblers, gulls, terns, herons and egrets also alight in this area from fall through early spring. In summer, American avocets, willets, black-necked stilts and several species of ducks nest here.

Mosquito repellent is a must on Pea Island from March through October. Ticks may also cause problems. Check your clothing before getting back in the car, and shower as soon as possible if you hike through any underbrush.

North Pond Trail

Pea Island, 4 mi. south of Oregon Inlet

A bird watcher's favorite, this handicapped-accessible nature trail begins at the visitors center parking area and is about a mile long — a 30-minute brisk walk to the sound and back. The trail runs along the top of a dike between two man-made ponds that were began in the late 19th century and completed by the Civilian Conservation Corps. The walkway includes two viewing platforms, marshland overlooks and mounted binoculars.

Wax myrtles and live oaks stabilize the dike — and provide shelter for scores of songbirds. Warblers, yellowthroats, cardinals and seaside sparrows stop here during their spring and fall migrations. If you whistle the correct calls into the brush and wait quietly, they'll answer in a symphony.

The U.S. Fish & Wildlife Service manages Pea Island refuge's ecosystem carefully. Workers plant fields with fescue and rye grass to keep the waterfowl coming back. Besides migrating birds, which don't occupy the island during summer, pheasants, muskrats and nutria live along these

Insiders' Tips

Each summer, volunteers at the Chicamacomico Life Saving Station re-enact beach rescue drills just like life saving station personnel used to perform for shipwreck victims at the turn of the century. These free, educational events are a great way to see how difficult — and treacherous — life used to be on the Outer Banks, especially for seabound sailors.

ponds year round. This short journey through a virtually unspoiled area will enhance any stay on the Outer Banks. If you crave quiet, fresh air, isolation and, above all, an opportunity to commune with wildlife, you'll want to walk the North Pond Trail.

Pea Island Refuge Headquarters

N.C. 12, 4 mi. south of Oregon Inlet 987-2394

A recently paved parking area, free public restrooms and the Pea Island Refuge Headquarters are 4 miles south of the Oregon Inlet bridge on the sound side of N.C. 12. Refuge volunteers staff this small welcome station April through November, Monday through Friday, 9 AM to 4 PM. They'll provide free information on bird-watching and nature trail maps. In summer months, they conduct special programs.

Hunting, camping and driving are not allowed in the refuge. Open fires also are prohibited. Dogs must be kept on leashes on the east side of the highway. Firearms are not allowed in the refuge — shotguns and rifles must be stowed out of sight even if you're just driving straight through Hatteras Island. Fishing, crabbing, boating and other activities are allowed in the ocean and sound but are prohibited in refuge ponds.

Pea Island Lifesaving Station

N.C. 12, 7 mi. south of Oregon Inlet

About 7 miles south of the Oregon Inlet bridge rest the remains of the nation's only all African-American lifesaving station. Pea Island was established with the rest of the U.S. Lifesaving outposts in 1879 and was originally manned by mostly white crews. Black men were confined to caring for the horses that dragged surfboats through the sand and other menial tasks.

The year after the station was set up, however, federal officials fired Pea Island's white crew members for mishandling the *Henderson* shipwreck disaster. Black personnel from other stations were placed under the charge of Richard Etheridge, who was of Native American and African-American descent. The new crew carried out their duties honorably.

Pea Island's surfmen rescued countless crews and passengers of ships that washed ashore in storms or sank in the seething seas. Etheridge became known as one of the best prepared, most professional and daring leaders in the service. One of the crew's most famous rescues was in 1896 when the captain of the *E.S. Newman* sounded an SOS off Hatteras Island's treacherous shores — beaches with so many shoals that sailors call the area the Graveyard of the Atlantic.

In 1992, the U.S. Coast Guard Service — a latter day version of the Lifesaving Service — dedicated a cutter to the Pea Island crew. About a dozen of the African-American surfmen's descendants witnessed the moving ceremony. A plaque on board the big ship commemorates the lifesaving crew's heroism.

Hatteras Shipwrecks

Northern Hatteras Island beaches

Big winter blows and even smaller summer storms often unveil incredible sunken treasures on the Hatteras Island beaches. Pirate gold and pieces of eight are few and far between. But shipwreck remnants, old bottles and beach glass abound. Each shift in wind seems to change the scenery for souvenir seekers who care to comb these quiet shores. You don't need a shovel or even a metal detector to unearth broken teacups, hand-blown whiskey bottles or the rotting remains of a cork.

Rodanthe

Chicamacomico Life Saving Station

East side of N.C. 12 987-1552

With volunteer labor and long years of dedication, this once decrepit lifesaving station is now beautifully restored and open for tours. Its white-washed buildings sparkle on the sandy lawn, surrounded by a perfect picket fence. Even the outbuildings and boathouse have been brought back to their former uses.

Chicamacomico was one of the Outer Banks' original seven lifesaving stations, opening in 1874 at its current site. The present boathouse building was the original station but was retained as a storage shed when the bigger facility was built. Under three keepers named Midgett, Chicamacomico crews guarded the sea along Hatteras Island's northern coast for 70 years. Between 1876 and the time the station closed in 1954, seven Midgetts were awarded the Gold Life Saving Award; three won the silver; and six others worked or lived at Chicamacomico. Perhaps the station's most famous rescue was when surfmen pulled crew members from the British tanker *Mirlo* off their burning ship and into safety.

Today, the nonprofit Chicamacomico Historical Association oversees and operates the lifesaving station. Volunteers set up a museum of area lifesaving awards and artifacts in the main building — and have recovered some of the lifesaving equipment for the boathouse. National Park rangers take school groups on tours of the station, showing them how the breeches buoy helped rescue shipwreck victims and explaining the precise maneuvers surfmen had to follow on shore.

In summer months, park rangers conduct beach apparatus drills when funding provides. Recently, volunteers have been doing the costumed re-enactments because of federal funding cutbacks. To help support the lifesaving station and the Chicamacomico Historical Association, send a check to P.O. Box 140, Rodanthe 27968.

Salvo

Salvo Post Office

West side of N.C. 12, southern end of Salvo

If you're heading south on N.C. 12 through Hatteras Island, slow down as you leave Salvo and try to spot a tiny whitewashed building with blue and red trim on the right side of the road. That's the Salvo Post Office, which was the country's smallest post office until an arsonist burned about half of it down in 1992. It sat atop low rails in the postmaster's front yard. Villagers moved it to in front of a new postmaster's house each time one came aboard.

The wooden structure had beautiful gilt post boxes surrounding the small glass service window. But it didn't have a bathroom, air conditioning or a handicapped-accessible ramp. So although community volunteers rallied and rebuilt their little post office quickly, the federal government refused to reopen the outpost — which was originally erected in 1901. Today, Salvo residents drive to Rodanthe to pick up their mail.

Avon

Canadian Hole

N.C. 12, 1.5 mi. south of Avon

If a breeze is blowing, pull off the west side of the road between Avon and Buxton into the big parking lot on the sound.

Insiders' Tips

If you climb the Cape Hatteras Lighthouse, look across the Atlantic, toward the south from the tower to see flashes from Diamond Shoals Light Tower set on rocks in the ocean.

Known as Canadian Hole, this is one of America's hottest Windsurfing spots — and a magnet for visitors from the great white north. Whether you ride a sailboard or not, this sight is not to be missed. On windy afternoons, more than 100 Windsurfers spread out along the shallow sound, their brightly colored butterfly sails gently skimming into the sunset. There's a nice bathing beach here, so bring chairs and coolers and plan to watch the silent wave riders — some of whom are famous in Windsurfing circles. See the related sidebar in our Watersports chapter.

Buxton

U.S. Coast Guard Station

Old Lighthouse Rd., Buxton 995-5881

A former U.S. Navy facility, this Buxton military outpost was turned over to the Coast Guard in 1982. It includes offices and personnel housing. Generally, it's closed to the public. But retired military employees, dependents and current military personnel are welcome to use the facilities. There's a limited commissary, a small exchange, mess hall, tennis court, basketball court and small dispensary. The station is open year round but usually closes at 5 PM.

The Monitor

Off Cape Hatteras, in the Atlantic Ocean

Launched January 30, 1862, the *Monitor* is one of the nation's most famous battleships. It's watery grave is the first National Underwater Marine Sanctuary. Divers sanctioned by the National Oceanic and Atmospheric Administration have spent four years trying to retrieve the four-pronged propeller from the ironclad boat, which rests upside down in 230 feet of water about 17 miles off Cape Hatteras.

The *Monitor* was owned by Union forces and was their counterpart to the Confederate ship *Virginia* during the Civil War. The *Virginia* was the world's first ironclad warship, built from the hulk of the Union frigate *Merrimac,* which southern forces captured and refitted. On March 8, 1862, the tent-shaped steamer *Virginia* cruised out of Norfolk to challenge a blockade of six wooden ships. By day's end, the *Virginia* had sunk two of those Union ships and damaged another.

Built by Swedish-American engineer John Ericsson and appropriately dubbed the "Cheesebox on a raft" for its unusual design, the *Monitor* was a low-slung ironclad that included a revolving turret to carry its main battery. This strange-looking ship arrived in Norfolk on March 9 and soon battled the *Virginia* to a draw. Retreating Confederates eventually destroyed the *Virginia*. The *Monitor* was ordered to proceed farther south.

The New Year's Eve storm of 1862 caught the Union ironclad off Cape Hatteras, far out in the Atlantic. The *Monitor* sank completely, taking its crew with it. Its whereabouts were unknown until university researchers discovered the *Monitor* in 1973.

Although they haven't been able to retrieve the heavy propeller, federally permitted scuba divers have brought a few small artifacts off the *Monitor's* waterlogged decks. They've recovered bottles, silverware and china pieces. In 1983, they even brought up the ship's distinctive four-blade anchor.

Cape Hatteras National Seashore

Hatteras Island Visitors Center

Off N.C. 12, Buxton 995-4474

About 300 yards south of Old Lighthouse Road, past the Texaco station and Sharky's eatery, a large wooden sign welcomes visitors to the Cape Hatteras National Seashore and Hatteras Island Visitors Center. Turn left if you're heading south, toward the split-rail fence. And follow the winding road past turtle ponds and marshes.

If you turn left at the fork in this road,

you'll head toward the Cape Hatteras Lighthouse and the National Park Service Visitors Center. Turn right, and you'll wind up at the Cape Point campground. Surf fishing, sunbathing, swimming, surfing and four-wheel driving are allowed along most areas of the beach here year round.

The visitors center is near the lighthouse, past a newly expanded parking area. It's in the former house of the assistant lighthouse keepers, which was built in 1854. This two-story, wooden frame home was renovated in 1986 and is adjacent to the smaller keepers' quarters. It houses an extensive museum of lifesaving artifacts and lighthouse memorabilia. Free exhibits include information on shipping, wars and Outer Banks heroes.

A small bookstore in the visitors center sells literature on lifesaving stations, lighthouses and Hatteras Island history. Clean restrooms also are available here. Volunteers offer a range of summer interpretive programs on the visitor center's wide, covered front porch. Activities change seasonally, with fall and spring programs also conducted. Call ahead for a schedule, or pick one up at the information desk inside.

The visitors center is open from 9 AM to 5 PM daily from September through mid-June and from 9 AM to 6 PM from mid-June through Labor Day. It's closed Christmas Day. Hours are subject to change in the off-seasons depending on federal funding cutbacks.

Cape Hatteras Lighthouse

Cape Point, Buxton *995-4474*

The nation's tallest brick lighthouse, this black and white striped beacon is open for free tours throughout the summer and is well worth the climb for hearty hikers. It contains 268 spiraling stairs and an 800,000 candlepower electric light that rotates every 7.5 seconds. Its bright beacon can be seen more than 20 miles out to sea.

The original Cape Hatteras Lighthouse was built in 1802 to guard the "Graveyard of the Atlantic." The tower sat near its present location, at Cape Point. Just off this eastern edge of the Outer Banks, the warm Gulf Stream meets the cold Labrador Current, creating dangerous undercurrents around the ever-shifting offshore shoals.

Standing 90 feet tall and sitting about 300 yards south of its current site, the first lighthouse at Cape Hatteras was fueled with whale oil — which didn't burn bright enough to illuminate the dark shoals surrounding it. Erosion weakened the structure over the years. And in 1861, retreating Confederate soldiers took the light's lens with them, leaving Hatteras Island in the dark.

The lighthouse that's still standing was erected in 1870 on a floating foundation and cost $150,000 to build. More than 1.25 million Philadelphia baked bricks are included in the 180-foot tall tower. A special Fresnel lens that refracts the light increases its visibility.

Although the lighthouse is still holding its ground, the beach around its octagonal base is eroding rapidly. Workers stacked sandbags around the structure and have added three rock groins in the ocean nearby to stop sand movement. But the National Park Service plans to move the lighthouse 1,500 feet inland — if the federal government ever finds the money.

Staffed entirely by volunteers, the Cape Hatteras Lighthouse is open all the way to the outdoor tower at the top. The breathtaking view is like looking off the roof of a 20-story building. And the free adventure is well worth the effort. The climb is strenuous — so don't attempt to carry children in your arms or in kid carriers. Climbing is permitted from 9:30 AM to 4 PM from May through Labor Day and from 10 AM to 2 PM, September 6 through Columbus Day. See our sidebar in the Hatteras Island chapter.

The Altoona Wreck

Cape Point, Buxton

Four-wheel-drive vehicle owners should enter the beach at the end of Cape Point Way on Ramp 44. Here, the Outer Banks jut out into the Atlantic in a wide elbow-shape curve near the Cape Hatteras Lighthouse. The beaches in this area offer some of the barrier islands' best surf fishing. Don't try this in a two-wheel-drive vehicle, and let a little air out of the tires on your sports utility vehicles when traversing sand.

If you can't drive on the beach, park on solid ground near the road and walk over the ramp to a foot trail. The path begins at the base of the dune and veers off at a 45-degree angle. At the edge of a seawater pond, about a 10 minute walk from the parking area, you'll glimpse the remains of the ancient shipwreck *Altoona*.

Built in Maine in 1869, the *Altoona* was a two-masted, 100-foot-long cargo schooner based in Boston. It left Haiti in 1878 with a load of dyewood bound for New York. On October 22, a storm drove it ashore near Cape Point. Lifesavers rescued its seven crew members and salvaged some of the cargo. But the ship was buried beneath the sand until a storm uncovered it in 1962. The sea has broken the big boat apart since then. But you can still see part of the bow and hull bobbing in the waves.

Diamond Shoals Light

Off Cape Point, in the Atlantic Ocean

You can't really visit this attraction — except in private boats. But you can see this unusual light tower from the eastern shore of Cape Point and from the top of the Cape Hatteras Lighthouse. Its bright beacon blinks every two seconds from a steel structure set 12 miles out in the sea.

Diamond Shoals once held a lighthouse. But waves beat the offshore rocks that held the lighthouse so badly that federal officials soon gave up the project. Three lightships have been stationed on the shoals since 1824. The first sunk in an 1827 gale. The second held its ground from 1897 until German submarines sank it in 1918. The third beamed until 1967 when it was replaced by the current light tower.

Diamond Shoals, the rocks around the tower, are the southern end of the treacherous near shore sandbars off Hatteras Island.

Buxton Woods Nature Trail

Cape Point, Buxton

Leading from the Cape Point Campground road about three quarters of a mile through the woods, the Buxton nature trail takes walkers through thick vine jungles, across tall sand dunes and into freshwater marshes. Small plaques along the fairly level walkway explain the area's fragile ecosystems. People who hike this trail will learn about the Outer Banks' water table, the role of beach grass and sea oats in stabilizing sand dunes, and the effects salt, storms and visitors have on the ever-changing environment.

Cottonmouths seem to like this trail too — so beware of these unmistakably fat, rough-scaled snakes that can be dull brown, yellow, gray or almost black. They're very rare. But if you see one, let it get away — don't chase it. If it stands its ground, retreat.

This hike is not recommended for handicapped visitors or young children. But picnic tables and charcoal grills just south of the nature trail provide a welcome respite for everyone. And the walk is well worth it for hearty nature lovers who don't mind mingling with the outdoor elements.

Frisco

Billy Mitchell Air Field

1 mi. south of N.C. 12, Frisco 995-3646

A small, no-frills airstrip near the en-

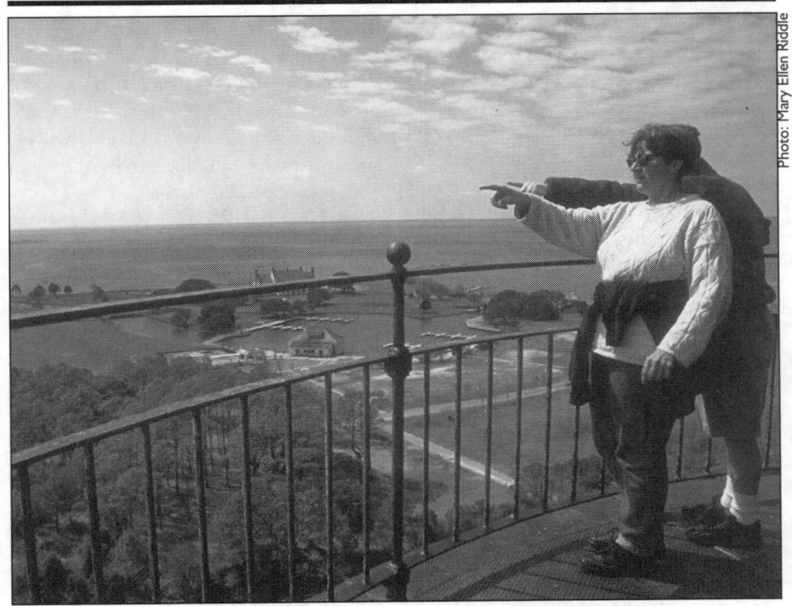

The Currituck Beach Lighthouse is a great place to view the beautiful scenery of the Outer Banks.

trance to the National Park Service's Frisco Campground, this Hatteras Island air field was named for a controversial aviator. Billy Mitchell conducted some of his bombing tests near here in 1921 to prove that airplanes could defeat Navy ships. An exhibit at the pilot's shed provides additional history on the subject.

The asphalt landing strip at this air field is 3,000 feet long, 75 feet wide, oriented NE/SW. Private planes are welcome. Outer Banks air tours conducted by Burrus Flying Service take off from this site from 10 AM until sunset Monday through Saturday. Half-hour tours of Cape Hatteras cost $25 per person for a party of two, $20 per person for a party of three. North and south tours of Hatteras Island also are available. These 45-minute air tours cost $37.50 per person for a party of two, $30 per person for a party of three. Call Burrus Flying, 995-6671 or 986-2679 (evenings), for schedules or more information.

Frisco Native American Museum

N.C. 12, Frisco *995-4440*

This small, family-owned museum on the sound side of N.C. 12 in Frisco houses a collection of Native American artifacts that Carl and Joyce Bornfriend have gathered all across the country. Hopi drums, pottery, kachinas, weapons and jewelry abound in homemade display cases with hand-lettered placards. A souvenir gift shop offers everything from antiques to Civil War uniforms.

With advance notice, the Bornfriends will give guided tours of their museum and lectures for school and youth groups. The museum property also includes some outdoor nature trails in the woods behind the building. Hours are 11 AM to 5 PM Tuesdays through Sundays, year round. Admission is free.

Hatteras-Ocracoke Ferry

End of N.C. 12, Hatteras Village to beginning of N.C. 12 on Ocracoke Island *986-2353*
(800) BY FERRY

The only link between Hatteras and Ocracoke islands, this free state-run ferry carries passengers and vehicles across Hatteras Inlet daily, year round, with trips at least every hour from 5 AM to midnight. A fleet of 10 ferry boats, some 150-feet long, carry up to 30 cars and trucks each on the 40-minute ride.

You can get out of your vehicle and walk around the open decks, or stay inside the car if it's cold. A passenger lounge a short flight of steps above the deck offers cushioned seats, wide windows and free 15-minute video depictions of the villages you're about to visit. On the lower deck, new telescopes give people a chance to see sea gulls and passing shorelines up close — for a quarter. Free, always clean restrooms also are on the deck. But there's no food or drink to be found on this 5-mile crossing, so pack your own picnic. Beware if you decide to break bread with the dozens of birds that fly overhead. After they eat, they, too, look for free bathrooms. And they'll follow — overhead — all the way to Ocracoke.

A souvenir shop opened at the Hatteras ferry docks in December 1995, selling everything from coloring books and Frisbees to sweatshirts and coffee mugs. Drink and snack machines also are on site.

A daytrip to Ocracoke is a must for every Outer Banks visitor, whether you're staying in Corolla or Kill Devil Hills. (See our Ocracoke chapter for details.) The free ferry is the only way to get there — except by private boat. In 1994, more than 750,000 people and 250,000 vehicles crossed Hatteras Inlet on the North Carolina ferry fleet. On summer days, more than 1,000 passengers ride the flat boats.

If you arrive at Ocracoke Island on the ferry, there's a 12-mile drive through open marshlands and pine forests before you get to the village. N.C. 12 picks up at the ferry docks and continues, two lanes, to the end of the island. On the left, some wide open beaches await avid four-wheelers and anyone who likes to have a piece of the seaside to themselves.

A National Park Service oceanfront campground is on your left just before you get to the village. Ocracoke itself is a quaint fishing village that has recently grown into a popular tourist destination. About 800 people live on Ocracoke Island year round. Boutiques, seafood restaurants, craft shops and other retailers line the quiet, twisting lanes, but most are open only during the summer season. We recommend you park your car somewhere near the waterfront and rent a bicycle to tour this picturesque, isolated island.

Ocracoke Island

Ocracoke Pony Pens

N.C. 12, on the soundside

According to local legends, ships carrying the first English colonists to America made their initial landing at Ocracoke Inlet in 1585. The flagship *Tiger* grounded on a shallow shoal. Sir Richard Grenville ordered the vessel — including a load of horses purchased in the West Indies — unloaded so the ship would float again. The horses swam ashore and some, it's said, escaped to run wild on Ocracoke Island.

Other theories say the ponies were refugees from Spanish shipwrecks. And a few practical people insist they were merely brought to Ocracoke by early inhabitants and allowed to roam freely because — on an island miles from anything else in the Atlantic — there is really no reason to fence in a herd of horses. In any case, Ocracoke's "wild" horses have survived on this Outer Banks island for at least two centuries. In the late 1900s, old-timers said, hundreds ran around eating marsh grass and splashing in the shallow salt marshes.

As populations grew, however, some of the animals were auctioned off. Boy Scout troops used to round up the wild horses annually. When the National Park Service began overseeing the federal seashore, they began managing the wild herd. Today, about two dozen ponies live in a large penned area off N.C. 12, about 6 miles southwest of the Hatteras-Ocracoke ferry dock. There's a small parking area off the road and a raised, wooden observation platform overlooking the mile-long fenced pasture. Sometimes the horses come right up near the road, posing for pictures. Other times, especially in bad weather, they huddle in shelters closer to the sound and can't be seen.

Don't climb into the horse pen or attempt to feed or pet the ponies. These are wild animals. They can kick and bite.

Hammock Hills Nature Trail

N.C. 12, opposite Ocracoke Campground

A three-quarter-mile nature trail north of Ocracoke Village, Hammock Hills covers a cross-section of the island. The 30-minute walk begins near the sand dunes, traverses a maritime forest and winds through a salt marsh. Hikers can learn how plants adapt to Ocracoke's unusual elements and the harsh barrier island weather.

Bring your camera on this scenic stroll. We highly recommend bug repellant in spring and summer months, and watch out for snakes in the underbrush.

Ocracoke Island Visitors Center

Near the Cedar Island and Swan Quarter Ferry Slips *928-4531*

This seasonal visitors center at the southern end of N.C. 12 is a clearinghouse of information about Ocracoke Island. It's run by the National Park Service across from Silver Lake. If you're arriving on the island from the Hatteras ferry, stay on the main road until you reach the T-intersection at Silver Lake. Turn right and continue around the lake, counterclockwise, until you see the low brown building on your right. Free parking is available at the visitors center.

Inside, there's an information desk, helpful staff, a small book shop and exhibits about Ocracoke. You can also arrange to use the Park Service's docks here. And you can pick up maps of the winding back roads that make great bicycle paths.

The visitors center is open Memorial Day through Labor Day from 10 AM to 5 PM. Rangers offer a variety of free summer programs through the center, including beach and sound hikes, pirate plays, bird-watching, night hikes and history lectures. Check at the front desk for changing weekly schedules. Restrooms are open to the public in season.

Ocracoke Coast Guard Station

Silver Lake *928-4731*
Emergency search and rescue only *928-3711*

This small station on the lip of Silver Lake is the southernmost Coast Guard outpost along the Outer Banks. It was built in 1938 to replace an older station on the same site. Today, about a dozen officers maintain a motorized lifeboat and provide services from search and rescues to law enforcement to maintaining channel markers.

Ocracoke Island Museum and Preservation Society

Silver Lake *928-7375*

Built by David Williams, the first chief of the Ocracoke Coast Guard Station, this two-story, white-frame house was moved to its present location on National Park Service land in 1989. It's east of the Park Service parking lot, on the same side of Silver Lake as the Coast Guard Station. It was recently restored and is now managed by the Ocracoke Preservation Society as a museum and visitors center. It's open daily

Photo: Mary Ellen Riddle

Hatteras Island is the site of annual East Coast surfing contests. This photographer is hoping to catch a big one too!

from 9 AM to 6 PM from April 1 through November 1.

Ocracoke Village Walking Tour

West end of N.C. 12, around the village

The easiest way to explore Ocracoke is by bicycle or on foot. The narrow, winding back lanes weren't meant for cars. And you miss little landmarks and interesting areas of the island if you try to drive through too quickly. People on Ocracoke are generally very friendly. You'll get a chance to chat with more locals, too, if you slow down your touring pace through this picturesque fishing village.

To take a walking tour of Ocracoke, park in the lot opposite the visitors center. Turn left out of the lot and walk down N.C. 12 around the shores of Silver Lake, past the sleepy village waterfront. You'll pass many small shops, boutiques and some large new hotels: the Anchorage, Harborside, Pirate's Quay and Princess Motel. Keep walking until you see a small brick post office on your right.

Opposite the post office, a sandy, narrow street angles to the left. This is Old Howard Street. It winds through one of the oldest and least changed parts of the village. Note the humble old homes, the attached cisterns for collecting rain water and the detached kitchens behind these historic structures.

Continue walking past Village Craftsman. After about 400 yards, Howard Street empties onto School Street. Turn left, and you'll see the Methodist church and K-12 public school that serves all the children on Ocracoke. With graduating classes of less than a dozen students, this is the state's smallest public school.

The church is usually open for visitors. But use discretion if services are in progress. And please wipe your feet as you go in. As you enter, note the cross displayed behind the altar. It was carved from the wooden spar of an American freighter, the *Caribsea*, sunk offshore by German U-boats in the early months of 1942. By strange coincidence, the Caribsea's engineer was Ocracoke native James Baugham Gaskill, who was killed when the boat sank. Local residents say that several days later a display case holding Gaskill's mate license, among other things, washed ashore not far from his family home. Ocracoke has had a Methodist Church since 1828. The current one was built in

1943 from lumber and pews salvaged from older buildings. A historical-sketch pamphlet is available in the vestibule for visitors.

Upon leaving the church, walk around the north corner of the school, past the playground, onto a narrow boardwalk. This wooden path leads to a paved road beyond it. Turn left. This was the first paved road on the island and was constructed by Seabees during World War II.

After walking less than a mile down this road, turn right at the first stop sign. A few minutes' walk along this narrow, tree-shaded street will bring you to the British Cemetery where victims of World War II are buried far away from their English soil. (See the subsequent listing in this section.) It's on your right, set back a bit from the road and shaded by live oak and yaupon. The big British flag makes it easy to spot.

To return to the visitors center, walk west until you reach Silver Lake, then turn right. You'll pass craft shops, a hammock shop and several boutiques along the way. (See our Shopping chapter for details.) If the weather's nice, we suggest a stop for an outdoor drink at the waterfront Jolly Roger, the Creekside Cafe upstairs above the bicycle stand, or Howard's Pub on the highway before heading back to the ferry docks.

See our Ocracoke chapter for additional information.

Ocracoke Inlet Lighthouse

SW corner of Ocracoke Village

The southernmost of the Outer Banks' four lighthouses, this whitewashed tower also is the oldest and shortest. It stands 75 feet tall, a good walk away from any water and has an iron-railed tower set askew on the top. The lighthouse isn't open for tours or climbing, but volunteers occasionally staff its broad base, offering historical talks and answering visitors' questions. Inquire about possible staffing times at the visitors center or National Park Service offices.

Ocracoke's lighthouse is still operating, emitting one long flash every few seconds from a half-hour before sunset to a half-hour after sunrise. It was built in 1823 to replace Shell Castle Rock lighthouse, which was set offshore closer to the dangerous shoals in Ocracoke Inlet. Shell Castle light was abandoned in 1798 when the inlet shifted south.

The beam from Ocracoke's beacon rotates 360-degrees and can be seen 14 miles out to sea. The tower itself is brick, covered by hand-spread, textured white mortar. The walls are five feet thick at the base.

On the right side of the wooden boardwalk leading to the lighthouse, a two-story, white cottage once served as quarters for the tower's keeper. The National Park Service renovated this structure in the 1980s. It now serves as the home of Ocracoke's ranger and the structure's maintenance supervisor.

To reach the light, turn left off N.C. 12 at the Island Inn and go about 800 yards down the two-lane street. You can park near a white picketed turnoff on the right. Visitors must walk the last few yards down the boardwalk to the lighthouse.

Silver Lake Marina

At the Visitors Center 928-4531

Run by the National Park Service near

Insiders' Tips

Sandboarding is allowed at Jockey's Ridge State Park during fall and winter with a special permit available from park rangers.

the end of N.C. 12, Silver Lake Marina is the only large marina on Ocracoke Island. There are low dockage fees and no reservations accepted for this 18-foot-deep basin. The marina has no slips — only 400 feet of frontage with tie-up facilities.

Docking is available on a first-come, first-served basis. If there's open space, just pull in and tie up. Boats are only allowed to tie up to other crafts if you've secured the permission of the vessels' owner. There's a 14-day stay limit in summertime. It's possible to get last-minute space even during the busiest in-season weeks, but it gets pretty crowded here on weekends. If the marina is full when you arrive, you can anchor out in the lake as long as you stay out of the channel and away from the ferry operations.

O'Neal's Dockside

Behind the Community Store *928-1111*

A friendly hunting and fishing center owned by Charlie O'Neal, this waterfront shop offers help with booking offshore fishing charters on the *Miss Kathleen*, *Seawalker*, *Bluefin* and *Outlaw*. O'Neal's employees also will help visitors charter daytrips to Portsmouth Island. O'Neal's sells a full line of supplies, boating gear and fuel.

Ocracoke Fishing Center

Silver Lake *928-6661*

Owned by the Anchorage Inn, this fishing center includes five 200-foot piers and a new building where customers can book charter boat trips to the sound, Gulf Stream and inshore areas (see our Fishing chapter). The Anchorage Inn is open most of the year (see our Accommodations chapter), but we advise calling ahead during December and January.

Styron's General Store

Ocracoke Village, near the lighthouse *928-6819*

One of the oldest establishments on Ocracoke Island, Styron's General Store opened in its present location in 1920. Owner Al Styron tore down his family's store on Hog Island — near Cedar Island — and loaded the cypress walls into his boat. He carted Styron's Store to Ocracoke and rebuilt the business there.

Today, Styron's grandson, James Barrie Gaskill, and Gaskill's daughter, Candy, run the family business. Gaskill also commercial fishes. The store stays open all year, catering to local customers and summer visitors. Each morning, when the weather is rough, watermen, retirees and old friends gather inside the wide front room of Styron's store to trade tales and drink strong, steaming, free coffee atop the pine-plank floors.

Ocracoke doesn't have a full-size grocery store, but Styron's stocks everything from chest waders to duck pâté. Wooden milk crates and apple boxes hold gourmet wines imported from Australia and France. Metal fish baskets are filled with fresh onions and red potatoes. Shelves along the sides are stacked with Chinese roast duck mix, Jewish matzos and Thai sesame oil. Of course, the simpler things such as Octagon soap and whole wheat flour are still sold here. But there's also an amazing mix of virtually everything anyone would need.

The store's been expanded over the years. A back room now contains commercial fishing supplies and all-weather gear. But the front room retains some of its past, proudly displayed amidst the newfangled fodder: Burgundy leather-bound ledgers contain records of every transaction made in the store since 1925. The antique, gilt cash register that Al Styron installed still occupies the prestigious front counter space. The former feed scale holds storeroom keys, and two 1950s-era meat coolers cradle Dutch cheeses and fancy deli meats. The original safe, a multi-drawer roll-top desk and a 1940 adding machine all are displayed — and used — as they have been for nearly a half-century.

Besides food and general merchandise, Styron's serves hot lunches made on the premises and homemade desserts to eat in or take out. Three wooden tables and a dozen ladder-backed chairs offer customers a place to sit a spell or sip one of Candy's locally famous fresh milk shakes. Styron's store sits on the corner of Point Road, about two blocks before the lighthouse. It's open from 8 AM to 5 PM Monday through Saturday, 10 AM to 5 PM Sunday. The store stays open later during summer months.

British Cemetery

British Cemetery Rd.

Beneath a stead of trees, on the edge of a community cemetery, four granite gravestones commemorate the crew of the British vessel HMS *Bedfordshire*. This 170-foot trawler was one of a fleet of 24 antisubmarine ships that Prime Minister Winston Churchill loaned the United States in April 1942 to stave off German U-boats. On May 11 of that year, a German submarine torpedoed and sank the British ship about 40 miles south of Ocracoke.

All four officers and 33 enlisted men aboard the Bedfordshire drowned. U.S. Coast Guard officers stationed on Ocracoke found four of the bodies washed ashore three days later. They were able to identify two of the sailors. Townspeople gave Britain a 12-by-14-foot plot of land and buried the seamen in a site adjacent to the island's cemetery.

Since then, Coast Guard officers have maintained the grassy area within a white picket fence. They fly a British flag above the graves. And each year, on the anniversary of the sailors' deaths, the local military establishment sponsors a ceremony to honor the men who died so far from their own shores.

Porstmouth Island

South of Ocracoke

Accessible only by private or hired boat

The only ghost town east of the Mississippi River, Portsmouth Village is about a 20-minute boat ride south of Ocracoke Island — and was once the biggest town on the Outer Banks. Today, the 23-mile-long, 1.5-mile-wide island is owned and managed by The National Park Service as part of Cape Lookout National Seashore. Wilderness camping, hiking, fishing and other activities are available on the wide beach. Free, self-guided walking tours of the village are an outstanding way to see how islanders lived in the 19th century.

Capt. Rudy Austin runs daily round-trip boat shuttles throughout the summer from Silver Lake on Ocracoke Island across the Pamlico Sound to Portsmouth Island. His boat leaves at 9:30 AM from the docks and picks up passengers on Portsmouth at 2 PM. Cost is $15 per person. Pets on leashes also are permitted. Call at least one day ahead for reservations, 928-4361 or 928-4281. See our Portsmouth Island sidebar in the Daytrippin' chapter.

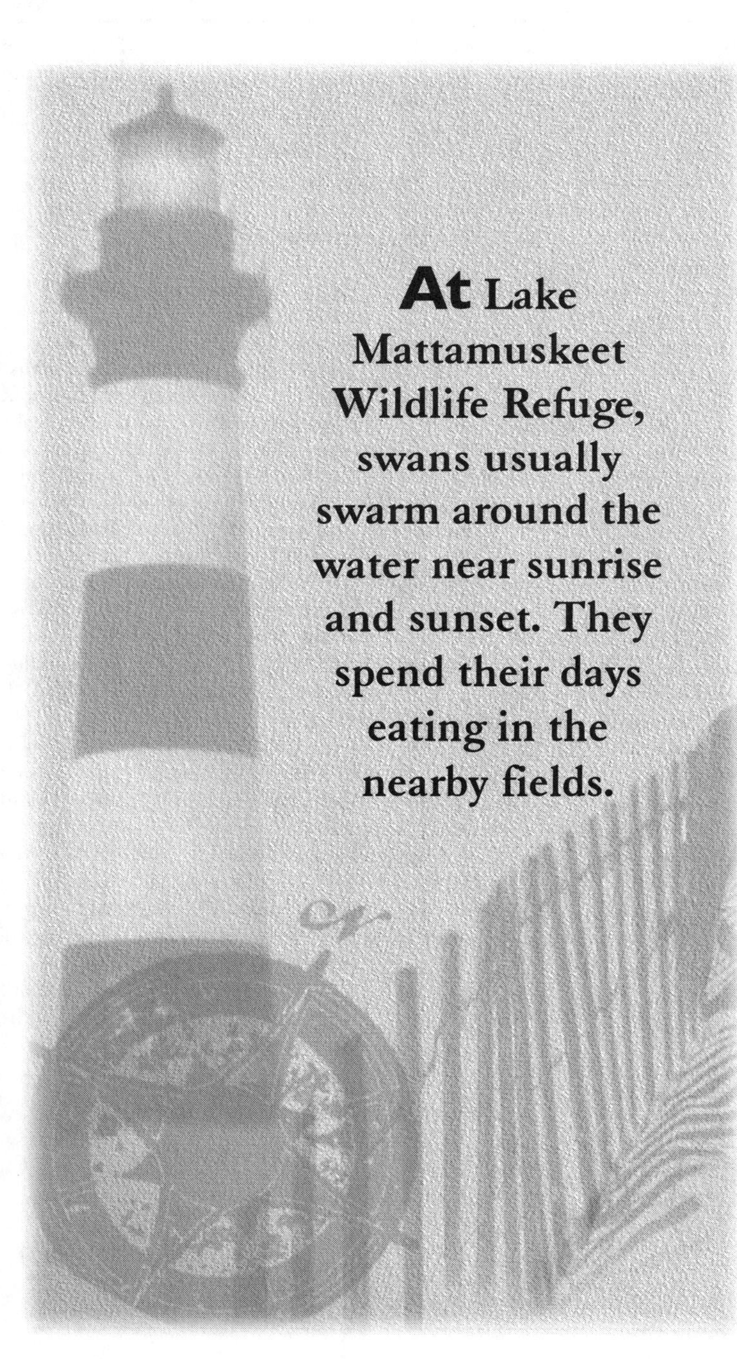

At Lake Mattamuskeet Wildlife Refuge, swans usually swarm around the water near sunrise and sunset. They spend their days eating in the nearby fields.

Inside Daytrippin'

With more than 100 miles of shoreline to explore, golden sandy shores that shift with the wind and over 400 years of history to ponder, the Outer Banks always offer new experiences. Sometimes, though, it's good to get onto solid ground again. The surrounding mainland — northeastern North Carolina's Albemarle area and the Central Coast area — offer wonderful nearby places to visit for daytrips and long, lovely weekends.

If you're itching for isolation, Portsmouth Island, the only ghost town east of the Mississippi River, has wilderness and waterfront campsites waiting for you to hike into. If antiquing is more up your alley, enjoy a day amidst colonial splendor along the shady streets of Edenton. Alligators and black bears, swans and shipwrecks await you in other nearby getaways.

Wildlife Adventures

Merchants Millpond State Park

Access from U.S. 158, N.C. 32 and N.C. 37
Gatesville *357-1191*

Less than a two-hour drive from the Outer Banks, Merchants Millpond is an isolated, undisturbed wonderland like no other place in the world. This scenic blackwater swamp boasts family and wilderness campsites, miles of well-marked hiking trails and canoe runs and some of the best largemouth bass fishing in eastern North Carolina.

Between the mid-1800s and early 1920s, the 760-acre millpond was a gathering place for farmers and merchants. A grist and sawmill sat on the edge on the pond. Water controlled by wooden gates in a spillway powered the mill. A general store, a post office and rough-hewn wooden houses also hugged the muddy shores. Today, only fragments of foundations can be found rotting among more than 2,918 acres of surreal state land in the western Albemarle area.

But picnic tables, ranger programs, fishing and at least 190 species of birds still cause people to flock into these boggy lowlands from early spring through late fall. More than 85,000 visitors tour the site each year. Poisonous snakes, mosquitos and ticks also inhabit the area — so beware.

Merchants Millpond became a state preserve in 1973 after Moyock nature lover A.B. Coleman donated 919 acres to North Carolina. The Nature Conservancy contributed another 925 acres, and additional land has been acquired over the years. The park tries to sponsor at least one activity per weekend throughout three seasons, ranging from talks and slide programs to moonlit hikes to spot stars or search for screech owls.

Reservations are taken in advance for 20 drive-in campsites with washouses, drinking water and grills. Three-quarters of a mile from the boat launching ramp are seven rustic canoe-in sites, and 3.5 miles into the woods are five primitive backpack sites. These sites offer more secluded camping and steel fire rings. The park also has three hike-in and three canoe-in sites — 1.25 miles from the launching site — for organized groups of up to 50 members. Camping permits are sold at the ranger station for $5 each. Group permits cost $1 per person. North Carolina requires anglers to have fishing licenses, and these are sold at nearby bait shops.

Even inexperienced boaters can manage to manipulate canoes around these serene, scenic waters. Canoes rent for $2.50 an hour or $10 per day. Both Merchants Millpond and the adjoining Lassiter Swamp — about a two-hour paddle away — have miles of water trails well marked by brightly colored buoys. The park is best observed by boat. But it's easy to get lost in this eerie area after dark.

With knobby knees sticking out of the coffee-colored water and long, spiraling Spanish moss beards, the bald cypress in this enchanted forest look like old, wizened wizards wading through the swamp. Some of the ancient trees here are more than 1,000 years old. Their gnarled trunks tower up to 120 feet, and grow up to 8 feet around.

Mistletoe has deformed the branches of tupelo gums into zigzags, circles, and fantastic spiderwebbing patterns. Pink swamp rose, white water lilies and purple pickerel weed form a floating garden around the edges of this murky millpond. Red and green duckweed weave weird mosaics across the center of the wide, winding waterway.

In canoes, your paddles make thick slurping noises as they drag through this flannel blanket — the only sounds disturbing the silence except for the croaking cricket frogs happily munching on mosquitos.

The deepest fishing spot in the state park is known as the "Polly hole." Here, at the most narrow part of the swamp, a makeshift boardwalk of cypress planks once ran from tree to tree. Legend has it that an elderly midwife named Polly drank too much whiskey, stumbled and fell in as she made her way home through the tangled tree trunks.

Beneath the still, dark waters, bluegill, chain pickerel, black crappie, catfish and primitive long-nosed gar lurk between the roots and reeds. Fly-fishing is probably the park's most popular pastime. River otter, beaver and mink also make the millpond their home. Mallards, swans and herons hover overhead. And turtles line up lethargically to sun themselves on logs.

There's plenty of free parking at the canoe, camping and picnic areas. The rangers supply paddles, life jackets and trail maps. You must bring your own food and drinks into the park. And don't forget your cameras. The strange sights in this secluded swampland speak thousands of unwhispered words.

Merchants Millpond State Park is open from 8 AM to 7 PM in March and October. Evening hours extend to 8 PM in April, May and September and to 9 PM June through August. The place closes at 6 PM November through February.

Alligator River National Wildlife Refuge

U.S. 64 near East Lake *473-1131*

Steads of six-foot-wide juniper stumps sparkle with the gray-green tentacles of sphagnum moss. Bobcats, wolves, bears, bald eagles and alligators thrive amidst these tangled thickets. And remnants of a century-old railroad track wind 100 miles through the thick forest, rotting tomb-ties of a 19th-century logging town that has long since been swallowed by the swamp.

On the Dare County mainland off U.S. 64 between East Lake, Manns Harbor and Stumpy Point — about a half-hour drive west of Manteo — Alligator River National Wildlife Refuge stretches across the Hyde County line into Alligator River. The U.S. Air Force owns a 46,000-acre Dare County Bombing Range in the center of the refuge. But the rest of this sprawling preserve is federally protected from development.

Endangered species including the peregrine falcon, red-cockaded woodpecker and the American alligator roam freely through the preserve. Dozens of red wolves, extinct in the wild less than two decades ago, have been re-introduced into this region. (See our sidebar in the Natural Wonders chapter.) The refuge also is reputed to have one of the biggest black bear populations in the mid-Atlantic region.

But only remnants of man remain. There are few traces of the town that once had two hotels, a school, general store, scores of moonshiners, a tavern, and more than 3,000 people living in the Albemarle area's largest logging town.

"This is one of the largest and wildest sections of land left on the Eastern Coast," said Bonnie Strawser, wildlife interpretative specialist for the U.S. Fish and Wildlife Service. "We have purchased additional land and now manage 151,000 acres. We're hoping to even open a visitors center soon."

The entire refuge is accessible to four-wheel-drive vehicles. Jeep trails traverse much of the flat, sandy marshlands. Two half-mile hiking trails and 15 miles of well-marked canoe and kayak trails also are open.

Activities are free, year-round and available throughout daylight hours. Parking is available at the Milltail Road paved lot or at the end of the dirt Buffalo City Road off U.S. 64. Two houses still stand alongside this dusty path leading to Milltail Creek.

Buffalo City thrived along the sandy banks of Milltail Creek from the late 1870s through the early 1940s. It was built by three men from Buffalo, New York, who bought 168,000 acres to begin a modest logging operation. Shortly after the turn of the century, they sold the remaining white cedars, cypress and juniper to the Dare Lumber Co. Loggers built wooden railroads through the slimy peat bogs and carted their plankings as far as New York and Atlanta. A thriving town grew up around the growing clearing.

When the trees ran out, the lumber company went broke, and townsfolk turned to making moonshine. It was the peak of Prohibition and the town had an isolated outpost with a built-in rail and water transportation system along the wide Alligator River, so inevitably the area became famous for its liquor. By 1936, experts estimate that East Lake had produced 1.5 million quart bottles of liquor, which showed up on the shelves of saloons from Philadelphia to Charleston.

Liquor became legal again, and the government took over small stills. After World War II, residents of what is now Alligator River Refuge returned to farming for awhile, but the swamp and snakes reclaimed the land too quickly. The government would not let people drain the marshes, so in 1984 then-owner Prudential Life Insurance donated 118,000 acres to the Nature Conservancy, who later turned that parcel over to the U.S. Fish and Wildlife Service.

Today, there are a variety of ways for

Insiders' Tips

The National Park Service leases abandoned homes on Portsmouth Island to people who want to help preserve the historic structures. Prices vary according to the cottages' sizes, and openings are only offered every few years. Contact Cape Lookout National Seashore headquarters for more information and see our sidebar in this chapter.

Photo: Philip S. Ruckle Jr.

Boat slips, such as these on the Manteo waterfront, are available in a number of locations on the Outer Banks.

visitors to see the refuge. About 4 miles west of the U.S. 64/264 split, travelers can stop at a wooden kiosk and pick up brochures about trails, wildlife and flora. Behind the kiosk there's a paved 15-space parking lot — where the old, dirt Milltail Road ends. Here, a half-mile paved walkway with a boardwalk overlooking the water begins. This Creef Cut Wildlife Trail and Fishing Area is wheelchair accessible. It opens at a public fishing dock and culminates in a 50-foot boardwalk atop a freshwater marsh.

Interpretive plaques depicting the area's unusual flora and fauna are nailed along freshly plowed pathways. Beaver cuttings, wood duck boxes, rare sun dew flowers and warbler nesting areas are among the hidden attractions. Look closely: In some places, the forest is so thick you can't see 20 feet ahead.

Refuge workers estimate there are about 100 alligators in this preserve, which marks the northernmost boundary of the American alligators' habitat. On the Milltail Creek Road, there's a platform winding around the creek. The waters surrounding that platform are supposed to be among the gators' favorite haunts. If you wait quietly, you might catch a glimpse of a scaly, dark green snout.

Sandy Ridge Wildlife Trail is a little more rugged. It starts where Buffalo City Road dead-ends off U.S. 64 about 2 miles south of East Lake. Rough, wooden pallets help hikers traverse swampy spots. But if rain has fallen during the past week, walkers are bound to get wet. Sweet gum, maple and pine trees reach 30 feet high around this path.

Canoe and kayak trails through Sawyer Lake and connecting canals include four main routes marked by colored PVC pipe. Trails range from 1.5 to 5.5 miles, all along a wide waterway that is smooth with no rapids. Boats are not available on site. But you can bring your own in and paddle for free. On the Outer Banks, several rental outlets lease canoes and kayaks by the day (see our Watersports chapter). Kitty Hawk Kayaks guides visitors through the trails in rental crafts towed to the site, 441-6800. And Melvin Twiddy of Manns Harbor also offers narrated canoe tours, 473-3270.

If you enjoy nature, isolation and abundant wildlife, there is no better place to spend a day away from the Outer Banks than at Alligator River National Wildlife Refuge.

Lake Mattamuskeet National Wildlife Refuge

Hyde County mainland *926-4021*

About a two-hour drive southwest of Manteo down lonely U.S. 264, more than half of the nation's tundra swans swoop into a rare wilderness refuge to feed, nest and wait out the winter.

From December through February, Lake Mattamuskeet National Wildlife Refuge is filled with thousands of the regal white birds. Their black beaks dip into the murky, shallow waters. Their wide wings flap noiselessly through the steely gray sky.

This sprawling marshland spans a man-dug lake that never dips deeper than 5 feet. Foliage and duckweed thrive atop the almost still waters, and swans creen their long, lovely necks through the surface, searching for supper.

Each fall, an estimated 100,000 tundra swans make a cross-continent trek from the wilds of western Canada and Alaska to the warmer waters of Carolina and the Chesapeake Bay. Biologists estimate that more than 90 percent of the nation's tundra swans winter in North Carolina. The state's most popular roosting area are these isolated flatlands surrounded by 400 acres of wheat farms.

An old hunting lodge near the center of the refuge is being restored with state funds. Hunters can still shoot the beautiful birds, but only 6,000 swan permits are issued throughout the state annually and a strict winter season has been established.

Photographers, bird watchers and people with only a casual curiosity can drive through the refuge, across the lake on a two-lane bridge to get a good glimpse of the migration. Swans usually swarm around the water near sunrise and sunset. They spend their days eating in the nearby fields.

Besides the big birds, who can live 20 years or longer, this U.S. Fish and Wildlife Service outpost also is famous for its crabs. The crustaceans creeping around this waterway are said to be more than twice as big as the Outer Banks variety. Some say that's because the crabs feed off the bottom of the lake, where rich fields of sweet potatoes grew before farmers flooded it.

If you make a trek to the refuge, be sure to buy some crabs at an area seafood shop and sample the sweet meat for yourself.

Columbia Waterfront and Marina

U.S. 64, Tyrrell County *796-0723*

Outer Banks visitors traveling to the beach from Raleigh used to be apt to overlook this isolated outpost in Tyrrell County. But if you're arriving at the beach via U.S. 64, you might want to stop and stretch your legs in this burgeoning new eco-tourist attraction. Columbia is a little more than an hour's drive west of Manteo on the main highway.

In the past three years, local and state officials have raised millions of dollars to revamp this waterfront community. A $1.1 million welcome station, visitors center and rest area opened in fall 1995 alongside the highway. A few months earlier, work was completed on a winding boardwalk that provides breathtaking views of the Scuppernong River as it slides slowly into Bull Bay. For thousands of feet along the river's edge tiny electric lights twinkle across the dark water, illuminating the walkway that creeps more than a mile through unspoiled timber wetlands.

Visitors are greeted with sounds from scurrying wildlife, jumping minnows and fat, quacking ducks. Bass bullfrogs clear their throats with resonating croaks. Possum, raccoon and nutria scuttle for cover beneath the reeds and marsh grasses. A black bear cub ambling along the boardwalk in broad daylight, apparently too lazy to struggle through the swampy un-

Portsmouth Island: A Wrinkle in Time

About a 20-minute boat ride south of Ocracoke — on an island inaccessible except by private passenger ferries — the only ghost town east of the Mississippi River offers daytrippers an isolated getaway and an opportunity to explore a well-preserved piece of the past.

Photo: Mary Ellen Riddle

This old church is one of the few structures on Portsmouth Island.

Porstmouth was the biggest, most bustling town on the Outer Banks for more than a century. By the Civil War, more than 700 people made this barrier island their home. About 1,400 ships docked at the rough-hewn wooden piers each year.

But now, the remote island is empty.

Twenty-five years have passed since the last permanent resident steered his homemade skiff toward Ocracoke, leaving this historic shipping port in its wake.

Today, Portsmouth Island's primary inhabitants are mammoth mosquitoes and biting, green-headed flies. Two dozen cottages still stand. Their faded curtains gather dust behind salt-sprayed window panes. The old post office remains. A rusty padlock knocks against its boarded doors.

But if you walk slowly through the sandy lanes of this Colonial community and peer carefully through the thick glass windows, you can still see how lovely and simple life once was.

From the docks at Silver Lake — next to Sharon Miller Realty on Ocracoke Island — Rudy Austin ferries travellers across Ocracoke Inlet at 9:30 AM throughout most of the spring, summer and fall. Reservations must be made at least a day in advance. Cost is $15 per person.

"Be sure to wear long pants and a long shirt, no matter how hot it might get," the ruddy faced captain tells travellers. "Pack a snack and something to drink — and bring your bathing suit. Most importantly, bring the insect repellent. There's no place to escape the bugs out here."

Owned by the National Park Service since 1976, Portsmouth Island is part of the Cape Lookout National Seashore. It's 23 miles long, 1.5 miles wide and abandoned except for two volunteer rangers who live in a restored cottage. Each year, about 10,000 people visit this isolated outpost.

Most come to fish, camp, watch birds, scan for seashells on miles of wide, empty beach, or just hike through the historic village and re-enter a long-forgotten world.

Chartered in 1753 by the Colonial Assembly, Portsmouth was the first village established on the Outer Banks. It was set up as a "lightering" center on the southern side of Ocracoke Inlet — which was, at the time, the major trade route from the Atlantic through the barrier islands. Hundreds of ships sailed across the shallow inlet each year. But some of the bigger boats drew so much water that they could not carry cargo across the shoals. So workers built wharves and warehouses on Portsmouth Island. There, they transferred goods from larger, ocean-going vessels to smaller sloops. Local captains carried the cargo from Portsmouth, across the sound, to the mainland.

Unlike other barrier island beach communities, which grew from single shacks to tiny towns as more people settled in the area, Portsmouth was planned from the start. The town was laid out in half-acre lots with wide, sandy streets cleared amidst the thick underbrush. Early inhabitants paid 20 shillings each for the land and were required to build "a good substantial habitable framed or brick house or good substantial warehouse," historian David Stick writes in his *The Outer Banks of North Carolina*. The first lot was sold in February, 1756.

Two decades later, Portsmouth boasted a permanent population of 246 residents. An academy for boys opened on the island by 1806, and by 1840, the growing coastal community had its own post office, which is still standing today. Two churches, a tavern, a one-room schoolhouse and more than a hundred houses also sprung from the sandy shores. More than 30 of those deteriorating structures still stand today.

The federal government erected a marine hospital in the village in 1846 to accommodate sick sailors who were passing through the bustling port. Later that year, however, a great storm spilled mountains of sand into Ocracoke Inlet, causing it to shallow considerably. The same storm opened Hatteras Inlet, between Ocracoke and Hatteras islands, and Oregon Inlet, between Hatteras Island and Nags Head. Shipping traffic quickly shifted routes to the deeper, more northern inlets.

During the Civil War, advancing Federal troops forced hundreds of Portsmouth residents to flee to the mainland. Many never returned. Businessmen tried to provide an industry for the island's remaining residents, including a whale oil extracting operation and a menhaden processing plant which was built in 1866. But without the steady stream of ships and cargo, work — and residents — began disappearing from the isolated island.

The U.S. Weather Bureau set up a station at Portsmouth that operated from 1876 to 1885. The U.S. Lifesaving Service established an outpost on the island in 1894. The boat house, crews' quarters and former station buildings all remain erect — if storm tattered — on the southern end of the village.

By 1950, severe weather, lack of work, electricity, running water and other amenities had driven all but 14 of Portsmouth's people to other areas. A real-estate developer was offering unoccupied houses for $495 each. Today, the National Park Service pumps an average of $60,000 annually into restoring and renovating two dozen historic homes.

About 250 acres of Portsmouth Island is a designated historic district, listed on the National Register of Historic Places. The village itself is set amid salt marshes and cedar-and-poplar hammocks on the sound side. Although most of the houses remain relatively healthy considering their exposure to the elements and years of uninhabitation, only one is open for public perusal: the turn-of-the-century Dixon/Salter House that now serves as the National Park Service Visitors Center.

The visitors center is one of the first places you'll arrive at if Austin drops you off at Haulover Point on the Pamlico Sound of the island. After a long, winding, walk through overgrown marshes, the tangled terrain opens into a clearing and tourists get their first taste of the town. The Dixon/Salter House is slightly to the right. The post office is straight ahead. And an old graveyard is tucked beneath the trees to the left, surrounded by broken white pieces of what once must have been a hand-hewn picket fence.

Closer to the center of town, if you walk past the cemetery, you'll come upon Henry's Creek. Here, a cluster of buildings includes the homes of Henry Pigott, Elma Dixon and Dixon's niece, Marian Gray Babb. These were the last three permanent residents of Portsmouth Island. The grandson of slaves, Pigott was said to have kept a bachelor's home so neat visitors could eat off his floor. He died in 1971 after a brief stay on Ocracoke. The women left that same year, finally abandoning the village they had struggled so hard to keep alive.

A short hike past these houses, the Methodist church is the most well preserved — and impressive — building on the island. Built in 1914 to replace a chapel that was destroyed by a violent storm, this white, simple structure with its tall steeple and sloping roof is always open — and an inviting escape from the biting bugs. Dozens of couples have walked the worn, wooden aisles to the altar in recent years, bringing their wedding parties by boat to the special ceremonies.

There's a sign-in book near the pulpit where people pen their impressions of the entire island: "Pray for cool breezes," said one summer visitor. "Back home again. Thanks to Jesus," read a separate entry. "Seen it. Done it. Love it every time," another repeat worshipper wrote.

Past the church — and several more shingled houses — the Lifesaving Station is the last structure you'll come to in the village, and — understandably — the closest one to the sea. It's still a long hike, however, to get to the beach. But the miles of wide, open sands and shallow ponds are well worth traversing to be beside the ocean.

Since so few people visit Portsmouth, the shells are almost untouched on this island. We've found briefcase-sized conchs — whole, pink and glistening; sand dollars and starfish fit for wholesale shipments; and Scotch Bonnets — the state shell — scattered on top of the sand. Even if you're not searching for them, shells seem to find you on this uninhabited Outer Banks island.

In an effort to keep up the houses and provide some sort of life in the windswept ghost town, the National Park Service now rents Portsmouth Island residences to private individuals. People can sign up on a long waiting list of wanna-be leasees. They pay a few thousand dollars each year — depending on the size and condition of the structure — and have to help restore the building to its 18th-century condition. Any money put into the house can be deducted from the rent. But there is still no electricity, no running water and no cars allowed on the island. Adventuresome, outdoorsy people who don't mind biting bugs and living without air conditioning are the only ones who need apply.

Portsmouth Island is an amazing, isolated, abandoned area of the Outer Banks that few people ever get to experience. If you enjoy history, aren't afraid of some inconveniences, and have a yearning to walk through yesteryear, plan to spend a day in this quaint seaside village.

If you love being away from it all and have ever dreamed of having an entire island to yourself, plan to camp in the wilderness sites for three or four nights at least.

derbrush below, astonished one walker on a recent trip.

A fountain, elegant gazebo and wide turnouts to accommodate wheelchair passengers are among the other attractions along this zigzagging boardwalk that twists around towering forest giants and squatty flowering bushes that would have soon disappeared in more chainsaw-oriented communities.

Columbia is a Tyrrell County townlet with a permanent population of about 900. The local folk have helped raise much of their own money for this waterfront revival project. Today, Columbia has one of the loveliest little marinas on the East Coast. The river has many miles of easily navigable routes for canoes and small boats, well marked with signposts offering directions and paddling advice. And the town leaders hope to enhance the area with additional eco-tourism opportunities in an attempt to utilize — and preserve — their unspoiled wilderness.

One state advisory board recommended that Columbia's development should never include "stores or restaurants that are so fancy or expensive that local people do not feel comfortable in them . . . The architecture should remain of human scale but eclectic, expressing the contradictory ideals and independent eccentricities of the town." So far, work at the waterfront has been extremely successful in meeting those aims.

Edenton National Fish Hatchery

U.S. 17 Bus.
(W. queen St. Ext.) *482-4118*

Run by the U.S. Fish and Wildlife Service on the grassy banks of the Chowan River, the Edenton National Fish Hatchery includes an expanse of outdoor ponds and a small aquarium.

Officials opened a waterfront walkway and pier at the facility in spring 1995, providing access to Pembroke Creek for people with disabilities. The 15-acre area also gives nature lovers a look at some of the native wildlife and waterfowl indigenous to the surrounding wetlands.

This $40,000 facility is open to the public. Tours are offered with advance reservations. And many programs are sponsored throughout the year for area school groups.

The most popular, "Pathway to Fishing," is a 12-station, one-hour tour that teaches youngsters the basics of fishing. Included are brief talks on angler ethics and safety, live baits and lures, ecology, rods and reels, knot-tying, casting and local fish species. Even old-time anglers often learn something at this pint-sized fish camp.

Cape Lookout National Seashore

Southern barrier islands of N.C. *728-2250*

Low, unpopulated and a lot less visited than the Outer Banks, the southern stretches of North Carolina's barrier islands extend 55 miles southwest from Ocracoke Inlet and include Portsmouth Island, Core Banks, Cape Lookout and Shackleford Banks.

These remote sand islands are untouched by development and linked to the mainland and other barrier island beaches only by private ferries or private boats. (Call the listed number for ferry schedules and reservations.) In 1966, they came under the control of the National Park Service when a separate national seashore was established south of the Cape Hatteras holdings. Each year, more than 300,000 nature lovers visit these sparse strips of beach.

If you have your own boat, you can get to get to Cape Lookout by launching from ramps at marinas throughout Carteret County or from Silver Lake on Ocracoke. The easiest access to Cape Point is from Shell Point on Harkers Island. Concession ferries and private boats for hire also are available from Harkers Island to the Cape Lookout Light area, from Davis to Shingle Point, from Atlantic to an area north of Drum Inlet and from Ocracoke to Portsmouth Village.

There are no roads on these islands, but four-wheel-drive vehicles can cruise north from where the southern sands connect with pavement near Atlantic Beach. The beauty of this pristine place can be a deterrent to travelers since there are few facilities along this sparse stretch of sand.

However, the islands are perfect for primitive camping year round, four-wheel driving, fishing, bird-watching and photography. Visitors must supply their own water and food.

Just stay alert for sudden storms because there is little shelter. A Coast Guard weather forecast often helps foreshadow bad squalls. Call 726-7550 before you set out on an excursion.

Deer ticks, chiggers, deerflies, mosquitoes, gnats and other annoying insects also are abundant around the islands, so bring repellent and wear long sleeves even in the summer months. Water is available from pitcher pumps around Cape Point. But campers are encouraged to bring their own supplies. Primitive camping is allowed throughout the park, but there are no designated sites.

The Cape Lookout grounds include a lighthouse that was first illuminated in 1859 and a small Coast Guard station that is no longer active.

For more information, call or write the National Park Service, Cape Lookout National Seashore, 3601 Bridges Street, Suite F, Morehead City 28557-2913. See our Portsmouth Island sidebar in this chapter, and pick up a copy of *The Insiders' Guide® to the North Carolina's Central Coast* from any area bookstore or by using the handy order form in the back of this book.

Historic Attractions

Museum of the Albemarle

1116 U.S. 17 S., Elizabeth City *335-1453*

About 50 miles inland from the Outer Banks, on the west side of Elizabeth City, a state-owned museum preserves the Albemarle area's past with exhibits, photographs and maps.

The Museum of the Albemarle includes permanent interpretive displays depicting Native American tribes and their tools and exhibits on the food, folk takes, crafts and hunting artifacts of early English speaking colonists. A 19th-century hearth exhibit allows visitors to contrast colonial living with modern American amenities. Other offerings trace the development of boating, logging and the U.S. Coast Guard in surrounding sites.

With two weeks notice, the museum can provide guided tours, lectures and audiovisual programs for groups and individuals. A small gift shop sells museum memorabilia, and admission to the handicapped-accessible building is free.

The museum is open Tuesday through Saturday from 9 AM until 5 PM and Sunday from 2 until 5 PM. It is closed Mondays and holidays. Call ahead for program schedules and reservations.

Historic Hertford

Intersection U.S. 17
and N.C. 1336 426-5657

One of the oldest towns in North Carolina, Hertford was incorporated in 1758 to serve as the Perquimans County seat and commercial center of the surrounding Albemarle area.

About 50 buildings dating from the early 1800s stand as stalwart sentries along the tree-lined lanes of the downtown. These magnificent mansions and well-kept gardens serve as reminders of the early inhabitants who spent their lives fishing, farming and felling trees for lumber. Later, cloth was manufactured in nearby factories.

This tiny town is easily toured by car. Walking around the shady streets is also advised for a closer perspective. Hertford is about an hour's drive from the Outer Banks.

The Newbold-White House

U.S. 17 S., Hertford 426-7567

About 60 miles from the Outer Banks in historic Perquimans County, North Carolina's oldest house was built in 1730, and is still open for tours today.

The Newbold-White House is an outstanding example of early American domestic architecture. It's set about a mile off the road across an expansive cotton field. Chimneys built with handmade bricks spring from the former plantation home's roof.

Joseph Scott, the original landowner, was a magistrate, legislator and Quaker. The original owner of the home was Abraham Sanders, who built this elegant brick abode on a 600-acre tract along the Perquimans River and surrounded it with tobacco fields. Tobacco was frequently used for payments during the 18th century. Later, peanuts and other products also were farmed in these fields.

Numerous other families occupied the house, and Thomas Elbert White bought it in 1903. In 1943, his heirs sold the property to John Henry Newbold, whose heirs

Insiders' Tips

If you're canoeing around Milltail Creek in the Alligator River National Wildlife Refuge, keep your eyes peeled for rope hanging from rotting piers along the water's edge. Moonshiners once tied bottles of homemade liquor beneath the logs to keep them out of eyesight of revenuers. Thousands of the big brown jugs are said to be still bobbing just beneath the creek's muddy surface.

in turn sold it to the Perquimans County Restoration Association in 1973. Since then, the house has been beautifully restored to its original condition.

Touring this three-century-old structure is well worth the trip. Sturdy and sophisticated, the dwelling is of English bond construction on the lower portions; Flemish bond-brick construction higher up. Its first floor consists of the traditional great hall and a more intimate parlor, both with cavernous fireplaces, great wooden mantles and superb original pine woodwork.

Winding wooden stairs tucked in the corner of the main first-floor room lead to two dormer-lighted, second-floor rooms. During restoration, leaded window casements with diamond-shaped panes were restored with glass shipped in from Germany. Artisans made these windows by copying a piece of the panes found on the floor of the Newbold-White House before restoration work began.

When you visit the house, be sure to stop at the Perquimans County Restoration Association headquarters on the way. This visitors center of sorts offers an informative audiovisual journey into the house's heyday and inhabitants. Hours are 10 AM to 4:30 PM Monday through Saturday from March 1 through Thanksgiving. The house is closed on Sundays. Special tours can be arranged in advance over the winter. Admission is $2 for adults. Children and students pay 50¢ each.

Albemarle Plantation

Hertford, N.C. (800) 523-5958
Golf pro shop 426-5555, (800) 535-0704

Albemarle Plantation, a golf and boating community, makes a great daytrip. This sprawling complex of recreational and dining facilities along the waters of the Albemarle Sound is part of an upscale residential development that also includes a swimming pool and fitness center. Sound Golf Links, an 18-hole golf course that's open to the public, is one of the most popular venues in the region for dedicated duffers. Call ahead for tee times. After a couple of rounds, you may be ready for lunch or dinner at the Soundside Grille, which has great views of the water.

The 200-slip marina, also open to the public, offers all the amenities and hookups a boater could wish for.

The 1,600-acre secured community is designed for 1,000 single-family homes, with a few townhomes and condominiums as well. If you're interested in staying for several days, call about the Albemarle Plantation's getaway packages.

Follow U.S. 17 from Elizabeth City to Hertford. Drive time from Kitty Hawk is just over an hour.

Historic Edenton

U.S. 17 S. in Chowan County 482-2637

Antique stores inhabit iron-gate sheltered alleys and bed and breakfasts offer extraordinary escapes in this 17th-century town that has managed to escape the trappings of tourism.

One of the oldest towns in America, Edenton was settled in 1660 along the shallow shores of the Albemarle Sound and Edenton Bay. This colonial community had its own tea party in 1774 when 51 women gathered at Elizabeth King's home and toasted their support of the American cause. A journey through town reveals the restored homes of James Iredell, an Attorney General during the Revolutionary War who served as a Supreme Court justice from 1790 to 1799; Samuel Johnston, a Revolutionary War-era senator; Dr. Hugh Williamston who signed the U.S. Constitution; Joseph Hewd who put his own John Hancock on the *Declaration of Independence*; and Thomas Barker, a North Carolina agent to England and reputed leader of the infamous Edenton Tea Party.

Other 18th-century buildings include

the Chowan County Courthouse, St. Paul's Episcopal Church and Iredell House — all with unsurpassed Colonial architecture. An easy walk along King Street uncovers a remarkable collection of Georgian, Federal and Greek Revival homes nestled among impeccably kept gardens and centuries-old trees. Barker House serves as a visitors center to the community, with guided tours of the town beginning there and an audiovisual presentation going on throughout the day.

From 1771 to 1776, Edenton was a prosperous port town. More than 800 ships linked Carolina and Virginia colonists with supplies from Europe and the West Indies. Blackbeard often sailed into Edenton Bay to unload — and pilfer — pirate goods. Sailors continue to cruise into this historic harbor today. Edenton is an easy day trip from the Outer Banks by boat or automobile.

And everything within this quaint waterfront village is readily accessible by walking. The Lords Proprietors' Inn at 400 N. Broad Street has three restored homes in the heart of the historic district. A total of 20 guest rooms are available for nightly accommodations, each with grand parlors and gracious front porches. Guests are served both breakfast and dinner Tuesdays through Saturdays. Reservations are available year round by calling (800) 348-8933.

Granville Queen Inn also offers exquisite accomodations in the historic district. This abode at 108 S. Granville Street features furnishings from around the world. Guest rooms are named for their individual themes, including the Queen's Cottage and Egyptian Queen bedroom. For more information, call 482-5296.

At the Captain's Quarters Inn, you get more than just a bed and breakfast. Guests are treated to two-night "sail and snooze" specials from March through November that include three-hour sailing excursions on the Albemarle Sound. On Saturday nights, dinner is served at this 1907 home in the historic district. Guests also may take a two-hour guided walking tour of the town or help solve a mock murder mystery by participating in parlor games. Reservations can be made at 482-8945.

Photo: Georgia Beach

A snowy egret searches for dinner.

The Trestle House Inn is on a private estate on Soundside Road outside Edenton. Built in 1972, this bed and breakfast inn features four guest rooms and redwood beams that were milled from old railroad trestle timbers. Guests can fish in a private lake or wander the inn's extensive grounds. Reservations must be made at least a week in advance and are available year round; call 482-2282.

Edenton can be reached from Roanoke Island via U.S. 64 W. by driving 40 miles until you come to N.C. 32 then turning right and following the signs. Tours of the town are offered from 9:30 AM to 2:30 PM Monday through Saturday and 1:30 to 2:30 PM on Sundays from April through October. From November through March, tour hours are Tuesday through Saturday 10:30 AM until 2 PM and Sundays at 1:30 PM. Group tours also are available.

SOMERSET PLACE

Pettigrew State Park
Off U.S. 64 *797-4560*

On the swampy stretch of marshland surrounding Phelps Lake, bordered by hand-dug canals and majestic stands of sycamore, Somerset Place is a historic plantation in Washington County where visitors can learn about antebellum lifestyles of wealthy plantation owners and slaves.

This state-funded site is 5 miles outside Creswell — about an hour's drive from the Outer Banks. Guides offer free tours and special arrangements for school groups. Grounds include isolated walking trails and wooden boardwalks to the water. Fishing nearby is excellent. About 25,000 people visit the park annually.

When a $1 million restoration is complete, this historic place will be the only plantation in the country that documents how both master and slave populations lived. Planning has begun to rebuild a two-story, four-bedroom house that the field laborers inhabited. Two families shared each small room — and helped to wrest the fertile farmland from the ever-encroaching swamp.

Once one of North Carolina's four biggest plantations, Somerset Place employed more than 300 slaves to grow corn and rice and work in the expansive wetlands. An incredible collection of the plantation's slave records is open at the house for genealogical research. In August 1986, more than 2,000 descendants of Somerset's slaves gathered for a homecoming among the twisted cypress tree trunks.

Josiah Collins built the elegant, 2½-story mansion in 1830 to entertain the cultivated elite of the state's planter aristocracy. Nearby, Noth Carolina's first Episcopal bishop-elect, Charles Pettigrew, his congressman son and Confederate brigadier general grandson lie buried beneath sprawling limbs of live oak. The plantation home itself has 14 rooms, six original outbuildings and is furnished with period furniture.

When students tour Somerset, they grind corn by hand, haul water from distant streams and make corn bread in a black iron skillet over an open fire. They wash dishes in homemade lye soap, gather broom straw and bind stalks together to clean wood floors. They dip wax and make candles two at a time, clean cotton by hand and sew pin cushions.

The idea, curator Dorothy Redford says, is to simulate experiences of the period slaves and see what it was once like to live on a Colonial plantation.

Somerset Place is open April through October from 9 AM to 5 PM Monday through Saturday and from 1 to 5 PM Sundays. From November through March, it's open Tuesday through Saturday 10 AM to 4 PM, Sunday 1 to 4 PM and closed Mondays. To make reservations for large groups, write Box 215, Creswell 27928.

HOPE PLANTATION

N.C. 308, Windsor *794-3140*

In the 1720s, the Lord Proprietors of the Carolina Colony granted abundant Albemarle-area acreage to the Hobson family. David Stone, a delegate to the North Carolina Constitutional Convention of 1789, began building an impressive plantation home on the site around 1800. About a two-hour drive west of the Outer Banks, this Federal period mansion is included on the National Register of Historic Places and is open to the public for guided tours.

Stone was a judge, representative, senator, trustee of the University of North Carolina and governor of the new state from 1808 until 1810. A contemporary of Thomas Jefferson, he shared many of his Virginia friend's enlightened interests, especially in books. When the Hope Mansion was completed in 1803, it included a 1,400-volume library. Copies of these works are being assembled from an inventory of Stone's belongings at the time of his death. They will be stored in a fireproof room inside a cedar heritage center on the site.

A well-preserved Federal residence furnished with period furniture, Hope Plantation reminds some visitors of Jefferson's Monticello estate, and reminds others of Scarlett O'Hara's beloved Tara. The Historic Hope Foundation purchased the home and 18 acres around it in 1966. Now restored, the property includes two smaller structures, the King-Bazemore and Samuel Cox houses. Lovely 18th-century style gardens surround the homesites. And the 16,600-square-foot J.J. Harrington Building nearby includes a museum-like center that promotes the area's history and culture.

To get to Hope Plantation, take U.S. 64 out of Roanoke Island west to its intersection with U.S. 13; go north on U.S. 13 and the house is 4 miles west of U.S. 13 Bypass. It's open March 1 through December 22, Mondays through Saturdays from 10 AM to 4 PM; Sundays 2 to 5 PM. It's closed in January and February. Adult admission is $6.50; students pay $2. Picnic facilities are available.

North Carolina Maritime Museum

U.S. 70 south of Cedar Island
Beaufort *728-7317*

More than a two-hour toll ferry ride west of Ocracoke, the state's maritime museum is in the historic port town of Beaufort. The North Carolina Maritime Museum offers free tours through a variety of exhibits depicting the history of the state's shipping and water transportation systems, its wildlife and its men and women who have made their living on the sea for centuries.

Visitors can trace the development of the nation's lifesaving stations and lighthouses along the Outer Banks, see old lifesaving artifacts and learn about early rescue techniques. They can marvel at the Watson Shell Collection, an exhibit of about 5,000 shells gathered from the oceans bordering more than 100 countries by Brantley and Maxine Watson. And they can learn about the making of the state vessel, the shad boat; the waging of the first battle between ironclad ships; and the sinking of thousands of others along what historians have dubbed "The Graveyard of the Atlantic."

North Carolina's treacherous coasts claimed their first recorded sailing ship in 1526 when a Spanish brigantine sank off the mouth of the Cape Fear River. Since then, about 2,000 ships have met a similar fate off the shallow shoals and shifting sands. The barrier island beaches boast one of the highest densities of shipwrecks in the world.

Among the most famous ruins is the rusting remains of the USS *Monitor*, which lie upside down beneath 230 feet of water about 16 miles southwest of Cape Hatteras. This Civil War ironclad was the United States' first iron warship. It was built in 147 days beginning in 1861 after the Confederacy captured the Gosport Navy Yard in Portsmouth.

Insiders' Tips

The U.S. Fish and Wildlife Service sponsors an annual celebration of migrating swans at Lake Mattamuskeet National Wildlife Refuge. Call ahead for reservations. Volunteers often are needed to help band the birds for identification projects.

The Confederates captured and refitted the USS *Merrimac*, renamed CSS *Virginia*, with an iron hull that was used as a battering ram against Union ships and threatened the Union blockade of the South. When launched in 1862, just two months later, the *Monitor* and the *Merrimac* fought in Hampton Roads in what historians describe as the first modern naval battle. After several hours of lobbing shells at one another, both ships withdrew and the battle was described by naval historians as a tie.

A few months later, in December, the *Monitor* was ordered to Charleston, South Carolina, by way of Beaufort, North Carolina, to participate in the Union blockade. As the 172-foot, 776-ton vessel rounded Cape Hatteras, it succumbed to seething seas and sank on New Year's Eve. At least 16 crew members went down with their ship.

In 1973, officials from the U.S. Navy and Duke University discovered the *Monitor* with side-scan sonar. There, they set up the country's first National Marine Sanctuary. Federally contracted divers hope to retrieve the ship's propellor some day.

Other artifacts, architectural and historical information about the boat are on display at the museum. The North Carolina Maritime Museum is open year round Monday through Friday, 9 AM to 5 PM; Saturday 10 AM to 5 PM; and Sunday, 1 to 5 PM. The museum is closed on major holidays.

Something Different

Currituck County's Produce Stands

Along U.S. 158 on the Currituck County mainland

If you're looking for a little lushness near the barren barrier island beaches — or if you're hungering for something sweet to eat on the long, last leg of your drive to the Outer Banks — Currituck County's mainland has the stuff to make your mouth water.

Visitors arriving from Hampton Roads areas travel through fertile farmlands on the last hour of their trip. Like an oasis in a boring desert of desolation, wooden produce stands pop out of the flatlands. Hand-painted signs hawk the home-grown wares: just-ripe melons, cucumbers, corn, blueberries, tomatoes, butterbeans and peaches so juicy that they should be sold with bibs.

About 20 markets are strewn in sporadic fashion from the Virginia border in Chesapeake to just west of the Wright Memorial Bridge. Each has a personality — and produce — all its own. Many are run by local families who began selling vegetables from the back of pickup trucks parked along the roadside. Some stands include frozen yogurt, dried flowers and even seafood stalls, and almost all sell produce grown within a few miles of the open-air markets.

Decor ranges from the hospitable deep-green awnings of Grandy Greenhouse and Farm Market to the baby-blue exterior of Tarheel Produce to the pink-

Insiders' Tips

At the end of the dirt Buffalo City Road, beneath waist-high tangled thickets, antique bottles are buried in the swampy peat bog — the most visible remnants of a turn-of-the-century logging town. These bottles of thick, hand-blown glass are wonderful finds. But they're often guarded by poisonous snakes lurking in the rotting leaves.

and-purple polka dots of S & N Farm Market. Margaret and Alton Newbern have been running the Hilltop Market for 42 years. Morris Farm Market is one of the larger outposts along the Currituck stretch. Rufus Jones Farm Market features colorful fruits stacked in tilted wooden troughs and large-wheeled carts. And Soundside Orchard specializes in peach sales beneath a pointy-roofed wooden gazebo.

Whether you know produce or not, local farmers and their families are always glad to give free advice. They can thump a watermelon or peruse a peanut shell or just feel a pumpkin and know how long ago it was picked. And they'll load you up with bursting berries, just-jarred apricot preserves and even local lore if you stick around long enough.

The produce of Currituck County is a far cry from the stuff grown amidst the sandy stretches of the Outer Banks. And the wooden markets are only a half-hour jaunt from the barrier island beaches.

Whether
represented as a
seascape, a pirouette,
symphonic melody or
dramatic performance,
culture thrives in our
seaside community.

Inside
Arts and Culture

Beware! The rolling waves, forceful winds and brilliant skyscapes of the Outer Banks may provoke a creative encounter. We, as art appreciators, want to take you on a cultural pilgrimage that promises to be as ever-changing and fresh as our climate. Whether represented as a seascape, a pirouette, symphonic melody or dramatic performance, culture thrives in our seaside community.

Thanks to the efforts of several organizations, including the Dare County Arts Council, Outer Banks Forum, The Theater of Dare and Roanoke Island Historical Association (producers of *The Lost Colony*), locals and vacationers on the Outer Banks enjoy ample exposure to the arts. The area has numerous galleries — including a concentration of excellent ones on Gallery Row in Nags Head — and individual artists' studios scattered from Corolla to Ocracoke. And while we do have a large group of landscape painters here, our visual art expressions are as individualistic as grains of sand.

Activity in the Outer Banks arts community has intensified in recent years with the establishment in 1995 of a permanent office for the **Dare County Arts Council** at Central Square in Nags Head. And artists and art representatives in the community have been trying to establish a center for the arts where folks can take classes, sell their wares and perform drama all under one roof, but so far finances have thwarted the project. Still, local artists offer private lessons — mostly in watercolor and other painting techniques — and you can call the local galleries in our listing for more information.

For a sampling of the very best of visual art on the Outer Banks, you'll want to make plans to attend several annual events. One of the longest-running of these is the Dare County Arts Council's **Frank Stick Art Show** — approaching its 19th year — held at the Ghost Fleet Gallery in Nags Head every February. (Frank Stick, 1884-1966, was a legendary illustrator and wildlife artist who moved to the Outer Banks in the 1940s.) The two receptions that mark its opening are always packed, and hundreds of local artists exhibit recent work during the event that lasts a little over three weeks. The show is so popular that art work hangs nearly from ceiling to floor, almost outgrowing its current setting (see our Annual Events chapter for more information).

For sheer fun, set aside the first weekend in October for the arts council's annual **Artrageous Art Extravaganza**, which features hands-on creative booths — bubble painting, hat creations, weaving, jewelry making, face painting and more — live music and performances, art demonstrations, public art collaborations and food. A children's auction on Saturday features fun gifts and surprises, and a Sunday auction is an elegant affair where fine art by adults and children is put on the block (see our Annual Events chapter). Volunteers who put the event together seem to outdo themselves year after year. It's never the same old thing!

Another must-see is the **New World Festival of the Arts** each August on downtown Manteo's waterfront, an ideal site for showcasing the talents of approximately 80 local and national artists and artisans. Eddie Green, longtime supporter of the arts in Dare County, heads the two-day event, which enters its 14th year in 1996. If you would like to show your work at the festival or would like more information about it, call The Christmas Shop, 473-2838, in Manteo.

The visual art scene is also enriched by the contributions of individuals, especially local gallery owners. For example, Glenn and Pat Eure, owners of the Ghost Fleet Gallery in Nags Head, represent the welcoming spirit of the Outer Banks at its best, helping many an artist gain exposure the good old-fashioned way: by word of mouth. If you have never spoken with Glenn and Pat, you must. It's an art happening all its own.

Another couple, Mitch and Christine Lively at the Morales Art Galleries, have made financial success a personal reality for many struggling artists by showcasing their work and producing fine art prints that are shown at their large gallery in Nags Head and at their second gallery in Duck (see the listing below for an in-depth description).

And Didi and Rick Tupper offer locals and guests a chance to experience exquisite fine crafts and paintings from American artists at their two Greenleaf Gallery locations in Duck and Nags Head. Didi, an Austrian native, has experienced art the world over and is a great person with whom to share "art thoughts."

The dramatic arts have a unique outlet on the Outer Banks in ***The Lost Colony*** outdoor drama, staged throughout the summer in a waterside theater on Roanoke Island (see our Attractions chapter). It's America's first and longest-running outdoor drama and is perpetuated by the Roanoke Island Historical Association (see below). Native North Carolinian and Pulitzer Prize-winning playwright Paul Green wrote the play for the association to commemorate the 350th birthday of Virginia Dare, the first English child born in the New World. The new genre, which premiered in 1937, was dubbed the "symphonic drama."

The play itself is steeped in tradition on the Outer Banks. The dress rehearsal is called Dare County Night, and area residents are admitted free by providing identification and a donation to the local food bank. The July 4 performance is enhanced by authentic fireworks, and the

August 18 performance commemorates the birth of Virginia Dare by including real infants in the christening scene.

We begin our cultural pilgrimage with a description of the area's major arts organizations and follow with a north-to-south excursion through the Outer Banks' best and brightest galleries and other creative venues.

Organizations

Dare County Arts Council

Central Square, Nags Head *441-5617*

After 21 years of uphill yet steady growth made possible by the efforts of countless volunteers, generous patrons and members, along with some state and county support, the Dare County Arts Council finally has an office of its own. Even without a telephone listing all those years, the all-volunteer, nonprofit group has had a tremendous impact on the community as a service organization.

The council is affiliated with the North Carolina Arts Council as the local distributing agency of the state's Grassroots funds. The DCAC not only subsidizes other area arts organizations but also sponsors arts programming throughout the year. The group's mission is to nurture and support excellence in all of the arts in Dare County, and it typically provides programming not supplied by other arts-related organizations. Students benefit through the council's cultural programs — everything from live opera brought in from the big city to creativity classes in a local middle school. The council also brings writers, dancers, actors and singers to the area to provide workshops, read poetry and perform for local audiences.

The arts council publishes a quarterly newsletter for members and is compiling a directory of artists. For more information write: Dare County Arts Council, P.O. Box 2815, Kill Devil Hills 27948.

Outer Banks Forum

P.O. Box 503, Kitty Hawk 27949 *261-8940*

The Outer Banks Forum is the area's primary performing arts presenting organization. Since 1983 the Forum has produced an annual calendar of events from September through May. It has sponsored performances by such notable regional groups as the U.S. Navy Jazz Band, Virginia Beach Community Symphony Orchestra, National Opera Company of Charlotte and Norfolk Savoyards. Each season represents a variety of musical and dramatic styles ranging from orchestral to bluegrass and opera to folk tales. Performances are held in January, March, April, October and December (see our Annual Events chapter). Call for an updated listing. The programs are held at Kitty Hawk Elementary School.

The Theater of Dare

P.O. Box 1927, Nags Head 27959 *441-3088*

The area's only community theater, The Theater of Dare was established in 1992 with a grant from the Outer Banks Forum. Its members bring quality live theater to the Outer Banks by taking part in all phases of production, from set design to performing. The Theater of Dare produces three main stage productions a year, in November, February and May.

To date, the organization has produced *California Suite*, a Neil Simon hit, and 14 Broadway classics including the 1994 season's acclaimed production of *Anastasia*. In this performance, the theater group showcased extraordinary dramatic talents.

The organization lacks a permanent rehearsal space. But most of its performances are held at Manteo Middle School. Discounted season tickets are available in 1996 for the first time. For more information about membership, volunteering, auditions or production dates, call Kathy Morrison at the above number or write to The Theater of Dare at the address given above.

Roanoke Island Historical Association

1409 U.S. 64/264, Manteo *473-2127*

The Roanoke Island Historical Association is the fund-raising organization for *The Lost Colony*, an outdoor drama that commemorates the 350th birthday of Virginia Dare, the first English child born in the New World (see our Attractions chapter).

In addition to its main production, the RIHA/Lost Colony also sponsors The Lost Colony Children's Theatre. Company members give children's presentations from early July through early August every Wednesday and Friday at 11 AM. Call for locations and information concerning the 1996 season. Admission fees are around $3 for children and $2 for adults. A full day of special events — free children's theater selections, interpretive park tours and special performances — take place on Virginia Dare's birthday, August 18. Call the Lindsey Warren Visitor Center at Fort Raleigh, 473-5772, for a schedule.

Galleries

John de la Vega Gallery

Ocean Tr. (N.C. 12)
Corolla Village *261-4964*

John de la Vega, a nationally recognized portrait painter and one of the Outer Banks' most accomplished artists, is an Argentine-born painter, sculptor, photographer and published poet. He has received the Distinguished Achievement in Portraiture Award; his winning entry was chosen from more than 600 entries from the United States and abroad. Some of his famous subjects include Lee Iacocca, Ronald Reagan and former Washington Redskins coach Joe Gibbs. Four of his portraits hang in the Wright Brothers Memorial in Kill Devil Hills.

The Corolla gallery is an intimate setting for the artist's portraits and scenes of nature, and many of his Corolla-inspired beach scenes are sold as prints. The gallery also features the work of seven other artists.

The artist is available to do commissioned portraits in pastels and oils. The gallery is open every day but Sunday during the summer and fall months and by appointment in the off-season.

Dolphin Watch Gallery

Ocean Tr., in Tim Buck II
Corolla *453-2592*

Dolphin Watch Gallery features the works of owner/artist, Mary Kaye Umberger, who moved to the Outer Banks from Tennessee. We are struck by Umberger's hand-colored etchings on handmade paper drawn from scenes indigenous to the Corolla area including wildlife, ducks and other waterfowl, seascapes and lighthouses. (Etchings are images created on a copper plate and reproduced on paper, yet no two etchings are exactly the same.) Other art pieces here include pottery, stoneware and wax sculptures (candles shaped by hand, with flower petals molded by the artist's fingertips). The gallery's dulcimers, bowed psaltery and lap harps are functional musical instruments that are also beautiful to look at.

Dunehouse Pottery

P.O. Box 926, Kitty Hawk 27949 *261-7367*

Dunehouse Pottery features the col-

Insiders' Tips

If you're interested in taking art classes while vacationing on the Outer Banks, call the galleries before you arrive to get a schedule of lessons offered.

Photo: Mary Ellen Riddle

Creative folk abound on the Outer Banks, from stained-glass artisans to decoy carvers.

laborative work of Shawn Morton and his mom, Lydi. Shawn creates the handthrown pottery, and Lydi glazes the many pieces. This is a new working studio, and the Mortons welcome your calls. Shawn especially loves creating "Pooh-like" honey jars of all sizes and shapes. His work is functional, but he also incorporates the artistic element in his pots. He will use lead glazes from time to time because he loves the colors, so these obviously would be used for decorative purposes only. There's lots to choose from here. His work is simple yet graceful. The studio is open year round; call for an appointment.

Greenleaf Art Gallery

1169 Duck Rd. (N.C. 12), Duck 261-2009
U.S. 158, MP 16, Nags Head 480-3555

The Greenleaf Art Galleries are a contemporary multimedia art showcase of only American arts and crafts. Approximately 150 artists and crafters are represented, offering a good geographic variation. The emphasis is on one-of-a-kind pieces including jewelry, stoneware, furnishings, sculpture, acrylic and watercolor paintings, etchings, lithographs, mixed-media pieces and more. At the Nags Head location you'll find a variety of paintings and prints by mid-Atlantic artists.

Greenleaf Art Gallery in Duck opened in 1995 in the former Duck Blind Ltd. gallery, which closed after 21 years of offering strictly original artwork. (Duck Blind owners Peggy Lewis and Anna Smith helped launch the careers of North Carolina artists Nancy Tuttle May, Majid Elbers and Rick Tupper.) Tupper, his wife Didi and partners, who own the Greenleaf Gallery in Nags Head, opened the Duck gallery with the featured work of Tuttle May, Majid and popular woodcarver Norton Latourelle, along with Tupper's own work and that of other artists.

The 1996 season promises some exciting shows, including a reprise of the successful 1995 glass show. In the works are a small sculpture exhibit and maybe a lighthearted coffee mug show.

Expect to find exquisite work at

Greenleaf, anything from a huge, whimsical praying mantis to the works of some of the nation's finest glass artisans. Check out Michael Capps' meticulous woodworking that's enhanced by authentic nomadic tapestries; the benches mark a successful collaboration by Capps and Majid.

The Duck gallery closes December 23 and reopens in mid-March. It's open daily the rest of the year, with extended hours in the summer. The Nags Head location has the same schedule but is closed on Sunday year round.

Marsh Ridge Studio

115 Ridge Rd., Kill Devil Hills *441-6581*

Award-winning watercolorist Chris Haltigan offers lessons and original art for sale in her private studio. She describes her work as impressionism and contemporary realism featuring scenes from the Outer Banks and general locale. The word "radiant" well descibes her work, which is characterized by irridescent sound waters and atmospheric early morning boat scenes. The passage of light gets special attention in her work. Call for an appointment. The studio is open year round.

Carol Trotman

Kill Devil Hills *441-3590*

Painter Carol Trotman specializes in floral watercolors. Her work is so spectacular she was invited to show her watercolors at the American Horticultural Society in the spring of 1996. Trotman's work is marked by bright colors and real feeling. Her complicated garden scenes as well as poetic profiles of single blossoms are exceptional. Her work has been reproduced on cards, and you can purchase these or original work by calling the artist for an appointment.

Shattered Dreams Stained Glass

Beach Rd., MP 4, Kitty Hawk *255-0364*

The original creations in stained glass here have an emphasis on nature. Jae Everett creates brilliant work that employs both subtle and bright colors. She specializes in custom-made panels and custom-design lamps. Special design contracts are welcome. The gallery is open year round, but hours fluctuate so call for a schedule.

The Wooden Feather

U.S. 158, MP 5, in Seagate North
Kill Devil Hills *480-3066*

The Wooden Feather presents award-winning, hand-carved decoys and shorebirds. More than 130 carvers are exhibited here, including Dr. Bob Couch, one of the owners, who has a passion for decoys and decoy carving. The driftwood sculptures are also interesting. The gallery features an outstanding collection of antique decoys and clocks that date back to the 1700s. The gallery is open Monday through Saturday during the summer season and is closed during January. Call for an off-season schedule.

Port O' Call Restaurant & Gallery

Beach Rd., MP 8, Kill Devil Hills *441-8001*

This popular restaurant and nightspot also has a gallery of original paintings and other works of art. The Port O' Call is open mid-March through December.

Lighthouse Gallery and Gifts

210 Gallery Row *441-4232*
Nags Head *(800) 579-2827*

Owners Cheryl and Bruce Roberts have put together a shop dedicated to the "Keepers of the Light." They've built their gallery as a replica of an original Victorian-style lighthouse that represents the U.S. Lighthouse Service at its prime at the turn of the 20th century.

Open year round seven days a week, this shop features lighthouse art and artifacts including hundreds of lighthouse models, collectibles, quality reproduc-

The Lost Colony Remembered

Marjalene Midgett Thomas first appeared in *The Lost Colony* as a flower girl in 1938. Five generations of her family have acted in the historical drama that continues to run today.

A Roanoke Island native, Thomas, 68, remembers attending a summer arts camp, Camp Seatone, situated on the very land where she now lives on the north end of the island. The camp was run by Mabel Evans Jones, whom Thomas credits with writing and producing the very first plays about the Lost Colony that predate by 16 years today's version written by Paul Green in 1937. It was through Jones that school children like Thomas learned to embrace the history of their island, and *The Lost Colony* production gave Thomas the opportunity to merge this very heritage with her love of acting and singing. Joining in the conversation is her husband, Harry.

"All of this property was owned by Mabel Evans Jones," says Thomas. "She was the first woman superintendent of schools in North Carolina, and she had always wanted to start a camp here.

"This was quite an innovative, brilliant woman who really wanted to do everything for the children in the state that she could possibly do. This camp was called Seatone. It use to be a small camp for children. It was quite an undertaking. It was a camp for the arts. You had dance — ballet, tap, gymnastics. Then it was also a camp for sports. You had tennis and swimming, rowing and sailing.

"And crafts. She had a whole first floor set up for all kinds of woodwork and metalwork and painting and anything in the craft line that you would like to do. And drama — so she really had quite an undertaking.

"I went to her camp as a child. I was a day camper. She had day campers and then full-time campers. For those of us who lived on the island she would send a big truck around in the mornings around eight-thirty — it was a great big truck with sides on it — and we'd all climb in the truck, and she'd bring us up here.

"At that time Paul Green's drama, *The Lost Colony*, hadn't started, but Ms. Mabel had been having her own productions of the *Lost Colony* on the north end of the island ever since 1921.

"And, oh, hundreds of people would go and take picnic lunches and spend the day. And there would be speakers, and it was costumed and staged, and it was quite an undertaking.

"But they were very successful performances. And from that the Roanoke Island Historical Association — they had another name at the time — decided for the 350th anniversary there should be a big celebration, they would have Paul Green write a drama, which he made into a symphonic drama — his first outdoor drama, by the way — and probably one of his most successful. But, ah, it was a lot of Ms. Mabel's ideas and her promoting."

"She talked the government into providing the funds to film a production of *The Lost Colony*, which she wrote herself and also played in," said

Photo: Mary Ellen Riddle

Marjalene and Harry Thomas reside on Roanoke Island.

Harry Thomas. "And this was so the schoolchildren throughout the state could get some idea of what the Lost Colony was all about."

Marjalene continued, "And when the kids came down to attend this camp, they would act it out, and in the later years, if the production was going, why, she would take them to see it.

"And when *The Lost Colony* came along — Paul Green's version — my grandmother was a costumer. The second year they decided to have three flower girls for Queen Elizabeth to come in with, and my grandmother said 'Well, I have a granddaughter who's very interested in music and theater. I think she would make a marvelous flower girl.'

"So because my grandmother was a costumer, she helped get me the part. There have been five generations of our family in *The Lost Colony*: my grandmother, my mother, myself, our son and daughter and Harry. He was in it for 14 years. And my son's son played the part of Virginia Dare on the 18th of August. So he was the fifth generation."

During World War II, *The Lost Colony* closed down, as did Mabel Evans Jones' Camp Seatone. The camp never reopened, and Ms. Mabel divided up her property.

"The play has changed quite a bit. The storyline is still the same, but it was necessary actually for it to change because people have become more aware of the arts and have an opportunity to see more live productions and, of course, excellent productions on TV, so it became necessary really to make the *Colony* more of a drama and a major production than a pageant.

"I know it did so much for our family. Our daughter, Barbara, started as Virginia Dare on the 18th of August and went from there to being a flower girl. She's 28 now, and they had flower girls when she was about 6, and so she was flower girl for a couple of years. Then she outgrew that and got to be a little colonist girl in the show.

"She was in the show until she started going to New York in the summer to study at the school of American Ballet. And she did very well in dance — and I can thank *The Lost Colony* for a lot of that, because even when she was little they let her go to the dance classes, and she'd stand on the back row and dance with *The Lost Colony* dancers. And she was in all the children's shows that they had.

"Our son, Hunt, was stage manager for *The Lost Colony* up until he started working in radio. He's been sound engineer for the show, and he played little boy parts, so, really, our kids just benefited from being in the show.

The Thomases' home is filled with Lost Colony memorabilia covering the walls, tables and scrapbooks. Holding an early playbill, she reflects on the old days.

"See . . . under flower girls? 'Marjalene Midgett Thomas.' So that was my first role, and then I did Joyce Archard, which was one of the supporting roles. But I'd always wanted to sing in the choir, and so when I went to college I majored in music. And at that time *The Lost Colony* was using all graduates from Westminster Choir School in Princeton, New Jersey.

"I auditioned and was accepted. So I was the first person from Dare County to sing with *The Lost Colony* choir as well as the first person other than a Westminster graduate to sing with the choir. From there I understudied Eleanor and played Eleanor Dare for seven seasons. I was Queen Elizabeth for two years, and I was production stage manager and served on the board.

"Harry was the lighting director [for six years] until he became superintendent of schools in Elizabeth City, and then he couldn't take the summers off," Marjalene said. He assisted with lighting for eight years prior to that.

tions, books, jewelry, prints, paintings from all over the United States and local artwork and T-shirts. You must see the special collection of lighthouse books with photography by Bruce, who offers unique and breathtaking views of these beloved sentinels. This year Bruce will be presenting the new edition of *Great Lakes Lighthouses*.

Add your name to the Outer Banks Lighthouse Society newsletter mailing list and look for special lighthouse interpretive events in the summer at the Bodie Island Lighthouse. You can also call the gallery for information about joining the Outer Banks Lighthouse Society, and you'll receive a Society newsletter.

Ipso Facto Gallery

206 Gallery Row, Nags Head *480-2793*

You won't find any theme collections here. The merchandise — antiques, curios and objects of art from all over the world — is quite eclectic, and it's reasonably priced too. Ipso is really more of an antique shop than a gift shop. It's a great place to browse, ooh and aah and, of course, find a treasure to take home. Ipso Facto Gallery is open year round; it's closed Sunday.

Morales Art Gallery

107 E. Gallery Row, Nags Head *441-6484*
Scarborough Faire, Duck *261-7190*
(800) 635-6035

Morales Art Gallery is the oldest art venue on Gallery Row — the late Jesse Morales first opened the doors 25 years ago. Today, Morales Galleries and Fine Art Print Shop carries fine original local, regional and nationally known art. Showcased are the works of Larry Johnson, Pat Williams, Dennis Lightheart, Pat Troiani, Tony Feathers, William "Red" Taylor, Carol Trotman and Liz Corsa. Expect to find limited edition prints by the Greenwich Workshop, Mill Pond Press, Hadley House, Somerset Publishing and Wild Wings. If you want to view a major collection of original seascapes, this is the place to come.

If you're searching for specific art or artists, the gallery's laser disc computer system stores more than 40,000 images that you can pore over to find the perfect piece. Featured in the print shop here are breathtaking fine art prints by premier nature painters.

Mitchell Lively, who owns the business with his wife, Christine, has been framing and publishing art for more than 21 years. The couple's dedication to the arts has been felt community-wide, especially in their generosity to the Dare County Schools. A member of the Professional Picture Framers Association, Morales Galleries offers a wide variety of choices in custom framing. Mitchell is also an inventor; stop by and ask him about the mat cutter he designed. Call for weekly show and exhibit information at their Scarborough Faire location in Duck.

The Nags Head Gallery is open year round, call for the Duck schedule.

B.J. Egeli Portrait Studio

Central Square, Nags Head *441-9696*

B.J. Egeli comes from a long line of artists who have concentrated on perfecting the portrait. At his Central Square Studio are portraits and landscapes done in a variety of media. He works in oils, watercolors, pastels and pencil to create images that capture the model's true spirit. Egeli prefers to work from life but if necessary will work from photos (he photographs his subjects himself).

This is a working studio so you can see B.J. in action while browsing for an original work of art to take home. Take your time — B.J. is an interesting chap to chat with. Call for an appointment.

Ray Matthews Photographer

P.O. Box 191, Nags Head 27959 *441-7941*

Ray has been living on the Outer Banks for 24 years during which he has developed a love for nature that is presented masterfully in his prints. While the Outer Banks is a real haven for the photographic arts, the height of excellence is represented in Ray's work. He is a consummate custom-slide printer as well as a commercial photographer. His work is shown at Browning Artworks in Buxton and The Christmas Shop in Manteo. Call for an appointment. He is available year round.

Glenn Eure's Ghost Fleet Gallery of Fine Art

Driftwood St., Gallery Row
Nags Head *441-6584*

Primarily a printmaker, Eure works in a variety of forms including etching,

woodcutting, collagraphy, serigraphy and relief carving and painting in addition to drawing, sculpture and oil, acrylic and watercolor painting, all of which are represented in a permanent exhibit at the Ghost Fleet Gallery.

Glenn and Pat Eure rotate other artists' work in the West Wing Gallery, and once a year Eure enters the ring with fellow artist Denver Lindley for "Mano a Mano," Spanish for "hand to hand." This exhibit includes works done by the artists over the course of the preceding year. The 1995 show featured shaped canvas paintings by Eure along with his traditional marine-related woodcut prints, collagraphs, and drawings. Lindley's work consisted mostly of drawings and paintings of mechanical devices and machinery, elevating the ordinary to a "work-of-art" status.

In the off-season Eure hosts two community shows: The first, the International Icarus Show in December, commemorates the Wright Brothers' first flight; the second is the Frank Stick Memorial Art Show each February sponsored by the Dare County Arts Council. Both shows draw more than 100 artists into the exhibition arena, and opening nights attract more than 800 art lovers to the gallery. Poetry readings are held year round (see our Annual Events chapter).

The Ghost Fleet Gallery is open from early spring through December. It's closed Mondays.

Jewelry by Gail

207 Driftwood St., Gallery Row
Nags Head *441-5387*

Gail Kowalski is a designer-goldsmith who has won national recognition for her creations in precious metals and stones. You'll want to see the unusual amethyst crystal chandelier created by Pennsylvania artist Michael Fornadley. Most of the jewelry designed and made here falls into the "wearable art" category. Gail's newest addition, Selections by Gail, 441-1547, is a department of very high quality but moderately priced handmade jewelry from all over the world. Gail personally selects each piece exhibited here.

The gallery is open Monday through Saturday and is closed in January.

Seaside Art Gallery

Beach Rd., MP 11, Nags Head *441-5418*
TimBuck II, N.C. 12, Corolla *453-0868*

Original etchings and lithographs by Picasso, Whistler and Renoir are among the thousands of original works of art on display at the Nags Head location of Seaside Art Gallery. Sculptures, paintings, drawings, Indian pottery, fine porcelains, seascapes and animation art from Disney are spread throughout numerous rooms in this expansive gallery.

The Seaside Art Gallery in Corolla is smaller than the Nags Head location but also offers a wonderful variety of original art, porcelains, pottery, sculptures, paintings, seascapes, drawings and cell animation.

The gallery hosts several international competitions annually including a Christian art show and a miniature art competition. Printmaking workshops are also held here each year. The Nags Head gallery is open seven days a week all year. The Corolla location is open daily beginning Memorial Day, but is open week-

Insiders' Tips

Unlike some museums in big cities, Outer Banks galleries are in the business of selling art. So while you can feel free to browse, most of what you see will be for sale.

ends only during the off-season and hours vary then so please call ahead.

Anna Gartrell's Art & Photography By the Sea

Beach Rd., MP 10½, Nags Head *480-0578*

Gartrell's artistry is evident in her expressive watercolors and photography. Her work seems to brighten every darkened recess in your spiritual being. Original is the key word here. A deeply spiritual woman, Gartrell revels in "God's explosive beauty frozen forever for you." Examine her series of jeweled and crystal wave photos, depictions of wild storms, sunrises and sunsets, ducks, dunes, wild stallions and lighthouses, crystal flounders and amazing sea angels. Take a bit of Outer Banks brightness home with you.

The gallery is open daily, but hours are flexible. The owner posts a note on the door daily with the day's operating hours.

Yellowhouse Gallery and Annex

Beach Rd., MP 11, Nags Head *441-6928*

Yellowhouse Gallery and Annex houses one of North Carolina's largest collections of antique prints and maps. Thousands of original old etchings, lithographs and engravings are organized for browsing in several rooms of one of Nags Head's older beach cottages. Established in 1969, the gallery features Civil War prints and maps; prints of botanicals, fish, shells and birds; and old views, antique maps and charts of the Outer Banks. Yellowhouse Gallery also offers a huge selection of decorative and fine art prints and posters as well as souvenir pictures and maps of the Outer Banks. If the picture you want is not in stock Uncle Jack, the genial proprietor, will order it for you.

Yellowhouse Annex next door offers fast, expert custom framing, matting, mounting and shrink-wrapping. Archival framing is also available. Yellowhouse Gallery and Annex are open daily except Sundays all year.

Island Art Gallery

U.S. 64, at The Christmas Shop
Manteo *473-2838*

The work of more than 100 artists is displayed in this adjunct to the popular Christmas Shop. The gallery, which is open daily year round, consists of several large rooms of paintings, sculptures and works in other media in a wide range of themes, including seascapes and other nautical subjects. Ask shop personnel for information on the New World Festival of the Arts held each August under the guidance of Christmas Shop owner Eddie Green.

Nick-E Stained Glass

813 Old Wharf Rd., Wanchese *473-5036*

The studio and gallery are a stained-glass wonderland featuring the original creations of Ellinor and Robert Nick.

Wanchese Pottery

107 Fernando St., Manteo *473-2099*

Customers can watch local potter Bonnie Morrill at work and learn about the stages of pottery-making from a display in the studio. Bonnie's husband, Bob, helps with the trimming and glazing. This shop is known locally for its beautiful, useful art — dinnerware, oil lamps, tumblers, lotion dispensers, hummingbird feeders, mirrors, soup mugs, pitchers and canisters. The shop also features some handmade baskets and fresh cooking herbs.

Manteo Gallery

The Waterfront, Manteo *473-3365*

This shop is relatively new, giving visitors more choices of where to go on the island for gallery purchases and browsing. Jack Hughes is offering limited-edition prints with an emphasis on maritime arts. Look for the aviation print collection and breathtaking antique map prints. The gallery also features the inspirational paintings and drawings of Ellie Grumiaux, who is on hand several days a week to demonstrate his skills.

Photo: Mary Ellen Riddle

The Dare County Arts Council brings in such national acts as the National Tap Ensemble from Washington, D.C.

The Manteo Gallery, located in Island Trading on the Manteo Waterfront, is open year round. Closed Sunday during the off season.

Upstairs Art Gallery

Pamlico Station, Rodanthe *987-1088*

The new Upstairs Art Gallery features works by James Melvin, Chris Haltigan, Glenn Eure and other Carolina artists. You can purchase limited edition prints, Black Hills gold jewelry, painted furniture, pottery and original watercolors. The gallery is above Lee's Collectibles.

Michael Halminski Studio and Gallery

Lillian Ln., Waves *987-2401*

Outer Banks seascapes and landscapes dominate the photography collection displayed at this studio. Call for an appointment. Halminski also has a fine collection of cards that feature his work.

Gaskins Gallery

N.C. 12, Avon *995-6617*

The focus at Gaskins Gallery is on original local art and custom framing. Artist and owner Denise Gaskins exclusively features original family art, including her own watercolors and those of her 82-year-old grandmother, who began painting several years ago. The gallery, which also has decorator prints and posters, is open year round.

Browning Artworks

N.C. 12, Buxton *995-5538*

This fine art and craft gallery, which opened in 1984, features the work of North Carolina artists exclusively. The collection includes the creations of 200 crafters who make blown-glass, porcelains, pottery, baskets, stoneware, fiber art, carved birds and jewelry. The gallery also exhibits paintings and prints, including the exclusive collection of Linda Browning's exquisite watercolor skyscapes and Dixie Browning's watercolor scenes as well as the photography of Ray Matthews and Michael Halminski. Antique tribal weavings by Majid are a beautiful attraction. Proprietors Linda and Lou Browning also maintain a bridal registry and will ship your selections.

Sunflower Studio

Back Rd., Ocracoke *928-6211*

Follow British Cemetery Road all the way around to find this little back street and the gallery. The Sunflower Studio combines contemporary and traditional arts and crafts. All of the artists are from Ocracoke, and some of the crafters are from other places. Only original art is exhibited. Other items here include custom deerskin shoes, custom moccasins, fused glass, stained glass, papermâché and handcrafted jewelry. Ethnic designs prevail.

Owner Carol O'Brien offers and participates in ongoing workshops for artists. Weekly summer workshops are held including classes in oil, acrylic and water color painting, plus pastels and drawing. A school of arts and crafts is offered January through April for adults and children. Shows start in June and run through the summer, changing biweekly.

Artists in Motion

Back Rd., Ocracoke *928-4535*

New in 1996, this gallery features the work of artist-in-residence, Russell Yerks, a Norfolk, Virginia, watercolorist. Local art is available including pottery by Rhonda Bates and decoys by Tom Leonard. Check out their on-the-premises coffee shop (see our Shopping chapter) for a relaxing spot to sip a cup and chat about art.

Village Craftsmen

Howard St., Ocracoke *928-5541*

The artwork in this well-known shop and gallery includes North Carolina pottery and other original items. The owner, Philip Howard, also sells his pen-and-ink and watercolor prints here. Turn to our Shopping chapter for more about this local landmark.

Steve Lautermilch

Colington Harbor *480-0060*

Steve Lautermilch is a professional photographer and poet who offers private and group classes in writing, dream work and meditation. His photography is displayed at Glenn Eure's Ghost Fleet Gallery in Nags Head. Lautermilch works mostly in color, but his subject matter encompasses both nature and people. His pictures have an ethereal feel, illustrating the absolute beauty of mother nature. He is a meticulous camera man, and believes that understanding your dreams and relaxing with meditation can enhance creativity. After viewing his work, you may think he's on to something. Call for an appointment.

Island Artworks

British Cemetery Rd., Ocracoke *928-3892*

Owner-artist Kathleen O'Neal has lived on Ocracoke for almost 20 years. This longtime local does all the copper enameling, and silver and goldsmithing work herself. "Art jewelry" aptly describes most of the finds here. The artwork is done by local and North Carolina artists mostly, such as Jack Willis, who handcrafts cedar boxes. Local photography, mixed-media art and paper-

Insiders' Tips

Don't forget to pack your paints and brushes before you head to the Outer Banks. The area has a way of stimulating creative juices by providing sunrises and sunsets on the water. You'll feel compelled to "dabble."

mâché items are just some of the exciting discoveries at Island Artworks. It's a real fine art experience.

Juried Art Exhibitions

The Outer Banks offers several juried art exhibitions each year. While the traditional definition of juried implies that work is selected for showing by judges, most shows here have an open-entry policy, and the work is judged for excellence and originality. Most shows have an entry fee that averages $10 to $15. We list the major shows in the area; for detailed information, call the galleries mentioned or the Dare County Arts Council, 441-5617. New shows are always cropping up, so keep in touch with the arts council. See our Annual Events chapter for more art happenings.

Frank Stick Memorial Art Show

Nags Head *441-5617*

This February show, held at Glenn Eure's Ghost Fleet Gallery, is open to Dare County residents and Dare County Arts Council members. One piece of work can be entered.

International Christian Art Show

Nags Head *441-5418*

Held in April at Seaside Art Gallery, this event is open to any artist.

International Miniature Art Show

Nags Head *441-5418*

Any artist may enter this May show, held at Seaside Art Gallery.

International Icarus Art Show

Nags Head *441-6584*

Open to any artist, this show is held in December at Glenn Eure's Ghost Fleet Gallery and the Seaside Art Gallery.

Dance Studios

Atlantic Dance Studio

Dare Center, Kill Devil Hills *441-9009*

This new studio run by Victoria Toms is a super addition to the Outer Banks creative scene. Toms brings with her an outstanding history of professional dance experience. She studied under the Martha Graham School of Contemporary Dance and performed with the Joffrey Ballet. Atlantic Dance Studio offers lessons for adults and children in tap, ballet, jazz, gymnastics and modeling. During the summer of 1996, the studio will offer a summer camp featuring those genres. Locals and visitors are welcome.

A dancer's boutique carries garments, bags and dance paraphernalia that will drive mothers of "little dancers" crazy.

Island Dance Studio

3017 Virginia Dare Tr., Nags Head *441-6789*

Sophia Sharp has been teaching dance on the Outer Banks for more than 15 years. She offers classes in ballet, jazz, tap and preschool movement. Sophia's studio closes during the summer, so she caters mostly to local folks. She teaches children and adults.

Inside Annual Events

Exciting events are always happening on the Outer Banks — from the annual Wines of the World Weekend in January to the Christmas Parade in Manteo every December. Retail stores, art galleries and historic sites also sponsor happenings such as drama vignettes, printmaking workshops and lectures. Your stay on the Outer Banks can be greatly enhanced by some of these state-of-the-art events.

In August, Dare County will host America's 1996 **Babe Ruth World Series Baseball Tournament**, which will bring eight teams of youths, ages 16 through 18, to the Outer Banks from across the country. Months of planning have gone into this event, scheduled for August 17 through 24. The 160 players will compete at the Manteo High School ball field, and 7,000 visitors are expected to attend the games. North Carolina's governor, James Hunt, will toss the first pitch in the double elimination series. You can purchase tickets at all Dare and Currituck county banks, and all Parks and Recreation Departments in Northeastern North Carolina. A weeklong family pass costs $50, individual passes cost $35 for the week. Daily passes will be sold, but prices were not set when we went to press in April. The event will commence with a parade at 10 AM in Manteo on August 17. Opening ceremonies start at 1 PM. Three games apiece are scheduled for Saturday and Sunday, and during the remainder of the week two games will be played every day through Friday beginning at 5 PM. To get to Manteo High School, head west on U.S. 64 and turn at

Photo: Mary Ellen Riddle

The Alice Kelly Memorial Ladies Only Billfish Tournament is highly competitive but leaves time for a breather on the way to each fishing stop.

the stoplight (it's the last light you come to as you're heading west out of Manteo) at the corner of Harriot Street. At the end of Harriot, the school is directly in front of you. Call Dare County Parks and Recreation, 473-1101, for more information.

During the summer months, the National Park Service offers free educational activities and programs at the **Fort Raleigh National Historic Site**, the Wright Brothers Memorial and Cape Hatteras National Seashore. Write to: National Park Service, Route 1, Box 675, Manteo 27954, or call 473-2111.

The following listings reflect events occurring during the 1996 calendar year. Most events are held on the same weekends or days each year.

January

Outer Banks folks and visitors can indulge in some events sure to warm the ol' January bones.

In mid-January, Pirate's Cove Yacht Club offers an annual **Wines of the World Weekend**, at the Marina, Manteo/Nags Head Causeway, 473-1451 or (800) 762-0245.

The **Outer Banks Forum** always schedules a January event, anything from a comedy act to a musical performance. These productions, brought in from out of town or state, are top-notch, 261-8940.

February

The **Frank Stick Memorial Art Show** at Glenn Eure's Ghost Fleet Gallery in Nags Head is held in early February featuring the work of over 150 artists (see our Arts and Culture chapter). If you want to submit work, you must be a local or a member of the Dare County Arts Council. You can stop in for the reception, always held on a Sunday, or leisurely view the show throughout the month of February. The event is sponsored by the Dare County Arts Council, 441-5617. Call the DCAC for an annual calendar of events. This group usually schedules a dance performance this month also.

Spend **A Literary Evening** at Glenn Eure's Ghost Fleet Gallery in Nags Head. Part of the month-long Frank Stick Memorial Art Show, members of the Dare County Writers' Group read from their original works-in-progress. This group, sponsored by the Dare County Arts Council, meets monthly. Call Phyllis Combs at 480-3808 for details.

March

Hungry? Check out **Taste of the Beach**. Local restaurants and beverage distributors provide the public with a taste of their best Outer Banks treats. Enjoy seafood and pasta specialties, fine wines and beers and a whole lot more. There is a $10 admission fee. We advise you to get there early. It's a very popular event with locals. For information, call Kelly's Outer Banks Restaurant and Tavern, 441-4116.

On the Sunday before St. Patrick's Day, the **Kelly's-Beach 95-Falcon Cable TV St. Patrick's Day Parade** begins at Nags Head Pier (11½ MP on the Beach Road) and proceeds north to about MP 10. Reputed to be the largest parade of its kind in North Carolina, the event is always fun for the whole family. Float participants throw candy, so wear pockets! Kelly's Restaurant, 441-4116, serves free hot dogs and sodas after the parade, and there's an evening of live entertainment at Kelly's under a tent.

Pirate's Cove sponsors an inshore/offshore **fishing school** this month. You can get information on the one- or two-day program — featuring North Carolina fishing experts — by calling 473-1451 or (800) 762-0245.

The **Outer Banks Forum** is on tap with a theatrical production. Members were still perfecting their calendar when we went to press, but you can call them at 261-8940 to get the scoop.

A Wolf Cries in the Wilderness

Without moon or stars, the night sky was black. The fog had lifted and heavy air hung over the still, silent wilderness on the eve of Halloween. Suddenly, out of the darkness, a low moan began to waver in the October night. Louder and louder it grew, becoming more high-pitched before reaching a crescendo in a piercing wail.

Quiet reigned for a moment.

Then the howling resumed, this time from a point about two-thirds of a mile south. A second voice took up the haunting call. Then a third.

And within 15 seconds a throaty chorus reverberated through the sky, sounding an eerie "Yiiieeeooooow" in various octaves.

"Oh my God!" a woman cried.

A dozen wolves were braying in the blackness.

Partly to celebrate Halloween, mostly to educate people about the endangered North American red wolf, the U.S. Fish & Wildlife Service sponsors an annual fall "howling" at Alligator River National Wildlife Refuge.

About 70 children and adults follow dirt roads and flick flashlights to find the wolves. But most people are content just to hear the Fish & Wildlife Service biologists howl — and listen to the animals' arresting voices answer.

"I think it's kind of scary, the way it is at night and dark and the way they wail," said Tim Bloker of Manteo, who kept close to his father all night. "In the zoo it's fun. But it sounds sort of spooky out here."

"I think it's neat because it's like knocking on the door of their house and waiting for them to let you in," said Tim's father, Jim Bloker.

In 1987, the U.S. Fish & Wildlife Service began a $200,000-a-year federally funded program to reintroduce red wolves to their natural habitat. The species was declared extinct in the wild in the mid-1980s. And to date there are fewer than 100 red wolves left in the world.

Workers breed wolves in outdoor pens on the 142,000-acre refuge on the Dare County mainland. Then, as puppies grow old enough, entire wolf families are let go into the wilderness of Alligator River National Wildlife Refuge. More than 50 wolves have been reintroduced near the Outer Banks so far.

"I saw a stuffed wolf in the aquarium. And I wanted to hear a live one howl," Tim Bloker said. "That's why I came: To know about the animals, and because I like to hear them howl."

(As appeared in The Virginian-Pilot.*)*

April

Please note that dates for Easter events, egg hunts and so forth will fluctuate, depending on when Easter occurs. Many stores and businesses offer egg hunts. They are usually advertised on radio and in the local paper or on individual marquees.

Kelly's Restaurant sponsors a "flashlight" midnight **Easter egg hunt** for adults, 441-4116.

Annual Easter Eggstravaganza, held

at The Promenade in Kitty Hawk and sponsored by the North Beach Kiwanis Club, goes from 9 AM until 1 PM. Lots of fun to be had here with an egg hunt, craftmaking, rides, races, food and more. Call 261-4900 for information.

The **Outer Banks Homebuilders Association's Parade of Homes** opens new and remodeled homes to the public from Corolla to South Nags Head and Manteo. There is a $5 fee; proceeds go to Habitat for Humanity and a scholarship fund. Write the association at P.O. Box 398, Kitty Hawk 27949, or call 255-1733.

Held in late April, **The Small Business Expo** is sponsored by the Outer Banks Chamber of Commerce. Write: P.O. Box 1757, Kill Devil Hills 27948, or call 441-8144.

The **Outer Banks Silver Arts Competition** takes place at the Thomas A. Baum Senior Center in Kill Devil Hills. This is the art section of the Outer Banks Senior Games, featuring an exhibition of talent and craftsmanship in the visual arts, 441-1181.

Also in late April, all ages will enjoy the fun at the **Blues Fishing Tournament and Music Festival**, off N.C. 12 in Rodanthe, Hatteras Island. Restaurants provide concessions — hot dogs, hamburgers, smoked fish, chicken and more — and the day includes plenty of blues music, a fish fry, arts and crafts booths and games. There are lots of children's activities, including an adult/child surf fishing tournament and distance casting competition, 987-2911. Admission is free.

The **Outer Banks Senior Games** competition includes shuffleboard, billiards, horseshoes, table tennis and much more. Dare County seniors age 55 and older are eligible to compete. All are welcome to watch and cheer for the competitors. Contact the Thomas A. Baum Senior Center, 441-9388, for information.

From the last week in April until mid-May, Soundings Factory Outlets, Nags Head, 441-7395 sponsors the **Great Escape Vacation Contest**. Stop by and become a contestant.

Outer Banks Forum, 261-8940, offers another special performance this month. All events are held at the Kitty Hawk Elementary School.

May

The **Small Business of the Year** luncheon is held in early May, sponsored by the Chamber of Commerce and Hutchins Allen & Co., CPA, 441-8144.

Call The Island Inn, 928-4351, on Ocracoke for information about the **Surf Fishing Invitational Tournament**.

For one weekend in mid-May, spectators and participants cover the dunes at Jockey's Ridge State Park, Nags Head, for the **Hang Gliding Spectacular**. It's the oldest continuous hang-gliding competition in the country (1996 marks the 24th year). Pilots from all over the United States compete in a variety of flying maneuvers. Beginning hang gliding lessons are given. A street dance and an awards ceremony adds icing on the cake! To preregister, call Kitty Hawk Kites, 441-4124 or (800) 334-4777.

Every May 10, the **British Cemetery Ceremony** on Ocracoke Island commemorates the 1942 sinking of the British Trawler *Bedfordshire*. A British official is sent to Ocracoke each year to attend this Coast Guard service. Call the U.S. Coast Guard, 928-3711.

The **Nags Head Woods 5K Run** is held at the Nags Head Woods Preserve, usually on a Saturday in midmonth. To participate, write: Nags Head Woods 5K Run 701 W. Ocean Acres Drive, Kill Devil Hills 27948, or call 441-2525.

The **Memorial Day Weekend Arts & Crafts Fair**, at the Ramada Inn, Kill Devil Hills, is sponsored by the Outer Banks Women's Club, 261-3196.

The **Hatteras Village Offshore Open Billfish Tournament** is a weeklong event in early May sponsored by the Hatteras

Village Civic Association, whose headquarters is at Teach's Lair Marina, 986-2460. This is a Governor's Cup-sanctioned event.

Outer Banks Outdoors Duck Cup Regatta is planned for mid-May. Enjoy a festival of sails and participate in classes including Flying Scot, catamaran, lidos and open class. Sail your own boat or charter one to compete for fun and prizes. Preregister at Kitty Hawk Kites, U.S. 158, MP 13, or call (800) 334-4777.

The **Virginia Beach Billfish Foundation Tournament** in late May takes place at Pirate's Cove Yacht Club, Nags Head-Manteo Causeway, 473-6800 or (800)537-7245.

Call 928-6711 for information about the **Arts and Crafts Festival** on Howard Street in Ocracoke.

USAir Fishing Tournament at Hatteras Harbor Marina is held the last weekend in May. Call 986-2166 for information.

June

Dare Day Festival in Manteo is always the first Saturday of June. It features arts and crafts, food and national and local musical entertainment. It's sponsored by the Town of Manteo and the County of Dare. Write: Box 1000, Manteo 27954, or call 473-1101, Ext. 319.

Pirate's Cove Invitational Offshore Tournament, at Pirate's Cove Yacht Club, Nags Head-Manteo Causeway, 473-6800 or (800) 537-7245, takes place in early June.

For information about **The Sport Fishing School** in Hatteras, write: Box 7401, Raleigh 27695.

The **Rogallo Kite Festival** on Jockey's Ridge is in its 14th year in 1996. This early June family fun fly celebrates the beauty of kite flying. It is open to kite enthusiasts of all ages and features stunt kites, home-builts and kids' competitions. Call Kitty Hawk Kites, 441-4124 or (800) 334-4777.

In mid-June, the **Outer Banks Outdoors Kayak Jamboree** takes place at the Waterworks Tower on the Manteo-Nags Head Causeway (U.S. 64). Try out new kayaks and explore Outer Banks salt marshes and channels from 9 AM until sunset, 441-4124 or (800) 334-4777. 1996 marks this event's third year.

The **Hatteras Marlin Fishing Tournament** is sponsored by and headquartered at the Hatteras Marlin Club. Write: Box 218, Hatteras 27943, or call 986-2454.

In mid-June, **Wil-Bear's Festival of Fun** takes place at Kitty Hawk Connection, Nags Head. The star of the day is Wil-Bear Wright, the colorful Kitty Hawk Kites mascot. Children of all ages are thrilled by action-packed workshops on kite flying, kite making, paper airplane making and T-shirt painting. Kids will also enjoy face painting, juggling and entertainment. Call Kitty Hawk Kites, 441-4124 or (800) 334-4777.

The **Arts and Crafts Show** takes place at the Outer Banks Mall, Nags Head. For information, call 441-5620.

The annual **Wanchese Seafood Festival** the last Saturday in June is in its 14th year in 1996. This event features the Blessing of the Fleet, arts and crafts vendors, educational displays, crab races, children's games and lots and lots of seafood. For information call 441-8144.

Insiders' Tips

If you're interested in watching the fireworks in Manteo on July 4, think about having an early dinner on the waterfront. This way you can secure a spot to watch the show before the crowds arrive.

Photo: Mary Ellen Riddle

The Sport-fishing School held annually on Hatteras Island draws students from around the country.

Beginning in mid-June (ending mid-August) **The Sunset Festival at Pirate's Cove and Arts on the Dock** occurs every Wednesday from 4 to 8 PM at Pirate's Cove Yacht Club on the Nags Head/ Manteo Causeway. Watch the boats come in with their daily catch and stroll the docks while taking in all the arts, crafts and live music. Kids games, food and drink are available. Call 473-6366 or (800) 762-0245.

On the fourth Saturday in June, Kitty Hawk Sports, 441-6800, sponsors its **Outer Banks Body Board Contest**. Competition is open to the public and features an exhibition by professional body boarders. The event is held behind the Ramada Inn, MP 9½ on the Beach Road in Kill Devil Hills.

Plan to be here the last weekend in June for the **Outer Banks Outdoors Sailing Jamboree** and **Windriders National Championships** sponsored by Kitty Hawk Kites and Outer Banks Outdoors, MP 13, Nags Head, 441-4124 or (800) 334-4777. The events feature free windsurfing and sailing demo lessons, plus races and a barbecue.

July

In early July, a breakfast meeting to honor **America's Birthday** takes place at the Ramada Inn, Kill Devil Hills. It's sponsored by the Outer Banks Chamber of Commerce, 441-8144.

On July 4, Outer Banks towns turn out in red, white and blue splendor for old-fashioned Independence Day observances. Here are a few to look forward to:

In picturesque Ocracoke Village, the **Independence Day Parade** makes its way through the streets starting at 3 PM. Call 928-6711. The **Sand Sculpture Contest** happens north of Ocracoke Village; call 995-4474.

Take part in the **Independence Day Celebration** at the Manteo Waterfront. Activities run from 1 to 9 PM and include a Wacky Tacky Hat Contest, children's games, food, concessions, musical entertainment and a street dance from 6 to 9 PM. A fireworks display begins at 9 PM. Call 473-1101.

Fireworks in Hatteras Village at the ferry docks occur at 8:30 PM, sponsored by the Hatteras Village Civic Association and the Volunteer Fire Department.

The historic Whalehead Club in Corolla is the backdrop for the **Fireworks Festival and Fair** from 4 to 11 PM. The Currituck County Board of Commissioners and the Corolla Business Association host this event. Expect fun, food, live music entertainment and, of course, pyrotechnics galore.

Call Newman's Shell Shop, 441-5791, in Nags Head for information about the **Hermit Crab Race**. Kids of all ages love this fun — and funny — event.

Held in early July, the **Youth Fishing Tournament** includes pier and surf fishing. Register at participating piers from Kitty Hawk to South Nags Head (see our Fishing chapter for locations). The cost is a mere pittance — 50¢ per person — and the experience is priceless. This event is sponsored by the Nags Head Surf Fishing Club, 441-5723 or (800) 850-0249.

Midmonth, sign up for **Seamark Foods/Oscar Mayer Children's Fishing Tournament** at Pirate's Cove Yacht Club (N.C. Special Olympics athletes are invited). Write: P.O. Box 1997, Manteo 27954, or call Barry Martin at 473-6800 or (800) 537-7245 for information.

Also midmonth, the **Annual Wright Kite Festival** takes to the skies for the 18th year in 1996 at the Wright Brothers National Memorial. This fun family event involves kite flying for all ages and also includes free kite-making workshops and children's games. Guests include the Revolution Kites, professional boomerang throwers and Wil-Bear Wright, 441-4124 or (800) 334-4777. The event is sponsored by Kitty Hawk Kites and the National Park Service.

August

On the first Sunday in August, make plans to be at the **Corolla Seafood Festival Fund Raiser**, sponsored by the Corolla Volunteer Fire Department, 453-3242.

Also in early August, the **Annual Wacky Watermelon Weekend and Windsurfing Regatta** takes place at the Kitty Hawk Connection and Kitty Hawk Sports, Nags Head. This is the 12th year for this watermelon-centered event, which begins with a parade led by the state's Watermelon Queen and includes an Olympic watermelon toss, big league watermelon bowling, carving, long-distance seed spitting and watermelon consumption. The most energized event of the day is the Kamikaze Watermelon Drop. Register at Kitty Hawk Sports' Nags Head store, or call 441-6800.

In early August, the **Annual Nags Head Woods Benefit Auction** for the Nags Head Woods Ecological Preserve is held at The Sanderling Inn in Duck; 1996 is the sixth year for this event. Call 441-2525 well in advance, as limited tickets are available for this major fund-raiser. The benefit features cocktails, jazz and a silent auction at 5 PM; the main auction featuring art and jewelry begins at 6:30 PM.

On the second Saturday, the **Annual Herbert Hoover Birthday Celebration** takes place at Manteo Booksellers. Write: P.O. Box 1520, Manteo 27954, or call 473-1221.

For the 23rd year, local senior citizens provide the crafts for the **Annual Senior Adults Craft Fair** at the Thomas A. Baum Center in Kill Devil Hills. It's a community project sponsored by the Outer Banks Women's Club, 441-9388.

The **Alice Kelly Memorial Ladies Only Billfish Tournament** takes place the second weekend of the month at Pirate's Cove Yacht Club, 473-6800 or (800) 367-4728. The tournament is in its seventh year.

In mid-August, the **48th Anniversary of the Rogallo Wing Invention** at Kitty Hawk Kites in Nags Head is a ceremony that honors Francis M. Rogallo, inventor of the flexible wing and the acknowledged father of hang gliding, who is usually present at this festive event. Call 441-4124 or (800) 334-4777.

Midmonth, Pirate's Cove Yacht Club hosts the **Pirate's Cove Billfish Tournament** for the 13th year in 1996. It's an official part of the N.C. Governor's Cup Billfish Series. Call 473-6800 or (800) 367-4728.

Come to the Manteo waterfront in mid-August for the **New World Festival of the Arts**, coordinated by Eddie Greene of The Christmas Shop. The outdoor show, which is in its 14th season, is a cultural event not to be missed. Write: Box 994, Manteo 27954, or call 473-2838.

In mid-August, **National Aviation Day** is observed at the Wright Brothers National Memorial in Kill Devil Hills. For information write: Route 1, Box 675, Manteo 27954, or call 441-7430.

Every August 18, the **Virginia Dare Day Celebration** at Fort Raleigh National Historic Site Visitors Center commemorates the birth of Virginia Dare, the first English child born in the New World. The celebration features a daylong series of special events including programs, singing and dancing. Call the National Park Service, 473-5772, for details.

Also on August 18, the **Virginia Dare Night Performance** of *The Lost Colony* celebrates the occasion by casting local infants in the role of Virginia Dare (see our Arts and Culture chapter). Call 473-3414 or (800) 488-5012 for information.

On Labor Day weekend, the **Labor Day Arts & Craft Show** takes place at the Ramada Inn, Kill Devil Hills, sponsored by the Outer Banks Women's Club, 261-3196.

Another Labor Day weekend event is the **Albemarle Challenge Cup Regatta**, sponsored by the Roanoke Island Yacht Club at the Colington Harbour Clubhouse. For entry fee information call 441-2059.

September

The **Labor Day Arts and Crafts Show** at the Hatteras Civic Center is sponsored by the Hatteras Island Arts and Crafts Guild, 995-5179.

The **Eastern Surfing Championships** take place in Buxton in September. Competition is open to association members only, but it's a fun spectator event. Write: Box 400, Buxton 27920, or call 995-5785.

During the first week in September, the Weeping Radish Restaurant and Brewery in Manteo hosts its 11th **Oktoberfest**, a family-oriented fun outdoors celebration featuring Bavarian-style food, the Oompah Band, children's games, specially brewed German beer and a chance to win a trip to Germany. Call 473-1157 for more information.

The 12-year-old **Outer Banks Triathlon** is held in early September on Roanoke Island. Entrants swim 6 miles, bike 15 miles and run 3.1 miles. Write the Dare Voluntary Action Center at P.O. Box 1213, Kill Devil Hills, or call 480-0500.

"The Allison" Crippled Children's White Marlin Release Tournament, now in its fourth year, takes place the first weekend in September at Pirate's Cove Yacht Club, 473-6800 or (800) 537-7245.

In mid-September, catch the **Carolinas' Shootout**, an annual North Carolina and South Carolina Governor's Cup finalists fishing tournament. This competition changes venue between North and South Carolina. The 1996 event is held at Pirate's Cove Marina on the Nags Head-Manteo Causeway. Call 473-6800 or (800) 537-7245.

Surf fishing fans will want to set aside the second weekend in September for the **Hatteras Village Civic Association Surf Fishing Tournament**. The event is in its 14th year in 1996. Call 986-2579 for information.

Outer Banks Outdoors Trashfest Regatta, held midmonth at MP 13, Nags Head, 441-4124 or (800) 334-4777, is an organized beach cleanup and sailing event with awards and festivities.

For the fifth year, Pirate's Cove Yacht Club sponsors the **Carolina 92-Pirate's Cove Small Boat Fishing Tournament**.

The event takes place the third Saturday of the month at the yacht club on the Nags Head/Manteo Causeway; call 473-6800 or (800) 537-7245.

Also in mid-September, the **Outer Banks Volleyball Championships** swing into action on the beach at the Pebble Beach Motel. For details, write P.O. Box 1209, Nags Head 27957, or call 441-5111.

The **North Beach Sun Trash Festival** includes Operation Beach Sweep and an afternoon festival in Duck. Beach Sweep participants receive a ticket to the festival for live music and a North Carolina barbecue dinner. Call the North Beach Sun at 480-2787.

On the fourth Sunday in September, put on your skates for the eighth **Flying Wheels Rollerblade Spectacular** and compete for gift certificates and prizes. It's for a good cause — the Corolla Wild Horse Fund — and is a fun time for the entire family. Contact Kitty Hawk Kites, 441-4124 or (800) 334-4777.

On the third Saturday of September, place your bids at the **Chamber of Commerce Auction** at the Ramada Inn, Kill Devil Hills. Bid on vacations, gifts, restaurant gift certificates and more. Enjoy heavy hors d'oeuvres and an open bar from 5:30 to 7:30 PM. The auction begins at 7 PM. Contact the Outer Banks Chamber of Commerce, 441-8144, for ticket information.

Also in midmonth is the **First Citizens Bank Big Sweep**, a statewide waterway cleanup from 9 AM until 1 PM on the third Saturday in September. This is the 10th year for this event; call (800)-27-SWEEP for details.

New in 1996 is the **"Women Only" Art Show and White Elephant Auction for Hotline**, a fund-raiser for the Outer Banks Hotline in Manteo. It will be held the third Saturday in September at Soundings Factory Outlets, Nags Head. Call 441-7395 for more information.

In late September, bring the whole family to The Promenade in Kitty Hawk for **Kids "Fun" Raiser Day**, sponsored by North Beach Kiwanis Club. The fun lasts from 9 AM to 1 PM and features a treasure hunt, minigolf, cake walks, costumed characters and train rides. For more information call 261-4900.

Also in late September, the **Dare County Jaycee's Golf Tournament Benefit** will take place at The Pointe Golf Course, in lower Currituck County. Write to: Dare County Jaycees, P.O. Box 3488, Kill Devil Hills 27948.

October

The **Nags Head Surf Fishing Club Invitational Tournament** is scheduled for the first week of October. Call 441-5723 for information.

The **Artrageous Art Extravaganza Weekend**, in its seventh year, is a community art festival and auction sponsored by the Dare County Arts Council and Youth Center Inc. (see our Arts and Culture chapter). A day of fun and color for everyone, children and adults are invited to spend Saturday painting, weaving and creating various arts and crafts. All art supplies are provided by the Arts Council. Listen to local musicians young and old, eat tasty food and witness art in the making by professionals. Artists sell their wares, lining the Arts Council parking lot

Insiders' Tips

Why not book a room in a Manteo bed and breakfast and celebrate Dare Day in June in style. Manteo's bed and breakfasts are within walking distance of the waterfront, and you will also be near the island's historic sites.

Photo: Mary Ellen Riddle

Test your sand-sculpting skills at the annual Sand Sculpting Contest on Ocracoke Island every July.

at Central Square in Nags Head. Collaborative paintings by children are auctioned on Saturday, and a more formal adult auction complete with hors d'oeuvres and cocktails takes place on Sunday (admission to Sunday's auction is $10).

Nags Head Woods Annual Oyster Roast and Pig Pickin' is a fund-raising event in mid-August for and at the Nags Head Woods Ecological Preserve, Kill Devil Hills, 441-2525.

The **Outer Banks Homebuilders Association's Home Show** presents exhibits about products, builders, lending agencies and services available to the consumer. Admission is free, and door prizes are distributed, 441-8600.

The 9-year-old **Outer Banks Stunt Kite Competition** at Jockey's Ridge State Park features novice, intermediate and expert challenges. Proceeds benefit First Flight schools. Contact Kitty Hawk Kites, 441-4124 or (800) 334-4777.

In mid-October, the American Lung Association **Golf Tournament** to benefit children with asthma will be held at Goose Creek Golf Course in Grandy (Currituck County). Entrant's fee is $50 per golfer; 18 holes, lunch and prizes round out the day. Call 261-4994 or (800) 443-4008.

Outer Banks King Mackerel Festival midmonth is held at Pirate's Cove Yacht Club, Nags Head/Manteo Causeway, 473-6800 or (800) 537-7245.

Kelly's Kup Regatta, a sailing race sponsored by Kelly's Restaurant and Roanoke Island Yacht Club, Colington Harbour, is held in late October. Call 441-2059 for information on entry fees.

Outer Banks Forum sponsors the **Virginia Beach Symphony** on October 19, 1996, at Kitty Hawk Elementary School, as part of the organization's annual cultural series. Call 261-8940 for ticket information.

The **Pacific Airwave Vision Classic**, at Jockey's Ridge State Park, features the latest hang gliders from California for a fun competition, barbecue and prizes. It's sponsored by Kitty Hawk Kites, 441-4124 or (800) 334-4777.

In late October, the **Red Drum Tournament** on Hatteras Island gears up. The official headquarters for this fishing competition is Frank and Fran's Fisherman's Friend in Avon, 995-4171.

Also in late October, tee off at the **Kelly's-Penguin Isle Charity Golf Tournament**. Proceeds benefit the Outer Banks Community Foundation, 441-4116.

A **King Mackerel Tournament** is held in Hatteras Village during October; call 986-2579.

The **Octoberfest** at Frisco Woods Campground in Frisco is another great way to enjoy autumn on the Outer Banks. The day's events include a pig pickin' (with all the trimmings), live music, crafts, a bake sale and a rummage sale. This event is sponsored by Ocean Edge Golf Course, Frisco Woods Campground and Bubba's Bar-B-Que. Call 995-5208.

Kids and Halloween are a magical combination, so head for the **Halloween Carnival for The Little Kids** at Outer Banks Mall, 441-5620, Nags Head.

Halloween Trick or Treat, 5:30 to 7:30 PM, brings out all the little ghosties and ghoulies to Soundings Factory Outlets, 441-7395, in Nags Head, on October 31.

November

Great food and good times are always on the menu at the **Celebrity-Waiter Heart Fund Dinner** at Kelly's Restaurant in Nags Head. Proceeds benefit the American Heart Fund, 441-4116.

In mid-November, **Mt. Olivet United Methodist Church Bazaar & Auction**, fills the church hall at 300 Ananias Dare Street, Manteo, with all sorts of goods. For information, call 473-2089.

Put on your dancing shoes, because late November is time to strut your stuff at the **Turkey Trot** fund-raiser for the Corolla Wild Horse Fund. It's held at the Corolla Volunteer Fire Department, 453-3242.

The **Invitation Inter-Club Surf Fishing Tournament and Open Invitation Tournament** in Buxton is sponsored by and headquartered at the Cape Hatteras Anglers Club. Write Box 145, Buxton 27960, or call 995-4253.

A **Christmas Arts and Crafts Show** at Cape Hatteras School in Buxton is sponsored by the Hatteras Island Arts and Crafts Guild, 987-2416.

In late November, stop by the **Christmas Arts & Crafts Show** at the Ramada Inn in Kill Devil Hills. The two-day show is sponsored by the Outer Banks Women's Club.

The **North Beach Seafood Festival** at the Barrier Island Inn in Duck is a full day of food and fun. Call 261-3901.

December

Watch the winter skies light up with **Kites with Lights**. This magical multicolored light show will be held at Jockey's Ridge State Park, MP 13. Call Kitty Hawk Kites to preregister and to obtain more information, 441-4124 or (800) 334-4777.

Christmas at the Aquarium is a nice occasion to visit the North Carolina Aquarium/Roanoke Island, 473-3494.

Outer Banks Hotline's Festival of Trees, an auction fund-raiser held at the Ramada Inn, Kill Devil Hills, takes place in early December. Businesses and individuals donate fully decorated Christmas trees and other holiday items to be auctioned and delivered to buyers. Proceeds benefit Hotline's Crisis Intervention Program and needy families in the area. The 1996 festival is the eighth; call 473-5121 for more information.

Also early in December is the **Christmas Parade** and **Christmas on The Waterfront** in Manteo, which includes food, Christmas crafts, entertainment and an appearance by Santa. The events are sponsored by the town of Manteo, 473-2774.

***Elizabeth II* Christmas Open House** at the state historic site on Ice Plant Island, Manteo, features Elizabethan-theme refreshments, music and free tours

Insiders' Tips

If you want to enter the local Frank Stick Art Show, but you're not a Dare County resident, just join the Dare County Arts Council (see our Arts and Culture chapter), and you'll qualify. You'll have a chance to win a cash prize, show your work and also help support the arts with your entry fee.

Photo: Mary Ellen Riddle

Call the Lost Colony office for information on special events held on site every summer.

of the ship. Call 473-1144 for information. The exact date is usually set by November.

In mid-December the Outer Banks Forum, 261-8940, continues its cultural series with the **Holiday Jazz Concert** by the North Carolina Repertory Orchestra, at the Kitty Hawk Elementary School.

Also in mid-December, the **Barbershop Chorus Christmas Caroling** adds a festive mood to Soundings Factory Outlets, 441-7395, Nags Head.

Man Will Never Fly Memorial Society Annual Seminar and Banquet — a tongue-in-cheek organization that tries to prove every year that man never really flew — imbibes, er, abides by the motto, "Birds

Fly, Men Drink." For information call (800) 334-4777.

One of the most notable annual occasions on the Outer Banks is the December 17 **Wright Brothers Anniversary of First Flight** at the Wright Brothers Memorial in Kill Devil Hills. Bands play, planes fly over and the monumental feats of Orville and Wilbur are recalled. Call 441-7430.

The **Christmas Parade** in Hatteras Village features floats, a bike-decorating contest and prizes for the best decorated home and business, as well as refreshments and caroling at the Community Center. Contact Belinda Willis, 986-2370.

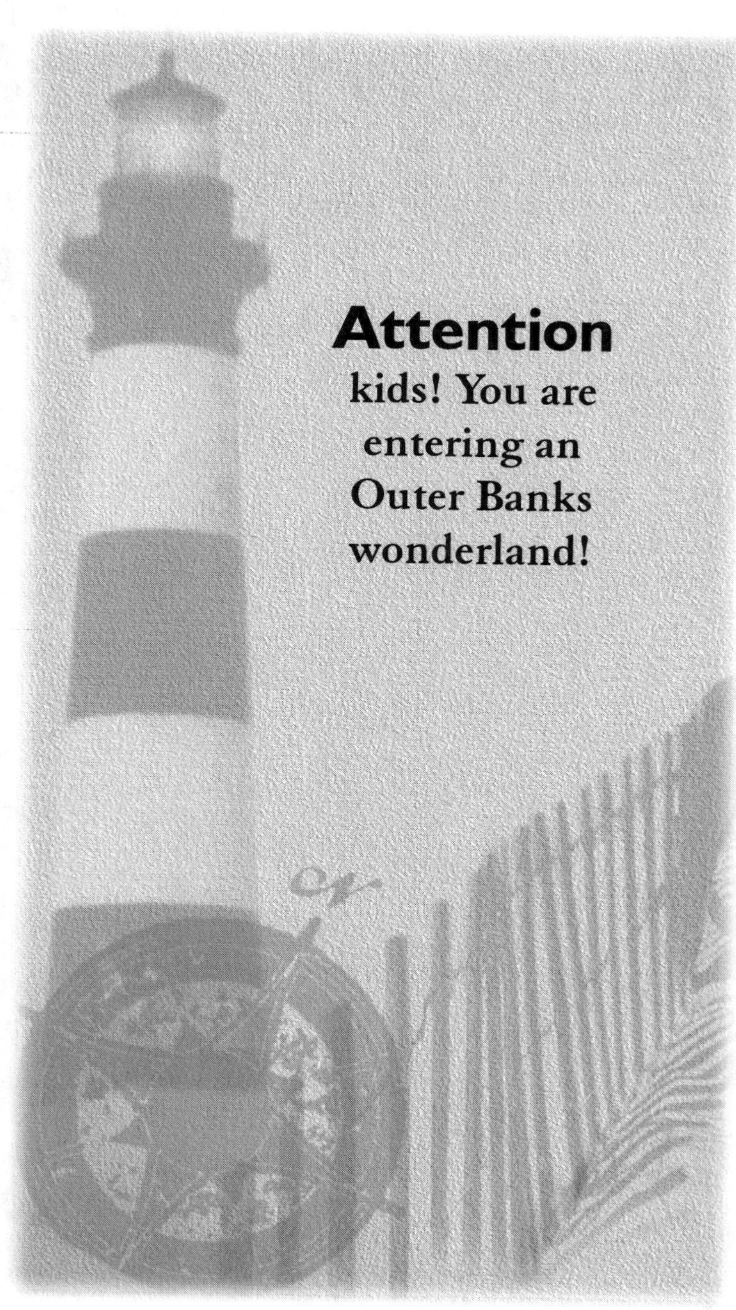
Attention
kids! You are
entering an
Outer Banks
wonderland!

Inside **Kidstuff**

So you've decided to come to the Outer Banks for a vacation. Unless you've been here before, you're probably expecting some fun mixed in with a little boredom. Isn't that what going on vacation means?

Wrong.

Attention kids! You are entering an Outer Banks wonderland! Once you step foot in our ecosystem, you find a zone that is different than any place you've ever been. The Outer Banks also has plenty of water slides, minigolf courses, horseback riding and games galore. You'll find information about these in our Recreation, Attractions and Watersports chapters. And check out our Fishing chapter for some inshore bottom-fishing boating trips. The costs are reasonable and perfect for the beginner angler. There are more fun ideas in our Annual Events, Arts and Culture and other chapters. Enjoy!

Beaches, Sand and Water

If you follow two rules during your stay on the Outer Banks, you are sure to have fun and will beg to return. First, you'll probably be spending a lot of time outdoors, so lather up with sunscreen. Second, always heed the red-flag warning system for ocean swimming, and choose a spot to swim that is lifeguard-protected (see our Beach Information and Safety chapter). If the red flags are flying, it is too dangerous to swim. This warning applies to swimmers of all skill levels. As Insiders, we know that even an award-winning swim team competitor has no business in the water when the surf is rough. Even if you see surfers in there, don't go in.

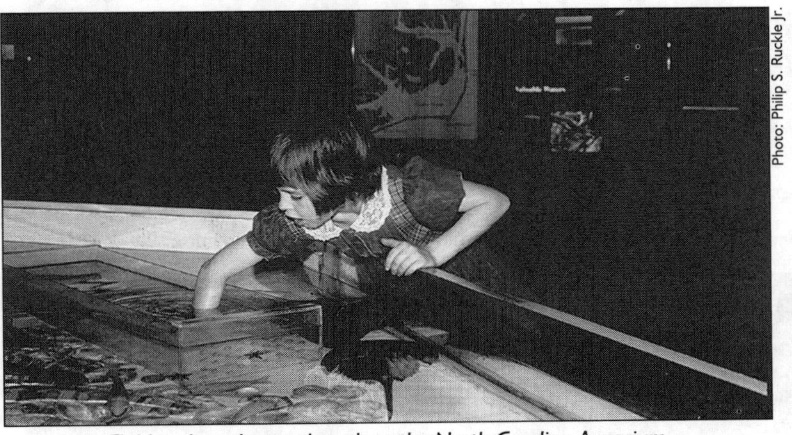

Photo: Philip S. Ruckle Jr.

Children love the touch tank at the North Carolina Aquarium.

When ocean conditions are favorable, you'll have plenty of choices to make.

The Outer Banks is heralded as the East Coast surfing capital of the United States. If you don't have a board, you can rent one at many surf shops; see our listing of them in the Watersports chapter. A Boogie Board can be a real blast, or you may want to stick to body surfing. Wave jumping is less rigorous but no less fun. In addition to surfing, you'll probably see lots of body boarding, skim boarding and sand boarding.

Not the active type? Wander along the beach and check out all the cool shells. The best time to go shelling is in the early morning following a storm.

Another Outer Banks favorite is sand sculpting. The sand found just above the really wet sand is just right for molding. If you like to draw, grab a stick and go at it in the hard, wet sand. We like to draw messages for the pilots flying overhead or leave a castle or sand figure behind for the ocean to claim.

You can always grab a good book and spend the day under an umbrella sipping cool drinks from your cooler. If you don't want to carry a lot of paraphernalia to the ocean but want to spend the day there, situate yourself near one of the piers that serves food. If you're weary of the sun, hop up and get some lunch. Or you could change speeds entirely and rent tackle to do some pier fishing. Anything biting? You can check out the fishing action from the sand if you sit close enough to the pier.

Corolla, Duck and Southern Shores all have several public beaches. Near MP 4 on the Beach Road in Kitty Hawk there is a public beach access with a bathhouse and parking facilities that are open from Memorial Day to Labor Day. The Town of Kill Devil Hills maintains 35 public beaches, many with parking, but only the one at Ocean Bay Drive has a bathhouse. Three of the 37 public access beach areas in Nags Head also have parking and bathhouse facilities.

The nice thing about the Outer Banks is when you're tired of the ocean, there's a flip side to play. Head over to the sound.

Nags Head maintains a wading beach on Soundside Road (south of Jockey's Ridge). Or you can try the Old Swimming hole on Airport Road on Roanoke Island. This area also features picnic tables under a roofed structure. When the wind is blowing just right, there are waves here that are fun to ride sitting in a big inner tube. Watch out for the metal piping that runs perpendicular to the shore into the water. This swimming hole can be a lot of fun if you can avoid banging your shins on the piping.

The "flip side" offers more than just a dip. How about a little crabbing? Try your luck in our sound waters.

There are soundside piers in Kitty Hawk on Kitty Hawk Bay (off West Tateway and Windgrass Circle) and in Kill Devil Hills on Orville Beach between Durham and Avalon roads. And the crabbing on Big Colington Island below the second bridge on Colington Road near the fire house is killer! There's a new parking lot there for about a half-dozen cars. The best time to crab is early in the morning or late in the evening when it's not so hot. You can buy a crab trap and bait, but frugal Insiders put a chicken neck on the end of a string to entice the crab then use

Insiders' Tips

Wear shoes to the beach in summertime — hot sand will burn bare feet.

Beach Reading for Kids

Enhance your Outer Banks vacation by reading books about our area. The Outer Banks is a haven for writers, photographers and artists. You'll find several collaborative children's series and a variety of history, folklore and natural history books in the local bookstores. A fun way to learn about Outer Banks nature is to read Suzanne Tate's children's nature series. Discover more about Spunky Spot and Freddie Flounder and the infamous Crabby and Nabby with the help of illustrations by James Melvin.

History comes to life in Mary Maden's *Flying High with the Wright Brothers* and the *Secret of Blackbeard's Treasure*. Get the real scoop from an animal's point of view in these new local books illustrated by Outer Banks artist Sara Hodder Daniels.

a long-handled net to bring it in. Or you can go to any of the marinas and ask for fish scraps. The crabs hang on real good to a fish head and tail.

History (really, it's fun stuff!)

Spend a day discovering the earliest known history of the Outer Banks through the story of the Lost Colony. Begin with a trip to **Fort Raleigh National Historic Site** off U.S. Highway 64 on Roanoke Island where there's a visitors center featuring artifacts, a gift shop and an earthwork fort authentically re-created to represent the first settlement.

The story of the colony that faded into memory — the first English settlement on Roanoke Island — is retold during America's longest-running outdoor drama, *The Lost Colony*. Performances begin in June, taking place nightly except Saturday at Waterside Theatre. The production is comic, tragic and quite educational. The ornate costumes are designed by former cast member and Tony Award-winner William Ivey Long. The production involves 117 cast members. President Franklin D. Roosevelt attended the premiere of *The Lost Colony* on August 18, 1937. The show is now in its 56th season.

The Lost Colony also produces a **Children's Theatre**. Cast members of the outdoor drama travel around the Outer Banks during the summer giving performances. For information on *The Lost Colony* call the box office, 473-3414, or for other programming information call the business office, 473-2127. Tickets for the outdoor drama are $14 for adults and $7 for children younger than 12. The show begins at 8:30 PM. Make sure you wear plenty of insect repellent — the mosquitoes will pester you to death otherwise!

Don't miss a chance to walk through the **Elizabethan Gardens**, off U.S. 64, north of Manteo at the Fort Raleigh Historic Site, created as a memorial to our first English Colonists. It is a beautiful spot year round, but if you're here, we suggest you hit the flowering of the bulbs and spring annuals in mid-April. The tulips are breathtaking! The gardens open at 9 AM seven days a week. Closing hours are: 8 PM during June, July and August; 7 PM during September; 6 PM in October; and 5 PM November through March. Admission is $3 for adults, $1 for children ages 12 through 17, and free for the younger ones.

If you want to completely immerse yourself in Elizabethan legends and lore,

Photo: Georgia Beach

You can become a pirate for a day on Ocracoke Island.

we recommend a visit to the ***Elizabeth II*** across Shallowbag Bay from the Manteo waterfront. The ship is an authentic reproduction of a 16th-century sailing vessel cast with a crew that speaks Olde Englishe. Hours are 10 AM to 6 PM daily April 1 to October 31, with the last tour starting at 5 PM. During the winter, hours are 10 AM to 4 PM Tuesday through Sunday, with the last tour starting at 3 PM. Adults pay $3, seniors pay $2, students just $1.50 and the little tykes 5 and younger are free.

There is no way you can come to the Outer Banks and not be curious about humankind's first powered flight. Head to the **Wright Brothers National Memorial**, on U.S. 158 at MP 8 in Kill Devil Hills, to learn more about Wilber and Orville Wright's incredible accomplishments, examine a replica of their *Kitty Hawk Flyer* and see the site of the first powered flight. Did you know these guys used to operate a bicycle shop? A half-million people visit the memorial each year. See our Annual Events chapter for a listing of their year-round events. The flyovers are pretty awesome. Call 441-7430 for more information. Admission is $2 per person or $4 per car, and the hours are 9 AM to 5 PM daily (sometimes it stays open until 6 PM in the summer).

If you caught the flying bug at the Memorial, you're in luck. Adjoining the Wright Memorial grounds is the **First Flight Airstrip**, headquarters for Outer Banks Airways, 441-7677. Advance registration is recommended but not always necessary for 50-minute air tours. The southern tour takes you over Jockey's Ridge and Nags Head Woods to the Bodie Island Lighthouse near Oregon Inlet. The northern tour carries you up toward Corolla. A two-person tour will cost $24 for each of you, and it's $19 per person if you have three.

On Hatteras Island, stop in the **Frisco Native American Museum**, 995-4440, on NC 12 in Frisco. Pore over Native American artifacts from across America or enjoy strolling on the trails behind the museum. This interesting place is open Tuesday through Sunday from 11 AM to 5 PM or on Monday by appointment. The folks here ask for a donation of $2 per person or $5 per family, but it's on the honor system (so be honorable or you'll feel like a heel!). Check out our Attractions chapter for more exciting Hatteras stops.

No matter where your family is staying, you're probably within an hour's drive of the **Cape Hatteras Lighthouse** in Buxton or the **Currituck Lighthouse** in Corolla. Both are open to the public. The famed Hatteras Light, with its stunning black and white spiral stripes, has been a beacon for mariners, a refuge for lifesavers and a magnet for surfers for the past 126 years. This lighthouse is the crown jewel of the entire Cape Hatteras National Seashore that extends from South Nags Head through Ocracoke Island. Several million folks visit the Cape Hatteras Seashore annually. (See the sidebar in our Hatteras Island chapter for more details.)

The Currituck Lighthouse in the heart

Tips For Kids From Kids

Miss Kathy Heinrich and her 5th grade class at Manteo Elementary School compiled the following suggestions for kids (of all ages!) visiting or moving to the Outer Banks.

- There are many groovy surf shops on the Outer Banks. Some of our favorites are Bert's, Backdoor, Whalebone, The Pit and Vitamin Sea. — Johnathan Draper, age 10
- Go to Queen Anne's Revenge for great food, great service and great prices! — Beach Gray, 11
- The Pioneer Theatre in downtown Manteo is a great place to go to the movies. The admission is low, the snacks are inexpensive, and the movies are current. It's a great place to go on a date for less than $10. — Vonnie Wescott, 10
- The Toy Boat Toy Store on the waterfront in Manteo has fun and educational toys. — Alice Bridge, 10
- The Outer Banks has a variety of music stores. If you are interested in reggae and underground music, go to Sundaze. If you like "hidden" tunes, go to Puffy's. Waves Music also has different styles. — Brian Jones, 10
- Dairy Mart is a one-of-a-kind food stop. Their ice cream is awesome! The sundaes are named after animals, and the owners are really nice. — Daniel Tugwell, 10
- Red's Army Navy store is a great place to get knives and camping supplies, and it's just fun to look and see the other things they have. — Evan Harrison, 11
- Jockey's Ridge is the place to go for sand-boarding, rolling down sand hills, hiking, hang gliding, kite flying and sunset watching. — Liddia Spencer, 11
- The *Elizabeth II* is a great place to learn about the ships and people's clothing of the late 1500s. — Alex Robinson, 10
- *The Lost Colony* is a fun play; you can learn about the history of Roanoke Island. — Brittney Midgett, 11
- If you need exercise, climb the Cape Hatteras Lighthouse. — Elizabeth Gamiel, 11
- If you need energy, go get some candy at the Christmas Shop in Manteo. — Omie Mann, 10
- Manteo Booksellers is a great place to find any kind of book. If they don't have what you want, Steve, the owner, will order it for you. — Jackie Gates, 11
- Diamond Shoals in Kill Devil Hills is a great place for the family: golf, a kids' pool, waterslides and chairs for mom and dad to sunbathe in. Their waterslides are the best! — Andy Holton, 10
- Wear a lot of 30 SPF or more sunscreen. — Mike Dough, 10
- Oregon Inlet Fishing Center is not only a great place to charter a boat for inshore or deep-sea fishing, it's also a great place to visit in the afternoon.

Miss Kathy Heinrich and her 5th grade class.

The deep-sea fishing fleet returns each day with its catch, unloading fish onto the docks once they've arrived. It's a lot of fun to watch each boat unload. Oregon Inlet Fishing Center also has a great selection of T-shirts. Before you go, call the center to ask the time of the fleet's return that day. — Miss Kathy Heinrich

of historic Corolla is open to visitors from April to October. Your reward for climbing the 212 steps is a bird's eye view of the Lightkeeper's House, the Whalehead Club, the marsh islands of the Currituck Sound and the Atlantic Ocean. Photographers will love the views inside looking down the spiral stairs and outdoors from the tower.

Environmental

If you'd like a close encounter of the crabby kind, The **North Carolina Aquarium** on Airport Road on Roanoke Island, 473-3494, offers a hands-on marine life exhibit for young children called *The Secrets of the Salt Marsh*. The large observation tank allows kids to examine horseshoe crabs, welks, hermit crabs, clams and starfish. Other permanent exhibits at the aquarium include regional fish, reptiles including real alligators plus the ever-popular shark exhibit. Check out the live video of an active osprey nest! Special exhibits on marine art, history, weather and flora and fauna are periodically displayed in the temporary exhibits area. Educational activities are offered for the whole family. Admission is $3 for adults, $2 for seniors and active military, $1 for kids ages 6 to 17 and free for kids younger than 6. Hours for summer '96 are 9 AM to 7 PM Monday through Saturday and 1 to 7 PM on Sunday. Off-season hours are 9 AM to 5 PM Monday through Saturday and 1 to 5 PM on Sunday. Call the center directly or pick up their seasonal calendar from the Aycock Brown Visitor Center in Kitty Hawk, the Outer Banks Chamber of Commerce in Kill Devil Hills or the Dare County Tourist Bureau in Manteo. While you're at the Aquarium, check out the gift shop. They have some beautiful nature posters and books and marine-related gifts to choose from.

Let's move from the water to the air. A fun stop down in Buxton is at the **Double L Bird Ranch and Petting Zoo** on Back Road, 995-5494. You can see anything from a small Zebra finch to a blue and gold McCaw. In the aviary you can hand feed the birds or scratch their heads. The larger birds perform in shows at 10:30 AM, 11:30 AM and 12:30 PM. The ranch is open year round. Summer hours are 10 AM to 1 PM then 5 to 8 PM Tuesday through Friday; 10 AM to 1 PM on Saturday; and closed Sunday and Monday. In spring and fall, Double L is open 10 AM to 1 PM, then 3 to 5 PM on Tuesday through Friday; the hours are the same on the other days as in the summer. Adults pay $5 and kids, $3 (this admission includes the bird shows).

Have we hooked you yet on the wild side of barrier-island living? "More, more," you scream!

Next stop: **Nags Heads Woods Preserve** on Ocean Acres Drive (turn toward the sound at the MacDonald's in Kill Devil Hills). What a rare wonder to find 1,400 acres of maritime forest that's protected by a ridge of ancient vegetation-covered dunes in the middle of a seaside resort. The woods offer a shady respite from sun and sand, with short and long trails. Nags Head Woods is a nesting area for more than 50 species of ducks. The forest is owned by the Nature Conservancy and is open on Tuesday, Wednesday, Thursday and Saturday in summer from 10 AM until 3 PM. There is no admission charge.

Nature camps are held in the summer for children who have finished the 1st through 8th grades. The courses are taught by resident interns, and the curriculum varies from year to year, but standard offerings include small mammal, insect, reptile and marine life identification as well as estuarine studies and canoeing. Call Nags Head Woods for more information about the woods or the ecology camp.

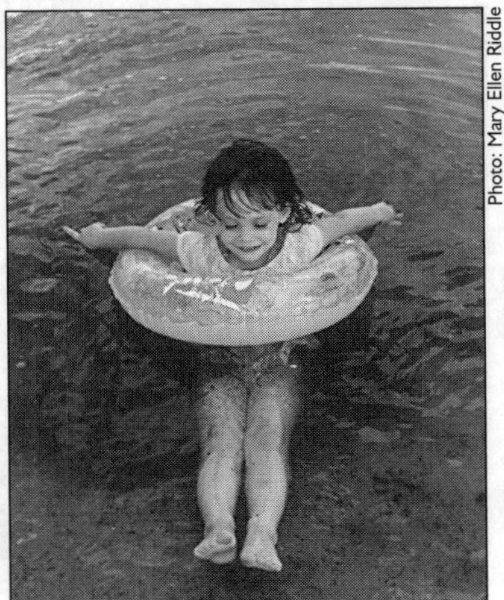
Photo: Mary Ellen Riddle

The sound waters off the tip of Roanoke Island offer kids a chance to cool off and still ride some small waves.

The very wind that inspired Wilber and Orville years ago still inspires kite enthusiasts today. **Jockey's Ridge State Park** in Nags Head is the ideal place to experience all kinds of wind-related fun. Try your hand at hang gliding, kite flying and sand boarding (sand boarding requires a permit, which you can get for free at the Park's offices, and is only allowed October 1 through May 31).

Kitty Hawk Kites sponsors a hang gliding school from the top of the 85-to-110-foot dune. State park rangers also offer more than 20 programs for children each summer including Beginner Astronomy, Seine the Sound and Tracks in the Sand. There are picnic tables here, and in case you can't climb the dunes, you can still get a good look from the boardwalk. The park headquarters are north of the dune and west of the U.S. 158 on Carolista Drive. For more information, call 441-7132.

Photo: Mary Ellen Riddle

Dowdy's Amusement Park in Nags Head is a fun stop for kids, especially on rainy days when you can go inside and play lots of games.

Other Fun Stuff

Well kids, as you can see there's a little bit of something for everyone here. When you're tired of sightseeing, think about taking in a movie. The **Pioneer Theater**, 473-2216, on Budleigh Street in downtown Manteo, shows only family movies for a reasonable price. Showtime is 8 o'clock every night.

Dowdy's Amusement Park, 441-5122, U.S. 158, MP 11, Nags Head, is a good old-fashioned amusement park complete with a tall Ferris wheel that gives you an incredible view of the Outer Banks. Kids and adults have a choice of fast-moving rides, including race cars. Take a break from the stomach-whirlers and relax in the arcade. It's filled with slot machines, pinball and video games. The park is not so big that it's overwhelming. It's open evenings from spring through Labor Day.

An exciting new shop you won't want to miss is the **Toy Boat Toy Store**, 473-6171, at The Waterfront in Manteo. The store is filled with toys from around the world including Playmobil, Alex Arts and Crafts, games, puzzles, outdoor beach toys, science stuff, plush animals and puppets. These creative shop owners are really into what they do. Both are actors and have performed locally for children so they just seem to have something extra when it comes to relating to kids. Hours are not set in stone yet but they will be open year round Monday though Saturday. They may be open on Sundays during the summer season.

For a cool — that is, air-conditioned — good time on a hot day, go to **Village Playhouse**, 441-3277, at MP 14 in Nags Head (between U.S. 158 and the Beach Road). This amusement center became the paintball capital of the Outer Banks when it opened in the summer of 1995. Adolescents — and adventurous adults — can shoot each other with pellets of paint in a long room filled with bunkers, fox holes and great hiding places. Headgear, camouflage clothes, a gun and 100 rounds of paint are provided for $15 per person. Toddlers will have a ball crawling through a room filled with rubber spheres. Older children will enjoy 30 minutes in the soft moon walk for $3 each. More, you say? Check out the video arcade, Skee-ball, air hockey and other games where winners can cash in paper tickets for prizes at a toy counter. This place is perfect for rainy afternoons, cold winter weekends and kids' birthday parties. A food court serves all sorts of appetizers and quick entrees. Parents can retreat to the quiet of an antique shop beneath the same roof. Village Playhouse is open Fridays through Sundays year-round. During the summer, it's open daily from 11 AM until 10 PM.

COROLLA LIGHT VILLAGE SHOPS • COROLLA LIGHT VILLAGE SHOPS
SWIMWEAR for the ENTIRE Family
We have the latest fashions in surfwear, swimwear & sportswear!
Billabong, Quicksilver, Rusty, Roxy, Oakley, Reef, and Mossimo.
Monteray Plaza, Corolla (919)453-0888
Corolla Light Shops, Corolla (919)453-8967
Outer Banks Mall, MP 14, Nags Head (919)441-8967
Ocean Threads
The Friendliest and Best Service on the Beach
HORSESHOE CAFE
COROLLA, N.C.
Seafood Steaks
SOUTHWESTERN CUISINE
Friendly Service
Breakfast Lunch Dinner
Tapas Bar
Beer & Wine
Corolla Light Shops
453-8463
Reservations Suggested
COROLLA LIGHT VILLAGE SHOPS • COROLLA LIGHT VILLAGE SHOPS

Inside Shopping

When you vacation on the Outer Banks, you enter a remote area known for its clean, uncrowded beaches. But remote does not apply to the shopping experiences you'll find here. After all, our buyers travel around the country and the world to bring back unique items that appeal to a wide variety of tastes, and handcrafted works by local artisans and artists are treasures found right here on the islands.

Many Outer Banks stores are eclectic, offering groceries, clothing and gifts under one roof. You'll discover antiques and collectibles in thrift stores, variety gift shops and home accessory stores. Gourmet food, environmentally oriented items and New Age products — a mix of ethereal tapes, books and knickknacks — are easy to find. And if you want to smell good, you'll find shops galore that carry fragrances, body lotions and bath herbs.

Traditional beach souvenirs are plentiful. In fact, a few shops get very creative with the marine theme, designing lovely lines of clothing with delicate watercolor-like patterns. Lighthouse models abound, from the locally carved to the popular designer lines.

Shopping on the Outer Banks can be a practical or very sensual experience. Aromatic gourmet coffees and tobacco excite the senses, cotton and silk fashions are caressable, handbags made from nomadic weavings are lush, and jewelry — from precious gems to new creations and estate pieces — are abundant. Artists offer pottery, basketry, painting, sculpture, carved decoys and carved ships (see our Arts and Culture chapter). Stained glass and handpainted furniture are available to embellish your surroundings. The adventurous will want to check out our surf and sport shops for windsurfing equipment, Rollerblades, team sporting goods and tennis and golf needs.

Our grocery stores are expanding to include more health-oriented foods and imported items — you can actually buy Greek Kalamata olives on the Outer Banks. Seamark Foods, for example, has two supermarkets (one next to Wal-Mart in Kitty Hawk and the other beside the Outer Banks Mall in Nags Head) that stock ample supplies of sometimes hard-to-find food items. And the Food Lion grocery chain has five stores spaced along the Outer Banks (no need to carry perishables from home if you're coming for an extended stay). Most seafood shops carry a line of fresh fish — tuna, dolphin, king mackerel and wahoo — crabs, shrimp and

Insiders' Tips

Many shops have seasonal hours, and some actually close down from December to March. During the height of the summer season, the majority are open seven days a week.

Manteo Booksellers is a relaxing place to stop and read a bit.

oysters in season. And for those who want to catch their own, tackle shops abound.

Whatever you may have forgotten to bring along — film, sunscreen, beach towels — you can find at several large department stores, including Wal-Mart and Kmart.

We can't forget books. The island stores specialize in North Carolina authors. Manteo Booksellers is an amazing shop that will order whatever they don't have. Several discount book outlets have great prices on big coffee-table art books and best sellers.

If you're thinking "gifts," visit one of our Christmas shops; The Christmas Shop on Roanoke Island is one of the best anywhere. Gift boutiques are tucked away in motel and restaurant lobbies and historic sites, including the North Carolina Aquarium on Roanoke Island and the Wright Brothers Memorial in Kill Devil Hills. The islands also have pet stores and toy shops — don't miss the new Toy Boat Toy Store in Manteo.

Many shops have seasonal hours, and some actually close down from December to March. During the height of the summer season, the majority are open seven days a week (some have extended evening hours). A good many shops in Southern Shores, Kitty Hawk, Kill Devil Hills, and Nags Head are open year round, though not every day. Corolla and Hatteras shopping tends to be more seasonal, but don't discount those shops in both spots that keep their doors open through the fall and winter.

Here are some of our favorite shopping spots on the Outer Banks, organized by communities beginning at the northern reaches of Corolla and Duck.

Corolla

Corolla vacationers can now have their cake and eat it too — the beauty of the beach and shopping for whatever their hearts desire — all without leaving the village. In what once was strictly four-wheel-drive territory, Corolla, about 10 miles north of Duck, now offers convenient and novel shopping, mainly along N.C. 12. If you haven't been to the northern beaches in a while, just climb to the top of the Currituck lighthouse and walk around the outside landing. Nowhere else is the area's dramatic development more evident.

Monteray Shores Shopping Plaza was built in 1991, and with it came **Food Lion.**

Folks no longer have to stock up quite so diligently or ride to Southern Shores to shop in a large supermarket. Among the stores here are **Gray's Department Store**, an Outer Banks clothing tradition for men and women, and **Ocean Annie's**, which has several locations on the Outer Banks and sells handcrafted functional and decorative pottery, jewelry, wind chimes, fine gifts and gourmet coffee. Monteray Plaza also has a four-plex cinema and a variety of other businesses, including the **Weeping Radish Brewery, Ambrose Furniture, Donna Designs**, one of three **Ocean Threads** shops on the Outer Banks (see our Corolla Light Village Shops listing), **TW's Bait and Tackle, Basnight Appliance, T-Shirt World, Just For The Beach, Sound and Video Systems, The Beaded Garden** and **Water's Edge Gifts and Books. Outer Banks Outdoors**, a sporting goods business operated by Kitty Hawk Kites, has an outdoor climbing wall in the courtyard.

Birthday Suits, featuring an extensive line of swimwear for the entire family, has a terrific shop here (see the Kill Devil Hills section for more information; there also a Birthday Suits in Duck).

Biking is an important Outer Banks pastime and the folks at **The Bike Barn** are here to help. The main store is in Kill Devil Hills, and a third is at Loblolly Pines in Duck.

Why not combine a bike trip with a picnic? Nearby, **Bacchus Wine & Cheese** can supply the "goodies." The shop carries one of the most extensive selections of domestic and imported wines on the Outer Banks as well as wine accessories and delicious deli sandwiches. Inquire about weekly wine tasting events. This shop also will put together special party platters and gift baskets. Add a little romance to your life with a "surprise" picnic gift basket!

Monteray Plaza has public restrooms and plenty of parking.

Ace Hardware has a store just across the road from the plaza.

Kitty Hawk Kites has two Corolla locations that offer all the colorful kites, windsocks, banners and apparel you'd expect from one of the Outer Banks' most popular businesses. Other shops are located in TimBuck II, Duck, Nags Head and Avon. In-line skates for sale or rent are big here.

About a quarter-mile south, the upscale **TimBuck II** shopping village features 60 shops and six restaurants, many of which are already familiar to shoppers because they have other locations along the Outer Banks. The center is the brainchild of Tim and Buck Thornton, developers of Ships Watch in Duck and Buck Island in Corolla. Ground-level parking, covered decks, public restrooms and a recreation area with playground equipment, hammocks, swings and a hang glider are features.

A branch location of **Kitty Hawk Sports** (the main shop is in Nags Head) carries equipment rentals. And **Gray's Department Store** here sells top-of-the-line swimwear (see our Duck write-up).

The Sophisticated Swan is a great find at TimBuck II. This shop sells jewelry, crystal, picture frames, toddlers' and women's apparel, cards and other wonderful gifts. Upstairs, there's a toy selection that will have your kids swearing

Insiders' Tips

The Island Pharmacy in Manteo has the best price on black and white Tri-X film on the Outer Banks.

they'll pledge their allowance to you for the next year if you'll just get them what they want. The staff here will gift wrap for free (we recently received a gift from here that was so beautifully wrapped we didn't want to open it) and ship your purchase to save you the hassle. This shop, unlike some of the others in this complex, is open all year.

Joan Estes of **Joan's** is returning for her fourth season at TimBuck II where she offers complete interior design and furnishing services. Her boutique offers home furnishings and accents including upholstery, dressers, nightstands, silk flower arrangements, lamps, pictures and wall hangings. At Joan's you can shop on the premises for goods but also request Joan's residential and commercial design services. Her style is varied from contemporary to traditional.

Another longtime Outer Banks favorite, **Surfside Casuals**, offers an extensive line of swimwear and casual attire here, which is one of multiple locations.

Tar Heel Trading Company (also in Duck and Kill Devil Hills) carries American handcrafted decorator items, accessories and serving pieces.

The Salt Marsh is for the conservation-conscious shopper (see our Nags Head write-up).

Corolla Book, Card & Gift has expanded into its own new building, still at TimBuck II, and now has a huge selection of beautiful gifts and items for the entire family, including posters, candles, Corolla souvenirs, greeting cards, florals, Jelly Bellies, jewelry and local T-shirts and hats. A large children's department sells hats, shirts, toys, books and games. And, as always, the store offers a wide selection of local books and best sellers in hard cover and paperback.

Another familiar name at TimBuck II is **The Cotton Gin**. Merchandise here includes quality clothing, unique bedding, bath and kitchen supplies. The store's primary location is a sprawling barn-red building on U.S. 158 on the Currituck mainland.

TimBuck II is the site of two art galleries: **Dolphin Watch Gallery**, which features the works of owner/artist Mary Kaye Umberger, who is well known for her beautiful hand-colored etchings on handmade paper, and **Seaside Art Gallery**, which has its main location in Nags Head (see our Arts and Culture chapter).

Just for the Beach sells just about everything you will need to enjoy a great day in the surf and sand: swimwear, casual clothing, beach towels, inner tubes, sunscreen and shades. Look for the other location in Duck.

Everything is ship-shape at **Sea Images**, which has nautical knickknacks and makes handcrafted wooden Outer Banks lighthouses.

No shopping destination on the Outer Banks is complete without a fudge shop, and TimBuck II is no exception with **The Fudgery** (see the section on Scarborough Faire in Duck).

Other TimBuck II merchants include **Kitty Hawk Kites, Earth Art, The Summer House by Surfside Casuals, Island Tobacco**, featuring imported cigars, tobacco, cigarettes, and clothing (with a Nags Head location too), a third **Island Gear** shop (the others are in Duck and Nags Head), **Dolphin Dreaming, Michael's Gems and Glass, Nags Head Hammocks, Horse Play, by Gayle, Rainbow Harvest**, with hand-crafted jewelry and gifts from more than 200 American artists and designers, and **Big Buck's Ice Cream**.

Additional shopping opportunities — as if that's not enough already! — include **Gourmet Kitchen Emporium and Confectionery, Jeanine's Cat House, Village Toy Store** and **Cap'n Woody's Fun Camp, Wild Horses, Match Point Golf and Tennis Shop** and one of our personal favorites, **Duck Donut and Ice Cream,**

one of four locations on the Outer Banks offering freshly baked doughnuts, bagels, breads and muffins and ice cream.

Other businesses here include **Brew Thru, Good Vibes Video** and **Green Acres**, a produce seller.

Corolla Light Village Shops is a collection of unique shops arranged in a quaint seaside setting. **Ocean Threads** (also at Monteray Plaza and in Nags Head), specializes in swimwear for the entire family including maternity, mastectomy and long-torso suits. Find names like No Fear, Air Walk, Rusty, Arnet, Quicksilver and Billabong. This shop is also packed with lots of sportswear for men and women including a good selection of tennis clothes and accessories plus Corolla and Duck T-shirts, sweatshirts, sunglasses and hats. A feature at this Ocean Threads location only is the **Gourmet Garage**, which sells gourmet foods, wine, bath salts, lotions, potpourri and everything you'll need to create a gift basket. Gift ideas abound; one of our favorites is the combination of wine, cheese, crackers and pâté — mm-mm, good!

Duck In Donuts is in its fifth season at Corolla Light Village Shops (see our Restaurants chapter). It's a nice place for a cappuccino and croissant break.

Mustang Sally's features ladies' and men's contemporary sportswear, accessories and handcrafted gifts.

Winks of Corolla, a general store with a few gas pumps, and the Corolla Post Office occupy a small strip north of the Currituck Beach Lighthouse. Corolla now has an **ABC Package Store** across the street from Winks and next to the new Sun Realty Building.

Just north of the Winks store is a row of shops and businesses known as **Whalehead Landing Station**. The **John de la Vega Gallery** here features works by John de la Vega and seven other artists (see our Arts and Culture chapter). And **Tackle 'n Tours** offers fishing equipment and more (see our Fishing chapter).

Duck

When vacationing families discovered Duck in the '80s, a few businesses — Wee Winks general store, Duck Blind Art Gallery and Bob's Bait & Tackle — and the Duck Methodist Church formed the core of the soundside hamlet. Today, after more than a decade of commercial growth, you can shop 'til you drop in Duck Village, which has maintained its quaint personality while adding numerous shops along the water's edge and among the shade trees across the narrow, winding Duck Road, which is N.C. 12. (Notice that we're changing directions briefly with our Duck shopping tour and describing shops from north to south, since most visitors encounter the village while traveling in this direction.)

The village of Duck unfolds just around the bend. On the right, past the woods where Duck Blind Ltd. once was, you'll find **Greenleaf Gallery**; the summer of 1996 is its second season in this location (see our Arts and Culture chapter).

Across the road on the sound side, you'll discover **Duck Soundside Shoppes**. Treasures that appeal to all ages await you at the **Sea Shell Shop**. For fine women's apparel, unique jewelry and accessories stop in at **La Rive Boutique**. Everything you need to add country charm to your home can be found at **The Farmer's Daughter** (there is another location in Nags Head), where T-shirts, decoys, crafts, Christmas decorations and gift items abound.

If you're looking for advice on where to catch that "really big one," stop in at **Bob's Bait & Tackle**. The old building is left over from Duck's early days, when a soundside dock out back was the distribution point for shiploads of fresh ocean fish.

Also in this set of shops is one of **Surfside Casuals'** locations, where you can buy women's swimwear and beach apparel for men and women.

Scarborough Faire and an adjoining complex, **Scarborough Lane**, a series of boutiques in a garden setting, are home to dozens of businesses. The facade of the latter is reminiscent of the architecture of vintage lifesaving stations. The building is set into grove of trees, and the shops are connected by a walkway through the woods, creating one of the shadiest spots in Duck in midsummer.

Gray's Family Department Store is the cornerstone of Scarborough Faire. This family-owned business, now operated by the second generation of Grays, is an Outer Banks tradition (other stores are in Corolla and Kitty Hawk). The Duck store has immortalized the official Duck T-shirt and sweatshirt, but also features famous-maker swimwear and sportswear. Gray's is one of the few places in town that carries everyday shoes.

Rainbow Harvest and G.G. Schnauzer's are next to one another (in fact, during the winter, if you want to visit G.G. Schnauzer's you have to enter via Rainbow Harvest). At **Rainbow Harvest** you'll find all made-in-the-USA items. The shop's jewelry line features gold and silver creations by Ed Levin. You can purchase candles and Christmas balls, posters and knickknacks with lighthouse and Corolla horse motifs. It's open daily all year.

G.G. Schnauzer's is an animal lover's paradise chock-full of animal figurines and gift items with animal motifs, of course. You'll find United Design Collectibles, a line of figurines including lions and tigers and teddy bears, plus penguins, frogs and lots more. Handcarved wooden marine mammals and animal mobiles abound. It's open all year.

Morales Art Gallery has a location here (see our Arts and Culture chapter).

Elegance-of-the-Sea features custom-designed wreaths from dry materials. In addition, the shop carries baskets, silk flowers, candles, oil lamps, collector's dolls and carvings.

The Flag Stand II sells state flags, American flags, nautical flags and decorative flags in miniature and full size.

Impromptu carries museum reproductions and original Mexican crafts pieces; the upper level features full-size handmade quilts.

Sharing an entrance with Impromptu is a charming boutique of handmade jewelry by local lapidarist **Sara deSpain**, who specializes in precious metals and stones.

A visit to **The Christmas Duck** reveals cherubs, angels, wreaths, collectibles and more.

Toy-rific is the Outer Banks' ultimate children's store for rain or shine activities. Top-of-the-line playthings for infants, toddlers and older kids include stuffed animals, puzzles, beach toys and kites.

While you're shopping, treat yourself to an ice-cream cone at **The Little Dipper**.

Nearby, **The Gourmet Kitchen Emporium** has a full line of specialty foods including pasta, jams, jellies, and hot spicy stuff. Look for unique culinary gadgets, gift baskets, linens and cookbooks.

The Fudgery at Scarborough Faire is the original storefront for this company that has locations around the country.

And the aroma of fresh coffee and the sound of wind chimes greet you every time you open the door to **Ocean Annie's**, another Outer Banks tradition (there are other outlets in Corolla, Avon and Hatteras Village). In addition to beans bought whole or ground to order, Ocean Annie's has functional handmade pottery, cookware, fine wood crafts, wind chimes and jewelry.

Motifs imports women's clothing from Mexico, Latin America, Africa and India. Jewelry, belts and other accessories complement these ethnic fashions.

Kid's Kloset is the one of the few children's clothing boutiques on the Outer Banks. You'll find summerwear and swimsuits sized for newborns to preteens.

Island Bookstore owners Bill and Ursula Rickman sell established works of fiction and discount hard-cover best sellers, a wide variety of nonfiction, children's books and specialty selections. The collection of works by Southern authors is extensive, and you can also find audiobooks and jazz and blues on compact disc.

Elizabeth's Cafe and Winery (see our Restaurants chapter) provides fine dining year round in two settings: outdoors under the trees or inside a cozy (smoke-free) country French dining room. Elizabeth's also has a wine shop, new for 1996.

The Solitary Swan features cherry, pine and walnut furniture and early accessories plus quality decoys and folk art.

Smash Hit offers a complete line of tennis and golf attire for men and women. Owner Sally Dowdy is one of the Outer Banks' most exuberant tennis enthusiasts and will strike up a conversation — or a match — at a moment's notice (see our Golf chapter).

Island Dyes displays a wide selection of hand-dyed garments, and **Head to Toe** offers a complete selection of souvenir T-shirts.

Scarborough Lane features **Michael's Gems and Glass; Get the Picture**, featuring quick photo turn-arounds; and **Island Trader** (also in Nags Head and Rodanthe), which sells sterling silver jewelry, treasures and gifts.

Other businesses here include **Exotic Cargo, Tar Heel Trading Company** (see our Kill Devil Hills listing), **Fish Bones Raw Bar & Grill** (see our Restaurants chapter), **Atlantic Shirts** and **Island Gear**, which sells T-shirts, souvenirs, swimsuits, sportswear and sweats and has other shops in Corolla and Nags Head.

Of the three locations of **The Salt Marsh** (the others are in Corolla and Nags Head), this one specializes in unique children's toys — from the educational to the just-plain-fun — in addition to carrying a line of conservation-oriented items. Look for the glow-in-the-dark playthings, stickers, puzzles, stuffed animals, baby gifts, collectibles, building toys and much more.

Scarborough Lane also has one of three **Birthday Suits** swimwear shops on the Outer Banks (the others are in Corolla and Kill Devil Hills).

Osprey Landing, a smaller shopping

area overlooking the sound as you continue north through the village, is another pleasant shopping destination. Look here for **Books & Things** — exactly that; **The Board Room**, featuring intellectual and challenging games; and **Osprey Gourmet**, a delightful cafe on the waterfront (see our Restaurants chapter). **Local Color T's** sells lots of souvenir T-shirts.

Farther north across the highway, **Loblolly Pines Shopping Center** is a complex of shops and eateries. Aromatic airs surround the entrance to **Scentuals Body and Bath** boutique. Owner Gayle Clark presents soaps, lotions, powders, sachets, bouquets, oils, sponges, brushes and candles for the bed, bath and the kitchen.

The **Duck Duck Shop and Post Office** features selected local North Carolina decoys, and **Yesterday's Jewels** carries an interesting collection of old but still fashionable jewelry. **TW's Bait & Tackle Shop** is probably the first door that opens every morning in Duck to provide all those necessary fishing supplies (see our Fishing chapter).

Just for the Beach comes close to being a general store for beach stuff and casual clothing.

Candy Cone Creations has scrumptious treats including homemade, hand-dipped ice cream and waffle cones and candy gift items.

Ready for a lunch break? **Pizzazz Pizzeria** cooks up great pizza and subs (see our Restaurants chapter).

The Phoenix offers high-quality fashions, jewelry and accessories — the hand-sewn hats are beautiful — and you will find other unique items here that you won't find anywhere else on the Outer Banks.

Loblolly Pines is also the home of the **Ocean Atlantic Rentals, T-Shirt World** and one of three locations of **The Bike Barn** (others are in Corolla and Kill Devil Hills).

Soundfeet Shoes, which has several locations on the Outer Banks, carries all the major brand names in athletic, casual and other styles of footwear for the entire family. This store and a new one at the new Nags Head shopping center, Croatan Center, are full-service shoe emporiums; the Outer Banks Mall location serves mainly as an outlet shoe store (see the great sales rack there!).

Duck Trading Company is another variety shop you won't want to miss in this part of Duck Village. If you like North Carolina-made products, you'll love the selection of Tarheel specialty foods, cookbooks, peanuts and other goodies. The staff will put everything together in a charming gift basket.

Herron's Deli is right up the road (see our Restaurants chapter), in case you're ready for a break from shopping.

Duck Village Square, on the southside of **Kellogg's True Value** in the heart of Duck, is home to several specialty shops, including **Duck Donut and Bakery**, a full-service bakery and doughnut shop with locations in Corolla and Kitty Hawk. This is a family-owned and -operated bakery with a very friendly staff; the Duck and Corolla locations also serve ice cream.

Mustang Sally's specialty clothing shop features outerwear for men and women and women's fashions and accessories. Look for Mustang Sally's other north beach shop in Corolla.

Another Duck Village Square shop, **Glitz**, features jewelry.

The **Village Wine Shop and Deli** offers an extensive variety of affordable wines and beers from all over the world.

Papa's Garden is a great dress shop here. It also carries incense and candles.

Kellogg's True Value is much more than a hardware store. It has a garden center, outdoor furniture and lots of other items especially for folks who enjoy working inside their house and outside in their yard.

Farther along Duck Road you'll find **Schooner Plaza**; it's the place with an ex-

Don't Miss Out Why Everybody
Is Flocking To The Lucky Duck
Many years ago a legend stated that "much happiness and good luck will come to those whose home shelters a duck." Our little duck offers a legend of happiness to the home in which it lives. May this happiness be yours.
Season Hours
9am-9pm
Winter Hours
10am-6pm
THE LUCKY DUCK
EST. 1984
Located in the
Village of Duck

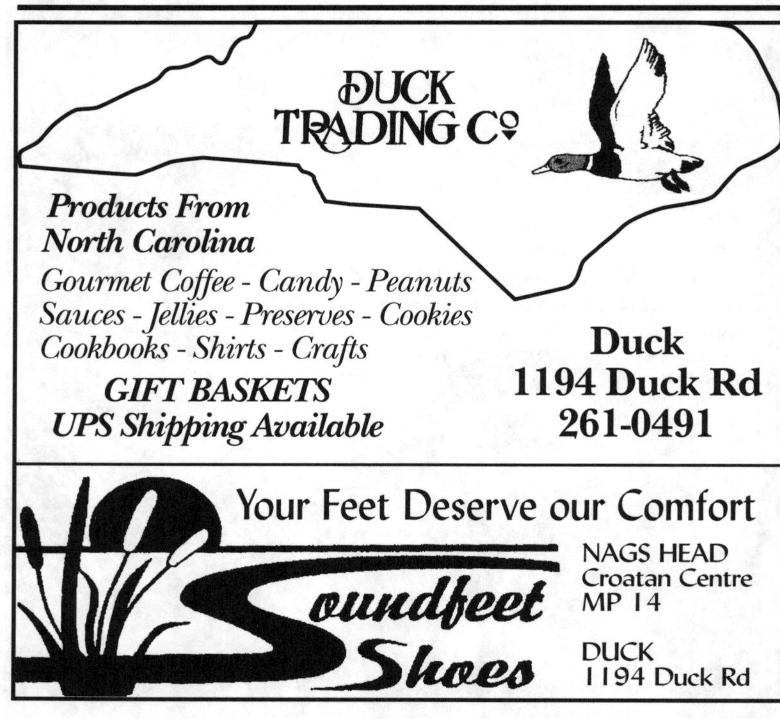

traordinary perennial garden. This is where you'll find **Confetti**, a unique boutique offering casual sportswear for men, women and children. Confetti stocks clothing made by small design firms so they avoid that mass manufactured look. But there's more to Confetti than designer threads. The shop carries novelty items and home accessories and has an interesting pet department complete with — you'll never guess — gourmet dog bones and catnip and an array of leash "apparel" with funny inscriptions. Also located in this plaza is the appropriately named gourmet shop called **Cravings** (see our Restaurants chapter). Once you take a sip of Northwest Market Spice Tea, you'll definitely have Cravings. Run by the folks who also operate Confetti, the shop features gourmet coffee and tea, capucino, blended ice drinks and ice teas. You can buy your favorite beverage already made or take home your own special package. They also sell fresh coffee beans.

Duck Road continues through the heart of Duck Village at **Wee Winks Square**. Here, one of several locations of **Kitty Hawk Sports** carries popular name-brand clothing, Boogie Boards, accessories and sunglasses (the main store in is Nags Head).

We dare you to make it through the charming shop, **The Lucky Duck**, without buying at least one remembrance of your visit to Duck. Here, every nook and cranny is filled with unique home accessories — local arts and crafts, pictures, shells, woven throws, bath items and more — plus books and even fudge. This store, which started out in a smaller location several years ago, is a must-see in Duck Village.

Beach Essentials carries virtually everything for a beach outing, including

Boogie Boards, lotions, rafts and lots more. Children are fascinated by the shop's hermit crabs.

In its third season, **Artisans Boutique** offers an eclectic combination of ladies' apparel, jewelry and accessories for the home, all of which bring to mind the artist's touch.

For a great selection of ready-to-cook seafood, visit **Dockside 'n Duck**. The shop also carries steamers, condiments, sauces and the finishing touches for the gourmet chef on vacation.

Lady Victorian is a stylish women's boutique filled with quality dresses, evening wear, intimate apparel, travel accessories and personal items such as bath products, soaps, powders and fabric clothes hangers. Outfits and suits are the emphasis here, and you'll find lots of cotton, silk and linen.

Wee Winks Square also includes an **ABC Package Store**.

Wee Winks Market is perfect for a quick stop for those last minute food and gas purchases, or for picking up a newspaper.

Green Acres Produce, open during the summer season, has the best fresh-from-the-farm vegetables and fruits in the village. The Duck location of **Kitty Hawk Kites** is next door (see our Nags Head write-up); it's a fun stop just to ogle bright colors and clever kite designs.

Tommy's Market is a place to pick up delicious, fresh-baked goods — pastries, turnovers, breads, bagels and doughnuts — in the early morning. You'll also find a complete deli featuring roast ham and chickens, ready-to-eat spiced shrimp, sandwiches, fresh salads, fresh-baked pies and daily luncheon specials. Tommy's maintains an extensive wine selection and carries lots of imported beers in addition to a full range of groceries.

Duck Waterfront Shops provide all kinds of great shopping opportunities. Stop in **Duck's General Store** and you'll find unique selections of cards, Outer Banks books, finely crafted jewelry, photography and candles. Popular items include Audubon Series books and environmental gifts such as endangered species books and T-shirts, bird feeders and birdhouses, binoculars for bird watching and instruments for gauging the wind. Look for specialty food items too.

Islands will tempt you with all kinds of merchandise that you would ordinarily have to go to the Caribbean and other exotic locales to find. Rain forest murals and bamboo fixtures accent this boutique, and African folk music plays in the background while you shop — all intended to create a total island feel. Unique items include coconut picture frames, artistic metalwork, Caribbean one-of-a-kind art, unusual Indonesian panels, 100 percent-cotton sleepwear, and killer straw bags. Women's fashions include wrinkle-free, lightweight resort wear for the beach or for dining out. The wrap skirts in batik prints are perfect for beach life on the Outer Banks. Don't miss the silver jewelry and a large selection of quality cotton T-shirts and tanks.

Barr-EE Station Catalog Outlet features some unbelievably low prices on name-brand clothing and shoes, and it's always stocked with lots of all-cotton, seersucker and linen and great outerwear, work wear, casual wear and dresses. And **Barr-EE Station Swimwear Outlet** sells discounted name-brand swimwear at up to 50 percent off. This outlet also carries beach accessories, flip flops, espadrilles, straw bags, hats and more.

For one-of-a-kind clothing for women and children, visit **Donna Designs**, a unique shop featuring airbrushed artwork — crabs, fish, turtles, flowers and pelicans, to name a few subjects — on 100 percent cotton T-shirts, sweatshirts, sundresses and French terry. The children's outfits are adorable, and the matching handpainted sneakers are a hit. The other retail location is at Kitty Hawk

Connection in Nags Head across from Jockey's Ridge State Park.

North Beach Sailing and Outfitters has a wide selection of quality outdoor clothing and accessories for men, women and children. You'll find name brands such as Gramicci, Royal Robbins, The North Face, Teva, Columbia, Revo and more. You'll also find ocean kayaks and accessories, windsurfing gear, shoes and sandals, swimwear and a tasteful selection of souvenir T-shirts.

The Kid's Store has toys for kids of all ages. The selection includes toys for the beach, craft kits, wildlife and museum replicas and infants and children's T-shirts in sizes ranging to preteens.

Cool treats await the weary shopper at Duck Waterfront Shops' ice cream shop, **Sunset Ice Cream**. While you sip or slurp your refreshments, the entertainment is provided by dozens of mallards and other web-footed friends paddling around in the Currituck Sound shallows just below the railings.

Southern Shores

The Marketplace in Southern Shores, which is the large shopping center on your left at MP 1 as you drive onto the Outer Banks off the Wright Memorial Bridge, is anchored by a **Food Lion** grocery store and **Revco** pharmacy. Food Lion, a large North Carolina-based chain, has five stores on the Outer Banks, and Revco has several additional locations as well.

Within this center are several boutique shops and **Carolina Flooring**. **Carolina Christmas** is a perennial Yuletide shop specializing in holiday decorations, gifts and decoys.

Coastal Cottage is a new shop featuring home accessories and furnishings, Christian books and "items for the heart and home."

Southern Bean coffee shop has opened up here (see our Restaurants chapter), and **Good Vibes Video** is the first video rental shop on the north beach to offer box-office hits and esoteric art films.

Paige's carries a full line of women's casual wear in sizes 2 to 24. The shop's forte is the original fashion statement tailored to customers' needs. The shop also helps sponsor several local benefit fashion shows.

Kitty Hawk

Shopping in Kitty Hawk is geared toward year-round residents. In Kitty Hawk, you'll find nationally recognized store chains plus local mom-and-pop shops. **Central Garden & Nursery**, MP ¼, is a family-owned and operated year-round business serving the Albemarle area for 30 years. The garden center sells indoor foliage plants, shrubs and trees. A landscape architect is available to assist with landscape planning. During the planting season, the center is open six days a week and part of the day on Sunday; it's closed on Sunday during the summer.

Islander Flags of Kitty Hawk, also at MP ¼, just before The Promenade, is the only flag maker on the beach. All of the designs are appliqued, including custom artwork and U.S., state and foreign emblems. You can also buy decorative banners, windsocks and flag poles and accessories. Another Islander Flags is in Corolla.

Wal-Mart and other franchise businesses, including **Radio Shack, Subway, The Dollar Tree, Cato's** and **McDonald's**, are located at **The Shoreside Centre** shopping center.

Seamark Foods, an upscale grocery store with a terrific bakery, deli and salad bar, has an extensive selection of cheese and wines as well as other gourmet foods not always available in other supermarkets on the Outer Banks. This Seamark location (there's another in Nags Head) also carries a large selection of fresh fish, shellfish — including live lobsters — and everything else you need to fix a seafood feast.

And while you're picking up goodies at Seamark, grab a couple of good movies at **Carolina Video** — and ask for a punch card to get discounts. The shop carries plenty of cartoons and kids' flicks too.

Situated on the lot in front of The Shoreside Centre is locally owned **Carawan Seafood**, which sells freshly caught local fish and shellfish in season. The store also carries a modest but excellent selection of wines and beers, gourmet food items, lures and tackle.

In the same area, **Three Winks Shops** has an **ABC Package Store** and **North China Express** eatery. **Teed Off**, a discount golf and tennis equipment shop, carries only new, top-quality merchandise at very low prices. The shop can also provide custom-built golf clubs.

Farther south on U.S. 158, past the Aycock Brown Welcome Center, is **Ambrose Furniture**, MP 2, a family-owned and operated furniture showroom that has been in business in the area for nearly 50 years. The year-round store has a free design service and a qualified staff to assist you with your selection of furniture, blinds and housewares packages.

Whalebone Surf Shop, MP 2½, U.S. 158, is jammed with all the hot looks in beach fashions, swimwear and surfwear. This is a real local's surf shop, and owner Jim Vaughn is popular with the area's top surfers. Surfboards, surfing supplies and travel gear are stocked here, and Whalebone signature T-shirts and sweatshirts have been top sellers for years. Whalebone Surf Shop sponsors a local team that competes each summer for Eastern Surfing Association awards. (Whalebone's other shop is in Nags Head.)

Cactus Tire, next door to Whalebone, offers bike sales, rentals and repairs and provides a delivery and pickup service for bike rentals during the season (see our Recreation chapter). Mountain bike video rentals are also available. The shop is open seven days a week in summer.

Wave Riding Vehicles, MP 2½, U.S. 158, is the largest surf shop on the Outer Banks. WRV has beach fashions, swimsuits and gobs of T-shirts in all the way-cool brands. WRV, which sponsors the largest professional surfing team on the East Coast, is well-stocked with surf boards and related gear.

Winks Grocery, MP 2, Beach Road, is what shopping is supposed to be like at a beach store: sometimes-sandy floors, beach music filling the air and a laid-back atmosphere. Winks has a deli and butcher shop and a good supply of other edibles and supplies. Get to know the good folks at Winks; the shop is open year round.

Kitty Hawk Thrift Consignment and Antiques is also in this stretch of the Beach Road, as is **Shattered Dreams** stained-glass gallery (see our Arts and Culture chapter).

Red's Army Navy Surplus in Kitty Hawk is the paintball outfitter for Outer Banks teenagers. Red's is quite a colorful character in his own right and personally shops military auctions to maintain his extensive inventory of camouflage shirts, pants, jumpsuits, jackets, helmets, hats, holsters, combat boots and camping equipment.

Seabreeze Florist, MP 3½, U.S. 158, specializes in fresh flowers and arrangements by designers on staff. Dried arrangements incorporate shells and flowers to create tasteful beach mementos. Nautical baskets are very popular, and Seabreeze delivers balloons, plants and flowers for all occasions.

Ace Hardware, MP 3½, U.S. 158, sells everything the do-it-yourselfer needs for home or cottage improvement projects. Other Ace Hardware stores are located in Corolla, Nags Head, Manteo and Avon.

A & B Carpets is practically next door to Ace, and its staff will assist you with your carpet, tile, vinyl floors and custom window treatments. **Pella Window &**

Door is a full-service company that shares the building with A & B Carpets.

Bert's Surf Shop, MP 4, U.S. 158, is one of two Bert's on the beach (the other is in Nags Head). Bert's carries a full line of swimsuits, T-shirts and other beachwear along with the obligatory surfing gear and souvenirs. You can rent a Boogie Board or surfboard here too.

COECO Your Office by the Sea, at MP 4, U.S. 158, is a complete office supply store.

TW's Bait & Tackle, MP 4, U.S. 158, next to the 7-Eleven, sells topnotch gear (see our Fishing chapter).

Kitty Hawk Plaza, MP 4, U.S. 158, offers quality shopping experiences beginning with **Gray's Specialty Department Store**, an Outer Banks legend (see our write-up in the Duck section). **Decor by the Shore** designs complete home furnishing packages assembled by a team of design specialists.

Daniel's Department Store, MP 4½, specializes in quality housewares and accessories.

Crafter's Gallery, MP 4½, across U.S. 158 from Daniel's, is a spacious year-round marketplace featuring only handmade one-of-a-kind crafts, pottery and jewelry, much of it created by local artists. This shop has a large inventory of contemporary and some country crafts including cloth baskets, angels, beach glass jewelry, handpainted gourds and furniture, condiments, bath herbs, mosaic candleholders and more.

Whitney's Bait & Tackle, MP 4½, U.S. 158, specializes in custom rods made by Whitney Jones (see our Fishing chapter).

Billy's Seafood, U.S. 158, offers the same fine quality Outer Banks seafood found at their Colington location.

Kill Devil Hills

Shopping is something to look forward to along U.S. 158 and the Beach Road in Kill Devil Hills — there's a little bit of everything along this stretch of the beach. (Kill Devil Hills is also a good place to head if you're hungry for fast foot: U.S. 158, here known as "Hamburger Alley," has Taco Bell, Burger King, Wendy's, McDonald's, Pizza Hut and Hardees.)

On the Beach Road across from the Avalon Pier, look to **Skippers** for all kinds of beach stuff. Farther south is **The Merry-Go-Round Thrift Store** featuring knick-knacks and lots of clothing.

On U.S. 158 at the north end of Kill Devil Hills is **Seagate North Shopping Center**, MP 6. Shops here include **T.J.'s Hobbies and Sports Cards**, which carries hobby and craft materials, model cars, airplanes and boats, radio control supplies for models and railroading supplies. The shop has metal detectors too. **Mom's Sweet Shop and Beach Emporium** will remind you of an old-fashioned ice-cream parlor. Choose from 24 flavors of ice cream and yogurt; they even make their own fudge. Browse around Mom's Beach Emporium for souvenirs.

Also in the center, **Charlotte's Web Pets and Supplies** is a well-stocked pet shop, and **Movies, Movies** rents videos and provides all the services you would expect from a video store. You'll find a large selection of shirts and prints at **T-Shirt Whirl. The Wooden Feather** presents a gallery of award-winning, hand-carved decoys and shorebirds (see our Arts and Culture chapter).

Hatteras Swimwear has custom-made swimsuits for our custom-made bodies. After you've been on the beach all day or played 18 holes of golf, you'll appreciate **East Coast Softspa** for a downright relaxing and hydrotherapeutic way to end the day. The company sells, services and rents Softubs and portable spas, which set up easily indoors or out and come in three sizes.

Country gifts, crafts and wood working can be found at **I Love Country**. The shop takes special orders. Shirl Caleo, owner of **Shirl's Gift Shop**, designs her own silk flower arrangements on driftwood and in baskets. **Lenscape Photos** is a full-service photography shop. **Nostalgia Gallery** specializes in antiques, vintage paper collection, antique advertisements, custom matting and framing. No reproductions found here!

The Shoe Doc sells footwear for adults, including both leather and canvas versions of Sperry Topsiders at hugely discounted prices. Fire, police and EMS personnel get a 10 percent discount. The folks here also can fix anything leather — shoes, pocket books, belts, golf bags and seat covers — and they'll also handcraft leather goods to order.

Vitamin Sea Surf Shop, just south of the Seagate North shops on U.S. 158, carries surfing gear — boards, supplies, wetsuits, leashes, you name it — but it's also a stylish boutique for men's and women's fashion beachwear and casual wear. You'll also find a good assortment of Boogie Boards and skim boards, sunglasses, No Fear clothing and unique women's clothing, including Too Hot Brazil bathing suits and skating attire.

Second Hand Rose Thrift Shop, MP 5½, U.S. 158, is brimming with consignment items, mostly old — some antiques — but some new items, jewelry, decorative items (with stories behind them) and clothing for the entire family. Prices range from 10¢ to $1,200. It's open Monday through Saturday.

Right across the street is the **Donut Factorie**, a family-owned and -operated doughnut shop that opened at that same location in 1972. The shop is open Memorial Day through September seven days a week.

The Dare Centre shopping center, MP 7 on the west side of U.S. 158, is anchored by **Belk** department store and **Food Lion**. **Hosanna**, featuring Christian books and cards, T-shirts and music with a Christian theme, is closed on Sunday. Among the bevy of eateries here are NY Bagels, Morgan's Seafood Grill and Petrozza's Deli (see our Restaurants chapter).

Team Kitty Hawk Sports specializes in — what else? — team sporting goods and active wear by such companies as Champion, Nike, Starter and Russell. The shop can also help your team or group with silk screening for uniforms and other items. Also here are **Clothing Liquidators**, which lots of clothes at very reasonable prices, and **Shoe Liquidators**, another discount shop.

At the **Sea Ranch**, MP 7, Beach Road, **Alice's Looking Glass** is a fine apparel shop for women featuring swim and sportswear and evening attire. The shop has plenty of hats, bags and belts to complete your outfit. Look for unique gifts and a selection of candles here in 1996.

North Carolina Books, MP 7½, U.S. 158, in the Times Printing building, is chock-full of secondhand paperback books and a selection of reduced-price hardcover books. You can bring in your old paperbacks and apply them as credit toward the purchase of other secondhand books from the store. The store also has new books and tapes.

A good general store to buy things you need for a day at the beach is **The Trading Post**, MP 8½, Beach Road. It carries T-shirts, souvenirs, swimwear and convenience grocery items and is also a branch post office.

Insiders' Tips

The homemade deli salads at Conner's Market in Buxton are mouth-watering.

Sun Daze, MP 9, U.S. 158, just past the post office — you can't miss the shop's Bermuda green color — features islandwear, recycled Levis and fine sterling silver jewelry. The shop also has Indian and Guatemalan apparel for men and women and a good selection of accessories including sunglasses, hats, belts, bags and scarves, plus incense, aromatic oils and candles.

The Bird Store is in a free-standing building at MP 9, U.S. 158. It carries a complete line of antique decoys and antique fishing gear, decoys, fish prints and original art.

17th Street Surf Shop, MP 9, U.S. 158, is a Virginia-based business carrying surf wear and gear including Pride surfboards.

Much more than just a pet shop, the **Pet Gallery**, MP 9, west side of U.S. 158, carries birds, reptiles, saltwater and freshwater fish and small animals, as well as everything you need to care for your pet. The reptile exhibits are fascinating, especially "Worm," a 15-foot-long python. You can also see iguanas, alligators, lizards, crocodiles, turtles and African clawed frogs.

Jim's Camera House, MP 9, U.S. 158, is a full-service photography store owned and operated by Jim Lee. Jim has a head full of knowledge about photography, so ask away. The store offers film developing (including one-, four- and 24-hour service) and is well-stocked with camera and black-and-white darkroom supplies. The shop also sells beautiful frames and albums and features the Outer Banks' only "Create-a-Print," a handy gadget that, with your help, creates enlargements in just five minutes. The folks here are happy to demonstrate.

If you like salt water taffy, stop at **Forbes**, MP 9, U.S. 158, for a box or three of the company's famous homemade gooey goodies; the shop also features a huge gift selection. **Pigman's Bar-B-Que**, right next door, has a selection of gorgeous Southwestern jewelry and gifts, plus homemade candies (see our Restaurants chapter for more about the tasty Southern cuisine here).

Look for the palm trees and lush landscaping around the expanded home of **Nags Head Hammocks**, MP 9, U.S. 158, which is famous for its durable, high-quality handmade hammocks, single and double rope rockers, footstools, single and double porch swings, "slingshot" swings, captain's chairs and double recliners. You can also purchase them via mail order year round by calling (800) 344-6433. The shop also has showrooms in Corolla and Avon.

The family-owned and operated **Viking Furniture**, MP 9, U.S. 158, specializes in rattan, wicker and casual furniture. Other furnishings include bedding, lamps, pictures and accessories.

The Bike Barn, MP 9½ behind Taco Bell on Wrightsville Avenue, sells and repairs 10-speed, recumbent and mountain bikes and carries a full line of parts and accessories. Serious bikers will appreciate specialized equipment including Caloi, Jamis, Giant, Trek and more. Skilled mechanics are on duty. The shop also rents 18-speeds and 21-speed hybrids, three-speed CBs, gear bikes and beach cruisers. The shop is open seven days a week in-season and weekends during the winter and has other locations in Corolla and Duck.

Look for the brick-red **Beach Barn Shops** at MP 10, on the west side of U.S. 158. **Carolina Moon** is a favorite place for finding unusual gifts, scents, pottery, stationery, greeting cards and audio tapes. The shop has an outstanding line of jewelry of all kinds, mostly pieces you've never seen before. Be sure to see the delightful Christmas ornaments, many with a whimsical touch — you won't be able to resist 'em. The shop has a New Age ambiance and a fine collection of esoteric gifts.

Another Beach Barn shop, **Birthday**

Suits, is a boutique of relaxed California and New York fashions for men and women. The shop carries mix-and-match bikini tops and bottoms so you can customize your fit, plus a nice selection of sunglasses, shoes, accessories, swim goggles, Big Mig socks and Fresh Produce T-shirts. Owners Gregg and Jill Bennett keep up with the times, and their shops reflect their desire to provide an extensive array of up-to-the-minute fashions that work for a wide variety of body types. Birthday Suits can also be found in Duck and Corolla.

Roanoke Press and Croatoan Bookery, MP 9½, U.S. 158, is owned by the same folks who publish the *Coastland Times* newspaper and operate Burnside Books in Manteo. Here you'll discover secondhand and new books; both bookstores carry an extensive line of books about North Carolina and the Outer Banks.

Seashore Shops, MP 9½, Beach Road, is another cluster of interesting places. Longtime tenant **Sea Isle Gifts and Lamp Shop** carries ceramic, wood, metal, shell-filled and empty lamps and a variety of shades, repair kits, shells, souvenirs, gifts, home accessories and jewelry. A picture frame shop and gallery, **Frames at Large**, is open year round. The shop provides custom framing services, and its gallery displays prints, watercolors, etchings and posters of seascapes, as well as Civil War engravings. **Dip-N-Deli** is also here (see our Restaurants chapter).

Stop by the **Lifesaver Shops** just down the road for a trip to **Nana's Thrift Store**, **Lifesaver Rentals** and **C & CT's**, which sells clothing, T-shirts and jewelry year round.

Sea Holly Square, MP 9½, is a complex of shops, boutiques and a restaurant connected by boardwalks around a central deck. **Tar Heel Trading Company** is filled with quality American crafts, many of which are made in Carolina (see the other locations in Duck and Corolla). If you're looking for a special collection of serving pieces, accessories and the like, Mary Ames' shop will have it.

Rhetty Made, The Country Store is a family-owned and operated craft shop featuring country accent furniture. Look for the life-size Granny and Gramps dolls and "nail art." The country candy counter is another attraction here.

Other shops at this shopping center include **Pottery by Sunny Fletcher**, **The Fudgery**, **Wright Kite Company**, **Cre-**

ative T's, **The Rain Forest**, **Hair Design Studio** and **Blue and Grey**, specializing in Civil War memorabilia. Skaters and bikers will want to check out **KDH Cycle and Skate** for bicycle and Rollerblade sales, rentals and repairs. The shop is open year round, daily in the summer.

If you own a cottage or other property on the Banks, you will appreciate the products and services provided by **Criner's Weatherdecks, Decks Inc.**, the Outer Banks' exclusive dealer for Weatherdek waterproof carpet and vinyl covering for exterior surfaces.

Nags Head

Nags Head is a shoppers' mecca on the Outer Banks with its many boutiques along the Beach Road, U.S. 158 and the Nags Head/Manteo Causeway as well as large shopping destinations such as the Outer Banks Mall and Soundings Factory Stores on U.S. 158.

A new shopping center, **Croatan Center**, opened in early summer 1996 at MP 13½ on U.S. 158. Shops here include **Lion's Paw**, **Soundfeet Shoes**, **Exotic Cargo**, **Creative T's**, **Darnells** and the **Sea Trader's Exchange**, featuring nautical gifts, home accessories, Yankee candles and jar candles. Also check out the all-new **Captain Marty's Tackle Shop**, which carries an incredible array of hunting and fishing goods, virtual reality archery, bait and much more. This shop boasts of being the largest of its kind on the East Coast, and the staff — including Marty himself — are all pros in the field.

The art galleries along Driftwood Street, Gallery Row and other Nags Head locations are discussed in our Arts and Culture chapter. They each offer creative options and hours of happy browsing.

Ben Franklin, MP 10, across the street from the **Food Lion Plaza**, carries clothing for all ages and everything you need for the beach. In the plaza itself you'll find **Nags Head News**, a well-stocked bookstore and newsstand. **Mrs. T's Deli** (see our Restaurants chapter) and a **TCBY** yogurt shop are here too. Another **Whalebone Surf Shop** is located in front of Food Lion Plaza (the other is in Kitty Hawk).

On Wrightsville Avenue, **Total Communications** is your Outer Banks source for pagers, cellular phones and two-way radios for individuals and businesses. Weekly rentals are also available.

On the Beach Road are few shops that bear noticing. **The Pit** is a hot surf shop (see our Watersports chapter).

At MP 10½, look for the new shop, **Something Fishy**, which is a fun shop swimming in the artistic fish-print clothing of Sherrie Lemnios, who has been creating fish prints for almost 10 years. Clothing, jewelry, toys and crafts all have a fish theme, plus crafts from the Outer Banks and all over. The shop is open seasonally, with extended hours in the summer.

Nearby you'll find a **Beach Mart**, a convenience store, and another location of **Island Dyes** (the other is in Duck). **Gulf Stream Gifts** features contemporary nautical gifts, jewelry and lighthouse and dolphin memorabilia. The store is open from Easter until Christmas.

Also on the Beach Road is **Nature's Exotics**, which features an incredible bunch of creatures ranging from hand-fed, domestically raised parrots, cockatiels and macaws to prairie dogs, hedgehogs, bunnies, ferrets, reptiles and freshwater and saltwater fish. If Nature's Exotics doesn't have what you're looking for, they'll help you find it. Also in stock is a full line of pet paraphernalia.

The Christmas Mouse, MP 10½, U.S. 158, is open all year, seven days a week, and is a delightful store brimming with Christmas collectibles, Cairn Gnomes, paper-mâché Santas, Snow Babies, porcelain dolls, unique ornaments and nautical and Midwestern theme trees and rooms.

Owner Steve Hess of **The Secret Spot**

Surf Shop, MP 11 on U.S. 158, has been shaping custom surfboards here since 1977 (see our Watersports chapter). Attached to The Secret Spot is **Nona's Nook**, operated by Steve's mother, Nona. Her intriguing collection of objects and antiques from the world over is equalled by Nona's vivacious and friendly ways. Even if you're not in the buying mood, stop in for a chat. Nona's Nook is open in the summer, but during the off-season Steve will let you in through his shop.

Across the highway from Secret Spot Surf Shop in **Central Square**, the weathered cottage-style complex of shops and offices, is **Hairoics**, the salon where the staff has a great sense of humor but takes your coiffure seriously. Hairoics is open year round Tuesday through Saturday.

If you enjoy a little deja vu with your dungarees, don't pass by **Twila Zone**, MP 11½, across from the Nags Head Fishing Pier on the Beach Road. Owner Jo Ruth Patterson stocks her shop with vintage clothing for the entire family plus hats, accessories, costume jewelry, dolls, dollhouses and fine-quality vintage furnishings.

Pirate's Quay, MP 11½, U.S. 158, is an eclectic grouping of clever boutiques, stores, offices and eateries. If anyone has every admonished you to "get a hobby," drop by the new year-round shop, **OuterRageous Hobbies**, and check out the shop's specialties: wooden ships and Nascar models. Another interesting stop is **Desirables**, an eclectic shop featuring tobacco, cigars and designer jewelry by goldsmith designer Cindy Krisa, who describes her work as organic free-form and says her inspiration comes from the soul. Desirables is open year round (Monday through Saturday in-season).

For jewelry that captures the feel of the sea, visit **Devi's**, also at Pirate's Quay. Tom Hampton, a goldsmith, and his wife, Anne, a designer, offer nautical and seashore jewelry priced for the locals, including their line of original shell jewelry. Look for traditional gems here along with a diamond line. The Hamptons also do repairs on the premises. The shop's open year round six days a week.

Island Magic sells contemporary fashions and wood crafts from Bali. The colorful wood masks, carvings, handpainted fish and jewelry are especially appealling.

Plan your shopping break around a stop at **Rollin' in the Dough** bakery and gourmet deli (see our Restaurants chapter).

Cloud Nine is an adventure in clothing, accessories and other discoveries from around the world. Owner Ginny Flowers has beads — and lots of them. Other finds include recycled glass, Grateful Dead merchandise, T-shirts made by locals and visitors, beautiful batiks and treasures from Africa and Nepal. Cloud Nine also carries gold and silver jewelry.

The Quacker Connection features decoys, country crafts, antiques and a large selection of country collectibles. Doug, the resident carver, is often carving or painting a decoy, so take a moment to see this classic craft in action.

Need a one-stop shop for all your vacation gear? Check out **Wings**, where you'll find bathing suits, beach chairs, umbrellas and fudge. During the summer, you can shop here until 11 PM. There's another Wings at MP 3½ in Kitty Hawk.

For the fly angler, John Dominick's **Outer Banks Fly Angler** is a must (see our Fishing chapter).

You'll have plenty of choices in T-shirts, sweatshirts and sportswear when you stop in **T-Shirt Whirl**, MP 12 (other shops are in Kill Devil Hills and Avon). This seasonal shop features more than 400 designs from infants to plus sizes.

Worn out? Sit a spell at **Hair Visions** while they create a new look for you.

At MP 13½ across from Jockey's Ridge, **Kitty Hawk Kites** and **Kitty Hawk Sports** are at opposite ends of the complex known as **Kitty Hawk Connection**. Kitty Hawk Kites, one of the most colorful shops on the Outer Banks, sells just about any kite, windsock and banner imaginable and can supply you with everything need for a great vacation on the Outer Banks, including quality men's and women's sportswear and outerwear, sandals, T-shirts and sweatshirts.

This complex also has **The Playport**, a big fun area for kids, and another location of **Donna Designs** (other locations are in Corolla and Duck Village). You can also browse through one of three locations of **The Salt Marsh** (the others are in Corolla and Duck Village), a conservation-conscious shop filled with irresistible gifts, T-shirts, clothing, jewelry, books and fun and educational toys. A portion of the profits are donated to wildlife and environmental associations.

Other businesses here include **The Stadium**, which has nostalgic clothing from your favorite sports teams; **How Sweet It Is**, for homemade ice cream and tasty deli sandwiches (and delicious ice-cream cakes); **Nags Head Pro Dive Center** (see our Watersports chapter); and **The Fudgery**.

The shops at **Surfside Plaza**, MP 13, U.S. 158, offer everything from comic books to contemporary clothing and crafts. **Surfside Casuals** has more swimsuits than just about any other store on the beach. This shop also carries an extensive line of casual wear for both men and women. Look for other locations in Rodanthe, Avon, Duck and Corolla.

Sea Holly Hooked Rugs, which has a beautiful display of finished pieces including small rugs, chair pads, coasters, seat cushions and more in traditional rug hooking rather than latch hooking, also sells rug hooking kits that are designed and put together by owner Jean Edmonds. All-wool fabrics are used throughout. This craft is true American folkart, and summer workshops are offered on Wednesday from 1 to 4 PM beginning in June.

Other shops here include: **Beach Peddler**, which sells everything you'd need at the beach and also has jewelry, shells, postcards, souvenirs, gifts hats and T-shirts; **Darnell's of Nags Head**, which stocks souvenirs, T-shirts, 20 flavors of homemade fudge, hermit crabs and seashells (look for their candy kiosk, **Sweet Sensations**, at the Outer Banks Mall); **Atlantic Shirt Company** (also in the Outer Banks Mall), a smart stop for year-round T-shirt buys; **Beauty and the Beach**, for cosmetics, nail and beauty products and costume jewelry; and **Joy by the Seaside** for plenty of needlework supplies.

For something to read or for an addition to your sports card or comic book collection, stop by **Outer Banks Cards and Comics**; it's open year round. Grab some lunch-to-go for a beach picnic at the **Country Deli** (see our Restaurants chapter) or **Yellow Submarine**. This plaza also has one of three **Island Trader** locations (others are in Rodanthe and Duck). **Bermuda Triangle**, a mecca for collectibles, used furniture, Civil War artifacts, jewelry, crystal and fine arts, is owned by Jim Fincher. Genuine Fiesta ware, Coca-Cola memorabilia, antique furnishings, vintage decorative accessories, costume jewelry and an extensive collection of cigarette cases, lighters and holders are but some of the treasures you'll find here.

For art lovers, **We're Art** is a year-round stop for posters, prints, local artwork and custom framing or ready-made frames.

The **Outer Banks Mall**, MP 15, U.S. 158, is open year round. **Seamark Foods** anchors the center of the complex, which is home to a mix of shopping, service, entertainment and dining businesses, including **Colony House Cinema**, **Video Andy** video rentals, **Donut Junction**, **New York Bagels** and **North China Restau-**

rant (see our Restaurants chapter), plus a dry cleaner, Laundromat, podiatry office and Outer Banks Animal Hospital (emergency nighttime number: 441-6066). **Soundfeet Shoes** has great sales rack here (there are two larger stores, one in Duck and another at new Croatan Center in Nags Head). And national chain **Heilig-Meyers** has a large selection of home furnishings and appliances.

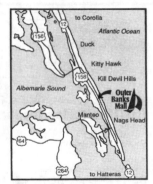

Other shops here include **United States Cellular** and **Peggy's Next to New Consignment Shop**, which features household goods, whatnots, jewelry, shoes and clothing for women and children.

Inside the mall you'll find the **Mule Shed**, a popular clothing and gift store featuring all-occasion, traditional and specialty items and a line of high quality apparel. **Ocean Annie's** (also in Corolla, Duck, Avon and Hatteras) has a large assortment of gifts from all over the country, with an emphasis on pottery and jewelry. The shop also sells gourmet, ground-to-order coffee (ah, the aroma!).

Lady Dare is a charming boutique for the fuller-figured woman and features clothing and accessories for the office and the beach, including the Outer Banks' largest selection of full-figure swimwear and sportswear. Mothers of brides will like this store too.

Waters Edge Books and Gifts is a full-service bookstore that also stocks greeting cards, baseball cards, stationery, framed and unframed prints and a large assortment of gifts.

If you have an interest in endangered species, you'll appreciate the selection at **Sea Witch Gifts**; the shop also has nautical gifts, pewter and stone critters, lanterns, wind chimes and a lot more.

For NASCAR Winston Cup souvenirs visit **T-Tops Racing**. Across the hall at **T-Tops Shirt Expo**, you can choose from T-shirts, shorts, hats, mugs and souvenirs.

Atlantic Shirt Company is another option for T-shirt shopping.

Ready for a break? Refreshments are available at several shops, including **Big Dipper Ice Cream**, **The Yellow Submarine** and **Sweet Sensations**, a candy kiosk. **Island Tobacco** (also in Corolla) stocks imported cigars, tobacco and cigarettes, smoking accessories such as imported pipes and pipe lighters, and darts and dart boards.

Habitat Earth carries "groovy" T-shirts, posters, Melrose necklaces, toe rings, belly chains, New Age music and

books and incense from around the world. You can even make your own sand bottle here.

For swimwear for all ages and a good selection of maternity and long-torso swimsuits, visit **Ocean Threads** (also in Corolla).

You can't miss **Out of the Woods** sign makers: Look for the perky pink flamingo and an authentic nag with lantern in the front window. The shop offers at least 150 designs of personalized wooden signs for all occasions. Ask for the latest color catalog.

Waves Music features a wide variety of CDs and cassette tapes. Other mall shops include **Professional Opticians, Peggy's Hallmark** and **Riddick Jewelers**.

The Chalet Gift Shop, MP 15½, Beach Road, is one of the nicest stores on the beach. The gifts, collectibles and souvenirs here are exquisite. Collectors will love the selection of David Winter Cottages, Sports Impressions, Lilliput Lane, Collectible Dolls, Legends, Michael Garman, Iris Arc Crystal and Emmett Kelly. The collection of 14 carat gold and sterling silver jewelry is gorgeous. The shop also carries fine home accessories and just about anything you'd need for the beach. Mail orders are welcome.

Seashore Stuffe, MP 15½, in the long yellow building on the east side of U.S. 158, is one of our favorite beach shops. You'll find a great selection of jewelry, including sterling silver with a nautical theme. The shop also has suntan lotions, rafts, seashore-theme gifts, homemade fudge, figurines, T-shirts, note cards, limited edition prints, lighthouses and pewter. It even has hermit crabs in season. The shop welcomes mail orders.

The Farmer's Daughter, MP 16, U.S. 158, is a browser's paradise of gifts and handcrafted home accessories; the shop has a nice selection of Christmas items too.

Greenleaf Gallery, at MP 16, U.S. 158, is another grand place to shop for fine arts (see our Arts and Culture chapter for details).

You haven't seen *every* souvenir of the Outer Banks until you've been to **Souvenir City**, MP 16, Beach Road, a family-owned shop run by Pat and Kathy Preston. (Woody, their friendly dog and official greeter, is often out front.) Possibly the most impressive collection of beach memorabilia around is joined by miles of T-shirts, jewelry, miniature lighthouses and hermit crabs. Going to the beach? Pick up your Boogie Boards, suntan lotion, hats and rafts here. Prices are reasonable too.

For 16 years the **Captain's Corner**, MP 16½ at Whalebone Junction, has offered a variety of local and North Carolina-made nautical gifts and crafts including lighthouses, lighthouse lamps and tide clocks.

The Dare Shops, MP 16½, Beach Road, has been in business since 1959, so they know what beachgoers love to wear. Here you'll find men's and women's sportswear, sweaters and other items as well as beautiful gold and silver jewelry.

One of the busiest shopping destinations on the beach is **Soundings Factory Stores**, MP 16½, U.S. 158, a discount outlet shopping center brimming with great buys in all sorts of merchandise, from clothes to dishes. Some of our favorites here are **Westport Ltd.** and **Westport Woman**, for clothing and accessories; **Pfaltzgraff Collector's Center**; **London Fog**, with a vast selection of coats; and **Rack Room Shoes**, which has good discounts on quality footwear. **Publisher's Warehouse** is jammed with books and computer software

at discount prices. **Cabin Creek** features Americana gifts, crafts and accessories, while **Jerzees** specializes in American sportswear and heat-transfer printing. Rock and glass collectors will be interested in **Michael's Gems**, and the kitchen fanatic is each of us will draw you into the **Corning/ Revere Ware Store**. Other big-name fashion names here are **Bugle Boy** (great sale prices on shirts, pants and sweats), **Bass**, **Polo/Ralph Lauren**, **Nine West** (we found fashionable short leather boots here), **Van Heusen**, **L'Eggs**, **Hanes**, **Bali** and **Playtex**, **Jones New York**, **Wallet Works** — it also sells gorgeous luggage — **Island Shirt**, **Sunglass Hut**, **Big Dogs**, **Fragrance Cove** and **Island Gear**. Whew! Take a food break at **Stone Oven Pizza** (see our Restaurants chapter).

Cahoon's, MP 16½, Beach Road, is a large family-owned variety store that's been around for more than three decades and is a nice change of pace from city-size supermarkets. Dorothy and Ray Cahoon bought the store shortly before the Ash Wednesday Storm of 1962 and, despite what must have been a rather wild start, continue to stock everything you need for your visit to the beach, plus good meats that butcher Robert Heroux cuts to perfection. The store is near Jennette's Pier, motels and cottages.

Nags Head has several seafood stores along U.S. 158. **Austin Fish Company** has been at MP 12½, U.S. 158, near Jockey's Ridge for many years. This store also serves as a gas station. **Whalebone Seafood**, MP 16½, is run by the Daniels family. The fish is always fresh, and they know how to cook every fish they sell.

If you follow U.S. 158 to its end, you'll see the big, new overhead signs designating U.S. 64/264 to Manteo. You're still in Nags Head as you cross the causeway, and a few stores are worth mentioning here. **Caribbean Corners** is the gaily painted cluster of buildings on the sound with plenty of parking in front. Music wafts across the breezy decks, where you can relax at the picnic tables between visits to the charming boutiques and businesses. **My Sister's Closet** features unique juniors and contemporary misses styles — definitely not your typical department store selection. Here, the motto is: "It's not an age, it's an attitude." **Adventure Travel** can satisfy your wanderlust. **Willows** specializes in gold and silver jewelry and gifts, and **Peachy Keen** is the place to find quality children's clothing from infants and toddlers to pre-teens. You'll find a full range of sizes in dress and sportswear for boys and girls. Peachy Keen also stocks newborn and shower gifts and accessories, games and jewelry. **Nuttun But Nuts** is a new addition in 1996, along with **Natures Treasures**, which features handcarved gourds and nature gifts, naturally. **What's Your Scoop?** will appeal to the tummy with ice cream, sandwiches and specialties from Petrozza's Deli and Garden Pizzeria. New to Caribbean Corners in 1996 is **Outer Banks Prints & Posters**, a shop slam full of nature-oriented prints and educational posters of dinosaurs, solar eclipses and atoms. These folks are the producers of the Apollo IX poster of the Outer Banks, which you can also purchase here. Another brand new shop here, **Pil Pel**, lives up to its motto, "A Bathing Suit for All," with an assortment of swimsuits to suit nearly every preference.

Vintage Wave offers vintage beaded wear, Levi's and glasses as well as estate jewelry, hats, purses, tie-dye T-shirts, leggings, shorts, headbands and recycled truck-tire backpacks and belts. Take your time while browsing through **Izit Emporium**, where owner Debbie Moore offers creative Outer Banks baskets and deck baskets filled with gourmet snacks, wine, beer and cheese. Aroma therapy and essential oils provide a sensual touch.

Also along this stretch is **Fishing Unlimited**, a tackle shop that specializes in fresh bait. You can also charter the inshore fishing boat *Fishing Unlimited* here. It's open Easter until Thanksgiving. The next causeway stop is **Blackbeard's Treasure Chest**, complete with a Christmas room, where you can buy a tree and ornaments. The shop also carries T-shirts, beach accessories and apparel, seashells, jewelry and local crafts.

Shipwreck, a short distance farther along the causeway, has local crafts, driftwood, nets, shells and other nautical treasures piled everywhere.

Anyone who loves fresh steamed crabs will delight in **Daniels Crab House**, which has a picking room and large steamers in the back. It's also on the causeway.

Roanoke Island

Shopping on Roanoke Island runs the gamut from small shopping centers and businesses along Main Highway (U.S. 64) to a collection of shops on and near the Waterfront.

Downtown and Greater Manteo

Pirate's Cove Ship's Store on the Manteo-Nags Head Causeway has a nice selection of active sportswear, including Kahalas, a Hawaiian line of beautifully hand-screened and batiked clothing — mostly shirts. The shop also carries gifts, picture frames, birdhouses, windup crabs, marina supplies and groceries as well as a line of 14-carat gold jewelry with a "fishy" flair.

Island Produce stand on U.S. 64 offers fresh seasonal vegetables and fruits. It also has flowering plants for the garden and home, including beautiful lilies, and pumpkins in season.

We covered **The Christmas Shop and The Island Gallery**, 621 S. U.S. 64, in our Attractions and Arts and Culture chapters, but a few items new in 1996 bear noting. Expect to find Christopher Radko glass ornaments and Polonaise glass ornaments from Poland, designed by American artists Patricia Breen and only available in 43 places in the country (they're usually displayed in museums). Other collectibles include: Byer's Choice Christ-

Photo: Mary Ellen Riddle

The Outer Banks is filled with quick stops and gas stations that supply a variety of goods, including this Nags Head station.

mas figurines dressed in the period of Dickens, a brand-new angel display and plenty of carolers. Parking is is plentiful in lots on both sides of the road.

The Chesley Mall and **Food-A-Rama** shopping center includes **Island Pharmacy**, an old-fashioned store where you can buy prescription and over-the-counter medicines, sundries, film and gifts and take advantage of the UPS and Airborne Express services in the back of the store. A Revco drugstore anchors the other end of the shopping strip; this store also carries school and holiday supplies, radios, clocks, calculators and phones, among other sundry goods. **Qwik Shot** can provide a fast turnaround on your vacation film; one-hour processing for 3½-by-5 and 8-by-10 prints is available. **J. Aaron Trotman Photographs** provides photography services for family reunions, weddings, portraits and commercial needs. Next door, **The Video Store** rents to visitors and has a huge array of first-rate movies. It also rents VCRs, 220 Nintendo and Nintendo games. **Susan's Hallmark** carries a wide variety of party supplies, religious products, candy — try the spicy jelly beans — cards, stationery and photo albums.

Also on U.S. 64/264 is **The Card Shed**, a sports fanatic's dream. The shop carries collectible sports cards — football, baseball, basketball, hockey and golf — along with hats bearing sports logos and pennants. You can also buy Marvel cards and browse through a big selection of those great old comic books you loved as a kid. Have a free minute or two? You can play pool, air hockey and a variety of video and pinball games here.

Across the street is **Crockett's Seafood Market**, selling right-off-the-boat fresh seafood and all the accompaniments.

There's a new shop in town. Occupying the building next door to Doug Saul's Bar-B-Que on U.S. 64 where Island Pharmacy once was is **Sybil's of Manteo** featuring women's apparel and a beauty parlor.

Burnside Books carries office and art supplies and a good selection of historical and children's books. Upstairs you'll find used hardback and paperback books and a North Carolina book section.

Lots of secondhand merchandise in good condition keep the customers coming to **Second Time Around**, on U.S. 64 west of the Dare County Public Library. This is a fund-raising shop for the Outer Banks Hotline, a crisis intervention service that also operates a shelter for bat-

Located on the Manteo Waterfront

Overlooking the Elizabeth II
on the way to the Lost Colony

Full Childrens Menu
Hours — 11.30am - 9.00pm Daily
Visa, MC, Discover accepted
473-MOON
Waterfront Shops • Manteo
Garden Courtyard Dining

Ye Old Pioneer Theatre

Downtown Manteo
on Budleigh Street

Movies Nightly

Call anytime 473-2216

ISLAND NAUTICAL

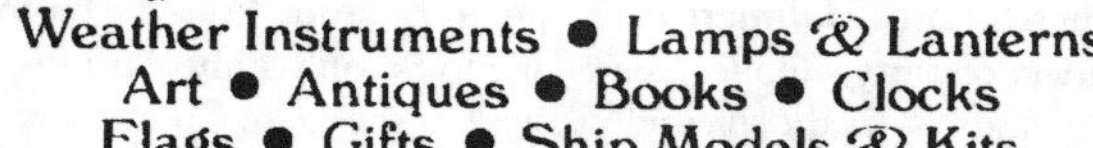

TOWN MANTEO

tered women and their children. The inventory includes furniture, toys, books, knickknacks and clothing.

Wanchese Pottery is a small shop near The Waterfront on Fernando Street where customers can watch local potter Bonnie Morrill at work (see our Arts and Culture chapter). This shop is known locally for its beautiful, useful art. The shop also features some handmade baskets and fresh cooking herbs.

Manteo Furniture, on Sir Walter Raleigh Street, stocks a large selection of home and cottage furnishings ranging from traditional to contemporary. The store, which has been in operation for nearly 51 years, offers down-home friendly service. Allow yourself plenty of time to browse through the many rooms of furnishings in this 48,000-square-foot showroom/wearhouse. The company sells a full line of GE appliances and offers financing and free delivery.

Accent on Flowers, on Sir Walter Raleigh Street across the street from the Green Dolphin Pub, is a full-service florist that will wire floral arrangements anywhere in the world. They also have beautiful silk and dried designs.

Nearby, **Manteo Booksellers**, housed in charming quarters dotted with wing chairs, cozy corners and quaint antiques, is a must-browse for every reader. Several rooms are packed with books — literary classics to delightful children's stories. The short story collection is excellent, as are the historical, self-help, Civil War and North Carolina fiction areas. The bookstore has a busy calendar filled with book signings and free readings by authors, poets and storytellers. This shop alone is definitely worth the trip to Manteo!

For the perfect gift for yourself or someone else, stop by **My Secret Garden**, by Plantiques Inc., next door to Manteo Booksellers. The Tiffany-style lamps, silk flowers you'd swear are real, unique garden accessories, Mary Engelbreit cards, gifts and much more will charm you.

Across the way, the **The Waterfront**, an attractive four-story complex of businesses, restaurants, residential space and covered parking, is home to several charming shops. **Shallowbags, Ltd.**, is a quality women's boutique that features contemporary fine clothing, accessories and gifts. You must see the beautiful sweater collection, including ones by designer Michael Simon. The helpful staff is attentive and professional.

Donetta Donetta is a full-service beauty salon for men and women, situated on the waterfront side of this shopping arcade. Pamper your nails, face and hair here.

Island Nautical is the Outer Banks' "headquarters for nautical gifts and decor." Owners Jack and Marilyn Hughes have devoted this shop exclusively to marine-related merchandise, including quality weather instruments, marine-style clocks and an array of tide clocks (23 styles), ship model kits, a ship-in-a-bottle collection and much more. This is the only place in the area to find out-of-print maritime titles as well as current selections. **Island Trading Company**, the Hughes' other venture, features fine pewter, crystal and English china gifts and accessories and more from such names as Woods of Windsor, Pimpernel, Vera Bradley Designs and Glassmasters. Island Trading Company includes **Manteo Gallery**, featuring original artwork and limited-edition prints. The gallery also showcases the work of notable local artist-in-residence Ellie Grumiaux. Drop by and peruse the myriad creations and collectibles.

Ken Kelley and Eileen Alexanian are the owners of **Diamonds and Dunes** jewelry shop. The "designing couple" produce fine handcrafted work, drawing on more than 21 years of experience in the jewelry business. Services include everything from setting a stone and sizing a ring to creating a one-of-a-kind keepsake. You'll find Outer Banks-oriented charms, including a new line of lighthouse charms, and unique custom pieces here. The shop hosts gem-of-the-month profiles in which the designers unveil a collection and give an informative lecture.

Roger and Cheryl Hannant opened **Candle Factory and Gift Shop** in December 1992. They have 17 years of experience making unique candles from molds. Aside from the owners' aromatic creations, including hand-rolled beeswax candles, you'll also find American brass (hard to find these days!), pewter and hand-forged iron candleholders, clocks and hand-blown glass. Check out their quality American-made gifts, including rope baskets, wind chimes, assorted wall decorations and the exclusive selection of locally made gyotaku print shirts. Young folks will enjoy the assortment of Discovery candles. Stop by and give them a look.

The Toy Boat Toy Shop is an exciting stop for high quality toys, both fun and educational. It's a fun shop for any age (see our Kidstuff chapter).

Two delightful restaurants — **Full Moon Cafe** and **Clara's Seafood Grill and Steam Bar** — are good choices for shopping intermissions (see our Restaurants chapter).

Returning to U.S. 64, head northeast, turning left onto Etheridge Road. Just a short drive and you'll be at **The Cloth Barn**, a store packed nearly floor to ceiling with fabrics, notions and patterns. Their selection of woven tapestry patterns is unbelievably beautiful. You'll want to wear it, cover your walls in it and just roll around in this eye-catching cloth!

Dare County Mainland

For travelers heading west from the Outer Banks on U.S. 64/264, Manns Harbor has two nurseries you won't want to miss. **Caimen Gardens**, a mile west of the William B. Umstead Bridge on Ina Waterfield Road, boasts a huge selection of top quality plants. The craft shop features garden and home accessories and gifts. Don't forget to take a peek at the live caimen.

The second stop is **Nature's Harmony**, 3 miles from the bridge on Shipyard Road. This is a full-scale nursery with three greenhouses specializing in herbs, perennials and wildflowers. It's a lovely, peaceful spot.

Wanchese

After you cross Roanoke Sound eastbound on the Nags Head-Manteo Causeway and pass Pirate's Cove, make a left turn at the next intersection onto N.C. 345, which will take you to the village of Wanchese. Large areas of marshlands and tall stands of pine trees create a beautiful scene as you drive along this road. **Added Touch**, a craft shop opened in 1979 by Maxine Daniels, is situated in a family home, so the atmosphere is comfortable. The shop carries needlework supplies and hand-knitted and hand-crocheted baby items along with machine-washable children's books. Other items here include

Insiders' Tips

Food Lion sells a great multigrain European batard in its deli.

baskets, seasonal decorations, wall hangings and woven darning-net placemats.

After you've turned around at the end of the road, return to Old Wharf Road and turn left to get to **Nick-E** studio and gallery, a stained glass wonderland featuring the original creations of Ellinor and Robert Nick (see our Arts and Culture chapter).

On the grounds of Queen Anne's Revenge (see our Restaurants chapter) is a lovely art and crafts shop, **Queen Anne's Lace**. The gifts here are displayed in a renovated house that originally sat on Jigsaw Road in Nags Head near Jockey's Ridge. The Ash Wednesday Storm of 1962 washed the house off its pilings, and it sat in disrepair for years before Wayne Gray had it moved to Wanchese. The shop sells pottery, candles, quality local crafts, decoys, jewelry, baskets and T-shirts and has a Christmas room. The shop caters to those who come for dinner and want to browse for gifts or unique crafts to take home. It's open during the season only.

Hatteras Island

Even though you may not find the large number of shops you'd find in Nags Head, Kill Devil Hills or Duck, the ones in the Hatteras area are unique in character and carry fine quality items. We love the selection of handmade goods that share space with the typical souvenir and gift items found all along the Outer Banks.

Every year, it seems that there are more shops on Hatteras Island. Some shops here are adopting year-round schedules, but most of them still close for at least a month or two during the winter.

Rodanthe

The **Island Convenience Store** is a one-stop shopping place. It has groceries, bait and tackle, gasoline and a deli featuring breakfast foods, sandwiches, pizza and fried chicken. You can take your food with you or eat at the tables that have been added for the 1996 season. The store also carries souvenirs, gifts and beach supplies and offers 24-hour AAA wrecker service and auto repair.

Rodanthe Surf Shop is one of the busiest businesses in this ocean-front town (see our Watersports chapter).

The Waterfowl Shop is a sports photography gallery featuring the work of Richard Darcey, award-winning former photographer for *The Washington Post*. The shop also offers gifts, such as new and used working decoys, tide clocks and wind speed indicators.

Collector Myrna Peters opened **The Sea Chest** more than 20 years ago. The shop offers a wide variety of antiques and gifts, including antique dolls and hand-carved decoys.

North Beach General Store is another interesting stop. This authentic general store stocks groceries, camping and fishing supplies.

You'll find a good assortment of general merchandise at **Jo Bob's Trading Post** including seafood, bait, groceries and fishing supplies.

Stop in the **Olde Christmas at Rodanthe Gift Shop** for one of the most complete cross-stitch departments on the Outer Banks. The shop has unusual gift items and a selection of nautical Christmas ornaments.

Next, you'll come to **Pamlico Station**, a two-story shopping center that sits on the east side of N.C. 12 in Rodanthe and houses a nice selection of shops and services as well as the post office for Rodanthe, Salvo and Waves. The **Village Video** here is northernmost of five locations on the Outer Banks. The shop rents TVs, VCRs, Nintendo systems, camcorders and movies. Also available are blank VHS tapes, head cleaners, rewinders, 8-mm film and VHS-C audio tapes.

At **Lee's Collectibles**, you'll find

North Carolina lighthouse T-shirts and figurines, beach supplies, unusual gifts, mugs, cards and antique bottles, shells, coral, toys and Hermit crabs. We could spend hours browing here. Visit the new **Upstairs Art Gallery**, featuring work by Lee, James Melvin, Chris Haltigan, Glenn Eure and other Carolina artists. You can purchase limited edition prints, Black Hills gold jewelry, painted furniture, pottery and original watercolors.

Pamlico Station also has **The Fudgery, Island Trader** and **Surfside Casuals**, each with several locations on the Outer Banks. **Hatteras T-Shirt Outlet** — the selection is terrific! — and **Ocean Gourmet & Gifts**, a specialty shop for gifts and coffee, teas, dressings and marinades are other popular shops here.

Just a short drive south brings you to **Bill Sawyer's Place**, which carries an assortment of general store items as well as bait and tackle and cold beer. The woodcrafts are intriguing; Sawyer also rents Boogie Boards.

Waves

Another **Hatteras T-Shirt Outlet** here offers design-your-own T-shirts and sweatshirts featuring Outer Banks designs. **Ocean Gourmet & Gifts** (there's another in Rodanthe) is another interesting shop here.

Hatteras Island Surf Shop and **Dare Building Supply** are also located in Waves.

Salvo

Salvo is also the home of the **Fishin Hole**, which in 1996 is marking its 20th year as a general tackle shop. The shop also sells beach supplies and is open from April through mid-December.

New in 1996 is the **Harbor Shops**, a collection of small businesses that include the **Wood Shop**, featuring antiques, gifts and decoys; **Sweet Sweets**, a candy emporium; and the **Blue Whale** grocery and T-shirt shop.

Stop at the **Mid-Atlantic Market** for groceries, cold beer, hot meals, sandwiches, subs, daily specials and a boat ramp!

Avon

On your right as you enter Avon are the **Island Shoppes**. Here you'll find delightful gifts and fun things to do. **Kitty Hawk Kites** has another colorful store here (others are in Corolla, Duck and Nags Head) featuring a 23-foot indoor climbing wall — great fun for kids on a rainy day or adults who want to stretch their physical skills (see our Recreation chapter).

Another **Ocean Annie's** craft gallery (others are in Corolla, Duck, Nags Head and Hatteras Village) has a nice selection of pottery, jewelry, chimes and other gifts.

Avon Waterside Shops complex is on the west side of N.C. 12 just south of the Island Shoppes. If nothing but the best will do, you must visit **Home Port Gifts**, one of the loveliest upscale gift shops on the Outer Banks. Here, original artwork, fine crafts and exquisite jewelry in fine silver and 14-carat gold — much of it with a nautical theme — will tempt you. You'll also find quality accessories for the home and nautical antiques. We especially like the custom Tiffany-style stained-glass pieces, nautical sculptures, hand-carved decoys, terra cotta sculptures and sea candles by Sally Knuckles. Ila's prints of sea turtles, pelicans and sandpipers are other unique items; the works of other local crafters are also well represented here. The gourmet chocolates and truffles are wonderful too.

Windsurfing Hatteras, also in Avon Waterside Shops, has everything you need for windsurfing including equipment sales, rentals and lessons (see our Watersports chapter). You'll also find a great selection of T-shirts and men's and women's swimwear and casualwear.

The Fisherman's Daughter features pottery from all over the United States. Local art and photography are also available in the upstairs room. Gift items include brass nautical items and furnishings, Christmas ornaments, a large line from Department 56 Christmas, T-shirts with Outer Banks themes, cotton afghans with various designs including lighthouses and lots of gold and silver jewelry.

The Wood Butcher offers quality handmade deck furniture.

Kitty Hawk Sports has another location here (see our Watersports chapter). The shop specializes in watersports lessons and rentals but also carries a nice selection of T-shirts and clothing.

Nags Head Hammocks operates another store in Avon (the main location is in Kill Devil Hills).

Avon Shopping Center is a local favorite stop for freshly cut meats, but they also have most everything else you'd expect from a general store, including souvenirs, beachwear, groceries, all kinds of fishing supplies, beach chairs, quick-serve foods, gas and free air. **Udder Delights** offers — what else? — ice cream by Edy.

Island Cycles offers bicycle rentals, sales and repairs plus plenty of accessories.

Frank and Fran's Fisherman's Friend is a full-service tackle shop, official weigh station and headquarters for the local Red Drum Tournament held every October.

New to Avon in 1996 is the **Summerwind Shops**, where you'll find **Island Spice and Wine**. This spicy shop is a little bit of wine heaven. Specializing in California, Italian and French wines, Island Spice and Wine has some tasty accompaniments, including gourmet foods and cheeses. How about a gourmet gift basket? You can sneak in some neat kitchen gadgets and gift items offered here. On the north side of the shops look for **Seafarer's Landing Gift Shop** and be prepared for a visual explosion! The shop has marble, limited-edition artwork, including seashell arrangements of driftwood done by local artists. The children's corner is filled with games, puzzles and books. The shop also carries gold and silver jewelry — mostly earrings and rings, with a few necklaces. Beeswax candles round out the selection, except, of course, for the "Zoo Doo." This is actually a fertilizer made from — you guessed it — that is formed into decorative shapes to put on house plants for a long-term fertilizing effect. And allow Summerwind to

carry you into **Brenda's Boutique**, where you'll find a nice selection of casual clothing, including women's sportswear, swimwear, T-shirts and sweats. The shop also has a line of sterling silver jewelry.

Carol's Seafood, just south of the stoplight in Avon, is a retail store offering some of the best local seafood around. Carol's also carries T-shirts, hats, coolers, charcoal, wine, beer and soda, assorted grocery items and ice.

If you turn right, heading south, at this stoplight — the only one south of Whalebone Junction — onto Harbor Road, you'll come across **Country Elegance**. Owned and operated by Lois and Dallas Miller, this store features wearable art, country collars, bonnets, handpainted shirts, antique quilted heirlooms, whimsical art, designer dolls and Southwestern decorator items.

Browse **The Sportsman's Corner** to find ducks and wildlife painted on magazine racks, hat and coat racks and saws. Ask about the "original Kinnakeet yaupon tea."

The Outer Beaches Realty Building is home to the **Gaskins Gallery** (see our Arts and Culture chapter).

Next door to Ocean Atlantic Rentals is another location of **T-Shirt Whirl** (others are in Kill Devil Hills and Nags Head).

Village Video's second location is in Avon (in case you missed them in Rodanthe). It's open year round.

Surfside Casuals/Suits Galore in the Hatteras Island Plaza features a mixture of juniors and misses swimwear and sportswear, men's sportswear and T-shirts.

The **Hatteras Island Plaza** in Avon is anchored by **Food Lion** (there are five on the Outer Banks). Another **Ace Hardware** is here as well. **Beach Bites**, a well-rounded bakery/deli, is the home of the Outer Banks Elephant Ear (see our Restaurants chapter).

Buxton

A 5-mile drive south of Avon brings you to the village of Buxton, where you'll discover that things are more spread out and range from a general store and bait and tackle shop to specialty boutiques.

One of our favorites, **Daydreams**, has earned a reputation for having stylish clothing and a selection of top name brands such as Patagonia and Birkenstock. The shop carries clothing for men, women and children and accessories and jewelry.

Hatteras Outdoors adjoins Daydreams and has all the coolest clothing for surfing enthusiasts. You can also find Cape Hatteras T-shirts, sweats and just about everything you need for the beach, including umbrella rentals and children's games and toys. The shop also rents and sells surfboards and Boogie Boards and provides surfing accessories too.

At **Dillon's Corner**, a terrific bait and tackle shop that carries all kinds of fishing rods, including custom-built ones, you'll find a charming little shop that features gifts, pottery and T-shirts.

Across the street, **Big A Auto Parts** offers automotive parts, gas and automobile service and repair.

The Silver Muse offers shells, gifts, music and island crafts.

Fox Water Sports features custom surf boards and sail boards and specializes in windsurfing equipment including boards, booms, sails, harnesses and more. Windsurfing lessons are also available. This shop also offers T-shirts and swimwear. You'll find just about everything you need for surfing including long boards and fun shapes.

Cape Yogurt Company serves ice cream, yogurt and the best shaved ice around.

Bilbo's Plaza is the location for **Moonshine Florist and Hallmark Shop**, which can help you celebrate special occasions

Dillon's Corner
Drum Fever Catch It
Buxton On Cape Hatteras

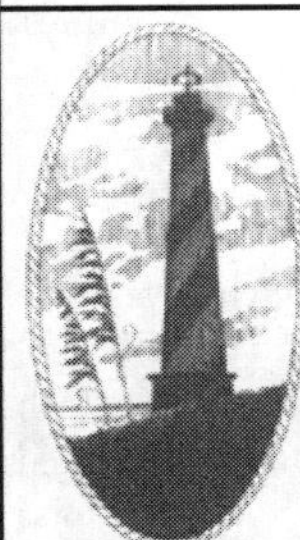

WATER SIDE REALTY
P.O.Box1088•Buxton,N.C 27920
(919)995-6001

while you're away from home with its selection of stuffed animals, balloons, candy and flowers (delivery service available).

Hatteras Wear is a seasonal shop filled with dresses, adult and kid Ts, swimwear, beach stuff, jewelry, sunglasses and suntan products.

You'll find all kinds of things at **Buxton Under the Sun Supply**, including movie and Nintendo rentals, jewelry, all kinds of beach equipment, clam rakes, fishing supplies, even four-wheel drive vehicles and cars.

Just south of Centura Bank on Buxton Back Road you'll find another **Village Video** (others are in Rodanthe, Avon, Hatteras and Ocracoke).

Natural Art Surf Shop is owned by Scott and Carol Busbey, two serious surfers who love the sport and the lifestyle. Over the 20 years the shop has been in business, it has gained the reputation for being "the surfer's surf shop," meaning they specialize in surfing rather than all water board sports. Surfers from everywhere and from all walks of life have been coming here for years. Scott, who has his own line of boards called In The Eye, manufactures custom boards and does repairs. Carol makes clothing — her hand-sewn women's tops and children's shirts and dresses are unique and colorful — and tries to find time to surf. The shop rents surfboards, Boogie Boards, swim fins, wetsuits and surf videos and sells all the necessary surfing gear, great T-shirts and Escher designs too. Call the shop's surf report at 995-4646.

Osprey Shopping Center, located behind Natural Art Surf Shop and the Great Salt Marsh Restaurant, has an ABC Package Store. Also, you'll find a little bit of everything at **Ocean Notions Gift Shop**. The shop has a nice selection of games for the beach or the beach house (for those rare rainy days), plus terrific souvenirs of your trip. Other items here include beach goods — chairs, rafts, towels — gold and silver jewelry, nautical gifts, beachwear, casualwear, swimwear, T-shirts, games, greeting cards and books.

Buxton's supermarket, **Conner's Cape Hatteras Market**, offers groceries and basic supplies.

Turn toward the ocean on Light Plant Road to find **The Old Gray House** gift shop. Baskets, woodwork, stitchery, miniatures, dolls, shells, potpourri and more fill the shelves in this old house, maintained as it must have looked at the turn of the century.

Ormond's, the oldest department store in Buxton, specializes in apparel and accessories for the entire family, including dresses, swimwear, casualwear, shoes, socks and hats.

Other Banks Antiques is a fun place to browse for plants, lampshades, lighting, local artwork and, of course, antiques.

Beach Pharmacy II can help with prescription needs and sundries; they also offer UPS shipping and Western Union services.

Comfortably nestled in what was once the summer kitchen of an island house, is open for its 13th year. Owner Gee Gee Rosell has packed this charming space with lots of good reads, including all the current best sellers as well as hard to find Southern fiction and saltwater fly fishing titles. In a room overlooking Pamlico Sound, you can browse over a delightful selection of notecards and stationery. The shop has a public fax machine; ask about the shop's new mail order catalogue.

Cactus Flower Gallery, next door to Buxton Village Books, carries an unusual collection of hand-cast plaster decorative pieces. Owner Mac Marrow, a longtime Hatteras Island resident and a former landscaper, began hand-cast plastering as a hobby and now makes his own molds. He does an excellent job of recreating marble, granite and wooden artifacts. All work is done on the premises. Pieces include sconces, brackets and decorative

wall hangings. Don't miss the pieces with mythological themes — cherubs and gargoyles — as well as human hands, angels, fish and lions.

Are you looking for original Outer Banks cross-stitch patterns? You'll find them — and lots more — at **Buttons N Bows**, just off N.C. 12. Owner Laurie Farrow's cute shop is growing by leaps and bounds — it's doubled in size — and we have never have seen so many Outer Banks-oriented cross stitch patterns in one place, including Farrow's own exclusive designs for beach scenes, local maps and birds. This shop also carries notions and other patterns and offers cross-stitch classes. The Outer Banks afghan is also available here.

Frisco

Scotch Bonnet Marina Gift Shop has great fudge, custom and silk-screened T-shirts, hermit crabs and other gifts. They also sell and rent boats, including Jet Skis. This shop and marina are located in a campground (see our Camping chapter).

Times Past Antiques, next to Arlyne's Hair Care, features antiques and newer items.

Pirate's Chest of Frisco opened in 1953, making it the oldest gift shop on Hatteras Island. If you've been searching for a coconut pirate head, you'll find one here. The shop also has exotic shells and coral, jewelry, handmade Christmas shell ornaments, T-shirts, scrimshaw, children's books and learning tools, cookbooks and lighthouse collectibles — a mountain of things to see for the whole family, including hermit crabs. And a new surf shop has opened next door.

Two other interesting shops are along this stretch. **Attic Memories**, featuring handmade gifts, and **Anne's Hope Chest**, a thrift and craft shop, are brimming with clever things to take home.

Browning Artworks, a fine art and craft gallery, is discussed in our Arts and Cultures chapter. Also, **The Gingerbread House Bakery** is a year-round stop for amazing goodies (see our Restaurants chapter).

All Decked Out is a furniture factory owned by Dale Cashman. Dale and his crew handcraft outdoor furniture — picnic tables, Adirondak chairs, benches, wooden recliners and hammocks — and will ship anywhere in the United States. Stop by and have a seat.

The **Frisco Market**, directly across from the entrance road to Ramp 49 and Billy Mitchell Air Field, and **Frisco Rod and Gun** are run by the same folks. The market stocks all sorts of groceries, beer, wine, reading material, gas and beach supplies. Frisco Rod and Gun specializes in fishing and hunting equipment. You'll find everything you need for a hunting or fishing trip on the Outer Banks. Offshore and inshore fishing equipment, fly fishing equipment, guns, ice, bait, tackle and one of the best selections of knives we've seen anywhere. They also carry camping supplies, name-brand outdoor apparel, Sperry Topsiders and T-shirts and offer free air.

Hatteras Village

Stop by the **Sea Witch** for gas, beach supplies, tackle, bait, auto and marine parts, silver jewelry, gifts, beach towels, books, hand-dipped ice cream and snacks. Another **Ocean Annie's** shop carries the same fine quality pottery and woodcrafts and wonderful gourmet coffee as the other Outer Banks locations.

Just behind Ocean Annie's is one of our favorite new stores of the 1996 season, **The Carolina Gourmet**. The colorful shop carries North Carolina specialty foods and imports such as super-hot hot sauce, incredible fat-free dressings and seafood marinades. You'll also find unique solid copper peppermills and a nice selection of North Carolina wines, smoked fish and pâtés and pastas along with gift baskets, unique BBQ equipment and kitchen utensils. We especially like the sushi fixin's — a great idea for the fresh Hatteras seafood. You won't want to miss this shop.

Village Video's fourth location as you head south on Hatteras Island is located here. Don't forget: In addition to videos, they rent TVs, VCRs and camcorders.

Burrus' Red & White Supermarket carries freshly cut meats and has a full-service deli and salad bar, 8 AM coffee and fresh produce. It also rents VCRs and videotapes. You can pay with a credit card.

Oceanside Bakery opens at 4:30 AM and closes around noon in the off-season (4 PM in the summer). The goodies are worth getting up early for (see our Restaurants chapter).

Next door is **Beach Pharmacy**, a full-service pharmacy for prescriptions, over-the-counter medications and vitamins as well as greeting cards. As in their Buxton location, this store also offers UPS shipping and Western Union services.

Nedo Shopping Center is really just one store, but it carries lots of things you'll need for fun and sun on the beach and beyond, including small appliances, kitchen and bath supplies, books, toys, sporting goods, fishing equipment, clothing and more. The store also has Makita tools and a new automotive section.

At **Summer Stuff** in Hatteras Village, you can buy everything from clothing to toys and gifts. Clothing selections include summer sportswear, men's and women's swimwear, lots of T-shirts and junior sportswear for young men. Souvenirs and gift items range from specialty food and North Carolina gourmet items and baskets to an extensive line of rain forest ecology and sea life items including plush and educational children's toys. Nostalgia items such as old-fashioned collectible wooden toys, dolls and teddy bears are just some of the great gifts found here.

Hatteras Harbor Marina Store Gift Shop has jewelry, name-brand quality sportswear, fishing supplies, unique gifts, deck shoes and other items. In addition, one of the largest charter fishing fleets on the island is here (see our Fishing chapter).

The original **Lee Robinson General Store** opened in 1948 but was replaced by a replica several years ago. We're glad it kept the old look, including the wide front porch and the wooden floors. Owners Belinda and Virgil Willis carry everything you need for a vacation at the beach, plus something you wouldn't necessarily expect to find at a beach general store: a great selection of fine wines. The store also carries groceries (including gourmet items), chocolates, fudge, books and magazines, T-shirts, sweatshirts, jewelry and gifts, plus sundries such as film, lotions, Boogie Boards and hats. You can rent a bicycle here too. We like to buy a Coke — in a glass bottle! — and something to snack on for the ferry ride to Ocracoke.

Stop by **Jeffrey's Seafood** for fresh retail fish, shrimp and crab. Ice is sold here too.

And a stop at **The Old Station** will fix you up just right with snacks and drinks to take with you on the Ocracoke Ferry ride.

And don't overlook the ferry terminal's **Ship's Store**, located in the lobby, for T-shirts, coffee mugs, coloring books and souvenirs.

Ocracoke Island

Shopping in Ocracoke is casual, interesting and easily managed on foot. Small shops are scattered throughout the village and along the main street, on sandy lanes and in private homes. You'll also discover that some dockside stores have the feel of a general store and carry everything you need. Ocracoke Village shops offer a variety of local crafts, artwork, quality accessories for the home, antiques, beachwear, books, music and magazines as well as the ubiquitous T-shirts and even a few souvenir mugs.

Let's start with the **Ocracoke Variety Store**, on N.C. 12 before you enter the village. Owners Hutch and Julia Hutcherson are almost always on hand to talk about the village and old times while you shop for groceries, beach wear, T-shirts, magazines, camping supplies, wine or beer. The couple keeps the menus of Ocracoke's cafes and restaurants on hand, so even if you're not shopping for anything specific, stop by and take advantage of this information. They're open all year. An **ABC Package Store** is adjacent to the Variety Store.

The **Ocracoke True Value Hardware Store** is an important part of life on Ocracoke, since the next closest one is a

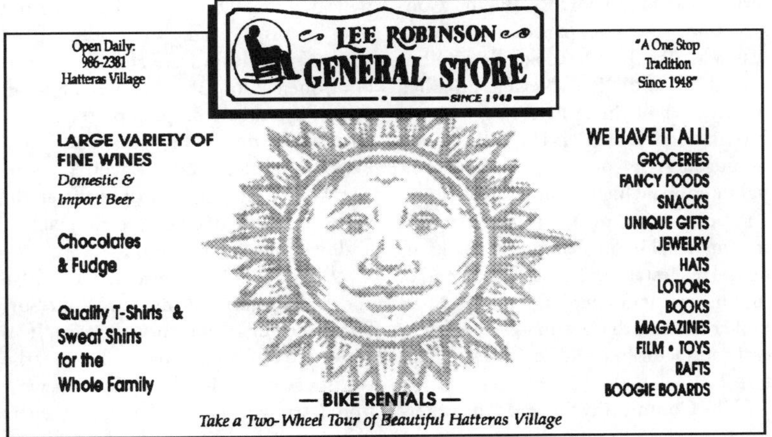

ferry ride away. It also has a generator to keep selling during power outages.

A short distance down the road is **Pirate's Chest Gifts and T-shirts**, and it's a must-stop just to peruse the variety of merchandise sold here: T-shirts, souvenirs, jewelry, craft supplies, local shells, prints, baskets, books, wooden lighthouses, scrimshaw, coral, driftwood sculptures and more.

Black Anchor Antiques & Collectibles is an interesting place to browse and select a favorite item from the past. In a far corner, you'll come upon an array of old clocks ticking away. No two are alike. Darrell and Sally Dudley have a large collection of weather vanes out on the porch and perhaps the only brass moose in North Carolina. Sally has an appealing collection of boat models, vintage jewelry, sterling silver jewelry, hand-shaped vases, hats and Victorian-era items.

Island Ragpicker will catch your eye with an attractive mixture of bells, baskets and handwoven rugs displayed on the porch and everywhere inside. Owners Mickey Baker and Carmie Prete offer fine quality crafts — some by local craftspeople — handmade brooms, cards, decoys, pottery, dishes, jewelry and casual cotton apparel. Look for local and nature books, short stories and self-help books along with an amazing assortment of easy-listening music. The Ragpicker has great cards too. It's one of the few Ocracoke boutiques open all year.

As you travel along the main street in the village, you'll see the **Merchant Mariner**. Freshly cut flowers, arrangements, potted plants and lots of hanging plant baskets accent this shop. Gift baskets and garden gifts are their specialties, but you also will find an assortment of children's and infants' toys, T-shirts, Balinese carved wood wall hangings and gift items.

No shopping experience is quite complete without a trip to the thrift store, and **Cork's Closet Thrift Store** is one of the best. The fun is in discovering unique island objects among the large inventory of new and used clothing, housewares, collectibles, books, antiques, toys and local crafts. Cork's Closet is located between Styron's General Store (see subsequent listing in this chapter) and Harbor Road.

Out back is **The Old Post Office Shop** building, which houses **Sally Newell In-**

teriors and **Homeport Realty and Construction**. The older part of the building was actually the Ocracoke Post Office from 1954 until 1967. Newell, an allied practitioner of the American Society of International Designers IMA allied practitioner, designs commercial and residential interiors, which includes furnishings and accessories, carpeting and window treatments. Her husband, Guy, looks after the real estate and construction end of the business at Homeport. He is a licensed broker and North Carolina-certified general contractor (see our Real Estate chapter).

The Community Store, on the waterfront, is a place to shop all year for essential items; you can also rent videos here. We like to grab an ice cream from the cooler for our Ocracoke visits.

Community Store proprietors David and Sherril Senseney also own **The Gathering Place** across the parking lot on the harbor. This century-old building boasts a front porch that is a great place to rest and look at the boats dockside. Inside, the shop has a collection of local crafts, decoys, toys, artwork, North Carolina pottery, Wise Woman pottery and antique collectibles such as old records, books, shoes and kitchenware. The sea glass and vintage glassware collection is especially nice. An upstairs art gallery features handpainted furniture and silver jewelry by Barbara Hardy and watercolors painted by Frans van Baars.

The T-Shirt Shop is right across the way, and next door is **The Fudge and Taffy Shop** where you'll find an abundance of sweet treats, enough to please even the most discriminating palate: 15 varieties of homemade fudge, 16 flavors of taffy and fresh frozen yogurt.

Tucked away on the back side of The Fudge and Taffy Shop, beside the big cypress tree, is **The Hole in the Wall**, where you can literally shop in, well, . . . a hole in the wall. This shop is seven feet wide by 23 feet long, and when the front door opens, it spans the width of the shop. You will find the entrance to this boutique as unique as its merchandise: one-of-a-kind clothing, imported batiks, hats, accessories, jewelry and handcrafted items from Brazil, India, Egypt, Afghanistan and Guatemala. Most of the clothing is unisex. Batik antique coin jackets and field hats are hot selling items.

Also on the harbor next to The Fudge and Taffy Shop is **Ride the Wind Surf Shop** (see our Watersports chapter). If all you're looking for is apparel, skip over the surfing gear and head for the activewear from J. Crew and Eddie Bauer (big sellers in the fall) and beachwear from Rusty, Quicksilver and Stüssy, plus a good assortment of sunglasses, dresses and bikinis, in the summer.

Do you see all those well-dressed mop and broom handles in the front yard of **Island T-Shirts & Gifts**? This clever shop is in the heart of the village and offers three distinct rooms of merchandise, including a great collection of T-shirts in a range of sizes and designs that's hard to beat anywhere. You'll also find beach souvenirs, books by local authors and flip flops for the entire family. The Christmas room features a wide selection of island- and beach-oriented handmade Christmas ornaments.

Kathy's Gifts & Clothing, on the waterfront, occupies the first floor space of the Princess Waterfront Suites Motel. Owner Joyce Barnette offers well-made, comfortable men's and women's apparel, including a very nice collection of classic, sophisticated clothing for women in sportswear and dressier island styles. The shop also carries lovely accessories for the home, such as collectors' items with frogs, cows, rabbits, fish, shells and teddy bears. Other great finds here: handcrafted fashion jewelry in all price ranges, mobiles, gifts, cards, stationery, wrapping paper and T-shirts with unique designs.

Discover the Hidden Treasures of Ocracoke Island

Distinctive Crafts

over the moon

Unusual Gifts

10-6 MON.-SAT.
(919) 928-3555

P.O.Box 153
British Cemetery Rd.
Ocracoke, NC 27960

Island Artworks

Handcrafted Jewelry &
Fine Art Crafts
Open 10-6 everyday

Kathleen O'Neal
British Cemetary Rd. Ocracoke, NC 27960
(919) 928-3892

TEACH'S HOLE

BLACKBEARD EXHIBIT
& Pirate Specialty Shop

Books • Video • Maps • Jewelry • Gifts
Toys • Costumes • Flags • Hats • Tee Shirts

Turn at Blue Medical Center Sign onto
Ocracoke's Back Road and we are 500 ft. on the left

(919) 928-"1718"
Call or ask about Mail Orders.
P.O. Box 276 • Ocracoke, NC 27960

The Sunflower Studio/Gallery 1

Fine Art, Handcrafted Jewwlry
Art Glass, Hand Painted Clothing

Carol Mugford-O'Brien
James O'Brien

P.O. Box 759
Ocracoke, NC 27960
(919) 928-6211

Ecotours with native guide, unique island photos & gifts

Hwy 12 and Silver Lake Rd.
919-928-7873

Michael O'Neal
Shirley Schoelkopf
Owners

P.O. Box 789
Ocracoke, NC
27960

Harborside Gifts is one of the pleasant surprises for visitors to Ocracoke. Quality sportswear for the family, as well as some gourmet foods, teas, cooking items, books and magazines, share the shop with an interesting collection of T-shirts and — look up! — a model train that chugs along overhead throughout most of the store.

Philip Howard's **Village Craftsmen** has become an Ocracoke landmark — it's been in business for 27 years — but it isn't as easy to find as, say, the local lighthouse. The shop is located on the narrow sandy lane known as Howard Street, a nice walk from the main street. The shop has an abundance of North Carolina crafts, including pottery, rugs, books, soaps, candles and jams. You can buy stoneware and tie-dyed T-shirts here too. Philip Howard, the owner, is an artist and sells his pen and ink and watercolor prints in the shop. Musical instruments, such as catpaws and strumsticks, help set a creative mood at this out-of-the-way place situated down a narrow lane. The instruments are lightweight and simple to play. You can pick up a mail-order catalogue at the shop or have one mailed to you by calling call (800) 648-9743.

On the road leading to the British Cemetery, you'll find a handful of great places. **Over the Moon** is a wonderful shop filled with celestial-inspired gifts. They also have beeswax impressions, porcelain ornaments, handpainted wooden music boxes, pottery, wooden items and all kinds of cards: batiks, pop-ups, pin cards and silkscreens. The Whole Earth, Earth Rare and constellation T-shirts are unique too. Browsers, pace yourself; this is a place to linger.

Just down the road from Over the Moon is **Island Artworks** (see our Arts and Culture chapter). It's a wonderful place for gift shopping or to add to your personal collection of favorite things, such as blown-glass balls, painted boxes, paintings by local artists and unique jewelry.

Just a stone's throw away is **The Village Bake Shop**, where early morning treats really hit the spot. Try the doughnuts, coffee cake, cinnamon buns, cookies, breads, muffins and the essential fresh-brewed hot coffee. Special occasion cakes and desserts are tempting too. The owners have added a **Village Video** movie rental shop at the same location.

If you overdid it on the doughnuts, you'll be ready for a break, so try out one of the lovely hammocks next door at **Ocracoke Island Hammocks**. These folks assemble their own 100 percent hand-woven hammocks on the premises, and you are welcome to come and watch the process. The shop also offers island mementos, lighthouse afghans, jewelry and unique candles. New in 1996 is a wide variety of Bath and Body and aromatherapy products and gourmet foods. Visit the **Heavenly Fudge Shoppe** and choose from 22 flavors of the rich island-made confection. The Rocky Road Chocolate Injection is filled with real marshmallows and lots of walnuts! Mail order service is available; write to Ocracoke Island Hammocks, P.O. Box 207, Ocracoke 27960.

Follow British Cemetery Road all the way around to find **Sunflower Studio/Gallery** (see our Arts and Culture chapter), on a back street known by locals as the Back Road. The gallery is rich with original mementos of your Ocracoke visit.

Come listen to the tales of the notorious Edward Teach, better known as Blackbeard the Pirate, at **Teach's Hole**, across the street from Sunflower Studio. The "piratical piratephernalia," as George and Mickey Roberson call their collection, includes a gift shop and exhibit. More than 900 pirate items, including a life-size re-creation of Blackbeard in full battle dress and artifacts from the

Photo: Philip S. Ruckle Jr.

The Elizabeth II is a nice stop for those interested in history and boats in general.

17th and 18th centuries, form the exhibit (there is a nominal fee to view it). Items in the gift shop include pirate toys, music boxes and movies and more than 100 pirate book titles, plus maps, flags, hats, T-shirts, costumes, ship models and treasure coins.

Styron's General Store, on the street as you approach the Ocracoke Lighthouse, dates back to 1920. Despite renovations, the store retains the appearance of an old general store. Make your purchases from a wide selection of cheeses, whole coffee beans, bulk spices and natural foods as well as beer, wine, T-shirts, crafts and general merchandise.

Located beside the community center on N.C. 12 is a stop you can't afford to miss. Open year round, the **Fig Tree Bakery** features homemade bread and desserts, deli meats and cheeses and salads (see our Restaurants chapter).

Ocracoke Adventures, at the corner of N.C. 12 and Silver Lake Road, is appropriately named. The merchandise includes Christmas gifts, birdfeeders, prints, shells, film and sundries. (You can also sign up for eco and kayak tours, educational programs and children's activities. Your kids will thank you for the memories!)

New in 1996 on Ocracoke Island is Charlie Bond's **Artists in Motion**, on the Back Road across from the firehouse (see our Arts and Culture chapter for details). Something special within the gallery is the **Ocracoke Coffee Company** — a great spot to relax and ponder the meaning of art. You can have gourmet coffee, espresso, cappuccino and bagels; desserts are available in the evening. The gallery/coffee shop is open daily through Thanksgiving and opens in March.

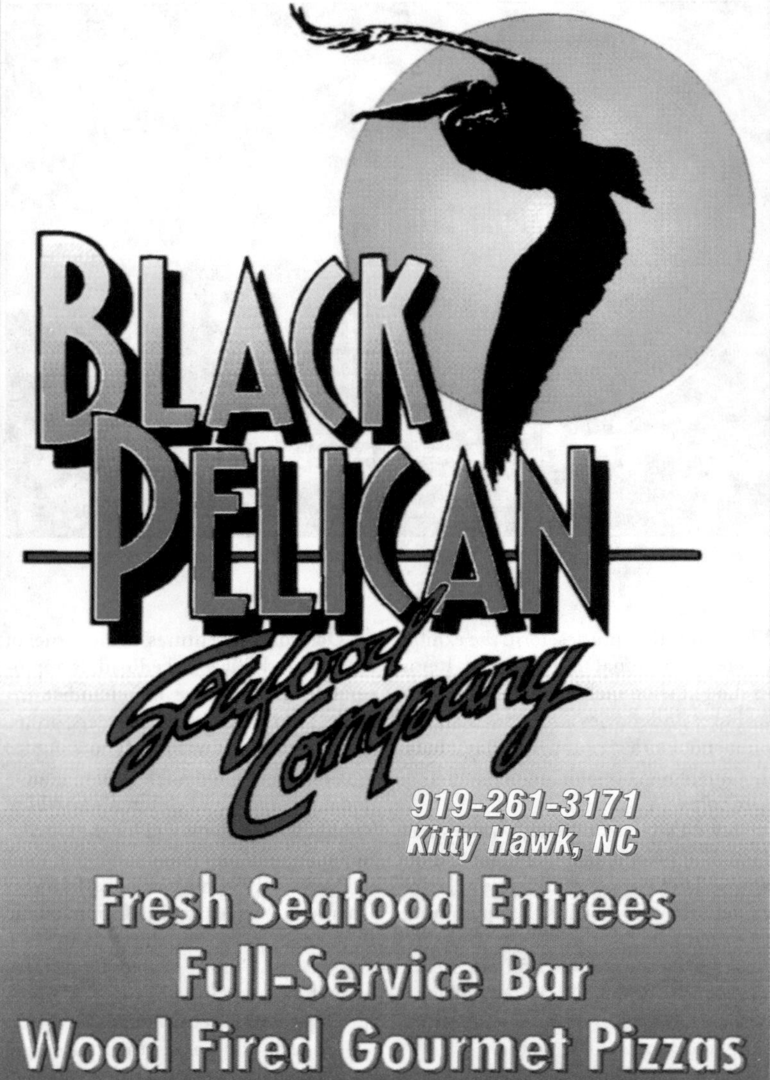

BLACK PELICAN
Seafood Company
919-261-3171
Kitty Hawk, NC
Fresh Seafood Entrees
Full-Service Bar
Wood Fired Gourmet Pizzas
Specialty Salads
Steamed & Raw Bar
Seasonal Entertainment

Inside Restaurants

Whether you're treating yourself to a delectable dinner while on vacation or just trying to find a quick, satisfying supper to fill your hungry family after a long day on the beach, dining out is one of the most enjoyable activities many people experience. The Outer Banks have a wide array of restaurants from which to choose, offering food to please every palate and price ranges to suit any pocket book. There are upscale cafes with European ambiance and unusual culinary creations and down-home fish houses where your meal may be caught only a few feet from the table you're consuming it on a fishing pier.

International fare, as well, has made its way to these isolated islands — with Mexican, Thai, Italian, Chinese, French and even Caribbean-style eateries springing from the sand in recent years. Ethnic cooking also has crept into even the most traditional restaurants. And many chefs have revised their menus for the summer season to reflect a wider variety of healthful alternatives and even vegetarian offerings.

Competition keeps increasing too. In addition to the dozen or more restaurants that changed owners or managers over the winter, at least 20 new restaurants between Corolla and Ocracoke have opened in time for the 1996 summer season. Newcomers and natives alike will find diverse dining styles and a wide range of entrees from which to choose.

Increasingly, restaurants are opening earlier in the spring and staying open longer into the fall each year. "The shoulder seasons really are becoming a popular time to dine out — especially for locals," Outer Banks Restaurant Association President Carol Ann Angelos says. "Vacationers, too, are finding that they can stay here cheaper in the off-season and get the same friendly service and great food — without ever having to wait for a table." Most eateries now open by Easter and don't close their kitchens until after Thanksgiving. Many even have decided to serve their full line of selections year round.

Although seafood has always been a mainstay for barrier island cooks and their customers, chefs schooled at culinary institutes around the world are making their way into Outer Banks restaurants — and changing the way we all eat out. Besides the traditional fried flounder, steamed shrimp and you-pick-'em blue crabs — which will never be removed from many area menus — bistros now serve poached salmon over beds of just-made saffron lin-

Insiders' Tips

The Red Apple food mart, inside the Amoco station at the corner of U.S. 158 and Colington Road, makes great donuts each morning, dripping with thick chocolate frosting.

guine; cafes coddle discriminating diners with everything from roasted duck breasts drizzled with raspberry cassias sauce to chick pea and black bean hummus dip with pita chips; and many eateries pride themselves as much on the food's artistic presentation as on serving the freshest, highest quality ingredients available.

Wine, too, is rapidly becoming one of our restaurants' biggest drawing cards. Several Outer Banks eateries host wine tasting weekends in the off-season. And many have decided to serve 12 or more types of wine by the glass for those who want to sample several types. Wine-by-the-bottle lists expand each season, and restaurants along the northern beaches sometimes offer 50 or more varieties of the world's finest wines.

Dinner isn't the only meal to eat out, of course. A variety of bakeries, diners and even seafood restaurants now serve big breakfasts and weekend brunches. Most places are open for lunch throughout the summer, and some even have decided to serve bathing suit-clad customers just off the beach. The majority of restaurants, however, still require you to wear shirts and shoes. Many cooks will package any meal to go, though, and some eateries even have started delivering — with menus offering much more than just pizza that can be dropped off at your door.

If you're eating an evening meal out, feel free to dress as comfortably as you desire. Even most of the expensive, elite establishments welcome sundresses, sandals and shorts. Some restaurant managers say everything from evening gowns and suits to jeans and T-shirts are acceptable at their linen-cloaked tables.

Reservations aren't taken at many restaurants. Others, however, suggest or even require them. The Blue Point in Duck, Ocean Boulevard in Kitty Hawk and Colington Cafe on Colington Island all get so booked up in the summer that you usually have to call at least three days ahead to secure a table. The fare at these fabulous places, however, is well worth the wait.

If sticking to a budget is more of a concern, you can have home-style meals from tuna steaks to North Carolina barbecue for less than $8 in many Outer Banks family-style restaurants. Western Sizzlin', Golden Corral and, of course, fast-food eateries from McDonald's to Wendy's all also offer their standard fare here. But for this chapter, we haven't included any chain restaurants — we think you already know what to expect from those spots.

Seafood is, and probably always will be, one of the biggest draws for Outer Banks diners. Caught in the sounds, inshore ocean and as far out as the Gulf Stream by local watermen, much of the fish served here lived or swam near the barrier islands — and often makes it to your plate less than two days after being landed. Some restaurants, however, are increasingly importing fish from foreign countries. So ask your waiter or waitress where the seafood came from if you're fishing for Outer Banks-only food. And if you want someone else to clean and cook your catch, Nags Head Pier Restaurant will gladly prepare your own "fish of the day" for you.

Raw bars always are great bets for relatively cheap — yet succulent — seafood. Oysters, clams, crab legs and shrimp are served on the shell or slightly steamed, and some places even include vegetables. Soft-shell crabs also are an Outer Banks speciality worth raving about, served from Easter through early July. Don't be put off by the spidery legs hanging off these crustaceans. Just consume the entire creature, shell and all — it's a whole lot quicker and easier than having to pick the meat out of a hard shell once the crabs stop molting later in the summer.

If you're into picking your own crabs, however, you'll probably want to spread some newspaper out at your cottage or find an outdoor picnic table to absorb the mess. You can buy the locally caught blue crabs

Photo: Mary Ellen Riddle

Owens' Restaurant is celebrating its 50th anniversary this year.

already steamed — or cook them yourself in a big kettle. Dirty Dick's Crab House in Kill Devil Hills even delivers them to your door already steamed, spiced and ready to eat. And you can catch your own crabs in area sounds, inlets and bays by dangling a chicken neck from a long string and letting the shellfish wrap its claws around the meat. Just be careful when you're taking it off the line to drop it in your bucket before it latches onto your finger. Always steam crabs while they're still alive. And don't eat the gray lungs or yellow mustard-like substance inside.

Most Outer Banks restaurants serve beer and wine — at least for dinner. But those in Corolla and on Colington, Roanoke, Hatteras and Ocracoke islands are forbidden by law to offer mixed drinks. Some establishments allow brown bagging, however, where you can bring in your own liquor. Call ahead to make sure that's OK. And ask if they provide setups.

For your convenience, we've included a pricing guide with each restaurant write up to give you a general idea of what to expect (see the Price-code Key gray box). The costs are based on entrees for two people, not including appetizers, desserts or alcoholic beverages. Many area eateries also have senior citizen discounts and children's menus to help families cut costs. Most entrees include at least one vegetable or salad and some type of rolls or bread. Prices vary if you select the most or least expensive items on the menu; this guide is a generalization hitting the mid-range prices of restaurants' most popular meals.

Price-code Key

Less than $25	*$*
$26 to $45	*$$*
$46 to $75	*$$$*
$76 and more	*$$$$*

Price ranges do not reflect North Carolina's 6 percent sales tax or the gratuity, which should be 15 percent to 20 percent for good service. Some restaurants offer early evening dining discounts to encourage patrons to avoid peak dining hours. Most have at least two or three daily specials that change depending on the availability of food and the whim of the chef.

Restaurants in this chapter are arranged from north to south — Corolla through Ocracoke. Seasons and days of the week each place is open are included with each profile. Unless otherwise noted, these eateries accept at least MasterCard and Visa, and many accept other major credit cards as well.

We've also added some primarily carry-out and outdoor dining establishments that offer quick, cheap eats, cool ice-cream concoctions and perfect items to pack for a picnic or offshore fishing excursion.

Whatever you're hungering for, you'll find it here. So eat up. Bon appetit!

Corolla

Corolla Pizza & Deli

Austin Complex, N.C. 12 *453-8592*
$

One of the only Corolla eateries that's open year-round, seven days a week, this take-out-only deli serves subs, sandwiches, Philly cheese steaks and pizza by the pie or slice for lunch and dinner. Each pizza is made to order on hand-tossed dough. Regular red sauce and gourmet white pizzas — including the ever-popular chicken pesto pizza — are available. During the summer season, Corolla Pizza offers free delivery. You can walk in or call ahead to have your order waiting.

Nicoletta's Italian Cafe

Corolla Light Village Shops *453-4004*
$$$

Since this small Italian cafe opened four years ago near the red brick Currituck Lighthouse, it has earned a fine reputation for a wide variety of well-prepared foods. This classy little bistro features tables covered in white linen and each adorned with a single, long-stemmed red rose. Waiters whisk about in crisp black and white uniforms. A thick burgundy floral carpet cushions their steps, while Frank Sinatra tunes often echo softly in the background.

Nicoletta's menu features a variety of fresh seafood, veal, chicken, pastas and salads. Special appetizers and dinner selections change each evening. And there's an abundance of authentic Italian dishes from which to choose, all with wonderful homemade sauces that seduce the palette.

A select wine list is available, and homemade desserts change weekly. A cup of espresso or cappuccino is a great way to end the evening. Reservations are highly recommended; a separate room is available for private parties. Dress is casual, and children are welcome (there's even a special menu to suit younger appetites). Nicoletta's is open seven days a week in summer. Call for off-season schedules.

Cosmo's Pizzeria

Corolla Light Village Shops *453-4666*
$

Open for lunch and dinner from April through November, this authentic New York-style pizza parlor features hand-tossed pies made right before your eyes. The decor is black and white, accented with old family photos from Italy and cooled by low-spinning ceiling fans. Calzones, stromboli and other Italian dishes are all homemade — and are as delicious as the pizza. An assortment of cold and hot subs and salads also is on the menu. Cosmo's serves beer and wine, and you can eat in or take-out. The restaurant is open seven days a week during the season. There is another Cosmo's Pizzeria in Kitty Hawk.

Horseshoe Cafe

Corolla Light Village Shops *453-8463*
$$

Four years ago, Horseshoe Cafe brought Southwestern cuisine to the northern Outer Banks. Here, you'll find homemade crab cakes, seasoned lightly with chili powder for that Tex-Mex flair. Vegetarian chili also is a stand-out. And there's plenty of good seafood, steaks, chicken and barbecue on the menu. All the desserts are homemade, from Key lime pie to crème brûlée to sopapillas drizzled with honey.

Choose from a variety of flavored coffee, mocha cappuccino and even hazelnut espresso to top off your meal.

The decor here fits the theme. Bull horns, wool rugs, cacti and, of course, horseshoes line the walls. A Mexican tile bar offers a cool place to sit a spell and sip one of 25 kinds of beer served. The wine list is extensive too.

Horseshoe Cafe serves breakfast, lunch and dinner in season. Sandwiches are available for a light supper in addition to the full entree offerings. A children's menu offers smaller portions and prices — and the wait staff even provides crayons to keep your tykes entertained. Reservations are suggested.

Tomato Patch Pizzeria

Monteray Plaza *453-4500*

$

The owners of Kitty Hawk Pizza offer northern beach-goers the same great home-style cooking found in their restaurant at Kitty Hawk. Tomato Patch features open spaces and wide tables that can handle large crowds. Greek foods from gyros to salads are made from family recipes. And pasta specials including spaghetti and lasagna are served daily. Besides the regular red sauce variety of pizza, diners here can choose from gourmet and white pizzas with such ingredients as bacon and fresh garlic. Desserts such as French silk pie, Snickers pie and — one of our favorites — Mediterranean-style baklava each will tempt you, even if you've already eaten your fill. Beer and wine are available. Bringing children is encouraged — the owners keep plenty of high chairs on hand. Tomato Patch Pizzeria is open for lunch and dinner March to October.

Smokey's Restaurant

Monteray Plaza *453-4050*

$

This down-home restaurant opened in 1991 and was one of the first in Corolla. Its specialties include barbecue, pork ribs, fried chicken, tuna steaks, fried and steamed shrimp and fried clams. They offer all the trimmings from cole slaw and baked beans to onion rings. We especially recommend the fried sweet-potato sticks for an unusual side dish — they're a nice alternative to the usual french fries and complement any meal. Appetizers range from jalapeño poppers to Buffalo wings, and sandwiches and salads also are available throughout the day.

Smokey's offers a children's menu and will package most of its items for take-out. Desserts, wine and beer also are available. This restaurant is open for lunch and dinner March through December. In season, it serves seven days a week; call for off-season hours. Reservations are not needed in this casual, family-style eatery.

Steamer's Restaurant & Raw Bar

TimBuck II *453-3344*
$$

This 50-seat restaurant and raw bar serves lunch and dinner year round. Lobster, shrimp, oysters, clams and mussels are available as well as lamb, veal, grilled beef, chicken and even sandwiches. Diners will enjoy the waterside view from this upscale but casual restaurant that boasts 28-foot vaulted ceilings. If you have to wait for a table, you can wear a "patron pager" and stroll through TimBuck II until you're beeped. Steamer's also offers desserts and appetizers as well as microbrewery beers, wine and Black and Tans to complement the fresh, local seafood.

For the summer of 1996, Steamer's will serve its ever popular steamer pots from a separate location at TimBuck II. These unusual "cook-it-yourself" meals offer hand-packaged live seafood and fresh vegetables to steam in the comfort and convenience of your home or rental cottage. Each pot includes lobster, shrimp, oysters, clams, mussels, vegetables and all the trimmings to make a huge meal. All you need is a stove-top burner. Of course, you can keep the steamer after you're done eating. Call ahead to have yours waiting.

Mane Street Eatery

TimBuck II, near the gasoline pumps *453-4644*
$

Under new ownership for 1996, Mane Street Eatery serves Southern-style cuisine with a heavy New Orleans influence. Here, you can choose from a variety of fresh Outer Banks seafood, sandwiches and combination platters. Daily specials vary, and beans and rice come with each entree. This is a family-style restaurant decorated in an "early stable" theme in honor of Corolla's herd of wild horses that recently were corralled onto a wildlife refuge north of the road's end.

Mane Street serves lunch and dinner in season and offers a separate children's menu. Beer and wine are available. The restaurant is closed Sundays. Call ahead for carry-out items. Reservations aren't accepted.

Neptune's Grill & Arcade

TimBuck II *453-8645*
$ *No credit cards*

Opened during the summer of 1995, this casual grill offers quarter-pound burgers, Philly cheese steaks, North Carolina barbecue, fried oysters, salads and veggie burgers and a variety of sandwiches to eat-in, carry-out or be delivered to your door. French fries, cheese fries, frozen candy bars and cookies also are available, as are beer and wine.

This is a low-key burger joint where you can sit at booths or tables. And it features the only pool table north of Duck; pinball and Foosball offer added family entertainment. Neptune's Grill is open for breakfast (sweet rolls, muffins and biscuit breakfast sandwiches), lunch and dinner year-round, and bring the kids — there's a special children's menu. In summer, it serves food seven days a week; call for off-season hours.

Leo's Bakery & Deli

TimBuck II *453-6777*
$ *No credit cards*

Reubens, pastrami sandwiches, deli creations and potato, pasta, tuna and Greek salads all are prepared here daily year-round for carry-out only. Leo's also has a huge array of ice cream, donuts, cookies, pies and cakes for any occasion except weddings. This combination bakery-deli serves beer and wine and is open for breakfast, lunch and dinner. Outdoor tables, however, are provided if you want to soak up some sun during summer.

Grouper's Grille & Wine Bar

TimBuck II *453-4077*

$$$

One of the best things to happen to the Outer Banks in years, this restaurant opened just in time for the 1996 summer season. Its owners also run Cafe Alpine in Breckenridge, Colorado, where they have earned numerous awards for their international eclectic menu and extensive wine list. Offerings at their Corolla location are similar, with cuisine hailing from Thailand, India and Greece, to name just a few locales. Local seafood is served with an international twist, and pastas, chicken and steaks also get a fresh treatment with unusual spices and sauces.

About one-fourth of the five-page menu is devoted to vegetarian dishes. Appetizers include such temptations as blackened shrimp salad with orange thyme vinaigrette dressing, baked peppercorn brie with fresh bread and fresh fruit, grilled marinated Portobello mushrooms with vegetable pesto and shaved Parmesan on a french roll. Olive oil pesto Parmesan pizzas, grilled New York strip steak sandwiches with caramelized onions and brandy dijon cream sauce, and spinach lasagna with seasonal vegetables and a white wine tomato marinara sauce all are available for lighter appetites.

Entrees come with a choice of gourmet soup or salad. All the dressings, breads, sauces and desserts are made from scratch. And dinner offerings range from crown roast of pork with apricot and sun-dried cherry compote and garlic mashed potatoes to pan-seared New Zealand lamb loins with coconut curry over rice. Having dessert is a *must* here — especially the chocolate bag filled with white chocolate mousse and raspberry sauce garnished with fresh fruit.

As if that's not enough of a selection, Grouper's also serves tapas (appetizer-size portions of entrees) that allow diners to sample an array of the magnificent offerings. This bistro sells 40 types of wine by the glass and more than 100 varieties by the bottle. There's also a wide assortment of domestic, imported and microbrewed beers served at the huge wine bar.

The atmosphere here is as delightful as the dinners, with open post-and-beam wooden ceilings, white tablecloths set with flickering candles and big windows all around the dining room. It's an upscale yet casual place where you'll fit right in wearing anything from a suit and tie to Levis. Reservations are recommended. Grouper's is open from March through November seven days a week.

Duck

Sanderling Inn Restaurant

N.C. 12, Sanderling *261-3021*

$$$

The restored lifesaving station at the Sanderling Resort just north of Duck houses one of the Outer Banks' most ac-

Insiders' Tips

If you like to sample a little taste of everything visit one of the Outer Banks' great buffet restaurants. Several of the most popular are Carolina Seafood in Kill Devil Hills and the Wharf and Seafare, both in Nags Head. New to the buffet scene is Flounders, formerly Waves Edge North, in Kitty Hawk on U.S. 158; it also serves a breakfast buffet.

claimed restaurants. Multiple dining rooms enhanced with rich woods and brass offer ocean or sound views from almost every table. Here, progressive Southern regional cuisine is served for breakfast, lunch and dinner. And a three-course, $14.95 Sunday brunch available from 11 AM to 2 PM is the best on the beach.

Start the morning with Chef Glen Aurand's blueberry walnut pancakes or orange cinnamon French toast. For lunch, try the grilled fish of the day or a seafood platter featuring mussels, clams and shrimp. The sun-dried tomato and goat cheese quiche flavored with Vidalia onions is fantastic. And vegetarians will appreciate the fresh vegetable strudel.

Dinner entrees include roasted rack of lamb, crab cakes made with all backfin meat and homemade pasta served with ambitious sauces. Five types of fresh local fish are served as specials each evening. And the desserts all are delectable — and worth saving room for. The Sanderling has a full bar that includes several California wine selections. A children's menu is available, and reservations are suggested. All three meals are served seven days a week throughout the year.

Duck News Cafe

N.C. 12 *261-1549*
$$

For a spectacular view of the sun setting over Currituck Sound, sample a dinner selection at this northern Duck restaurant. Selections nightly include Italian entrees, shrimp served three ways, crab imperial, marinated locally caught tuna and aged beef tenderloin. Chicken with special sauces, soft-shell crabs in season, crab cakes, clam chowder and Caesar salads are other options.

Key lime pie, brownies à la mode and a Lady Godiva — ice cream drowned in chocolate liquor — all are delightful desserts. The full bar has four types of beer on tap. This is a casual, family-oriented restaurant (there's a children's menu); it sits across from the Sanderling Inn. Reservations are recommended. Dinner is served here from early spring through fall, and lunch and dinner are offered in summer.

Cravings Coffee Shoppe

Duck Common Shopping Center *261-0655*
$

Opened during the summer of 1995, this delightful eatery is the perfect place to pop by for a quick breakfast before hitting the beach or to indulge yourself in a delectable dessert and coffee after dinner. You can eat inside, on an open air deck or take the tasty treats home with you. Table service is not available; you order and pick up your food from the counter.

Order a fresh New York-style bagel with one of six flavored cream cheeses. Homemade pastries, breads and muffins also are baked each day. And out-of-town newspapers are available each morning if you miss browsing through big city dailies such as *The New York Times*, *Washington Post* and *The Wall Street Journal*.

For lunch, try an Italian sandwich on just-baked bread. And, of course, every type of coffee drink you can concoct is available, from four types of brewed coffee that change daily to espresso, cappuccino, mocha drinks and other fancy combinations. You can also buy gourmet coffee beans, gift baskets and other items at a small shop inside Cravings.

Cravings serves breakfast, lunch and dinner seven days a week, and the cafe only shuts down in January.

Barrier Island Inn and Tavern

Duck Rd. (N.C. 12) *261-3901*
$$

The first restaurant in Duck, Barrier Island Inn is situated on the Currituck Sound — and there's a large waterfront deck out back with both covered and open-air portions that offer great views of the sunset and sparkling water. Osprey, ducks and windsurfers testing their sails on the Currituck Sound afford constant

Photo: Philip S. Ruckle

Come sail away on the Outer Banks.

entertainment during the day. At night, live music is offered throughout the summer (see our Nightlife chapter).

Outer Banks seafood is a speciality, along with pasta, steaks, crab cakes, lobster and chicken. A light fare, including homemade pizza and sandwiches, is available in the tavern late into the night. Appetizers, desserts and separate selections for children are also on the menu. The restaurant serves lunch and dinner year round; a weekend breakfast buffet is available.

Elizabeth's Cafe & Winery

Scarborough Faire *261-6145*
$$$

Well known across the East Coast for its wine and wonderful food, Elizabeth's has earned international acclaim from *The Wine Spectator* magazine from 1991 through 1995. For the past three years, this cafe was one of only five restaurants in North Carolina to win Best of the Award of Excellence. For the 1996 season, owner Leonard Logan has added a walk-in wine cellar and retail sales area and expanded the restaurant to accommodate additional patrons. A new jazz bar features live music most summer evenings, and local favorite Laura Martier will grace this fabulous eatery with her sultry blues tunes during Sunday deck parties outdoors.

Elizabeth's is a delight — from ambiance through entrees. It's warm and casual inside, with a fireplace that's usually lit on chilly evenings. Service always is excellent. And the owner will personally select a vintage wine to complement any meal. Wine makers from around the world are featured here during special dinners each Thursday.

In addition to the regular menu offerings, which include country French and California eclectic foods that change continually, prix-fixe dinners — six-course meals and accompanying wines — for $75 per person are available. All the dishes are made with fresh ingredients, from seafood and steaks to unusual pastas. A new wine bar with steamed shrimp, cheeses and croissants serves dining delights all afternoon. And a pastry chef creates different desserts daily: Elizabeth's Craving especially is sinfully delicious.

This cafe is small and popular so reservations are highly recommended. On some summer weekends the owner has had to turn away more than 200 potential diners. The restaurant has a covered gazebo and deck outdoors. Microbrewery beers are served in addition to all the fine wines. Elizabeth's is open on weekends for dinner year round and for lunch and dinner seven days a week in season.

Fish Bones Raw Bar & Grill

Scarborough Lane Shoppes *261-6991*
$$

Specializing in locally caught seafood, this raw bar and grill opened in the summer of 1995 and won the Outer Banks chowder cook-off with an original recipe during its first year in business.

Midday items include sandwiches, crab cakes, fried seafood and creamy soups such as tomato conch and, of course, chowder. Dinner entrees offer pastas with fresh clam sauce, lobster tails, crab legs and more than a dozen raw bar selections. The hot crab dip, barbecue shrimp and shrimp rolled in coconut all are outstanding appetizers. This is a casual place with a full bar, four types of beer on tap, a wine list and several microbrews from which to choose. Desserts also are available.

Fish Bones serves lunch and dinner seven days a week year round, and specials change daily for both meals. Reservations are not accepted.

The Blue Point Bar & Grill

The Waterfront Shops *261-8090*
$$$

This waterfront bistro is one of our favorite places to dine on the Outer Banks. It's been open for lunch and dinner since 1989 and consistently receives rave reviews from magazines such as *Southern Living* and *Gourmet* as well as admiring local audiences. Here, regional Southern cooking brings a cosmopolitan flair to the area. A 1940s-style interior with bare floors, low ceilings and shiny black and white tables and chairs provides an upbeat, bustling atmosphere indoors. An enclosed porch offers an alternative dining experience closer to the Currituck Sound. There's also a small bar facing the aromatic kitchen where you can watch your appetizers being prepared while sipping a cocktail as you wait for a table.

The Blue Point's menu is creatively nouvelle and changes weekly. Starters range from scallops to escargo — each artistically arranged and flavored with the freshest combination of seasonings. Entrees include homemade soups, unusual seafood dishes, steaks, salads and perfect pastas. And there's a new pastry chef in 1996 — although we can't believe the divine desserts this eatery has become known for could possibly improve.

If you're into creative cooking that's sure to tantalize every taste bud — and awaken some you might not even have realized you had — this restaurant is a must-stop on the Outer Banks. It's open for lunch and dinner year round, and reservations are highly recommended. During the winter, The Blue Point closes on Mondays, but the rest of the year it's open seven days a week. Good thing — we're addicted.

Roadside Raw Bar & Grille

Duck Rd. (N.C. 12) *261-5729*
$$

Occupying a renovated 1932 cottage, this year-old restaurant is warm and homey, with hardwood floors inside and a patio dotted with umbrella-shaded tables out front. In the summer, live blues music is performed here two nights a week (see our Nightlife chapter).

A casual, fine dining establishment, Roadside offers pork loin sandwiches and crab cakes for lunch. The chef's chili won the Outer Banks chili cook-off this year. And the clam chowder is chock-full of shellfish. A raw bar serving all sorts of shrimp, oysters, clams and shish kebab combinations is open all afternoon.

For dinner you can choose from fresh salads with mangos and other exotic fruits, loads of locally caught seafood, just-sliced steaks, whole lobsters and poultry platters. Other specials change daily for lunch and dinner. Desserts include chocolate bread pudding with Jack Daniels caramel sauce and steaming slices of Mom's Apple Pie. A children's menu is available, and the full bar has a nice selection of microbrewed beers.

The restaurant is open year round seven days a week. Reservations are not accepted.

Duck Deli

Duck Rd. (N.C. 12) *261-3354*
$ *No credit cards*

This casual deli on the east side of the highway opened nine years ago primarily to serve locals lunch. Since then, it's expanded to offer breakfast, lunch and dinner seven days a week, 11 months of the year (the eatery closes during January).

Barbecue pork, beef, chicken and ribs are the specialities here. And the cooks will smoke fish you catch — or ones landed by local watermen. Sandwiches, Philly cheese steaks and subs are served all day, as are side salads, garden burgers and coleslaw. A full breakfast menu includes everything from eggs and pancakes to omelets. And for dessert, you can get sweet on cherry and peach cobblers, homemade brownies or a frozen yogurt bar with plenty of toppings. Beer is served at Duck Deli, and everything is available to eat in or take-out.

Herron's Deli and Restaurant

Duck Rd. (N.C. 12) *261-3224*
$

With a full menu available for carry-out or to eat in, this casual deli serves breakfast and lunch seven days a week all year and adds dinner hours in the summer. Booths and tables are available indoors, and picnic tables offer outdoor dining. Hot and cold Italian subs, cheese steaks, cheeseburgers and crab cakes are among the most popular items in the afternoon and evening. We recommend the soups — from chili specials to she-crab bisque and Hatteras-style chowder.

A big breakfast menu features French toast, sausage gravy, omelets, eggs and homemade biscuits. And desserts range from cakes and brownies to homemade strawberry pie. Beer and wine also are available.

Swan Cove

Duck Rd. (N.C. 12) *255-0500*
$$$

One of the Outer Banks' newest upscale restaurants, this elegant establishment opened in 1995 and already has revamped its menu for the 1996 summer season. Unbelievable views are available from the soundfront dining room, where tablecloths and cut flowers grace each and crystal glasses sparkle during sunset hours. And there's a separate lounge with a full bar and an extensive wine list upstairs.

Chef Mac Ritter of the Culinary Institute of America describes his cuisine as seasonal/regional. And he says the menu changes frequently to incorporate new offerings. "I use all local produce, seafood and fresh herbs," says Ritter. "And I specialize in low-fat, light cooking." Entrees include duck, pastas, French-cut pork chops, three kinds of Outer Banks fish, seafood bouillabaisse over saffron fettuccine, tenderloin steaks and fresh salads. Warm rolls and garden vegetables come with each dinner.

Great bets: Hot and cold appetizers such as avocados stuffed with lump crabmeat and tequila mayonnaise and andouille sausage served with hot mustard sauce. For dessert, try choosing between a chocolate layer cake, peanut butter pie and seasonal fresh fruits drizzled with fabulous sauces.

Swan Cove is open seven days a week in season, serving lunch and dinner; dinner only is served in spring and early fall. There is a children's menu. Reservations are suggested.

Pizzazz Pizza

Loblolly Pines Shopping Center 261-8822
$ No credit cards

Celebrating its 11th season in Duck, this small pizza parlor serves subs and pizzas to eat in or take out. Another Pizzazz Pizza is located in Kitty Hawk; see that description for more details on the menu. Pizzazz is open March through November seven days a week for lunch and dinner. Reservations are recommended for parties of six or more.

Kitty Hawk

Southern Bean

The Marketplace 261-JAVA
$ No credit cards

Opened in September 1995, this gourmet coffee shop has been the talk of the northern Outer Banks towns all winter. Southern Bean serves breakfast and lunch year round — and adds dinner hours in the summer. Three types of just-brewed coffee always are simmering here, filling the air with amazing aromas.

It's a very casual place that has every type of speciality coffee drink imaginable, from espresso and cappuccino to iced lattes — even in decaf varieties. More than 30 flavors of freshly roasted coffee beans are sold by the pound here. You can eat inside at Southern Bean, sip a warm blend from an outdoor table or order your drinks and food to go. All menu items are either vegetarian or seafood, and sandwiches range from hummus to peanut butter-and-honey; try the bean bagel topped with sun-dried tomatoes, pesto, red onion slices, cream cheese and sprouts. Muffins, croissants, cinnamon rolls and other bakery items also are available. No sandwich costs more than $5.

Southern Bean is open seven days a week in season and closes on Sundays the rest of the year.

North China Express

In front of Wal-Mart
shopping center 261-5511
$ No credit cards

This Chinese restaurant serves take-out meals only, with nine items on the lunch and dinner menu. Both Thai and Kung Pao chicken are spicy selections. See our write-up of North China Restaurant in the Nags Head section. This eatery is open year round and closed Sundays.

Kitty Hawk Pier Restaurant

Beach Rd., MP 1 261-3151
$ No credit cards

One of the most popular breakfast places on the beach, this ultra-casual restaurant, which opened in 1954, is somewhere you'll feel comfortable just rolling out of bed and rolling into. Pancakes, eggs, sausage, French toast, omelets, biscuits, hash browns, grits, sausage, bacon and anything else you could desire for a filling first meal of the day are cooked up beginning at 6 AM.

Lunch specials change daily and include such local favorites as ham and cabbage, trout, shrimp, crab cakes, meat loaf, and turkey with dressing and yams. For dinner, try a seafood platter of flounder, scallops, oysters, dolphin or Spanish mackerel — each served with a choice of two sides: hushpuppies, rolls, cole slaw, beets, peas, beans or other vegetables.

Kitty Hawk Pier Restaurant is a down-home place with lots of local patrons — and flavor. You can find out what's biting here and may even see your dinner being reeled in off the nearby wooden planks. "A lot of our fish is caught from the pier here, within 200 feet of where you eat it," said the owner. "You can come as you are to our restaurant. Hey, it's the beach. Even bathing suits are OK by us."

Desserts include homemade cobblers (peach, apple, blueberry and cherry), strawberry shortcake and a variety of pies. Beer is served in cans. And a children's menu is offered for small fries. Everything is available to take out, but you'll enjoy eating in this oceanfront restaurant where salt spray stains the wide windows.

The restaurant serves three meals a day, seven days a week from April through November.

Rundown Cafe

Beach Rd., MP 1 *255-0026*
$$

Opened in 1993, this Caribbean-style cafe is owned by the same friendly folk who run Tortuga's Shellfish Bar and Grill in Nags Head. It's been a big hit with locals who live on the northern end of the beach — and offers some spicy, unusual alternatives to traditional Outer Banks seafood. Named for a Jamaican stew, Rundown serves island entrees flavored with African and Indian accents. Try the conch chowder for an appetizer, or one of several wild soups that change seasonally.

Specials shift nightly. Some of our favorites are blackened pork tenderloin, spinach-and-feta stuffed chicken with roasted red pepper sauce and freshly grilled tuna topped with sesame-vinaigrette. The steam bar here serves shellfish of all sorts, vegetables and steamed dinners. All the regular menu items also are terrific.

There's a full bar — and the bartenders can come up with some pretty potent concoctions. This is a casual, happening place that features live blues and jazz at least twice a week in summer (see our Nightlife chapter). A rooftop deck is a great place to soak in the sunset, catch a few rays or just linger over a cool cocktail after a hot day in the sun. Lunch and dinner are available year round seven days a week.

Ocean Boulevard

Beach Rd., MP 2 *261-2546*
$$$

This warm, cozy, upscale eatery gives you a great feeling from the second you walk into the gold-walled dining room until you leave full and relaxed after consuming a fabulous meal. It opened in September 1995 and has quickly become one of the most popular places on the Outer Banks. Manteo

Insiders' Tips

In addition to the dozen or more restaurants that changed owners or managers over the winter, at least 20 new restaurants between Corolla and Ocracoke have opened in time for the 1996 summer season.

residents even drive 30 miles each way to treat themselves to a midweek dinner here. No wonder — it's owned by the same culinary masters who brought us the Blue Point in Duck. Ocean Boulevard has a lot more intimate atmosphere, however, and the food is slightly more sophisticated.

This restaurant occupies the former 1949 Virginia Dare Hardware store — and you won't believe what the builders and decorators have done with the place. It's accented with warm woods, burgundy fabrics and forest green chairs. Cobalt blue glasses — and water pitchers — grace every table top. There's even an open-air kitchen where you can watch the chefs work.

Selections all are prepared with locally grown herbs, spices, produce and just-caught seafood. Influences and ideas from around the world give the food here a flavor all its own. For appetizers, try poached oysters with creamy horseradish risotto and fresh dill. Or sample the chilled terrine of three cheeses served with smoked salmon, wild mushrooms, chive vinaigrette and toast points. Four meal-size salads — one with seven types of lettuce — also are outstanding.

Our favorite entree is the avocado and pistachio crusted mahimahi, which comes with herbed basmati rice, roasted tomato and black bean sauce. The pepper-seared breast of moulard duck with walnut and gorgonzola polenta, savory turnip greens and black currant-port wine jus is also amazing. And you can't go wrong by ordering any of the pastas, beef, shrimp with Portobello mushrooms or pork chops served with blue cornmeal onion rings.

Ocean Boulevard's wine list contains more than 100 selections, at least a dozen of which are served by the glass. Microbrewed beers and a full bar also are on hand. And six dessert offerings each are to die for. We especially crave the flourless chocolate espresso bean torte with seasonal fruit sorbet and the praline-crusted butterscotch torte served with a scoop of pistachio ice cream. A full line of after-dinner coffee drinks and herbal teas also are served.

This elegant eatery will please even the most discriminating diners. It's open year round for dinner only. During summers, doors are open seven days a week. Call for off-season hours. Reservations are highly recommended.

Art's Place

Beach Rd., MP 2½ *261-3233*
$ *No credit cards*

Serving good, basic meals for 17 years, this tiny eatery across from the ocean is a Kitty Hawk standby well known among locals. The food here isn't fancy, but it's cheap, filling and all-American. Sausage gravy is the most popular breakfast entree, although Art's also serves the usual eggs, pancakes and biscuits. The same entrees are available for lunch and dinner, with daily specials such as fried chicken, shrimp and clam strips and cheeseburgers each served with french fries, cole slaw and a cucumber and onion salad. Jalapeño poppers are a hot bet for an appetizer. And calamari also is available most of the time. The eatery is open seven days a week year round. Reservations are accepted — but seldom necessary.

Insiders' Tips

Oyster shooters — raw oysters splashed with Tabasco sauce — are terrific, especially when washed down by a cold beer.

Argyle Bake Shop & Deli

U.S. 158, MP 2½ *261-7325*

$

Formerly located on the beach road in Nags Head, this scrumptious bake shop now includes a sit-down restaurant and full delicatessen. Argyle Bake Shop is our favorite place for gooey baked-goods breakfasts — and it serves hot pancakes, eggs, hash browns and sausage as well. The cinnamon rolls are giant and sticky, smothered with just enough frosting to guarantee you'll lick your fingers. Eclairs, croissants, muffins and breakfast biscuit sandwiches all are sure to satisfy and keep you coming back for more.

For lunch, Argyle serves hamburgers, french fries, chicken tender strips, prime rib, seafood platters, Philly cheese steaks and a full line of huge deli sandwiches — all made on freshly baked bread with the finest Boar's Head meats and cheeses. The chicken salad here is the best on the beach. And you can also choose from loads of meal-size chef and garden salads, cole slaw, pasta salad, potato salad and veggie burgers. The owners are glad to accommodate special diet needs.

But when you see the dessert case, you'll forget about your figure. Cannolis, cookies of all shapes and sizes, at least a half-dozen flavors of cheesecake, turtle and Snicker's pie, mousse tortes and an array of other unreal sweets are available — like the meals — to eat in or take out. Argyle's cooks also cater parties and weddings and will make special cakes for any occasion. You can get beer and wine here too. Dinner is served only until 6 PM. Argyle is open year round every day but Sunday.

Pizzazz Pizza

U.S. 158, MP 3½ *255-0050*

$

This fun pizza parlor is owned by the same people who run the Duck location. But here, delivery is offered as well as eat-in and take-out meals. Pizzazz has a casual, family atmosphere and a full bar. Menu items include California white pizzas with spinach, pesto, vegetables, seafood and at least two dozen other toppings. Traditional red sauce pies also are offered — and you're welcome to create your own combinations to spread across the hand-tossed dough.

Pasta dishes, lasagna and subs are served on freshly baked rolls. Appetizers and desserts such as cannoli, ice cream sundaes and brownies also are offered. Pizzazz's Kitty Hawk location is open year round, seven days a week for lunch and dinner. Reservations are recommended for parties of six or more.

Keeper's Galley

U.S. 158, MP 4 *261-4000*

$$

Over the winter of 1996, Keeper's Galley changed hands. It's now run by the same people who own the Dunes Restaurant in Nags Head. But the menu is slightly different here — and Keeper's Galley serves breakfast, lunch and dinner year round seven days a week.

Breakfast, which is available until noon, features waffles, eggs, pancakes, country ham, grits, toast, biscuits, vegetarian breakfast sandwiches and fish roe stirred into eggs. For lunch, try a Reuben, cold plate, shrimp or tuna sandwich, homemade seafood stew or a big bowl of clam chowder. Dinner entrees change daily but include such regular offerings as prime rib, crab cakes, seafood fettuccine, chicken and a surf and turf platter. For dessert, the turtle cake is simply scrumptious. Keeper's Galley has a children's menu and a full bar. Reservations aren't accepted.

Black Pelican Seafood Company

Beach Rd., MP 4½ *261-3171*

$$

This casual restaurant is in an old Coast Guard station and includes a newly enclosed deck overlooking the Atlantic. It's roomy and wide, with three separate levels, and features a huge bar with 12 TVs (see our Nightlife chapter). Hardwood floors, tongue-and-groove appointments, light gray accents, burgundy carpet and black bentwood chairs all add to the comfortable ambiance of this moderately priced eatery.

Here, gourmet pizzas are cooked before your eyes in a wood hearth oven. Steamed shellfish fresh from the sea are served at a raw bar. And an extensive selection of appetizers are made from scratch. Dinner offerings include pasta and seafood specials, grilled or blackened to suit your taste. Children's portions also are available. Black Pelican serves lunch and dinner year round, seven days a week in summer. During the off-season, the restaurant is closed Tuesdays.

Frisco's Restaurant

U.S. 158, MP 4½ *261-7833*
$$

Chefs at this restaurant pride themselves on using only fresh local seafood, choice beef, poultry and pasta. Entrees include traditional Outer Banks fish, great crab cakes and a locally popular blackened prime rib. Dinner specials change daily. And all the desserts — including three types of cheesecake — are homemade. Frisco's dining room is light and open, with greenery throughout. Well-tended terrariums and aquariums filled with fascinating tropical fish line the walls and gargantuan bar (see our Nightlife chapter). Dinner is served seven days a week during the summer. Call for off-season hours, because this restaurant is open year round. A children's menu is available, and early bird prices are offered from 4:30 to 6 PM.

John's Drive-In

Beach Rd., MP 4½ *261-2916*
$ *No credit cards*

Home of the planet's best milk shakes, John's has been an Outer Banks institution for years. Some folk even drive two hours from Norfolk just to sip one of the thick fruit and ice cream concoctions — some of which won't even go through the straw. Our favorite is the chocolate-peanut butter-and-banana variety. But you'll have to sample a few first — and create some of your own combinations — before making that call for yourself.

You can't eat inside here. But plenty of picnic tables across from the ocean are scattered around the rundown-looking building. And everything is served in paper bags to go. While you're waiting for your food, check out the faded photographs of happy customers that line the salt-sprayed windows of this diner. You may even recognize a few local friends.

Besides the milk shakes and ice cream sundae treats, John's serves delicious dolphin, trout and tuna sandwiches or boats with the fish crispy-fried alongside crinkle fries. Dogs love this drive-in too. If your pooch waits patiently in the car, the worker behind the window probably will provide him or her with a free "puppy" cup of soft-serve vanilla ice cream. Ours can't think of a better treat on a hot summer afternoon.

John's drive-in is open from May through October for lunch and dinner. It's closed Wednesdays, unfortunately — we could eat there seven days a week. Call in take-out orders ahead of time.

Capt'n Franks

U.S. 158, MP 4½ *261-9923*
$ *No credit cards*

If it's been a while since you tried a real Southern hot dog, Capt'n Franks will rekindle that enjoyment. The Hess family has been serving hot dogs on the Outer Banks for more than 22 years. Just walk up to the place and you'll experience an assault on your senses you won't soon forget. The assortment of hot dog toppings here stretches the imagination. And the french fries drenched with cheese offer a different, delicious twist.

Frisco's
RESTAURANT & LOUNGE
• Courtesy Van
• Karaoke
• Great Dinner Specials
• Early Bird Menu
• Children's Menu
• Open Year Round
(919) 261-7833
Milepost 4½, 158 Bypass Kitty Hawk, NC 27949

Steamed shrimp is available by the pound during the evening. And the grilled tuna dinners with hushpuppies and coleslaw also are popular options. Capt'n Franks has picnic tables outside and booths, tables and a bar inside, or order any item for take-out. Call ahead for carry-outs to help save time at this busy place. This extremely casual eatery is open all year — except Sundays in the winter. It's open for lunch and dinner in season and closes at 3 PM the rest of the year. Beer is served.

Kitty Hawk Pizza

U.S. 158, MP 4½ *261-3933*
$

Serving lunch and dinner year round seven days a week, this pizza joint caters to couples and crowds. It offers great pizza with all sorts of toppings and home-cooked Greek gyros and salads. Spaghetti and lasagna are other favorite entrees. A point of interest: The giant plants will boggle even botanists' minds.

This year, a new tavern opened inside Kitty Hawk Pizza, serving more than 50 kinds of microbeers in addition to imported and domestic varieties. Cheesecake, lemon pie and real Mediterranean baklava also are delicious options for dessert. The atmosphere here is comfortable — and all the people are friendly. The same family runs Tomato Patch Pizzeria in Corolla.

Tradewinds

U.S. 158, MP 4½ *261-3052*
$

If you're in the mood for Chinese food, Tradewinds serves tasty Mandarin-style dishes. The chef here is willing to cook each meal to your specification — whether you prefer lightly steamed vegetables without a sauce or a variation on the seafood, chicken and beef entrees, which are always available. Carry-out is popular here, as it is at many Chinese restaurants, but the generous portions of succulent spicy and mild meals are best enjoyed in this dimly lit eatery. Tradewinds has a full bar and is open for lunch and dinner all year.

La Fogata Mexican Restaurant

U.S. 158, MP 4½ *255-0934*
$

The Outer Banks' only traditional Mexican restaurant, La Fogata got its name from the Spanish word for "campfire." All the owners, waiters and cooks are Mexican natives, but they speak fluent English. We think they serve the best ethnic food for the price on the beach. After two years, people still wait in line to eat here on weekend nights.

Airy, bright and decorated with paper piñatas, the interior of this ultra-casual eatery usually hums with Latin tunes; an authentic mariachi band plays here frequently. Tables and booths all are set with bowls of slightly spicy homemade salsa, and the waiters never stop filling the baskets of crispy tortillas they serve as soon as they distribute the menus. Beware: We often fill up on chips and this authentic salsa before the meals arrive. All entree portions are generous, so save some room for the main course. Other appetizers we enjoy include the hot queso (cheese) dip and stuffed jalapeño peppers.

Specialties here are fajitas, beef and chicken tacos, enchiladas and chile rellenos. The cooks make the dishes hot or mild, depending on your desire. And selections come in every possible combination, vegetarian varieties and à la carte if you want to try one of everything. (Actually, that's impossible here. The menu has more than 36 dinner selections — many starting at $6.) A full bar offers a wide selection of Mexican, American and imported beers. And mixed-drink and Margarita prices are among the lowest on the beach. La Fogata is open for lunch and dinner year round, seven days a week.

Da Kine Hawaiian Kitchen

U.S. 158, MP 4½ *261-3169*
$

With one wall covered by a mural of a Hawaiian bay and the rest flecked with surfing photos and memorabilia, this year-old eatery offers a glimpse and taste of the Pacific islands for which it's named. Japanese breaded chicken strips, Korean beef barbecue and several authentic Hawaiian rib, chicken and shrimp dishes are among the menu's most popular items. The cook also serves crispy fried wontons, Hawaiian-style Kahlua pig, Phillipino flavored egg rolls and good old American hamburgers. Shaved ice in a variety if exotic flavors is a cool, refreshing dessert after the well-spiced food. You can eat in here or take any item to go. Lunch and dinner are served year round on disposable plates. This Hawaiian kitchen is closed Sundays. Reservations aren't accepted.

Primavera's Pastaria

East Kitty Hawk Rd., between the highways *261-1198*
$$

White tablecloths on every table, Frank Sinatra tunes playing softly in the background, bunches of grapes, ivy vines and thick burgundy carpet add to the casual yet upscale ambiance for this new pastaria. And there's a low, intimate bar where eight types of draft beer and an extensive selection of wines are available and speciality coffee drinks are made after dinner.

Specializing in Italian pasta dishes, Primavera's serves three tortellini entrees, three types of seafood lasagna, fresh veal, chicken, homemade ravioli, meatballs, fresh-made Italian sweet sausage, clams, antipasto and all sorts of sauce over all styles of made-on-the-premises pasta. Each entree can be tailored to vegetarian tastes. And the pesto ravioli appetizer with ricotta cheese or fried calamari strips are sure palate pleasers from the appetizer list. For dessert, try the best lemon icebox pie in town. All portions are big enough to fill even the heartiest appetite — and usually a take-out container too. Reservations are accepted. Dinner is served seven nights a week year.

Stack 'em High

U.S. 158, MP 4½ *261-8221*
$

Hearty breakfasts served cafeteria-style off steam tables await patrons of this Outer Banks pancake house. See our write-up of the Kill Devil Hills location. Breakfast is served until noon from early spring through Thanksgiving. A limited sandwich menu also is offered.

Hushpuppies

Many seafood restaurants on the Outer Banks serve a basket of hushpuppies with each entree. Hushpuppies are a traditional Southern deep-fried cornmeal bread with a crispy coating on the outside. A batter of corn meal, flour, baking powder, salt, sugar, egg and milk is dropped by the spoonful into deep hot fat and allowed to fry until it turns golden brown.

In some Southern areas, cooks add finely chopped onion to the mix, and the hushpuppies are fried in the same oil used to fry fish. But quintessential Outer Banks hushpuppy cooks forego the onion and fishy hint in favor of a sweeter, almost cake-like quality achieved by increasing the flour and sugar ratio and frying in oils reserved just for hushpuppies.

Hushpuppies vary in diameter as well as sweetness. Some cooks believe the size of the round crispy breads is the secret to their texture and taste. Others guard their batter recipes in the conviction that they have discovered the perfect hushpuppy formula. Many restaurants on these barrier islands have loyal followers who are convinced their favorite eatery's hushpuppies are the best around. To tell the truth, few restaurants make hushpuppies from scratch anymore. There are excellent commercial mixes that get "doctored" so that the cook can claim it as his or her own. The quantitative and qualitative difference actually is often very small.

Hungry hunting dogs would hang around the kitchen and bark for their share of the food. The harried cooks, trying to finish supper for a waiting family, attempted to appease the dogs with bits of corn bread batter dropped into the hot frying fat. They tossed the little fried dough balls out the door to the dogs, admonishingly adding, "Hush, puppy!"

After dining out, we still like to bring a few hushpuppies home to our pets in doggie bags that most waitresses will provide. Instead of quieting the pooches, however, these tasty morsels often leave our happy dogs barking for more.

Kill Devil Hills

Coastal Cactus

Seagate North Shopping Center
U.S. 158, MP 5 *441-6600*
$

Three years ago, Jim and Deby Curcio opened this casual eatery to bring authentic, affordable Southwestern cuisine to the Outer Banks. They prepare all their food from scratch daily using fresh vegetables and meats and hot-off-the-stove tortillas. Start your meal with nachos piled high on the plate and covered with cheese and homemade salsa. Or bite into a crab and cheese quesadilla to get your taste buds ready for treats still to come.

For an entree, select their signature dish: sizzlin' fajitas — served still smoking in a cast iron skillet. You can choose from shrimp, steak, tuna, chicken or vegetarian combinations to fill them. Other offerings include tacos, enchiladas, burritos, chiles rellenos and tequila-lime shrimp. Desserts all are tempting — and retain the Tex-Mex theme. Fried ice cream, banana chimichangas and coconut caramel flan are just some of the sweets from which you can choose.

Drinks are among our favorite features at the Cactus. The golden

Margaritas are marvelous. And there are several other fresh-fruit varieties to sample. Wine, beer and other mixed drinks also are available in this peach and teal colored restaurant accented with Southwestern pottery, wicker, piñatas and colorful blankets. A children's menu is provided. A Southwestern general store here features Navajo pottery, Hopi jewelry, hot sauces and other unusual gift items. The Coastal Cactus is open year round seven days a week for lunch and dinner.

JK's Ribs

U.S. 158, MP 5¼
at the Grass Course *441-9555*
$

Long-known for serving the best pork ribs on the beach, JK's originally opened in the early 1980s — but the restaurant burned down several years later. Now, JK and his gang are back in a tiny eatery located at the Grass Course. And they're again serving those baby back ribs that have made mouths water for years. There's no table service here — you have to call in carry-out orders or pick up your own plate from the counter. A few tables allow you to eat inside, and outdoor tables are available too. Besides ribs, which are smothered in his famous dry spice so you don't have to deal with sloppy sauce, JK's serves grilled and roasted chicken, hamburgers, cold salads, cole slaw, red beans, freshly baked corn bread and thick brownies. Beer and wine are available. You can eat lunch and dinner here year round — including late night suppers. Delivery also is available. Reservations are not accepted.

Henry's Beef & Seafood Restaurant

U.S. 158, MP 5½ *261-2025*
$

Locals love this low-priced, homey restaurant that has been serving breakfast, lunch and dinner for seven years. Omelets, hot cakes and egg combinations are filling ways to start the day, and they're served until 1 PM for late-risers. Lunch entrees include hamburgers, a variety of sandwiches, seafood platters and several homemade soups. For dinner, there's prime rib, fried oysters, chicken dishes, pasta, shrimp, scallops, soft-shell crabs in season, flounder, trout, clam strips and daily specials. The hot fudge cake, apple pie and cheesecake all are rich and decadent dessert options.

There's nothing fancy about Henry's.

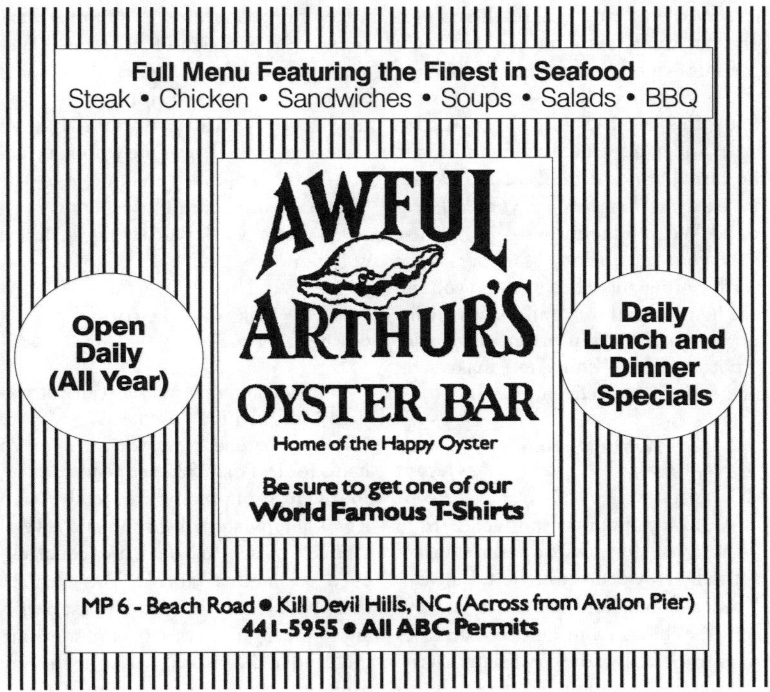

Diners eat at low booths lining the walls or on paper placemats spread across bare table tops. But the food is hearty and filling, and the prices are extremely affordable. Beer, wine and mixed drinks are served here. Reservations are accepted for large parties. And all-you-can-eat dinners are offered daily for $10.95. Henry's is open year round, seven days a week.

Chilli Peppers

U.S. 158, MP 5½ *441-8081*
$$

Southwestern fusion cooking comes alive in this fun, always bustling restaurant. Owners Bryan Oroson and Jim Douglas have worked in Outer Banks eateries for years. Finally, they teamed up their talents in 1993 to bring some of the most creative cooking around to their own tables. If hot and spicy is your style, you'll be wowed by their wild collaborations. If you prefer a more mild meal, they can do that too — and still tickle some untapped taste buds. The menu here changes frequently, with daily lunch and dinner specials sometimes stunning even regulars. Some of our favorite entrees are the scallops, steak, shrimp, pork and quail combinations, each as tastefully presented as they are tasty. Chef Damon Krasauskas, who graduated from the Baltimore International Culinary College, always comes up with something exciting. The nachos appetizer is a meal in itself.

A full bar separate from the cozy dining room offers fresh-fruit Margaritas, a nice wine selection and more than a dozen varieties of bottled beer. Nonalcoholic fruit smoothies also are a great bet in the early afternoon. Try sipping one on the outdoor deck. Steamed seafood and veggies are served until closing. And there's usually something going on here late night (see our Nightlife chapter). Chilli Peppers is an extremely progressive restaurant with a laid-back feel. Cacti, wooden chairs and handpainted accents all add to the casual atmosphere. Lunch and dinner are served here seven days a week year round. Weekend brunches — featuring a make-your-own bloody Mary bar — are worth getting out of bed for. And you can take home a bottle of Chilli's award-winning original hot sauce, barbecue sauce or hot salt. The T-shirts, too, make great memorabilia of a delicious meal.

Awful Arthur's

Beach Rd., MP 6 *441-5955*
$$

An always-popular spot across from Avalon Pier, this raw bar and restaurant is usually crowded throughout the year. Wooden booths and tables are laid out along the oblong room, and a bar stretches the entire length of the downstairs eatery. Upstairs, a separate lounge offers an ocean view. A live lobster tank and huge saltwater reef tank also offer interesting sea creatures to watch as you dine.

Arthur's is an incredibly casual place where you won't mind peeling seasoned shrimp or picking the meat from succulent crab legs with sticky fingers. Seafood is the speciality here: Everything from scallops and oysters to clams, mussels and homemade crab cakes. The bartenders are some of the fastest shuckers in town. Bass Ale and several other varieties of beer are on tap, or you can order from a full line of liquor and speciality drinks. And for landlubbers, several non-seafood sandwiches are served.

At night, Arthur's is almost always packed (see our Nightlife chapter). A late-night menu is available. And Mondays are Locals' Nights, featuring drink and food specials all day. Arthur's T-shirts have been seen all over the world and account for a good percentage of the restaurant's income. This eatery is open seven days a week year round for lunch and dinner.

Carolina Seafood

Beach Rd., MP 6½ *441-6851*
$$$

For an elaborate, all-you-can-eat seafood buffet where "fried has died," try Carolina Seafood. Here, you can enjoy 25 items for less than $25 per person: salad, soups, hushpuppies, garlic crabs, crab legs, scallops, stuffed shrimp and several types of fish served baked, broiled, blackened, steamed or sautéed. You even see the whole loin of fish here. Roast beef is cut to order, and a variety of desserts are included in the price. If you're not feeling hungry enough to tackle the buffet, Carolina Seafood serves crabs, scallops, shrimp and other seafood by the basket too. A children's menu also is available. This restaurant is open seven nights a week from April through November.

Jolly Roger Restaurant

Beach Rd., MP 7 *441-6530*
$$

Serving some of locals' favorite breakfasts, this lively restaurant is open for three meals a day 365 days a year. Besides the traditional eggs, pancakes, sausage, bacon and toast, Jolly's has an in-house bakery that cooks up some of the biggest muffins

Insiders' Tips

John's Drive-In on the Beach Road in Kitty Hawk serves the world's best milk shakes. Some are so thick you can't even suck them through a straw.

and sticky buns you've ever seen. For lunch, choose from sandwiches, local seafood or daily $3.95 specials. Dinner entrees include homestyle Italian dishes, steaks, broiled and fried fish and a popular $8.95 prime rib special each Friday. All the desserts are homemade, and special orders are accepted for items to go. The food isn't fancy, but the portions are enormous. You'll have no excuse if you leave here hungry. Jolly's also offers steamed spiced shrimp in the separate bar area each afternoon and has live entertainment throughout the year (see our Nightlife chapter).

Morgan's Seafood, Grill & Yogurt

Dare Centre, U.S. 158, MP 7 *441-8267*
$ *No credit cards*

This mom-and-pop eatery is family-owned and run and has been serving breakfast, lunch and dinner from a small strip mall store for three years. Breakfasts include omelets, Danish pastries, pancakes and traditional egg offerings. For lunch, try a fresh flounder sandwich or half-pound burger that comes with french fries, cole slaw and hushpuppies. Dinner selections include seafood platters with shrimp, oysters and clams. Baskets of steamed shrimp piled high with fries also are great bets. Two types of frozen yogurt — with a full topping bar — change daily. And beer and wine also are available. Morgan's has a few booths and tables inside, and offers everything in carry-out containers too. It's open seven days a week from February through December.

New York Bagels

Dare Centre, U.S. 158, MP 7 *480-0990*
$

With 11 types of bagels baked fresh daily and seven varieties of flavored cream cheese from which to choose, this eatery serves the only authentic New York bagels on the beach. For lunch you can pile the delicious bagels high with turkey, roast beef or lox. Or try a tasty tuna melt or pizza bagel for something a little more filling. Potato and pasta salads also are served on the side. And muffins, cinnamon buns and donuts are available as breakfast alternatives. You can eat in this small, casual, counter-service style restaurant or buy a bag of bagels to go. It's open daily year round for breakfast and lunch.

Petrozza's Deli and Cafe

Dare Centre, U.S. 158, MP 7 *441-2519*
$$

Our favorite place for sandwiches, desserts and take-home dinners, Petrozza's also offers the option of eating in its casual cafe — complete with table service. Lasagna, Italian sausage with peppers, whole roasted chickens, stuffed peppers, tortellini treats, vegetarian entrees and a numerous other delicious dinners are always on hand. At least three daily specials also are served with soup or salad and huge slabs of just-baked garlic bread. For a light lunch or side dish, don't miss the sesame noodles with carrot and green pepper slivers. The cucumber and tomato salad also is fantastic. And you can't go wrong with any of the dozens of deli sandwich options. The bread is baked each day, the variety of top-quality meats and cheeses is enormous, and the cooks will be glad to create your own favorite combination if you don't see it on the extensive menu. Lunch specials, too, change daily — and start at $3.95.

Even if you're trying to squeeze into a new swimsuit, you won't want to miss dessert here. The cream cheese brownies are big enough to satisfy at least two chocoholics. The flourless chocolate torte is the richest treat in town. Carrot cake, cheesecake, pies and other delights you've never dreamed of also line the glass case out front. Trying not to drool on it is as challenging as selecting just one slice from within. Petrozza's serves several types of unusual beers and wines by the bottle and a full line of cappuccino and espresso coffee drinks. The small gourmet store here carries deli meats and cheeses, and catering is available. Daily specials are recorded on a special telephone line, 441-1642. This outstanding eatery is open seven days a week in season for lunch and dinner. Call for winter hours.

Mako Mike's

U.S. 158, MP 7 *480-1919*
$$

Opened during the summer of 1995, this is the most outrageously decorated dining establishment on the Outer Banks. The fluorescent shark fins outside, decorated with swirls, stripes and polka dots, don't even give a glimpse into what you'll see once you step inside. Some patrons have described the experience as being under water. We think it's almost like visiting an Octopus's garden — complete with three separate levels of dining, fish mobiles flying overhead, painted chairs, bright colors exploding everywhere and murals all along the deep blue walls.

The menu is big and varied. Entree salads — Greek, Thai, spinach, Caesar and fruit flavors — are popular choices. Appetizers include crab-stuffed wontons, hot crab dip and calamari. For lunch choose from seven types of wood-oven baked pizzas, a variety of hot and cold sandwiches and small seafood platters. Dinner offerings are seasoned with Mediterranean, Cajun, Oriental and other exotic spices and include nine varieties of fresh pasta, chicken, several sorts of fish, beef, pork, vegetarian stir-fries, mixed grills, scallops, shrimp and dozens of other options. For dessert, try chocolate coconut cheesecake, white chocolate mousse or the chef's special: bread pudding.

This huge restaurant caters to couples, families and large groups. A small meeting room is available for business lun-

cheons and private parties. And a separate bar serves daily frozen drink specials — in addition to dozens of bottles of beer and wine. A children's menu is provided. Lunch and dinner are available here seven days a week year round. Mako Mike's owner, Mike Kelly, also operates Kelly's Restaurant and Tavern, George's Junction and is part owner of Penguin Isle — all in Nags Head.

Third Street Oceanfront Grille

Beach Rd., MP 7, in the Sea Ranch Hotel — *441-7126*
$$$

Third Street Oceanfront Grille offers one of the few true oceanfront dining rooms on the Outer Banks. A wall of glass overlooks the Atlantic, allowing patrons at any table to get caught up in the rhythm of the waves. The menu features traditional Outer Banks seafood and steaks prepared with a Southern regional flare. Appetizers include fried green tomatoes with a remoulade sauce; grilled shrimp and grits with sautéed sweet peppers and red-eye gravy; and puff pastries filled with sautéed scallops, country ham, mushrooms and spinach in a chardonnay shallot cream sauce.

A children's menu and nightly specials are available. Our favorite entrees include fresh egg fettuccine with scallops and shrimp tossed with bacon, sweet peas and a garlic cream sauce; grilled center-cut pork chop with an apple pecan compote; and sesame seed-crusted wahoo with a wilted spinach and soy ginger beurre blanc. The selections and service here are superb. A traditional breakfast also is served daily. Third Street isn't open for lunch, and reservations are recommended for dinner. The restaurant is open seven days a week year round.

Goombay's Grille & Raw Bar

Beach Rd., MP 7½ — *441-6001*
$$

A fun place for food, drinks and just hanging out, Goombay's is owned by John Kirchmier, a 14-year veteran of Outer Banks restaurants and bars. This island-style eatery is light and bright inside, with plenty of cool artwork, an outrageous fish tank and a wall-size tropical mural in the dining room. The ambiance is upbeat and casual, with wooden tables and chairs and a bare, tile floor. The horseshoe-shape bar, which is separate from the eating area, is a great place to try some of the delicious appetizers or drink specials Goombay's serves. We especially recommend the spicy crab balls and sweet coconut shrimp. And some of the drink offerings — both alcoholic and children's cocktails — come with zany toys to take home.

For lunch or dinner, try a fresh pasta entree, locally caught seafood, a juicy burger topped as you wish, Southwestern sampling or one of the half-dozen daily specials that range from pork to barbecued shrimp and steak stir-fry. Everything here is reasonably priced and flavorful. A raw bar is open until 1 AM, serving steamed shrimp, oysters, vegetables and other favorites. Key lime pie is always a smart choice for dessert. Other great goodies change daily. Goombay's is open for lunch and dinner year round, seven days a week (see our Nightlife chapter).

Quagmire's

Beach Rd., MP 8 *441-9188*

$$

With two oceanfront decks, an upstairs snack bar and large downstairs dining room overlooking the Atlantic, Quagmire's opened just in time for the 1996 summer season. It's in the old Croatan Inn, where Papagayo's used to be. And it's owned and operated by John Kirchmier, who's already locally revered at Goombay's Grille.

This casual restaurant caters to almost every dining whim. If you're sunning yourself on the beach midday and start to hear your stomach grumble, you can get lunch to go from the upstairs grill without even putting on shoes or throwing a shirt over your wet bathing suit. If you'd rather wait to dress for dinner, you'll feel well cared for — and fed — in the casual downstairs dining room. The giant U-shape bar upstairs provides a great place to watch the waves — and sip some of the best Margaritas on the beach. There's a kid's menu and special treats just for the little ones. A volleyball court, horseshoe pit and even ring toss are set up in the sand behind this eatery in case the younger set gets bored while their folks dawdle over dinner. Don't be misled, though: Those games also are open to adults.

The menu here features Papagayo's famous fiesta dip and 10 of John's favorite items from the former tenant's Southwestern seafood fare. Crab enchiladas, broccoli and almond quesadillas, veggie burritos and several daily specials range from $5 to $17. John also said he has some surprises in store with newfangled fare designed just for Quag's. Fresh, fabulous desserts change often. And live acoustic music is offered throughout the summer (see our Nightlife chapter). Quagmire's is open seven days a week for lunch and dinner in season. Call for winter hours.

Port O' Call Restaurant & Gaslight Saloon

Beach Rd., MP 8 *441-7484*

$$$

This antique-adorned restaurant offers continental cuisine with entrees such as broiled shrimp stuffed with crabmeat and an array of seafood, veal, chicken, pasta and beef. Blackboard specials change nightly. Each dinner comes with fresh baked bread, fruit and salads. The soups and chowders here are hot and succulent, and all the desserts are decadent. A children's menu also is offered.

Frank Gajar opened the restaurant 20 years ago, decorating it with a collection of Victorian furnishings. The dining room is warm and romantic, with flickering gas

Insiders' Tips

Soft-shell crab sandwiches are a delight in spring and early summer. Just eat them, spidery legs and all. You don't have to do any picking to get at the meat in these crustaceans.

lights and brass accents. Port O' Call doesn't serve lunch, but there's a Sunday brunch buffet that lasts until 1:30 PM and special early bird dinners are served from 5 to 6:30 PM. Live entertainment is offered in a large, separate saloon (see our Nightlife chapter). A full bar is available, and the gift shop/art gallery carries unusual, eclectic items (see our Arts and Culture chapter). Port O' Call is open from mid-March through December.

The Thai Room

Oceanside Plaza, Beach Rd.
MP 8½ *441-1180*
$$

Jimmy lets his patrons choose their own level of spice — from mild to blow-your-brains-out. When he asks, "Very hot?" think twice. He means it. In addition to the daily specials, the cooks have added a new buffet dinner so you can sample several of the wonderful offerings. More than a dozen American-style desserts are available. As for decor, it is unlike any other on North Carolina's barrier islands: authentically Thai with paper lanterns, Oriental portraits and red-tasseled lamps. Family members prepare and serve each delectable meal — and they'll be happy to make suggestions if you're overwhelmed by all the options. The Thai Room is open for lunch and dinner March through December. All items also are available for carry-out. And the restaurant has a full bar where you can indulge in exotic drinks and Chinese beer while you wait for a table or take-out order.

Four Flags Restaurant

Beach Rd., MP 8½ *480-3733*
$$

Located in the former Mex-Econo building, which also once served as the Kill Devil Hills town hall, this family-owned eatery offers filling, reasonably priced meals for breakfast, lunch and dinner. Eggs, pancakes, hash browns and other early morning staples are available until 1 PM for late sleepers. Lunch and dinner entrees include Italian-style recipes of seafood, chicken, spaghetti, lasagna and other varieties of pasta. Prime rib is available every night, and daily specials include lobster, tuna and crab imperial.

Children have their own menu here. Vegetarian offerings are always available. The decor is casual and comfortable. There's a full bar — complete with kiddie cocktails. Four Flags is open seven days a week year round.

Van's Pizza

U.S. 158, MP 9 *441-5534*
$

Van's has been serving subs, spaghetti and a variety of pizzas to its Outer Banks customers for more than 20 years and offers the only lunch and dinner pizza buffet on the beach. This ultra-casual eatery also has a full salad bar and offers wine and beer. Desserts include pineapple cheesecake, cookies-and-cream cheesecake and apple pie. All items can be eaten in or carried out. Lunch and dinner are available seven days a week year round.

Bob's Grill

U.S. 158, MP 9 *441-0707*
$ *No credit cards*

The Outer Banks' only all-night grill, Bob's is open year round for breakfast, lunch and dinner. During the summer it also stays open from dinner straight through breakfast the next day from Wednesday through Saturday. Bob serves big, cheap breakfasts year round seven days a week until 3 PM daily — and that's hard to find around here. The blueberry pancakes are so big they fill a whole plate. Eggs are made any way you want 'em. And the hash browns flavored with onions and peppers are some of the best around.

For lunch, try a hamburger, tuna steak or one of several traditional hot and cold sandwiches. Owner Bob McCoy cooks much of the food himself. Dinners feature the biggest cuts of prime rib on the

Outer Banks, Cajun beer batter-dipped shrimp and fresh mahimahi caught just offshore. The selection of salads is also good here. And you gotta save room for the hot fudge brownie dessert.

Bob's is a low-key, casual place with vinyl booths and a few posters tacked onto the walls. Service is fast and friendly, beer and wine are available and everything can be ordered for carry-out. This grill closes from 3 to 5 PM daily, but it's open for three meals a day every day all year.

Chardo's

U.S. 158, MP 9 *441-0276*
$$

A quiet, fine restaurant specializing in seafood and meats with regional flavors of Italy, Chardo's serves an array of entrees and plenty of homemade pasta. Veal chops are a speciality here, cut to order on the premises. There's a $9.95 steak and pasta special each Tuesday, Thursday and Saturday. And a pasta buffet is open throughout the winter for $7.95 per plate. Fresh sautéed or steamed vegetables and warm bread accompanies every entree.

Salads here are prepared with originality and flair. They include an interesting combination of garden vegetables and flavorful homemade dressings. The tableside Caesar salad especially is delicious. A full bar is set apart from the dining area. Chardo's wine list features top California and Italian varieties, and a coffee bar also is on hand for after dinner speciality drinks. And all the desserts are made daily; try a cannoli, tiramisu or napoleon for the perfect ending to a delightful dinner. Children can purchase half-portions of any entree for half-price. Several smaller rooms set off from the main dining area provide an intimate atmosphere for special occasions.

Chardo's is open all year for lunch and dinner. Cooking classes are offered sporadically here as well. Call for winter hours.

Stack 'em High

U.S. 158, MP 9 *441-7064*
$ *No credit cards*

This 15-year-old pancake house serves breakfast 'til noon daily from early spring through Thanksgiving. Owned by Kiki and Perry Kiousis, who also have a Kitty Hawk location, Stack 'em High serves several varieties of pancakes, blueberry muffins, seasonal fruit selections, Danish pastries, cereal and eggs however you like them. Juice and coffee also are available.

Dirty Dick's Crab House

Beach Rd., MP 9 *480-3425*
$$

Celebrating its second summer on the beach, this unusual carry-out-only eatery also delivers everything on the menu. If you're tired of calling in for pizza or subs, why not try a dinner of steamed blue crabs, shrimp, snow crab legs, crab cakes or clams tonight — cooked and spiced to order and brought directly to your door? Clam chowder, jambalaya, corn on the cob, hushpuppies and even soft-shell crabs are served in season. Crabs can be bought by the bushel too. And owner Mark Bradford even caters large parties. All the seafood (except the snow crab legs) is caught around the Outer Banks, so you know it's fresh. All meals are cooked on site. Dirty Dick's is open seven days a week for lunch and dinner in summer. Call for off-season hours.

Dare Devil's Authentic Pizzeria

Beach Rd., MP 9 *441-6330*
$

This pizza parlor has been in business for more than a decade and is known for its superb strombolis and hand-tossed pizzas. Chicken wings, mozzarella sticks, nachos, Greek salads and pizza bread also are available here. And Dare Devil's has four types of beer on tap — served in frosty glass mugs. The interior is low-key, with wooden tables and a long bar where you can eat. A big-screen TV in the corner features whatever hot sporting event happens to be going on. And you can also order any item to take out. Dare Devil's is open seven days a week for lunch and dinner from March through November.

Dip-n-Deli

Beach Rd., MP 9¼ 441-4412
$ *No credit cards*

The perfect place for a healthy, quick, inexpensive lunch, this deli serves fresh tuna salad chock-full of chunky white fish, homemade chicken salad with just enough mayonnaise, veggie pitas with hummus and sprouts, chef's and Greek salads and a variety of cold plates. The Sou'wester — a thick sandwich of grilled wheat bread loaded with smoked turkey, Muenster cheese, mustard and hot peppers — is one of our favorites. And all their homemade soups could make a meal in themselves. The jalapeño poppers here are stuffed with three types of cheese.

And the homemade cookies, Key lime pie and old-fashioned milk shakes are fantastic. For an unusual dessert treat, try the locally revered bumbleberry pie, bursting with rhubarb, apples, blackberries and raspberries. It's a taste sensation. Several flavors of hand-dipped Breyer's ice cream also are on hand. Dip-n-Deli serves beer and wine, and everything in this casual eatery is available to eat in or take out. You can even get boxed lunches for fishing trips or beach picnics, and party platters are made to order. This enjoyable diner is open seven days a week for lunch year round. Dinner hours are offered through the summer.

Etheridge Seafood Restaurant

U.S. 158, MP 9½ 441-2645
$$

The Etheridge family has long been synonymous with Outer Banks seafood, operating a commercial fishing fleet and wholesale fish company from the deep-draft docks in Wanchese. This 10-year-old restaurant serves almost all its fish right off the boats — so you know it's fresh. The casual, round dining room is nautically themed as well.

This is a real family-style restaurant where the waitresses never stop pouring iced tea and the food — though cooked to order — always seems to come fast. This is an ideal place to sample traditional Outer Banks-style seafood. For lunch, try a seafood pizza served with red or white garlic sauce. The Mill Landing egg rolls won the Wanchese Seafood cook-off several years ago and will win your approval too; it's stuffed with black olives, scallops, shrimp and fresh vegetables rolled into a slightly crisp shell. Crab cakes here are divine, filled with fresh white meat and bursting with flavor. The sweet hushpuppies are, in our opinion, some of the best on the beach.

For dinner, a five-course early bird special is served for $13.95 each day. Blackened Cajun crawfish with tomato basil sauce, broiled or fried platters with a sampling of several types of seafood and any of the traditional fish specials are sure to please. Landlubbers, too, will find something to their liking here with several beef and chicken entrees from which to choose. The soups make great starters. And each evening meal comes with a basket of crackers, a crock of cheddar cheese and the best seafood cheese spread you've ever tasted. There's even a children's menu, and a full bar is set off from the dining area. Etheridge's is open for lunch and dinner seven days a week from March through December.

Pigman's Bar-B-Que

U.S. 158, MP 9½ *441-6803*
$

Pigman's rib-man, Bill Shaver, is locally famous for his corny cable television commercials. He's also known for serving succulent North Carolina-style barbecue — and walking his pet potbelly pigs around town. At this counter-service eatery, you can get beef, pork, turkey, chicken, tuna, ribs and even buffalo barbecue. Each entree comes with cole slaw and skinny fries and is served on disposable plates with plastic utensils. Pigman's is open for lunch and dinner seven days a week, year round.

Madeline's Restaurant

Beach Rd., MP 9½ *441-6333*
$$

Located within the Holiday Inn, this restaurant serves steaks and locally caught seafood. It's a casual place that's been recarpeted, renovated and updated for the summer of 1996. A children's menu is available, and breakfast and dinner are served daily in season. Holiday Inn guests may order room service. Madeline's staff can cater banquets for up to 325 people.

Peppercorns

Beach Rd., MP 9½, in the Ramada Inn *441-2151*
$$

With a wide, open dining room overlooking the Atlantic, Peppercorns includes a new team of chefs that Ramada Inn Food and Beverage Director Michael Sullivan assembled for the 1996 summer season. Adrian Swicegood, a local culinary icon for years, is the sous chef. Mark Pennington offers multi-ethnic foods and aromatic Mediterranean dishes as the chef de cuisine. And Executive Chef Erik Speer brings a cosmopolitan flair to the entire menu with innovative appetizers, healthy, grilled entrees and an array of finely crafted desserts.

Outer Banks favorites including Hatteras-style chowder, locally caught shrimp and crab cakes top the menu. But unusual dishes flavored with saffron, curry, Thai spices and chiles also will tempt those with extraordinary tastes. Pork, tender chicken and imported fish such as talapia are available. And each meal is served with several artfully prepared vegetables and a basket of interesting breads. Vegetarian entrees always are offered. There's a full bar here, and a children's menu. You'll especially want to save room for Erik's painted-plate desserts, some of which are so carefully manicured they appear as masterpieces after the artistically arranged meals. Peppercorn's provides take-out food and room service for Ramada guests. This restaurant is open daily year round for breakfast, lunch and dinner. Custom catering also is available for events of any size.

Impacciatore's Italian Cafe

Sea Holly Square, Beach Rd.
MP 9½ *441-1533*
$$

Fresh seafood, veal, beef, poultry and gourmet pastas all are served here in an elegant Italian atmosphere. Appetizers and breads are fresh and innovative. And daily specials augment the intriguing menu. Impacciatore's has a full bar, and it serves a variety of wines by the glass or bottle. Impacciatore's is open seven days a week in season for dinner only.

Miller's Seafood and Steakhouse

Beach Rd., MP 9½ *441-7674*
$$

A family-style, moderately priced restaurant, Miller's serves breakfast and dinner daily from March through November. Breakfasts include a 99¢ special of two eggs and toast. Pancakes, hash browns, sausage and other early morning standards also are on the menu. For dinner, there's a full raw bar with a wide range of shellfish, crab cake entrees, rib eye steaks, filet mignon, prime rib and all sorts of fish. Salads, bread, potatoes and fresh vegetables come with each meal; desserts are homemade and plentiful. The restaurant has a full bar and a children's menu.

Flying Fish Cafe

U.S. 158, MP 10 *441-6894*
$$

Opened just in time for the summer 1996 season, this delightful new restaurant is owned by George Price, who helped manage Penguin Isle for the past eight years. Price purchased the former Osprey Island Grille, sandblasted off its pink and teal exterior and added his own special touches — and dishes — to create an island eatery serving an array of American and Mediterranean dishes. The interior is spruce green and adobe white with purple accents. Brightly colored tablecloths adorn each table, illuminated by sconce wall lights crafted from wine boxes and by candles set in the center of each table or booth.

Chefs at Flying Fish roll their own pasta daily and offer an array of seafood, vegetarian and non-traditional toppings for the scrumptous noodles. In addition, gourmet pot pies, salmon and roasted chicken are always on the menu. Fresh fish is served four ways each night. And there's an Angus filet mignon and pork chops with carmelized onions for meat lovers. All entrees come with a starch of the day, vegetables and just-baked bread. Appetizers include Portobello mushrooms stuffed with shrimp, two types of soup, oysters Florentine, hot seafood dip and a pizza of the day. For dessert, try to resist the Grecian Urn — a waffle filled with ice cream and topped with glazed fresh fruit and whipped cream. Chocoholics will love the chocolate hurricane, a bed of white chocolate with dark chocolate swirled through the top.

Lunch specials are served daily. And more than 40 types of wine are served by the bottle or glass. A children's menu also is available. Early-bird dinner specials are discounted from 5 to 6 PM. The Flying Fish offers lunch and dinner every day year round. Reservations are recommended for dinner at this casual, innovative restaurant.

Ship's Wheel

Beach Rd., MP 10 *441-2906*
$

Home of the world's largest pancakes — and breakfast combinations served on cafeteria-sized trays — this down-home eatery only serves the first meal of the day. But the low-priced portions on these gargantuan plates will fill you up until supper. French toast, eggs, omelets, sausage, bacon and good, strong coffee are offered until noon seven days a week from March through October.

Colington Island

Colington Cafe

Colington Rd., 1 mile west of U.S. 158 — *480-1123*

$$

Step back in time at this cozy Victorian cafe, nestled among live oaks on Colington Road. This popular restaurant is only a mile off the Bypass. But once you've arrived, you'll feel worlds away from the bustling beach. It's tranquil and absolutely lovely in this restored old home set high on a hill. This is our favorite place to come for an intimate dinner — and the chefs prepare some of the most marvelous meals around for extremely reasonable prices. Three small dining rooms each are adorned in tasteful decor. There's a separate bar upstairs where you can sip a glass of wine or imported beer while waiting for your table. Even the black painted plates are unusual and artistic.

Hot crab dip slathered on buttery crackers and bowls of homemade crab bisque are each outstanding appetizers. Daily specials include wonderful pasta dishes, a mixed grill with hollandaise and the freshest filet mignon available. Seafood entrees change depending on what's just been caught. Only fresh herbs and vegetables are used in cooking and as side dishes. Salads are served à la carte. Owner Carlen Pearl's French heritage permeates her restaurant's delicious cream sauces. And Carlen makes most of the irresistible desserts herself — from blackberry cobbler to chocolate tortes and crème brûlée. Colington Cafe is open for dinner only seven days a week in summer. The restaurant closes in January and is open on weekends during the spring and fall. Reservations are highly recommended.

Zanzibar

Colington Rd., 2 miles west of U.S. 158 — *480-3116*

$$$

This upscale fondue eatery offers an entire evening of entertainment. It's the perfect place for a couple — or two — to enjoy each other's company and some unusually prepared food. The view of Kitty Hawk Bay is fantastic from the covered front deck, especially at sunset. We suggest you get there a half-hour before you're ready to eat so you can enjoy one of the rare microbrews or sample some wine outdoors before dining.

Inside, there's a quiet, intimate atmosphere with fondue pots and hot stone grills in the center of the tables. Waitresses and waiters help cook the chicken, tuna, shrimp, beef and fresh vegetables in herb bouillon poured into your pot, but you have to select one of the dozen or more specially devised sauces that come with every meal. It's great fun to find different taste sensations with each bite. And owner Trisha Krolick changes her sauce combinations nightly, so no two dinners are ever quite the same.

We like to make a meal of the cheddar and Swiss cheese fondue appetizers, served with a half-dozen types of bread. That way, we've got plenty of room left for the dark, white or milk chocolate fondue desserts. Slices of bananas, pineapples, pound cake, strawberries and marshmallows each come up dripping with the rich chocolate. It's the perfect way to end an enjoyable meal.

Zanzibar, which gets its name from a place on the African coast where strange spices are exported all across the globe, is open for dinner only seven days a week in season. It's open weekends during the fall and spring.

Bridges Seafood Restaurant

Colington Rd., 3 mile west of U.S. 158 — *441-6398*

$$

Kristina Bridges offers some of the freshest seafood around in this small frame house surrounded by a rose garden on Colington Road. No wonder. Her father,

Kid Friendly Restaurants

Here is a list of Outer Banks spots we've found to be especially kid-friendly, whether it's for the menu or the atmosphere.

The Full Moon Cafe

The Waterfront, Manteo *473-MOON*

While this is a small restaurant, it is definitely kid-friendly, with a menu that features children's selections including the noodlehead, grilled cheese, Mexican grilled cheese, pita pizza and black beans and rice. The proprietor, Sharon Enoch, is a mom so she has a lot of patience with a cafe full of children. When dining here you also have the option to eat on the patio out front. This allows the children some room to wander.

The Seafare Restaurant

U.S. 158 MP 13½ *441-5555*

If you have to wait to be seated here, you'll have no problem with the children. The restaurant features a wonderful outdoor play-yard that will supply plenty of distraction. Adults can sit under umbrella tables and chat while kids burn off excessive energy.

Horseshoe Cafe

Corolla Light Village Shops *453-8463*

It's hard to wait for food no matter how old you are. Horseshoe Cafe makes it easier by supplying crayons and coloring material for the kids. A children's menu is available at this Southwestern Tex-Mex Cafe.

Tortuga's Lie

Beach Rd., MP 11 *441-RAWW*

Kids will enjoy their stop at Tortuga's Lie for the ceiling covered in license plates — a great little distraction. But it will be those exciting Shark Bite drinks that keeps them coming back! Sitting upright in the juice drink is a toy shark filled with grenadine — hence the shark bite!

Goombay's Grille & Raw Bar

Beach Rd., MP 7½ *441-6001*

Kids can order drinks here that are Goombay's version of classics. The Shirley Shark, for example, is a typical Shirley Temple with a shark added to it. Prehistoric Punch (fruit juices) comes with a toy dinosaur. And don't miss the Elephant's Foot filled with orange soda.

The Weeping Radish

U.S. 64, Manteo *473-1157*

Kids will want to stop at The Weeping Radish restaurant's great playground, situated under a cool canopy of trees. Nearby is the bright red Gingerbread House where you can buy ice cream and goodies.

Murray Bridges, runs one of the biggest crab and seafood dealerships on the Outer Banks from the lot next door. So she gets the cream of his crustacean crop to cook up at her restaurant. There's a covered, outdoor porch off the side of the restaurant — a perfect place to have a drink while waiting to dine. Inside, seafood is served with a French and Italian flair, with nine nightly dinner specials in addition to the regular menu. Pasta entrees especially are always inventive. And steaks, chicken and children's portions also are served. Desserts, too, are worth saving room for. Bridge's is open from April through November seven nights a week for dinner.

Nags Head

The Fish Market

U.S. 158, MP 9½ *441-7889*
$

Serving traditional Outer Banks seafood in a down-home fish house atmosphere, this low-key restaurant has some of the friendliest employees in town. It's been open for 17 years and has always been a favorite with locals and watermen. Lunch specials such as meat loaf, fish cakes and chicken and dumplings all taste just like Grandma used to make 'em. Dinner entrees from shrimp to tuna to mahimahi each come with hushpuppies and two vegetables. The clam chowder is among the best on the beach. And you won't want to skip dessert: chocolate turtle cake, Key lime pie and apple crunch are our favorites.

Besides the restaurant, which is lined with wooden chairs and tables, The Fish Market has a seafood market in its front foyer. One of the owners is a commercial waterman, so the seafood's usually fresh out of the ocean. And there's a great Nags Head flavor about this place. A children's menu is offered. An L-shaped bar stretches around the wide room and serves all sorts of beer and mixed drinks. Live acoustic music is performed here on weekends year round (see our Nightlife chapter). This inexpensive restaurant is open for lunch and dinner seven days a week all year.

The Sands

U.S. 158, MP 10 *441-1649*
$$

You won't soon forget the cable TV commercials for this local favorite, and once you dine here, you'll understand why the spokesman — and woman — look so well fed. This restaurant features country cooking for lunch and dinner year round seven days a week. It's been serving ham and cabbage, stewed chicken, roast pork and seafood specials for seven years. Dinner entrees include Delmonico steak, prime rib, lobster tails, shrimp, tuna steaks, lemon pepper trout and daily specials. Each meal comes with unlimited trips to the salad bar, a baked potato, cole slaw, hushpuppies and a basket of rolls. Desserts such as hot fudge cake, peanut butter pie, turtle cheesecake and three types of cobblers are made each day. And a full bar and children's menu are offered. This food isn't unusual or artistic, but it's well prepared and oh-so-filling. The Sands is very casual with wide wooden tables and booths. The thing we like best about this restaurant is that it serves thick, creamy she-crab soup every day — enough to make a meal in itself.

Mrs. T's Deli

U.S. 158, MP 10, in the
Food Lion shopping center *441-1220*
$

Owned and operated by a little local lady, her sweet daughter, Shirley, and at least two grandchildren when school lets out, this homey deli is a great bet for quick, satisfying lunches and some of the friendliest chatter in town. A big color TV plays year-old movies constantly, and the largest collection of antique cookie jars we've ever seen lines three walls. You serve yourself drinks here out of a wall of coolers stocked with everything from beer and Snapple to sodas and exotic fruit drinks. Menu items are scrawled in thick magic marker strokes on paper plates and cardboard squares hung behind the cash register.

Mrs. T's soups are laden with vegetables, pulled chicken and rich broth. Most of her three dozen sandwiches are named after friends and family members who eat here. We like the Stacy sub — dripping with four types of cheese. And the three varieties of veggie burgers always get rave reviews. Club sandwiches are stacked so high they barely fit in your mouth. And all the meats and cheeses are fresh out of the deli counter — which also offers items by the half-pound or more to take home. The Outer Banks curly fries, lightly seasoned and made to order, are wonderful. And each entree comes with ripple chips and a pickle. Cakes, pastries and gourmet jellybeans are available for dessert. And lots of Kosher food, including Matzos, can be found all year. Mrs. T's serves lunch and dinner seven days a week from mid-March through early February. Everything here also can be packaged to go.

Sweetwaters

U.S. 158, MP 10½ *441-3427*
$$

Celebrating its 12th anniversary on the beach, Sweetwaters is open for breakfast, lunch and dinner from mid-March through November. It's located next to the Cineplex 4 movie theaters, so it's a convenient place to have supper before taking in a flick. Airy, bright and decorated with hanging plants and brass railings, Sweetwaters has a separate bar area where live music is performed in summer (see our Nightlife chapter).

Breakfast items include eggs Benedict and omelets filled with a half-dozen options. For lunch, there are lots of hot sandwiches, burgers, quiches, a great taco salad and daily specials such as fried chicken and fish. The onion rings are light and served in ample portions. Dinner entrees range from grilled seafood and steak to pasta dishes. Wednesdays and Sundays are prime rib nights, featuring huge cuts for $9.95. Desserts are rich and ample: Key lime pie, apple pie and hot fudge cake usually are the best bets. There's also a children's menu here.

Kelly's Outer Banks Restaurant & Tavern

U.S. 158, MP 10½ *441-4116*
$$$

Kelly's is an Outer Banks tradition and one of the most popular restaurants year round. Owner Mike Kelly gives his personal attention to every detail, so the service and selections are always first-rate. This is a large, upscale eatery and a busy place. The decor reflects the area's rich maritime heritage and includes abundant examples of fish, birds and other wildlife. The tavern is hopping seven nights a week — even during winter (see our Nightlife chapter).

Dinner is the only meal served here, and it's offered in several rooms upstairs and downstairs. Kelly's menu offers fresh seafood dishes, chicken, beef and pastas. There's a raw bar for those who enjoy feasting on oysters and other steamed shellfish. And an assortment of delicious homemade breads accompanies each meal. Kelly's sweet potato biscuits espe-

Insiders' Tips

Tortuga's Lie Restaurant in Nags Head makes the best french fries we've ever tasted.

cially are succulent — we usually ask for a second basket. Desserts are flavorful and filling. A separate children's menu is available — complete with crayons and special placemats to color. Kelly's also caters private parties, weddings and any style event imaginable. The restaurant and lounge are open seven days a week.

THE CAROLINIAN RESTAURANT

Beach Rd., MP 10½, in the Carolinian Hotel *441-7171*
$$

Serving Outer Banks guests since 1946, the Carolinian offers continental breakfasts and dinner daily during the season. Fresh seafood and nightly specials are available for supper. The restaurant has early bird discounts and a children's menu. The big dining room can easily accommodate large groups and conferences. And the outdoor tiki bar has all sorts of beer, wine and tropical drinks. Free, live music is performed here six nights a week through the summer. Dinner patrons also receive priority seating at the Carolinian's comedy club (see our Nightlife chapter).

MULLIGAN'S OCEANFRONT GRILLE

Beach Rd., MP 10½ *480-2000*
$$

Serving seafood, filet mignon and an array of pasta dishes, Mulligan's is a great place for lunch or dinner. For the summer of 1996, this restaurant is under new ownership. Occupying the old 1949 Miller's Pharmacy building, the eatery is divided in half lengthwise by wooden and glass partitions. The south end is flanked by a long, low bar reminiscent of the TV show *Cheers*. Scores of old Outer Banks photographs, painted mirrors and other memorabilia decorate this comfortable, full-service bar — where appetizers and light dinners are available.

The north half of Mulligan's is the restaurant, where excellent oysters, crab cakes, teriyaki chicken and scallops roumaki are available. Bread, a salad and potatoes or rice complete the main course, but be sure to save room for cheesecake and other delightful desserts. Live entertainment is featured here year round (see our Nightlife chapter). Mulligan's is open seven days a week all year.

IT'S PRIME ONLY

Beach Rd., MP 10½ *480-1400*
$$$

The Outer Banks' classiest steakhouse, It's Prime Only opened on New Year's Eve 1993. Owner Russell Poland has created an upscale, intimate ambiance here, complete with a beautifully furnished den-style lounge that's an elegant place to sip a glass of brandy or coffee after enjoying a marvelous meal. Comfortable couches and armchairs are arranged near a fireplace. In the dining area, tiny white lights sparkle against green plants. And candle lamps illuminate every table top.

The mainstay here, of course, is beef — from a petite filet to porterhouse, served sizzling hot on a 450-degree platter. The meat is literally crackling when it reaches your table. Other scrumptious selections include chicken, pasta, tuna, baby back ribs, lobster and salmon. Side dishes such as broccoli, creamed spinach, mushrooms and mashed potatoes are served family-style so everyone can share. It's Prime is open year round for dinner only seven days a week in season; call for winter hours.

GEORGE'S JUNCTION

Beach Rd., MP 11 *441-0606*
$$

Outside, George's Junction has a slightly exotic mystique, thanks to the unusual architecture of the former Restaurant by George. Inside, a country-western theme prevails and the food is as all-American as it gets. The dinner buffet offers 36 hot items for $17.95 per person and includes hand-carved roast beef, ham, chicken, ravioli, a variety of local seafood, a full salad bar, several varieties of bread and rolls baked daily and a delicious dessert bar. A limited menu with steaks, crab legs and pastas also is available, and breakfast is served seven days a week during summer. This place is nicely decorated and includes a large lounge with a full bar. Patrons will feel comfortable in everything from jeans to evening gowns. You can take free line dancing lessons most nights in season on a huge dance floor and listen to live country bands (see our Nightlife chapter). George's opened in June 1995 and serves dinner from March through November. Reservations are requested for parties of 10 or more.

CW's

U.S. 158, MP 11 *441-5917*
$

For more than 23 years, CW's has been serving food on the Outer Banks. Wayne Blackburn has owned this Colonial-style restaurant with the tall white columns since 1982. He offers traditionally prepared local seafood, steaks and baby back ribs for dinner only during the summer. Breakfast, which is available year round, includes pancakes, eggs, bacon, hash browns, sausage and other early morning staples starting at $1.50 per meal. There's full bar service here and separate smoking and nonsmoking rooms. Original art, on loan from Seaside Art Gallery, adorns the walls.

Tortuga's Lie

Beach Rd., MP 11 *441-RAWW*
$

Our hands-down favorite haunt on the Outer Banks, this small, upbeat eatery is housed in a turquoise and white cottage across from the ocean — near a great surf break. It's been remodeled for 1996, with an enclosed porch furnished with handmade wooden booths; an expanded bar seats more than two dozen people. There's a sand volleyball court out back where pickup games always are being played — and watched from the outdoor picnic tables. This is one of the only places around where it's truly comfortable to eat alone. The bartenders and wait staff are the friendliest folk we know. And all the food is fabulous, creatively concocted and priced incredibly reasonably. The atmosphere inside is fun and casual, with turtle-themed batiks hanging from the white walls and more than 100 license plates from across the country tacked to the low ceiling beams — some with pretty unusual personal messages.

The menu here offers everything from 'gator bites — yes, the real thing — and delicious sandwiches to scrumptious seafood flavored with outrageous spices and a full raw bar that always has something steaming. The french fries are the best we've ever had. And the coco loco chicken entree (a big breast smothered with coconut, served with a side of lime curry dipping sauce for lunch and dinner) is something we crave at least once a week. Other dinner entrees include pork medallions, steak stir-fries, just-off-the-boat tuna steaks, succulent shrimp and pasta plates. Most meals come with finely flavored rice and beans, but the cooks will substitute fries if you ask. And the full lunch menu is offered until 10 PM. Sushi is served during the off-season on Wednesday nights — and the place usually is packed with locals. Desserts also are creamy, delicious and change daily. Some of our favorites are turtle cheesecake and Tortuga's gargantuan chocolate chip cookies.

There's a full bar here with loads of speciality drinks. We also enjoy the Black and Tans — a combination of Bass Ale and Guiness — poured to almost overflowing in pint-sized glasses. If you're a beer lover and haven't discovered this duo yet, be sure to order one on your next trip to Tortuga's (see our Nightlife chapter). This hip, laid-back eatery is open seven days a week for lunch and dinner from late February through December. Call for winter hours.

Rollin' in the Dough

Pirate's Quay, U.S. 158, MP 11½ *441-6042*
$ *No credit cards*

A combination bakery and gourmet deli, this 3-year-old eatery primarily caters to take-out customers, but there are a few tables outside if you want to eat nearby. Breakfast items include French pastries, croissants, moist muffins and eight types of bread — all baked fresh each morning. The Cajun chicken salad spread on thick slices of pumpernickel is one of our favorite lunches. Other combinations, including those you dream up yourself from the fancy deli offerings, also are outstanding. And special sauces are served with almost every sandwich. An array of unusual side salads beckons patrons from the glass cases. Wine, flavored coffee and speciality cakes also are available. Catering is offered for any occasion. And you can call in orders ahead of time to have them waiting. Rollin' in the Dough is open from March through early December.

Woody's Good Time Bar & Grill

Pirate's Quay, U.S. 158, MP 11 *441-4881*
$$

One menu is available for lunch and dinner at this casual two-story eatery. Selections include steamed and smoked seafood, burgers, seafood platters, salads and more. The hot wings are spicy and tasty, and the chocolate decadence dessert is to die for. Children's items also are available. And there's a full bar here. It's open daily year round.

Pier House Restaurant

Beach Rd., MP 11½ *441-5141*
$

Offering the best ocean view on the beach, this family-style restaurant allows patrons to sit right above the ocean. You can feel the salt spray if you dine on the screened porch. And even inside the air-conditioned building, waves sometimes crash beneath the wooden floor's slats. This is a great, laid-back place to enjoy a big breakfast before a day of fishing or to take a break from angling on a hot afternoon. The staff is friendly. And all three meals of the day are traditionally prepared — Outer Banks style — and good. Lunch includes sandwiches, soups and seafood specials. All-you-can-eat dinners also are popular picks. Each entree comes with cole slaw, hushpuppies and french fries or baked potato. And you can have your fish grilled, broiled or steamed. The folks here will even clean and cook fish you catch for you. Appetizers and desserts also are available. Free sightseeing passes come with supper so you can stroll along the long pier after your meal and watch the anglers and surfers. Pier House Restaurant is open seven days a week from March through November.

The Snowbird

Beach Rd., MP 12 *480-0000*
$ *No credit cards*

This locally loved ice cream and quick-eats carry-out originally was near the old Nags Head Casino, then disappeared for a while after that hot spot shut down. The Snowbird re-opened at its current location as the Outer Banks' first Dairy Queen more than 20 years ago, and took its present name in the early 1980s. For 1996, it's under new ownership by a local couple who just moved up the beach from Manteo.

Ice cream continues to be the main draw here, with strawberry, banana, beach and pineapple shakes topping the list of fresh fruit concoctions. Parfaits, banana splits and turtle, hot fudge and brownie sundaes also are sure palate-pleasers. If you need some sustenance to supplement your sundae, try a fresh tuna, dolphin, shrimp or oyster boat, which comes with french fries. Soft-shell crab sandwiches are served here in season. And the quarter-pound "Snowburger" with mozzarella cheese is a daily special. Even Greek salads are available for vegetarians. You can carry-out any item from The Snowbird. And outdoor picnic tables shaded by umbrellas are strewn along the parking lot if you'd rather eat on the premisis. The Snowbird is open seven days a week from 11 AM to 11 PM, mid-May through September. During the peak part of summer, breakfast muffins, danishes, donuts, cereal and sausage biscuits also are served.

The Wharf

Beach Rd., MP 11½ *441-7457*
$$

You can't miss this popular beach restaurant across from the Atlantic: It's the one with the long, long line of people out front. Folks arrive early for the ever-popular all-you-can-eat seafood buffet of steamed shellfish, fried shrimp, scallops, chowder, broiled catch of the day, clam strips, barbecue, prime rib, homemade yeast rolls, loads of vegetables and desserts — all for less than $14 per person. The atmosphere is very informal. A new $4.95 children's menu offers hamburgers, hot dogs, peanut butter and jelly sandwiches, pizza, chicken tenders, a drink and all-you-can-eat dessert served on a souvenir Frisbee. Kids 3 and younger eat for free. The Wharf is open from Easter through October. Doors open at 4 PM during the summer. The Wharf is closed Sundays. Alcoholic beverages are not served here.

Country Deli

Surfside Plaza, between the highways, MP 12 *441-5684*
$ *No credit cards*

A laid-back eatery with items only available for take-out, Country Deli offers some of the biggest sandwiches on the beach. The Killer is always a hit, with ham, turkey, havarti and Muenster cheese and hot peppers spread on a sub roll. Our favorite is the Goesway, where five kinds of cheese are melted on thick slices of toast and topped with crispy strips of bacon. There's a full deli counter here, so you can create your own sandwiches. Side salads of macaroni, pasta, potato and vegetables also are served. The owner offers several types of chips à la carte, but sour pickles come free with every option. Brownies and cheesecake are tempting dessert selections. And don't leave without checking out the philosophical ponderings employees leave on the blackboard behind the cash register — they could change the way you think about the world while you're trying to decide what to order. Country Deli is open for lunch and dinner seven days a week during the summer and offers free delivery to Nags Head and Kill Devil Hills. This eatery is open for lunch only during the off-season (call for hours and days).

Jockey's Ribs

Beach Rd., MP 12½ *441-1141*
$$

This casual, family-oriented eatery serves steaks, barbecue and broasted chicken, pork chops, seafood, filet mignon, shrimp, gumbo, French onion soup, she-crab soup and, of course, delicious racks of all-pork ribs that have been pleasing patrons for more than a decade. Each entree comes with a baked potato or hash browns, rolls, salad, cole slaw and baked beans. There's a full bar here. And tasty desserts include chocolate mousse, cheesecake and peanut butter pie. Reservations aren't accepted.

Midgett's Seafood Restaurant

U.S. 158, MP 13 *480-0810*
$$

Midgett is a legendary name among Outer Banks lifesavers and watermen. The menu at this 100-seat restaurant, which opened six years ago and was built by a father-and-son team, features family recipes dating to the 1920s. The atmosphere is quiet and nautical — there's a definite family feel to the place.

Jeffrey Wade Midgett put away his tools after helping his dad, Jeffrey Gray Midgett, build the old Coast Guard-style building. He's creating equally authentic traditional beach treasures in the kitchen. From a bounty of fresh seafood entrees to ribs, chicken and beef, all the food is homestyle and hearty. Desserts also are homemade (you'll especially love the Key lime pie). Midgett's offers a separate early bird menu from 4 to 6 PM daily, and a senior citizens' menu is available too. There's a big porch along the wooden building's north side and a nice gazebo out front in case you have to wait for a table. There's also a full bar. Reservations aren't accepted. Midgett's is open for dinner seven days a week from March through Thanksgiving.

Dairy Mart

Beach Rd., MP 13 *441-6730*

$

Soft ice cream reminiscent of the 1960s is served by the barrel-full here on summer afternoons — in cups and big cones. There also are 17 scrumptious sundae combinations, including some with fresh fruit and big brownies. The "Crunchy Cougar" and "Devil Made Me Do It" are two of our favorite ice cream delights.

This is a drive-in-style eatery where you order from walk-up windows and eat at umbrella-covered picnic tables out front — or take your meal to go. Owners Ron and Carol Rodrigues also serve excellent sandwiches, grilled tuna and shrimp and clam boats, which come with fries or onion rings. Make sure you have an appetite before tackling a "Big Daddy Burger." You won't want to fill up before consuming a cool dessert. The ice cream could make a meal in itself here. Dairy Mart is open from May to October every day except Wednesdays.

Seafare Restaurant

U.S. 158, MP 13½ *441-5555*

$$

This family-owned and operated business began in Nags Head in 1959 and has been nationally known for its she-crab soup for more than 50 years. The exceedingly popular nightly buffet features a 40-item salad bar, four homemade soups, 12 vegetables, 15 types of seafood, four varieties of meat, homemade rum rolls and just-baked bread, fresh cobbler, made-from-scratch chocolate chip cookies and ice cream. Steamed shrimp, crabs, mussels, clams and scallops also are served. Snow crabs legs are one of the most popular items. And a full menu is available if you don't feel up to tackling the tantalizing buffet. The Seafare has a small bar with complete service. Dinner is served nightly from March through November. Call for off-season hours. Reservations are not accepted here, but a new outdoor playground will keep the kids entertained while you wait for a table. Be sure to ask about children's and senior citizens' discounts.

Lance's

U.S. 158, MP 14 *441-7501*

$$

Lance's is the shocking-pink restaurant on the Bypass in Nags Head. In business since 1985, Lance's is under new management in 1996. Although it's been redecorated inside and appears lighter and brighter, you'll still see lots of Outer Banks memorabilia here: decoys, trophy mounts of billfish and a 735-pound blue marlin. A new 125-gallon tropical fish tank flanks one wall, and a wood-carver often is on hand creating some of the lovely cutouts displayed around the restaurant. This is a popular spot with locals.

A new cook offers soft-shell crabs in season, fresh gamefish daily, crab imperial, oysters, clams, hard crabs, shrimp, prime rib, steak, chicken, pastas and Lance's famous whole lobsters. There's a full bar here and plenty of dessert options. A separate menu is available for kids. Lance's is open for lunch and dinner daily in the summers and only for dinner in the off-season.

Maione's

U.S. 158, MP 15 *480-3311*
$$

Owned by a New Jersey family who decided to relocate its popular Northern beach eatery to Nags Head, this new restaurant opened in 1995 and serves a variety of homemade, traditional Italian offerings. Linguine with clam sauce, fresh-baked lasagna and seafood specials are among the best selections. A huge array of pastas with flavorful sauces are always on the menu. And each entree comes with salad and bread, and you have a wide range of appetizers from which to choose. The tiramisu is sinfully delicious — and authentic — for dessert. A full bar and lounge area is separate from the dining room. Lunch and dinner are available throughout the summer seven days a week; dinner is served sporadically in the off-season. Call for fall and winter schedules.

North China Restaurant

Outer Banks Mall, north wing
U.S. 158, MP 15 *441-3454*
$

Fast, hearty Chinese food is offered here to eat in or take out. Appetizers range from hot and sour soup to crunchy egg rolls. Entrees include sweet and sour pork, kung pao chicken and Hunan delight — which includes beef, chicken and shrimp. Rice comes with every meal, and fortune cookies are given out for dessert. North China is open year round for lunch and dinner (closed Sundays). A take-out-only eatery run by the same owners is situated in front of the Wal-Mart shopping center in Kitty Hawk.

New York Bagels

Outer Banks Mall, north wing
U.S. 158, MP 15 *480-0106*
$

Owned by the same couple that runs the Kill Devil Hills operation, this storefront eatery offers take-out only and doesn't serve sandwiches. Bagels also are served by the bag for breakfast and lunch daily most of the year. Call for winter hours.

The Links Room

Off U.S. 158, MP 15½
at Nags Head Golf Links *441-8076*
$

This restaurant on the Village at Nags Head golf course offers a splendid sound view — and a chance to watch people tee-off on the links. The spacious dining room with a plate glass window wall is open year round for lunch only. There's a nice fireplace here, and classy lunches of pasta, Reubens and steak sandwiches are served daily. A full bar also is available for final rounds at the 19th hole.

Penguin Isle Soundside Grille

U.S. 158, MP 16 *441-2637*
$$$

As night falls, waterfowl begin fluttering across the low-lying marshlands of Roanoke Sound, right outside the windows of this elegant soundside restaurant. Windsurfers in the distance cruise by beneath colorful sails. And brilliant sunsets abound. The sights outside the dining room are as lovely and tranquil as the ambiance inside. Penguin Isle is truly a peaceful place to enjoy a relaxing, intimate meal.

Here, the decor is tasteful and creative, with displays of local art, hand-carved decoys, lighted authentic ship models, enormous mounted wine bottles and light wood accents around the airy dining room. White linen tablecloths cover every table, and the lights and slow jazz music are soft and low.

Penguin Isle is not only a premier place to dine — it's also a wine destination. The staff is very knowledgeable, and the much heralded *Wine Spectator's* Award of Excellence identified this restaurant's wine list as "one of the best in the world" for the past four years. Seasonal wine dinners also are offered in the off-season with advance registration. To be placed on the mailing list, call or write: Penguin Isle, P.O. Box 1898, Nags Head 27959.

A separate window-walled lounge with full bar, an abbreviated menu and small tables overlooks the sound. Patrons can also have a cocktail before dinner on the outdoor deck, and a lobby with comfortable couches affords an alternative place to await your table. Owners Mike Kelly and Doug Tutwiler combine their talents here to create a truly distinctive restaurant. Chef Lee Miller is one of only a handful of certified working chefs on the Outer Banks. And all the staff are friendly and professional.

Penguin Isle serves fresh local seafood, handmade pasta, certified Black Angus beef, chicken, duck, fresh-baked breads and many other appetizing offerings. Creative food pairings — also called fusion cookery — is the chef's specialty. But the seafood trio platter featuring fresh fish, shrimp and scallops is hard to beat. We also recommend grilled Gulf Stream tuna over homemade fettuccine. And the seafood gumbo and bean cakes are delicious

Photo: Mike Booher

Reel in your dinner at the pier. Some eateries will cook what you catch.

for starters here. Penguin Isle's portions are generous, especially for such an upscale restaurant. All the desserts, of course, are delectable.

Only dinner is served here from March through early December. Employees also will cater private parties, wedding receptions and almost any occasion on-site. A children's menu is available, and early dining specials are offered from 5 until 6 PM.

Soundside Pavilion

U.S. 158, MP 16½ *441-0535*
$$$

Upstairs in this wide, open eatery with a great view of the Roanoke Sound, an all-you-dare-to-eat surf and turf buffet is served nightly throughout the summer for $21.95 per person. Fresh fish, chicken, pasta, barbecue, oysters, clams, crab legs, vegetables, rolls, fresh-baked breads, fruit, a salad bar, homemade desserts and soft-serve ice cream all are included in the price. Prime rib is available à la carte for an additional charge. A $4.95 breakfast buffet has been added for 1996 offering eggs, pancakes, sausage, fruit, bacon, grits, French toast sticks, biscuits, sausage, ham, corned beef hash and other items — with bottomless cups of coffee — until noon. Cocktails, beer and wine are served nightly. Buses and large groups are welcome.

Windmill Point

U.S. 158, MP 16½ *441-1535*
$$$

Magnificent views of the sound at sunset, marred only by the colorful sails of windsurfers, delight diners here. Famous for its memorabilia from the elegant ocean liner SS *United States*, this restaurant provides excellent cuisine to match the outdoor sights. There are two dining areas, tastefully furnished down to the tablecloths, linen napkins and comfortable chairs that hug rather than support you. Service is fast and unobtrusive. The upstairs lounge, which features the authentic kidney-shape bar from the ship — complete with plaques from famous 1950s statesmen and actresses who sipped cocktails there — is a pleasant place to await your call to dinner.

Favorites from the menu include a seafood trio, poached or grilled with a succulent sauce; and a seafood pasta entree of lightly seasoned scallops. The chefs also prepare roasted prime rib, sautéed duck, fettuccine primavera and cappelli con scampi. Cooked with fresh herbs and creative sauces, the entrees get better each season. Windmill Point's menu features heart-healthy selections. And a children's menu is available. A private dining room was added in 1995. Dinner is served seven nights a week throughout the year.

The Island's Eye

Beach Rd., MP 16 *480-1993*
$$

This family-owned and operated restaurant opened in 1991 and offers a warm, soothing atmosphere and abundant greenery. Island's Eye is open for dinner only, serving selections such as seafood broiled, pan fried, blackened or baked; and combination platters of beef, poultry and pasta. The barbecue shrimp is great for starters. A children's menu is available, and early dining specials are offered from 4:30 to 6 PM. The restaurant has a full bar. The Island's Eye is open from early spring through fall. Call for off-season hours.

Miller's Waterfront Restaurant

U.S. 158, MP 16 *441-6151*
$$

A gorgeous sound view and moderately priced dinners are available at this two-level, waterfront restaurant. Miller's serves fried, broiled, steamed and sautéed seafood and steaks as well as raw bar staples. All the desserts are homemade. And a children's menu is offered — as well as a full bar. There's even a separate lounge for folks waiting for a table. Miller's is open March to November seven days a week.

The Dunes

U.S. 158, MP 16½ *441-1600*
$

When a large crowd or big family is gathering for a meal, this 14-year-old restaurant can accommodate everyone in its three huge dining rooms. Breakfast at The Dunes is a locals' favorite — you can tell by the packed parking lot — where every early morning entree in every imaginable combination is offered. There's also a popular breakfast bar here during weekends in the off-season and daily in the summer. Lunches include great burgers and homemade crab cakes served with fries and cole slaw. The rib-eye steak sandwich is a good choice if you've gone without breakfast — or if your beach appetite has grown.

Dinners feature local, well-prepared seafood at moderate prices and a huge salad bar. All-you-can-eat specials are selected often. And there are plenty of desserts to choose from — if you're not already too full. The Dunes serves beer and wine and has a children's menu for small fries. The service is fast and friendly. The restaurant is open from mid-February through Thanksgiving seven days a week in season (call for winter hours).

Owens' Restaurant

Beach Rd., MP 16½ *441-7309*
$$$

The oldest Outer Banks restaurant owned and operated continuously by the same family, Owens' is a local legend. In 1996, this upscale eatery is celebrating its 50th anniversary — marking a half-century of good food and good service, which are well appreciated by loyal patrons who return year after year.

Clara and Bob Owens first owned a small hot dog stand in Manteo. In 1946, they opened a 50-seat cafe in Nags Head on the deserted strip of sand that's now filled with hotels, rental cottages and thousands of vacationers who arrive each summer. The Owens raised their two children, Bobby and Clara Mae, in the restaurant — serving breakfast, lunch and dinner during those early days. Today, Clara Mae and her husband, Lionel, run the family restaurant. R.V., Clara Mae's nephew, owns a restaurant by the same name on the Nags Head-Manteo Causeway. Clara Mae's daughter, Clara, runs a self-titled eatery on the Manteo waterfront. Together, this food-loving family serves some of the best traditional Outer Banks-style seafood on the beach.

Owens' Restaurant now seats more than 200 people and offers only evening meals. More than 90,000 dinners are served from this beach road eatery each season. But the atmosphere is still homey, the food is still fresh and homemade, and the large lobby overflows with memorabilia of the barrier islands' — and Owens family — heritage. Even the building's architecture is reminiscent of the Outer Banks' past, patterned after an old Nags Head lifesaving station. The menu, however, combines modern tastes with traditional recipes.

Locally caught seafood, often fresh off the boat, is broiled, fried or grilled each evening. Coconut shrimp, "Miss O" crab cakes and pasta are among the most popular entrees. There's a mixed grill for patrons who prefer prime rib with their fish. And live Maine lobsters that you pick from the tank are steamed just before they're placed on your plate. Homemade soups, including Hatteras-style clam chowder and lobster bisque, are delicious ways to start a meal. And all the homemade desserts are well worth saving room for.

There's a full bar upstairs in the Station Keepers' Lounge where beer, wine, mixed drinks and special coffee concoctions are available. Owens' is open from mid-March through New Year's Eve. Dinner is served seven days a week.

Fatboyz

Beach Rd., MP 16½ *441-6514*
$ *No credit cards*

Known for its delectable ice cream, this eatery across from the Atlantic also offers fabulous flurries, sinful hot fudge cake and thick, meal-size milk shakes. But, since "you can't have any pudding if you don't eat your meat," Fatboyz serves sandwiches too.

Insiders' Tips

Raw oysters taste best with a little Tabasco sauce sprinkled on top.

There's fresh-grilled tuna steak topped with mild pepper cheese and a Big Mama featuring spicy Italian sausage. The Fatboy burger is a 6-ounce hand-pressed patty made fresh daily. And the new bacon cheeseburgers, chili cheeseburgers and a variety of grilled sandwiches round out the lengthy menu. Golden onion rings are a great side dish to select. And everything is served from a walk-up menu to go or to eat at one of the outdoor tables. Fatboyz is open from Easter to Labor Day seven days a week for lunch and dinner. Call for off-season hours.

Stone Oven Pizza

Soundings Factory Outlets
U.S. 158, MP 17 *441-7775*
$

Serving some of the best pizza on the Outer Banks, this counter-service-only pizza parlor has round and raised tables for dining in, or they'll box everything to go. Traditional red and California white pizzas are served in round pies or Sicilian-style with toppings from sweet sausage to spinach and pepperoni to pineapple. Daily specials change often, and you can call in orders ahead of time to have them waiting. Stone Oven employees toss all their dough by hand and bake each pizza to order. The salads here are meal-size. And you can have hand-dipped ice cream for dessert. Bottled beer and serve yourself soft drinks are available. Stone Oven is open year round for lunch and dinner.

There's also a carry-out-only branch of Stone Oven at the intersection of U.S. 158 and Colington Road, beside Metro Rentals. Call 441-3339 to place an order from this northern location at MP 8¼.

Sam & Omie's

Beach Rd. at Whalebone Jct. *441-7366*
$$

Started as place where early rising anglers could indulge in a big breakfast before the Oregon Inlet charter fishing fleet took off, Sam & Omie's has been an Outer Banks tradition for more than a half-century. Omie Tillett still captains a boat from the inlet. But he's long-since sold this little wooden building at Whalebone Junction. The restaurant, however, retains its old beach charm — and still serves hearty, homemade food cooked with traditional local recipes for breakfast, lunch and dinner.

This is a very casual place, with wooden booths and tables, a full-service bar and an always lively pool table in a separate, back room. Here, local fishermen congregate to contemplate the day's catch. And families flock to enjoy the low-priced, filling meals. Photographs of famous Gulf Stream catches line the walls, and the TV is usually tuned in to some exciting sporting event. For breakfast, omelets are our favorite option. We like to make a meal of the rich she-crab soup and red pepper poppers for lunch. Salads, sandwiches, hamburgers, fish fillets, turkey clubs and daily specials also are served. For dinner, try a soft crab sandwich in season or a prime rib entree on Thursdays. Sam & Omie's is open from early March through December, at least — call for winter hours. Recently, workers added a handicapped ramp outside the screened porch and adjusted the restrooms to accommodate disabled patrons.

Dune Burger

Beach Rd. at Whalebone Jct. *441-2441*
$ *No credit cards*

This dilapidated drive-in with the walk-up window has been an Outer Banks eatery since 1950. It serves lunch and dinner seven days a week from March through November and offers quarter-pound hamburgers, hot dogs, barbecue sandwiches, french fries and onion rings in addition to ice cream cones and milk shakes. Picnic tables are scattered outside Dune Burger; there's no indoor seating — or even a bathroom — here. You can get anything to go; call in orders ahead of time to have them waiting.

Tale of the Whale
Specializing in Seafood
Steaks & Prime Rib
Home of the Peanut Pie
Manteo/Nags Head Causeway
Nags Head, NC 27959
Phone: 441-7332

R.V.'s

Nags Head-Manteo Causeway *441-4963*

$$

R.V.'s is one of the most constantly popular places on the beach for lunch and dinner. Just check the parking lot if you don't believe us. Owner R.V. Owens often stops by your table to greet you, offering his warm smile and firm handshake as an appetizer to an abundant meal. You can eat at the full-service bar in this casual restaurant or sit at a table in one of the soundfront dining rooms. The seafood stew is extremely tasty and filled to overflowing with shrimp and scallops. Marinated tuna is a must for fish lovers. There's also a gazebo raw bar on an attached deck overlooking the water that takes on a life of its own in the evening — and stays open late. Prices here are really reasonable, and the atmosphere is lively and fun. RV's is open from mid-February through Thanksgiving seven days a week.

Tale of the Whale

Nags Head/Manteo Causeway *441-7332*

$$

This family restaurant is a friendly place to stop in for seafood — and the service is always fast and good. It's dark inside, decorated in a nautical theme, and the views of Roanoke Sound are delightful at any time of day. Specials feature everything from a mixed grill to broiled shellfish. Combination platters can be served fried or broiled. The salad bar is excellent, and it comes with meals. Desserts are wonderfully cool and tasty. A gazebo deck outside offers a gorgeous view across waterfowl-laden marshlands. Diners can enjoy cocktails while they wait or just stop by to see the sunset. Tale of the Whale is open from April through October for dinner. During summer months, lunch also is served.

Lone Cedar Cafe

Nags Head-Manteo Causeway *441-5405*

$$

One of the newest Outer Banks restaurants, Lone Cedar Cafe opened in the spring of 1996 to serve lunch and dinner. The Basnight family of Manteo operates this casual, upscale eatery where diners wearing everything from shorts to suits are welcome. Checkered green-and-white tablecloths cover every table, and the hunting motif with duck decoys and fishing memorabilia in honor of the former barrier island hunt club for which the eatery is named.

Appetizers are plentiful, ranging from spicy Wanchese chicken wings to clam chowder, seafood bisque, clam and oyster fritters, hot crab balls and hot crab dip,

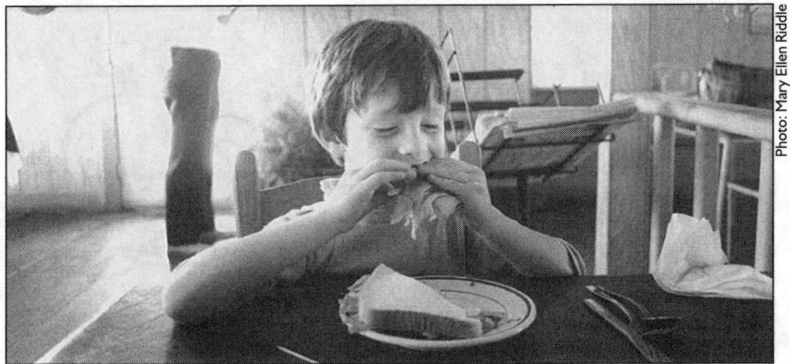

There are plenty of good fixin's on Ocracoke Island.

plus soups and other specials of the day. Lunch entrees start at $3.95 and include sandwiches and fresh local seafood. For dinner, try black Angus beef, homemade pasta, sliced duck breast or fried, broiled or blackened seafood — or order any of the evening specials. Each meal is accompanied by a salad, choice of potato, rolls and homemade corn bread. There's a full bar and an extensive wine list here. And desserts include pumpkin and pecan praline cheesecakes; pecan, peanut butter, lemon or Key lime pie; and ice cream drizzled with Grand Marnier and surrounded by fresh strawberries.

This cafe offers a view of the water from every table and is open for lunch and dinner daily from February through November. Vegetarian and children's offerings are available. Reservations are not accepted.

The Oasis

Nags Head-Manteo Causeway *441-7721*
$$

This waterfront building was constructed as a restaurant in the 1940s, making it one of the oldest continuously operated eateries on the beach. Violet Kellam bought the building in 1950, and her grandchildren — Mike, Mark and Kellam France — took the place over several years ago, spruced it up and renamed it The Oasis. Framed black and white photographs of barefoot 1950s-era waitresses still flank the front lobby.

Open for breakfast, lunch and dinner April through Christmas, this restaurant offers a panoramic view of the sound. Breakfast includes traditional eggs, bacon and pancake options. Fresh seafood and hearty sandwiches are served for lunch. For dinner, try a daily special or featured entree such as peppered salmon, blackened tuna or prime rib. The steam bar serves oysters, shrimp, clams, crab legs and vegetables. A full breakfast buffet and an à la carte menu are available on weekends. The Oasis has a children's menu, and a full bar service is available evenings. A new 10-foot pier has been added for boaters to tie up at. And acoustic entertainment is offered Wednesday nights and Sunday afternoons.

Roanoke Island

Manteo

Pirate's Cove Restaurant & Raw Bar

Manteo-Nags Head Causeway *473-2266*
$$$

Situated high atop Pirate's Cove Marina, overlooking the Roanoke Sound, this upscale restaurant offers magnificent views and tasty food. Chef Ron Davidson serves appetizers such as grilled Portobello mushrooms and baked oysters, great crab cakes for lunch and dinner entrees including shrimp Aristotle and pork Carolina stuffed with lump crabmeat and drizzled with hollandaise sauce. Loads of delicious desserts are prepared daily. And the wide windows give you a view of the charter fishing fleet returning to the marina each afternoon. In the spring of 1996, the dining room at Pirate's Cove Restaurant was remodeled. A children's menu is available. A nice selection of beer and wine are served, and brown bagging is allowed. Lunch and dinner are served daily throughout the summer. Call for winter schedules.

The Weeping Radish Brewery & Bavarian Restaurant

U.S. 64 *473-1157*
$$

Located next to the Christmas Shop on the main highway in Manteo, this large Bavarian restaurant includes an outdoor beer garden, separate pub, children's playground and two-story dining room. A European flavor prevails throughout. Traditional German meals include veal, sauerbraten and a variety of sausages. Homemade noodles — also called spaetzle — and cooked red cabbage are flavorful side dishes offering unusual tastes you won't find elsewhere on the Outer Banks. Continental cuisine also is available.

The restaurant's name comes from the radish served in Bavaria as an accompaniment to beer. Cut in a spiral, it's sprinkled with salt and packed back together. The salt draws out the moisture and gives the radish the appearance of weeping. Beer isn't served with radishes here — except by special request — but the brews are certainly the best part about this place. A microbrewery opened at The Weeping Radish in 1986 offering pure, fresh malt German brews without chemical additives or preservatives. You can watch this "nectar of the gods" being brewed on site. Or take home a pint or small keg to enjoy later. The Weeping Radish is open all year seven days a week for lunch and dinner.

Garden Pizzeria

U.S. 64 *473-6888*
$ *No credit cards*

Shaded by pine trees, this tiny restaurant has a breezy outdoor deck perfect for summer dining. Here, New York-style pizzas are cooked to order — and packaged to go, if you wish. White pizza, one of our favorites, is topped with ricotta, mozzarella, provolone and Romano cheeses, broccoli, pepperoni and minced garlic. Traditional red sauce pizzas with vegetables and pepperoni also are offered. And the Philly cheese steaks, burgers and a wide assortment of deli sandwiches, homemade salads and antipasto salads all are enjoyable. Fresh tuna and chicken salad plates are just right for a light lunch or dinner. All the soups are homemade, as are the desserts. Garden Pizzeria's employees offer free evening delivery to Roanoke Island and Pirate's Cove. The restaurant is open for lunch and early dinners during summer; winter schedules vary. Garden Pizzeria is closed on Sundays.

Darrell's

U.S. 64 *473-5366*
$$

This down-home restaurant started as an ice cream stand more than 30 years ago and has been a good family-style eatery for the past two decades. Daily lunch specials such as popcorn shrimp are accompanied by salad and vegetables. Darrell's fried oysters are among the best in town. Daily seafood specials are served for dinner; a children's menu is available. The hot fudge cake is a must for dessert. Beer and wine are served. Darrell's is open for lunch and dinner year round (closed Sundays).

Dock of the Bay Cafe

U.S. 64 *473-6845*

$$

This casual, comfortable waterfront restaurant offers a full menu featuring fresh local seafood. Crockett's Seafood Market is right next door, so it would be hard to get any fresher fish. The steam bar serves shrimp, clams and oysters along with soups and sandwiches. One of the things we like about this spot is the huge back deck overlooking the sound — there's usually a breeze to keep things cool here even in summer. Live entertainment outdoors is a draw on Friday evenings, weather permitting, during the season (see our Nightlife chapter). Wine and bottled beer are available including more than 50 varieties of microbrews.

The Dock of the Bay serves lunch and dinner seven days a week in summer. Call for winter hours.

Doug Saul's Bar-B-Q and Family Buffet

U.S. 64 *473-6464*

$ *No credit cards*

The atmosphere is casual and the food is spicy at this family-style restaurant known for its Carolina-style barbecue. The all-you-can-eat lunch and dinner buffets include fried chicken, cole slaw and other vegetables — in addition to the barbecue, of course. Rose Bay oysters are available all summer, and the popcorn fried shrimp is great. The ambiance is friendly — Doug enjoys his customers as much as they enjoy his ribs and sandwiches. Eat in or call for take-out. Doug Saul's also caters off-site pig pickin's and family barbecues. It's open Tuesday through Saturday for lunch and dinner in season. Call for winter hours.

Clara's Seafood Grill and Steam Bar

On the Waterfront *473-1727*

$$$

Overlooking Shallowbag Bay and the state ship, *Elizabeth II*, this is one of our favorite Manteo eateries where diners can watch boats on the water and see birds diving for fish. A casual, relaxing restaurant with good service and equally admirable food, Clara's lunch menu has delicious sandwiches and salads, hot soups and an ever-changing specials board. We order the black beans and rice most frequently. All the dinners are excellent, especially the mixed grill of shrimp and scallop kabobs, filet mignon and tuna. Caesar salads are a cool alternative on warm summer evenings. And the steam bar showcases local seafood of all sorts.

Historic photos lining the walls will remind you of what Manteo's waterfront looked like in the early days. And since this restaurant is less than a 10-minute drive from *The Lost Colony* amphitheater, it's a good place to take in an early meal before the outdoor drama begins. Beer, wine and champagne are available, and brown bagging is allowed. A children's menu is provided. Lunch and dinner are served here year round.

Full Moon Cafe

On the Waterfront *473-MOON*

$$

A cozy cafe overlooking Shallowbag Bay from its second-story vantage point, this eclectic eatery opened in late 1995 and already is overflowing with local and visiting patrons. Tablecloths line every table. And a plate glass window wall opens onto the water. The innovative cuisine here has a somewhat Southwestern flair. But most of the entrees and specials are so unusual we haven't seen them anywhere else on the Outer Banks.

Hummus spread, baked brie and mushroom caps stuffed with shrimp each are succulent appetizers. Lunch specials include gourmet sandwiches to satisfy everyone's tastes, vegetarian offerings, seafood, chicken and homemade soups such as Hungarian mushroom, curried spinach and spicy tomato that change daily. Each entree is served with chips and Full Moon's own salsa. A separate dinner menu offers enticing seafood dishes, stuffed chicken breasts, roasted eggplant with other vegetables smothered in marinara sauce and provolone cheese and beef Charron covered in Portobello mushrooms and a gorgonzola cheese sauce. All the desserts are delightful. Beer and wine are available. You can eat inside the lovely little dining room, dine outdoors in the covered courtyard or take any meal to go. Reservations aren't accepted.

Full Moon is open for lunch and dinner seven days a week in summer. Hours are more limited in the off-season so call for specific schedules.

Poor Richard's

On the Waterfront *473-3333*
$ *No credit cards*

Richard Brown owns and operates this cheery and convenient sandwich shop overlooking the sound and the *Elizabeth II*. Despite his eatery's popularity, he says he's still poor. But that never seems to get this smiling man down. Locals love Poor Richard's at lunchtime for its great selection of made-to-order sandwiches and daily specials — all cheap and filling. Soups, meatless chili, salad plates, cookies and ice cream also are available. Eat inside at a wooden booth or table or take your meal out on the back porch and enjoy the waterfront view. Poor Richard's also serves scrambled-egg and bacon sandwiches, bagels and cream cheese and other early morning fare for breakfast. This comfortable, friendly restaurant is open all year. Winter hours vary, so call ahead.

1587

Queen Elizabeth St., at the Tranquil House Inn *473-1587*
$$$

The owner of this critically acclaimed restaurant makes your mouth water just by reading his menu aloud. The offerings are unusual, extremely upscale cosmopolitan and certainly the most ambitious of any Outer Banks establishment. Ambiance is elegant and romantic: the soft glow of intimate lighting, a gleaming copper-topped bar in a separate lounge area and polished wood and mirrors that reflect the lights sparkling off boats anchored in Shallowbag Bay. Executive Chef Donny King creates a constantly changing menu that's always as fresh and fabulous as the food.

Homemade soups prepared each day include Mediterranean mussels and crayfish with spring vegetables and feta cheese in a light tomato broth. For appetizers, select sesame-encrusted colossal scallops with spicy vegetable slaw and soy-Wasabi cream or grilled Portobello mushroom on a zucchini podium with balsamic-sautéed julienne vegetables. Salads, served à la carte, offer Boston Bibb, romaine and baby lettuce leaves with spring vegetables and herb-shallot vinaigrette.

Dinner entrees, each of which is an artistic masterpiece, range from crispy

Insiders' Tips

Outer Banks chowder — also known as Hatteras- or Wanchese-style — consists of clams cooked in their own broth or liquor with other ingredients such as diced potatoes, chopped onions, celery, parsley and the chef's choice of spices that enhance the shellfish flavor.

cornmeal rockfish with Louisiana-style crayfish butter sauce and chile-fried rice to an ocean panache of tiger prawns, mussels, scallops and fish tossed with vegetables and orzo pasta, finished with feta cheese. Another excellent choice is grilled filet mignon fanned with roasted garlic mashed potatoes and a wild mushroom and goat's cheese and Cabernet Ragout.

A children's menu offers simpler dishes for younger tastes. Vegetarian requests are welcome. And the exquisite dessert creations are well worth saving room for — and photographing, they're so beautifully arranged.

Named for the first year English colonists attempted to settle on Roanoke Island, 1587 serves a wide selection of wine and beer and permits brown bagging. This outstanding restaurant is open for dinner daily in the summer. Call for off-season hours. Reservations are requested.

The Green Dolphin Pub

Sir Walter Raleigh St. *473-5911*
$

This downtown Manteo eatery has been a popular pub for more than 15 years. It's casual and dark inside, with wooden booths and tables fashioned from the hatch covers taken off old ships. Other nautical memorabilia lines the walls, and a long bar stretches along the back of the restaurant. Food here is simple, cheap and satisfying. Hamburgers, she-crab soup, crab cakes, lasagna, manicotti, Italian sausage and french fries are just a few of the offerings served for lunch and dinner. Appetizers and desserts also are available, and the pub serves pizzas and small fry portions for the kids. The Green Dolphin is open year round daily except Sundays.

Anna Livia's Restaurant

U.S. 64, at the Elizabethan Inn *473-2101*
$$

Opened in 1995, this restaurant already is earning acclaim for its moderately priced, contemporary and traditional Italian cuisine and a generous selection of seafood. Anna Livia's features specials such as seafood fra diablo, chicken scarpariello and lasagna Bolognese for supper. The lunch menu offers daily specials, sandwiches and seasonal fresh salads. Desserts are homemade, and beer and wine are served. A variety of breakfast entrees and a weekend breakfast buffet also are available. Other features include a children's menu, seniors' discounts, daily early bird dinner specials from 4 to 5:30 PM, a separate nonsmoking section and full carry-out menu. Banquet rooms are reserved for private parties. Anna Livia's is open daily year round; on Saturday, breakfast and dinner only are served. Call for winter hours.

Wanchese

Queen Anne's Revenge

Old Wharf Rd. *473-5466*
$$

Named after one of Blackbeard's famous pirate ships that plied the waters off Carolina's coast during the early 1700s, Queen Anne's Revenge is snuggled in a grove of trees in the scenic fishing village of Wanchese. It's one of our favorite Outer Banks restaurants, well off the beaten path at the end of a winding lane. Wayne and Nancy Gray, and Jim and Donald Beach have operated this outstanding restaurant since 1978. They use only quality ingredients, and their attention to detail really shows.

The restaurant has three dining rooms, one with a fireplace that provides a cozy ambiance during cold winter months. A large selection of appetizers is offered, including bouillabaisse (chockfull of fresh seafood) and black bean and she-crab soups. All the seafood here is excellent, from Blackbeard's Raving to the locally landed shellfish and fish served with the Wanchese platter. There's even Châteaubriand for two, carved at your

table. Queen Anne's chefs make their own pasta — their fettuccine is a staple around Wanchese. All the desserts are homemade and served in generous portions. This lovely restaurant offers a children's menu and a nice selection of beer and wine. The dining room serves dinner only seven days a week during the summer. Queen Anne's is open all year, closing on Tuesdays during the off-season.

Fisherman's Wharf

Near the end of N.C. 345 *473-5205*
$$

Overlooking the fishing port of Wanchese, the dining room of this family-owned restaurant offers the best views around of the Outer Banks' commercial fishing fleet. Windows form an entire wall of the dining room, so diners can see the seafood they might be served this evening being unloaded from the boats in the afternoon. The fish here is as fresh and local as it gets.

The Daniels family, of Wanchese fishing history fame, opens this restaurant for lunch and dinner from late March through November. Seafood plates complete with homemade hushpuppies and good cole slaw are the best selections from a variety of items on the menu. There's a new grill for 1996, and landlubbers can order pasta and chicken entrees. You'll want to save room for the homemade desserts. This is a casual eatery where families feel right at home. A children's menu is available. Fisherman's Wharf is closed Sundays.

Hatteras Island

Rodanthe, Waves and Salvo

Casual Clam II

Pamlico Station, N.C. 12
Rodanthe *987-2700*
$

Featuring 10¢ shrimp, 30¢ clams, pizza, sandwiches, soft pretzels, hot wings and nachos, this second-story restaurant offers some of the cheapest eats on Hatteras. You can get cold beer in bottles and on tap. Fun diversions include a Foosball table, pool tables and arcade games galore (see our Nightlife chapter). You can't really eat a huge dinner in the booths or at the bar, but if quick seafood and a lively atmosphere are what you're looking for, step inside the Casual Clam. Happy hours are from 4 to 8 PM nightly. This eatery is open from March through

Thanksgiving for dinner and for lunch and dinner during summer months.

Lisa's Pizza

N.C. 12, Rodanthe *987-2525*
$ *No credit cards*

Speciality pizzas, deli sandwiches, subs, hoagies, chicken Parmesan, stuffed shells and salads are among the most popular items at this 11-year-old restaurant. Lisa's also serves bread sticks, hot wings, garlic and cheese bread — and New York-style cheesecake for dessert. Beer and wine are available. There's also a separate children's menu. Lisa's offers lunch and dinner seven days a week from early April through November. All items can be eaten inside this casual restaurant or carried out.

Down Under Restaurant & Lounge

Rodanthe Pier, off N.C. 12 *987-2277*
$$

Ocean views are spectacular at this Australian-style restaurant, perched high over the pilings of Rodanthe's pier. Here, you'll find crabmeat and Western omelets for breakfast. Lunch specialties include the Great Australian bite — similar to an Aussie burger — made with hamburger, a fried egg, grilled onions, cheese and bacon. Spicy fish burgers, Vegemite sandwiches and marinated chicken sandwiches are good authentic options too. And since the owner shot a lot of kangaroos while visiting his homeland over the winter, he'll be serving 'roo stew, 'roo burgers and kangaroo curry for the summer of 1996.

Dinner selections include Down Under shrimp stuffed with jalapeño peppers and cream cheese wrapped in bacon. We also enjoy a side order of the foot-high onion rings and a tall can of — what else? — Foster's lager. Happy hour at the separate bar is from 3 to 6 PM daily in season. Steamed, spiced shrimp are 10¢ each. This unusual restaurant serves breakfast, lunch and dinner through the summer. Lunch and dinner are available during the spring and fall. Parents will appreciate the children's menu. And everyone will enjoy the view. Down Under is open seven days a week from April through November.

Surfriders Grill

N.C. 12, Rodanthe *987-2220*
$

This upbeat, happening eatery opened just in time for the 1996 summer season. It's already the grooviest grill on Hatteras Island. Owned by local surfers and their pals, it's decorated with antique surfboards and photographs of historic boardheads. The bar is shaped like two waves crashing into each other, and surfing laminants line its broad top. The bar is unusually low so patrons can sit on the stools, eat at the counter — and still keep their feet on the ground. At least 20 types of beer always are on tap here. And surfing videos and tunes play continuously.

Families will feel comfortable at Surfriders — even if they've never ridden a wave. A variety of appetizers and foods feature flavors from around the world. Mexican, Italian, Chinese, Japanese and Neuvo-American are just some of the influences you'll recognize. Speciality salads, vegetarian dishes, fish tacos, personalized pizzas, gourmet sandwiches and California-style cuisine are on the menu for lunch and dinner seven days a week from April through November. "We use only local seafood and the freshest, finest ingredients," says part-owner Steve Hess, who shapes surfboards in the off-season from his Secret Spot Surf Shop in Nags Head. "When we make you a burger, we'll grind you a steak." Delectable desserts change daily. See our Nightlife chapter for more about Surfriders Grill.

Top Dog Cafe

N.C. 12, Waves 987-1272
$ *No credit cards*

New for the summer of 1996, this small gourmet hot dog stand offers all items to take out, eat inside surrounded by dolphin photographs and reggae tunes, or enjoy outdoors on a deck under blue-and-yellow striped umbrellas. Top Dog serves all-beef Oscar Mayer wieners with chili, spicy onions, green peppers and almost any other topping you can think of. Half-pound burgers smothered in bacon, cheddar cheese, mushrooms and Swiss cheese are thick and juicy. The owners here also make Philly cheese steaks, chicken fingers, onion rings, jalapeño poppers and Italian sausages and serve beer and wine. The restaurant is within walking distance of the KOA and Camp Hatteras campgrounds. This comfortable cafe is open from March through November for lunch and dinner and serves food seven days a week during the summer. Call for off-season hours.

Mid-Atlantic Market, Restaurant & Marina

N.C. 12, Salvo 987-1520
$

Serving some of the best hot lunches on Hatteras, this take-out-only eatery is open year round seven days a week, and it also serves dinner in the summer. Lunch specials, which are amazingly popular with local construction crews and watermen, include hot roast beef sandwiches with mashed potatoes and green beans, meat loaf made that morning, ham and cabbage, fried chicken, pork chops, hamburgers and barbecue. And all the regular sandwiches — including fresh tuna and chunky chicken salad — are available. Popular side dishes are french fries and onion rings, and beer and wine can be bought to go. Mid-Atlantic also sells gasoline and has a boat ramp, travel trailer park and dock space for fishing boats.

Avon

The Froggy Dog

N.C. 12 995-4106
$$

This casual seafood restaurant serves big breakfasts, fast affordable lunches and a variety of dinner specials that change daily. Traditional early morning fare here includes eggs, hotcakes and sausage. Grilled sandwiches and cool salads always are available for lunch, and The Froggy Dog has earned our vote for the best burger in Avon. Regular dinner entrees range from broiled, fried or sautéed seafood to steaks and chicken. Other features include children's portions, senior citizens' specials and early bird dinners from 5 to 6

PM. The gift shop upstairs sells the famous Froggy Dog T-shirts. And the separate Lily Pad Lounge is a popular Hatteras nightspot (see our Nightlife chapter). The Froggy Dog is open year round for all three meals. Call for winter hours.

Sea Robin Restaurant

Waterside, off N.C. 12 *995-5931*
$$

This popular soundside restaurant offers wonderful, waterfront views and it's off the main highway — a lot quieter than many Hatteras eateries. The Sea Robin serves eggs Benedict, steak and eggs, waffles and several other traditional breakfasts. For lunch, try oysters, clams, mussels, shrimp or crab legs from the steam bar — then order an appetizer to augment your seafood. A sampling includes Buffalo wings, cheese sticks and jalapeño poppers. Dinner menus feature a full list of entrees, from the Sea Robin seafood platter and surf 'n turf to Cajun fish and crabmeat saute. Wine and beer are served here, and a children's menu is available. This restaurant is open from March through November for all three meals. Call for off-season schedules.

Beach Bites Deli & Bakery

Food Lion Shopping Center
N.C. 12 *995-6683*
$

Breakfast sandwiches, sticky buns, eclairs, muffins and croissants are just a few of the tasty choices at this delightful bakery. Your best bet for breakfast is to order an Elephant Ear — a foot-wide crispy pastry loaded with cinnamon and brown sugar. For lunch, you can select any deli sandwich combination made on whatever type of bread you like. Philly cheese steaks, roast beef, Reubens, ham, turkey and vegetarian options are among the choices, complemented by a variety of homemade soups and luncheon salads. All lunch entrees come with a pickle wedge and chips. Dinners include Beach Bites' own chili served in an edible bowl made of Italian bread and topped with shredded cheese. Seating is limited inside this small deli. Carry-out is available for any item. You can buy one of 10 types of bread to go, and don't leave without trying a soft, just-baked six-ounce cookie — they come in several flavors but only one size. This casual eatery is open seven days a week for three meals a day from early April through late December. The bakers also will create special cakes for any occasion.

Nino's Pizza

N.C. 12 *995-5358*
$

Serving pizza and authentic Italian entrees since 1979, this low-key restaurant lets patrons dine inside or carry any item out. Besides red sauce pizzas, Nino's offers spaghetti, lasagna, chicken Parmesan, meatball subs, manicotti and eggplant Parmesan. Only dinner is served in the off-season; lunch and dinner are available through summer. Nino's is closed in December but is open daily otherwise.

Blue Parrot Cafe

N.C. 12, in the Castaways Motel *995-6993*
$$

Serving breakfast and dinner daily from April through November, this casual cafe is adorned with an artistic surf theme and provides diners with a view of a marshy pond. Here, cooks offer Belgian waffles, eggs Benedict, blueberry pancakes, hash browns, toast, bacon and French toast for breakfast. Dinner entrees include steaks, seafood, chicken, pasta, vegetarian dishes and a special kids' menu. The tempura shrimp and she-crab soup are great appetizers. And for dessert, we recommend French silk pie or chocolate pecan pie. Early bird specials of prime rib or blackened tuna are less than $10 between 5 and 7 PM. California and Australian wines — as well as domestic, imported and microbrewed beers — are available.

Reservations are recommended for parties of five or more. Every item can be packaged to carry out or to be delivered to the hotel's rooms. Blue Parrot's staff also caters private parties or banquets.

The Mad Crabber Restaurant & Shellfish Bar

N.C. 12 *995-5959*
$$

This lively place offers dinner nightly from April through November. It's not a fancy restaurant by any means, but you'll find good, fresh seafood here — and reasonable prices. Steamed crabs and shrimp lead the way on the menu. Locally caught blue crabs, snow crabs, Dungeness crabs from the Pacific Northwest and Florida golden crabs also are on hand. Of course, delicious crab cakes are the speciality.

If you're not feeling "crabby," try a pasta dish, the vegetarian platter or — for meat-lovers — a thick burger or juicy steak. All-you-can-eat specials are served on "Fat Tuesdays," along with $1 draft beers. Wine also is available. And there's a special menu just for kids. A separate game room attached to the Mad Crabber has two pool tables for low-key fun.

Big Wave Diner

N.C. 12 *995-4966*
$$

A fun place to go for casual dining and tasty food, this diner has a back deck overlooking a pretty pond that's a great place to relax and enjoy spectacular sunsets. Chef Eric Anglend, formerly of Waves Edge Restaurant, is cooking up some new Italian entrees in the 1996 season, including vegetarian and pesto lasagna, a pasta bar, fish of the day entrees and new Fricos — crust-less pizzas that taste more like a cheese torte and are topped with tantalizing vegetables, meats and sauces. Chicken and steak also are served here. There's a children's menu, homemade desserts and beer and wine. Full catering is available. The restaurant is open seven days a week for lunch and dinner in season (call for winter hours). Big Wave is open mid-March through mid-December.

Buxton

Cape Sandwich Company

Daydreams Shopping Center
N.C. 12 *995-6140*
$ *No credit cards*

A popular spot with both tourists and locals, Cape Sandwich Company serves breakfast, lunch and dinner during summer months to eat at an umbrella-shaded table outdoors or for take out. Owners Bryan and Sylvia Mattingly are now into their third season and continue serving a consistently good array of salads and sandwiches, daily specials and enticing desserts. Imported beer and cappuccino are available, as are picnic items for the beach. Call for off-season hours.

Diamond Shoals Restaurant

N.C. 12 *995-5217*
$$

The parking lot at this casual eatery, which is within walking distance of several Buxton motels, always seems to be crowded around breakfast time. Here you'll find one of the best breakfasts on Hatteras Island, featuring all your early morning favorites. Diamond Shoals is closed for lunch; dinner offerings include plenty of seafood choices, featuring fried and broiled seafod and some good nightly specials. For the 1996 season the new owner has renovated the dining room and hired a new chef. His specials are sure to please. Diamond Shoals is open from March through November.

Sharkey's Eatery

N.C. 12 *995-3861*
$$ *No credit cards*

For the 1996 season, the owners of this casual place re-carpeted the dining

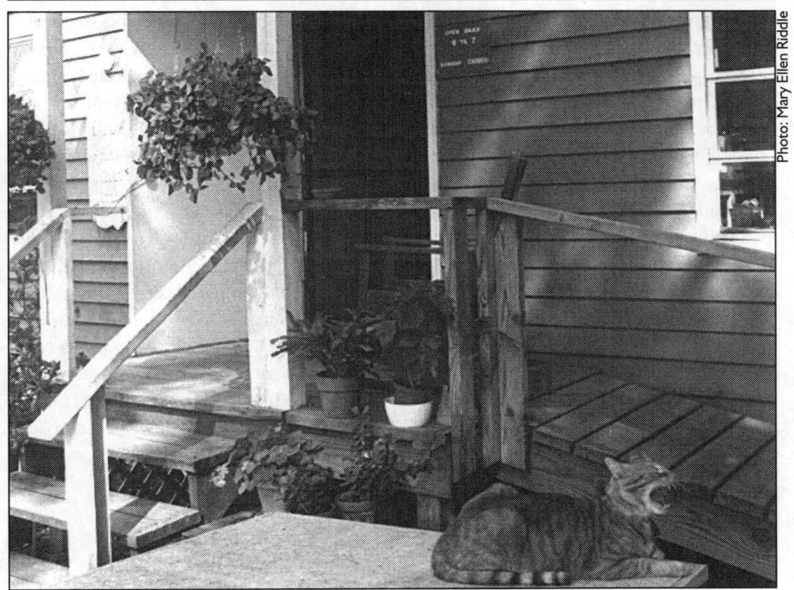

Photo: Mary Ellen Riddle

Buxton Books is a relaxing stop for folks and cats alike.

room, completely renovated the interior and eliminated the game room and front counter to accommodate table-service dinners. Dinners include speciality pizzas, lasagna, manicotti and spaghetti, and there's a full salad bar. Everything is available to eat in or take out; Sharkey's offers free delivery throughout the village. And domestic and imported beers are served. Sharkey's is open daily during summer. Call for off-season hours.

Tides Restaurant

Off N.C. 12 *995-5988*
$$

The driveway for this family-style restaurant is just south of the entrance to the Cape Hatteras Lighthouse, on the sound side. Traditional breakfasts are served here, with tasty homemade biscuits and blueberry and pecan pancakes. Dinner selections include a fresh catch of the day, steaks, chicken and ham. The stuffed potatoes are super. And although the Tides is closed for lunch, sandwiches and burgers also are served for supper. All the portions here are large, and the service is attentive. Beer and wine are available; brown bagging is allowed. This restaurant is open daily from March through November.

The Great Salt Marsh Restaurant

N.C. 12, beside the
Osprey Shopping Center *995-6200*
$$$

This unique California-style grill is our favorite fine dining establishment on Hatteras Island. It's worth the hour's drive from Nags Head just to enjoy the excitement of this innovative cuisine. *Gourmet Magazine* and *Southern Living* each have praised this restaurant's fine taste. And we know you'll enjoy anything you select off the ambitious menu. The ambiance, too, is upscale and original: black and white tile floors offset laminated black tables. It's a lot more contemporary and cosmopolitan than any other eatery on the southern Outer Banks.

For appetizers, we suggest scallop puffs, shrimp cheesecake or smoked Gouda cheese with Cajun spices. The big Caesar salad is plenty for two. Pan-sautéed crab cakes are succulent for supper. Soft shells sautéed over a bed of garlic-laced spinach makes a wonderful signature dish, Soft Shells à la Salt Marsh. Vegetarian entrees include penne with sun-dried tomato pesto or a grilled vegetable and mozzarella salad. Prime rib and pasta creations also are marvelous. For dessert, try homemade mile-high pies — both Key lime and lemon are luscious. A select wine list is available. And reservations are welcome. The Great Salt Marsh is open for dinner only every day except Sunday through the summer. Call for off-season hours.

Orange Blossom Cafe and Bakery

N.C. 12 *995-4109*
$$ *No credit cards*

Henry and Michel Schliff started Papagayo's Restaurant in Nags Head in 1978 — then relocated to Buxton where they opened the Orange Blossom. Now in its fifth year, this wonderful cafe serves the best Mexican cuisine on Hatteras. And the sandwiches made with thick, homemade Italian bread always are a good bet. This little spot also caters to vegetarians, serving a wide selection of meatless salads, sandwiches and entrees. The Orange Blossom starts the day offering an array of baked goods and keeps serving through the late afternoon. The famous Apple Uglies — huge apple fritter-style pastries piled high with fruit — are our favorite early morning treats. This restaurant is open daily from 7 AM until late afternoon in the summer and offers take-out or eat-in. Call for off-season hours.

Billy's Fish House Restaurant

N.C. 12 *995-5151*
$$

Can you tell that this always bustling eatery occupies a former fish house? If the simple wooden architecture and wharf-front location didn't give it away, you might notice something fishy when you glimpse down and see the slanted concrete floors — sloped for easy washing so the fish scales could flow back into the sound. Billy's is now a down-home restaurant where everything is casual and easygoing. It also serves some of the best Outer Banks seafood prepared with traditional, local recipes. The tile fish is a popular choice, and we highly recommend the homemade crab cakes. All the seafood is fresh. Each entree comes with your choice of vegetables and hushpuppies. Most of the foods are lightly fried with peanut oil (except the new pasta offerings, of course). And everything is served on disposable plates with plastic utensils. Billy's is open for lunch and dinner daily from early April through mid-November.

The Pilot House

N.C. 12 *995-5664*
$$$

Set well off the road to capture spectacular, panoramic views of the sky, water and sinking sun, The Pilot House offers soundside dining amid a decor that's unobtrusively nautical. A separate upstairs lounge serves beer and wine. Capt. Bernice Ballance serves fresh local seafood such as oysters Rockefeller and clams casino for appetizers and homemade soups and bisque.

Dinner entrees include a catch of the day, a variety of shellfish and grilled steaks hand-cut to order. Salad and bread accompany each meal. Desserts all are delicious, especially the hot fudge cake and fresh fruit cobblers. Both children's and senior citizens' menus are available. The Pilot House serves only dinner seven days a week from mid-April through late fall.

Nino's Pizza

N.C. 12, in the Village *995-6364*
$

Now in its third year of operation, this pizza place has limited seating in a few small booths — so most meals are served to go or delivered. Calzones, subs, spaghetti, lasagna, manicotti and eggplant, veal and chicken Parmesan are among the most popular offerings. Several salads and antipasto plates also are available. And you have your choice of 17 toppings to put on the hand-tossed pizza dough. Nino's is open for lunch and dinner daily through the summer; the rest of the year, it serves dinner only.

Smokin' Chicken

Osprey Shopping Center
off N.C. 12 *995-5502*
$ *No credit cards*

Breakfast, lunch and dinner are offered daily year round for eat-in or takeout. Homemade biscuits, hash browns, eggs, toast, sausage, bacon and cheese teasers all are great ways to start the day. Five lunch specials are served each afternoon for $3.95, usually including at least two of the following: chicken breasts, roast beef, barbecue or Philly cheese steaks. Each comes with french fries; the two- or three-piece chicken dinners also include two vegetables (baked beans, mashed potatoes, cole slaw or green beans). Chicken nuggets, onion rings, hot dogs and livers and gizzards are available throughout the day. For dessert, there's ice cream to enjoy on hot summer evenings.

Soundside Restaurant

N.C. 12 *995-6778*
$$

With 30 to 50 items served for all three meals daily, year round, this casual waterfront eatery has something for everyone. It's not a fancy place, but the food's good and filling. And manager Candy Quidley says shirts and shoes are all you need to get served.

Breakfasts include eggs, pancakes, five kinds of omelets, sausage and chipped beef gravy and, of course, bacon and coffee. Popcorn shrimp, oysters and clam strips are our picks for lunch — unless you prefer Hatteras-style chowder, gumbo or beef stew. For dinner, you can choose between prime rib cut to order, rib eye steaks, fresh trout, crab legs or dozens of other entrees. Each comes with a trip to the salad bar, two vegetables and rolls. Desserts are a changing selection of cake and pie slices. Children can order off their own separate menu. And senior citizens receive a 10 percent discount.

For 1996, Soundside's owners added a new lounge and raw bar downstairs (see our Nightlife chapter). Here, you can enjoy shellfish while drinking beer or wine. Or bring your own bottle of liquor in a brown bag.

Frisco

Quarterdeck Restaurant

N.C. 12 *986-2425*
$$

Fresh, local seafood served broiled or fried, crab cakes packed with jumbo lump meat and ham-bone vegetable soup are among the most popular offerings here. The Quarterdeck also has an 18-item salad bar and gives 10 percent off all dinners to folk who eat between 5 and 6 PM. For dessert, the coconut cream, lemon meringue and Key lime pies are delicious. Beer and wine are available — as well as a children's menu.

This low-key spot occupies a 70-year-old building that housed Hatteras Island's original bar. For the past 17 years, the same family has owned and operated the Quarterdeck, which is open for lunch and dinner daily from mid-March through late November.

Gingerbread House Bakery

N.C. 12 *995-5204*
$ *No credit cards*

From this tiny cottage flanked by gingerbread-style fencing, breakfast and dinner are served seven days a week in season. To start the day, sample egg biscuits, French toast, omelets or waffles. If you'd rather indulge yourself in delicious baked goods, try a frosted donut, cookie or still-steaming bagel. By early evening, you can order a gourmet pizza — made on the bakery's own homemade dough. Pan and hand-tossed thicknesses are offered in regular and whole wheat varieties. A whopping 16 toppings to choose from should satisfy virtually any craving. Ice cream, brownies and sweet breads all are great dessert options. You can eat inside this low-key little house, or get your pizza and sweets to go. During the summer, the Gingerbread House also delivers from Buxton to Hatteras Village. And its bakers make super speciality cakes for any occasion. Call for off-season hours.

Frisco Sandwich Shop

N.C. 12 *995-5535*

$

In the past 19 years, Frisco Sandwich Shop has grown from a drive-in to a full-service restaurant by continuing to offer a quality selection of fresh local seafood and reliable service. We suggest trout sandwiches and baskets for lunch. And the cheeseburgers here are fat and juicy. Daily specials and desserts are always delicious, and beer and wine are available. Frisco Sandwich shop is open for lunch until 4 PM every day but Sunday year round. During the summer, this homey eatery stays open for supper seven days a week.

Bubba's Bar-B-Q

N.C. 12 *995-5421*

$

If you're in the mood for some genuine Carolina barbecue, you won't be able to miss Bubba's — just follow your nose to his famous roadside joint. The hickory fires start early here so the pork, chicken, beef, ribs and turkey can cook slowly over an open pit behind the counter. Larry "Bubba" Schauer and his wife, Julie, brought their secret recipe from West Virginia to Hatteras Island more than a decade ago — and the food has been drawing locals and tourists to their eatery ever since. Homemade cole slaw, baked beans, red-skinned potato salad, french fries and corn bread round out the meal — and diners' bellies.

The homemade sweet potato and coconut custard pies, cobblers and other desserts are delectable. Mrs. Bubba's Double Devil Chocolate Cake is approaching celebrity status. Bubba's has a children's menu and a nice selection of beer and soft drinks. All items are available for eating in or taking out. Bubba's Sauce is now a hot commodity with barbecue fans and is sold at retail and specialty shops across the Outer Banks. Like Bubba says, "Once you try my barbecue, you'll throw stones at everyone else's." We agree. Bubba's is open daily for lunch and dinner during the summer. Call for winter hours. You'll find a second Bubba's, 995-4385, farther north on N.C. 12 in Avon, near the Food Lion.

Hatteras Village

Gary's Restaurant

N.C. 12 *986-2349*

$$

In recent years, this restaurant has grown from a fast-food style eatery to a small cafe. You can relax over a cup of coffee and a great breakfast here — or enjoy a nice lunch any day of the week year round. Breakfast treats include crabmeat omelets, Belgian waffles, steak and eggs, homemade biscuits and fresh fruit cups. For lunch, there's steamed shrimp, clams, deli or sub sandwiches and a variety of seafood entrees. Homemade cheesecakes and fudge cakes are divine desserts. Beer and wine are available, and carry-out is an option for any item. A separate smoking area is set aside inside.

The Channel Bass

N.C. 12 *986-2250*

$$

Owned by the Harrison family, well

known for its fishing heritage, this canal-side restaurant has been a Hatteras Village institution for more than 30 years. And you'll notice all of Mrs. Shelby Harrison's fishing trophies in the foyer. The Channel Bass has one of the largest menus on the beach, loaded with seafood platters, no-filler crab cakes, veal and char-broiled steaks that the chefs slice in-house. An old family recipe is used for the hushpuppies, and all the salad dressings are homemade. Make sure you try the homemade coconut, Key lime and chocolate cream pies. A private dining room is available, and large groups are welcome. The Channel Bass has early bird discounts and different dinner specials here every night. A nice selection of beer and wine is served; brown bagging also is allowed. A children's menu is available. Dinner is served seven days a week from mid-March through November.

Harbor Seafood Deli

N.C. 12, at Hatteras
Harbor Marina *986-2331*
$

Harbor Seafood Deli serves breakfast and lunch, including daily seafood specials, homemade pasta, seafood salad and a wonderful shrimp pasta salad. Homemade desserts are delicious and can be enjoyed on the enclosed porch. This porch gets very busy in the late afternoons, when charter boats return to the adjacent marina. Steamed shrimp and other munchies are available during the late afternoon hours if you want to watch all the activity. And hand-dipped Breyer's ice cream is a favorite dessert to sample while sitting in the hot sun.

The best aspect of this deli, in our opinion, is that the owners will pre-pack breakfasts and lunches that you can pick up the next day to take on a charter fishing trip. Just call in the afternoon or early evening before you're scheduled to depart — and a hearty meal will be ready to go, probably even before you are. Harbor Seafood Deli opens at 6 AM daily. There's a $15 minimum purchase if you want to pay by credit card. Call for off-season hours.

Breakwater Island Restaurant

N.C. 12 *986-2733*
$$

If dining in a comfortable atmosphere with a stunning view of Pamlico Sound or relaxing with some live music on a deck at sunset sounds good, then this restaurant is the place for you. Here, a second-story dining room, deck and bar overlook a small harbor and stone breakwater, providing a unique feel to this locally loved outpost.

The dinner menu features fresh, progressive seafood dishes, prime rib, veal and pasta, all served in generous portions. Entrees are accompanied by a selection of vegetables, salad and fresh-baked breads. Live entertainment is performed atop the deck on summer Sunday evenings between 8 PM midnight. Dinner is served seven days a week during the season. A good selection of beer and wine is available. Children's items are also offered. Check for winter hours.

Oceanside Bakery

N.C. 12 *986-2465*
$ *No credit cards*

Serving fresh baked good on Hatteras Island for more than a decade, this little bakery opens at 4:30 AM daily from March through December to accommodate local fishermen. Sausage biscuits, blueberry scones and muffins and old-fashioned eclairs are among its most popular selections. Apple fritters, Key lime cake, bread pudding and assorted pies also are available. A few tables allow diners to eat in, but most people take their goodies to go. In 1996 Oceanside Bakery has added an ice cream and candy shop to round out its line of sweets. This eatery is open through early evening each day.

Rocco's Pizza

N.C. 12 *986-2150*
$

Calzones, subs, pasta, ravioli and antipasto are available here in addition to a variety of pizzas. This is a casual place where you can eat in. Rocco's employees also will package any item to go. Beer and wine are served here, and desserts such as tiramisu, cheesecake and Key lime pie are fantastic. A children's menu is offered. And reservations are accepted for large parties. Rocco's is open for dinner only every day except Monday. It closes during the month of December.

Sonny's Restaurant

N.C. 12 *986-2922*
$$

This incredibly casual, family-run eatery serves three meals a day seven days a week year round. Breakfast begins at 5:30 AM for fishermen and includes hash browns, grits, Western omelets, ham and cheese omelets and hot cakes — just a few of Sonny's specialties. Lunch includes an array of sandwiches, crab cakes, hot dogs and hamburgers. There's an $18.95 dinner buffet each evening, with an 18-item salad bar, breads, crabmeat bisque, soft-shell crabs in season, sea scallops, popcorn and regular shrimp, prime rib, clams, oysters, macaroni and cheese, fettuccine alfredo and desserts such as carrot and chocolate cake, rice pudding and a soft serve ice cream bar.

Regular menu items range from steaks to seafood to pasta. Alcoholic beverages aren't served here. But you're welcome to bring your own. Sonny even will provide frosty beer mugs and wine glasses for you. Senior citizen and children's menus are offered. Reservations are accepted for large parties.

Ocracoke Island

The Fig Tree

N.C. 12 *928-4554*
$

The Fig Tree, a tiny delicatessen offering carry-out cuisine only, packs picnics for ferry boat rides and serves a variety of light lunches and baked goods. Veggie pockets here are stuffed to overflowing with lettuce, tomatoes, cucumbers, carrots, mushrooms, sprouts and feta cheese and topped with a choice of homemade dressing. Shrimp and tuna salad are made with just-off-the-boat seafood. Or you can design your own sandwich from numerous selections of meats and cheeses to be served on bakery-fresh bread, a hearty bagel or inside a pita. Baked delights include jumbo cinnamon rolls, doughnuts, scones, fruit and nut breads, breakfast biscuits and gourmet cookies. Heavier dessert items — also outstanding — range from chocolate swirl cheesecake atop brownie crumb crust to Ocracoke's own fig cake, each served whole or by the slice.

Trolley Stop Restaurant

N.C. 12 — *928-4041*

$

Serving breakfast and lunch all year — and adding dinners during the summer season — this cheap little eatery has counter-service only and pretty basic, non-gourmet food. Diners can eat inside on the long picnic tables after serving themselves drinks, or the staff will package any meal to go. Breakfasts start at 99¢ for biscuit sandwiches. French toast, scrambled eggs, bacon, pancakes and grits are other offerings. For lunch, you can order all your favorite sandwiches from Italian subs to six-ounce hamburgers to hot pastrami, barbecue and crab cakes. French fries, hushpuppies and chips are served à la carte. The seasonal dinner menu is the same as the lunch fare. Large groups can call ahead here to order boxed lunches, complete with sandwiches, chips and a cookie.

Cockle Creek Restaurant

N.C. 12 — *928-6891*

$$

Opened in January 1995, this lovely Italian seafood cafe is located in the building that used to house Maria's Restaurant. It's owned by Hyde County Commissioner David Styron and his wife, Kari. The couple does much of the cooking themselves, and they produce some delightful, moderately priced dinners and offer a range of entrees. Linen tablecloths and oil lamps are attractive table appointments in the three-level dining room, with soft jazz music piped in to create added ambiance. Dress is casual, but you could come for a special evening out and still feel intimate and elegant here.

Dinner entrees include grilled swordfish, homemade lasagna, pizzas and fresh-cut steaks. The ravioli special, stuffed with flavorful cheeses, is superb. And each meal is accompanied by a baked potato or fries and salad or soup. A nice wine list and plenty of scrumptious desserts are added features, as are raw bar selections of all sorts of shellfish. Cockle Creek is open seven days a week for dinner only from late January through late November.

Pony Island Restaurant

N.C. 12 *928-5701*
$$

A casual, homey place that lots of people come back to time and again, this restaurant features big breakfasts of biscuits, hot cakes, omelets and the famous Pony Potatoes — hash browns covered with cheese, sour cream and salsa. Dinner entrees range from Chinese and Southwestern cuisine to a variety of interesting fresh seafood creations. The folks here even will cook your own catch of the day for you, as long as you've cleaned the fish first. Beer and wine are served. And homemade desserts add a great finishing touch to a tasty meal. The Pony Island Restaurant is adjacent to the Pony Island Motel. Breakfast here begins at 7 AM. The restaurant closes during lunchtime then reopens for dinner nightly from early April through late fall.

The Back Porch

1324 Country Rd. *928-6401*
$$$

Whether you dine on the wide, breezy screened porch, eat in this quaint restaurant's small nooks or get seated in the open dining room of this well-respected restaurant, you'll find that dinners at the Back Porch are some of the most pleasant experiences on the Outer Banks. Owners John and Debbie Wells renovated this older building and refurbished it to blend with the many trees on their property. It's off the main road, surrounded by waist-high cacti, and is a quiet place to enjoy appealing entrees and comfortable conversation. Overall, it's one of our favorite restaurants on the 120-mile stretch of barrier islands. It's well worth the two-hour trip from Nags Head — including the free ferry ride — just to eat here.

The menu is loaded with fresh herbs, vegetables and seafood, most of which is caught nearby. All sauces, dressings, breads and desserts are made right in the Wells' huge kitchen. And they hand-cut every piece of meat. In addition to the quality ingredients, these chefs come up with some pretty outrageous taste combinations — and all of them seem to blend perfectly. The crab cakes with red pepper sauce are outstanding. And you won't want to miss the smoked bluefish or crab beignets appetizers. Non-seafood dishes are a tasty option as well. Our favorite is the Cuban black bean and Monterey Jack cheese casserole. Reduced prices and smaller portions are available for children and senior citizens. And all the desserts are divine. Freshly ground coffee is served here, and the wine selections and imported beers are as ambitious as the menu. If you get hooked — like we are — you can try your hand at some of the Wells' recipes at home after buying a *Back Porch Cookbook*. Be prepared, however. Some of these menu items are quite involved. After reading the recipes you'll be even more impressed with the upscale culinary concoctions served in this laid-back island eatery. Dinner is offered nightly here in season.

Cap't. Ben's

N.C. 12 *928-4741*
$$

Serving Ocracoke locals and guests for 26 years, Cap't. Ben's is a casual restaurant that offers lunch and dinner every day from April through November. Owner and chef Ben Mugford combines Southern tradition with gourmet foods to achieve a well-balanced menu. Ben is especially revered for his crabmeat, prime rib and seafood entrees. He also serves a mean Caesar salad and comes up with some good pasta and chicken creations as well. Sandwiches, crab cakes and shrimp salad are good bets for lunch, each served with chips or fries. Dinners come with soup and salad. And all the desserts are delicious and homemade. A large variety of domestic and imported beers is available, and the wine list complements the menu. The decor in this family eatery is nautical and friendly. The lounge is a comfortable place to relax if you have to wait for a table.

Island Inn Restaurant

Lighthouse Rd. *928-7821*
$$

This family-owned and operated restaurant at the Island Inn is one of the oldest establishments on Ocracoke. Its main dining room and airy porch are furnished in a traditional country style, with blue and white china to dine on and bright, nautical touches throughout. Breakfast and dinner are served here daily except in the dead of winter. Owners Bob and Cee Touhey make sure everyone — not just Inn guests — are welcome to eat here. Standard breakfast fare, such as pancakes, eggs and hash browns, is available. And the cook also comes up with some unusual creations, such as oyster omelets with spinach and bacon, and shrimp omelets drenched with melted Jack cheese, green chiles and salsa.

For dinner, locally landed seafood and shellfish entrees can be grilled, fried or broiled to your liking. Beef, pork, lamb, pasta and stir-fry dishes also are available, as are vegetarian offerings. All the breads and soups are made daily at this restaurant. And homemade desserts from gingerbread with lemon sauce to chocolate chess pie and even pineapple layer cake are innovative and sweetly sinful. A selection of wines is served here, and a children's menu is available. Reservations are needed for large groups; the owners are happy to accommodate private party requests. Call for off-season hours.

Creekside Cafe

N.C. 12, across from Silver Lake *928-3606*
$

Overlooking Silver Lake Harbor from a second-story vantage point, the views from this year-old restaurant are wonderful. A covered porch around two sides of the wooden building has ceiling fans and breezes to cool afternoon diners. Inside, the eatery is casual and friendly, serving brunch items daily and lunch and dinner from a single menu between April and early November. Soups, salads, seafood and pasta dishes are the afternoon and evening fare here. The blackened chicken sandwiches already have gone over so well that the owners decided to package and sell the spices for the 1996 season. French dips, fresh fish sandwiches, fried oyster burgers, crab cakes and Greek-style linguine with feta cheese and black olives all are great choices. For brunch, we recommend the Tex-Mex: scrambled eggs, onions, peppers, tomatoes and salsa served in a tortilla shell with a dollop of guacamole. Desserts include parfaits, cheesecakes, Key lime pie, tollhouse pie and pecan pie — all homemade. Beer and wine are available, and four champagne drinks offer unusual alcoholic creations.

Howard's Pub & Raw Bar Restaurant

N.C. 12 *928-4441*
$

A fun, friendly place to go for a meal, conversation or to try one of more than 175 different types of beer, Howard's Pub is the only Ocracoke establishment that can boast it's open 366 days this year. Owners Buffy and Ann Warner hail from West Virginia, where he was a senator and she worked for the governor as director of economic development. Their lifestyles have changed a bit since purchasing this pub. And you can tell they love it. This is a must stop for everyone on Ocracoke, with great local flavor and guaranteed good times (see our Nightlife chapter). You can relax on the screened porch that stretches the length of this long, wooden restaurant. Or sit inside the ultra-casual eatery at a wooden table.

Howard's is the only raw bar on the island — and home of a spicy oyster shooter. We love these raw oyster and Tabasco combinations, especially when washed down with an unusual Australian beer. Howard's appetizers range from soups and salads to jalapeño poppers and hot wings. Lunch and dinner items include subs, burgers, fish sandwiches and, new for 1996, prime rib. Also in 1996, Howard's is adding a dishwasher. So instead of dining on paper plates with plastic utensils, real china and silverware now will be available. Buffy Warner also ordered his own wine label for red and white varieties to be served in his hip, always lively pub.

There's a wide-screen TV, several smaller ones, free popcorn and games from chess to Barrel of Monkeys to Trivial Pursuit to play with. You have lots of room for dancing to live bands in the evenings. And food and drinks are served every day beginning at lunchtime and continuing into the wee hours.

Cafe Atlantic

N.C. 12 *928-4861*
$$

This traditional beach-style building was opened a few years ago by Bob and Ruth Toth. But there's not much traditional about their innovative, fantastic food. Views from the dining room look out across marsh grass and dunes. The gallery-like effect of the restaurant is created with hand-colored photographs by local writer and artist Ann Ehringhaus. There's a nonsmoking dining room upstairs and a smoking section downstairs. Lunch and dinner are served at this upscale yet casual eatery seven days a week in season. And the Sunday brunches from

11 AM to 3 PM are the best we've found south of Duck. Brunch menus change weekly, but champagne and mimosas always are served. We're partial to the blueberry pecan pancakes, chicken and broccoli crepes and the huevos rancheros served over black beans in a crisp tortilla shell. Hash browns come with almost every entree. And the flavorful food will fill you up at least until supper.

The Toths make all of their soups, dressings, sauces and desserts from scratch. Lunches feature a variety of sandwiches and salads. Dinner entrees include caciucco — a combination of fresh fish, shrimp, scallops and mussels in marinara sauce served over linguine; and a wide range of beef, chicken, lasagna and other excellent seafood and pasta plates fill out the menu. Each meal is served with salad, rice or potato and steaming rolls just out of the oven. You've gotta leave room for dessert here — or take one of their outrageously ornate cakes, pies or cobblers home. A children's menu is available, and the restaurant has a nice selection of wine and beer. Cafe Atlantic is open from early March through October. Inquire about on- and off-site catering. This cafe — though isolated on tiny Ocracoke — is certainly among the best the dining experiences the Outer Banks have to offer.

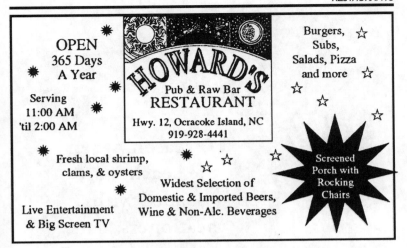

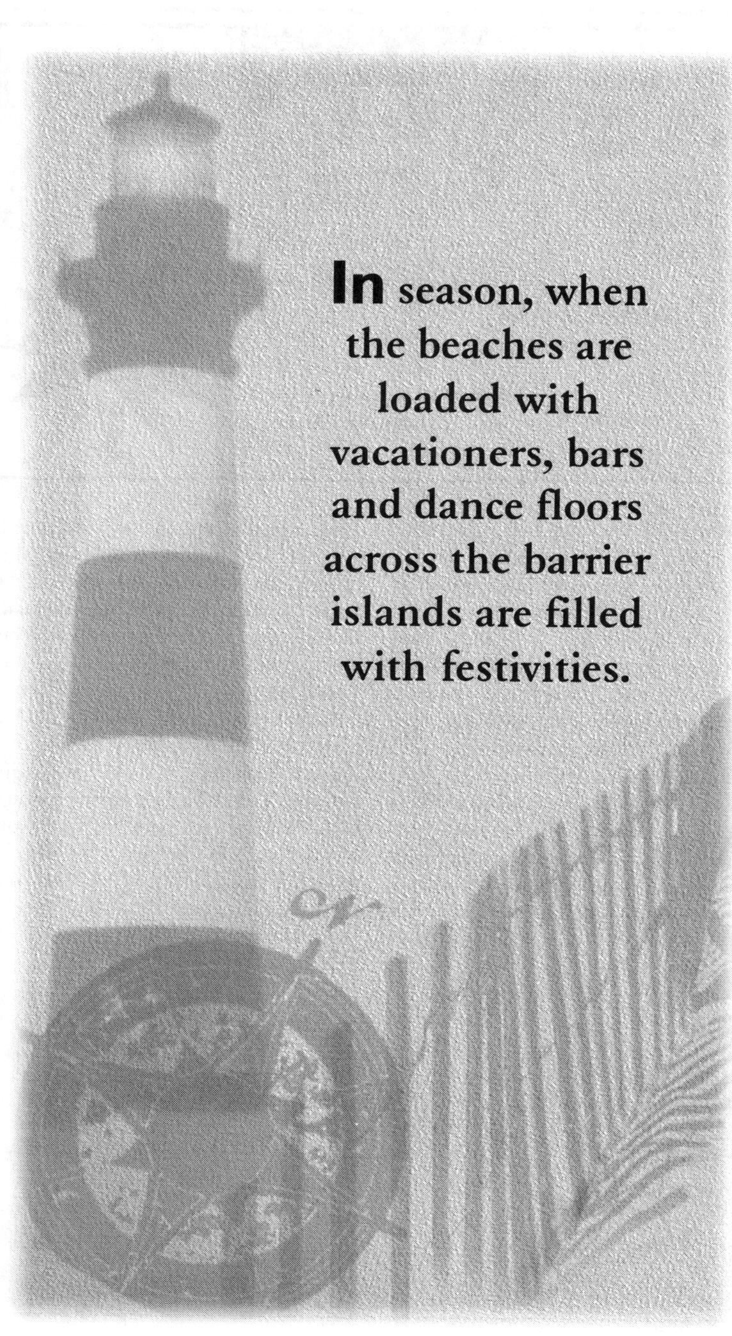
In season, when the beaches are loaded with vacationers, bars and dance floors across the barrier islands are filled with festivities.

Inside Nightlife

When the sun starts to sink into the silvery sounds and sparkling stars emerge across a darkening sky, nightlife begins to awaken along the Outer Banks — especially during summer. In recent years, many hot spots have begun hosting entertainment year round on weekends and holidays. But in season, when the beaches are loaded with vacationers, bars and dance floors across the barrier islands are filled with festivities.

The Outer Banks after hours aren't like other resort areas. So many families come here — and so many early-rising anglers — that many people are bedded down for the evening by 9 PM. But if you're a night owl, or at least like to stretch your wings a bit on vacation, there's always fun and frolic to be found in dozens of establishments from Corolla through Ocracoke.

Families also can enjoy a variety of early evening entertainment here. Miniature golf, go-cart tracks, movie theaters, bumper boats, even an amusement park and bowling alley are listed in our Recreation chapter. And don't forget *The Lost Colony* outdoor drama that's written up in our Attractions chapter.

But if what you want to do is unwind — or gear up for a really good time — there are plenty of places to shoot pool, watch sporting events on big-screened TVs, play interactive trivia, throw darts, learn to line dance, listen to low-key acoustic music or boogie the night away to a rocking live band.

Local musicians play everything from blues to jazz to rock to hard-core alternative and country tunes. Outer Banks and out-of-town cover bands and those with original songs also take the stage often during the summer season. Several nightclubs on the Outer Banks assess nominal cover charges at the door, usually ranging from $1 for dueling guitar duos to $10 for national acts that grace these sands between mid-May and Labor Day. Many of the acoustic acts, however, can be heard for free.

If live music is what you're listening for, check *The Virginian-Pilot's* weekly *Carolina Coast* magazine — available free at area grocery and general stores — for an up-to-date listing in its "Club Hoppin'" section. Local music lover Linda McBreen also operates a service noting all the hippest entertainment happenings. Call her recorded message at 480-CLUB for updates on which bands are playing where. WVOD FM 99.1 and

Insiders' Tips

Taxis wait outside most Outer Banks nightclubs, and bartenders will be happy to call you a cab if you can't find one on your own. Local police often are on the prowl for drunk drivers after midnight — and lives are at stake — so don't risk it.

WERX FM 102.5 also give daily concert updates on their evening radio broadcasts.

Drinks are available at most Outer Banks lounges until around 2 AM. Beer and wine are offered throughout the barrier islands. But in Corolla and on Colington, Roanoke, Hatteras and Ocracoke islands, mixed drinks aren't allowed to be sold — by law. With the exception of Colington Island, however, ABC stores sell liquor in each of those areas. And most nightclubs on those islands allow people to brown bag — bringing in their own alcohol for the evening. Call ahead to make sure that's okay.

Several restaurants on the Outer Banks offer late-night menus or at least raw and steamer bar food until closing. Every nightclub operator will be glad to call a cab to take you home or to your hotel or rental cottage after an evening of imbibing. Beware: The legal drinking age in North Carolina is 21, and the blood-alcohol content for a drunk driving citation is only .08. So even if you've only had a couple of cocktails, play it safe and take a taxi. It's a whole lot cheaper than court costs.

Although several area restaurants offer happy hour specials — and most have bars inside their establishments — we've only included those that are open until at least midnight in this chapter. Check our Restaurants chapter for early bird bar specials and sunset entertainment schedules. Several spots also feature outdoor acoustic music until dark — but this section is for those who like to come out with the stars.

Corolla

Neptune's Grill & Arcade

Timbuck II Shopping Center
off N.C. 12 *453-8645*

A laid-back burger joint offering dine in, take-out and delivery of good, cheap eats, this year-old establishment has the only pool table north of Duck. Pinball, Foosball and a variety of video games also are available here, and beer and wine are sold until late in the evening. Neptune's is open year round, seven days a week in season. Call for winter hours.

Duck

Barrier Island Inn Restaurant and Tavern

Duck Rd. (N.C. 12) *261-8700*

A favorite nightspot in Duck Village, this tavern is upstairs, separate from the restaurant. Folks enjoy fabulous sunsets overlooking Currituck Sound and indoor recreation including a pool table, dart board and tabletop shuffleboard. There's an outdoor deck where you can stargaze until closing time, and live acoustic music or bands can be heard here most summer nights. The tavern offers interactive TV trivia nightly year round, and QB1 interactive football is fun for armchair quarterbacks — especially those who enjoy the free buffalo wings that the tavern serves during fall football season. Steamed shrimp, sandwiches and pizza are available late at the bar or around tables sized to accommodate any party. Barrier Island is open seven nights a week. Call for summer schedules of entertainment.

Fishbones Raw Bar & Restaurant

Scarborough Lane Shops
Duck Rd. (N.C. 12) *261-6991*

Opened in the summer of 1995, this raw bar and restaurant is fast becoming one of Duck's most popular evening hangouts. It's open every day year round and features a full bar including four beers on tap, a variety of domestic and microbrewery beers and a wine list. Live music is performed here at least three days a week, with blues artists being Fishbones' speciality. In the summer, deck parties are held outdoors in good weather. It's a casual place to catch up on conversation with old acquaintances — or make new ones.

Roadside Bar & Grill

Duck Rd. (N.C. 12) *261-5729*

Low-key, casual and offering great food year round, Roadside is another new Duck establishment that's been receiving rave reviews from locals and tourists alike. There's a full bar in this restored 1932 cottage, and an outdoor patio where live blues music is performed twice a week in season. Appetizers and cocktails can be consumed under the stars, and you'll enjoy the hardwood floors and homey feeling inside as well. Roadside is open seven days a week.

Kitty Hawk

Rundown Cafe

Beach Rd., MP 1 *255-0026*

If you're looking for summertime blues and jazz — or just want to sip some frothy brews — this Caribbean-style cafe is always an exciting spot to hang out on the north end of the beach. It's owned by the same friendly folks who run Tortuga's Lie restaurant in Nags Head, and it's a great place to relax with friends, listen to some of the best music on the Outer Banks several nights a week or just sit a spell at the long bar. You'll even be comfortable coming in here alone. A rooftop deck was added in 1995, affording great views of the ocean and the opportunity to catch some cool breezes and cool conversation. There's a variety of domestic and imported beers on hand and a full line of liquor — including specialty rum and tequila drinks. The steam and raw bar serves seafood and vegetables until closing. By the way, Rundown is a traditional Jamaican stew, and the decor reflects the cafe's unusual name. Call ahead for a rundown of the evening entertainment, or just stop by and check out this happening haunt.

Frisco's

U.S. 158, MP 4 *261-7833*

A popular nightspot for locals year round, this restaurant features a huge, three-sided bar and beautiful terrariums and aquariums throughout the dining area. It's open seven days a week, and karaoke offers everyone a chance to take the stage Wednesday through Sunday evenings. Groups are welcome and encouraged here, and singles and couples will find a good time, too. There are tables of all sizes in the lounge, and drink specials are served late into the night. There's even a wide-screen TV for sports fans. The best part about Frisco's, in our opinion, is that the managers here offer a free courtesy van to drive you home if you've been drinking.

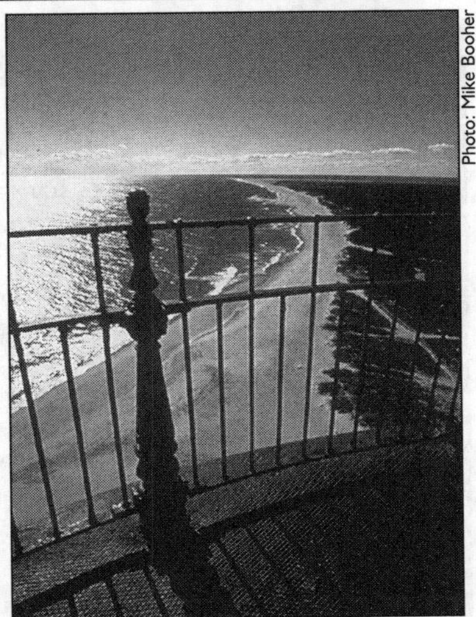

Photo: Mike Booher

A view from the top of the Cape Hatteras Lighthouse — it's worth the climb.

Black Pelican Seafood Company

Beach Rd., MP 4½ *261-3171*

With 12 TVs and an enclosed porch overlooking the ocean, this Kitty Hawk hangout is a fun place to catch up on sporting events or just sit a spell at the bar. It's in a former Coast Guard Station and still features hardwood floors, tongue-and-groove appointments and light gray accents reminiscent of days gone by. In

Meteor Showers

While we can't actually put the stars in our vacation brochures as Wonders of the Outer Banks, as Insiders we know we have the best seats in the house when it comes to star gazing. You can still find beaches here that are isolated enough to provide darkness, and the shore is a great place to lay down and gaze upward. Think of the sand molding to your body. No cricks in the neck. No chairs to carry.

Throw a blanket down on a personally made sand chaise and even a pregnant woman will be comfortable. Instantly you have an outdoor amphitheater with the ocean providing original background music. If you drive down N.C. 12 toward Hatteras, you'll be headed into a more isolated part of the Outer Banks beaches located in the National Park, away from oceanfront development. Coquina Beach is a good place to stop the car and head toward the sand. There's plenty of parking too.

The nice thing about sky-gazing is that it's free and you don't need any optical aid other than the naked eye. And if you're really into doing it up right down by the seaside, choose one of the summer showers to witness. While January has a spectacular show called the Quadrantids where you can see 40 meteors per hour, it could be too cold for oceanfront seating.

There are nine major meteor showers you can look for from January through December. The average hourly count for meteors ranges from 15 to 50, depending on the time of year. Mark your calendars with these dates. The specific date marks the peak day of the shower, the quantity marks the average hourly rate an observer can see.

January 4th — The Quadrantids, 40
April 21st — The Lyrids, 15
May 4 — The Eta Aquarids, 20
July 29 — The Delta Aquarids, 20
August 12 — The Perseids, 50
October 20 — Orionids, 25
November 5 — Taurids, 15
November 16 — Leonids, 15
December 14 — Geminids, 50

Before approaching the beach, let your eyes adjust to the dark. This way you'll be less apt to turn on a flashlight, which will surely disturb other watchers already in place. If you absolutely must use one to get to the beach, try putting a dark handkerchief over it. Arriving early will also solve this problem.

Leave the music home. This will give you an opportunity to really commune with nature, plus you won't be able to hear all the oohs and ahs of your fellow sky watchers if the radio is blasting.

Lazily gaze to the heavens. The meteors can be seen in all parts of the sky. We hope you enjoy the show — Outer Banks style!

the evenings, its upbeat atmosphere is anything but antique. Live music is offered sporadically throughout the summer season, and gourmet pizzas are a great treat for late-night munchies. The Black Pelican is open year round. Call for entertainment schedules.

Kill Devil Hills

Chilli Peppers

U.S. 158, MP 5½ *441-8081*

Southwestern fusion food from the fiery to mild is served at this small, innovative restaurant year round. The separate bar area out front always is teeming with partying people. In the off-season, live entertainment and open-mike nights are featured, but it gets too crowded in the summer to pack a band in here. A full bar offers fresh fruit Margaritas, a nice wine selection and dozens of domestic and imported beers seven nights a week. Bartenders also serve nonalcoholic beers and fruit smoothies that complement any meal. There's an outdoor patio if you want to sip your drinks under the stars, and steamed seafood and vegetables are served until closing.

Awful Arthur's

Beach Rd., MP 6 *441-5955*

Loud, packed with people and about as popular as it gets on the Outer Banks, this rustic restaurant features a live lobster tank and long bar downstairs and a separate upstairs lounge that affords patrons an ocean view. Live bands perform downstairs on Monday nights throughout the off-season, and during the summer, live music is featured in the upstairs lounge area. Locals love to hang out here — especially on Mondays when there are food and drink specials all day. There's a full bar, lots of cold beer on tap and raw or steamed seafood served late into the night. The TVs always seem to be tuned into the day's most popular sporting event. The T-shirts here sell as well as the steamed shrimp. College students especially seem to enjoy Arthur's atmosphere, but people of all ages will find a good time here seven nights a week year round.

The Sea Ranch Lounge

Sea Ranch, Beach Rd., MP 7 *441-7126*

A longtime tradition for Outer Banks' shaggers, this lounge in the Sea Ranch hotel features local musician Buzz Bessette Tuesday through Saturday nights year round. He plays a variety of dance music from the '50s to the '90s — and there's almost always someone cutting a rug on the dance floor. A full bar is open seven nights a week and a large-screen TV is always on for added entertainment. Recorded beach music is played here Monday nights. The low-key atmosphere seems to attract a more mature crowd than other Outer Banks establishments.

Jolly Roger Restaurant

Beach Rd., MP 7 *441-6530*

Adorned with hanging plants and colorful lights, the lounge at this restaurant is separate from the dining area. This is a casual place with a long, wooden bar and there's almost always something going on here late into the night. Most summer evenings, there's live acoustic entertainment or a band. Outer Banks folk favorite Jamie Jamison plays a variety of country, rock and blues every Thursday night — and usually brings some musician friends with him. The Wilder Brothers (Kevin Roughton and Tom Scheel) perform often throughout the year, and the bar is open seven nights a week. Interactive TV featuring games from sports to movie trivia draws a regular audience. Prizes are even awarded to some of the big winners. Locals love this place and you'll find people from their early 20s to late 60s hanging out here year round.

Paradise Billiards

The Dare Centre, U.S. 158, MP 7 441-9225

The Outer Banks' only private club, Paradise's owners decided to take that step in 1995 so they could serve mixed drinks in addition to the beer and wine that's available at other pool halls. Annual memberships cost $5 and state law requires a three-day waiting period between the time you apply and get your pass. But if you know when you plan to arrive, you can call or mail in a request ahead of time — and your membership will be waiting for you at the door. There are six pool tables here and play is by the hour. The 50-inch TV includes a satellite system with a special sports package that provides plenty of nationwide events that patrons wouldn't be able to watch elsewhere. Dart boards, pinball and free interactive trivia also are on hand until 2 AM. For 1996, in addition to liquor, bartenders will be serving an expanded late night menu featuring steak sandwiches, burgers and deli offerings until midnight. You must be 21 or older to come to Paradise after 7 PM — and if you're younger than 21 and want to shoot pool in the daytime, you have to bring an adult with you. To order a membership by mail, write: Paradise Billiards, P.O. Box 3307, Kill Devil Hills 27948.

Goombay's Grille and Raw Bar

Beach Rd., MP 7½ 441-6001

This popular nightspot teems with tourists and locals year round and is open seven nights a week. It's fun and colorful with a tropical island flair and flavor — and the bartenders all are local characters. Goombay's is Caribbean and casual, the kind of hangout where you're sure to feel right at home even if you've never visited the Outer Banks. On Wednesdays during the off-season, live bands play here for an increasingly crowded "Locals' Night." During the summer, acoustic entertainment is offered several nights a week. The horseshoe-shape bar is set off to the side from the dining area, so you can lounge on a stool or high-backed chair in the bar area or have a seat at a nearby table after the dining room closes at 10 PM. Goombay's serves lots of imported and domestic beer, wine and mixed drinks until 2 AM. Be sure to try some of the special rum, vodka and tequila combos that come with toys to take home. Steamed shrimp and veggies are served until closing.

Quagmire's

Beach Rd., MP 8 441-9188

The newest addition to Outer Banks nightclubs, this fun-loving place opened in the former Papagayo's Restaurant — also the site of the old Croatan Inn — just in time for the 1996 summer season. It's owned by the same groovy guy who runs Goombay's, so you know once you step inside or out onto one of the biggest open-air oceanfront decks on the beach, you're bound to have a great time. A horseshoe-shape bar faces the Atlantic — so everyone sitting on a stool is guaranteed a gorgeous view. Frozen drinks are served outdoors or in, and the bartenders even pour pitchers of margaritas here so you don't have to keep getting up to fill your thin-stemmed, salt-encrusted glass. Beer, wine and mixed drinks are available, and there's a whole line of appetizers and munchies to sample through the night. Quagmire's is open seven days a week year round and features live acoustic music throughout the summer season. On the sand below the bar, horseshoes, a ring toss and beach volleyball court beckon people to come play if they need a break from partying in the lounge.

Dare Devils Authentic Pizzeria

Beach Rd., MP 8½ 441-6330

With a big-screen TV and four types of beer on tap, this wide, airy pizza joint is a cool place to kick back and enjoy an evening with friends. Dare Devils some-

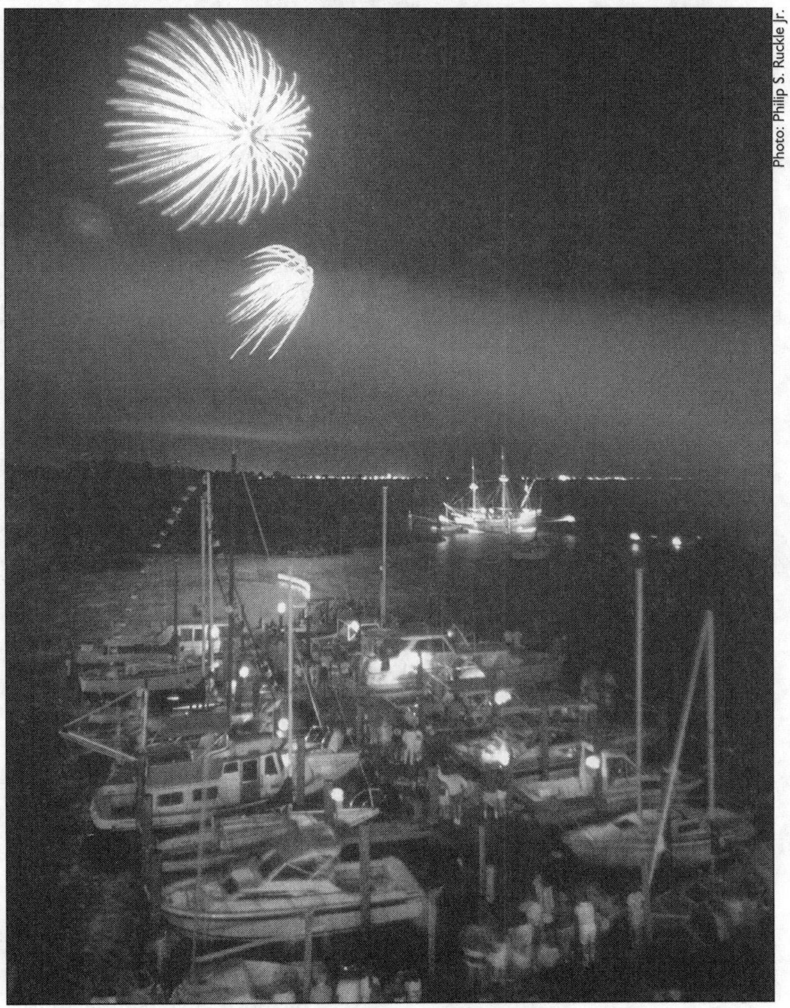

Photo: Philip S. Ruckle Jr.

Fourth of July in downtown Manteo.

times offers live music in season. There are plenty of domestic and imported beers served in heavy glass mugs, a wine list and mixed drinks to sip at a table or while sitting at the bar. Each pizza is cooked to order and there also are a variety of appetizers, from plates piled high with nachos to hot wings sure to set your mouth on fire.

Port O' Call Gaslight Saloon

Beach Rd., MP 8½ *441-7484*

One of the area's most unusual places to hang out — and one of the only nightclubs that attracts national bands in the summer — the Gaslight Saloon is decorated in an ornate Victorian style complete with overstuffed arm chairs, antique wooden tables and a long mahogany bar.

There's a nice dance floor here and an upstairs lounge with a separate bar that overlooks the band stage. Port O' Call features live entertainment seven nights a week in season and every weekend while the restaurant is open from mid-March through December. There's usually a cover charge here for the bigger name bands. Beer, wine and liquor are served until 2 AM.

Shucker's Pub and Billiards

Oceanside Plaza
Beach Rd., MP 8½ *480-1010*

This pub and billiard room serves more than 75 types of beer and features the only nine-foot pool tables on the Outer Banks. A dozen billiard tables offer people the chance to play by the game or the hour. Darts, Foosball and pinball also are popular pastimes, and there are plenty of TVs for sports fans. Shucker's is open year round, seven nights a week until 2 AM. Wine is available, and Shucker's serves pizza and sandwiches until closing. You must be 21 or older to play in this pub after 9 PM.

Crocker's Ocean Reef Cafe

Ocean Reef Motel
Beach Rd., MP 8½ *441-4080*

An upstairs bar featuring "monumental sunsets" behind the Wright Brothers' Memorial, this small cafe is a late-night haunt for locals. It's quiet and subdued, with a variety of games and Jimmy Buffett music usually playing in the background. Crocker's serves beer, wine and liquor. The restaurant offers sushi on Mondays and Thursdays, 50¢ tacos on Tuesdays, and pizza, deli sandwiches and shrimp throughout the week.

Madeline's at the Holiday Inn

Beach Rd., MP 9½ *441-6333*

A disc jockey spins Top 40 tunes here most summer nights, and live bands sometimes take the stage. Every Thursday night from Memorial Day through August, there's a bikini contest offering cash prizes. Madeline's often charges a cover at the door. The lounge serves beer, wine and mixed drinks year round and is a convenient place for guests of the hotel who don't want to worry about having to drive anywhere after enjoying an evening out on the town.

Peppercorn's at the Ramada Inn

Beach Rd., MP 9½ *441-2151*

Enjoy a breathtaking ocean view out of the plate-glass window wall while visiting with friends and listening to acoustic soloists or duos in the Ramada Inn's expanded lounge area. Live music is performed frequently throughout the summer and often starts earlier here than elsewhere on the Outer Banks — sometimes at 8 PM. This is an open, laid-back place with booths, tables and a full bar. The music is never too loud to talk over. But if you'd rather listen, some of the best guitar talent on the beach shows up here in-season.

Colington Island

Blue Crab Tavern

Colington Rd.
1½ miles west of U.S. 158 *441-5919*

A favorite early afternoon and evening haunt for this island's watermen, Blue Crab includes an indoor bar, pool tables, video games and one of the best soundfront decks in the area. Fishermen often pull their boats up to the rectangular deck and tie onto the wooden pilings to sip a few beers outdoors after work. Lots of local characters hang out here, and if you sit a spell, you're sure to hear what's biting where. Liquor is not available, but brews are cold — and among the cheapest you'll find. There's a horseshoe pit out front if you feel like tossing a few around after you've tossed a few down.

Nags Head

The Fish Market

U.S. 158, MP 9¾ *441-7889*

A local hangout popular with fishermen and Outer Banks natives, this low-key restaurant includes an L-shape wooden bar and great barrier island flavor. The Fish Market serves all sorts of beer, and the bartenders shake and stir mixed drinks to suit any taste. On Sundays, step into a NASCAR speedway cheering section and prepare to get caught up in the fast-paced action broadcast from overhead TVs. The Fish Market features live acoustic music year round on Friday and Saturday nights and serves great locally caught seafood throughout the evening.

Mulligan's Oceanfront Grille

Beach Rd., MP 10 *480-2000*

Under new ownership for 1996, Mulligan's is still heralded as a popular evening hot spot and retains its image — and feel — of the Outer Banks own version of TV's *Cheers*. A wooden partition separates the long, three-sided wooden bar from the dining room, and loads of local memorabilia adorns the walls. Mulligan's serves beer on tap or from iced-down bottles. Wine and liquor also are available.

Atlantis Nightclub

U.S. 158, MP 10 *480-3757*

In early 1996, this always rockin' nightspot moved from its rundown oceanfront location into the former Night Flight Restaurant building on the Bypass. It's brighter, much bigger and has renovated, well-working bathrooms now. Even the air conditioning is guaranteed to crank all summer. The same owner, Jerry "Chopper" Dowless, runs the place — so you're still sure to see great bands. After all, he was the one who first brought Hootie and the Blowfish, Live and the Dave Matthews Band to the Outer Banks.

The 1996 summer lineup promises to feature national, regional and local acts as well, with groups playing everything from classic rock to reggae to alternative to progressive and blues music already booked. There's a much bigger dance floor in the new building, a two-story lounge and lots more room to enjoy all the entertainment. Former Mex-Econo Restaurant owner Chris Campbell even cooks up some surprises in the Atlantis' new vegetarian restaurant — housed in the same white building as the nightclub. This place can pack in crowds of up to 500 people and is probably the biggest club between Greenville and Norfolk. Be prepared to pay a cover charge here, with prices dependent on the band's popularity. Call for a summer schedule.

Sweetwaters

U.S. 158, MP 10½ *441-3427*

Separated from the restaurant by a wide entry way, this split-level bar includes booths, tables and plenty of stools. Sweetwaters features live acoustic entertainment throughout the summer, and has two TVs for viewing enjoyment. The bar serves the restaurant's complete menu until 10 PM and a light menu after that time. This is a comfortable place to come with a date or a group of people.

Insiders' Tips

Some nightclubs charge a cover, and most bars only accept late-night patrons age 21 or older. Call ahead for specific costs and rules about underage people. If you're age 40 or younger, bring your driver's license with you and prepare to get carded.

The Comedy Club at the Carolinian Lounge

Beach Rd., MP 10½ *441-7171*

This is the oldest oceanfront summer comedy club in the country, featuring soon-to-be stars for more than 12 years. Favorite television comics Sinbad, Brett Butler and Drew Carey all have tickled people's funny bones from this eclectically adorned stage. National comedians are booked for the summer of 1996 as well. Reservations are recommended — although the room is big, it often gets packed in the season. There's a full bar here, and cocktail servers offer tableside service throughout the show. One cover charge includes three comics who each appear separately and always put on hilarious acts — many that demand audience participation. Doors open at 9 PM seven nights a week in season and the laughter begins around 10. During the fall and spring, the comedy club is open only on weekends. Before the show, you can enjoy your favorite beverages from a bar on the outside, oceanfront deck. The Carolinian features free live music on the deck six evenings a week in season — weather permitting. Priority seating in the comedy club is given to those who dine in the Carolinian's restaurant.

Kelly's Tavern

U.S. 158, MP 10½ *441-4116*

Probably the most consistently crowded tavern on the Outer Banks, Kelly's offers live bands six nights a week in season and a lip-sync contest with cash prizes on the only off-night, Monday. Even during the fall and winter, rockin' bands take the stage, and fun people always fill this place. There's a full bar serving everything from suds to shots — and folks often line up around its three long sides two or three people deep. The big dance floor is usually shaking after 10 PM. If you're in the mood just to listen and watch, secluded booths surround the dance floor a few steps above the rest of the lounge, and tables are scattered throughout the tavern. A dart board and fireplace adorn the back area, and beach memorabilia hangs from every corner. Featuring a tasty variety of foods served late into the night, a lounge menu offers appetizers and steamed shellfish. An old-fashioned popcorn popper even provides free munchies in wicker baskets throughout the evening. Singles seem to really enjoy this tavern.

George's Junction

Beach Rd., MP 11 *441-0606*

The Outer Banks' only all-country saloon, this high-steppin' hot spot opened in the summer of 1995 and has kept line-dancing locals lively ever since. It's open from March through November seven days a week, featuring twanging tunes to dance to throughout the summer season. A Dixie disc jockey plays oldies, disco and, of course, country music. Live country bands often kick up their heels here. Karaoke contests also are held — with cash prizes awarded for the best performances. Free line-dancing lessons are offered until 2 AM most summer nights. There's a full bar and separate lounge area if you'd rather relax and take it all in. Call for a summer schedule of entertainment.

Tortuga's Lie Shellfish Bar and Grill

Beach Rd., MP 11 *441-7299*

Our favorite place to meet friends for a laid-back evening — or hang out alone to chat with long-lost local pals — Tortuga's offers sporadic acoustic entertainment in summer and probably the most comfortable atmosphere you'll find on the Outer Banks most of the year. Owners Will Thorpe and Bob Sanders often are on hand to greet guests themselves. They renovated their restaurant just in time for the 1996 season — regulars will notice the closed-in screened porch that now includes custom-made wooden booths and ceiling fans. The bar also got bigger —

winding around a corner, allowing at least a half-dozen more stools to slide under the redone countertop. Don't worry, however, if you loved Tortuga's just as it was: All the old license plates still perch on the low, wooden ceiling beams and the sand volleyball court remains ready for pickup games out back all summer. Bartenders serve the ever-popular Black and Tan brews in pint-size glasses — that's right, they have Guinness and Bass Ale on tap. Longneck beers are served by the bottle or by the iced-down bucket. Shooters, mixed drinks and tropical frozen concoctions are sure to please any palate. The steamer is open until closing, so you can satisfy late-night munchies with shellfish or fresh vegetables. Whether you're new in town or here to stay, Tortuga's is one place you won't want to miss. Most nights, it remains open until 2 AM. Tortuga's closes for a brief spell in January and early February.

Lance's Seafood Bar and Market

U.S. 158, MP 14 — *441-7501*

Live bands don't play here often, but when they do, this pink building on the Bypass is packed. Lance's has a full bar and lots of wooden tables. The people here are down-to-earth and regulars seem to return each season. It's unpretentious, decorated with duck decoys, mounted gamefish and beach memorabilia. When music is offered, chairs are pushed away to form a dance floor near the center of the lounge.

Maione's

U.S. 158, MP 15 — *480-3311*

Across from the Outer Banks Mall, this authentic Italian restaurant has a separate lounge area featuring a full bar. Light, contemporary live music often is performed on summer evenings, and a late-night menu complements the entertainment.

Roanoke Island

Dock of the Bay Cafe

U.S. 64, Manteo — *473-6845*

This cozy cafe has a long bar serving steamed shrimp, clams and oysters into the night along with sandwiches and homemade soups. Dock of the Bay offers more than 50 microbrews — and plenty of other domestic and imported beers and wines — at the bar and tables. There's a wide, outdoor deck overlooking the Roanoke Sound, where cool breezes complement cold drinks on hot summer nights. Food and beverage specials often are featured in season. Live acoustic musicians perform here on summer Fridays, weather permitting. Anyone would feel welcome in this friendly, locally owned-and-operated establishment.

The Green Dolphin Restaurant and Pub

Sir Walter Raleigh St., Manteo — *473-5911*

Acoustic entertainers perform here on Fridays year round, featuring rock, folk, blues, beach and even light jazz tunes. There's a big bar serving a variety of beer, and there's never a cover charge for live music. This pub is warm and dark, with wooden floors, booths and tables made from old ship hatch covers. The staff is friendly, and locals like to hang out here. It's a fun, sometimes rowdy place with

Insiders' Tips

Bob's Grill on U.S. 158 in Kill Devil Hills is the Outer Banks' only all-night restaurant, serving burgers, appetizers, sandwiches and even breakfast all night Thursdays through Sundays in season. It's a great place to satisfy late-night munchies — or just unwind after a night on the town.

pool tables and pockmarked dart boards set in a separate room. The restaurant serves appetizers and sandwiches late into the night. Call for seasonal schedules of entertainment.

Hatteras Island

Casual Clam II

Pamlico Station
N.C. 12, Rodanthe *987-2700*

Cold beer, cool bartenders and some of the cheapest seafood on the Outer Banks are highlights here from March through November seven nights a week. The restaurant serves 10¢ shrimp, 30¢ clams, pizza, sandwiches and nacho platters late into the night. Foosball, pool tables and a variety of video and arcade games offer added entertainment. There's an outside deck and gazebo that afford both sound and ocean views. Live acoustic performers play here every other weekend in summer. This is one of the only late-night establishments on northern Hatteras Island.

Surfriders Grill

N.C. 12, Rodanthe *987-2220*

Newly built in 1996 and operated by Outer Banks surfing enthusiasts, this upbeat restaurant has 20 types of beer on tap — all served in frosty glass mugs. The bar is shaped like two large waves, laminated with surfing logos from around the country, and is built so low you can sit on stools and still have your feet touch the ground. Walls here are adorned with — what else? — surfing memorabilia, enough to qualify it as Hatteras Island's own surf museum. Appetizers from all over the world are cooked up in the kitchen, including loads of vegetarian and health-food selections. It's a casual place where you can stop in wearing shorts and sandals. Surfriders shows surfing videos on TVs most nights and hosts some live music in season. Although it just opened, we predict Surfriders will quickly become one of Hatteras Island's most popular places to eat, drink and philosophize about the sea. Ride this wave while it's still breaking . . .

The Froggy Dog

N.C. 12, Avon *995-4106*

The Lily Pad Lounge inside this Hatteras Island restaurant is open seven nights a week year round. A disc jockey plays tunes Friday nights, and live acoustic solo guitarists and duos perform each Saturday — all for free. Karaoke, for the aspiring star in everyone, is offered Sunday through Thursday nights. For 1996, there's an expanded appetizer menu served at the bar as well as a variety of beer, wine and the ever-popular steamed shrimp.

Soundside Restaurant

N.C. 12, Buxton *995-6778*

New for the summer of 1996, this waterfront eatery is the only Hatteras Island hot spot south of Avon that caters to a late-night crowd. There's a separate lounge area that just opened in the downstairs level where acoustic guitar musicians perform most weekends in season. Soundside serves a variety of beer and wine — and brown-bagging is welcome.

Insiders' Tips

Longtime Outer Banks guitarist Jamie Jamison performs at a variety of clubs across the area year round. This talented musician plays everything from country to rock to blues tunes — and sounds a lot like Willie Nelson, although he has a charm all his own.

Ocracoke Island

Howard's Pub & Raw Bar Restaurant

N.C. 12 *928-4441*

Our absolute favorite place to hear live bands — featuring the friendliest crowd of locals and visitors around — Howard's Pub has an atmosphere and feeling all its own. Once you've visited, you'll plan to make at least a yearly excursion to this upbeat but laid-back place. We try to return at least once a month to get a fix of fun and to get away from it all. In 1996, Howard's is open 366 days a year until 2 AM — the only place on the Outer Banks that can make that claim. It's also the only restaurant on Ocracoke open year round.

The pub serves more types of beer than any place we know of — at least 175 different bottles line the top shelf above the bar, showing an unusual array of offerings from around the world that are always available at this oasis on the isolated island. There's an outdoor deck here for catching sunsets or stars. A huge screened porch — complete with Adirondack rocking chairs for relaxing in the evening breezes — wraps around one side of the spacious wooden building. A wide-screen TV offers sports fans constant entertainment, and six other TVs usually tune into a variety of events. Howard's has a dart board, backgammon, chess set, checkers, Trivial Pursuit, Barrel of Monkeys and card games available for free to playful patrons. Bartenders serve pizza, sandwiches and raw bar-style food until 2 AM, and offer free chili Monday nights during football season.

Bands play at least three nights a week in season — and can be heard here even on winter weekends. Music ranges from rhythm and blues to bluegrass, jazz, rock and originals. Open-mike nights and karaoke are favorite events with locals and visitors alike. The cover charge at Howard's is never more than $2. Even when electricity fails the rest of the island, this pub is equipped with a generator so employees can keep on cooking — and keep the beer cold.

Photo: Mary Ellen Riddle

The Outer Banks' very own nightingale, Laura Martier, sings jazz regularly when she's not recording a CD or traveling to New York to perform.

Jolly Roger Pub

N.C. 12, Ocracoke Village *928-3703*

A waterfront eatery overlooking Silver Lake, this pub has a huge outdoor deck that's covered in case of thunderstorms. Local entertainers often perform live acoustic music here — with no cover charge. Jolly Roger serves beer, wine and finger foods throughout summer.

From the off-road wilderness of Currituck's National Wildlife Refuge in Carova — north of where N.C. 12's pavement ends — to the quaint hammocks of live oak that line Ocracoke Island, rental cottages are scattered along almost every mile of the Outer Banks.

Inside Weekly and Long-term Cottage Rentals

Unlike other beach resorts, where vacationers arrive to spend a day or two at a time, most Outer Banks visitors enjoy these isolated barrier islands so much that they choose to stay a week or more each summer. Hotels, motels, efficiency apartments, inns and bed and breakfast establishments all cater to short-term lodgings, from a day to weekend to even a week. Listings for those units are included in our Accommodations chapter.

But if you crave a longer getaway — usually from a week to a month at a time — rental cottages probably will be more to your liking. And if, like most locals, you decide you never want to leave this vacation paradise, this chapter also includes long-term rental options to help you stake out a year-round place in the sand. A few rental companies even will lease properties by the month or season in case you just want to be here for the warm weather — or during the deserted months when most other visitors have left the beach.

From the off-road wilderness of Currituck's National Wildlife Refuge in Carova — north of where N.C. 12's pavement ends — to the quaint hammocks of live oak that line Ocracoke Island, rental cottages are scattered along almost every mile of the Outer Banks.

"Cottage" options range from small beach bungalows that sleep two to four people amidst wooden crate-style furnishings to huge oceanfront mansions that sleep at least 20 — complete with columns, Jacuzzis, fireplaces, decks, porches and custom, upscale interior decorations. If you plan early enough and do your research, you can find short-term rentals to suit any taste, budget or size party in just about any place you wish to be.

Weekly rentals are the most popular options, followed by seasonal and monthly leases. In the off-seasons, many cottage management companies also allow vacationers to rent homes for three- or four-day weekends. And they cut the rates at least in half. The peak season here is summer — from mid-June through August. Most companies rent cottages at least from Easter through Thanksgiving. And many offer year-round short and long-term leases.

In this chapter, we've tried to help you plan any vacation — or long-term stay — you might desire. Information is included on reservations, deposits, regulations, equipment rentals and, of course, cottage rental companies throughout the Outer Banks. Your best bet is to reserve that vacation getaway early, often by late March. It's almost impossible to secure a weekly

Insiders' Tips

If you don't want to carry sandy towels, bathing suits and clothes home with you, call ahead to see whether the cottage you're renting has laundry facilities.

cottage rental after schools let out in June. But sometimes, rental managers can squeeze you in if there's a cancellation.

Planning Your Cottage Vacation

Demand and prices for rentals vary according to the area of the beach you want to be on, proximity of the property to the ocean, amenities offered, number of people the unit sleeps and the time of year during which you plan to stay. Traditionally, oceanfront properties book first. Cottages that are semi-oceanfront and between U.S. 158 and the Beach Road in the central areas of the Outer Banks typically book up next. Soundfront and soundside properties and those west of U.S. 158 tend to be reserved at a slower rate simply because they are farther from the ocean.

Descriptions of Locations

Rental properties right on the beach — with no homes or lots between the cottages and the Atlantic — are called "oceanfront" and are, by far, the most popular option for vacationers. In these houses, you can walk out your door onto the sand, eat lunch at home without driving to another destination and fall asleep to the rhythm of the waves. You'll pay for those privileges, though — these are the most expensive properties.

Semi-oceanfront cottages usually lie one lot behind an oceanfront lot or oceanfront house. Distance to the Atlantic varies. And some views are blocked by high sand dunes. Oceanside properties are those from which you can walk to the beach without having to cross a major street or road. There will be other rows of houses along roads or lanes between your cottage and the ocean. But sometimes you can still watch the waves from these homes' upstairs windows.

Many cottages from Kitty Hawk through Nags Head are between the highways, located west of the Beach Road but east of U.S. 158. You don't have to traverse the five-lane highway that way to get to the beach. But you can count on at least a five- to 15-minute hike to the sea. And you'll have to cross the two-lane Beach Road to get there. Traffic travels at a slow pace on this road: 35 mph. A word of caution: The pavement gets scorching hot in the summer sun, so don't venture out without wearing shoes when walking from a cottage between the highways to the ocean.

Soundfront or soundside locations generally mean that the homes face the waters of the sound on the western reaches of the Outer Banks. Families with young children — or those who don't mind a short drive to the ocean — often select these cottages because the sound is a shallow, warmer body of water to swim in than the Atlantic. And these rental units are considerably cheaper than those east of U.S. 158. You have to cross the five-lane highway to get to the Atlantic from these cottages. But you often can still reach the waves by walking or biking less than a mile.

West side rentals are those west of U.S. 158 but probably not too near to the sound. These are the least expensive cottages to rent. Most year-round rentals also are in this location.

Reading chapters on each area of the Outer Banks in this book should help you

Insiders' Tips

Cribs, highchairs, strollers and other baby equipment can be rented from most equipment rental companies along the Outer Banks so you don't have to carry all that gear with you on vacation.

choose which places on the beach you'd prefer to visit. Whether it's upscale, elegant homes loaded with amenities in Corolla or quiet, cloistered neighborhoods in South Nags Head or off-the-beaten-path fishing villages in Frisco — each town and village has its own personality and price range. Once you know, generally, where you'd like to be and when you plan to arrive, call the rental companies in that area and request a brochure. Many rental companies cover wide expanses of the barrier islands and offer an array of options. Most have toll-free telephone numbers and will gladly send a free brochure to you. Read the cottage and location descriptions carefully so that you'll know exactly what you're renting. And make sure to confirm rates and extra expenses you might incur with your rental agent.

Reservations

When you make an advance reservation for a rental cottage, be sure you can provide a portion of the rent to secure your spot. Rental brochures are mailed between Thanksgiving and mid-January, in plenty of time for you to make informed choices about accommodations. Traditionally, most summer reservations are received by March or April. However, if you are unable to book as early as you would like, or you decide at the last minute that you need an Outer Banks getaway, don't be discouraged. Rental managers say some cottages almost always can be found at the last minute.

Most cottages are equipped with full kitchens — complete with pots and pans and dishes — color cable TVs, telephones and air conditioning. Many, however, require guests to provide their own towels and sheets. And, of course, you'll almost always need to bring toiletries. Before booking your cottage, ask about what things you should pack to insure that your rental unit is as comfortable as possible when you arrive. Rental managers also can answer questions about whether they can accommodate special needs — such as provisions to bring pets, nonsmoking units or handicapped accessible houses.

If you vacation at the Outer Banks annually, most companies also offer the option of reserving time in the same property for the following year. It's not uncommon for visitors to rent the same cottage year after year. Some families even think of these weekly rentals as a second home at the beach.

Renting a cottage near the seashore is a good vacation strategy.

Minimum Stays

During the off-season, some options exist for partial weeks and weekend rentals in cottages. During the summer, it's practically impossible to rent for less than a full week. Most weeks run either Saturday to Saturday or Sunday to Sunday. Long-term rentals are by the month, season or year. Hotels and motels are much more flexible for short-term stays — but sometimes end up costing more if you want to spend a full week at the Outer Banks.

Remember, the off-season — especially September through November — is a much cheaper time to rent cottages for the week or long-weekend on these barrier islands. Fewer people are around then. And most restaurants and shops stay open through Thanksgiving, at least.

Cancellations

Rental brochures and lease agreements spell out each company's specific cancellation policy in detail. Most cancellations or transfers of any confirmed reservations are required in writing. You will probably lose all or part of your deposit and advance rent if the property you already have reserved is not re-rented. Forfeiting money is never fun. Make sure you read the small print and know what will happen if you decide you have to cancel.

Advance Rents

Money paid in advance is no longer considered a deposit. It's usually called advance payment or advance rent. Laws of the North Carolina Real Estate Commission involving renting or leasing property now govern most of these practices.

Details, explanations and rules are spelled out in rental brochures and again in your lease. Read the fine print and save yourself a potential headache. Personal checks are usually accepted for these advance rents. And some rental companies allow credit card transactions. In most cases, rent balances, taxes and other applicable fees and deposits are due 30 days prior to arrival. Final payments made upon check-in are usually required in the form of certified checks, travelers' checks or cash. Most rental companies do not accept personal checks at check-in.

Security Deposits

In addition to advance rents, most rental companies also require people to pay security deposits when they lease a cottage on the Outer Banks. The deposit can be as much as $500 for a week's stay. Some properties do not require a deposit.

Security deposits generally are refundable if the cottage you've rented passes inspection. If anything is damaged or missing, expect a smaller refund or no refund at all. Rental company agents have the final word on this. So take as good care of your vacation property as you would of your own home. Cottages that accept pets, especially, almost always charge high security deposits.

Hurricane Evacuation Refunds

Each rental contract has different specifications about whether you'll get your money back if the Outer Banks are evacuated for a hurricane. In many cases, partial or complete refunds are provided if a mandatory evacuation has been issued by the Dare County Emergency Management Control Group. Adjustments to your bill are made according to the number of days you were unable to occupy the property due to the mandatory evacuation.

Most rental managers say refunds are not provided for days you don't occupy the property once re-entry is permitted. Ocracoke property management companies also make special provisions for refunds in case the free state ferry boats can't run from Hatteras or Cedar Island to their island. Since it's almost impossible to visit Ocracoke without the ferries — unless you own a private plane — most rental companies will refund your rent and deposits if you can't get to Ocracoke because of interrupted ferry schedules. These policies also vary by business.

Handling and Inspection Fees

Almost all rental companies charge a handling fee for processing information and an inspection fee to check out the cottages after you've gone. The total for both generally ranges from a few dollars to $50. This is a nonrefundable fee assessed on top of advance rents and security deposits.

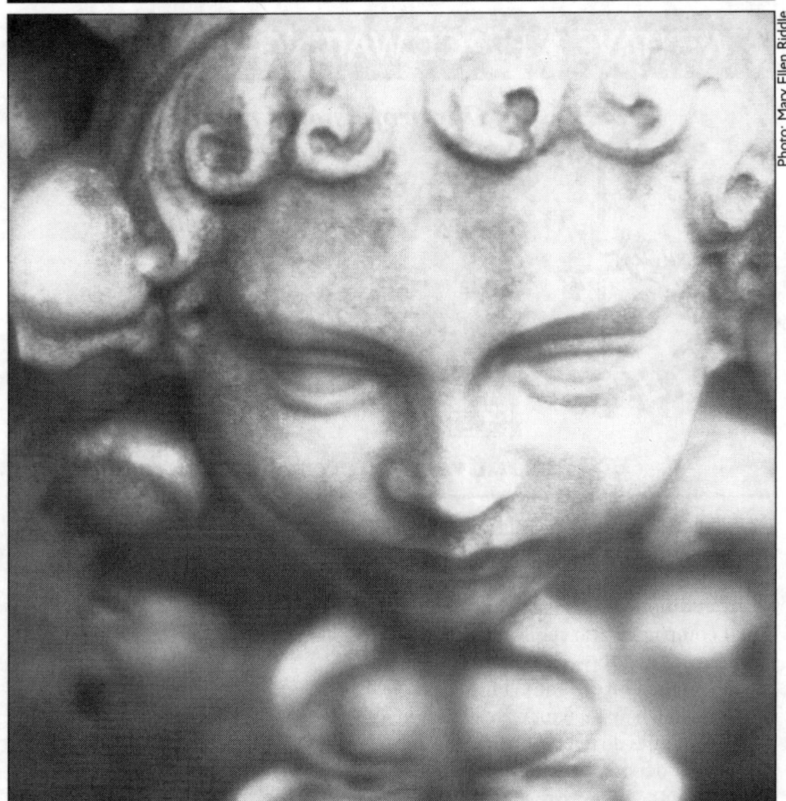

Photo: Mary Ellen Riddle

This is one of the many statues that greets visitors at the Elizabethan Gardens.

Taxes

On the Outer Banks, all tourism fees are taxable. Rental charges and handling fees are taxed. If cleaning, pet or extermination fees are applicable, they are taxable, too. Deposits are not taxable since they're generally returned. The N.C. State use tax rate is 6 percent. The local/county lodging tax rate is 4 percent. Combined, the tax rate is 10 percent on rental charges and fees.

Pet Rules and Costs

Some rental cottages allow guests to bring along their pets. Most of the companies that manage these properties, however, require additional deposits and, often, additional fees. These extra costs help cover charges for spraying for fleas, ticks and other pests. Fees vary depending on the type of pet, type of house, and management company. Pet fees generally are not refundable.

Check-In, Check-Out Times

Check-in times vary between companies. Most rental cottages allow you to get inside your temporary home between 3 and 6 PM. Guests check-in at the rental company before taking occupancy of the cottage. Be prompt. But don't be early. Cleanup crews need sufficient time to get your cottage in tip-top shape. Rental managers urge you not to try to occupy the cottage before it is ready. They understand your eagerness to settle into your cottage, in many cases after a long drive, but they simply are unable to let you do so.

Most checkouts occur between 9 and 11 AM. Again, it is important to check out on time to allow for necessary maintenance. Late fees may be imposed if you stay too long. Don't forget to return your keys or you may lose your key deposit.

Almost all Outer Banks cottages that rent by the week go from Saturday to Saturday. In recent years, however, some property managers have been trying to steer renters toward Sunday rentals and checkout instead. If you have this option — and hate sitting in traffic — you may want to consider this alternative check-in time when fewer people are trying to get to the beach and pick up their keys.

Occupancy

The number of people each rental cottage can accommodate is listed in the rental brochure for each individual property. Often, this limit is determined by the number of beds available — including sleeper sofas. Septic and water capacity, however, also dictate how many people can stay in each unit. So don't exceed the maximum occupancy or you may find yourself with more problems than you care to handle on vacation. Groups who try to get around rules governing occupancy stand to lose their money — and risk eviction.

What's Furnished

Most rental cottages are fully furnished homes with appliances, TVs, toasters, microwaves, telephones and other necessities. Some also include extra amenities such as VCRs, stereos, board games, beach chairs, beach umbrellas, hammocks and outdoor grills. Kitchens generally are fully equipped with dishes, silverware and pots and pans.

Almost all rental companies, however, require guests to bring their own sheets and towels, paper products, detergents and personal toiletries. You can rent towels from many equipment rental companies (see the "Equipment Rentals" section of this chapter). And you also can lease bicycles, in-line skates and other recreational equipment to take back to your cottage for the day or week.

If it's important to keep track of the time, bring a clock or radio. Otherwise, judge time by the sun and relax. After all, you're on vacation!

Mail and Phone Service

Some rental company agents will take phone or mail messages for you while you're vacationing on the Outer Banks. But it's better to take care of these requirements before you arrive. When you reserve a cottage, ask for the phone number at that location to leave with close friends, colleagues or relatives in case they need to contact you.

Some older cottages don't have telephones. So ask ahead if you really need one. All rental companies require their renters to foot the bill for long-distance charges.

Trash Pickups and Recycling

Town or county garbage collectors gather the trash from in front of most rental cottages at least twice a week during summer. Just put your bags in the bin or receptacle in front of the property and make sure it sits beside the road before you leave. Recycling, however, is the renters' responsibility. You can carry bottles, cans, plastics, cardboard, newspapers and other items to a variety of Outer Banks recycling collection points located at town halls, fire stations and shopping centers. You have to rinse out all items and sort them according to material.

Many beach accesses also have recycling bins for you to deposit cans or bottles in as you leave the sandy seashore for the day. If there isn't one at the spot you choose to sun yourself, please pack up your trash and take it off the beach with you. For a complete list of recycling centers on the Outer Banks, see our Services and Information Directory.

Equipment Rentals

If you'd rather not pack everything with you, equipment rental companies along the Outer Banks can provide almost everything you need except clothing. Strollers and wheelchairs with large wheels for easy movement in the sand, beach chairs, umbrellas, bikes, videos, VCRs, camcorders, cribs, highchairs, cots, fishing gear, linens, grills, camping equipment, watercraft . . . you name it, and you can probably rent it by the day, week or month.

Businesses that lease surfboards, Boogie Boards, Jet Skis, kayaks, boats, windsurfers, canoes and other watersports equipment are listed in our Watersports chapter. In this section, we've included companies that rent a wider range of items. Some rental companies even will deliver large equipment to your home, hotel or rental cottage. A few of these businesses are only open seasonally. So if you need to rent items during the off-season, call ahead to check on availability and hours.

Beach Outfitters

At Ocracoke Island Realty *928-6261, (800) 242-5394*

Beach Outfitters is open all year and accepts reservations. Free delivery and pickup is available on Ocracoke Island with full-week rental and prepayment.

Island Rentals

Ocracoke *928-5480*

Affiliated with Sharon Miller Realty, Island Rentals leases beach equipment, croquet sets, Nintendo games, cottage supplies and watersports equipment.

Lifesaver Rent-Alls

Information *(800) 635-2764*
Three Winks Shopping Center
U.S. 158, MP 1, Kitty Hawk *261-1344*
Lifesaver Shops, Kill Devil Hills *441-6048*

Delivery is available. Beach equipment, bikes, baby supplies, linens, fishing supplies and beach wheelchairs are among the items this company leases.

Metro Rentals

U.S. 158 and Colington Rd.
Kill Devil Hills *480-3535*

This company specializes in party supplies, construction equipment and beachcombing devices such as metal detectors.

Money's Worth Beach Home Equipment Rentals

Information *(800) 833-5233*
Corolla *453-4566*
Kitty Hawk *261-6999*

With a minimum rental order of $20, all items are delivered to your vacation home on your check-in day and picked up after you check out. This company is the only one that services the real estate companies directly. You do not have to be present for delivery or pickup service.

Ocean Atlantic Rentals

Information *(800) 635-9559*
Village Shops, Corolla *453-2440*
Scarborough Faire, Duck *261-4346*
N.C. 12, MP 10, Nags Head *441-7823*
N.C. 12, Waves *987-2492*
N.C. 12, Avon *995-5868*

If you've prepaid with advance reservations, Ocean Atlantic will deliver from any location. Beach umbrellas and chairs, bikes, cribs, TVs, VCRs, kayaks, linens, skates, grills, videos and watersports equipment are among the items this company leases.

Rental Companies

In this section, we've listed rental companies, their physical locations, mailing addresses, telephone numbers, geographic areas in which they lease properties and the number of cottages these companies maintain. We've also provided information about what types of rentals are available, whether the companies rent by the year — or by the week year round — whether they offer weekend rentals in the off-season, whether they have cottages that can accommodate pets, whether they rent handicapped-accessible units and other notable details such as Internet addresses. For your own benefit, call each rental company you may be interested in leasing from as soon as possible to get someone to mail you a brochure with other specific information.

Insiders' Tips

Towels, sheets and other linens aren't provided at most rental cottages.

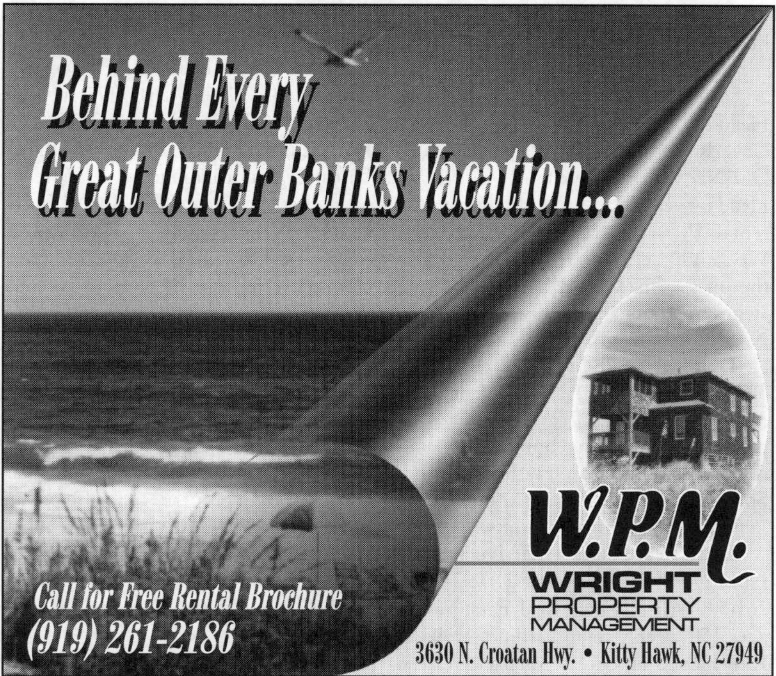

Atlantic Realty, U.S. 158, MP 2½ (4729 N. Croatan Highway, Kitty Hawk 27949), 261-2154 or (800) 334-8401, and TimBuck II Shopping Village (100-M Sunset Boulevard, Corolla 27927), 453-4110 or (800) 669-9245. This company manages 216 properties from Corolla to South Nags Head for year-round and seasonal rental. Pets are accepted in some units. Atlantic Realty can be contacted electronically at ATLANTIC @interpath.com.

B&B on the Beach, Brindley & Brindley Realty and Development Building — Corolla Light (P.O. Box 564, Corolla 27927), 453-3033 or (800) 962-0201. B&B manages 290 properties from Carova to Pine Island and Buck Island. Weekly rentals are available all year. And weekend rentals are offered during the off-season. Pets are accepted in some units. Handicapped-accessible cottages also are available. Linens and toiletries are provided in these units.

Bodie Island Rentals, Bodie Island Beach Club Timeshare Resort, Beach Road, MP 17 (P.O. Box 331, Nags Head 27959), 441-2558 or (800) 862-1785. This R.C.I. affiliate manages 23 timeshares and four wholly owned units in the Bodie Island Resort for weekly rental all year. Three-night rentals are offered during the off-season. An elevator is located in one building.

Britt Real Estate, N.C. 12 north of Duck Village (1316 Duck Road, Kitty Hawk 27949), 261-3566 or (800) 334-6315. Britt Real Estate manages 225 properties, including two handicapped-accessible homes, from Corolla to Southern Shores. Pets are accepted in some units. Weekend rentals are offered in the off-season. Contact Britt Real Estate electronically at BRITT-DUCK@aol.com or http://www.infi.net/britt.

Cove Realty, between the Beach Road and U.S. 158, MP 14 (P.O. Box 967, Nags Head 27959), 441-6391 or (800) 635-7007. Cove Realty manages 140 properties in Old Nags Head Cove and South Nags Head for year-round, weekly and student rental. Pets are accepted in some units. Weekend packages are available during the off-season. Guests have access to a swimming pool and tennis courts in Old Nags Head Cove.

Dolphin Realty, N.C. 12 (P.O. Box 387, Hatteras 27943), 986-2241 or (800) 338-4775. This company manages 70 properties, including homes and one-room efficiencies on Hatteras Island. Some are available for year-round rental. Pets are accepted in some units.

Duck Real Estate, (1232 Duck Road, Duck 27949) 261-4614 or (800) 992-2976, 261-5408 (fax). Duck Real Estate manages 150 weekly rentals from Corolla to Kitty Hawk. Three-day golf packages also are available. Pets are accepted in some units. Some cottages are equipped for handicapped guests. Duck Real Estate can be contacted electronically at http://wmi.cais.com/white/index.html.

Hatteras Realty, N.C. 12 (P.O. Box 249, Avon 27915), 995-5466 or (800) HATTERAS. Hatteras Realty manages 220 properties on Hatteras Island for weekly rental only. Units may be rented by partial weeks during the off-season. Pets are accepted in some units. Handicapped-accessible cottages are available. More than half of this company's units are furnished with hot tubs.

Karichele Realty, TimBuck II Shopping Village (P.O. Box 100, Corolla 27927), 453-4400 or (800) 453-2377. Karichele Realty manages 75 properties from Carova to Pine Island that may be rented by the week. During the off-season, weekend packages are available. Pets are accepted in some units. Handicapped-accessible cottages also are available.

Kitty Dunes Realty, (P.O. Box 275, Kitty Hawk 27949), 261-2171 in Kitty Hawk, 453-DUNE in Corolla, 441-DUNE in Colington, (800) 334-DUNE for catalog information; 261-2326, reservation hotline; and (514) 376-4382 for the Canadian representative. Kitty Dunes manages 430 rental properties from Carova to Oregon Inlet. Some can accommodate up to 20 people. Most properties rent by the week. Long-term rentals are offered in Colington Harbour, call the Kitty Hawk office. Three-night weekend packages are often available — even during the summer. Pets are accepted in many units. A few cottages are handicapped-accessible. Some properties include private pools and spas.

Kitty Hawk Rentals/Beach Realty & Construction, U.S. 158, MP 6 (P.O. Box 69, Kill Devil Hills 27948), 441-7166 or (800) 635-1559; N.C. 12 (1450 Duck Road, Duck 27949), 261-6605; and TimBuck II Shopping Village (790-B Ocean Trail, Corolla 27927), 453-4141. This company manages 575 properties, a few of which are handicapped-accessible, from Ocean Hill to South Nags Head. Some are available for year-round rental, but most rent by the week. Pets are accepted in some units. Outer Banks Golf Getaways, a new division, offers weekend golf/accommodation packages in area homes and hotels. Call (800) 916-6244 for more information.

Joe Lamb Jr. & Associates, U.S. 158, MP 2 (P.O. Box 986, Kitty Hawk 27949), 261-4444, 261-3720 (fax) or (800) 552-6257. This company manages 200 properties, including year-round rentals, from Whalehead to South Nags Head. Three-night packages also are offered during the off-season. Pets are accepted in some cottages. Handicapped-accessible rentals also are available. Units in some developments include pool access.

Frank Mangum Realty, U.S. 158, MP 10.3 (P.O. Box 655, Nags Head 27959), 441-3600 or (800) 279-5552. Frank Mangum manages weekly rental properties from Corolla to South Nags Head. Weekend packages are available. Some cottages accept pets. Contact Frank Mangum electronically at http://www.mangumrealty.com.

Midgett Realty, N.C. 12 (P.O. Box 250, Hatteras Village 27943), 986-2841, 986-2745 (fax) or (800) 527-2903. Midgett Realty manages 300 properties from Rodanthe to Hatteras Village for weekly rentals. Three-night rentals are available during the off-season. A few properties accept pets. Two handicapped-accessible units are offered.

Sharon Miller Realty, off N.C. 12 (P.O. Box 264, Ocracoke Island 27960), 928-5711. Sharon Miller Realty manages 112 Ocracoke Island properties, one of which is handicapped-accessible. Only weekly rentals are available. Pets are accepted in some units. Contact this company electronically at OCRACOKE @outer-banks.com.

Nags Head Realty, U.S. 158, MP 10 (P.O. Box 130, Nags Head 27959), 441-4315 or (800) 222-1531. Nags Head Realty manages year-round and weekly rentals from the Crown Point development in the north beaches to South Nags Head. Three-day rentals are offered during the off-season. Some units accept pets.

Ocean Country Realty, N.C. 12 (P.O. Box 806, Avon 27915) and N.C. 12 in Waves, 995-6700, 995-6800 or (800) 444-5459. Ocean Country Realty manages 51 properties on Hatteras Island for weekly rental. Three-day packages also are offered during the off-season. Some cottages are handicapped-accessible. Some accept pets. Swimming pool access is available with all rentals.

Ocracoke Island Realty Inc., (P.O. Box 238, Ocracoke 27960), 928-6261, 928-7411. Ocracoke Island Realty manages 95 weekly rental properties on Ocracoke. Three-night packages are available during the off-season. A few of these cottages allow pets. One cottage is handicapped-accessible.

Outer Banks Ltd., U.S. 158, MP 10.2 (P.O. Box 129, Nags Head 27959), 441-5000 or (800) 624-7651. Outer Banks Ltd. manages 275 weekly rental properties from Duck to South Nags Head. Three-day packages are offered year-round as well. Pets are accepted in some units.

Outer Banks Resort Rentals, Pirate's Quay, U.S. 158, MP 11, Nags Head, 441-2134. Marvin Beard represents the sales and rentals of timeshares only from Duck to South Nags as well as a few in Hatteras.

Outer Beaches Realty, (P.O. Box 280, Avon 27915), 995-4477 in Avon and 987-2771 in Waves, (800) 627-3250 (fax) or (800) 627-3150. Outer Beaches Realty manages 414 rental cottages from Rodanthe to Hatteras Village. Weekly and three-day rentals are available. A few allow pets. Some handicapped-accessible properties also are offered. Contact Outer Beaches Realty at OBR@vdsys.com or http://www.beachsurf.com/obr.

Pirate's Cove Realty, Roanoke Island (P.O. Box 1879, Manteo 27954), 473-6800 or (800) 537-7245. Pirate's Cove Realty manages properties in the Pirate's Cove development for weekly rentals. Two-

Insiders' Tips

Some of the larger rental properties include sinks in each room to accommodate several families or couples who share the same house.

night weekends also are offered during the off-season. Some cottages accept pets. All units include access to an outdoor swimming pool, tennis courts, a playground and free boat slips.

R & R Resort Rental Properties Inc., N.C. 12 (1184 Duck Road, Duck 27949), 261-4498 or (800) 433-8805 in Duck; or (800) 849-6189 in Corolla. R & R manages more than 300 weekly rental properties from Corolla to Southern Shores. Three-day off-season packages are available. Some cottages allow pets. A few units are equipped with elevators. Many of these rental properties have private swimming pools — including indoor, heated pools. Contact R&R electronically at RR-udeservit@outer-banks.com or http://www.RR-udeservit.com.

Real Escapes Properties, N.C. 12 (1183 Duck Road, Duck 27949), 261-3211, or (800) 831-3211 for brochure requests. Real Escapes manages more than 180 weekly rental properties from Corolla to Southern Shores. One unit includes an elevator. Contact Real Escapes at VACATIONS@outerbanks.com or http://www.real-escapes.com.

RE/MAX Ocean Realty, U.S. 158, MP 6 (P.O. Box 10, Kill Devil Hills 27948), 441-3127 or (800) 548-2033 or (800) 334-6436. RE/MAX manages more than 300 units from Whalehead through South Nags Head. Year-round and weekly rentals are available. Three-night packages are offered during the off-season. Some allow pets. Some are handicapped-accessible. For 1996, RE/MAX manages properties formerly affiliated with The Young People Realty.

Resort Central Inc., U.S. 158, MP 2½ (P.O. Box 767, Kitty Hawk 27949), 261-8861 or (800) NAG-HEAD (624-7432). Resort Central manages 70 year-round and weekly rental properties from Corolla to Nags Head. Some weekend packages are available. Some cottages allow pets. Some units are equipped with elevators.

Resort Realty, (P.O. Box 1008, Kitty Hawk 27949), 261-8383 or (800) 458-3830; 261-8888 in Duck. Resort Realty manages 340 weekly rental properties from Corolla to South Nags Head. Some three-night packages are available with a maximum of five days notice. A few cottages allow pets.

Salvo Real Estate, N.C. 12 (P.O. Box 56, Salvo 27972), 987-2343; fax number is the same. Salvo Real Estate manages 35 weekly rentals in Rodanthe, Waves and Salvo. Three-night rentals are offered during the off-season. A few of these cottages allow pets.

Sea Oats Realty, U.S. 158, MP 11½ (P.O. Box 3399, Kill Devil Hills 27948), 480-2325 or (800) 933-2325. Sea Oats Realty manages 40 weekly rentals from Duck to South Nags Head. Pets are allowed in some units.

Seaside Realty, U.S. 158, MP 3. (4425 N. Croatan Highway., Kitty Hawk 27949), 261-5500 and (800) 395-2525. Seaside Realty manages 140 year-round and weekly properties from Corolla to South Nags Head. At least 300 additional timeshares also are offered in that area. Three-night packages are available during the off-season. Some of these units allow pets. Some accommodations have elevators.

Southern Shores Realty, N.C. 12 (P.O. Box 150 Kitty Hawk 27949), 261-2111 or 261-4968 (fax) or (800) 334-1000. Southern Shores Realty manages 425 year-round and weekly rentals from Duck to Kitty Hawk. Weekend packages also are available year-round. Dogs are accepted in some units. Ramps and elevators are offered in some cottages. Contact Southern Shores Realty electronically at http://www.soshores.com/soshores.

Sun Realty, U.S. 158, MP 9 (P.O. Box 1630 Kill Devil Hills 27948), 441-7033 or (800) 334-4745. Satellite offices are at Corolla, Duck, Kitty Hawk, Salvo and Avon. Sun Realty offers the largest inventory of rental properties on the Outer Banks, managing 1,100 properties from Corolla through Hatteras Island. Weekly and year-round rentals are available. Special weekend packages and sports packages for golf, kayaking, hang-gliding, offshore fishing and fly fishing are available. A special program for handicapped guests — with a separate brochure — is offered. Pets are accepted in some units.

Surf or Sound Realty, N.C. 12 (P.O. Box 100, Avon 27915), 995-5801 or (800) 237-1138. Surf or Sound Realty rents properties from April through early December. This company offers 120 cottages on Hatteras Island. Pets are accepted in some units. Handicapped-accessible rentals also are available.

Twiddy & Company Realty, (1181 Duck Road, Duck 27949) 261-3521 or (800) 489-4339 in Duck; 453-3341 or (800) 789-4339 in Corolla; 261-1628 (fax). Twiddy & Company manages more than 400 rental properties from Carova to Southern Shores. Pets are accepted in some units. Some units offer private pools and hot tubs.

Village Realty, U.S. 158, MP 15. (P.O. Box 1807, Nags Head 27959), 480-2224 or (800) 548-9688. Village Realty manages 215 rental properties in the development of the Village at Nags Head. A few year-round rentals are offered. But most lease by the week. Special weekend and golf packages are available. All units include access to a beach club with an outdoor swimming pool, tennis courts, a game room and family activities. Golf and tennis lessons are available. A golf course, private oceanfront access and two private soundside piers also are on the premises. Some cottages allow pets. Some have el-

Insiders' Tips

Ask about Sunday-to-Sunday rental homes if you hate sitting in long lines of traffic waiting to get on or off the beach in the summer. Some real estate companies are now offering this option.

evators and can accommodate handicapped vacationers. Contact Village Realty electronically at OAKIWON @aol.com.

Water Side Realty Inc., (P.O. Box 1088, Buxton 27920), 995-6001 or (800) 530-0022. Water Side Realty manages 40 year-round rentals and 18 cottages that rent by the week on Hatteras Island. Special midweek prices are offered with three-night minimum stays.

Stan White Realty, U.S. 158, MP 10½ (P.O. Drawer 1447, Nags Head 27959; 1232 Duck Road, Duck 27949), 441-1515 or (800) 338-3233, Nags Head; 261-4614 in Duck; 441-1208 (fax) Stan White manages 350 weekly and year-round rentals from Corolla to South Nags Head. Pets are allowed in some weekly rentals. Handicapped-accessible units are available. Corporate retreat and golf packages are offered. Contact Stan White electronically at http://wmi.cais.com/white/index.html. Stan White is now managing rental properties formerly run by Gardner Realty.

20/20 Realty, (516 S. Main Highway, Manteo 27954), 473-2020 or (800) 520-2044. This company manages primarily year-round rentals from Kitty Hawk to Manns Harbor. At least eight weekly rentals also are offered on Roanoke Island.

Wright Property Management, U.S. 158, MP 4¾ (3630 N. Croatan Highway, Kitty Hawk 27949), 261-2186, 261-5773 (fax). Wright Property manages 150 year-round and weekly properties from Ocean Sands to South Nags Head. Weekend rentals also are offered. Some units accept pets. Contact Wright Property electronically at WPM@interpath.com.

Year-round rentals

Because the Outer Banks is primarily a vacation destination, not all rental companies will lease their properties to year-round residents. Some houses, apartments, duplexes and other units, however, are available for monthly, seasonal or year-round rentals. Most of these accommodations are located from Duck to South Nags Head and on Colington, Roanoke and Hatteras islands.

The majority of long-term rentals are between the highways or west of U.S. 158 in Kitty Hawk, Kill Devil Hills and Nags Head; or on Colington, Roanoke and Hatteras islands. It's easiest to sign a year-round lease between October and March. If you're looking for a seasonal, summer rental, make arrangements through a real estate agent as early as possible — at least before Easter.

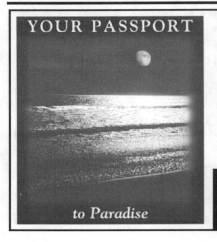

Check with rental agents to determine specific occupancy rules regarding rates, deposits, pets, furnishings, washing machines and dryers or other issues. Most companies require one month's rent plus a security deposit equalling one month's rent, and, often references from previous employers and landlords. Pet deposits can be hefty around here.

The following companies manage year-round rentals. Most of these companies are listed above in greater detail. Also check local newspapers for classified listings of year-round rentals available:

Atlantic Realty, 261-2154, Colington, Kill Devil Hills and Kitty Hawk.

Cove Realty, 441-6391 or (800) 635-7007, Old Nags Head Cove and South Nags Head.

Dolphin Realty, 986-2241 or (800) 338-4775, Hatteras Island.

Family Inn, 480-0874 Beach Road, MP 8½, Kill Devil Hills. This establish-

You Want it? You Got It!

A vacation is supposed to be fun, right? So who wants to spend hours in a grocery store checkout line — or tied to other chores that eat up your precious beach time? At Your Service, a growing 8-year-old business on the Outer Banks, will take on those tiresome chores by acting as your personal concierge — acquiring babysitters (it's the oldest babysitting and eldercare service on the Outer Banks), stocking your vacation cottage with groceries and other necessities before you arrive, providing linens and cleaning service, ordering flowers and theater tickets and seeing to details to make a vacation run smoothly. Pamela Price, a former teacher and public relations professional, is the energetic owner of At Your Service, and she has a well-trained and competent staff of around 50 employes. Phone or fax the company at 261-5286.

ment includes eight furnished one-bedroom apartments and efficiencies — all that rent on a month-to-month basis year-round. Private accesses, outdoor decks. fully equipped kitchens and cable television are included in each unit. Phone jacks are available — but tennants have to install their own phones. Efficiency units rent for $500 per month. Apartments rent for $600 monthly. The owner prefers quiet couples and does not accept pets.

Kitty Dunes Realty, 261-2171, Colington Harbour, Kill Devil Hills and Kitty Hawk.

Kitty Hawk Rentals/Beach Realty & Construction, 441-7166 or (800) 635-1559, Duck, west of U.S. 158, and between the highways in the central areas of the beach.

Joe Lamb Jr. & Associates, 261-4444, Kitty Hawk to Nags Head.

Nags Head Realty, 441-4315 or (800) 222-1531, Kitty Hawk to South Nags Head.

Jim Perry & Company, 441-3051 or (800) 222-6135, Duck to South Nags Head.

RE/MAX Ocean Realty, 441-3127 or (800) 548-2033, Kitty Hawk to Manteo.

Resort Central Inc., 261-8861 or (800) 334-4749, Kitty Hawk to Manteo.

Seaside Realty, 261-5500, Kitty Hawk to Nags Head.

Southern Shores Realty, 261-2111 or (800) 334-1000, Duck to Kitty Hawk.

Sun Realty, 261-1152 or (800) 334-4745, Corolla through Hatteras Island.

20/20 Realty, 473-2020, (800) 520-2044, Kitty Hawk through Roanoke Island.

Water Side Realty Inc., 995-6001 or (800) 530-0022, Hatteras Island.

Stan White Realty & Construction Inc., 441-1516 or (800) 338-3233, Kitty Hawk to Nags Head.

Wright Properties, 261-2186, Ocean Sands to South Nags Head.

Surf Side
MOTEL

OCEANFRONT

ON THE OCEAN AT MILEPOST 16

You'll discover vacation fun for the whole family in this superb oceanfront setting. The Surf Side is conveniently located within walking distance of scenic and historical attractions, outlet malls, local shops and restaurants.

- INDOOR POOL AND SUN ROOM
- OCEANFRONT OUTDOOR POOL
- ALL ROOMS HAVE BALCONIES WITH OCEAN VIEW
- HONEYMOON SUITES WITH JACUZZI
- MINI CONVENTION ROOM
- OCEANFRONT JACUZZI ROOMS
- OCEANVIEW EFFICIENCIES

P.O. Box 400 • Nags Head, NC 27959 • (919) 441-2105

1-800-552-SURF (7873)

See listing in MOTELS Beaches North of Oregon Inlet

Inside Accommodations

Short-term accommodations on the Outer Banks range from small family-owned and operated seaside motels to multiple-story franchises of national lodging chains. In recent years, upscale elegant inns and a variety of bed and breakfast establishments also have opened their doors — offering a little more luxury and personal attention than the traditional barrier island hotels.

Many families and friends also choose to rent one of the thousands of cottages along the Outer Banks for a week's vacation or longer. Companies that lease those properties are included in our Weekly and Long-term Cottage Rentals chapter. The pages here outline only places that allow people to stay for a night or two at a time.

A few of these motels and hotels require two-night minimums on the weekends, however. And many accommodations managers request at least three-day stays for Memorial Day weekend, July 4 weekend and Labor Day weekend — since those are, by far, the busiest times on these barrier islands. A lot of Outer Banks hotels also have suites, efficiency apartments and cottage units that rent by the day, the week or longer. And, of course, you can stay in any room in any of these accommodations for a week or longer if you wish.

If you're planning a summer stay on the Outer Banks you should call early for reservations. Most accommodations are filled to capacity from mid-June through August. Usually, you can find walk-in rooms during the week. But if you know a week — or weekend — that you're planning to visit, your best bet is to go ahead and book a room now.

Locations are indicated by milepost and town. Most of the hotels, motels and inns are scattered along the Beach Road. A few line U.S. 158, also called the Bypass. And Roanoke and Ocracoke islands have several tucked beneath the trees off the beaten paths. If you're looking for a more private accommodation, we suggest you check out the bed and breakfast inns listings, especially.

Pricing Information

Rates vary dramatically from one area of the Outer Banks to another, from oceanfront rooms to those across the highway, between in- and off-season times and especially depending on the amenities offered with each unit. In general, however, fall, winter and early spring prices are at least one-third lower than midsummer rates — often as little as $25 per night.

Insiders' Tips

If you're planning a summer stay on the Outer Banks you should call early for reservations. Many accommodations are filled to capacity from mid-June through August.

The most expensive season, of course, is between mid-June and mid-August, when rates in general range from $50 a night for two people with two double beds to more than $150 per night in some of the fancier establishments.

Many hotels and motels honor AARP and other discounts. And children stay free with paying adults in several of these accommodations.

For your ease in checking out price ranges, we've created a dollar-sign key (see chart) showing a range of the average summer cost for a one-night stay for two people with two double beds in the room. Extra charges may apply for special weekends, additional people in the room, efficiency apartments or pets. These prices do not include local and state taxes. Unless otherwise indicated in the description, accommodations accept major credit cards such as MasterCard and Visa.

Pricing Key

$55 and less	$
$56 to $75	$$
$76 to $95	$$$
$96 and more	$$$$

Many accommodations owners have decided to keep their doors open all year to cater to fall fishing parties, spring visitors and people who like the Outer Banks best in winter — when few other folk are around. If you prefer isolation at the beach and don't mind wind and temperatures in the 40s and 50s, November through February would be a good time to come. September and October, however, are our favorite months. The ocean is still warm enough to swim in, the daytime temperature seldom drops below the mid-60s, most restaurants, attractions and retail shops are still open — yet the prices are much cheaper and most of the bustling feeling is gone once school starts up again.

Deposits and Check-in Times

Most motels and hotels require deposits to hold advance summer registration. Policies vary between properties, but the average amount is 25 to 35 percent of the total reservation cost or one night's rate. Ask about specific provisions when reserving your room. And always call before you come to the Outer Banks to confirm your reservation.

Many proprietors require the balance of your bill to be paid upon arrival. Be prepared with cash, travelers' checks or a credit card. Personal checks often are not accepted for this final payment. Again, ask ahead when booking your room. Automated teller machines also are available at most Outer Banks banks, but the majority of them have a $200 per day withdrawal limit and not all accept all bank cards.

If you've booked an efficiency, inn or motel unit for several days and decide not to stay the whole time, you may not be able to get your money back. Policies change between managers and rental companies. Even during some mandatory evacuations due to hurricanes, some guests have been left to foot the bill for the entire stay — despite the fact that they may have been forced off the islands early by Mother Nature. Ask ahead to learn the particular rules of your accommodation.

Check-in times also vary among accommodations. Most places won't allow you into their rooms before 2 PM but can hold them for you until 10 or 11 PM if necessary. If you know you'll get here earlier, ask about early check-in provisions — or go ahead and just spend that first morning out on the beach. Public showers are even provided at some beach accesses so you can clean off before getting into your hotel room. And several motels, inns and bed and breakfast establishments also offer outdoor showers for their guests. Check-out times in general are between 10 AM and noon. Sometimes, later stays

Photo: Philip S. Ruckle Jr.

Bed and breakfast inns are becoming more prevalent in this area.

can be accommodated. Ask ahead if you know you'll want to linger that last day.

Locations and Amenities

In this chapter, oceanfront means that the property has at least some rooms facing the ocean, right on the beach. Most of these units have balconies and picture windows. Rooms on the ground level or behind sand dunes, however, may not have views of the Atlantic — even if they're just off the sandy shore. Ask about what's available. And clarify which type of location you'd prefer. Remember, you'll almost always pay more to watch the waves from your room.

Conveniences and luxuries included in rooms at motels, hotels, inns, efficiencies and bed and breakfasts usually vary — even within the same structure. Some include kitchenettes, king-size beds and Jacuzzi units. Others may have double beds and an extra sleeper sofa for the kids. All have air-conditioning. And places that remain open in the fall and winter also include heat.

Many motels and hotels — especially the older beachfront structures and newer high-rise units — also have meeting facilities, conference rooms and large common areas to accommodate family reunions, business workshops and tour groups. Some have federally approved handicapped-accessible units and are fully accessible to wheelchair users. Others even allow you to bring a pet on vacation.

Amenities span the gamut from the most basic — bed and shower only — to places that provide microwaves, refrigerators, televisions with free movie channels or videocassette recorders, telephones, fluffy bathrobes, fancy soaps, free coffee, cocktails and afternoon tea, gourmet breakfasts, bicycles and even golf clubs. A few hotels offer "big-city" advantages such as room service, assistance with luggage and wake-up calls. But most don't. So read the descriptions carefully if you require such services and call ahead with other specific questions.

All Outer Banks accommodations provide free parking for at least one vehicle per unit. Keep valuables with you rather than leaving them locked in the car. Theft and vandalism are rare around here, but it's not even worth taking the chance. Some hotels offer safes in the main office for their guests to stow special stuff.

Many motel, hotel and inn managers

will provide recreation packages with your room — especially during the off-season. Golf courses, tennis facilities and health clubs are almost all open year round. Call about these special combinations. Or ask the proprietor of your particular accommodation about special discounts that might be available to guests. Walk-in or weeklong memberships are even offered at most private facilities. And some accommodations include volleyball courts, horseshoe pits, picnic tables, gas grills and small putting greens on site for their guests.

Area Profiles

Accommodations in the northern beaches are much more upscale than on the rest of the Outer Banks — although you'll find a few luxury inns and bed and breakfast inns in Kill Devil Hills, Nags Head, Roanoke Island and on Ocracoke too. Corolla only has one place that allows people to stay for a night at a time; Duck boasts two such establishments. All three are extremely elegant and guaranteed to make their guests feel comfortable and well cared for. But most travelers who stay in these villages rent individual cottages by the week.

Nearly all accommodations in the northern beaches area are along the main artery, N.C. 12, which is known as Ocean Trail in Corolla and Duck Road in Duck.

Kitty Hawk was one of the first Outer Banks beach towns to develop a tourist trade, and some of the hotels and motels there are reminiscent of the early cottage courts. These primarily family-run businesses are small, clean and often cheaper than nationally-known hotels. There's also a Holiday Inn Express on U.S. 158 (the Bypass) here and a bed and breakfast inn on a golf course west of the highway.

Kill Devil Hills is probably the most central — and most populated — place on the barrier islands. Many of its accommodations are within walking distance of restaurants, shopping and recreational attractions. Quaint motels with fewer than two dozen rooms are common here. And big chain establishments with conference centers and bellhops are just across the street. Public beach and sound accesses abound in this town.

The Outer Banks' first resort destination was Nags Head. So here, you'll find everything from a 1930s-era inn to the tallest hotel on the Outer Banks. Some accommodations retain the old-timey feel of cedar-shake-shingled cottages, while others have gone for the ultramodern, multiple-floor look — complete with elevators and room service from the in-house restaurant. Like Kill Devil Hills — but a lot more spread out and slightly less populated — Nags Head abounds with restaurants, retail shops and recreation.

Roanoke Island's accommodations range from cheap cottage courts to fine, fabulous inns. None are more than a bike ride away from the historic waterfront. And many are perfect for a romantic weekend getaway or cloistered honeymoon stay. Rental cottages aren't prevalent here because the large majority of even the summer population is made up of permanent residents. But if you want to get away from the bustle of the beach — and still be close to the sound, wetlands and wonderful historic attractions this island has to offer — you won't have difficulty finding a room to suit your tastes here.

Motels and hotels on Hatteras Island are, in general, more laid-back than on other parts of the barrier islands. Recently, a national chain has opened a unit in Buxton and Hatteras Village. But family-owned and operated places still dominate the accommodations here. Many of these units are no-frills — without phones in the rooms or fancy furnishings. But if you're looking for an affordable place to stay along quieter stretches of beach, don't overlook Hatteras Island's short-term room, inn and efficiency options.

Ocracoke Island's lodgings are, in general, the most personal on the Outer Banks. Here, you'll find old inns, newer motels, upscale bed and breakfast inns, efficiency apartments and even a few folk who'll rent you a room in their house — sometimes right next to their own. This laid-back little island is separated from the rest of the world by free ferry boat rides. It's a great place to escape from it all. And there are plenty of accommodations, quaint boutiques and great restaurants to please almost anyone here.

Corolla

The Inn at Corolla Light

1066 Ocean Tr. 453-3340, (800) 215-0772

$$$$

At the luxurious Inn at Corolla Light, guests can plan their days around an incredible array of recreational activities available nearly at their doorstep — or they may wish simply to relax in full view of the sparkling waters of Currituck Sound and bask in the serenity of this beautifully appointed facility. The year-round inn opened during the 1995 season in the ocean-to-sound resort community of Corolla Light. The upscale development is laced with wooded walking and biking trails and offers every leisure amenity a vacationer could dream of: an indoor sports center with an Olympic-size pool, hot tub, saunas, clay tennis courts, racquetball courts and fitness equipment; an oceanfront complex that boasts two outdoor pools, a video game room, restaurant and exclusive access to the beach; play areas for basketball, shuffleboard, tennis, horseshoes and more; and terrific shops and restaurants nearby (see our Shopping and Restaurants chapters). Guests of the inn have free unlimited access to all of the resort's facilities.

Guests may also use the inn's own soundfront swimming pool, hot tub and private 400-foot pier on Currituck Sound. And two stocked bass ponds give anglers an almost guaranteed opportunity to catch some supper. The inn also furnishes bicycles to guests so they can take a leisurely tour of the resort's landscaped grounds.

Sailing excursions, guided kayak trips, windsurfing, parasailing and personal watercraft — Jet Skis, Waverunners and others — are available at a watersports rental site on the resort. A golf course is nearby.

The inn's 17 guest rooms include kitchenettes, color cable TVs, radios,

VCRs and private baths. Many also have fireplaces and whirlpool tubs. The rooms are designed for single or double occupancy, and most are equipped with sleeper sofas too. Guests can enjoy a free continental breakfast daily.

The Inn at Corolla Light has a two-night minimum stay on weekends and charges $10 per night for each additional person. Ask about special rate packages offered throughout the year, especially in the off-season.

Duck

Sanderling Inn Resort and Conference Center

1461 Duck Rd. 261-4111, (800) 701-4111
$$$$

The Sanderling Inn Resort is situated on 12 acres of oceanside wilderness, about 5 miles north of Duck Village. Here, heavy strands of beach grass, sea oats, pines, fragrant olives and live oaks provide a natural setting for an elegant, enjoyable vacation. The Sanderling was built in the style of the old Nags Head beach homes with wooden siding, cedar shake accents, dormer windows and porches on each side. Rocking chairs line the wide porches, providing a relaxing way to pass sultry afternoons while overlooking the ocean or sound.

All 86 rooms at the Sanderling are comfortable, lush and oh-so-accommodating. The inn provides all its guests with lounging robes, Caswell Massey soaps, toiletries and complimentary fruit, wine and cheese. A continental breakfast and afternoon tea also come with each room.

The main lobby and gallery of the Sanderling offer a warm welcome to weary travelers. Decorated in an English country theme, they're adorned with contemporary finishes and accented by polished wood floors and wainscotting. The inn's main building has 28 rooms, all with kitchenettes. Audubon prints and artwork line the walls. Another 32 rooms in Sanderling Inn North are filled with wicker furniture and equipped with a refrigerator and wet bar. The 26 rooms in the newest South Wing each have a king-size bed, double sleeper sofa, wet bar, refrigerator, microwave, two televisions with video cassette recorders — one in the bedroom, one in the living area, a stereo with compact disc player and 1½ baths. Some suites also have Jacuzzis. All Sanderling rooms have telephones and televisions with remote control and cable.

Accommodations here are designed for the comfort and privacy of two guests per room. But sleeper sofas and cribs are available for an additional charge.

A separate building at the Sanderling houses excellent conference and meeting facilities including the Presidential Suite, complete with Jacuzzi bath, steam shower and two decks — one overlooks the ocean and the other, the sound. For an additional charge, the inn's housekeeping staff provides laundry service with a 48-hour turnaround time. Room service is provided by the on-site, upscale Sanderling Inn Restaurant (see our Restaurants chapter).

This is a complete resort with private beaches, a health club with two exercise rooms, an indoor pool, a separate whirlpool room, locker rooms, saunas, an outdoor pool, tennis courts and a natural walking or jogging trail. The Audubon Wildlife Sanctuary and Pine Island Indoor Tennis and Racquet Club are nearby.

Full package deals are available for New Year's Eve, Valentine's Day, honeymoons and winter escapes. Packages generally include one or more meals at the Sanderling Inn Restaurant, full use of the health club and indoor pool, welcoming gifts and other extras. Some seasonal discounts are available. Weekend guests must stay both Friday and Saturday nights during the summer, and a three-day minimum stay is required for in-season holidays. Pets are not allowed here. Wheelchair access is provided for all buildings on the property, and handicapped-acces-

sible rooms are available. The Sanderling Inn is open year round.

Duck

Advice 5¢

111 Scarborough Ln., in Sea Pines Subdivision, Duck *255-1050*
$$$$

Starting its second season in 1996 as the only bed and breakfast north of Kitty Hawk, Advice 5¢ offers four guest rooms and one suite and exudes an air of casual simplicity. Here, Nancy Caviness and Donna Black provide all their guests with private baths, rocking chairs and decks. The suite also includes color cable TV, a stereo and Jacuzzi. Hardwood floors and juniper appointments, comfy Lexington cottage furniture, quilts, colorful bath towels, linens and greenery galore make this place feel just "like Grandma's house."

A common area with a fireplace for those chilly off-season evenings is a popular gathering spot for guests. A continental breakfast buffet of fresh fruit salad and just-baked breads and muffins is served daily in the common room. Afternoon tea tempts guests with more homemade delights as well as hot and cold beverages. At day's end — or when the weather doesn't cooperate — you can try your hand at a puzzle or round up some folks for an intense game of Scrabble. If quieter pursuits are what you crave, the den on the guest floor level is the perfect place to delve into one of a variety of good books available here.

Two outdoor showers allow beachgoers to wash off after a long day in the sun. And a locking storage shed provides protected shelter out of the elements for storing bicycles, Boogie Boards, golf clubs and other gear. No wonder Nancy and Donna have already had so many repeat guests after only one year in the bed and breakfast business.

All rooms at this establishment are nonsmoking. Young children cannot be accommodated here. Advice 5¢ is open year round.

Kitty Hawk

3 Seasons Guest House

Off U.S. 158, MP 2 *261-4791*
at Seascape Golf Course *(800) 847-3373*
$$$$

This bed and breakfast inn is tucked away from the ocean and highways at Seascape Golf Course on the west side of the Bypass. Golf enthusiasts find this location ideal: The putting green is in front of the property, and the 9th hole is behind it. You barely have to get out of bed before bellowing, "Fore!"

Just 2½ blocks from the ocean, 3 Seasons sits on a high sand hill, so guests can enjoy views of the Atlantic. Even if you've never swung a 9-iron, you'll enjoy unwinding and relaxing at this charming establishment. Susie and Tommy Gardner have been operating the bed and breakfast since 1992. It's a five-bedroom house, and four of the rooms are available for double occupancy. Each guest room has a private bath and TV. The decor feels like home — comfortable and "beachy." Guests can enjoy the common area with a fireplace. And the Jacuzzi on the deck creates a big splash.

Complimentary cocktails are served afternoons on the enclosed patio. Guests can also enjoy a full breakfast cooked to order daily between 8 and 10 AM. Bicycles are available for a ride to the beach or along trails nearby. And the entire establishment is nonsmoking — although smoking on the outdoor deck is fine. Pets aren't allowed here. And 3 Seasons is not equipped to accommodate children younger than 18. Two-night stays are required on summer weekends, and a three-day minimum is requested for holiday weekends. This quaint inn is open April through November.

Sea Kove Motel

Beach Rd., MP 3 *261-4722*
$$$ *No credit cards*

This family-owned and operated establishment rents 10 one-bedroom efficiency units, 10 two-bedroom units and one cottage by the week only from April through November. It's across from the ocean and includes full-size kitchens and televisions in each apartment. A playground and outdoor pool also are available.

Beach Haven Motel

Beach Rd., MP 4 *261-4785*
$$

This small motel sits across the road from its own beach access and includes two buildings with a total of six semi-efficiency units. A practical, homey atmosphere prevails at the Beach Haven, where items such as coffee makers (with free coffee), refrigerators, microwaves, hair dryers, televisions and porch chairs are provided. Telephones aren't available in each room, but owner Joe Verscharen will let you take his portable phone back to your room for private conversations.

Each unit sleeps one to four people comfortably, depending on which one you choose. Cribs also are provided for infants. And the decor throughout reflects a contemporary beach look with rattan furniture and pastel colors. A grill and picnic table are on the premises. And you're welcome to play croquet in the yard or try your hand at the on-site putting green. Joe lives at this motel and promises to make your stay here as pleasant as possible. Guests have referred to these accommodations as an "oasis" on the Outer Banks. Beach Haven Motel is open April through October.

Holiday Inn Express

U.S. 158, MP 4½ *261-4888, (800) 836-2753*
$$

Situated on the east side of the By-

Insiders' Tips

A new Holiday Inn Express will open in late June 1996 in Hatteras Village at the southern tip of the island by the ferry docks.

pass, Holiday Inn Express has an outdoor swimming pool and is a short walk to lifeguarded Kitty Hawk Beach, where guests can use the motel's private access and oceanfront deck. All of the motel's 98 rooms are spacious and have color cable TV, telephones and refrigerators. Some also have couches, and half have microwaves. Most offer queen-size beds, and all are attractively furnished in soft beach decor.

The inn provides a complimentary continental breakfast bar for guests each morning in the lobby.

Nonsmoking and handicapped-accessible rooms are available at this Holiday Inn Express. The rates are very reasonable. Children 17 and younger stay free if accompanied by an adult. Meeting rooms accommodate up to 10 people, and year-round group rates are available. This motel is within walking distance to shopping and several restaurants. It's open all year.

Buccaneer Motel and Beach Suites

Beach Rd., MP 5¼ *261-2030*
$$ *(800) 442-4412*

The Buccaneer is an older, well-maintained, oceanside family motel. Owner Keith Byers has operated this friendly establishment for more than 13 years. Here, overnight travelers have their choice of one- and two-bedroom units, and efficiency apartments with one to four bedrooms are available for those who wish to stay longer. Each unit has a refrigerator and cable TV. As with many older Outer Banks properties, the rooms do not have telephones; however, pay phones are on the premises for personal calls.

While the Buccaneer is across the highway from the beach, there are no other buildings between it and the ocean. Guests only have to cross a small sand dune to reach the surf. A dune-top deck and private beach access make enjoying the Atlantic from this accommodation almost as easy as if the motel were on the ocean. Other amenities provided include a large, outdoor swimming pool with adjoining deck; a children's playground; basketball and volleyball courts; a horseshoe pit; charcoal grills and a fish-cleaning station.

Handicapped-accessible rooms are available at the Buccaneer. Ten percent discounts are offered on all weekly stays, and AARP and other discounts are honored during the off-season. The Buccaneer is open March through November.

Kill Devil Hills

Tanarama Motel Apartments

Beach Rd., MP 6 — *441-7315*
$$$

Two regular motel rooms and 33 one- and two-bedroom efficiency units are offered at this oceanside motel. Most of the rooms have ocean views, but a few of the efficiencies are across the street, on the west side of the beach road. Four upstairs oceanfront suites each include a separate bedroom with two double beds, a sitting room with a double bed and a full kitchen. Courtside efficiencies have two double beds plus a sitting room and kitchen. A beachfront room is available, as is a unit with a double bed, small refrigerator, microwave and coffee maker. Phones and color cable TVs are provided in all units.

Guests of the Tanarama will enjoy its outdoor pool. And the Avalon Fishing Pier is on the north side of this motel. Kids 6 and younger stay free here. This motel is open March through November.

Driftin' Sands Motel

Beach Rd., MP 6½ — *441-5115*
$$ — *(800) 237-1083*

Six rooms and three efficiency apartments are available in this well-kept motel across from the Atlantic. Each room has a refrigerator and television. A two-night minimum stay is required during summer weekends. The Driftin' Sands is open from April through November.

Days Inn Mariner Motel

Beach Rd., MP 7 — *441-2021*
$$$ — *(800) 325-2525*

A total of 70 units — 58 of which are on the ocean — comprise the accommodations here: 33 offer two double beds in a single room and 37 are one- and two-bedroom apartments with complete kitchens. Each room and apartment includes a telephone, refrigerator and cable TV. And all the rooms were refurbished recently with a fresh, contemporary beach look.

There's easy access to the Atlantic. And the units are spacious enough to offer flexible living arrangements for families or groups. This motel's recreation area has facilities for volleyball, and an outdoor swimming pool and showers are just off the ocean. Nonsmoking rooms are available here. All Days Inn programs are honored, and AARP discounts are available. The Mariner is open mid-February through November.

Quality Inn Sea Ranch Hotel

Beach Rd., MP 7 *441-7126*
$$$$ *(800) 334-4737*

The Sea Ranch was one of the Outer Banks' first resort properties to include recreational amenities, a restaurant, lounge and retail shops. This hotel is family-owned and operated, with a five-story oceanfront tower and a two-story building that contains 50 motel-style rooms and 28 luxury apartments with full kitchens. Each unit has a cable TV and HBO, a refrigerator, microwave and telephone. The apartments have glass-enclosed oceanfront balconies, two bedrooms and two baths. They typically rent weekly, but some also can be rented nightly depending on occupancy. About 25 of the hotel rooms have oceanfront views. Nonsmoking rooms are available.

Amenities at the Sea Ranch include room service — a rare find on the Outer Banks — from the hotel's upscale restaurant, Third Street Oceanfront Grille (see our Restaurants chapter). The lounge has a dance floor and nightly entertainment (see our Nightlife chapter). If you're in the mood for exercise, the Sea Ranch has a heated indoor pool that's open year-round on the premises. Across the road, a recently expanded Nautilus fitness center is frequented by locals and visitors. A women's boutique and hair salon also are on site (see our Shopping chapter). The Sea Ranch is open all year.

The Chart House Motel

Beach Rd., MP 7 *441-7418*
$$$

The hosts of this 18-unit motel, David and Kristin Clark, live in the large oceanfront brick Colonial beside it — close enough to offer their personal touch. Built in 1966, the Chart House is a popular spot with six efficiency apartments and 12 motel rooms. Each unit has two double beds, a color TV, refrigerator, microwave and coffee maker. The one-room efficiencies also have fully equipped kitchens. And five of these units connect with regular motel rooms to accommodate larger groups and families. Nonsmoking rooms are available.

The Chart House sits perpendicular to the ocean, so direct ocean views are not available. A small pool and patio are situated away from the road. The motel is open mid-March through November.

Nettlewood Motel

Beach Rd., MP 7 *441-5039*
$$

Locally owned and operated for more than 20 years, the Nettlewood is a favorite of the older set who like to come to the beach in small groups and who appreciate a small, clean motel. The Nettlewood has 22 rooms with one or two double beds and 16 efficiency units with two double beds and complete kitchens. All rooms have refrigerators and color TVs with remote controls and cable. They rent by the day during the week. But three-night minimum stays are required during summer weekends.

Across the street, four 1,500-square-foot apartments each offer three bedrooms and two baths and can accommodate up to eight people. These larger units rent weekly. There's a large in-ground swimming pool on site for guests. The Nettlewood is open year round.

Hampton Inn

Beach Rd., MP 7¾ *441-0411*
$$$$ *(800) 338-7761*

This 97-room, four-story hotel has exterior and interior corridors and was recently renovated inside and out. It's across the street from the ocean, so some guest rooms here have views of the Atlantic — while others afford glimpses of the Wright Brothers National Monument. Twelve of the first-floor guest rooms open directly onto the outdoor courtyard and pool.

Each room has a microwave, refrigerator, color TV with remote control, cable and free HBO, a telephone and private balcony or patio. Nonsmoking and handicapped-accessible rooms are available. A complimentary continental breakfast — cereals, pastries, juices, coffee, tea and fresh fruits — is served daily in the lobby from 6 until 10 AM. Discounts are available to AARP members. Children 18 and younger stay free in their parents' room. Pets are welcome here for a $5 per day additional charge. During summer holidays, three-night minimum stays are required. The Hampton Inn is open all year.

Comfort Inn North

Beach Rd., MP 8 — *480-2600*
$$$$ — *(800) 854-5286*

One of the newer oceanfront motels on the Outer Banks, this three-story property includes 120 rooms that open along exterior corridors. They're filled with natural light and decorated with mauve and teal accents. The building is T-shaped, so not all rooms have views of the Atlantic. Oceanfront units, however, also offer private balconies.

Some rooms at this Comfort Inn have refrigerators and microwaves. All have full baths, cable TV and HBO, telephones and coffee makers. Nonsmoking and handicapped-accessible rooms are available. Guests here can enjoy the hotel's oceanfront pool. And a hospitality room is available for meetings. Other amenities include a game room and coin-operated laundry facilities on-site. A complimentary breakfast is provided. Children 18 and younger stay free with an adult. A three-night minimum stay is required on summer holiday weekends. Managers honor AARP discounts. The Comfort Inn is open all year.

Cherokee Inn Bed and Breakfast

Beach Rd., MP 8 — *441-6127*
$$$ — *(800) 554-2764*

This historic bed and breakfast inn owned by Kaye and Bob Combs was originally operated as a hunting and fishing lodge. Guests can still imagine the feasts that must have been held here a half-century ago at day's end around a grand table. The Cherokee has been operated as an inn for the past 18 years and has been a bed and breakfast for the last nine years. If you stay here, you'll learn about your lodging's history from its second-generation proprietors — who are surrounded by four generations of family just a short distance away.

Six guest rooms are available on the second floor of this three-story building. Wicker furniture and floral accents in each room help create a bright, homey atmosphere. All units include private baths, remote color TVs and ceiling fans. Five of the rooms offer queen-size beds, and one room has a double and a twin bed. Although telephones aren't in each room, there is a phone in the first-floor common area that's reserved for inn guests. A wraparound porch with picnic table allows guests to catch cool ocean breezes during the heat of summer.

A continental breakfast is included in room rates. And bicycles, beach chairs, golf clubs and an outdoor shower are available for all guests. No smoking is allowed in this inn. In July and August, two-night minimum stays are required on weekends. The Cherokee Inn Bed and Breakfast is open April through October.

Sun & Sand Motel

Beach Rd., MP 8 *441-7319*

$

Single and double rooms are available in this 15-unit motel across the street from the Atlantic. In addition, you can rent one- and two-bedroom apartments with full kitchens if you prefer to cook meals yourself. Each room includes a refrigerator and cable TV. Telephones, however, are not provided. Handicapped-accessible rooms are available. And pets are welcome. The motel has a two-night minimum stay during summer weekends. Sun & Sand Motel is open from April through mid-October.

Tanglewood Motel

Beach Rd., MP 8¼ *441-7208*

$$$$

A two-story oceanfront motel offering 11 one- and two-bedroom vacation apartments, the Tanglewood has upper-level accommodations with ocean views and lower level units tucked behind the sand dunes. Each apartment is unique, but all have complete kitchens with microwaves, refrigerators, cable TV and full baths. One-bedroom apartments also have sleep sofas, so they accommodate up to four adults. A phone is available by request. Most two-bedroom units sleep five or six people, and one can accommodate up to 10. Linens are provided here. Maid service is offered midweek for weekly rentals.

This family-oriented motel has an outdoor swimming pool, boardwalk to the ocean with a deck for sunbathing and an enclosed outdoor bathhouse with hot and cold water for a relaxing shower after a day at the beach. Other amenities include a fish-cleaning station, picnic tables and grills. The Tanglewood is open April through October. Weekly rentals are preferred during the summer; daily rentals are also available.

Cavalier Motel

Beach Rd., MP 8½ *441-5584*

$$$

A variety of rooms is available at this courtyard motel on the oceanfront. Three one-story wings enclose the two swimming pools, a volleyball court, children's play area and shuffleboard courts. The Cavalier has 40 rooms with double and single beds and six one-room efficiency units with two double beds and kitchenettes right on the beach. Some rooms have full baths, while others just have shower stalls. All are equipped with telephones, refrigerators, microwaves, cable TV and free HBO.

In addition to these units, the motel offers 13 cottages that rent by the week. Pets are allowed in the cottages only.

Photo: Mary Ellen Riddle

The First Colony Inn was relocated in the mid-1980s to its current spot in Nags Head. It was completely restored and today is a thriving bed and breakfast inn.

Parking is available outside each room. And the covered porch with outdoor furniture is just right for relaxing with a free cup of coffee while watching the sunrise. An observation deck sits atop the oceanfront section. This is a well-maintained, family-oriented property and is reasonably priced for daily or weekend rentals. Children 5 and younger stay for free in their parents' rooms. The Cavalier Motel is open year round.

Days Inn Oceanfront Wilbur & Orville Wright

Beach Rd., MP 8½ *441-7211*
$$$ *(800) 329-7466*

An oceanfront property situated on a wide stretch of beach, this facility opened as an Outer Banks motel in 1948. It was built to resemble an old mountain lodge and boasts an inviting lobby decorated in the nostalgia of Old Nags Head where guests can read the newspaper and sip a cup of free coffee. The room is further enhanced by Oriental rugs on polished hardwood floors and a fireplace large enough to take away the chill on cold beach evenings during the off-season.

Guests here enjoy balconies with old-fashioned furniture and nice views. All 52 rooms have been renovated and furnished with 1990s decor. There are singles, doubles, kings, king suites and efficiency units that sleep six and include a living room, adjoining bedroom and complete kitchen. All rooms have telephones, cable TV and refrigerators. Oceanfront rooms also have microwaves. Nonsmoking and handicapped-accessible rooms are available. The hotel has interior and exterior corridors, and suites have entrances to both.

A complimentary continental breakfast is available throughout the year. Hot apple cider and popcorn are served around the fireplace during the winter, and lemonade and cookies are served in the summer. Leisure amenities include a large outdoor pool, sun deck, volleyball court, barbecue pit for cookouts and a boardwalk to the beach.

Children 12 and younger stay for free here. AARP discounts also are honored. There's a three-night minimum stay for summer holiday weekends, and Saturday check-ins aren't allowed unless you plan to stay for a week. Daily and weeklong rentals are available throughout the year.

OCEAN REEF-BEST WESTERN HOTEL

Beach Rd., MP 8½ — *441-1611*
$$$$ — *(800) 528-1234*

All 70 one-bedroom suites in this newer oceanfront hotel are decorated and arranged like luxury apartments with a contemporary beach decor. The views are great. And you'll find everything you need for a truly luxurious beach vacation. Each room has a telephone, cable TV, free coffee and a fully equipped galley-style kitchen. A nice touch: The bath area has a double vanity.

Nonsmoking and handicapped-accessible rooms are available. Upper-floor rooms have private balconies overlooking the ocean. Some first-floor units open onto the oceanfront pool and courtyard, while others offer a private patio. The Ocean Reef is one of the few facilities on the beach to have a penthouse suite; this one boasts a private Jacuzzi and rooftop deck. A heated, seasonal outdoor pool and a whirlpool are available to guests in the courtyard, and the exercise room features the latest equipment and a sauna. Other amenities include a laundry facility on the premises and year-round bar and food service available in the cafe. Children 17 and younger stay free with adults here. A two-day minimum stay is required on summer weekends. Ocean Reef is open all year.

COLONY IV MOTEL

Beach Rd., MP 9 — *441-5581*
$$$ — *(800) 848-3728*

This modern family-owned and operated oceanfront motel is well maintained and offers lots of amenities. Managers Cindy and Tom Kingsbury provide ample hospitality for moderate prices — as well as an outdoor heated pool and patio, a nine-hole miniature golf course, two picnic areas with grills, a children's playground, a dune-top gazebo, a video game room, horseshoe pits, a private beach with lifeguard and other outdoor activities. A complimentary continental breakfast is served every morning. Laundry facilities are also available on the premises.

The motel has 87 units, 14 of which are efficiencies. Most offer two double beds, although three oceanfront rooms have king-size beds. Telephones, refrigerators, microwaves, color TV with remote control and cable and clock radios also are provided in each unit. Some rooms have direct access to the beach while others have a small balcony overlooking the ocean. One room even has a Jacuzzi. The efficiencies have an eating area and, when combined with adjoining rooms, create a good arrangement for family vacationers. Nonsmoking units are available.

Children 12 and younger stay free here. Discounts of 10 percent are provided for AARP and active military members. A three-night minimum stay is required on summer weekends. The Colony IV Motel is open February through November.

Budget Host Inn

U.S. 158, MP 9 *441-2503*
$$$ *(800) BUD-HOST*

This motel is on the Bypass, about two blocks from the ocean. All 40 rooms are tastefully furnished and well-maintained, with either king-size beds or extra-length double beds. Each unit has a telephone, cable TV and tub/shower combination. Refrigerators and microwaves are not available in the rooms, but the lobby has a guest refrigerator and microwave. A coin-op laundry room also is on the premises.

Nonsmoking and handicapped-accessible rooms are available here. The motel also offers two family rooms that sleep six to eight people comfortably. The property maintains an indoor heated pool for year-round use. And a small picnic area is just south of the motel. Free coffee and tea are available in the lobby each day. Pets are accepted. Cribs are provided free of charge, and children 16 and younger stay free. The Budget Host Inn is open year round.

Ramada Inn Hotel

Beach Rd., MP 9½ *441-2151*
$$$$ *(800) 635-1824*

This five-story, 172-room oceanfront hotel was built in 1985. It's popular with tour groups and hosts many meetings throughout the year. All rooms have balconies or patios, cable TV with pay-per-view movies, small refrigerators and microwaves. Bellhop and room services — rarities on the Outer Banks — are available here. Nonsmoking and handicapped-accessible rooms also are offered. Meeting facilities are on the third floor overlooking the ocean. Several suites are available as well to fit a variety of conference and workshop needs.

For guests, an indoor swimming pool and Jacuzzi are just off the second floor, atop the dunes and surrounded by a large sun deck. A flight of steps takes you onto the beach where volleyball is a popular pastime. Food and beverage services area available at the oceanfront Gazebo Deck bar, adjacent to the pool.

Peppercorns, the hotel's fine oceanview restaurant, serves breakfast and dinner year round and offers lunch on the deck during the summer (see our Restaurants chapter). The Ramada Inn is open all year.

First Flight Inn

Beach Rd., MP 9 *441-5007*
$$

Of the 55 units at this oceanfront inn, 25 are efficiency apartments. Most have two double beds per room, and five have one double bed. Each room has cable TV and a refrigerator. Microwaves are available in 20 rooms. And although telephones aren't in each guest room, there are two pay phones on the premises. This is a family-oriented inn with an outdoor swimming pool and deck, fish cleaning station and outdoor showers. Free coffee is always brewing in the office. And children 12 and younger stay free. On summer holiday weekends, there's a three-day minimum stay. First Flight Inn is open from April through October.

Insiders' Tips

From Corolla through Hatteras Island, cable television includes five pay-per-view movie channels.

See Sea Motel

Beach Rd., MP 9 *441-7321*
$$

A small, family run motel across the street from the ocean, See Sea offers 20 rental units, including 11 motel rooms, five efficiencies, three two-bedroom apartments and one three-bedroom cottage. The motel rooms and efficiencies rent by the day (the apartments and cottage require a one-week minimum stay in season). All units have a refrigerator and cable television. Rooms do not have telephones, but there's a pay phone on the premises. A coin-op laundry facility also is on site. And free coffee is provided.

Amenities here include an outdoor swimming pool, fish-cleaning facility, fish freezers, a picnic area and gas grill. Nonsmoking rooms are offered. And children 14 and younger stay free. See Sea Motel is open from April through mid-October.

The Anchorage

Beach Rd., MP 9 *441-7226*
$$

All 17 units at this oceanfront motel include full kitchens and cable TV. There are nine efficiencies and eight cottages that rent by the day or week. Pets are accepted here, and nonsmoking rooms are available. The Anchorage is open year round.

Holiday Inn

Beach Rd., MP 9½ *441-6333*
$$$$ *(800) 843-1249*

This oceanfront hotel has 105 rooms — many with spectacular ocean views. Banquet and conference facilities here can accommodate 10 to 300 people. An on-site restaurant and lounge provide room service (see our Restaurants chapter). Guests may use the on-site video arcade game room and coin-op laundry. An outdoor pool, Jacuzzi and outdoor oceanfront bar are other features.

All rooms include telephones and cable TV with remote. Some also have microwaves and refrigerators. This Holiday Inn has a nonsmoking floor and handicapped-accessible rooms. Children 18 and younger stay free here, and AARP members receive a 10 percent discount. Holiday weekends require three-night minimum stays during summer. The Holiday Inn is open all year.

Tanya's Ocean House Motel

Beach Rd., MP 9½ *441-2900*
$$$

This seaside motel is an Outer Banks legend offering unique, individually designed accommodations the owners call "Carolina Collection Rooms." Legend has it that original owner, Tanya Young, and a designer friend decided to do a theme room at the motel. Their ideas got a little out of hand, and they ended up selecting separate themes for each room. There's the Carolina Party Room, Jonathan Seagull's Nest and dozens more. No two rooms at this motel are alike.

Tanya's has 47 rooms, including a few "normal" rooms that have to been converted back from the original designs over the years. All units have refrigerators and cable TV with HBO. Oceanfront rooms also offer microwaves. Telephones are not provided.

Guests here can enjoy a 40-foot outdoor pool surrounded by umbrella-shaded picnic tables. Free coffee is provided throughout the day. During summer, there's a two-night minimum stay on weekends. The seventh night is free if you stay a week. Children younger than 18 stay free at this motel, and AARP discounts are honored. Tanya's is open April through mid-October.

Miller's Outer Banks Motor Lodge

Beach Rd., MP 9½ *441-7404*
$$$

An oceanfront motel with 30 efficiency units and eight regular rooms, Miller's Outer Banks Motor Lodge only rents its oceanfront units by the week during the peak season. Other units, however, can be occupied by the day. Each room has cable TV, a refrigerator and microwave. Handicapped-accessible units are available. Also on-site are a washer and dryer, a playground, outdoor swimming pool, a restaurant and a video arcade room. Children 9 and younger stay free here. Miller's is open from March through November.

Quality Inn John Yancey Motor Hotel

Beach Rd., MP 10 *441-7141*
$$$$ *(800) 367-5941*

This older family hotel is on a wide beach that's guarded during the summer. Shuffleboard courts, an outdoor pool and a playground are on the premises. The main building has been stripped, rebuilt and redecorated recently.

The hotel has 107 rooms — most of them doubles — housed in three buildings. The oceanfront units each have balconies so you can watch — and hear — the waves from your room. Cable TV with pay-per-view in-room movies, small refrigerators and telephones are in each room. Ten units also offer microwaves, five have fully equipped kitchens, and three include hot tubs. About half of the rooms are nonsmoking, and one is a handicapped-accessible unit.

Other features here include a coin-op laundry. VCRs, movies and free coffee are available in the lobby. This Quality Inn has 24-hour front desk and maintenance service — a rare find on the Outer Banks. Children 12 and younger stay free here, and you can rent roll-away beds to accommodate additional kids. A two-night minimum stay is required on summer weekends. AARP and other discounts are honored. The Quality Inn John Yancey is open all year.

The Ebb Tide

Beach Rd., 10½ *441-4913*
$$

The ocean is just across the road from this family-run motel, which has 34 rooms with refrigerators, microwaves and cable TV. Three seaside apartments across the street are right on the beach. The apartments accept pets, but the motel itself doesn't. Guests have full use of the outdoor pool, picnic table and restaurant on the premises. Children younger than 12 stay free. The Ebb Tide is open from mid-March until early October.

Nags Head

Ocean Veranda Motel

Beach Rd., MP 10½ *441-5858*
$$ *(800) 58BEACH*

A well-maintained oceanfront property, Ocean Veranda offers 16 standard rooms, 14 efficiencies and one honeymoon suite with a king-size, canopy waterbed. Standard rooms are large and have two double beds, refrigerators and cable TV. Efficiencies have complete kitchens with microwaves and can adjoin other rooms to accommodate larger families of up to five people. Rollaways and cribs are available for a small charge. Some rooms on the second level offer partial ocean views.

Complimentary morning coffee is offered in the office. Other amenities include an outdoor pool and two gazebos, a children's playground, picnic area and barbecue. Children younger than 6 stay free. A small charge for extra persons in the rooms is applicable. Ocean Veranda is open January through November.

Beacon Motor Lodge

Beach Rd., MP 10¾ *441-5501*
$$$ *(800) 441-4804*

Visitors will find lots of options for seasonal and off-season stays at this family-oriented, comfortable oceanfront lodge. The James family has owned the 47-room Beacon Motor Lodge since 1970, offering one-, two- and three-room combinations that include motel-type rooms and efficiencies, plus two cottages. Nonsmoking rooms are available. The attractive rooms, finished in mauve, turquoise and peach, are all equipped with small refrigerators, phones and cable TV with remote control. Many units also have microwaves.

Guests can gather on the oceanfront patio — a grand place for enjoying the beach scene from a comfy lounge chair. Oceanfront rooms open onto a large, walled terrace affording wonderful views of the ocean from early morning until moonrise. Amenities include two children's pools, a large fenced-in, elevated outdoor pool with tables and umbrellas, a playground, patios with grills, an electronic game room and laundry facilities. Some provisions have been made for handicapped guests, including a ramp for beach access.

Inquire about discounts and weekly rentals (credit cards are not accepted for some discounts). The Beacon Motor Lodge is open late March through late October.

Colonial Inn

Beach Rd., 11½ MP *441-7308*
$

The Colonial Inn sports some oceanfront rooms, efficiencies with full kitchens and nine apartments with separate bedrooms, kitchens and full baths. All 38 rooms have televisions. And while you're only a short distance from the ocean, you can also choose to take a dip in the Inn's outdoor pool. Colonial Inn is open from April through November.

Old London Inn

Beach Rd., MP 12 *441-7115*
$

The Old London Inn is split in two sections with some efficencies on the west side and the rest on the east side of the Beach Road. A good many units are also oceanside. These are larger than the westside group and feature two double beds and a rollaway, plus a full kitchen; they accommodate up to five people. Smaller rooms are available with a double and a single bed to sleep up to three. All remaining rooms offer two double beds. All rooms have cable TV and full-size refrigerators. The westside effiencies are not heated. Children younger than 12 stay free. Prices reflect single or double occupancy; for each added person you pay $6. The Inn is open from the last week of March until mid-October.

Sea Spray

Beach Rd., MP 12 *441-7270*
$

This down-to earth beachfront establishment has a little bit of everything including eight rooms, 16 efficiencies and four cottages. All rooms feature two double beds, and some efficiencies have queen beds. All units have TVs. The cottages with two and three bedrooms are located across the street from the main establishment. Sea Spray is open March 1 through November.

Nags Head Inn

Beach Rd., MP 14 *441-0454*
$$$$ *(800) 327-8881*

This sparkling white stucco building with blue accents and plush Bermuda lawns is a tasteful contrast to the older Nags Head-style cottages nearby. Designed for family enjoyment, the oceanfront inn features a sunny lobby where greenery thrives. Also at ground level are offices and covered parking for guests.

Guest rooms begin on the second floor of this five-story building, and all oceanside rooms afford panoramic ocean views from private balconies. Rooms on the street side do not offer balconies, but the view of the sound from the fifth floor rooms is notable. All rooms have small refrigerators, Supercable TV with HBO, phones and full baths. Nonsmoking rooms are available, and there are handicapped-accessible rooms on each floor. The Nags Head Inn also features one suite with adjoining sitting room, wet bar and Jacuzzi — a perfect honeymoon setting.

A small conference room with adjoining kitchen/sitting area can accommodate about 30 people comfortably. The heated, all-weather swimming pool is on the second floor with a deck overlooking the ocean. During the summer months, the glass doors are removed providing a completely wide open lounging and sitting area for your enjoyment. Of course it's nice and toasty in the pool area in the winter months, so don't forget to pack bathing suits; the kids will love you for it.

Tour groups are welcome, and rates are seasonal. The inn is open all year.

Silver Sands Motel

Beach Rd., MP 14 *441-7354*

$$

Silver Sands, which sits across the road from a beach access, has 26 rooms that offer simple, basic decor — rustic pine walls and crate furniture — along with such amenities as refrigerators and cable TV with HBO. Guests are offered either two double beds or one queen-size bed. One handicapped-accessible room is available. Rooms do not have telephones.

A separate two-story building offers rooms on the upper level with balconies for ocean views. The main building offers 16 units near the outdoor swimming pool. Complimentary coffee is provided for guests. For the location, you can't beat the price. Off season rates go as low as $29. It's open Easter through November.

Oceanside Court

Beach Rd., MP 15½ *441-6167*

$$

There's nothing like an oceanside stay on the Outer Banks! That's what you'll get here, and you can choose from a room, efficiency or cottage. This small establishment offers six effiencies with cable TV and full kitchens; two rooms with microwaves, refrigerators and cable TV; and seven cottages. Phones are not available in any of the units.

The Oceanside Court is open from March 1 to November 30.

Surf Side Motel

Beach Rd., MP 16 *441-2105*
$$$$ *(800) 552-7873*

This attractive five-story motel is situated on the oceanfront, and rooms face north, south and east for ocean views. Some rooms have views of the sound as well. All oceanfront rooms have private balconies and are attractively decorated in muted beach tones. Refrigerators, cable TV and phones are standard room features, and the honeymoon suites feature king-size beds and private Jacuzzis. An elevator provides easy access, and handicapped-accessible rooms are available. An adjacent three-story building offers rooms and efficiencies with either ocean or sound views.

Complimentary coffee and sweets are provided for early morning convenience, and the staff hosts an afternoon wine and cheese social hour for guests. You can choose between an indoor pool and Jacuzzi that is open all year and an outdoor pool for swimming in warm weather. The Surf Side is open all year.

If you're interested in deep-sea fishing, Surf Side charters a boat for expeditions from Oregon Inlet. Call Oregon Inlet Fishing Center, 441-6301, for reservation information.

Sandspur Motel and Cottage Court

Beach Rd., MP 15¾ *441-6993*
$$

At the Sandspur you can choose from a room, efficiency or cottage stay. All rooms feature two double beds, cable TV, ceiling fans, refrigerators and microwaves. The efficiencies also have stoves. The rooms have no phones, but a pay phone is located on the premises. The motel also has a coin-operated washer and dryer. The Sandspur closes in December and reopens March 1.

First Colony Inn

U.S. 158, MP 16 *441-2343*
$$$$ *(800) 368-9390*

Back in 1932, this gracious old structure was known as Leroy's Seaside Inn. Today, the landmark hotel has been moved and refurbished, but it's still a favorite for those who like the ambiance of a quiet inn. The old Nags Head-style architecture, resplendent under an overhanging roof and wide porches, has been preserved and now is listed in the National Register of Historic Places. This is as close as you'll come to what it must have been like 64 years ago when the little hotel first opened. The First Colony received a historic preservation award from the Historic Preservation Foundation of North Carolina.

The Lawrence family, with deep roots in the area, rescued the hotel from demolition in 1988. The building was sawed into three sections for the move from its oceanfront location to the present site 4 miles south between the highways. It took three years of rehabilitation to return the inn to its original appearance. The interior was completely renovated and now contains 26 rooms, all with traditional furnishings and modern comforts.

In the sunny breakfast room, you can

Insiders' Tips

Bring extra beach towels so you don't have to borrow bath ones from your hotel.

enjoy a complimentary deluxe continental breakfast and afternoon tea. Upstairs, an elegant but cozy library with books, games and an old pump organ is a favorite place to read the paper or meet other guests. A great selection of jazz and classical music wafts throughout the reception area.

Each room is individually appointed in English antique furniture. Special touches — tiled baths, heated towel bars, English toiletries, telephones, TVs, individual climate control and refrigerators — are standard. Some rooms offer wet bars, kitchenettes, Jacuzzis, VCRs and private balconies; some also include an additional trundle bed or day bed for an extra person. The first floor is wheelchair-accessible, and one room is designed for handicapped guests. Smoking is not permitted in the inn.

Guests are invited to relax at the 55-foot swimming pool and sun deck behind the inn or to follow the private boardwalk across the street to the oceanfront gazebo.

This magnificent year-round inn provides easy access to the ocean and is close to many shops and restaurants in Nags Head. Discounts and group rates apply under certain conditions, and the inn has a policy of one night free for stays of five weeknights or longer.

Islander Motel

Beach Rd., MP 16 — *441-6229*

$$$

The Islander is a small, popular oceanfront property, due in part to its attractive landscape and well-maintained rooms. Most rooms have an ocean view, and some have private patios or balconies.

Some of the first floor units do not offer ocean views because they are tucked behind the dunes. The rooms are large and frequently refurbished. All have sitting areas and refrigerators. Some first-floor units offer kitchenettes.

Guests will enjoy the pool and private dune walk to the ocean. This property is convenient to all Nags Head restaurants, shops, recreational outlets and attractions. You'll find the comforts of this attractive motel more than adequate. The Islander is open April through October.

Blue Heron Motel

Beach Rd., MP 16 — *441-7447*

$$$

The Blue Heron Motel is considered one of the Outer Banks' best-kept secrets of the small motels in the area. The family-owned facility provides reasonably priced oceanfront rooms, a year-round indoor swimming pool, a spa and two outdoor pools. The Gladden family lives on the premises and pays careful attention to the management of the property. It's located in the midst of fine Nags Head restaurants and offers plenty of beach for those who come here to relax.

Nineteen rooms offer double or king-size beds, and 11 efficiencies sleep up to four people and provide full kitchens. All units have refrigerators, microwaves, coffeepots, cable TV, phones and shower/tub combinations. One handicapped-accessible room is available. Second- and third-floor rooms offer private balconies. The Blue Heron Motel is open all year and offers weekly rates.

Vivianna

Beach Rd., MP 16 *441-7409*
$$

You can't beat the views at the oceanfront Vivianna, and with the number of folks who return here year after year, something must be going right. The Midgett-Senf family has owned the motel since 1960. Expect to find 15 rooms here that are mostly apartments with kitchens and grand ocean views. All rooms have cable TV and microwaves. The motel is open March 1 through December 1.

Owens' Motel

Beach Rd., MP 16 *441-6361*
$$

The Owens family has owned and operated this attractive motel — one of the first on the beach — for more than 40 years. Adjacent to the family's famous restaurant, which is observing its 50th anniversary in 1996 (see our Restaurants chapter), this property across the highway from the ocean is well-maintained. You'll love the family atmosphere!

The Owens' three-story oceanfront addition includes efficiencies with large, private balconies. Each room has two double beds, a tile bath and shower and a kitchen. Cable TV also is standard in the guest rooms.

The motel swimming pool on the west side of the property offers guests an alternative to the ocean. Easy access to Jennette's Fishing Pier and a comfortable oceanfront pavilion with rocking chairs also will entice you. Owens' Motel is open April through October.

Sea Foam Motel

Beach Rd., MP 16½ *441-7320*
$$$

Twenty-nine rooms, 18 efficiencies and two cottages make up this attractive oceanfront motel. Efficiencies accommodate two to four people, and cottages sleep up to six comfortably. The efficiencies and cottages rent weekly; inquire about rates. Rooms are tastefully decorated in mauve and green, some with washed-oak furniture. All rooms have cable TV with HBO, refrigerators, microwaves and phones. Some have king-size beds, and each has a balcony or porch with comfortable furniture. Some units in the one- and two-story buildings have ocean and poolside views.

Children are welcome, and they will enjoy the playground. Other features include a large outdoor pool, children's pool, sun deck, shuffleboard area and a gazebo on the beach for guests' pleasure. Sea Foam Motel is within walking distance of restaurants and Jennette's Fishing Pier. Free coffee is provided until 11 AM, and a special family plan allows children younger than 12 to stay free with parents. Sea Foam Motel is open March through mid-December.

Quality Inn Sea Oatel

Beach Rd., MP 16½ *441-7191*
$$$$ *(800) 441-4386*

This year-round Quality Inn has an excellent oceanfront location near restaurants, recreation, shops and Nags Head attractions. Each of the 111 rooms is tastefully furnished; nonsmoking and handicapped-accessible rooms are available.

This inn is one of the nicest places

to stay on this end of Nags Head. The front desk is open 24 hours a day, and all rooms conform to Quality Inn's high standards. Each room has a telephone and cable TV with HBO. You'll also find a coin-operated laundry, snacks and ice. A sheltered gazebo is located on the beach. Inquire about *Lost Colony* and other package options. The inn is open all year.

Dolphin Motel

Beach Rd., MP 16½ *441-7488*
$$

The Dolphin Motel features 46 rooms and 12 efficiencies. Some rooms have queen-size beds, but most have double beds. Two nice features are the breezeway to the beach and an outdoor pool. All rooms and efficiencies have cable TV. The Dolphin Motel is open March 29 through October 26.

Whalebone Motel

Beach Rd., MP 17 *441-7423*
$$

The Whalebone Motel is open year round and has standard motel rooms and efficiencies divided among three buildings. All efficiencies offer one double and two single beds, and some units have two double beds. All accommodations feature microwave ovens and cable TV with HBO.

Comfort Inn South

Beach Rd., MP 17 *441-6315*
$$$$ *(800) 334-3302*

The Comfort Inn South, a seven-story oceanfront hotel situated in a quiet residential neighborhood, is one of the few accommodations in this area, and the tallest building on the Outer Banks. The light peach-and-teal exterior gives this hotel a clean, contemporary beach look. The 105-room hotel has deluxe oceanfront rooms

Photo: Mary Ellen Riddle

Ye Olde Pioneer Theatre in Manteo is a favorite spot for viewing family movies.

with magnificent views from private balconies; oceanside and streetside rooms are available too. All rooms have remote cable TV and phones. Rooms with refrigerators and microwaves are also available. Nonsmoking rooms are offered too. A honeymoon suite with Jacuzzi is popular, as are rooms with king-size beds. Corporate meeting rooms can accommodate groups of up to 450 people.

The in-season guest lounge and the outdoor oceanfront pool and deck are favorite gathering places. Other amenities include a children's pool, game room and playground. These features make this hotel appealing to families and business groups alike. A deluxe complimentary continental breakfast is offered in the lobby. Jennette's Fishing Pier is only a block away. The Comfort Inn South is open all year.

Fin 'N Feather Motel

Nags Head-Manteo Causeway *441-5353*
$$

A popular small motel along the water's edge, the Fin 'N Feather is popular with those who come to the Outer Banks to fish or hunt. If you're planning to come in the fall or spring, call well in advance for reservations. This motel's proximity to Pirate's Cove Fishing Center is convenient for anyone headed out for a day on the open seas. There's a boat ramp here too.

Housekeeping units are available year round, featuring single- and double-bed efficiencies. Each efficiency has a stove and refrigerator and is equipped with cooking utensils. The renter takes care of all his/her needs here. The rooms are clean and comfortable with blue and white decor. Large windows open onto the water from either side and offer stunning views of the sound.

Roanoke Island

Manteo

The Elizabethan Inn

U.S. 64 *473-2101*
$$ *(800) 346-2466*

The Elizabethan Inn is a year-round resort facility with spacious shaded

grounds, country manor charm and Tudor architecture that reflects the area's heritage. Only 7 miles from the beach, the hotel consists of three buildings providing more than 80 rooms, efficiencies and apartments, plus conference facilities, a health club, gift shop and a restaurant. Nonsmoking and handicapped-accessible rooms are available. All rooms have cable TV with HBO, refrigerators and direct-dial phones. Rooms are available with a king-size bed or two queen-size or standard double beds, and two rooms have whirlpool baths. All rooms are comfortable and well suited for a quiet, Roanoke Island-style vacation.

Anna Livia's Restaurant, on the premises, features excellent contemporary and traditional Italian cuisine and a bounty of seafood dishes (see our Restaurants chapter). The lobby is filled with interesting antiques, and a friendly staff makes you feel welcome. A small shop offers a selection of fine gifts plus local books, souvenirs and personal items.

The inn's Nautics Hall Fitness Center, the largest and most complete health club in the area, is available for guests of the inn (see our Recreation chapter). Guests may also use the small outdoor pool and a heated, competition-size indoor pool. Another nice touch: Guests have free use of bicycles to tour the nearby village or travel the paved bike path.

Inquire about special rate packages. The inn is open all year.

Roanoke Island Inn

305 Fernando St. *473-5511*
$$$$

With the sparkling Roanoke Sound and quaint Manteo waterfront just a stroll away, you'll find yourself easing into the relaxed village pace the moment you step up to this attractive inn. The distinctive white clapboard inn with dark green shutters offers the atmosphere of a gracious, restored residence with the comforts of a small, well-designed bed and breakfast. The furnishings are handsome, reflecting the meticulous care of the innkeeper, designer-architect John Wilson IV. And the ambiance is laid back and friendly.

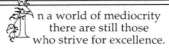

An eight-room addition designed for the guests' privacy gives each room a private entrance, private bath, TV and phone. You'll enjoy browsing through a collection of Outer Banks-related books and artwork in the lobby, and a light breakfast is offered in the butler's pantry.

The grounds are private and landscaped with gardenia, fig bushes and other native plants. Dip nets are provided so guests can experience netting crabs along the water's edge. Bicycles are furnished for touring the town and nearby historic attractions, including the *Elizabeth II* and the Outer Banks History Center. The pond out back provides "nature's music" to soothe and relax guests.

The inn opens in the spring, usually around Easter, and closes in the fall when the innkeeper and staff get tired.

The White Doe Inn

Sir Walter Raleigh St. *473-9851*
$$$$ *(800) 473-6091*

The White Doe Inn retains the charm of its Queen Anne-style heritage and offers guests an elegant escape in its rooms and hideaways. The inn offers six guest rooms and one suite, each with its own personality. Each room has a private bath and fireplace. The large, wraparound porches are the perfect place to relax and be pampered. Guests have full use of the study-library, formal parlor-living room, foyer and dining room of this stately old home. Afternoon tea and coffee are served. Bob and Bebe Woody work hard to fulfill their guests' every need. The inn serves a full Southern-style breakfast every morning, a good time for guests to gather to read the newspapers, enjoy the fine food and prepare for a day of exploring historic Manteo and Roanoke Island.

The White Doe is in a quiet neighborhood of downtown Manteo and is a perfect point of departure to explore the town on foot. Everything is within easy reach. The inn is truly beautiful, and guests won't be disappointed. Special events for up to 30 people can be accommodated — a perfect place for weddings, anniversaries, reunions or retreats. The inn is open all year, and off-season rates are available.

Scarborough Inn

U.S. 64 *473-3979*
$$

Located across from The Christmas Shop, this small inn is a delightful and friendly place to stay. Owners Rebecca and Fields Scarborough have taken over the family business for 1996. (Fields' parents, Phil and Sally Scarborough, now operate Scarborough House; see below.) With the help of designer-architect John Wilson IV — who, by the way, owns and designed the beautiful Roanoke Island Inn — the two-story structure was modeled after a turn-of-the-century inn. Each of the guest rooms is filled with authentic Victorian and pre-Victorian antiques and other interesting furnishings — mostly family heirlooms refinished by Field's mother.

Each room and piece of furniture has a story, and the Scarboroughs create a casual, comfortable atmosphere as they relate the history behind some of the pieces. The inn's six rooms are set away from the street. Each has a double bed, cable TV, phone, private bath, small refrigerator and coffee maker. Tasty muffins for the morning are delivered the night before, an especially nice treat for early risers.

Rooms in the two-story inn have exterior entrances and open onto a covered porch. The four rooms in the Annex offer two suites with two separate rooms as well as two smaller rooms; all are tastefully furnished, and one is handicapped-accessible. The Barn has two king rooms that are light and airy. All six rooms are equipped with wet bars, double vanities and small storage spaces for kitchen utensils and miscellaneous items.

Complimentary bicycles are available, and there's a glider swing in the backyard. Travelers will appreciate the owners' care and attention. We're sure your stay here will be most pleasant. It's open year round.

Scarborough House

Fernando and Uppowac Sts. *473-3849*
$$

If the Scarborough Inn is all booked, plan to stay at the Scarborough House, which Phil and Sally Scarborough opened in 1995. Relax in one of five tasteful guest rooms, each with its own refrigerator, microwave and private bath. Like its counterpart, this inn is appointed with period antiques and other fine furnishings. A continental breakfast is served daily. Bicycles are available for guests' enjoyment — in our opinion, the best way to discover downtown Manteo. Everything about this accommodation reflects the owner's care and personal touch. The Scarborough House is open year round.

Duke of Dare Motor Lodge

U.S. 64 *473-2175*
$

Located on the main street and only a few blocks from the Manteo waterfront, this small L-shaped motel provides the basics in accommodations: clean rooms with full baths, cable TV and phones. All rooms have queen-size beds. Handicapped-accessible rooms are available. The lodge also has an outdoor pool.

The Creef family has owned and managed the motel for almost a quarter of a century. The Duke of Dare is an inexpensive, family-oriented motel that's close to shopping, restaurants and attractions. It is open all year.

Tranquil House Inn

On the waterfront *473-1404*
$$$$ *(800) 458-7069*

You will be charmed by this lovely, 25-room country inn on Shallowbag Bay that's modeled after an old hotel that stood on this site from just after the Civil War until the 1950s. Although the inn looks authentic, it is only 9 years old, so all sorts of modern conveniences are included: TVs with HBO, telephones and private baths. Two of the 25 rooms, which are on the second floor, are one-bedroom suites that feature a queen-size bed, a separate sitting room with sofa and two TVs. All are individually and delightfully decorated.

Large rooms on the third floor have high ceilings. Nonsmoking rooms are available, and the inn has one handicapped-equipped room. A ramp to the first floor makes rooms on that level accessible to all. You're sure to enjoy the hospitality and fine surroundings.

The spacious second-floor deck faces east toward the bay. The *Elizabeth II* sailing ship is docked across the water. Shops along the waterfront are just a few steps away, and a marina out back is convenient for those arriving by boat.

The inn's exquisite restaurant, 1587, specializes in gourmet cuisine and offers an extensive selection of wines (see our Restaurants chapter). A fully appointed conference facility is available to groups on an hourly or daily basis. Guests have free use of bicycles. Tranquil House Inn is open all year.

Dare Haven Motel

U.S. 64 *473-2322*
$

The Dare Haven, a family-run motel suited to the cost-conscious vacationer, is located toward the north end of Roanoke Island and is a favorite place for families and fishing enthusiasts — there's enough room here to park your own boat and trailer. Visitors planning to attend *The Lost Colony* or visit any of the other Roanoke Island attractions and historic sites of Fort Raleigh will find this location very convenient. The motel also is close to the beaches and many other Outer Banks attractions.

The 26 motel-style rooms are basic,

clean and comfortable and have cable TV and telephones. Most rooms are decorated in traditional Outer Banks-style, with paneled walls and wraparound porches. All rooms are on ground level.

Crafts-lovers will want to visit the on-site Crafts Galore shop, which offers craft supplies for plastic and canvas needlework, stenciling, dolls and other handicrafts as well as displays works by local artists and crafters.

Call for special rates for groups and extended stays. The motel is open all year.

Wanchese

C.W. Pugh's Bed and Breakfast

Old Wharf Rd. *473-5466*
$$

A truly charming bed and breakfast, C.W. Pugh's occupies a renovated house that is more than 100 years old. Situated next door to Queen Anne's Revenge (see the Restaurants chapter), the inn has three guest rooms. Baths are located on the first and second floors, and a parlor and seating area is the setting for a complimentary full breakfast. Antique furniture and some reproductions add to the appeal of the bed and breakfast.

The spacious lawn is appealing for those who like some elbow room, and the winding lanes of Wanchese are perfect for bicycle rides. This bed and breakfast is situated near the end of the road where, at one time, Mr. Pugh was a lighthouse keeper at Marshes Light, a house built on pilings in the water. Pugh's duty was to help keep the channel waters open and safe for passing ships in an area where shifting sands fouled the entrance to the harbor. These days, there's is an electric light out on the sound instead. Nancy Gray, whose husband, Wayne Gray, is one of the operators of Queen Anne's Revenge, has managed this bed and breakfast for nine years.

This country setting, not far from historic Manteo and the beach, is a good choice for anyone looking for quiet relaxation. Children are welcome. It's open from Easter through Thanksgiving.

Island House Bed and Breakfast

104 Old Wharf Rd., Wanchese *473-5619*
$$$

This old home, built in 1902, is in its second year as a bed and breakfast in 1996.

Furnished in period antiques with Oriental rugs and cabana fans, the small but cozy establishment offers many comforts including private baths, cable TV and radios in every room, beach towels and chairs, complimentary bikes and a hot tub for guests. All rooms have one double bed.

Of course, a bed and breakfast would not be complete without a hearty morning meal, and Island House serves a full breakfast. Island House is open April through November. Summer rates apply from May 15 to September 15.

Hatteras Island

Rodanthe

Hatteras Island Resort

N.C. 12 *987-2345, (800) 331-6541*
$$

Plenty of leisure activities await guests at this large oceanfront resort next to the Hatteras Island Fishing Pier. The two-story building includes 18 motel-type rooms, each with two double beds, a dressing room and shower and 14 efficiencies featuring queen beds and full kitchenettes. Each of the eight oceanfront rooms and efficiencies offers an ocean view. A second building behind the dune offers 10 additional motel-type rooms.

The 25-acre oceanside property also has 35 two-, three- and four-bedroom cottages arranged in clusters. Cottages rent weekly; inquire about rates. All units are comfortably furnished and have cable TV. In-room phones are not available, but pay phones are located on the premises.

Families will enjoy the outdoor oceanfront swimming pool, kiddie pool, large patio area, volleyball and basketball. The Hatteras Island Fishing Pier is right out front on the Atlantic and draws a lot of people to the resort. The motel is open April through November.

Many restaurants will deliver to Outer Banks hotel rooms.

Insiders' Tips

Avon

Castaways Oceanfront Inn of Cape Hatteras

40393 N.C. 12 *995-4444*
$$$ *(800) 845-6070*

The hallmark of this year-round oceanfront establishment is the spaciousness of its 68 rooms, spread over five floors and offering oceanfront, ocean or dune views. Rooms feature king and queen size beds. Most rooms have wet bars, refrigerators and private balconies. Only first floor rooms do not offer ocean views because they are tucked behind the dunes. Nonsmoking connecting rooms, microwaves, rollaways and cribs are available. Meeting and conference facilities accommodate up to 200 people.

Amenities here include a heated, competition-size indoor swimming pool and hot tub. The wide, unspoiled beaches at the Castaways are beautiful and perfect for swimming, sunbathing and beach recreation. A boarded walkway leads you across the dunes and onto the beach.

The on-site Blue Parrot Cafe (see our Restaurants chapter) is attractively decorated in a tropical island motif. The ambiance, delicious fresh seafood and leisurely pace put guests into a real vacation mood.

The Castaways is closed in December. Inquire about special rate packages.

Buxton

Cape Hatteras Motel

N.C. 12 *995-5611*
$$$$ *(800) 995-0711*

When you arrive in Buxton, you'll see the Cape Hatteras Motel situated on both sides of the road. Owners Carol and Dave Dawson maintain this motel, parts of which have been here for more than 30

Insiders' Tips

Bring along a camera when heading for the kayak or canoe. The Outer Banks is threaded with canals that take you to where the wildlife is. A long lens will help get you close in and still not disturb the bears, deer, birds, alligators, fish and turtles.

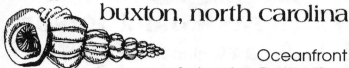

years. The 28 efficiency units are popular with anglers, surfers and folks who just plain enjoy Hatteras Island's beaches. Windsurfers especially like this facility because it is near some of the best windsurfing conditions on the East Coast at the nearby Canadian Hole (see our Attractions chapter).

Efficiencies sleep up to six comfortably, offer double beds as well as queens and kings and have full kitchens. The newer, more modern townhouses and efficiencies are located on the ocean. The motel has an outdoor swimming pool and spa. The motel's position at the north end of Buxton is convenient not only to pristine uncrowded beaches but also is near restaurants and services, making this a very popular place in the busy summer season.

Efficiencies rent weekly, but nightly rentals may also be available, depending on supply. Book reservations early. Cape Hatteras Motel is open year round.

Outer Banks Motel

N.C. 12 *995-5601*
$$

Situated next to the Cape Hatteras Motel, this establishment offers 11 motel-style rooms, six efficiency units and 17 two- and three-bedroom cottages. Units accommodate from one to nine people comfortably, and about 80 percent of the units provide an ocean view. Rooms and efficiencies offer enclosed porches with sliding windows and screens, perfect for a relaxing evening listening to the ocean. The pine-paneled rooms have tiled baths, microwaves, toasters and small refrigerators. Efficiencies have fully equipped kitchens. All units have cable TV and telephones.

The owners also have 14 additional cottages in the village of Buxton, a mile from the ocean near Connor's Market. Because these units are not oceanfront, rental rates are quite a bit lower. If you rent one of these cottages, you are welcome to use the motel pool and beach facilities. These cottages are clean, simply furnished and provide the basics for family vacationers, including cable television.

The motel has a coin-operated laundry, fish-cleaning station and a guest freezer to store your big catch. If you enjoy soundside crabbing — or if you just want to paddle around on the sound — the motel has several row boats that guests may use free of charge. There's even a library in the office in case you want to grab a good book on your way to the beach.

This motel is open year round.

Lighthouse View Motel

N.C. 12 *995-5680, (800) 225-7651*
$$$

Lighthouse View is easy to find on the big curve in Buxton, where the Hooper family has been serving vacationers for more than 36 years. The 73 units include a choice of motel rooms, efficiencies, duplexes, villa units and cottages. Most units are oceanfront, and all are oceanside. (The rate guideline above pertains to motel rooms.) The well-maintained complex has an outdoor pool and hot tub, and surfers, windsurfers and fishing enthusiasts like the proximity to ocean and sound.

Rooms have cable TV, phones, full baths and daily maid service. Efficiencies accommodate two to six people and are equipped with complete kitchens. The oceanfront villas offer balconies on both the oceanside and soundside, so you can enjoy sunrises and sunsets. The six duplexes offer two decks and sleep up to six people each. Efficiencies and villas rent on a weekly basis, but they can be rented nightly when available.

A three-night minimum stay is required for the efficiencies and villas. Cottages are rented by the week only. Efficiencies, duplexes, villas and cottages are fully furnished and have linen service (linens can be exchanged, but daily maid service is not provided). Handicapped-accessible one-room efficiencies are available.

Falcon Motel

N.C. 12 *995-5968, (800) 635-6911*
$$

The Falcon offers some of the best prices for accommodations on the Outer Banks. The traditional Outer Banks-style rooms here appeal to family-oriented guests who appreciate moderate prices, accommodations with character and the peaceful environment of Hatteras Island. The Falcon, owned by Doug and Anne Meekins, is known for its attention to detail, which is apparent in the clean, well-maintained rooms and grounds.

This motel includes 35 units with 30 rooms and five fully equipped apartments, all at ground level. Nonsmoking rooms are available. The spacious rooms have a light, airy feel and include cable TV with HBO. Many rooms have refrigerators and microwaves. Some have wooden deck chairs on a wide, covered porch. Park right outside your door.

Guests have use of the swimming pool and boat ramp as well, and you'll

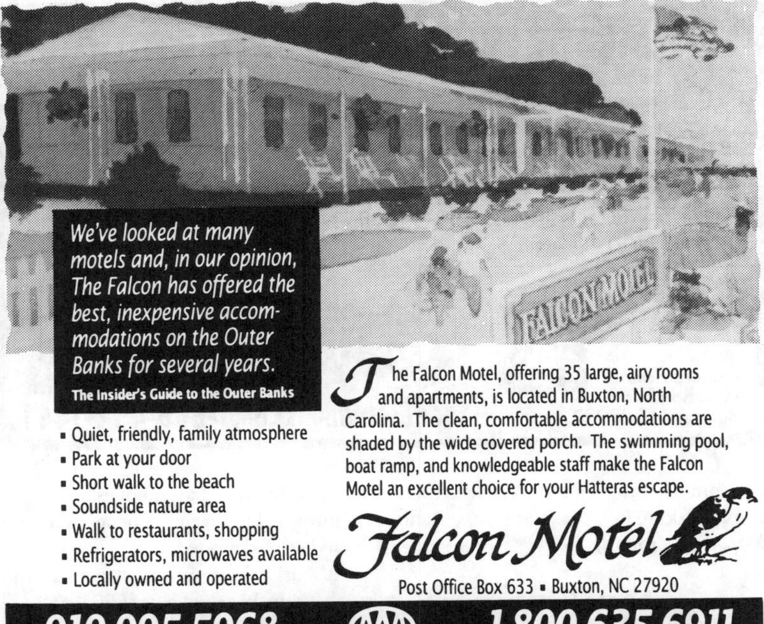

find a shaded picnic area with barbecue grills amidst mature oak trees, away from the road. The landscaping includes martin and bluebird houses and planted shrubs and flowers that attract the local bird population. Don't miss seeing the osprey platform on the soundside area beyond the trees. As you can tell, Anne Meekins is a devout bird lover and enjoys sharing her interests with guests.

The Falcon Motel is located in the heart of Buxton within easy walking distance of several shops and restaurants, including Diamond Shoals Restaurant (see our Restaurants chapter) across the street. The beach is a short walk away.

The rate guideline above pertains to the rooms; apartments rent mostly on a weekly basis. The motel is open from March through mid-December.

Comfort Inn of Hatteras

N.C. 12 *995-6100, (800) 432-1441*
$$$$

The Comfort Inn is located in the heart of Buxton, close to the beach and shops. The 60 units with exterior access are standard motel-style rooms decorated in attractive, soft beach colors; all have cable TV with HBO, refrigerators and direct-dial phones, and some offer microwaves. Nonsmoking and handicapped-accessible rooms make this property attractive to all visitors of the island.

Free ice and complimentary guest laundry is available. A complimentary continental breakfast is served in the lobby. Guests have use of the outdoor swimming pool, gazebo and the three-story watch tower — the latter two providing panoramic views of the ocean, the sound and nearby Cape Hatteras Lighthouse (see our Attractions chapter).

Comfort Inn of Hatteras Island has ample parking for boats and campers and is open year round.

Tower Circle

Old Lighthouse Rd. *995-5353*
$ *No credit cards*

This small motel, just off N.C. 12, is the closest lodging to the Cape Hatteras Lighthouse (see our Attractions chapter) and is one of the friendliest spots on the Outer Banks. The Gray family, which has owned Tower Circle for 24 years, treats their guests like old friends — which many of them are. Guests sit on the porch, swap stories and enjoy the atmosphere.

The 15 units, including eight duplexes, five suites and two efficiency apartments, all open onto the porch, have cable TV and sleep from two to six people comfortably. All suites and apartments have complete kitchens, and some have two bedrooms while others are two-room efficiency apartments. None of the units have phones. All linens are furnished for the apartments, and fresh linens can be delivered.

It's just a short walk to restaurants and stores or the beach. Tower Circle is open April through November.

Surf Motel

Old Lighthouse Rd. *995-5785*
$$$

The ocean is only a 1½-block walk from this motel managed by Bea and Jack Goldman, which is one reason it's so popular with surfers, windsurfers, anglers and family vacationers. Four motel-style rooms, eight efficiencies and one apartment are available here. The rooms offer double or single beds; the efficiencies sleep two or four comfortably and have full kitchens; the apartments, featuring two separate bedrooms and 1½ baths, are popular with families of up to five people. The decor features carpet-

Insiders' Tips

The Outer Banks Medical Center has physicians on-call 24 hours a day, year round, at the west end of Barnes Street, Milepost 11, near Britthaven elder care facility.

ing and traditional Outer Banks-style wood paneling.

Amenities include an outdoor, enclosed hot and cold shower, a horseshoe pit, barbecue grills, fish-cleaning stations and a freezer for your daily catch. There also is a handicapped-accessible ramp. Daily maid service is provided.

The Surf Motel is open March through December.

Cape Hatteras Bed and Breakfast

Old Lighthouse Rd. *995-6004*
$$ *(800) 252-3316*

This bed and breakfast inn is popular with windsurfers — the owners are both windsurfing enthusiasts — surfers and couples who just want to get away. The two-story inn offers several styles of accommodations from which to choose. All six units are nonsmoking and located on the first floor, and each has its own entrance opening onto a covered porch that runs the length of the building. Two of the rooms offer two double beds and the rest have queen-size beds. The inn has two efficiency units: The two-room unit features a bedroom with a queen-size bed, a living room with a queen-size sleeper sofa and a full kitchen; the one-room unit has a queen-size bed and kitchenette. All units have cable TV and private baths. A refrigerator and phone are available to all guests in the common room.

Amenities include a common dining and living area upstairs where a complimentary full breakfast is served, color cable TV, VCR, stereo and a small library. Outdoor showers are an appealing feature. Beach chairs, coolers, picnic bags, bicycles, fishing rods and beach toys are available along with lockable storage for surf and sailboards. Weekly rentals are available. Special accommodations are available for honeymooners! It's open year round, but we recommend that you call after November to be sure.

Cape Pines Motel

N.C. 12 *995-5666*
$

Cape Pines Motel, in the center of Buxton just a mile south of the Cape Hatteras Lighthouse, is a nicely maintained one-story facility with private exterior entry to each room. Steve and Hazen

Totton have owned this property since 1988.

Each of the 26 rooms offer cable TV and a full bath. Furnishings have a contemporary beach look. Some rooms have queen-size beds, and nonsmoking rooms are available. Microwaves are available for rent. Guests will also find three apartments, each offering separate bedrooms, a living room and a full kitchen. In the summer season, the apartments rent on a weekly basis only.

Stretch out and relax around the pool and the lawn. The flowers and landscaping are some of our favorites on this end of the island — a splash of color along the main road through Buxton all summer. You'll also find picnic tables and charcoal grills. Fish-cleaning tables are nearby, and there's a pay phone on the premises. Cape Pines is close enough to walk or bike to shopping, attractions and the beach. The motel is open year round.

Pamlico Inn

Buxton, 1 mi. south of Cape Hatteras School on the sound — *995-6980*
$$$

New in 1996, the Pamlico Inn features three suites overlooking the sound. A large wraparound deck, hammock and gazebo on the sound are pleasant places to enjoy the outdoors, or guests can gather in the common room to watch TV or videos, play games or browse through an extensive library. Scott and Brenda Johnson, the owners, both grew up on the island, and they want to help you enjoy their native home like an Insider so they are making watersports equipment — Waverunners, a sailboat and canoes — accessible for free to their guests and offering complimentary boat rides on the sound, fishing trips and windsurfing lessons.

Rooms have queen-size beds and private baths.

The inn offers special packages, including ones for anniversaries and honeymoons. The inn is open year round.

Hatteras Village

Durant Station Motel

N.C. 12 — *986-2244*
$$$$

Durant Station Motel caters to families and fishermen as well as outdoor enthusiasts. Amenities include an outdoor pool and fish-cleaning stations for the day's catch. Limited handicapped access is available.

This property offers one motel room and 29 apartments, each individually owned and furnished. The one-, two- and three-bedroom apartments rent weekly or nightly depending on availability. The apartments have a minimum two-night stay in season. The motel room rents nightly only. Each of the apartments is comfortably furnished. All rooms have cable TV, and two rooms have phones. Linen service is provided. Daily maid service is not available, and pets are not allowed.

Durant Station is open April through November.

Sea Gull Motel

N.C. 12 *986-2550*
$$

Most nights at this motel, you can just raise the window, catch the ocean breezes and listen to the breaking waves about 125 yards away. The Sea Gull is a well-maintained motel at the northern end of scenic Hatteras Village, and patrons will enjoy the quaint, quiet charm and friendly ambiance of this popular, established accommodation. Guests enjoy walking on the beach and along nearby Pamlico Sound or relaxing in the shade on a lazy afternoon. Sea Gull Motel has spacious grounds and walkway to the beach.

Other amenities include an outdoor pool, a wading pool for the kids, picnic tables, grills and fish-cleaning tables. A few shops are within walking distance, and Gary's Restaurant, just across the street, serves three meals daily (see our Restaurants chapter).

Guests will find a variety of accommodations, including 35 motel-style rooms. Six apartments and four efficiencies offer fully equipped kitchens. Handicapped-accessible rooms are available. The large, comfortable rooms rent nightly, while the apartments and efficiencies require a three-day minimum stay. Phones are available. All rooms have cable TV.

The motel is open March through November.

General Mitchell Motel

N.C. 12 *986-2444, (800) 832-0139*
$$

This motel is named for Billy Mitchell, the aviation pioneer of the U.S. Air Service, who proved the value and power of airplanes against naval vessels by sinking two retired battleships off Cape Hatteras from his plane. The 30-year-old facility, on the left as you enter Hatteras Village from the north, is typical of smaller motels built to accommodate fishermen who don't need a lot of extras. The rooms are clean and comfortable and do not face the ocean. The two buildings house 33 motel-style rooms and 15 efficiencies. Rooms offer two double beds, cable TV and telephones. Most of the efficiencies have full kitchens, although some have mini-kitchens. A two-day minimum stay is required for the efficiencies.

Amenities include an outdoor pool and Jacuzzi, and it's a short walk to the beach. Avid anglers will appreciate the freezer to store the day's surf catch.

General Mitchell Motel is open March through December.

Atlantic View Motel

Off of N.C. 12 *986-2323*
$$ *(800) 986-2330*

The office of Atlantic View is close to the main road, but the motel itself is situated down a quiet paved lane. The beach is just a few minutes' walk away. The motel offers 20 motel rooms and eight efficiencies. The rooms are larger than standard, and all are fully carpeted and have two double beds and cable TV. Efficiencies have fully equipped kitchens. Handicapped-accessible rooms are available. Phones are located near the office. High dunes prevent ocean views.

This is a particularly nice place for families. Guests and their children will enjoy the play area, in-ground swimming pool, smaller kiddie pool, volleyball nets, basketball hoop and complimentary bikes.

Shankie and Donna Peele, owners of the Atlantic View, cater to small families, but some rooms connect to accommodate larger groups. For travelers on a tight budget, this motel is a good choice. The Atlantic View is open year round.

Hatteras Harbor Motel

N.C. 12 *986-2565*
$$

This soundfront motel in the heart of Hatteras Village is convenient to restaurants, shops and services and is situated adjacent to the Hatteras charter boat fleet. Visitors can park their cars and walk or bike to most places in this sleepy community. We like this motel because of its location and its cheerful staff.

Hatteras Harbor Motel has 15 rooms (each with two double beds and a full bath), four two-bedroom efficiency apartments and two studio efficiencies. All rooms have cable TV and telephones. Daily maid service and fresh linens are provided. Guests will enjoy the in-ground pool — complete with kiddie wading pool — and the long, shaded porches that are perfect for watching the daily village activities.

The Hatteras Harbor also allows pets, although there is a fee to cover pest control and any damages that might occur.

The motel, a longtime favorite of fishermen and budget-minded travelers, is open year round. Inquire about off-season rates.

Hatteras Marlin Motel

N.C. 12 *986-2141*
$$

Hatteras Marlin Motel, owned and operated by the Midgett family, is within sight of the harbor fishing fleet, restaurants and shops. The 40 units are divided between three buildings and consist of standard motel rooms and one- and two-bedroom efficiencies. A newer building situated near the back of the property away from the road offers a pair of two-bedroom suites with combined living, kitchen and dining areas. From this building, built along a canal, you can often see ducks waddling around in the grassy areas of the yard.

The two older buildings near the road share parking with Midgett's gas station and convenience store. All rooms are well-maintained and have cable TV and telephones. Accommodations sleep one to six people comfortably and rent weekly or nightly depending upon availability. The motel has an in-ground swimming pool and sun deck. Hatteras Marlin Motel is open all year.

Ocracoke

Berkley Center Country Inn

N.C. 12 *928-5911*
$$$ *No credit cards*

Two buildings, situated on 3 acres, house this nine-room bed and breakfast on Ocracoke Harbor. The Manor House, built in 1860, was remodeled in 1950. The Ranch House dates from the mid-1950s, and the architecture and cedar exterior create an impression of age and quality. Both buildings are furnished in reproduction antiques. All interior walls, floors and ceilings of the Manor House are made of hand-carved wood panels of redwood, pine, cypress and cedar.

Berkley Center is adjacent to the Park Service offices and ferry dock but away from the congestion that one might anticipate from seasonal visitors. Lots of trees provide comfortable privacy. A complimentary continental breakfast consisting of fresh breads, fruits, preserves and coffee is available in the breakfast room of the Manor House. A guest lounge also is located here and offers the only television at the inn — a real opportunity to get away from the hustle and bustle of everyday life. Guests also have a choice of relaxing on one of the porches overlooking the lovely lawn and enjoying the company of other guests.

All rooms are spacious and have been furnished in classic fashion. Doubles sinks in the baths and large closets are among the nice features here. The inn has nine rooms, seven with private baths (two rooms share a large bath, ideal for a family). Phones are not provided in the rooms. Berkley Center is open April through October.

Princess Waterfront Motel

Silver Lake *928-6461*
$$$

Situated on the edge of Silver Lake, the Princess Waterfront Motel is an older building that features the quaint charm typical of Ocracoke Village structures. The first floor includes retail shops, and the second offers spacious efficiency apartments.

Its six units are equipped with modern furnishings, full kitchens, phones and remote-controlled cable TV with Showtime. The motel sits perpendicular to the waterfront, so not every room has a full view of the harbor. A private dock at the end of the parking lot is available for guests, who also have pool privileges at The Anchorage Inn across the street. Princess Waterfront Motel is open from April to November.

The Anchorage Inn and Marina

Silver Lake *928-1101*
$$$$

The Anchorage Inn overlooks Silver Lake and the village and is more like a small resort. In addition to accommodations, the inn has a marina and fishing center, recreational amenities, an outdoor grill and gift shops nearby. The attractive five-story red brick building with white trim has elevator access to each floor.

Accommodations here offer some of the best bird's-eye views available of the harbor and Ocracoke Village, especially from upper-floor rooms. Most of the rooms have some view of Silver Lake Harbor. Each of the motel-style rooms has king- or queen-size bed or two double beds, full bath, direct dial phone, and cable TV with

Insiders' Tips

You can rent a boat to take you to Portsmouth Island from Ocracoke. But take insect repellent — the mosquitoes on the island are fierce.

the Movie Channel. The fourth-floor units are nonsmoking rooms.

The Anchorage Inn offers its guests a complimentary continental breakfast, a private pool with a sun deck situated on the harbor and an on-premises boat dock and ramp. The gazebo at Silver Lake is a perfect place to watch an early evening sunset. Guests can walk to restaurants, shops and the historical sights on Ocracoke Island, or bike rentals are available. Fishing charters, which depart from the dock across the street, can be booked with the Inn's receptionist or from your room. The motel is open year round.

Pony Island Motel

Near Silver Lake Harbor *928-4411*

$$

At the edge of Ocracoke Village, a short distance from Silver Lake Harbor, Pony Island Motel offers 50 units.The grounds are spacious and inviting. For nearly 23 years, owners David and Jen Esham have hosted families and couples in search of peace and solitude on Ocracoke Island.

The Pony Island Motel has served visitors for more than 30 years. Most of the units have either single or double occupancy, but the motel offers some rooms that accommodate up to five people. Each room has color cable TV with Showtime, and the efficiencies provide fully equipped kitchens. Rooms are refurbished regularly, but maintain a traditional decor with paneled walls.

They have recently remodeled by adding bedroom suites featuring from one to four additional rooms per suite. The rooms are spacious and have wet bars and refrigerators.

The motel is within walking distance of the Ocracoke Lighthouse and other island attractions. Bike rentals are available. The large pool, deck, picnic tables and lawn offer plenty of room for family activities. The Pony Island Restaurant, a locals' favorite, is right next door (see our Restaurants chapter). The motel is open year round.

Edwards Motel

Pony Island Rd. *928-4801*

$

This older motel, away from the center of Ocracoke and off the main route near The Back Porch Restaurant, consists of eight motel rooms, three efficiencies and two cottages. The 13 units have screened porches and cable TV, and some open onto a veranda. Phones are not available in any of the units. The cottages rent weekly, and the efficiencies require a three-day minimum stay. (The rate guideline above pertains to nightly rentals of the motel rooms only.)

The Edwards Motel has been family-owned and operated for more than 25 years. Current owners Ruth and David Sams bought it from Ruth's sister, Mary, and her husband, Bernie Edwards. The motel offers inexpensive accommodations in a family setting with a carefully landscaped green lawn, flower beds and pine trees. Pets are not allowed. The motel is open Easter through mid-November.

Bluff Shoal Motel

N.C. 12 *928-4301, (800) 292-2304*

$$

Bluff Shoal Motel, a small seven-unit facility on the village's main street, has carpeted and paneled rooms that open onto a long porch. Each room has a private bath, small refrigerator, telephone and cable TV with Showtime. A two-bedroom efficiency apartment also is available. Bluff Shoal Motel is across the street from The Pelican Restaurant and is within walking distance of the post office, community store and village shops. Owners Jennifer and Wayne Garrish keep the motel open all year.

Pirate's Quay

Silver Lake *928-3002*

$$$$

This extraordinary hotel directly across from the Coast Guard Station in Ocracoke Village opened in 1987 and provides some

of the most luxurious accommodations available on a nightly basis anywhere on the Outer Banks. The hotel is made up of six individually owned condo suites, each with living room, dining room, full kitchen, two bedrooms and 1½ baths. Units on the top floor have cathedral ceilings. Two decks off each suite, a waterfront gazebo and docking facilities make the most of the harborfront location.

Each condo suite accommodates four adults and children and has a Jacuzzi and cable TV with Showtime. All suites are beautifully furnished and have kitchens stocked with all the dishes, cookware and gadgets you need.

From Pirate's Quay, guests can walk or bike to quaint nearby shops, restaurants and other attractions. The hotel is open year round.

The Island Inn

Silver Lake *928-4351*
$$$

The Island Inn, owned by Cee and Bob Touhey, provides a variety of accommodations suitable for single adults, couples and families with children. Originally built as an Odd Fellows Lodge in 1901, the main building has served as a school, a private residence and naval officers' quarters. It was restored by former owners and has been recognized in *Country Inns of the Old South*, *Southern Living*, *Cuisine* and *The Saturday Evening Post*.

The owners had their first date on Ocracoke Island and vacationed here for many years; they have returned to live and work. Many of the 35 rooms have been refurbished, reflecting the inherently romantic style of this country inn. The main building houses individual rooms and suites, all uniquely furnished with antiques and quilts, as if they were separate guest rooms in a private home, providing a restful ambiance. The adults-only rooms and suites accommodate a wide range of needs. If you're looking for a contemporary feel, ask for the Crow's Nest, which offers spectacular views of the postcard-pretty village.

Across the street, a much newer 19-unit, two-story structure includes two honeymoon rooms with king-size beds and bay windows affording views of beautiful sunsets over Silver Lake. Families with children will find these casual accommodations a welcome retreat. The inn also rents a number cottages, some of which accommodate pets, and has a heated swimming pool that is kept open as long as weather permits. Cable TV with free Showtime is available in every room. The inn has an on-site restaurant (see our Restaurants chapter), a large lobby for lounging and a covered porch with rocking chairs. The inn is open year round.

Oscar's House

One block from Silver Lake Harbor *928-1311*
$$

Oscar's House was built in 1940 by the keeper of the Ocracoke Lighthouse and was first occupied by the World War II commander of the Ocracoke Naval Base. Stories abound about Oscar, who lived and worked on the island for many years as a fisherman and hunting guide. This four-room bed and breakfast guesthouse is managed by Ann Ehringhaus, a local fine art photographer and the author of *Ocracoke Portrait*.

Insiders' Tips

While Ocracokers may use the legend of Blackbeard to enhance tourism some, one local said Ocracokers prefer not to romanticize the pirate who was really nothing more than a rotten scoundrel.

Boyette House
A TRADITION IN INNKEEPING
BOYETTE HOUSE I
est. 1981
Offering the amenities and privacy of a small hotel with the ambiance of an Inn. Comfortable and clean. Modern convenience at moderate cost.
BOYETTE HOUSE II
est. 1995
In-room breakfast bars; steam baths & whirlpools. Decks & balconies, porches with rocking chairs & ceiling fans. Hammocks under the trees. A new standard in beach accommodations.
Inquire about our luxury suites
919-928-4261
Ocracoke, North Carolina 27960

The house retains the original beaded-board walls, and all rooms are delightfully furnished. One upstairs bedroom has a loft that creates a comfortable setting. You won't find private baths, but sharing is easily managed. The large kitchen with a big table is available to guests; however, the stove is off limits. Ann serves a complimentary full breakfast to all guests and will gladly adhere to special preferences for vegetarian or macrobiotic meals. Smoking is allowed on the back deck only.

In addition, Oscar's House offers an outdoor shower (there's one inside, too), a dressing room and a deck area complete with barbecue grills. Meals can be eaten inside or outdoors. Oscar's House is within walking distance of all village shops and restaurants, and bicycles are free for guests. Ann will also gladly transport guests to and from the Ocracoke Airport, which is open to single- and twin-engine planes. This bed and breakfast is open from April to October.

Boyette House

Ocracoke *928-4261*
$$

Lanie Boyette-Wynn and her son, a third-generation Ocracoker, preside over this very pleasant motel that opened more than 16 years ago. The atmosphere suggests a quaint bed and breakfast, although the 12-unit, two-story wooden structure offers comfortable hotel-style rooms. The Boyette House has more than doubled in size since 1994, and Boyette House II is now open.

At Boyette House I, rocking chairs line the wide upper and lower decks fronting all rooms — nice places to read and relax. The lobby is a comfortable reading area as well, and visitors can borrow from the house selection of books. Guests will enjoy the complimentary coffee bar in the mornings.

Each room has a private bath, remote-controlled cable TV with Showtime and a refrigerator. Ten of the rooms have two double beds, and the other two offer one double bed. The five units on the first floor have ramp access, and wheelchairs will fit through the doors into the rooms.

Boyette House II, new in 1995, offers wide porches and wicker furniture, which create a comfortable atmosphere, and ceiling fans stir the air on warm summer evenings. Each of the rooms in the new section is well-appointed with a queen-size bed, breakfast bar, microwave, refrigerator and coffee maker. Most rooms also have wet bars and steam baths; all rooms have phones and cable TV with remote control. Boyette II offers a special room that meets all handicap requirements for convenience. The two luxury suites on the third floor each have a private porch, picture windows on three sides, a Jacuzzi and steam bath.

Whether you're staying at Boyette House I or II, the sun deck in the back is perfect for sunbathing. And, you can arrange to be picked up at the boat docks or the airport free of charge. Boyette House is within walking distance of Silver Lake and the restaurants in Ocracoke.

The motel is open most of the year, but its best to call ahead during the winter months just to make sure.

Sand Dollar Motel

Sand Dollar Ln. *928-5571*
$$

This quaint establishment is located in the heart of Ocracoke Village behind the Back Porch Restaurant (there are no street signs). The Sand Dollar has 11 rooms and a two-bedroom cottage. Two of the rooms are efficiencies featuring small microwaves and coffee makers; all rooms have refrigerators and cable TV. One special room is connected to the pool and has a private deck and two-double beds. All guest can enjoy a continental breakfast and a dip in the pool. The inn is open from April 1 to mid-November.

Silver Lake Motel

N.C. 12 *928-5721*
$$

Silver Lake Motel sits among a grove of trees along the main street of Ocracoke Village. The Wrobleski family built the two-story, 20-room motel in 1983 and has added another building since then. Featuring long porches and rooms paneled in California redwood, this motel is well-known for its rustic appeal and comfort; most of the furniture in the older rooms was built by the owners. Wooden shutters, pine floors and wallpapered baths create a cozy atmosphere.

The 12 suites in the newer building feature private porches with hammocks and wicker furniture, affording views of the lake. Rooms adjacent to these suites can be opened to provide for larger families. Suites, which offer living rooms and full kitchens, have wood floors, wallpapered baths and Victorian-style furnishings and wall coverings. End units have their own 7-foot-wide Jacuzzis overlooking Silver Lake — a relaxing environment indeed. All the rooms have cable TV with Showtime. A common area on the second floor of the main building serves as a dining room and lounge.

The Silver Lake Motel offers families comfortable and attractive rooms. A deep-water dock is provided for those arriving by boat. Handicapped-accessible rooms are available. It is open year round.

Harborside Motel

Across from Silver Lake Harbor *928-3111*
$$

This charming motel offers 18 rooms and four efficiencies, all well-kept and comfortable. All rooms have cable TV, phones and refrigerators. Guests can use the waterfront sun deck, docks and boat ramp across the street. Nonsmoking rooms are available.

Harborside has its own gift shop offering a wide selection of clothing, books, gourmet foods and small gifts. Other shops and restaurants of Ocracoke Village are within walking distance. The Swan Quarter and Cedar Island ferry docks are nearby. This property has been owned by the same family since 1965, and its hospitality and service are well-established. All rooms are refurbished on a regular basis.

A complimentary breakfast of homemade muffins, coffee, juice and tea is provided. The motel is open Easter through mid-November.

Blackbeard's Lodge

Back Rd. *928-3421, (800) 892-5314*
$$$$

Bob Martin and his family have owned and operated Blackbeard's Lodge for 14 years. This two-story motel is right across the street from The Back Porch Restaurant.

This family-oriented property offers a wide variety of accommodations to suit almost anyone's needs. The 36 units, which accommodate from two to 10 people, all have private baths, cable TV with Showtime, linen service and daily maid service. Eight of the units are efficiency apartments, some with adjoining rooms. All of the apartments offer fully-equipped kitchens but no microwaves. Among the amenities at this 36-room motel, which includes suites, are refrigerators, whirlpool baths, king-size beds and wet bars. A 7-foot-deep above-ground heated pool and bicycle rentals are also available.

Some units require a minimum stay of three nights, and others rent nightly and by the week. Ask about group rates and special rates for school trips. Blackbeard's Lodge is open April through October.

Eugenia's Bed and Breakfast

N.C. 12 *928-1411*
$$

Proprietor Eugenia "Jean" Fletcher lived in Swan Quarter for about 20 years before retiring from teaching and relocating to Ocracoke six years ago. This 5-year-old establishment, furnished with antiques and collectibles, offers four guest rooms. One room has a queen-size bed; others have two three-quarter-size beds and two double beds. Each of the rooms has a private bath.

Guests are served a full breakfast, including homemade breads, jams and casseroles. The lounge is a great spot to relax or watch television, and the porch swing and rocking chairs are perfect places to reflect upon your Ocracoke vacation.

Look for Eugenia's on the southside of Cafe Atlantic as you enter town. The airport is only a half-mile away, and shuttle/van service is free. Eugenia's is open April through October.

Crews Inn Bed and Breakfast

Back Rd. *928-7011*
$ *No credit cards*

The Crews Inn is a great place to really get away from it all. No phones or TVs will disturb your privacy here. Each of the five rooms sleeps two adults. Three rooms have private baths and two share a bath. The wraparound porch is an especially nice spot for guests to gather because the bed and breakfast is surrounded by large live oaks and is far enough away from traffic to make chatting easy. The inn serves a continental breakfast. Crews Inn is open year round.

Pelican Lodge

Across from fire station *928-1661*
$$

Built as a lodge, the Pelican features a full sit-down breakfast. The four rooms — one with two double beds and the others with one double bed — are spacious, carpeted and have private baths. Amenities include cable TV, a small pool and free use of bicycles. The lodge is open year round.

Between
mid-March and late
October, the weather
along the barrier
islands often is ideal
for outdoor
accommodations.

Inside Camping

Whether you're sleeping in style in an air-conditioned Winnebago or snoozing under the stars in a sleeping bag, the Outer Banks are among the prettiest places on earth to go camping. Waves, wind and wildlife provide night symphonies and create long lost lullabies that just can't be heard inside hotel rooms. Between mid-March and late October, the weather along the barrier islands often is ideal for outdoor accommodations — and the soft sand of most area campsites makes a much more comfortable bed than the hard dirt floor of other campgrounds.

Even local Insiders like to get away for a weekend, leave their nearby homes, pitch a small tent and enjoy the Outer Banks as nature intended. Each year, more than 100,000 people camp in the National Park Service campgrounds. Thousands of others spend memorable vacations outdoors at privately owned facilities.

In its early days as a summer tourist destination, the Outer Banks overflowed with campgrounds. Fishermen, boaters and hunters seemed to prefer sleeping outdoors. And there wasn't such an abundance of motels and rental cottages back then.

Recent development, however, has encroached on some of the formerly wide open spaces. Several of the area's original campgrounds have long since closed. But 20 campgrounds, some with hundreds of sites, still are available on Colington, Roanoke, Bodie, Hatteras and Ocracoke islands. Many of these facilities are right off the ocean, behind high dune walls, open to the sun and wind. Others are secluded along the sound or in wooded hammocks.

Several Outer Banks campgrounds are seasonal, open only during warm weather and offering only cold showers. Others are year-round, residential parks that include electric and water hookups, sewage disposal, cable television, laundry facilities, swimming pools, game rooms, full bathhouses — even on-site general stores. A few campgrounds also rent fully furnished recreational vehicles that sleep up to six people — as well as renting lots for travellers to park their own RVs on. And, of course, tents are accepted at almost every camping facility.

All Outer Banks campgrounds have drive-up sites and roads suitable for any vehicles. Wilderness camping is not allowed anywhere — including open, undeveloped areas such as Kitty Hawk

Insiders' Tips

For other camping options within a two-hour drive of the Outer Banks, see our Daytrippin' chapter.

Woods, Nags Head Woods and Buxton Woods. Camping also is prohibited on the beach.

But if you're looking for the ultimate back woods escape, wilderness camping is permitted on Portsmouth Island — about a 20-minute boat ride south of Ocracoke. This uninhabited, isolated island has no permanent residents and is inaccessible except by boat. It's the perfect place to get away from it all and experience the barrier islands the way they once were.

Campgrounds along the Outer Banks are either privately owned or managed by the National Park Service. Unless otherwise noted, private campgrounds accept major credit cards. Many take advance reservations. And we recommend making reservations if you plan to stay in July or August.

Summer is certainly the warmest time to sleep outside. Some people actually find it too hot to stay in a tent. We suggest coming back to camp in spring or fall, too, when the barrier islands seem a different place and the air is crisp and cooler. If you're going to camp in season, however, bring lots of bug repellent. Many campgrounds are in wooded areas or along the sound where mosquitoes sometimes outnumber people by the millions. Also bring long-sleeved, loose-fitting shirts and long pants to wear after the sun sets. And you'll need shoes to traipse across sandbur-infested dunes on your way to the beach.

Be alert to sudden storms and get a weather report before setting up camp for the night. Hurricanes are prevalent in the late summer. And other squalls can wash across the area in a matter of hours.

All National Park Service campgrounds on the Outer Banks operate under a common policy and charge the same fees, except for the Ocracoke campground that is on the Mistix Reservation System between Memorial Day and Labor Day (see the Ocracoke section for details). Other Park Service campgrounds accept only cash upon arrival — and don't take reservations. Sites are assigned on a first-come, first-served basis. Call the Park Service at 473-2111 for additional information about any of their Outer Banks campgrounds.

During the summer season of 1996, the National Park Service plans to provide lifeguards at Coquina Beach, the Cape Hatteras Lighthouse, south of the Frisco Pier at Sandy Bay, and on Ocracoke Island. Swimming, shelling, surfing, fishing and sunbathing are allowed virtually everywhere on the Outer Banks. So pack your duffle bags and coolers, pull out those hiking boots and tent stakes, and get ready to really enjoy all the outdoors has to offer.

North of Oregon Inlet

Colington Park Campground

Colington Rd., Little Colington Is. 441-6128

Less than 3 miles west of the Bypass, past the first Colington Road bridge by Billy's Seafood, Colington Park Campground is situated on the quiet, calm waters of the sound — a stone's throw away from the best crabbing bridge on the Outer Banks. Heavily wooded, tucked beneath tall pine trees, this campground originally was a tent-only area but has since been redesigned to accommodate recreational vehicles too. It's open year round, and reservations are accepted. Tent campers, however, are limited to two-week stays at a time.

Insiders' Tips

If you're pitching a tent in sand, bring along tent stakes designed to hold fast in sand. Otherwise, you may find yourself sleeping under the stars on a windy night.

Photo: Georgia Beach

Camping is one of the favorite pastimes on the Outer Banks.

All 55 sites at this facility have water, power and picnic tables. Grills, however, are not provided. And open fires are prohibited. So bring your own grill or camp stove if you plan to cook. Hot showers, toilets, laundry facilities and a swing set on the property offer amenities to campers. There's also an on-site general store.

Fishing, crabbing and boating opportunities abound in the areas around this campground.

Pets are allowed on leashes. And air conditioning is available to recreational vehicles for $2 a night. Camping rates start at $14 per night for tents with two people and $16 a night for RVs with two people. The campground accepts personal checks.

Joe & Kay's Campground

Colington Rd. *441-5468*
Little Colington Is. *No credit cards*

About a mile west on Colington Road — before you get to the first bridge — Joe & Kay's Campground has 70 full hookup sites that are rented on a yearly basis. An additional 15 tent sites also are available from April through November. Rates are $12 a night for two people, with a $2 per night charge for each additional person. Reservations aren't accepted, so sites are secured on a first-come, first-served basis. Personal checks are not accepted.

Oregon Inlet Campground (NPS)

N.C. 12 *473-2111*
Bodie Is. *No credit cards*

The northernmost National Park Service campground on the Outer Banks, this facility offers 120 sites along the windswept dunes just north of Oregon Inlet. If you're arriving from the north, look for the campground entrance on the east side of N.C. 12 just before you cross the Bonner Bridge. It's almost directly across from the Oregon Inlet Fishing Center, on the ocean.

Water, cold showers, modern toilets, picnic tables and charcoal grills are available here. But there aren't any utility connections. Dumping stations, however, are nearby.

Most of these sites are in sunny, open areas on the sand. So Park Rangers suggest that campers bring awnings, umbrellas or other types of shade. You also may need mosquito netting and long tent stakes here.

Oregon Inlet Campground is open from Easter weekend (April 5) through September. Campers are limited to a two-week stay. Reservations are not accepted.

Sites are assigned on a first-come, first-served basis. And only cash is taken. Fees begin at $12 per night. Golden Age Passport holders receive a 50 percent discount.

Roanoke Island

Cypress Cove Campground

U.S. 64/264 — *473-5231*
Approx. 1 mi. south of downtown Manteo

Cypress Cove is a wooded, year-round, family-vacation campground across from the Christmas Shop on Roanoke Island. A total of 60 sites are available, including 27 tent sites with shade and 33 sites with hookups for RVs. Reservations are accepted. And pets are allowed on leashes.

Amenities at Cypress Cove include a playground, basketball court, horseshoe pits, a nature trail with an osprey lookout and a fishing pond stocked with bass, bream and catfish where no fishing license is required. Hot showers, restrooms, picnic tables, grills and drinking water also are on the premises. There's an on-site dump station here. And laundry facilities are within walking distance at a nearby shopping center.

Rates are seasonal, with fees going up in the summer. Tent sites begin at $16 a night. RV sites start at $20 a night. Additional charges apply for additional people and sewer hookups.

Besides providing camping accommodations, Cypress Cove also rents 15 fully furnished trailers and "Kamper Kabins" that sleep one to six people. Rates run from $35 to $75 per night, depending on which cabin is used and how many people sleep there. Some units have up to three bedrooms and efficiency-style kitchens. Weekly rentals also are available.

Hatteras Island

Cape Hatteras KOA

N.C. 12 — *987-2307*
Rodanthe — *(800) 562-5268*

A large campground about 14 miles south of the Bonner Bridge across Oregon Inlet, Cape Hatteras KOA has 269 sites with water and power and 66 sites with sewer connections. There are also 33 tent sites with water only. The campground is open March 15 through November and accepts reservations.

Besides hot showers, drinking water and bathhouses, Cape Hatteras KOA offers campers a dump station, laundry facilities, two pools, a hot tub, a playground, a game room, a restaurant and a well-stocked general store. The ocean is just beyond the dunes for fishing and swimming. And a 200-foot soundside pier is the perfect place to fish, crab, or just sit and watch spectacular sunsets. Soundside swimming in shallow water without waves also is convenient for small children. There's even a recreation director at this campground in the summer.

Rates are seasonal. Summer charges for tent sites with two campers are $26.95 per night. Sites with water and electric hookups cost $29.95 per night for two people. Full hookups are $31.95 nightly.

Cape Hatteras KOA also rents one- and two-room "Kamping Kabins." These cabins aren't fully furnished. But they do have beds. Rates are $39.95 per night for

Insiders' Tips

Always bring a cooler with you when camping. Some of the campgrounds do have on-site stores that sell ice and essentials. But others are miles away from the nearest convenience mart.

one-room units and $49.95 nightly for two-room cabins.

Lisa's Pizza Shoreline Campground

N.C. 12 *987-2525*
Rodanthe *No credit cards*

This soundside campground is open from Easter through Thanksgiving for recreational vehicles and tents. Six sites have electrical and water hookups and cost $14.50 per night. Tent sites also include water and cost $11.50 nightly. Hot showers and picnic tables are on site. But grills aren't provided, so bring your own camp stove if you plan to cook. This campground is within walking distance of Rodanthe restaurants. Pets are allowed. Reservations are accepted — but not required. Personal checks are accepted. Windsurfers especially enjoy this campground because they can sail right up to some sites.

North Beach Campground

N.C. 12, Waves *987-2378*

In the village of Waves, North Beach Campground sits alongside the ocean south of the Chicamacomico Lifesaving Station. Here, 110 sites, all with water and electric hookups, offer campers both tent and RV accommodations and a wide range of amenities. Hot showers, bathhouses, picnic tables, a laundry facility, an outdoor swimming pool and a pump-out station are available on site. But there aren't any grills here. And open fires aren't allowed. So bring your own grill or campstove if you want to cook.

North Beach Campground also has a grocery store that sells LP gasoline, kerosene, regular gas and virtually any convenience store item you might need. Pets are allowed on leashes. Reservations are accepted.

The campground is open from March through November. Rates begin at $14.50 a night for tents. Full hookups start at $19.50 a night.

Camp Hatteras

N.C. 12, Waves *987-2777*

A 50-acre, world-class campground, Camp Hatteras is a complete facility that's open year round and offers every amenity campers could desire. Nightly, monthly and yearly reservations are accepted. And the site includes 1,000 feet of both ocean and sound frontage.

Most of Camp Hatteras' 275 sites have full hookups, concrete pads and paved roads. There's also a natural area near the Atlantic available for about 50 tents. Campers will find laundry facilities, hot showers, full bathhouses, picnic tables and grills on the premises.

For recreation, this campground provides three swimming pools, a club house, a pavilion, a marina, fishing, two tennis courts, a nine-hole miniature golf course, volleyball, basketball and shuffleboard on site. The grounds are extraordinarily well kept and more organized than most comparable facilities. Sports and camping areas are separate, so sleeping outdoors is still a quiet experience here — even if you're napping midday.

Rates vary throughout the year, with full hookups running from $22 per night to $35 per night. Tent sites cost between $17 and $25 nightly. Personal checks are accepted. Pets are allowed on leashes.

Ocean Waves Campground

Off of N.C. 12, Waves *987-2556*

Open mid-March through mid-November, Ocean Waves Campground is a seaside resort with sites for RVs as well as tents. There are 64 spaces with full hookups. Twenty-five of those sites are concrete paved.

Three bathhouses, hot showers and laundry facilities are available. Campers also will enjoy the game room, picnic tables and an outdoor pool.

Rates for a family of four, with two children younger than 12, begin at $18 per night for a full hookup and $13 per night for a tent site. Cable television hookups also are offered for $2 per night.

Kinnakeet Campground

Off of N.C. 12, Avon *995-5211*

A soundside campground geared toward families, Kinnakeet Campground is open year round and offers RV as well as tent sites. Reservations are recommended. And a dump site is available.

This Avon outpost has 53 full hookup sites and 15 tent sites. Each site has a picnic table, access to hot showers, toilets, drinking water and electricity. No grills are available. And open fires are prohibited. So bring your own grill or campstove if you plan to cook. A laundry facility is on site.

Rates for two people begin at $12 a night year round for full hookups and $10 a night for tents. The cost for each additional person is $5 per night. Pets are allowed on leashes.

Sands of Time

Harbour and North End Rds. *995-5596*
Avon *No credit cards*

This year round Avon campground has 36 sites with full hookups, 15 with electricity and sewer connections and 25 tent sites — some with full shade. Water is available at every site. Hot showers, flush toilets, laundry facilities, a dump site — even a pay telephone also are offered to all campers.

Besides swimming, fishing and sunbathing at the nearby beach and sound, visitors at Sands of Time will enjoy volleyball, horseshoes and picnic tables. Cable television connections also are available for $2 extra per night. Grills aren't provided, however. And open fires aren't allowed. So bring your campstove or small grill if you want to cook.

Pets are allowed on leashes here. Residents are permitted to live in this campground year round. And reservations are accepted and recommended for summer stays. Rates for tent sites are $16 a night in-season and $14.50 a night off-season. Rates for full hookups are $18.50 a night in-season and $16.50 a night off-season. The campground accepts personal checks.

Cape Woods Campground

Back Rd., Rt. 1232, Buxton *995-5850*

This off-the-beaten-path campground sits on the south side of Buxton in stands of poplar, pine and live oak trees. It includes 120 sites, 25 for tents, 29 with electric and water hookups, and 66 sites with full hookups. Cape Woods is open from March through November and accepts reservations.

Campers at this full-service facility will find two hot showers, fire pits, grills, picnic tables and two bathhouses — one of which is handicapped accessible. There's also a laundry room, outdoor swimming pool, playground, volleyball court, video game room and horseshoe pits. A general store on site sells fire wood, ice and LP gas. Freshwater fishing is allowed in the canals that run around this campground, where bass frequently are found. And pets are permitted as long as they're leashed.

In-season rates for a family of four begin at $16 a night for tents, $18 a night for water and electric and $20 a night for full hookups. Cable television also is available for $2 extra per night. And if you prefer sleeping in a bed, Cape Woods

Insiders' Tips

Don't leave valuables — or even shoes — on the beach unattended. Lock them in the trunk of your car or bring them with you.

Campground rents a furnished "Park Model" trailer that sleeps four people for $350 per week. Monthly and seasonal rates are available for all sites, and the campground accepts personal checks. Good Sam discounts are honored too.

Cape Point Campground (NPS)

Off N.C. 12 *473-2111*
Cape Hatteras *No credit cards*

The largest National Park Service campground on the Outer Banks, Cape Point is about 2 miles south of the Cape Hatteras Lighthouse, across the dunes from the Atlantic. This campground has 202 sites — none with utility connections. It's open from Memorial Day Weekend through Labor Day Weekend, but does not accept reservations.

Flush toilets, cold showers, drinking water, charcoal grills and picnic tables are provided here. Each site has paved access. A handicapped-accessible area also is available. And a dumping station is nearby.

The campground is a short walk away from the ocean where world-class fishing and surfing abound. Most of these sites sit in the open, exposed to the sun and wind. So bring some shade, long tent stakes and lots of bug spray. Cost is $12 a night. Pets are allowed on leashes.

Frisco Woods Campground, Inc.

Frisco Woods, off N.C. 12, Frisco *995-5208*

This 30-acre campground in Frisco Woods is one of the best privately owned facilities on the Outer Banks. Developed by Ward and Betty Barnett, the soundside property boasts abundant forest and marshland beauty — and at least 300 sites in a wooded wonderland.

Electricity and water are available at 150 campsites. Full hookups are offered at 35 other sites. And there are 90 tent sites in this shady spot.

Amenities include an in-ground swimming pool, picnic tables, hot showers, a small country store, propane gas and public phones. Windsurfers prefer this campground because you can sail right to the sites on the sound. Crabbing, fishing and hiking through the woods also are enjoyable activities for campers staying at Frisco Woods.

Photo: Philip S. Ruckle Jr.

Even dogs enjoy the beaches on the Outer Banks.

In-season rates for two people begin at $17 a night for tent sites, $20 a night for electric and water and $22 a night for full hookups. Each additional person costs $4 per night. Cable television is available for an extra $2 per night. And air conditioners and heaters are available for $3 a day.

Frisco Woods is open March through November. Pets are allowed on leashes. Reservations are accepted.

Frisco Campground (NPS)

N.C. 12 *473-2111*
Frisco *No credit cards*

Our favorite spot for tent camping on the Outer Banks, Frisco Campground is operated by the National Park Service and sits about 4 miles southwest of Buxton. Just off the beach, next to Ramp 49, this is the area's most isolated campground. Its undulating roads twist over dunes and around small hills, providing privacy at almost every site. Some tent areas are so secluded in stands of scrubby trees that you can't even see them from the place you park your car. This campground is a welcome find for folks who like to camp away from civilization.

Frisco Campground has 127 no-frills sites, each with a charcoal grill and picnic table. Flush toilets, cold water showers in bathhouses and drinking water are available. There aren't any hookups here. But RVs are welcome. A wooden boardwalk crosses from the campground to the ocean.

As in all National Park Service campgrounds, reservations aren't accepted, and only cash is taken. Cost is $12 per night. Pets are allowed on leashes. Frisco Campground is open from Memorial Day weekend through Labor Day weekend. Golden Age discounts are honored.

Hatteras Sands Camping Resort

Eagle Pass Rd., Hatteras Village *986-2422*

A well-maintained campground near the Hatteras Village ferry docks, Hatteras Sands is about a 10-minute walk from the ocean and is open March through November. Reservations are accepted up to a year in advance. Pets are allowed on leashes.

This campground has 104 sites with water and electricity, 41 sites with full hookups and 25 tent sites. Pull-through sites for people who don't want to unhook their campers from their cars also are available. Each site has drinking water and a picnic table. But grills aren't provided and open fires are prohibited. So bring your own grill or campstove if you plan to cook.

Hot showers, five-star bathhouses and laundry facilities are on site here. There's also an Olympic-size swimming pool, a game room and a mini mart that stocks all sorts of camping supplies. A canal winds through this campground, offering fishing and crabbing opportunities. Campers also can walk to village shops and restaurants from this Hatteras resort.

Rates for tent sites run from $20.95 nightly in the off-season to $22.95 nightly in the summer. Sites with hookups range from $24.95 through $33.95 per night. Hatteras Sands also rents six RVs, called "Camping Condos" that include beds and water. Electricity is available outside these units. Cost is up to $45 per night. In addition, there's a mobile home with two bedrooms and two baths that sleeps four. The fully furnished mobile home rents for $675 per week or $100 per night. The minimum stay at the mobile home is four nights. No other sites at this campground have minimum stays. Some special rates and a 10 percent discount are available to Good Sam Park members.

Village Marina Motel & Campground

N.C. 12 *986-2522*
Hatteras Village *No credit cards*

Open from May through November, this soundside campground includes six tent sites as well as 30 hookups with electricity, water and cable TV for recreational vehicles. A bathhouse with hot showers, a boat ramp, a small store, boat slips, picnic tables and grills are on site. Even tent sites, which cost $15 per day for two adults, include electrical outlets. Recreational vehicle sites cost $17 per day for two adults. Additional adults cost $2 per person per site. Children younger than 12 are free.

Insiders' Tips

Check weather forecasts before setting up camp. Sudden storms can spring up quickly — washing out outdoor adventures and wreaking havoc on small tents.

One small pet per site is permitted, as long as it's leashed. Personal checks are accepted.

Ocracoke

Teeter's Campground

Cemetery Rd. 928-3511, 928-5880
Next to the British Cemetery No credit cards

Near the heart of Ocracoke Village, tucked in a shady grove of trees, Teeter's Campground offers nine full-hookup sites, 16 sites with electricity and water and 10 tent sites. Rates for two people begin at $12 a night for tents, $15 a night for electric and water and $20 a night for full hookups. Almost an anomaly on the Outer Banks, green grass lines this semi-wooded campground, creating a soft bed beneath thin tent floors.

Hot showers are available here. And a picnic table sits at every site. But there aren't any laundry facilities on Ocracoke — so don't plan to wash any clothes on this island.

Teeter's Campground is open year round for self-contained units. But as soon as the weather gets cold enough to freeze water, the grounds are closed to other campers.

Beachcomber

N.C. 12 928-4031

Less than a mile from Silver Lake and the nearest beach access, Beachcomber campground has 29 sites with electricity and water and six tent sites. Rates for two people begin at $15 a night for tents and $18 a night for electric and water hookups. There's a $2 charge for each additional person.

Hot showers and fully-equipped bathrooms are available here. Picnic tables and grills also are on the premises. But there aren't any laundry facilities on all of Ocracoke Island.

Pets are allowed at Beachcomber — as long as they're leashed. The campground is open from late March through late November, depending on the weather. Reservations are recommended if you plan to camp here during the summer.

Ocracoke Campground (NPS)

N.C. 12 (800) 365-CAMP
3 mi. east of Ocracoke Village No credit cards

An oceanfront campground just behind the dunes, this National Park Service campground maintains 136 campsites. No utility hookups or laundry facilities are available here. But there are cold showers, a dumping station, drinking water, charcoal grills and flush toilets. As in all Park Service campgrounds, there's a 14-day limit on stays at Ocracoke Campground. The facility is open from Easter Weekend (April 5, 1996) through September.

Since most of these sites sit directly in the sun, we suggest bringing awnings or some sort of shade to sit under. Long tent stakes also are helpful to hold down tents against the often fierce winds that whip through this campground. The constant breeze, however, is a welcome relief from summer heat. Bug spray also is a must here to ward off mosquitoes in the summer.

Ocracoke is the only National Park Service campground on the Outer Banks that operates on the Mistix reservation system. From Memorial Day weekend through Labor Day, you must either write Mistix Corporation at P.O. Box 85705, San Diego, California 92186, and include a check or money order, or call the listed toll-free number — where Visa, MasterCard and Discover are accepted. Since the phone number is almost always busy, we recommend reserving your campsite in writing. Reservations are not accepted during the off-season, so sites are assigned on a first-come, first-served basis — with cash only. All sites at Ocracoke Campground cost $13 per night in the summer, $12 nightly during the off-season.

The maximum speed for beach driving is 25 mph, but even that can be too fast on a crowded day. Look out for children, pets, sunbathers and anglers.

Inside Beach Information and Safety

In some ways, the Outer Banks seems to be a very simple place. While traveling down U.S. 158 in either direction you can see glimpses of the sound on one side and the ocean on the other. There was a time when development was so sparse, you only had to drive around and look for where friends' cars were parked to locate them without an address. Even though the Outer Banks appear uncomplicated — minus huge cityscapes and a complex web of roads — you need to be aware of safety and environmental issues in this sandy area sandwiched between sound and sea. Here are a some tips we've gathered to help make your stay a comfortable one.

Beach Driving

Off-road access is possible on the Outer Banks but only in designated spots and at certain times of the year. Checking with each township for specific rules is necessary, and some places even require a permit. Generally you can ride on the beach in Kill Devil Hills and Nags Head from October 1 through April 30. You must have a permit to do so in Nags Head. Southern Shores and Kitty Hawk prohibit driving on the beach at all times. As far north as Corolla and Carova in Currituck County, there are designated spots where you can drive on the beach. Hatteras Island operates under the guidance of the National Park Service, 473-2111, so any questions you have concerning off-road driving can be referred to them. Driving is not allowed on the beach at Pea Island National Wildlife Refuge, but as you move south, you will see access areas marked by a picture of a Jeep where you can travel on the beach. Obviously those Jeeps with an X marked through them are spots where beach driving is prohibited.

Beach Speed Limit

The maximum speed for beach driving is 25 mph, but even that can be too fast on a crowded day. Look out for children, pets, sunbathers and anglers. Many folks fall asleep on the beach and are groggy as a result. Expect the unexpected.

Beach drivers follow the same rules they use on the asphalt: Keep to the right, pass on the left, etc.

You are not allowed to drive on, over or in between the dunes for any reason at any time. The dunes and their fragile vegetation create our protective barrier and are vital to the environment.

Insiders' Tips

To report an emergency, call 911.

Driving On Sand

Drive carefully. It is so easy to get stuck in the sand. We've assembled a list of essential gear you'll want to have on hand in case you have such a problem. Read on for some driving tips too!

- shovel
- tire pressure gauge
- tow rope
- fire extinguisher
- flashlights (two or more)
- bumper jack (with some boards to place beneath it)
- blankets
- drinking water and snacks

Many drivers get stuck because they don't let air out of their tires before driving on the beaches. The National Park Service says its rangers generally drive with 15 to 20 pounds of pressure in their tires. Rangers advise reinflating tires when you return to the paved roads. We usually drive with 22 to 25 pounds of pressure, and we don't bother to reinflate for local driving — say, a drive of 20 miles or less. Please don't block the beach ramps to lock hubs or deflate tires. We suggest pulling well off to the side of the ramp or using the parking areas found at most vehicle accesses.

Hazards

Try to drive on the firm, wet section of the beach below the high tide line and follow in someone else's tracks if you can. Areas that don't have any tracks might have been avoided for good reason. Watch out for areas of the beach with shell-laden, reddish sand and depressions where there is just a bit of standing water. These areas can be very soft.

Anglers

It's considered rude and unsafe to drive (or walk) under an angler's line. Stay on the dune side when you approach someone who's fishing, and there won't be any confusion. Also keep an eye out for surf-fisherman getting ready to cast. You may not be ready for a dip just yet!

Pedestrians

Pedestrians have the right-of-way at all times on the beach. When leaving the sand, please keep your eye on pedestrian traffic on the beach road also. The edge of the beach road sometimes grabs the car a bit and can pull you to one side or another abruptly. Just make sure you give a wide berth to anyone walking near you. And a note to pedestrians themselves: Wear light clothing at night if you intend on walking near car traffic. While most folks respect driving safety rules, some come to the beach to really let their hair down. The pedestrian needs to be as conscientious as the driver as a result on both sand and road.

Restricted Areas

Please obey all of the area designations that you'll find on the beaches. Often, portions of the beach are roped off to allow shorebirds and turtles to nest. These areas change throughout the seasons, so ar-

Insiders' Tips

Lifeguard Beach Service Inc., a member of the United States Lifesaving Association, has been providing beach service and ocean rescue to Dare County since 1958.

eas that were open in April could be closed in August. On rare occasions, through traffic is curtailed by these closings, especially at high tide. Stay alert for the changes and respect the limitations. There are substantial fines for violators.

Litter

If you're getting ready to throw down a soda pop bottle or candy wrapper, it might help if you remember that while you may be staying at the ocean, which essentially belongs to everyone on the planet, you are also littering in a year-round community. Inevitably what is tossed in one backyard winds up gracing the lawn of another due to the wind factor. With that in mind, you'll want to secure all trash and trash bags carefully so the wind can't make mischief. Feel free to pick up any stray trash. It's not uncommon to see locals doing just this. Don't be shy — after all we've already established that the ocean is yours too!

If you can't find a trash can that isn't already overflowing, please find another appropriate spot to dispose of potential litter. A good idea too is to look into our recycling efforts when you first get to the Outer Banks (see our Services and Information Directory).

The Ocean

Very few folks come to the ocean and don't get in. Here are a few water safety points to bear in mind.

Backwash Current

A backwash current on a steeply sloping beach can pull you toward deeper water, but its power is swiftly checked by incoming waves. To escape this current, swim straight toward shore if you're a strong swimmer. If you're not, don't panic; wait and float until the current stops, then swim in.

Littoral Current

The littoral current is a "river of water" moving up or down the shoreline parallel to the beach. It is created by the angled approach of the waves. In stormy conditions, this current can be very powerful due to high wave energy.

Losing Control in the Waves

If a wave crashes down on you while you are surfing or swimming, and you find yourself being tumbled in bubbles and sand like a sheet in a washing machine, don't try to struggle to the surface against it. Curl into a ball, or just go limp and float. The wave will take you to the beach or you can just swim to the surface when it passes.

Rip Currents

Rip currents often occur where there's a break in a submerged sandbar (see the diagrams in this chapter). Water trapped between the sandbar and the beach rushes out through the breach, sometimes sweeping swimmers out with it. You can see a rip; it's choppy, turbulent, often discolored water that looks deeper than the water around it. If you are caught in a rip, don't try to swim against the current. Instead, swim across the current parallel to the shore and slowly work your way back to the beach at an angle. Try to remain calm. Panic will only sap the energy you need to swim out of the rip.

Undertow

When a wave comes up on the beach and breaks, the water must run back down to the sea. This is undertow. It sucks at your ankles from small waves, but in heavy surf undertow can knock you off your feet and carry you offshore. If you're carried out, don't resist. Let the undertow take you out until it subsides. It will only be a few yards. The next wave will help push you shoreward again.

Jellyfish

Watch for jellyfish floating on the surface or in the water. While some can give little more than an annoying stinging sensation, others can produce severe discomfort. The Portuguese man-of-war is sometimes blown onto Outer Banks beaches and can be recognized by its distinctive balloon-like air bladder, often exhibiting a bluish tint. Man-of-war stings can be serious. Anyone who is stung by the tentacles and develops breathing difficulties or generalized body swelling should be transported to the nearest emergency facility for treatment. In extreme cases, death can result from anaphylactic shock associated with man-of-war toxin exposure.

Treatment for jellyfish stings includes vinegar or meat tenderizer applied to the affected area. Don't rub the wound site, since rubbing can force toxins deeper into the skin. Pain relievers can also allay some discomfort.

Services

Emergency Assistance

Many areas of the Outer Banks don't have lifeguards or flags systems (a red flag means "don't enter the water." Keep in mind that help can be a long way off, and an emergency is not the time to learn about ocean safety. Review some of our reminders and watch your surroundings. Accidents can and do occur. Be prepared. If you have an emergency and need the rescue squad, dial 911 for help. Please remember that this number is for emergencies only. Please refer to our Service and Information Directory for the local, non-emergency numbers and services in your area.

Lifeguards

Lifeguards are provided by Lifeguard Beach Service Inc. and Nags Head Ocean Rescue at fixed sites along the Outer Banks.

Lifeguard Beach Service guards are on the beach from Memorial Day weekend through Labor Day weekend. Their hours at the designated sites are 9:30 AM to 5:30 PM daily, but hours and locations (see below) are subject to change without notice. Always use caution before entering and/or swimming in the ocean and be alert for red warning flags and red-and-white warning posters.

Ocean Rescue Services, 441-5909, are provided by the town of Nags Head to that town's beaches. This service is also provided to Kitty Hawk and Southern Shores through a contracted arrangement. Lifeguarded beaches are available daily beginning Memorial Day weekend through Labor Day, 10 AM 'til 6 PM.

In 1996, ocean lifeguard stands will be located at the following Dare County beaches:

In Duck: Ocean Pine, North Snow Geese Drive, Barrier Island and Plover Drive

In Southern Shores: Hillcrest and Chicahawk

In Kitty Hawk: Kitty Hawk Public Beach

In Kill Devil Hills: Helga Street, Haymen Street, Fifth Street, Third Street/ Sea Ranch, Second Street, First Street, Ashville Drive, Woodmere Avenue, Raleigh Street, Sutton Avenue/Comfort Inn, Ocean Bay Boulevard, Oregon Street, Cavalier Motel, Clark Street, Outer Banks Beach Club, Martin Street, Atlantic Street, Holiday Inn/Ramada Inn and John Yancy Motel.

On Roanoke Island: Old Swimming Hole (10 AM to 6 PM), on the sound at the Airport.

In Nags Head: Bonnett Street, Epstein

RIP CURRENTS

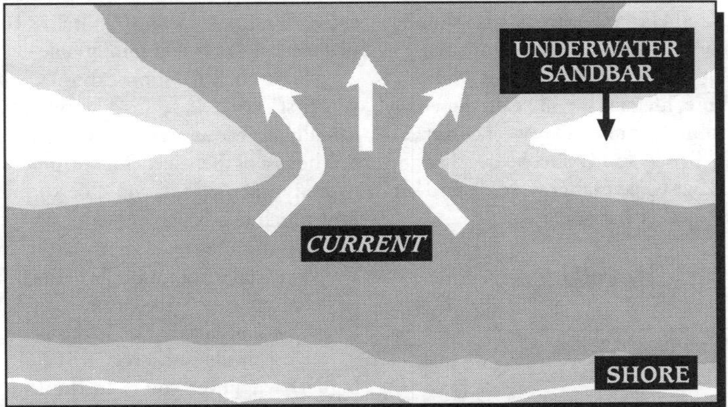

Rip currents form when water breaks through a nearshore sandbar (see figure above) or is diverted by a groin or jetty (see figure below) and rushes out to sea in a narrow path.

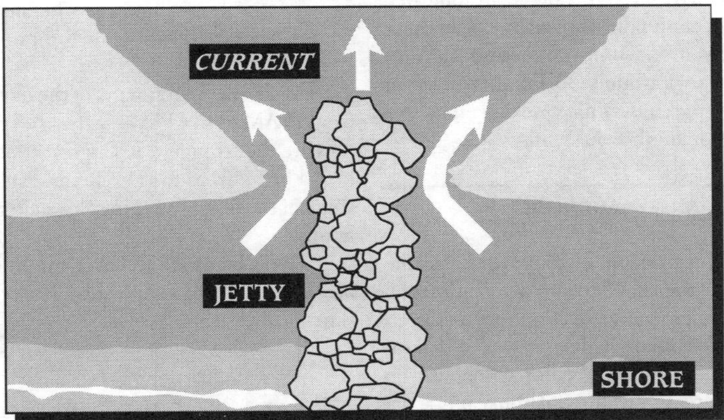

Rip currents can extend 1,000 feet offshore and travel up to 3 miles an hour.

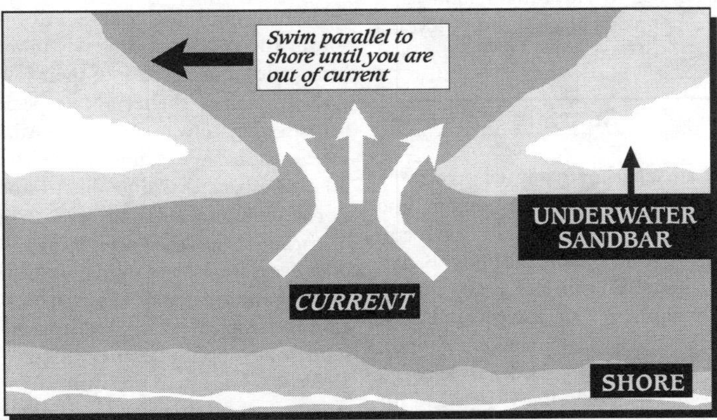

If caught in a rip current, don't panic. Do not swim against the current. Swim parallel to shore until you are out of the current, or float calmly until it dissipates.

Street and Hargrove Street (LBS supplies lifeguards at the Nags Head Inn area)

Within the **Cape Hatteras National Seashore**, lifeguards will be on duty daily beginning Memorial Day weekend at Coquina, Frisco and Ocracoke beaches and June 21 at Cape Hatteras. Lifeguard service ends after Labor Day.

Miscellaneous

Pets

Dogs must be on a leash unless they are in the water. Park Rangers do patrol the beaches regularly, and they will approach you if your dog is running free. Voice command control is not enough. Save yourself some money and leash up; fines range around $50. For that price, you could purchase a nice meal, a fancy souvenir or another dog!

Alcohol

The effects of alcohol can be amplified by the heat and sun of a summer afternoon, so be aware. It's illegal to operate boats or motor vehicles if you've had too much to drink, and enforcement officers keep an eye out for violators, so practice moderation. Alcohol and swimming can be a potentially deadly combination. Even small amounts of alcohol can give you a false sense of security.

Suntans

It's amazing how many red-bodied folk we see lying on the beach, limping into restaurants or, worse yet, waiting in medical centers while visiting the Outer Banks. Yes, we know. The sun feels so good. Combined with the sea air, it seems to have a rejuvenating effect. Actually any form of tan or burn is now considered damaged skin. While we can't stop visitors and Insiders alike from toasting themselves, these tips will help keep you comfortable.

• Start out with short exposure when you first arrive. It seems like most folks initially overdo it and have to be careful for the rest of their stay. The summer sun is pretty intense, and you'd be surprised how much of a burn your skin can get in 20 or 30 minutes on a afternoon in July. We always take our umbrella to the beach to keep our exposure within reasonable levels. You might want to do the same.

• Use ample sunscreen (SPF 15 or higher) whenever you're in the sun for any length of time. We always put an extra coat on our noses, cheeks, lips and any other high-exposure spots. We also apply sunscreen at least 20 minutes before we go out, since it takes a while for it to become fully effective.

• Avoid the hottest parts of the day — from 10 AM until 2 PM — when the sun's rays are the strongest. It's a great time to take a break from the beach and explore some of the other fun things listed in this guide.

• Don't be afraid to cover up on the beach. Just remember: Healthy, protected skin is a sign of good sense.

Storm and Hurricane Procedures

June through November is hurricane season on the Outer Banks. All of the southeastern United States is prone to hurricanes, but because of their low elevation, lack of shelter and, especially, because they're way out in the Atlantic Ocean, the barrier islands of North Carolina are especially vulnerable to storms. Forecasters and almanac writers say a hurricane strikes the Outer Banks about once every nine years. A major one tears through the area every 42 years, on average. And tropical cyclones spin across the sand dunes about every five years.

When Dare County officials order evacuations off the islands, everyone —

Water Sense

Water conditions here call for unusual vigilance. Listen to local radio stations or call municipal headquarters for daily water conditions anytime you plan to enter the ocean, regardless of the season.

Here are a few other precautions for swimmers:

• Never swim alone.

• Observe the surf before going in the water, looking for potentially dangerous currents.

• Non-swimmers should stay out of the water and wear a life jacket if they're going to be near the water.

• Swim in areas with on-duty lifeguards, or use extreme care.

• Keep non-swimming children well above the marks of the highest waves. Keep an eye on children at all times and teach them never to turn their backs on the waves while they play at water's edge.

• Don't swim near anglers or deployed fishing lines.

• Stay 300 feet away from fishing piers.

• Watch out for surfers.

from vacationers who already have paid for their week's stay to permanent residents who don't want to leave their homes behind — must leave the Outer Banks. Radio, newspaper and television announcers will notify the public about mandatory evacuations and when bridges into the area may re-open for people to return. Make plans early to take pets and elderly people off the islands — and scope out a shelter or safe place to stay on the mainland. Watch the Weather Channel (channel 25 in the local cable listings) for early warnings or signs of a storm, and then obey your common sense: Stay off the beach and out of the water, especially during electrical storms.

For more information about emergency storm procedures, call 473-3355 (Dare County), 232-2115 (Corolla) or 928-1071 (Ocracoke).

Tornadoes spawned by hurricanes are among the worst weather-related killers. When a hurricane approaches, listen for tornado watches and warnings. (A tornado watch means tornadoes are expected to develop. A tornado warning means a tornado has actually been sighted.) When your area receives a tornado warning, seek inside shelter immediately, preferably below ground level. If a tornado catches you outside, move away from its path at a right angle. If you don't have time to escape, lie flat in the nearest depression, ditch or ravine.

Hurricane watches mean a hurricane could threaten the area within 24 hours. Evacuation is not necessary at that point. If a hurricane warning is issued, visitors should leave the Banks and head inland using U.S. 64/264 or U.S. 158, following the recently installed green and white "Hurricane Evacuation Route" signs. Always heed instructions of local authorities.

The Dare County Civil Preparedness Agency officials issued these guidelines:

Hurricane Safety Rules

1. By late May of each year, recheck your supply of boards, tools, batteries, nonperishable foods and the other equipment you will need if a hurricane strikes.

2. Keep a battery-powered radio close by to listen to the latest weather reports and official notices. When you hear the first tropical cyclone advisory, listen for future messages. This will prepare you for a hurricane emergency well before watches and warnings are issued.

3. If your area comes under a hurricane watch, continue normal activities. But stay tuned to the Weather Channel or to local radio stations (see "Media" in the Services and Information Directory). Keep alert. Ignore rumors.

4. If your area receives a hurricane warning, keep calm until the emergency has ended. Leave low-lying areas that may be swept by high tides or storm waves. If time allows, secure mobile homes with heavy cables anchored in concrete footings. Then leave mobile homes for more substantial shelter. If possible, move automobiles to high grounds too as both sound and sea can flood even central spots on the Outer Banks.

5. Moor boats securely before the storm, or haul them out of the water to a safer area. Once boats are secure, leave and don't return to them until the wind and waves have subsided.

6. Board up windows or protect them with storm shutters or tape. Danger to small windows is mainly from wind-driven debris. Larger windows may be broken by wind pressure. Secure outdoor objects that might be blown away, uprooted or propelled into the house. Garbage cans, garden tools, toys, signs, porch furniture and other harmless items become missiles of destruction in hurricane winds. Anchor outdoor items or store them inside before the storm strikes.

7. Store drinking water in clean bathtubs, jugs, bottles and cooking utensils. Water supplies can be contaminated by hurricane floods.

8. Check battery-powered equipment. A radio may be your only link with the world outside. Emergency cooking facilities, lights and flashlights also are essential if utilities are interrupted.

9. Keep automobiles fueled. Service stations may be inoperable for several days after the storm strikes.

10. Remain indoors during the storm. Keep pets and children inside and don't attempt to travel by foot or vehicle. Monitor weather conditions on the radio or television.

Once the hurricane has truly passed (don't be fooled by the relative calm that may return as the hurricane's eye passes):

1. Seek necessary medical care at the nearest Red Cross disaster station or health center.

2. Stay out of disaster areas. Unless you are qualified to help, your presence might hamper first-aid and rescue work.

3. Unless you're injured or are transporting someone who is injured, do not travel until advised by the proper authorities.

4. If you must drive, be careful along debris-filled streets and highways. Roads may be undermined and could collapse under the weight of a car.

5. Avoid loose or dangling wires and report them immediately to North Carolina Power or the nearest law enforcement officer.

Insiders' Tips

The most fixed lifeguard stands in Dare County are strewn along Kill Devil Hills beaches. Lifeguards here also rent umbrellas and Boogie Boards from their stands. They abandon their posts before dark each day.

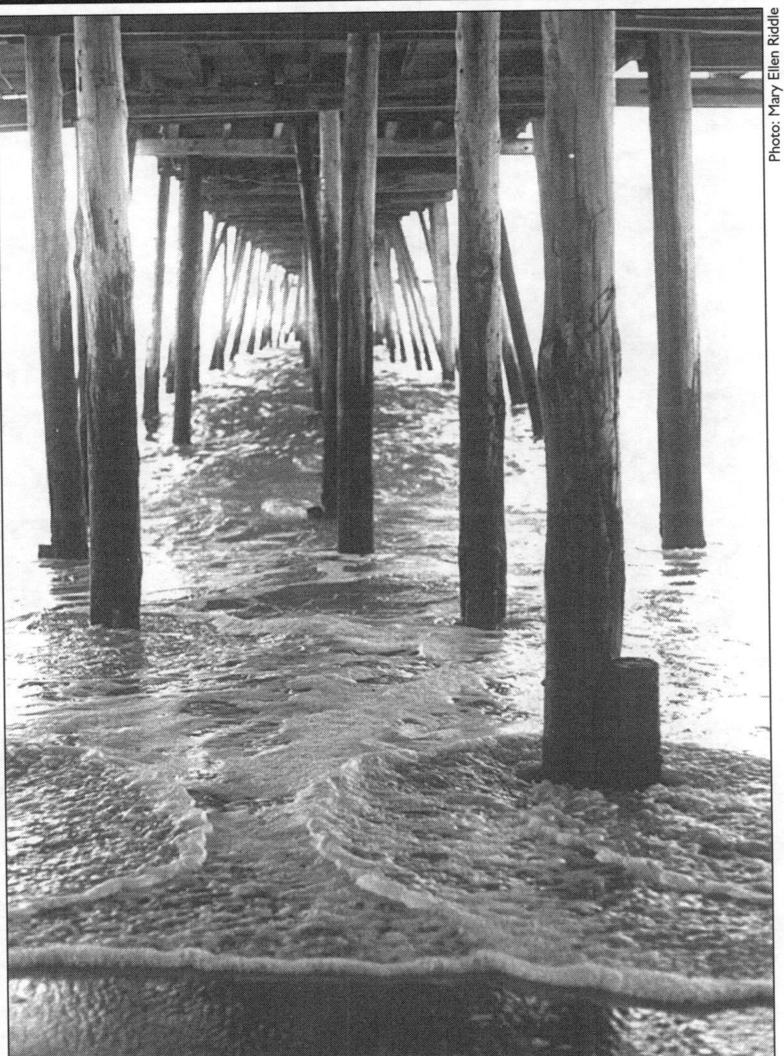

Photo: Mary Ellen Riddle

Surfers need to be careful of surfing too close to the piers. There are ordinances in place to enforce this safety rule. You don't want to get hooked by a pier angler!

6. Report broken sewer or water mains to the county or town water department.

7. Prevent fires. Lowered water pressure may make fire-fighting difficult.

8. Check refrigerated food for spoilage if power has been off during the storm.

9. Stay away from river banks and streams.

10. Check roofs, windows and outdoor storage areas for wind or water damage.

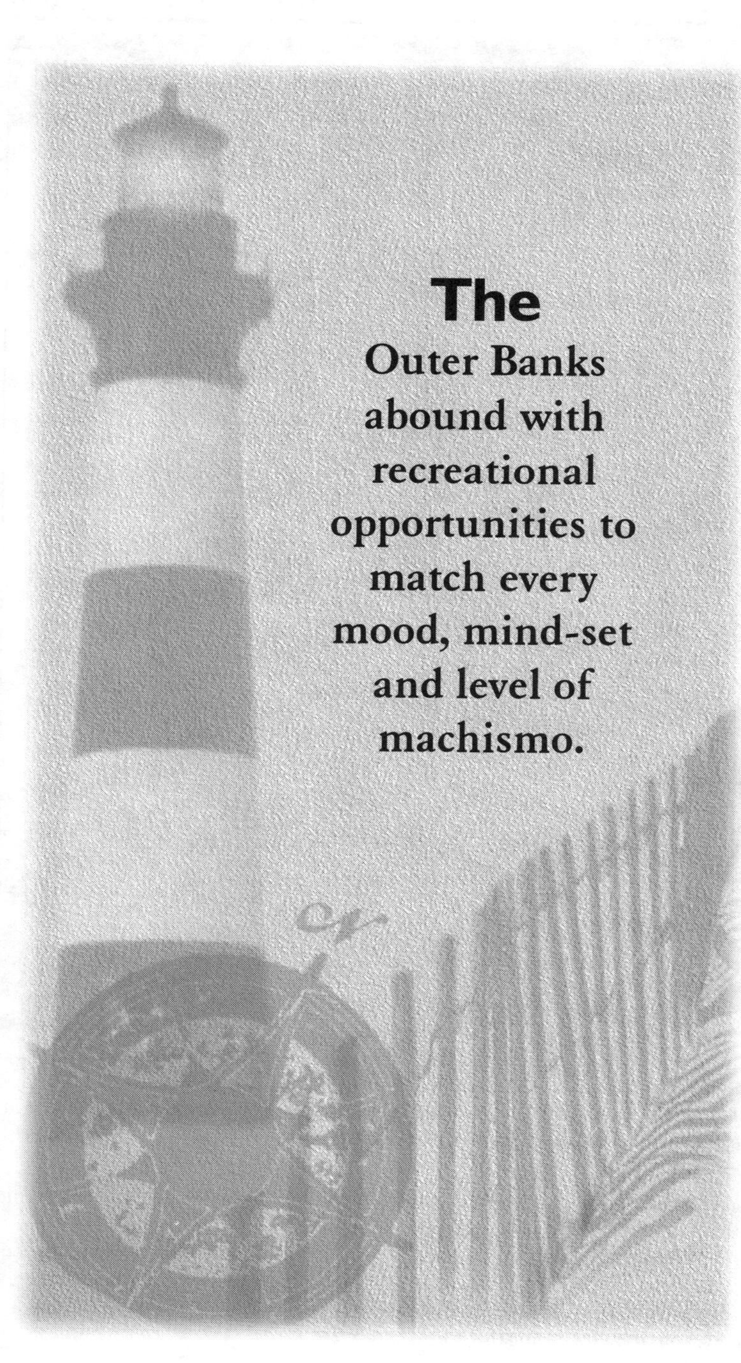
The
Outer Banks
abound with
recreational
opportunities to
match every
mood, mind-set
and level of
machismo.

Inside Recreation

Whether you're looking for a way to loll away a sultry afternoon with your sweetheart, seeking some form of entertainment for a troop of teenagers or hankering to try your wings on a solo hang gliding flight across the East Coast's tallest sand dune, the Outer Banks abound with recreational opportunities to match every mood, mind-set and level of machismo.

You can spend an afternoon walking the wide beaches searching for shells and pieces of bright cobalt beach glass that have been polished smooth by the sand and seasons of waves. You can buy the kids a cheap kite and help them send it soaring atop the wafting winds. Bird-watching opportunities abound in the wildlife refuges north of Duck and south of Pea Island. Nags Head Woods offers a shady respite during the heat of summer — and secluded hikes through one of the most marvelous maritime forests preserved on the Atlantic seaboard.

Public libraries and well-stocked bookstores are air-conditioned and staffed with helpful employees if you're seeking quieter pursuits. Horseshoes and pickup volleyball games are scattered along many public beach accesses for those who prefer working up a sweat and finding a little friendly competition. And if you just need to get to sea for a while and see the Outer Banks from a vantage point off its sandy shores, riding the state ferry to Ocracoke Island is one of our favorite year-round pastimes. Best of all, each of those activities is free!

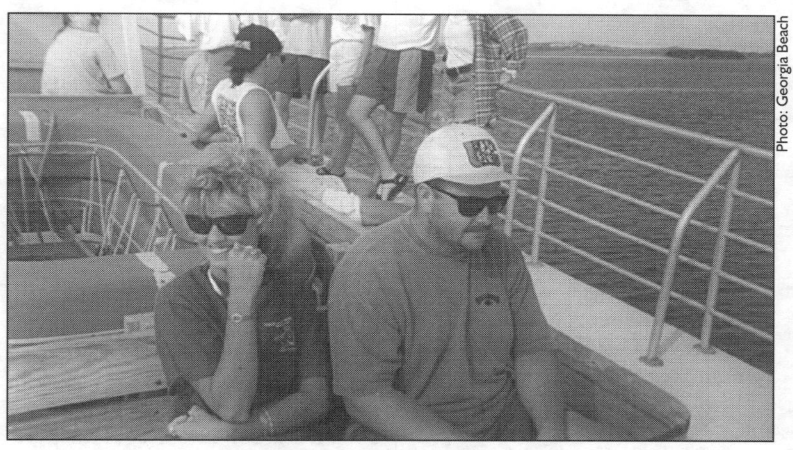

Photo: Georgia Beach

Take a cruise on a headboat.

If you'd don't mind dropping a little dough to try something different, we've devoted entire chapters in this book to Watersports — from surfing and windsurfing to sailing and scuba diving; Fishing — from Gulf Stream charter trips that allow you to hook huge tuna to inshore headboat expeditions and casting a lure off one of our many public piers; and Golf — where new courses are cropping up each season to test your skills and, perhaps, even try your patience.

This chapter includes overviews on all the other recreational opportunities and adventures we could think of. Sections on tennis, biking and in-line skating, athletic clubs, horseback riding and go-carts are guaranteed to get your blood flowing. Write-ups on hang gliding, Parasailing and airplane tours promise to set even the most landlocked spirits soaring. If you want to get your feet wet, try slipping down a twisting waterslide, seeking a school of dolphin on a boat trip or watching a pirate play from the deck of a vessel as it cruises around the Pamlico Sound. Miniature golf courses abound here — from par 3 natural grass greens to crazy-themed courses complete with moving obstacles and horrific clowns. You can tour beaches north of where N.C. 12's pavement ends on a rented all-terrain vehicle. Or, if you've had a little too much fun in the sun, there are sections on indoor activities such as bowling, movie theaters and noisy, state-of-the-art video arcades.

For organized sports and athletic endeavors, Dare County's Parks and Recreation Department has adult and youth soccer, softball, basketball and other leagues that play throughout the Outer Banks towns seasonally. Sign-up fees for these refereed games are nominal. And anyone is welcome to join for a season. You can even form your own team and get in on the lineup. For more information, call 473-1101 for the main Manteo office; 441-2143 to reach the beach satellite office; 995-4401 on Hatteras Island; or 473-5070 during nights, weekends and holidays.

If bingo is your bag, several fire stations and civic clubs along the barrier island host regularly scheduled sessions in the early evenings throughout the summer. Colington Island's Volunteer Fire Department off Colington Road, 441-6234, and Nags Head's Fire Department on U.S. 158 just south of the Outer Banks Mall, 441-5909, are home to two of the area's more popular part-time bingo parlors.

Video rental stores for stay-at-home nighttime entertainment also are scattered from Corolla through Ocracoke. Most managers don't require memberships. And almost all rent video cassette recorders you can take home to your hotel room or vacation cottage for a night or week.

Each season, it seems, some new pastime springs from these sandy shores. The area's first paintball war zone opened in 1995. At least two new minigolf courses are opening their greens for the 1996 season. Even Insiders who have lived here for years have not yet experienced all the recreational opportunities the Outer Banks have to offer. But we sure have fun trying . . .

Tennis

Many cottage rental developments throughout the Outer Banks have private tennis courts for their guests. Outdoor public tennis courts are located near the Kill Devil Hills Fire Station, at the Baum Senior Center in Kill Devil Hills, behind Kelly's Restaurant in Nags Head, at Manteo Middle School, at Manteo High School and next to Cape Hatteras School in Buxton. If you don't own a racquet — or left yours back on the mainland — you can lease one by the day or week from Ocean Atlantic Rentals in Corolla, 453-2440; Duck, 261-4346; Nags Head, 441-7823 or Avon, 995-5868.

ADVERTISER'S SHOWCASE

PINE ISLAND INDOOR RACQUET CLUB

N.C. 12, Duck *453-8525*

Offering the Outer Banks' only indoor tennis courts, Pine Island is part of the Sanderling Inn's athletic package and is open to the public year-round for recreational or competitive play. Here, three hard-surface courts are under a vaulted roof for air-conditioned or heated comfort. Two clay courts and a platform tennis court are outdoors. There are also squash and racquetball courts inside and an upper-level observation deck overlooking all indoor courts that can be reserved for private parties. Restroom, locker and shower facilities are included. And Pine Island recently added two ball machines, a radar gun to time your serves and a video tape analysis machine to see what areas of your game might need work. Resident professionals Rick Ostlund and Betty Wright teach clinics for adults and children and offer individualized instruction at any skill level. There's a pro shop that sells racquets, clothes, tennis accessories and has stringing services. Several tournaments are held here each season.

Reservations are suggested for indoor and outdoor courts. Cost is $14 an hour for outdoor facilities. Indoor courts cost $16 to $20 an hour, depending on the season. Pine Island is open every day except Christmas from at least 9 AM to 6 PM. During the summer, it's open from 8 AM to 9 PM.

Biking and Skating

With two lanes of N.C. 12 stretching along more than 100 miles of blacktop from Corolla to Ocracoke — and hugging the seaside almost all the way — cyclists and in-line skaters can cruise comfortably throughout the Outer Banks and get almost anywhere they want to go. The flat terrain on these barrier islands makes the area perfect even for beginners. Three new off-road, paved paths on Roanoke Island, South Nags Head and Kill Devil Hills provide safer routes for everyone to follow (see the listing in our Getting Around chapter). Also, **Wheels of Dare** bicycle club schedules sporadic tours and treks throughout the year; call Charles Hardy, 473-3528, for details.

Kill Devil Hills officials restrict in-line skating along U.S. 158 and the beach road. You can get a ticket in this town for recreating in an improper area. But most other places allow biking and skating almost anywhere off the five-lane highway. Just be careful cruising over the narrow bridges, where there's not much room for motorists to move aside.

OCEAN ATLANTIC RENTALS

Corolla *453-2440*
Duck *261-4346*
Nags Head *441-7823*
Avon *995-5868*

Bicycles and Rollerblades of all shapes and sizes can be rented by the day, weekend and week from each location of Ocean Atlantic Rentals. Adult bikes rent for an average of $10 a day or $25 per week. Children's cycles lease for $7 a day, $20 per week. And in-line skates rent for $15 a day or $25 for three days. In addition, these rental outfits lease volleyball and croquet sets and other recreational equipment. Most Ocean Atlantic outposts are open seven days a week, year-round from 10 AM to 6 PM in the off-season and 10 AM to 9 PM throughout the summer.

KITTY HAWK KITES — OUTER BANKS OUTDOORS

Corolla *453-8845*
Duck *261-2900*
Nags Head *441-4124*
Manteo *473-2357*
Avon *995-6060*
Toll-free *(800) 334-4777*

This recreational haven on the Outer Banks sells and rents Rollerblades by the day or week from its Manteo, Nags Head and Corolla locations. In-line skating clinics, lessons and festivals also are held throughout the summers. Skates rent for $10 a day or $25 for three days. Lessons cost $15 and require advance reservations. The Nags Head store is open-year-round from at least 9 AM to 6 PM, with extended hours in the summer. Other outposts are open seasonally.

Bicycle tours of Roanoke Island and Corolla also are offered on your own cycle or a beach cruiser you can rent from Kitty Hawk Kites at the Manteo and Corolla stores. Two-hour tours cost $20 per person and are offered during the summer, Tuesdays through Saturdays at 10 AM. Bike rentals are $6 for the first two hours, $2 each additional hour or $12 per day. Child seats are available for an additional $2.

Additionally, sport climbing walls are available at Kitty Hawk Kites locations in Corolla, Nags Head and Avon. Rappelling equipment, climbing shoes and ropes are all part of the package. Three climbs and basic instruction cost $7 per person. Corolla's TimBuck II location has a 22-foot-high indoor wall with four main routes and an overhang for extra challenges. At Monteray Plaza, there's a 25-foot outdoor wall with six main routes and an overhang. In Nags Head, try the 21-foot indoor climbing wall with four main routes and an overhang. Avon's location includes a 21-foot indoor wall with three main routes and an overhang.

The Bike Barn

Corolla *453-0788*
Duck *261-2276*
Kill Devil Hills *441-3786*

For more than 10 years, The Bike Barn has sold and repaired various makes and models of bikes on the Outer Banks. This shop also rents bikes and stocks a range of accessories. The Bike Barn sells equipment from name-brands such as Giant, Specialized, Trek, Cannondale and Diamond Back. The Kill Devil Hills shop is open year round Monday through Saturday. Hours are 10 AM to 5 PM in spring, 9 AM to 6 PM in summer and 11 AM to 4 PM in winter. The Duck and Corolla shops open May 1 and operate throughout the summer season; please call for additional information.

Cactus Tire Bike Shop

U.S. 158, MP 5½, Kill Devil Hills 480-0222

This full-service shop sells, repairs and rents all types of bikes year round. Summer hours are 9 AM to 7 PM Mondays through Saturdays and from 11 AM to 3 PM Sundays. Beach cruisers and mountain bikes rent for $8 a half-day, $15 for a full day or $35 a week. Kids bikes also are available. And kid carriers for bicycles lease for an additional $5 per day. Free delivery is available in most central areas of the Outer Banks.

K.D.H. Cycle & Skate

Beach Rd., MP 9½, Kill Devil Hills 480-3399

Open year round, this full-service cycle and skate shop offers free delivery between Duck and Oregon Inlet. Single-speed bikes rent for $10 a day or $30 per week. Mountain bikes with 21 speeds rent for $18 per day or $45 a week. Children's bicycles, child seats and tandem bikes — built for two — also can be leased. In-line skates lease for $10 per day or $30 per week. Employees here also sell and service all sorts of bikes (Fischer, Specialized and Mongoose to name a few brands)

Insiders' Tips

Most Outer Banks video stores don't require memberships and will rent VCRs to vacationers by the night or week.

and skates — and sell any supplies you might need. Free tour maps of the Outer Banks are available here.

K.D.H. Cycle & Skate is open from 8 AM to 8 PM, seven days a week in the summer.

Family Life Center

U.S. 158, MP 11½, Nags Head *441-4941*

A recreational facility for the Outer Banks Worship Center, this Christian-affiliated roller-skating rink behind the Ark is open to the public on Friday evenings from 7:30 to 10 PM year round. Here, kids can rent regular, old-fashioned roller skates for $2 and cruise around the slick floor. Ping-Pong and video games also are available.

Kitty Hawk Sports

U.S. 158, MP 13, Nags Head *441-6800*

Bike rentals are not available here, but two-hour tours on 18-speed mountain bikes are given every summer morning and afternoon. The $24 cost includes bikes, helmets, water bottles and the guided tour. Tours depart from Kitty Hawk Woods, Nags Head Woods and Roanoke Island. Call for off-season schedules.

Island Cycles

N.C. 12, Avon *995-4336*

This all-encompassing bicycle shop is located next to the Dairy Queen and is open from mid-March through mid-December from 9 AM to 6 PM. During summer, the store stays open slightly longer. Sales, repairs and advice are offered here — as well as bicycle rentals. Cyclists can lease six-speed beach cruisers for $15 a day or $45 a week; single speed beach cruisers, mountain bikes and road bikes for $10 a day or $35 a week; or higher-end bikes for slightly higher prices. Kids bikes lease for $7 a day or $25 a week. Cycles also can be rented by the hour for $4 or $5, depending on the style.

Lee Robinson's General Store

N.C. 12, Hatteras Village *986-2381*

Here, bikes can be rented year-round, seven days a week for cycling tours around the southern end of Hatteras Island. Bikes rent for $2 an hour, $10 a day or $35 per week. Lee Robinson's is open from 8 AM to 11 PM in the summer, with abbreviated hours during the off-season.

Slushie Stand

Across from Silver Lake, Ocracoke *928-1878*

You can't miss the bike racks spread out in front of this old-fashioned slushie stand just across from Silver Lake Harbor. Here, traditional coaster and kids bikes rent by the hour, day or week from April through October. And special tandem bicycles and tricycles also can be leased. Bikes rent for $4 an hour, $10 a day or $35 a week. Hours are 9 AM to 5 PM during the off-season, and the stand stays open until 9 PM during the summer. After a long ride through Ocracoke Island, be sure to sample a hand-dipped ice cream cone or old-fashioned slushie at the snack bar.

Insiders' Tips

You can bead your own jewelry at Cloud 9 — an eclectic, artsy shop at Pirate's Quay Shopping Center in Nags Head where owner Ginny Flowers is glad to help her customers string together something special to suit any taste.

Bicycle Safety

Since the Outer Banks have some great spots to ride your bicycle, you might want to arm yourself with some safety tips. A little bit of prevention goes a long way and you'd be surprised how many folks don't know the bicycle safety rules.

Also, while there is little crime on the Outer Banks, bicycles do disappear. Lock up carefully and never leave your bike parked overnight in a front yard or in an easy access spot. If your bike gets stolen, call the local police (see our Services and Information Directory). Sometimes the bike has been taken on a nocturnal "joy ride" and has been picked up by local police department, so call them before you panic. It's a good idea to mark down your bike's serial number for identification purposes.

Remember to:

- Use designated bike paths when available (see our Getting Around chapter for path locations).
- Wear safety helmets.
- Ride on the right side of the road with the flow of traffic.
- Always maintain a single file.
- Obey all traffic rules.
- Use hand signals for stops and turns.
- Don't double up unless the bike is made to ride more than one.
- Keep your hands on the handlebars.
- Observe pedestrian's right-of-way on walks, paths and streets.
- Look out for soft sand that can cause a wipe out.
- Use a front lighted white lamp and a rear red reflector when riding at night.

Motorists should pass with at least two feet between bicycle and motor vehicle.

Island Rentals

At Sharon Miller Realty, Ocracoke 928-5480

Adult and kids bikes can be rented by the day, three days or week from this Ocracoke Island outpost. Weekly rental rates are $23 for children's cycles and $27 for adult bikes. Reservations can be made in advance for weekly rentals.

In addition, Island Rentals leases volleyball, horseshoe and croquet sets for recreation at your rental cottage. And clam rakes rent for $12 a week if you want to try to dredge up your own dinner from the muddy shores along Ocracoke Island.

Bowling

Sometimes even the most dedicated sun-worshippers need an afternoon or evening in air-conditioned comfort. When you've caught too many rays — or the weather just won't cooperate — bowling is an alternative way to wile away the hours on the Outer Banks.

Beach Bowling Center

U.S. 158, MP 10, Nags Head 441-7077

Open for year-round league and recreational excitement, this is the Outer Banks' only bowling center. Here, 24 lanes are available for parties of one to six players. There's also a pro shop, video arcade and restaurant serving snacks, sandwiches, wine, beer and hamburgers. Bowling costs $2.75 per game and shoes rent for $2. Beach bowling is open from noon to midnight Sundays through Fridays and from 10 AM to midnight on Saturdays. Call for league information.

All-terrain Vehicles

One of the most exhilarating ways to see the off-road areas of the Outer Banks is on an all-terrain vehicle. Whether you're cruising over sand dunes, blasting along the beach or chasing a sunset up the marshy sounds, you can't get closer to nature than on one of these low-to-the-ground, open-air, gasoline powered dune buggies. With these babies, you can go where most Jeeps don't even dare!

Corolla Outback Adventures

Wee Winks Shopping Ctr., Corolla 453-4484

This outpost for northern Outer Banks adventures rents ATVs for individual excitement or guided off-road tours. Take your vehicle north of where N.C. 12's pavement ends — into the Currituck National Wildlife Refuge where you can see herds of wild horses, flocks of rare waterfowl and even feral hogs wallowing along the muddy marshlands. Vehicles seat two people and rent for $49 an hour. Two-hour sunset tours are offered for $85 per vehicle. Corolla Outback Adventures is open seasonally, from May through September. Call for off-season hours and varying tour times. All rentals are weather dependent.

Horseback Riding

Our favorite way to experience the Outer Banks is without gasoline or motors — on the back of a gentle horse clopping through the sand. Some folk in Kitty Hawk and Wanchese villages keep their own horses for private rides. And we envy their freedom to roam these barrier islands on the backs of such beautiful animals. But if you don't own your own horse, you can still enjoy riding one. Year-round trips are offered on Hatteras Island.

Buxton Stables

Off N.C. 12, Buxton 995-4659

Brown, gray, black, white and chestnut horses take riders on unforgettable tours from these wooden stables year-round. No experience is necessary for one-hour trail rides through the maritime forest of Buxton Woods. But you have to have at least ridden a horse before to enjoy the three-hour beach ride that winds through the woods onto the wide sand, into the surf. One-hour rides are offered in the afternoons and cost

Insiders' Tips

Shellfish enthusiasts take note: You can try your hand at recreational clamming — and rake your own dinner — at Hatteras Village Aqua Farm, off N.C. 12 less than a mile north of Hatteras Village, 986-2249 or (800) 986-2249. Equipment and instructions are provided, and clamming success is guaranteed. Like a pick-your-own vegetable farm, you can rake until your bucket is full. If you'd rather not rake, you can buy fresh seafood from the on-site retail shop. The farm is open daily for clamming from 9 AM to 7 PM, mid-April to October 1; the retail shop remains open throughout October.

$25 per person. The three-hour trips cost $60 each and leave at 8 AM. The stables are open every day except Sunday from 7 AM to 8 PM — but rides are scheduled for certain times so call for afternoon tour times. Weather affects these lovely animals, so make reservations — but call ahead to ensure the trip will take place.

Photo: Georgia Beach

Horseback riding on the beach is a great way to spend the day.

Movie Theaters

On some sultry summer afternoons — or rainy Saturday nights — there's no better place to be than inside a dark, air-conditioned movie theater catching the latest flick with a friend. First-run movies are offered at most Outer Banks theaters. And, of course, popcorn, candy and sodas are sold at all movie houses.

Colony Cinema, Corolla

N.C. 12, Monteray Plaza *453-2399*

The Outer Banks' newest theater, this year-old establishment includes four wide screens and is open from May through December, seven days a week from 11 AM to midnight. Tickets cost $7 for adults; $5 for children. Call 441-5630 for recorded featured information.

Colony Cinema, Southern Shores

U.S. 158, MP 1, The Marketplace *261-7866*

Two screens show first-run movies in this theater year-round, seven days a week. Evening only shows are offered during the off-season weekdays. Movies begin at 11 AM on weekends and throughout the summer. Tickets cost $6 for adults, $4 for children. Call 441-5630 for recorded feature information.

Colony Cinema, Kitty Hawk

U.S. 158, MP 4 *261-7949*

Open from Memorial Day weekend through Labor Day, this movie house has two screens that show films seven days a week from 11 AM until midnight. Tickets are $6 for adults and $4 for children. Call 441-5630 for daily feature information.

Cineplex, Nags Head

U.S. 158, MP 10½ *441-1808*

Offering four screens and first-run movies year-round, this large movie house shows films all day on weekends and throughout the summer and evenings only in the off-season. Admission is $6 for adults, $4 for children. Call 441-5630 for recorded daily features and times.

Colony Cinema, Outer Banks Mall

U.S. 158, MP 14 *441-3900*

Two wide screens feature films here throughout the year. During the summer and on weekends, they're shown from 11 AM until midnight. On off-season weekdays, the movies only run in the evening. Tickets are $6 for adults, $4 for children. Call 441-5630 for daily features and times.

Ye Olde Pioneer Theatre

113 Budleigh St., Manteo *473-2216*

The nation's oldest theater operated continuously by one family, the Pioneer is our favorite place to see films on the Outer Banks. It's filled with nostalgia — and smells of just-buttered popcorn. And it's been showing great flicks since 1934. For the $3 admission price — and the feel of the place — it can't be beat. Even the popcorn, sodas and candy are a great deal. The Pioneer is open year round. All movies start at 8 PM daily. Listings change weekly on Fridays. See the Attractions and Roanoke Island chapters for more information.

Miniature Golf Courses

No beach vacation is complete without putting a brightly colored ball through a windmill, under a pirate's sword or across a slightly sloping hill into a small metal cup. On the Outer Banks, more than a dozen minigolf courses await fun-loving families and friends from Corolla through Hatteras Island. Themed fairways featuring African animals, circus clowns and strange obstacles await even the most amateur club-swinging couples. Small children will enjoy the ease of some of these holes. And even good golfers can get into the new par 3 grass courses that have been growing in numbers over the past three years.

You can tee off at most places by 10 AM. Many courses stay open past midnight for night owls to enjoy. And several of these attractions offer play-all-day packages for a single price. Almost all minigolf courses operate seasonally. And, since they're all outside, their openings are dependent upon the weather.

The Grass Course

N.C. 12, Corolla *453-4198*

The Outer Banks' first natural grass course, these soundside greens are open throughout the summer season. This 18-hole course includes par 3s, 4s and 5s. And the undulating hills winding around natural dunes will provide intriguing challenges for beginning and better golfers. Cost is $7 for adults, $4 for kids 6 and younger. The course is open from April to November. Summer hours are 10 AM to midnight daily; weekends only in the off-season.

The Promenade

U.S. 158, MP ¼, Kitty Hawk *261-3844*

This family fun park includes Victorian-style buildings, turn-of-the-century streetlights, waterside recreation, a children's playground and an 18-hole themed minigolf course called Waterfall Greens where the cost is $4 per game. There's also a 27-hole, par 3, natural grass putting course — complete with separate putting greens and a target driving range; cost is $5 per game. A snack bar and picnic tables are on site. The Promenade is open Easter weekend through early October. Summer hours are 8:30 AM to midnight seven days a week.

Bermuda Greens

U.S. 158, MP 1¼, Kitty Hawk *261-0101*

This lovely, landscaped course is situated at the intersection of U.S. 158 and N.C. 12 — straight ahead if you're going east from the Wright Memorial Bridge, between the turnoffs to Duck and Kitty Hawk beaches. Two 18-hole miniature golf courses are open here from Easter through Thanksgiving. Cost for one round, on one course, is $7 for adults, $5 for children 10 and younger. During the summer, the greens stay open from 10 AM until midnight daily. There's also a video arcade on site and a TCBY yogurt stand for cool, creamy refreshments after a heated game of golf.

The Grass Course

U.S. 158, MP 5½, Kill Devil Hills *441-7626*

More challenging than the usual minigolf fairways, this natural grass course includes two 36-hole, par 72 courses. Most holes are 110 feet from the tees. The courses are open from 9 AM until 1 AM daily during summer, with the last tee time being midnight. Cost for one 18-hole game is $7 for adults and $5 for children younger than 10. If you play a second round of 18 holes in succession, discounts are offered. JK's Ribs is on site offering great lunch and dinner specials in case you work up a hunger (see our Restaurants chapter).

Diamond Shoals Family Fun Park

U.S. 158, MP 9¾, Kill Devil Hills *480-3553*

Two 18-hole miniature golf courses await putters here from Easter through October. All the grass is natural. Cost is $7 for one game for adults, $5 for children. In addition, there's a video arcade, batting stadium where you can slam a softball or baseball up to 250 feet, paddle boats, waterslides and a snack bar. Diamond Shoals is open from 9 AM to midnight during the summer.

Pink Elephant Mini Golf

Beach Rd., MP 11, Nags Head *441-5875*

Colorful circus animals in bright cages surround 36 lighted holes of minigolf at this popular Outer Banks course across from the Atlantic. You can't miss this place because the world's freakiest clown presides over its grassy greens, mocking would-be putters to try to sink one in. Pink Elephant is open on weekends in April, early May, September and October — and daily throughout the summer. In-season hours are 10 AM to midnight. You can play all day here for $4 per person. Kids age 12 and younger pay $3 each. The price doesn't change after dark, as it does on many minigolf courses.

Forbes Candies and Mini Golf

Beach Rd., MP 12, Nags Head *441-7293*

A giant pirate peers across this themed course, where 36 holes are open daily from April through September. Hours are 9 AM to 7 PM during the shoulder seasons, 9 AM to 10:30 PM in summer. You can play as many games as you like until 6 PM for $4 per person. During the evenings, each 18-hole game costs $5.

Blackbeard's Miniature Golf Park

U.S. 158, MP 15, Nags Head *441-4541*

The Outer Banks' most infamous pirate wields his 6-foot sword above these greens. Open daily summers only until at least 10 PM, Blackbeard's includes a video arcade if you're tired of putting around.

King Neptune Golf

U.S. 158, MP 16, Nags Head *441-6841*

Two 18-hole courses wind through caves, across man-made streams and around strange figurines on these fairways. King Neptune is open weekends from Easter through Memorial Day and during September, and daily throughout the summer. Hours are 9 AM until midnight. Cost is $4.75 to play all day during the off-season. In-season, you can play from 9 AM to 5 PM for the same price. But after 5 PM in summer, it costs $4.75 to play one 18-hole game and $1 extra to play the second course.

Avon Golf

N.C. 12, Avon *995-6159*

Adjacent to the Avon Pier, this 18-hole, natural grass course is open from noon to midnight, seven days a week all summer. You can play as many games as you can squeeze in from noon until 6 PM for $6. After 6 PM, each round costs $7 for adults, $5 for children.

Cool Wave Ice Cream Shop and Miniature Golf

N.C. 12, Buxton *995-6366*

One of the Outer Banks' only minigolf offerings with moving obstacles, this nine-hole course is open from Easter through Thanksgiving. Summer hours are noon until 10 PM seven days a week. Cost is $4 for adults, $3 for children 12 and younger. If you play one round of nine holes, the second time around is free. Ice cream, milk shakes and the best banana splits on Hatteras await players after a good game.

Trent Woods Golf Center

Off N.C. 12, Frisco *995-6325*

Set between tall pines, live oaks and freshwater ponds, this 18-hole minigolf course is open April through September, seven days a week. Mondays through Saturdays, hours are noon until 11 PM. On Sundays, Trent Woods is open from 3 to 11 PM. Each round costs $6 per person. Video games, picnic tables and soft ice cream are additional amenities offered here.

Airplane Tours

The best way to get a feel for how fragile these barrier islands are is to take a plane ride above the Outer Banks. Small planes offer tours daily most of the year from Corolla through Ocracoke. And pilots are always pleased to dip their passengers over a school of dolphins frolicking in the Atlantic, circle one of the four lighthouses beaming from these beaches or cruise around the Wright Brothers National Monument where Wilbur and Orville flew the world's first successful heavier-than-air flights. Bring your camera. These treetop adventures provide great photo opportunities of both sea and sound shores of the islands and a true glimpse at these waterlogged wetlands. Trips can be catered to fit any desire — and are well worth the reasonable rates to obtain a bird's-eye view of these skinny ribbons of sand.

Reservations are strongly recommended at least a day in advance of takeoff. All flights are weather and wind dependent. Charter flights to Norfolk and other areas of the Outer Banks also are offered through most of these companies. And several offer flight instruction to obtain a pilot's license and certification.

Kitty Hawk Aero Tours

Wright Brothers Airstrip, Kill Devil Hills 441-4460

Based just behind the Wright Brothers National Monument, off Colington Road, these air tours offer half-hour flights in Cessna aircraft year-round. Trips take you soaring south over Oregon Inlet, flying above the waves to see shipwrecks, over Jockey's Ridge and Roanoke Island and back to circle the monument. Cost is $24 per person for parties of two; $19 per person for three- to six-person parties. Tours are offered from 10 AM to 5 PM in the off-season, from 9 AM to sunset during the summer.

If you're up for more high-flying excitement, try a trip in a 1941 Waco biplane — where the cockpit is open and you're head is literally in the clouds. Twenty-minute trips take two passengers around the central Outer Banks for a total of $98. Leather helmets and old-fashioned Red Baron-style goggles are included in the price. Biplane tours are offered from May through September from 9 AM until sunset. Reservations are preferred for both types of flights.

Southeast Air Tours

Dare County Airport *473-1566*
Roanoke Island *473-3222*

Three separate air tours are offered in high-wing Cessnas from Easter through September with this aviation company. Half-hour tours take passengers over Roanoke Island, to the Wright Brothers' Monument and over Bodie Island Lighthouse for $15 per person if you have at least three passengers in your party. The Oregon Inlet tour is slightly longer and includes glimpses of sunken shipwrecks off the Atlantic Coast for $20 per person. If you're up for a little longer hang time, try the 45-minute flights to the Currituck Beach Lighthouse in Corolla and back for $25 per person. Each aircraft can accommodate three to five passengers. Reservations are suggested. Ask about summer biplane rides too.

Burrus Flying Service

Billy Mitchell Airstrip *995-6671*
Frisco *After hours: 986-2679*

Three flight-seeing tours leave daily all year from the small airstrip near Frisco Campground. Flying above Hatteras Island, you can get aerial views of Cape Hatteras' spiral-striped lighthouse, Diamond Shoals, Hatteras Inlet, Canadian Hole and wide expanses of Pamlico Sound. Trips to Ocracoke and Portsmouth islands also are available. Cost is $20 to $25 per person for a 30-minute flight, depending on how many people are in your party; $30 to $38 per person for a 45-minute tour. Flights leave from 10 AM to sunset Mondays through Saturdays. On Sundays, these exciting air adventures depart from 2 to 6 PM.

Pelican Airways

Ocracoke Airstrip, Ocracoke Island 928-1661

Half-hour trips above Ocracoke and Portsmouth islands are available any time year round in this Aero-Commander plane piloted by an Ocracoke resident. Trips can be tailored to suit individual interests or narrated to explain interesting aspects of the southern Outer Banks area. Cost is a total of $55 for two people; $75 for three people. Flight instruction also is available. Call for an appointment.

Go-carts

If you're looking for a way to race around the Outer Banks — without fear of getting a ticket — five go-cart rental outlets offer riders a thrill a minute on slick, curving tracks. Drivers have to be at least 12 years old to take the wheel at most of these places. But younger children often are allowed to strap themselves in beside adults to experience the fast-paced action.

Dowdy's Go-Karts

Beach Rd., MP 11, Nags Head 441-5122

This is one of the area's oldest go-cart tracks, located across from the ocean next to Tortuga's Lie Restaurant. But all the cars are less than 3 years old and can take tight turns at more than 40 miles per hour around the oval track. Outdoor bleachers provide a perfect place for parents to spectate this noisy sport. These motorized carts can be rented daily throughout the summer from midmorning until 11 PM.

Dowdy's Amusement Park

U.S. 158, MP 11, Nags Head 441-5122

A second go-cart track, owned by the same family, awaits riders at the Outer Banks' only amusement park. This long, oval track is open evenings only from May through early September. There's also an indoor video arcade and snack bar here (see our Kidstuff chapter).

Speed-n-Spray Action Park

U.S. 158, MP 15, Nags Head 480-1900

This year-old racetrack treats drivers to wild rides around quick curves that twist back toward the blacktop just as you think you might slip off into the sound. It's open from early May through September daily.

Nags Head Raceway

U.S. 158, MP 16, Nags Head 480-4639

Speed demons and thrill-seekers will revel in this new roadway, complete with two-seater carts and slick new racers. A five-minute spin around the track costs

Insiders' Tips

On Wednesday nights just before sunset throughout the summer, head to the parking lot of K.D.H. Cycle & Skate, Beach Road, MP 9½, Kill Devil Hills, for pick-up games of roller hockey. Nets, sticks and pucks are available for free. You can bring your own skates or rent them here — the shop is open until 8 PM in summer.

$6 in a single cart, $8 for a double. Drivers can time themselves, trying to beat the clock — or sprint against their friends in hurried heats. Nags Head Raceway is open from April through September. Summer hours are from 10 AM until 11 PM seven days a week.

Waterfall Park

N.C. 12, Rodanthe *987-2213*

This sound-to-sea amusement area offers the biggest selection of go-cart tracks on the Outer Banks — and more recreational opportunities in a single spot than anywhere else on Hatteras Island. Here, kids of all ages will enjoy six separate race car tracks where drivers can test their skills on a different style vehicle at each pit stop. Wet racers are great for hot afternoon sprints against the wind — and other boaters. Bumper boats, two minigolf courses and a snack bar also are open from 11 AM to 10 PM daily from May through October. Each ride costs $6 per person.

Parasailing

If you've always wanted to float high above the water, beneath a colorful parachute, opportunities for such peaceful adventures await you at a variety of locations along the Outer Banks. This is one of the most enjoyable experiences we've had during summer. Our only regrets are that the incredible rides don't last longer. We could stay up at these lofty heights, strapped comfortably into a climbing harness, swinging beneath billowing air-filled chutes for hours. Although a boat pulls you from below — allowing the wind to lift you toward the clouds — you don't get wet on these outdoor adventures over the sounds — unless you want to. Riders don't even have to know how to swim to soar with the sea gulls above whitecaps and beach cottages. Anyone of any age, without any athletic ability at all, will enjoy parasailing and find it one of their most memorable pastimes.

Kitty Hawk Kites — Outer Banks Outdoors

Corolla *453-8845*
Duck *261-2900*
Avon *995-6060*

From these soundside locations, licensed captains and parasailing experts will help you float above the water at heights up to 1,000 feet. Parasailing is offered during summers only.

Kitty Hawk Watersports

TimBuck II Shopping Center
Corolla *453-6900*

Parasail flights are offered daily throughout the summer at this TimBuck II shop, owned by Kitty Hawk Sports.

The Water Works

N.C. 12, Duck *261-7245*
U.S. 158, MP 17, Nags Head *441-8875*

Whatever height you wish to reach, parasailing captains from The Water Works can take you there. Uplifting experiences are offered daily from 8 AM to 5 PM in Duck and Nags Head from May through September. These eight- to 15-minute flights allow you to float at 300, 600, 900 or 1,200 feet and cost $38 to $98 per person — depending on how high you want to fly.

Willett's Wetsports

Nags Head-Manteo Causeway
Nags Head *441-4112*

This new watersports station in the bright pink building provides parasailing experiences daily during the summer.

Island Parasail

N.C. 12, Avon *995-4970*

All summer long, you can soar over the Pamlico Sound beneath a rainbow-colored parachute based at this Avon outpost. Ten-minute flights are offered from 9:30 AM to 6:30 PM daily at heights of 300, 500, 700, 1,000 or 1,200 feet. Costs range from $40 to $75 per person, depending on what lofty level you wish to reach.

Skateboarding is always popular with the young crowd.

Go ahead — as long as you're strapped in and sitting on air, take it to the top. You'll be glad you saw everything you can see from high above the salty marshes and shallow sound.

Hang Gliding

The closest any human being will ever get to feeling like a bird is by flying beneath brightly colored wings of a hang glider, with arms and legs outstretched and only the wind all around. Lessons are available for flight enthusiasts ages 8 to 80. Just watching these winged creatures soar atop Jockey's Ridge or catching air lifts above breakers along the Atlantic is enough to make bystanders want to test their wings.

Corolla Flight

N.C. 12, Corolla *453-4800*

Open from April through October, this northern flight school is operated by Greg DeWolf who piloted his own hang glider across the United States several years ago, landed at the Wright Brothers National Monument in Kill Devil Hills, and decided to stay.

DeWolf and other instructors take novice hang gliders on tandem flights over the ocean and Curritck Sound. A pick-up truck tows the tandem team down the beach, then cuts them free to soar into the sky. You're strapped to your instructor the entire time. One flight to 1,500 feet of altitude costs $75. A 2,500-foot flight costs $100. Three flights and a lesson cost $160. It takes 10 lessons to qualify for a solo flight. Photos and videos of you under wings are offered for an additional $20.

Kitty Hawk Kites — Outer Banks Outdoors

U.S. 158, MP 13 *441-4124*
Nags Head *(800) 334-3777*

The country's most popular hang gliding school, this Nags Head training center across from Jockey's Ridge State Park offers a variety of ways to learn to fly — or just enjoy the thrill of being airborne while strapped onto an experienced instructor. Whether you want to soar solo five feet above a sand dune or cruise through the clouds after taking off from the shoreline, teachers here can help you meet your goals. After all, they've taught more than 200,000 people how to fly since first opening their doors on the Outer Banks more than 22 years ago.

Beginning dune training programs probably are the most often chosen methods of learning to hang glide. In these classes, you learn how to launch a rental craft by foot from the undulating sand dune of Jockey's Ridge State Park — and you never have more than 15 feet to fall. These are solo flights, where you and the hang glider are alone in the air. No experience is necessary. Group and private lessons are offered. Basic instruction and three flights off Jockey's Ridge cost $49 and are available most of the year. Two additional flights can be purchased for $20 more.

Aerotow training programs are based at Maple Airport in Currituck County. With these flights, you're strapped behind an ultralight plane with an instructor who helps you take off after the aircraft tows you to a safe altitude. You never have to go it alone in one of these gigs. One tandem flight to 1,500 feet costs $85. A tandem flight to 2,000 feet costs $100.

If you'd rather take off from the water, boat tow training programs take place at the Outer Banks Outdoors Watersports Center in Duck. Again, you and an instructor are strapped together — but a boat tows you to the proper altitude before you begin to soar off the long line. One tandem flight to 1,500 feet costs $99. Take it to the top — 2,000 feet — for $114.

Paragliding is the fastest growing form of individual aviation in the world, featuring an elliptical shaped, completely flexible parachute-like wing that operates more as a hang glider. These easy-to-operate crafts are launched by running until the chute fills with wind and air. Then, you control the fate of your own solo flight by using handles that change the shape of the wing. These chutes are slower and easier to maneuver than hang gliders. And they're so light you can stuff them into a backpack. Paragliding training takes place at Maple Airport in Currituck County and allows students to fly from 500 to 1,000 feet into the air. A three-hour lesson costs $75.

Although most sportsmen — and women — seek out these activities during the summer, you can achieve most of these high-flying thrills year-round. Reservations are required for most adventures. And discount packages offer more in-depth instruction — and a shot at certification.

Water Slides, Arcades and Other Amusements

On those hot afternoons when you just can't stand the smell of saltwater or scratch of sand in your bathing suit any longer, slip on down to a waterslide and splash into one of their big pools. Most of these parks are open daily during summer — some well into the evening. Water slides generally close on rainy days.

Among the recreational outposts, many include video arcades with their offerings. But the Outer Banks' oldest — and newest — amusement centers also offer bright computerized games as well as other unusual activities. We can't list everything the owners of these establishments include — so you'll have to experience these places for yourself to discover all the surprises in store.

Diamond Shoals Family Fun Park

U.S. 158, MP 9¾, Nags Head 480-3553

The Outer Banks' newest and most upscale water park, this enormous wet playground includes three twisting, twirling waterslides — complete with tunnels and mats — that drop frolicking bathers into a wide, waist-deep pool. Parents will enjoy splashing afternoons away with their kids here.

Diamond Shoals is open from 9 AM until midnight daily during the season. There's also a kiddie pool for little tykes. All-day passes are $10 to slide, $4 for spectators and the kiddie pool only. Season passes cost $35.

Paddle boats, a video arcade, batting cage, snack bar, sunbathing deck with lounge chairs and minigolf courses also are on the premises.

Dowdy's Amusement Park

U.S. 158, MP 11, Nags Head 441-5122

A sure sign of summer is when the area's oldest recreational attraction begins gearing up for the season. Insiders often mark the arrival of visitors by when workers at Dowdy's begin bolting the rides back together. This is the only boardwalk-like place on the Outer Banks — although it's at least three blocks from the ocean. Step inside the wire fence and you're sure to feel as if you've stumbled into a county fair or carnival. Traditional Midway rides like the Scrambler, Tilt-A-Whirl and merry-go-round spin to peppy, piped in music. Cotton candy, caramel apples and popcorn aromas waft through the blinking lights. There's even a little roller coaster here — its hills and dips barely more than the geographic variations on these flat barrier islands. Tickets for each ride are sold separately. Dowdy's is open daily from May through early September, in the evenings only.

Surf Slide

U.S. 158, MP 10½, Nags Head 441-5755

Two yellow waterslides allow people to cool off on sultry summer afternoons — and race fellow riders down the long chutes. Surf Slide is open daily from Memorial Day through Labor Day from 10 AM until 10 PM. Mats are provided — but bring your own towels. It costs $6 to slide all day.

Village Playhouse

Between U.S. 158 and Beach Rd.
MP 14, Nags Head 441-3277

Paintball blasted its way onto the Outer Banks during the summer of 1995 when this indoor Nags Head amusement center opened its doors across from the Outer Banks Mall. Here, toddlers will have a ball crawling through a room filled with rubber spheres. Older children will enjoy 30

Insiders' Tips

For an unusual indoor recreational experience, try climbing the wall at Kitty Hawk Kites. Rappelling equipment and basic instruction is provided. This is a great way to reconcentrate stress if you're already climbing the walls.

minutes in the soft moon walk for $3 each. Adolescents — and adventurous adults — can shoot each other with pellets of paint in a long room filled with bunkers, fox holes and great hiding places. Headgear, camouflage clothes, a gun and 100 rounds of paint are provided for $15 per person. There's also a video arcade, Skee-ball, air hockey and other games where winners can cash in paper tickets for prizes at a toy counter. This place is perfect for rainy afternoons, cold winter weekends and kids' birthday parties. A food court serves all sorts of appetizers and quick entrees. And an antique shop beneath the same roof gives Mom a place to shop — and escape from the gleeful squeals. Village Playhouse is open Fridays through Sundays year-round. During the summer, it's open daily from 11 AM until 10 PM.

Waterfall Park

N.C. 12, Rodanthe *987-2213*

In this palm-tree lined playground, two waterslides are open daily from May to October. Hours are 11 AM to 10 PM. Each slide is a different shape.

Dolphin Tours, Boat Rides and Pirate Trips

Most Outer Banks boat cruises are included in our Watersports and Fishing chapters. But a few unusual offerings are worth mentioning here as well. These trips, of course, are weather dependent and available only during warmer spring and summer months. Reservations are recommended for each of these tours. But unlike sailing and more participatory water adventures, you don't have to be able to swim to enjoy these activities — and you probably won't even get wet on board these boats that slip along the shallow sounds.

Bumper boats also are available on the Beach Road in Kill Devil Hills at Wet-n-Wild Bumper Boats, 441-0264, and on U.S. 158 at Nags Head Watersports, 480-2236.

The Water Works

Nags Head-Manteo Causeway
Nags Head *441-6822*

If you'd like to get a glimpse of dolphins up close, take a one-hour cruise through schools of the gentle creatures who will leap and dive alongside your boat. Trips are offered daily throughout the summer. Cost is $22 per person.

Airboat rides also are available from Water Works — and are almost guaranteed to get you wet. These expeditions through the sound cost $15 per person. They last about a half-hour.

The Crystal Dawn

Pirate's Cove Marina, Manteo *473-5577*

Sunset cruises around Roanoke Island are offered every evening except Sunday throughout the summer on this beautiful, two-story vessel. Trips include commentary about the Outer Banks and depart at 6:30 PM, returning about 90 minutes later. Adult admission is $8 per person, children 10 and younger cost $5 each.

Moonlight trips around Roanoke Island also are available aboard *The Crystal Dawn*. They last from 8:30 to 10 PM and are offered on summer Thursdays and Fridays. Cost is $8 per person.

Captain Clam

Teach's Lair Marina
Hatteras Village *986-2460*

Three-hour dolphin tours around Hatteras Inlet are offered each Thursday afternoon at 1 PM throughout the summer aboard this inshore headboat. Passengers aboard *Captain Clam* are virtually guaranteed to see dolphin because the crew constantly communicates with spotter planes on radios. Cost is $20 per person.

Additionally, *Captain Clam* crews clad in pirate garb put on plays about Blackbeard and other Outer Banks renegades from 5 to 7 PM each Thursday in-season. As you cruise around the pirate's haunts — wearing complimentary eye patches and swords — you'll be treated to tales of mutiny on the high seas, buried treasure and other local lore. Cost is $15 per person.

Athletic Clubs

Despite all the outdoor activities the Outer Banks have to offer, many locals and visitors still crave vigorous indoor workouts at traditional gyms and health clubs. These three fitness centers are open year round and include locker room and shower facilities. Both are open to the public for annual, monthly, weekly and walk-in daily membership rates.

Outer Banks Nautilus Athletic Club

Beach Rd., MP 7, Kill Devil Hills 441-7001

A full line of Nautilus and Paramount exercise equipment is available here, as well as free weights. Exercise bikes, stair machines and treadmills offer other workout options. And a wide range of aerobic classes are offered throughout the day. There's a whirlpool here, small pro-shop where vitamin supplements and fitness apparel are sold, and towels are included with your admission charge. Cost is $10 per day or $25 a week for aerobics classes and gym privileges. To use the gym only, memberships cost $50 per month, $125 for three months and $299 per year. For aerobics and gym use, memberships cost $65 per month, $150 for three months and $399 annually.

Outer Banks Nautilus is open Mondays through Fridays from at least 7:30 AM to 9 PM and Saturdays from 8 AM to 5 PM. This facility is closed Sundays.

Nautics Hall Health & Fitness Complex

U.S. 64, in the Elizabethan Inn
Manteo 473-1191

A competition-size, indoor, heated pool is the centerpiece of this health club where water aerobics, swimming lessons and lap times are offered throughout the year. There's also a workout room with Nautilus equipment, free weights, aerobicycles and Stairmasters. Low-impact and step aerobics instruction is available daily. Other amenities include an outdoor pool, racquetball court, sun decks, a sauna and massage therapy on the premises. Even a nursery is often provided — call for hours. Nautics Hall is open from 6:30 AM to 9 PM, Mondays through Fridays and from 9 AM to 9 PM on summer weekends. Off-season weekend hours are 9 AM to 5 PM. Monthly memberships cost $50 per person. Daily passes cost $6 each.

Frisco Fitness Works

Off N.C. 12, Frisco 995-3900

This newly renovated athletic club is open year round from 7 AM to 9 PM Mondays, Wednesdays and Fridays; from 7 AM to 7:30 PM Tuesdays and Thursdays; and 9 AM to 4 PM Saturdays. It's closed on Sundays. State-of-the-art 5X weights, free weights, exercise bikes, treadmills and stair machines are offered here. There's a changing facility on site, but showers are not available. Aerobics are taught at 7 PM Mondays, Wednesdays and Fridays and 9 AM Tuesdays and Thursdays. Cost for aerobics and the gym is $37 per month. Aerobics-only packages cost $27 a month. Weekly memberships are $27 each. Daily passes cost $8.

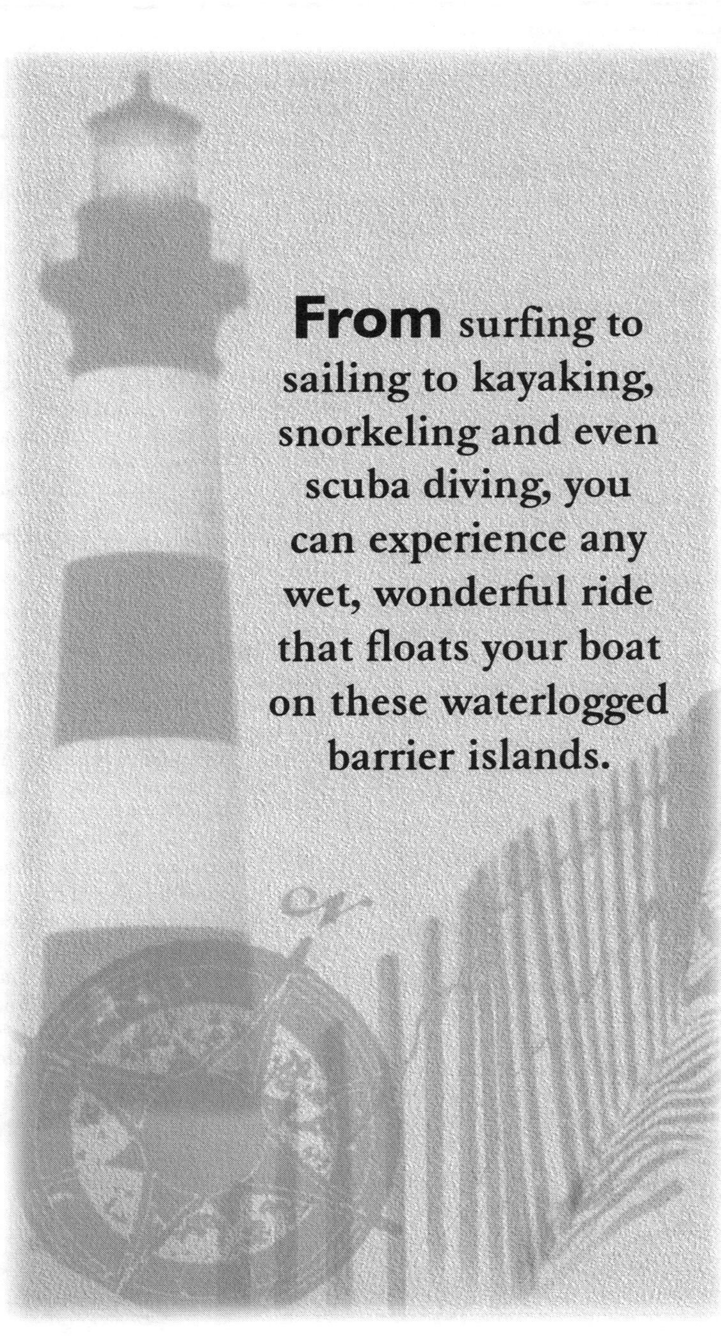
From surfing to sailing to kayaking, snorkeling and even scuba diving, you can experience any wet, wonderful ride that floats your boat on these waterlogged barrier islands.

Inside Watersports

Water, water everywhere! . . . While the Outer Banks certainly qualify as a hydrophobe's nightmare, there's no denying these barrier islands are a promised land for anyone who loves to be near, on or in the water. Head 5 miles due east or west from any point between Carova and Ocracoke Island, and you'll either cross over water while traversing a bridge or end up taking a dip. Whether you've a yen for "hanging ten," crave a sail across the sound, want to whip along on a windsurfer, dream of jetting into white caps on a Jet Ski, or prefer paddling along the brackish backwater bays, the Outer Banks is the perfect place to satisfy the watersports fanatic in you.

Surfing and windsurfing are among the area's most popular watersports. Each summer season, thousands of novice- to expert-level athletes arrive at the Outer Banks to whet their appetites for those outdoor adventures. Dozens of other folk move to Dare County annually to be closer to the waves and shallow sounds year round.

Personal watercraft — Jet Skis, Sea Doos, Wave Runners, et al. — have been growing in popularity recently, with rental outposts opening all along the sound shores. Kayaking, canoeing and sailing also are coming into their own, as eco-tours and sunset cruises become increasingly popular pastimes. For more unusual endeavors, the National Park Service offers occasional snorkeling expeditions for families. Some Outer Banks surf shops have begun leasing skimboards to dare devils who like to slide along the sand amid the ocean's shore break. And a few marinas along the barrier islands are even renting power boats for near-shore fishing and water-skiing.

Weather plays a big factor in whether a particular watersport is available. Some area sports stores offer surfing hotlines or wave updates. And even when temperatures begin to drop, you can heat things up in the ocean or sound with increasingly warm wetsuits sold just for watersports fans at almost all Outer Banks surf shops.

Some water workouts require special training and equipment. But shops and sports schools in almost every area of the Outer Banks rent and teach whatever you need to know. (Also, see our Beach Information and Safety chapter for information about rip tides and other hazards.)

From surfing to sailing to kayaking, snorkeling and even scuba diving, you can experience any wet, wonderful ride that floats your boat on these waterlogged barrier islands.

Surfing

Warmer than New England waters, wielding more consistent waves than most Florida beaches, the Outer Banks has the best breaks on the East Coast, scores of surfers say. The barrier islands are set far out into the ocean, in deeper parts of the Atlantic than most vacation destinations. Such a location allows area beaches to pick up more swells and wind patterns than any place around. Piers, shipwrecks and offshore sandbars also offer unusual wave patterns. And the beaches from Duck through Hatteras are some of the only spots left that don't have strict surfing regulations: As long as you keep a leash on your board and stay at least 300 feet away from public piers, you won't get a surfing citation.

Although California's surfing subculture didn't really surface until the late 1950s, Outer Banks historian David Stick said he saw the first local surfboard in the 1930s, when Tommy Fearing built one after hearing about guys riding waves on big boards in Hawaii. "It took six men to handle that board. It was very big, very clumsy, 8 or 9 feet long and made of juniper," Stick recalled. "I'm not sure anybody ever stood up on it."

By the late 1960s, Stick said, surfing had become popular along the still sparsely populated barrier islands. Station wagons laden with teenagers — and their boards — skirted the soft sands each weekend, traveling from Virginia Beach and Ocean City, Maryland, to hang in the Outer Banks' huge waves. Hatteras Island native Johnny Conner Jr., who runs Buxton's only supermarket, said boys sold their boards when they ran out of money. He bought several. Then, he turned around and rented those surfboards to local friends and newcomers who also wanted to ride the waves.

Cape Hatteras' black-and-white striped lighthouse, set in the elbow of the barrier islands, had become known as a magnet for East Coast swell seekers by the early 1970s. Jim Vaughn opened one of the Outer Banks' first surf stores at Whalebone Junction in Nags Head in 1975. Today, his Whalebone Surf Shop on U.S. 158 E. is one of more than 20 such outposts along the barrier islands.

In the late 1970s, the East Coast Surfing Championships started here. The U.S. Championships were held on the Outer Banks in 1978 and 1982. Each summer — and during winter storms — famous surfers can be seen riding the competition circuit along the Atlantic or just riding waves with hundreds of other "boardheads."

Surfers at shops along the barrier islands design, make and sell their own boards, with prices ranging from $100 for used models to $600 for custom styles. Some stores, including Secret Spot in Nags Head, offer lessons for beginning surfers. And many rent boards for as little as $10 a day — plus a deposit. Make sure your board is waxed, however, or you'll slide all over and off it.

Surfing is a strenuous sport. You need to be able to swim well in wicked waves. But with a variety of board lengths — and 90 miles of oceanfront to choose from — there are usually breaks to accommodate almost every surfer's style and stamina.

Since the beaches have been getting increasingly crowded with summer surfers, some folk won't reveal secret spots where they like to ride "rad" waves. But we'll share some of the favorite haunts with you here: Kitty Hawk Pier and Avalon Pier in Kill Devil Hills each boast ample parking and pretty rideable waves. The public beach access at Barnes Street in Nags Head, with plenty of parking, provides some steady swells. Nags Head Pier also is a favorite haunt. If you don't mind hiking across the dunes with a board under your arm, Pea Island and Coquina Beach both have waves worth the walk. Recently, Rodanthe has become a popular destination, with the pier there producing waves even when almost everything else around is flat. Ramp 34, just north of Avon, is another good location, as are the turnout north of Buxton, Ramp 49 in Frisco, Frisco Pier and the public beach access area between Frisco and Hatteras.

The best and biggest waves by far, however, hover around the Cape Hatteras Lighthouse. Here, beaches north and south of The Point face in two directions, doubling the chances for good conditions. But concrete and steel groins jut out into the Atlantic near the beacon's brick base, so beware of being tossed toward one of these head-bashing barriers.

Waves along the Outer Banks average two to three feet high in the summer. Winter swells usually double those heights. Many areas along the barrier islands also have strong rip currents and strange sandbars — so always surf with a friend and stay alert of water, weather and beach conditions. You'll need a wetsuit for surfing in the spring, fall and winter. But if you can stand the sea's cold shock, winter rides are well worth that frigid first dive.

In 1995, surfers estimated, waist-high swells came ashore along the Outer Banks at least 60 percent of the time. Even California surfers brought their boards to North Carolina's barrier islands to ride the radical waves. If weather patterns continue sending hurricanes and other summer storms skirting just off the coast, visitors and locals alike should be able to keep standing on swells — and doing some soul surfing with the scores of other area wave riders.

How to Surf

If you've never tried to surf, you might want to begin on a boogie board. Area surf shops also rent these shorter, lighter boards and they'll allow you to get the feel of the waves without having to get whacked in the head. You can't stand up on a boogie board. But most first-time wave riders can't stand up on a surfboard anyway. Boogie boards also are a lot cheaper to buy and easier to maneuver than real surfboards.

Strong swimming skills are a prerequisite for any surfer. Like most sports, the younger you start, the easier it is to learn. If you feel confidant braving waves 100 yards off the beach — and you're patient enough to learn to work with, rather than against, the Atlantic — you can learn to ride waves on the Outer Banks.

Start off in small swells that are breaking cleanly and evenly. You'll probably want to work in uncrowded areas at first because it's difficult to maneuver surfboards around other people. And good surfers won't want you getting in their way.

Paddling is the first step. Lie on your stomach, with your chest across the thickest part of the surfboard. Then paddle your arms in a freestyle stroke, practicing until you can really control the board and find a good balance spot. Paddle around in the shore break. Then, when you're comfortable, stroke on out into the real waves.

To ride a swell, you have to get slightly ahead of it and travel at almost the same speed as it's moving. Paddle out past where the waves are breaking. Then, turn around until you're facing the beach and watch your back until you see a swell forming. Waves are cyclical. So once you've watched a few, it will be easier to gauge the timing you'll need to paddle with the wave and let it crest beneath you. You'll know when the wave begins to carry you. Just as in body surfing, you can feel it carry you forward fast.

When you're positioned in the breaking wave, stand up as if you're doing a push up on the speeding board. Don't try to get to your knees first. Just pop up on your feet and keep your arms outstretched for balance. Place one foot in front of the other, about a shoulder length apart, and enjoy the ride.

Surf only until you've had enough. Don't get too tired because this sport takes incredible stamina and strength — and can get the best of you if you've been out in the Atlantic too long. Once you've gotten good enough to hang with other boardheads, respect their space. Always watch out for swimmers. And try to stay out of others' way — or, at least, share the waves.

Photo: Philip S. Ruckle Jr.

Come sail away.

Surf Shops

From Corolla through Ocracoke, the Outer Banks are inundated with surf shops. Each summer, surf shop managers post competition schedules for beginners through surfing circuit riders near the store fronts. Most shops stock gear, and many provide instructors in season. A Kitty Hawk and a Buxton surf shop also offer 24-hour daily updates on surfing conditions, and a Corolla shop sponsors a daily summer report on a regional radio station (see our "Surf Lines" gray box).

Surf Lines

Wave Riding Vehicles, Kitty Hawk 261-3332
Natural Art Surf Shop, Buxton 995-4646
Daily summer report on WERX-Rock 102.5FM, sponsored by Corolla Surf Shop, Corolla, 453-WAVE

In Corolla, you can rent surfboards and boogie boards — and take a surfing lesson — at **Corolla Surf Shop**, 453-WAVE; and rent surfboards at **Kitty Hawk Sports**, 453-4999. **Ocean Atlantic Rentals** in Corolla Light Village Shops rents surfboards, wetsuits and related apparel, boogie boards and skim boards, 453-2440. Duck surfers also can stop in at another **Kitty Hawk Sports** location on the west side of N.C. 12, 261-8770; or rent boards at **Waterworks Too** near the Duck Landing Water Tower, 261-7245.

In Kitty Hawk, **Wave Riding Vehicles**, MP 2 on the west side of U.S. 158, rents surfboards and boogie boards, 261-7952; **Whalebone Surf Shop** is next door at MP 2, 261-8737; and **Bert's Surf Shop**, MP 4 on the east side of U.S. 158, 261-7584, rents surfboards and boogie boards.

Kill Devil Hills has four surf shops: **Back Door**, MP 6 on U.S. 158, 480-3055; **Vitamin Sea Surf Shop**, on the east side of U.S. 158 at MP 6, 441-7512, rents surfboards and boogie boards; **17th Street Surf Shop**, MP 9 on the west side of U.S. 158, 441-1797; **New Sun Surf Shop**, where custom-made surfboards are a speciality, is west of U.S. 158 at MP 10 in the Ocean Commerce Park, 441-3994.

In Nags Head, **Whalebone Surf Shop** is at MP 10 on the west side of U.S. 158, 441-6747; **Bert's Surf Shop** is on the east side of U.S. 158 at MP 11, 441-1939; **Secret Spot**, about a block south on the same side of the highway, 441-4030, rents foam-core boards with hard plastic shells and can teach you how to use them; **The Pit**, on the beach road at MP 12 (across from some good breaks), 480-3128, rents surfboards and boogie boards and offers lessons; **Kitty Hawk Sports** offers rentals from its shop on the east side of U.S. 158 at MP 13, 441-6800; **Cavalier Surf Shop**, one of the Outer Banks' earliest outposts, on the beach road at MP 13½, 441-7349, offers lessons and surfboard and boogie board rentals; **The Waterworks**, on the west side of U.S. 158 at MP 16½, rents surfboards and boogie boards, 441-8875.

On Hatteras Island, you can rent surfboards and boogie boards at **Rodanthe**

Surf Shop (the northernmost surfing haven), on N.C. 12 in Rodanthe, 987-2412, and **Hatteras Island Surf Shop,** also on N.C. 12, Waves, 987-2296. In Avon, **Kitty Hawk Sports**, N.C. 12, 995-5000, offer rentals; and **Ocean Atlantic Rentals** rents surfboards, boogie boards and all sorts of wetsuit equipment from its outpost on the west side of N.C. 12, 995-5968. Buxton boasts three surf shops, all on N.C. 12: **Hatteras Outdoors**, 995-5815; **Fox Water Sports**, which rents boogie boards, soft boards, surfboards and wetsuits, 995-4102; and **Natural Art Surf Shop**, where the owners also offer great advice, 995-5682. **Hatteras Island Rentals**, also in Buxton, rents surfboards, 995-6363.

If you're looking for big breaks on Ocracoke Island, stop into **BW's Surf Shop** on N.C. 12, near Silver Lake, 928-6141; or **Ride the Wind Surf Shop**, also on N.C. 12, 928-6311, which rents surfboards and boogie boards. **Ocracoke Adventures** offers surfing and boogie board instruction from its location on N.C. 12 near Silver Lake, below Creekside Cafe, 928-7873.

Windsurfing

Since the early 1980s, windsurfing has grown from a relatively obscure sport to one of the most popular activities on the Outer Banks. Each year — especially in autumn — thousands of northern visitors descend on the barrier islands to skim the shallow sounds or surf the sea's whitecaps on brightly colored sailboards. When the wind is whipping just right, hundreds of neon-striped sails soar along the shores of Hatteras Island, silently skirting the salty water and looking like bright butterflies flitting near the beach.

Many sailboarders swear by the Outer Banks, calling it the best windsurfing spot on the Atlantic seaboard — and one of the top three locations in the country. International windsurfing magazines say an Avon soundside beach dubbed "Canadian Hole" is one of the continent's best sailboarding spots. Canadians, especially, come in droves, driving more than 30 hours at a clip to catch the warm October breezes in their Mylar sails.

Ted James moved to Hatteras in 1972 to surf and fish, "looking for what Florida lost years ago." He runs a commercial fishing boat in the winter and has been making his Fox sailboards in Buxton and Florida since 1968. James was one of the first people to put a sailboard in the Outer Banks surf — and he was instrumental in improving both boards and rigs.

"People have been cussin' the wind here since there was wind. But with sailboards, the more wind the better," James says. "You don't have to be athletic to windsurf. Though it's easier to teach people who sail, in a way, because they know the wind. We've had people uncoordinated, overweight, and they catch on. For a lot of them, it's the first athletic success they've ever had."

Whether you're an expert athlete or novice who knows nothing about wind and water, windsurfing is not an easy sport. Once you get the hang of it, however, it is one of the most intoxicating experiences imaginable. It's clean and quiet. You can do it alone or with friends. With the proper equipment, sailboarders can control their speeds — sliding slowly into a sunset or cruising more than 40 miles an hour across choppy breaks. On the Outer Banks, sailboarders can usually find some wind to ride year round. And windsurfing is permitted any place you can set your sails. This sport truly lets you feel like a part of the natural surroundings — and it's an incredible rush to be able to maneuver with the wind.

Canadian Hole, on the west side of N.C. 12 between Avon and Buxton, is undoubtedly the most popular windsurfing spot on the Outer Banks. Formed in the early 1960s, it was created after a storm cut an inlet across Hatteras Island, just north of Buxton, and workers dredged sand from the sound to rebuild the roadway. Dredging activities carved troughs just offshore in the Pamlico Sound. The deep depressions, which extend to about 5 feet, help create ideal conditions for sailboarders. Additionally, Canadian Hole flanks one of the skinniest strips of sand on the barrier islands. So windsurfers can sail the sound then walk their boards across to cruise in the ocean in fewer than five minutes.

Besides the sound and the Atlantic, Canadian Hole offers other amenities many windsurfers find helpful. There's a 100-space paved lot to park big vans and trailers in, four Porta-johns, a phone booth and a half-dozen metal trash cans. Even the beach at Canadian Hole is much wider than other soundside stretches of sand — about 50 yards wide and able to accommodate sunbathers, coolers and plenty of spectators.

"The sound is so wide and flat, you can sail for miles without turning," said Michel St.-Jean, from Quebec, who traveled 18 hours to windsurf at The Hole. "There are no signs or buildings to see when you're sailing. That's really what we like best about this place."

Nags Head's soundside beaches also provide great sailboarding — and are more shallow than Canadian Hole thus safer for beginners. In spring and fall, tourism officials estimate, as many as 500 windsurfers a week arrive at the Outer Banks. Dozens of other visitors try the sport for the first time while vacationing in Dare County.

Learning to Windsurf

From Duck through Ocracoke Island, there are more than a dozen outposts that sell windsurfing gear and sailboards. Many of those shops offer windsurfing lessons for less than $40. We recommend receiving professional instruction if you're just starting out. It's also better to learn if you like this sport on rented equipment, because even beginning rigs cost about $500. Windsurfing is free once you're outfitted — but the equipment can be quite expensive.

Anyone who's patient enough to learn to understand wind and wave patterns can eventually learn to ride a sailboard. James said he's taught more than 1,000 people ages 12 to 60 to windsurf — and only one failed completely. Most beginners, he says, can get good enough to at least enjoy the challenges of the sport within two hours.

Even sailboarders who have been skimming the seas for 20 years say they still haven't mastered all the complexities windsurfing offers.

"The equipment you use is a board and a rig. The heart of the system is a 'universal' that swivels and pivots in every direction. That allows you to position the mast, boom and sail, and determine your direction," says James. "Basically, to sail crosswind, the mast is up and down. To sail downwind, tip the mast forward, and that turns the front of the board downwind. Mast back turns the board upwind."

Some sailboard instructors, such as the those at Kitty Hawk Sports on the sound in Nags Head, let their students start out on land, on specially made boards that let you feel how to balance and move before ever getting wet. Learning how to work with the wind is the toughest part. And you also need some arm strength to hold up the sail.

Sailboarders are strapped onto their masts in a sling-like contraption similar to those used in rappelling or rock climbing. You control the board with your feet, the sail with your hands. And you have to learn to upright yourself in case you fall — but even standing the sail up again is difficult when it fills with water.

If you're just starting out, don't sail too far from shore at first. If your rig breaks, or the wind dies down, you won't have as far to walk back with your board that way. One of the best ways to learn windsurfing maneuvers is to watch the good sailboarders who make this challenging sport seem so effortless.

Along the Outer Banks, several windsurfing competitions and speed trials are held each year. James runs the Hatteras Wave Classic in October and the Pro-Am each spring. Kitty Hawk Sports sponsors an Easter Dash for Cash, the August Watermelon Regatta and the Thanksgiving Classic Regatta (see our Annual Events chapter for related information).

Windsurfing Shops

Whether you're looking for a lesson, need a sail of a different size or want to ask for advice about sailboarding, more than a dozen shops from Corolla through Ocracoke stock windsurfing supplies, and many provide instructors in season.

Outer Banks Outdoors, at the Inn at Corolla Light, rents windsurfing rigs, 453-8602; at another location, 2 miles north of the Duck Fire Station, Outer Banks Outdoors offers windsurfing lessons and rentals, 261-2900. **North Beach Sailing**, in the Waterfront Shoppes on the west side of N.C. 12 in Duck, 261-6262, rents gear and provides instruction. The sailing site for that center is at Barrier Island, 261-7100 or toll-free from Corolla, 453-4414. **Waterworks Too**, near the Duck Landing Water Tower, also rents sailboards — and teaches beginners how to use them, 261-7245.

Kitty Hawk Sports has two locations in Nags Head, at MP 13 on the east side of U.S. 158, 441-6800; and at a soundside watersports site near Windmill Point Restaurant, MP 16, 441-5240 — where multiple levels of lessons are offered. **The Waterworks**, south of Soundings Factory Stores at MP 16½ in Nags Head, also has windsurfing lessons and rentals, 441-8875.

On Hatteras Island, Waves has one windsurfing shop, **Hatteras Island Surf Shop** on N.C. 12, 987-2296, where you can rent gear and take a lesson. **Hatteras Watersports** in Salvo offers sailboard rentals, 987-2306. The tiny village of Avon sports five windsurfing shops, all on N.C. 12: **Windsurfing Hatteras** sells, rents and gives instructions on windsurfing, 995-4970; **Avon Windsurf Company**, 995-5441, rents equipment; **Hatteras Island Wind Gear**, 995-4819; and **Kitty Hawk Sports**, 995-5000, offers rentals. Farther south, Buxton boasts **Fox Water Sports**, which offers windsurfing lessons, wetsuit rentals — and custom-made sailboards — also on N.C. 12, 995-4102 or 995-4372.

Ocracoke Island sailboarders can stop into **Ocracoke Outdoors** on Oyster Shell Lane, 928-4061.

Kayaking and Canoeing

The easiest, most adaptable and accessible watersports available on the Outer Banks — kayaking and canoeing — are activities anyone of any age or physical ability can enjoy. These lightweight paddlecrafts are extremely maneuverable, can glide almost anywhere along the seas or sounds, and afford adventurous activity — as well as silent solitude. They're also relatively inexpensive ways to tour uncharted waterways and see sights you'd miss if you stayed on shore.

Insiders' Tips

You can make a beautiful T-shirt by painting the scales of the fish with different colored permanent paints and pressing down a cotton shirt on top of it.

In the past five years, more than a dozen "eco-tour" outlets have opened on the barrier islands. Stores offer everything from rent-your-own kayaks for less than $40 a day to guided, day-long and even overnight tours around abandoned islands. With no fuel to foul the estuaries, no noise to frighten wildlife, and little skill needed to chart your own course, kayaks and canoes offer a sport as strenuous or relaxing as you want it to be — and an outdoor activity that will make a splash with the entire family.

Unlike the closed-cockpit kayaks used in whitewater river runs, most kayaks on the Outer Banks are a sit-on-top style that stretch from 7 to 10 feet long. They're molded in bright colored plastic, are light enough for even adolescents to carry to a launch site and come in one- and two-seat models. A double-blade paddle and a life jacket are the only other equipment you'll need, and these are included with all rentals and lessons.

Canoes are heavier and harder to get into the water — but slightly more stable than kayaks. They seat two or three people and include a more sheltered hull to haul gear or picnic lunches inside. Single-blade paddles — usually two per boat — are needed to maneuver these traditional watercraft.

Perhaps the best aspect of kayaking and canoeing is the versatility. You can perform these paddle sports in any weather, with or without wind, in calm or rough seas, shallow sounds and narrow creeks. You can creep around alone, just communing with nature. Or you can share the sights with a single friend in the same boat — or a group along for a guided ride.

Thrill-seekers can splash kayaks through frothy surf in the Atlantic, or paddle past the breakers and float alongside schools of dolphin. For more tranquil times, kayakers and canoeists can slip slowly through marshy creeks at the isolated Alligator River National Wildlife Refuge, explore narrow canals that bigger boats can't access, or slip alongside an uninhabited island in the middle of the shallow sound. There are historical tours around Roanoke Island, nature tours through maritime forests, and self-guided trails with markers winding through a former logging town called Buffalo City, on the Dare County mainland. Virtually anywhere there's 2 feet of water or more, you can take a kayak or canoe.

Learning to Paddle

Unlike other watersports, little to no instruction is needed to paddle a kayak or canoe. It helps to know how to swim — in case you capsize. But since most of the sounds are only 4 feet deep, you can walk your way back to shore if you stay in the estuaries — or, at least, jump back in your boat from a standing position.

Different strokes are required for each type of craft. Kayakers' double-blade paddles are designed to be used by one person. The blades are positioned at opposing angles, so you can work across your body with a sweeping motion and minimal rotation and still paddle on both sides of the boat. The trick is to get into a rhythm and not dig too deeply beneath the water's surface. Canoeing is done with one person paddling on each side of the boat — if there are two passengers — or a single operator alternating sides with paddle strokes.

Most kayak and canoe rental outfits also offer lessons. And even if you prefer to be on your own, rather than with a guided group trip, people renting these watercraft are happy to share advice and expertise with you. If you have any questions, or need directions around the intricate waterways, just ask.

Paddling Places

All of the sounds around the Outer Banks are ideal for kayaking and canoeing: shallow, warm and filled with flora

Canadians Flock to World-class Windsurfing

When winter winds begin whipping across the Pamlico Sound and forecasters predict big blows for the beach, thousands of Canadians head for "The Hole."

They come to Hatteras Island in custom-built vans. They fill roof racks with masts, boards and quivers of flamboyant Mylar sails. And they drive up to 24 hours to reach a shallow spot on the western shore of North Carolina's Outer Banks where windsurfers have been clocked cruising 42 miles per hour.

Like their country's geese that fly south each winter, Canadian sailboarders often arrive in flocks. Their annual migration begins in October and extends almost until Christmas. But Thanksgiving week is one of the busiest times for windsurfers who frequent this glassy stretch of sound known throughout the world as Canadian Hole.

International windsurfing magazines tout "The Hole" as one of North America's best sailboarding destinations. On blustery days, the 100-space parking lot just north of Buxton overflows and vehicles vie for spaces along the two-lane highway. On warm afternoons, the 50-yard-wide soundside beach resembles a scene from a West Coast surfer movie: Boomboxes, lounge chairs and festivities abound.

"The high-performance windsurfers all like the late fall down here best," said Michael Grundy, a windsurfer who manages a retail sailboarding shop in Avon. "The winds come from all sides. Some blows last for days. And the warm weather brings loads of people from the north."

A decade ago, anglers were among the only tourists who traveled to Hatteras Island during autumn months. But since the mid-1980s, droves of windsurfers have made the trip from Canada, California, Mexico and the Midwest. Many stop to sightsee along the way. But almost all are bound for the same place.

Located about a five-minute drive north of Cape Hatteras' spiral-striped lighthouse, Canadian Hole is a deep depression a few hundred yards offshore in the Pamlico Sound. The National Park Service constructed a parking lot nearby several years ago to accommodate the throngs of watersports enthusiasts coming to sail the silvery sound. Now, four mocha-colored porta-johns, a half-dozen metal trash cans and a shiny scarlet phone booth grace the blacktop.

"In the early 1960s, a storm cut an inlet across Hatteras Island just north of Buxton. Workers dredged sand from the sound to rebuild the roadway. And that created troughs — holes — just offshore in the Pamlico Sound," said longtime Buxton windsurfer Art Dervaes.

"In the early 1980s, locals began windsurfing in that area pretty regularly. But they all rode waves in the ocean," Dervaes said. "Then, Canadians started coming on holiday to sail the sound. They hung out near the hole — even before there was a parking lot there. I guess that's how it got its name. Now, everyone knows about it."

Most of the vehicles parked at Canadian Hole bear Canadian license plates. French conversation wafts from all quarters. Sailboarders squat on the sand, fixing masts and eating peanut butter to keep up their energy.

"We drove 18 hours straight through from Quebec to sail here," said Michel St.-Jean, who traveled to the barrier islands with 39 other French-speaking Canadian sailboarders. "At home, it's too cold to windsurf. Here, we had three weeks of sailing already. One more after this. We go out four or eight hours a day when it's good."

Dressed in shorts and a cotton T-shirt proclaiming "Life Begins at 40 Knots," St.-Jean said Canadian Hole was well worth his 10th annual trip.

Besides the smooth sound, which attracts beginners and speed-seeking slalom sailors, the ocean waves are only 70 yards away. Canadian Hole abuts the thinnest strip of sand on Hatteras Island.

"The sound is so wide and flat you can sail for miles without turning. Then, right on the other side of the road is the sea. You can really do wave stuff here as well as speed," St.-Jean said. "And it's wild. Natural. There are no signs or buildings to see when you're sailing. That's really what we like best about this place. It probably is the most popular spot for us from Canada who windsurf."

(As appeared in The Virginian-Pilot*)*

and fauna. There are marked trails at Alligator River National Wildlife Refuge; buoys around Wanchese, Manteo and Colington; and plenty of uncharted areas to explore around Pine Island, Pea Island, Kitty Hawk, Corolla and the Cape Hatteras National Seashore. Unlike other types of boats, you don't even need a special launching site to set a kayak or canoe in the water and take off.

On the northern Outer Banks, **Corolla Outback Adventures** offers guided kayak eco-tours and rents such watercraft from its location at the Winks Shopping Center on N.C. 12, 453-4484. **Kitty Hawk Sports** has a Corolla kayaking center, 453-4999, with rentals and in-season tours. **Outer Banks Outdoors**, a branch of Kitty Hawk Kites based at the Inn at Corolla Light, conducts nature tours and rents kayaks, 453-8602. **North Beach Sailing Center** in Duck also has kayak and canoe rentals and tours embarking from Barrier Island, 261-7100 or toll free from Corolla, 453-4414. **Waterworks Too** rents kayaks and canoes from Duck Landing, 261-SAIL. **Outer Banks Outdoors** also has a Duck site 2 miles north of the Duck Fire Station that rents kayaks and offers nature tours of Pine Island, 261-2900.

Kitty Hawk Kayaks has a storefront location in Kitty Hawk, at the MP ¼ of U.S. 158 on Jean Guite Creek, where kayaks are rented, kayak nature tours of Kitty Hawk Woods are offered, and beginning to advanced paddling lessons are available 261-0145. **Promenade Water Sports**, also in Kitty Hawk on U.S. 158, near the Wright Memorial Bridge, rents kayaks and canoes, 261-4900.

In Nags Head, would-be paddlers can rent kayaks at **Kitty Hawk Kites**, across from Jockey's Ridge State Park at MP 13 on U.S. 158, 441-4124; or next-door at

Kitty Hawk Sports, 441-6800. Kitty Hawk Sports also has a soundside launching site at MP 16, 441-2756. All three of those locations also offer a lessons and a variety of guided paddling tours around the area. **The Waterworks** rents kayaks and canoes from its MP 16½ location on U.S. 158, 441-8875 and from a waterfront site on the Nags Head-Manteo Causeway, 441-6822. Nearby, **Willett's Wetsports** at Caribbean Corners on the Nags Head-Manteo Causeway rents kayaks and canoes too, 441-4112.

Roanoke Island also has gotten into the kayaking scene recently. In Manteo, you can rent kayaks or take tours from Kitty Hawk Kites' **Outer Banks Outdoors** location on the waterfront, 473-2357. From there, you can paddle around Ice Plant Island, near the state ship *Elizabeth II*, or just tour the quaint, historic waterside community and see Dare County's seat from the shore.

Melvin Twiddy, in Manns Harbor on the mainland, conducts canoeing and kayaking wilderness adventure tours around Alligator River National Wildlife Refuge, through the former frontier town Buffalo City. Call 473-1960 to make a reservation, or for more information. **Kitty Hawk Sports** also conducts guided kayak tours of the refuge, 441-6800.

Hatteras Island Surf Shop rents kayaks from its N.C. 12 shop in Waves, 987-2296. **Kitty Hawk Kites**, 995-6060, and **Kitty Hawk Sports**, 995-5000, both offer kayaking tours and rentals in Avon. **Ocean Atlantic Rentals** in Avon rents single- and double-seat sit-on-top kayaks, 995-5868. **Avon Water Sports** also rents kayaks and has a convenient launch site for tours of Pea Island National Wildlife Refuge, 995-4970.

On Ocracoke Island, paddlers and those who want to learn can stop by **Ocracoke Adventures**, under the Creekside Cafe, where custom trips of the area are offered in the ocean or around Portsmouth Island. This shop also rents sit-on-top, self-bailing kayaks in single- and double-seat varieties, 928-7873. And **Ride the Wind Surf Shop**, N.C. 12, 928-6311, offers kayak rentals and three tours daily.

Scuba

Cloudier and cooler than waters off the Florida Keys and the Caribbean Islands, offshore areas along the Outer Banks offer unique scuba-diving experiences in "The Graveyard of the Atlantic." More than 500 **shipwrecks** — at least 200 named and identified — are strewn along the sand from Corolla through Ocracoke. Experienced divers enjoy the challenge of unpredictable currents and always seem to find something new to explore beneath the ocean's surface. From 17th-century schooners to World War II submarines, wreckage lies at a variety of depths, in almost every imaginable condition. After each storm, it seems, a new shipwreck is unearthed somewhere near the barrier island shores. Many of these wrecks haven't been seen since they sank beneath the sea.

Some underwater archaeological shipwreck sites are federally protected and can be visited — but not touched. Others offer incredible souvenirs for deep-water divers: bits of china plates and teacups, old medicine and liquor bottles, even brass-rimmed porthole covers and thick, hand-blown glass that's been buried beneath the ocean for more than a century. If you prefer to leave history as you find it, waterproof cameras are sure to bring back even more memorable treasures from the mostly unexplored underwater world.

Shark, whales, dolphin and hundreds of varieties of colorful fish also frequent deep waters around these barrier islands. There's even a coral reef off Avon — the northernmost one in the world. And submerged Civil War forts are scattered along the banks of Roanoke Island in much more shallow sounds.

While dive boat captains will carry

charter parties to places of their choosing, some shipwrecks have become popular with scuba divers and are among the most frequently selected sites. The freighter ***Metropolis***, also called the "Horsehead Wreck," lies about 3 miles south of the Currituck Beach Lighthouse off Corolla, 100 yards offshore, in about 15 feet of water. This ship was carrying 500 tons of iron rails and 200 tons of stones when it sank in 1878 — taking 85 crewmen with it to a watery grave. Formerly the Federal gunboat *Stars and Stripes* that worked in the Civil War, this is a good wreck to explore in the off-season. If you have a four-wheel-drive vehicle, you can drive up the beach and swim out to this shipwreck site.

Off Kill Devil Hills, an unidentified tug rests about 300 yards south of Avalon Pier, about 75 yards off the beach, in 20 feet of water. Two miles south, the **Triangle Wrecks** *Josephine*, *Kyzickes* and *Carl Gerhard* sit about 100 yards offshore, about 200 yards south of the Sea Ranch motel, in about 20 feet of water. These vessels sank in 1915, 1927 and 1929, respectively. They, too, can be reached by swimming from the beach.

Nags Head's most famous dive site is the ***USS Huron***, a Federal gun ship that sank in 1877, bringing 95 crew men to the bottom with it. This wreck is about 200 yards off the beach at MP 11. It rests in about 26 feet of water and includes many salvageable artifacts. The tug boat ***Explorer*** is nearby.

Long known as the East Coast's most treacherous inlet, Oregon Inlet between Nags Head and Hatteras Island has claimed hundreds of ships — and scores of lives — through the ages. The liberty ship ***Zane Grey*** lies about a mile south of this inlet in 80 feet of water. A German sub ***U-85*** sank northeast of the inlet in 100 feet of water in 1942. The ***Oriental*** has sat about 4 miles south of Oregon Inlet since sinking there in 1862; its boiler is visible above the surf. Most of these dive excursions can be accessed only from boats.

About a mile north of Rodanthe Fishing Pier, 100 yards offshore, the ***LST 471*** sits in about 15 feet of water. This ship sank in 1949 and is accessible by swimming out from shore. Nearby off Rodanthe, about 22 miles southeast of Oregon Inlet, the tanker ***Marore*** is about 12 miles offshore. It sank after being torpedoed in 1942 and lies in about 100 feet of water.

More experienced deep water divers enjoy the ***Empire Gem***, a British carrier which sank in January 1942 after being torpedoed by a German U-boat. This shipwreck sits about 17 miles off Cape Hatteras in 140 feet of water and was one of the first vessels to go down in World War II. It, too, must be reached by boat.

Learning to Dive

Unlike other water sports, scuba diving isn't something you can learn on your own. You have to be certified in order to do deep dives. This takes special training by certified instructors — and, sometimes, weeks of practice in a pool. Average recreational dives are 80 to 100 feet deep. Extreme divers reach depths of more than 300 feet. But there are dangers associated with such deep dives. Almost every diver has heard horror stories about people they've known who died during underwater cave dives, friends they've had who were attacked by sharks and days they've spent in hospital recompression chambers, waiting for their bodies to readjust after swimming over the ocean floor. Divers universally agree, however, that the thrill — and tranquility — of deep wreck diving are well worth the risks.

"It's exploring history, being along in another, undiscovered world and finding a haven below the sea's surface," said diver Ron Wallace who explored the *Empire Gem* wreck off Hatteras in summer 1995. "If you

Stop by Canadian Hole and watch the windsurfers in action.

walk in the forest, all the animals disappear. They run away from you. You can't really experience their world because once you've entered it, you've altered it. Under water, though, all the fish come right up to you. Those sea creatures aren't scared. It's the most wonderful experience in the world."

Four Outer Banks dive shops offer lessons, advanced instruction and all the equipment you'll need to get started. This is a relatively expensive sport. Divers say it takes at least $1,500 just to get the necessary tanks, hoses, wetsuits and other paraphernalia to take that first plunge. Dive boat charters, which all dive shop workers will help arrange, begin at about $550 per day — depending on how far offshore you want to go.

Some dive shops also can recommend shallow dive spots that you don't need a boat to get to as well as near shore or sound areas you can explore with just a face mask and snorkel. **Ocean Atlantic Rentals** in Corolla, 453-2440, and Avon, 995-5868, rents fins, masks and snorkels. **Ride the Wind Surf Shop**, on Ocracoke Island, N.C. 12, 928-6311, offers an afternoon snorkeling trip daily in season. And the **National Park Service** also offers sporadic snorkeling adventures along the Cape Hatteras National Seashore in the summer. Call 473-2111 for tour times and information.

If you're going scuba diving, you'll need to call ahead for a National Weather Service forecast, (800) 697-7374. You'll also need to know these important emergency numbers:

USCG Stations:

Oregon Inlet 995-6411, 987-2311, 441-1685
Hatteras Inlet 986-2175
Ocracoke Inlet 928-3711
Diver Alert Network (DAN) 684-8111
Ocean Rescue Squad (helicopter available) 911

Dive Shops

Nags Head Pro Dive Center

U.S. 158, MP 13 (In Kitty Hawk Connection)
Nags Head 441-7594

The oldest dive shop on the Outer Banks, Nags Head Pro Dive Center opened 17 years ago and is now on the bypass across from Jockey's Ridge State Park. This full-service facility offers everything you'll need to get started scuba diving — from PADI-certified lessons and advice to equipment sales and rentals. Diving experts can give airfills to 5,000 psi and charter boats for interested parties. Employees even run trips from their own 50-foot customized dive boat *The Sea Fox*, which takes scuba enthusiasts to historic wrecks all along the Outer Banks. Commercial diving also is done from this central site. Nags Head Pro Dive Center is open seven days a week from 9 AM to 9 PM from Memorial Day through Labor Day. Hours vary during the off-season.

Sea Scan Dive Centre

Beach Rd., MP 10
Nags Head *480-3467*

On the west side of the beach road, Sea Scan Dive Centre in Nags Head is a full-service NAUI Pro facility offering scuba equipment sales, rentals, repairs, tank refills and instruction. Employees also will give guided tours of Outer Banks wreck sites and charter private boat captains to carry divers to any underwater site they want to explore — whether near or offshore. Snorkeling lessons also are available — and much more easily accessible for vacationers who only have a few days to spend at the beach. Sea Scan is open year round. Hours are generally from 7 AM to 7 PM in season.

Hatteras Divers

N.C. 12
Hatteras Village *986-2557*

Just west of Hatteras Harbor Motel on the waterfront, Hatteras Divers is a specialized scuba shop. Employees here will plan charter trips to most Hatteras Island offshore sites, including the Tarpon, Abrams, Dixie Arrow, Proteus and Box-Car reefs and other popular destinations. They'll also rent you gear, fill your air tanks and arrange special excursions. Hours are 9 AM to 6 PM Monday through Saturday from June to October.

Ocracoke Divers Inc.

Oyster Creek Rd.
Ocracoke Village *928-1471*

Ocracoke Divers Inc. includes a full-service marina, air, gear, gas and equipment. Scuba specialists here can arrange guided shallow- and deep-water diving tours, and PADI-certified divers guide parties to century-old wrecks off the barrier island. Accommodations also can be provided. And advance reservations are required.

Sailing

With wide, shallow sounds and more than 90 miles of easily accessible oceanfront, the Outer Banks have been a haven for sailors since Sir Walter Raleigh's explorers first slid along these shores more than four centuries ago. Private sailboat owners have long enjoyed the barrier islands as a stopover en route along the Intracoastal Waterway. And many sailors have dropped anchor beside Roanoke or Hatteras Island — only to tie up at the docks permanently and make Dare County their year-round homes.

Until recently, however, you had to have your own sailboat to cruise the area waterways. Now, dozens of shops from Corolla through Ocracoke rent sailboats, Hobie Cats and catamarans to weekend water bugs. Others offer introductory and advanced sailing lessons. And some even take people who have no desire to learn to sail on excursions across the sound aboard multi-passenger sailing ships. Eco-tours, luncheon swim-and-sails and sunset cruises have become increasingly popular with vacationers who want to glide across the waterways — but not necessarily steer their own vessels. From 40-passenger catamarans captained by experienced sailors to pirate-like schooners carrying up to six passengers to single-person Sunfish sailboats, you can find almost any type of sailing vessel you desire on these barrier islands.

Unlike motorized craft, which pollute the water with gasoline and cause passengers to shout over the whirr of engines, sailing is a clean, environmentally friendly sport that people of all ages can enjoy. You can sail slowly by marshlands without disturbing the waterfowl or cruise at 15-mph clips in stiff southern breezes. It all depends on your whim — and the wind.

If you've never sailed before, don't rent a boat and try to wing it. Breezes around the Outer Banks are even more tricky than elsewhere, subject to blow up out of nowhere and shift direction without a moment's notice. And if you get caught in a gale, you could end up miles from land if you don't know how to maneuver the vessel. A two-hour introductory lesson is well worth it to learn basic sailing skills from knot tying to sail rigging to steering.

Sailors with even some on-water experience, however, can usually manage to navigate their way around the shallow sounds. All boats come with life jackets. But it's best to be comfortable swimming in case your sailboat capsizes.

Sailboat Cruises, Courses and Rentals

Prices for sailboat cruises depend on the amenities, length of voyage and time of day. Midday trips sometimes include boxed lunches or at least drinks for passengers. Some sunset tours offer parties wine, beer and appetizers. And almost all of the excursions let people bring their own food and drink aboard. Some even accept dogs on leashes aboard the decks. And special arrangements can be made for handicapped passengers. Prices generally range from $25 to $55 per person. Some captains will rent themselves out with the sailboats too — beginning at $50 per hour per vessel, and allowing the renter to fill the craft with its capacity of passengers.

Lesson costs, too, span a range — depending on how in-depth the course is, what type of craft you're learning on and whether you prefer group or individualized instruction. Costs can be from $10 to $50 per person. Call ahead for group rates if you've got more than four people in your party.

If you'd rather rent a craft and sail it yourself, dozens of Outer Banks outfitters lease sailboats by the hour, day or week. Deposits generally are required. Costs range from $20 to $50 per hour and $45 to $100 per day. Most shops accept major credit cards.

In Corolla, you can rent sailboats from **Outer Banks Outdoors** at the Inn at Corolla Light, 453-8602. Duck has become one of the Outer Banks' busiest sailing hubs — and is among the easiest places in the Albemarle area to learn to sail or take a calm cruise. **North Beach Sailing** rents 19-foot Flying Scots and 16-foot Hobie Cats (with or without captains), offers guided cruises, group and private lessons and rents a variety of other sailing vessels. At Barrier Island Inn, this popular sailing site can be contacted at 261-7100, or toll-free from Corolla, 453-4414. The retail store in Duck can be called at 261-6262. From its N.C. 12 location north of the Duck Fire Department, **Outer Banks Outdoors** offers sailing lessons, sailboat rentals and charter sailboat cruises, 261-2900. **Waterworks Too** also offers summer sailboat lessons and rentals from its Duck Landing Water Tower location, 261-7245.

Insiders' Tips

Carova Beach, between Corolla and the Virginia border, is the best place to bring dogs to run on the sand.

At MP ¼ on U.S. 158 in Kitty Hawk, **Promenade Water Sports** offers sailboat lessons and rentals. Call 261-4400 or 255-0272.

Nags Head has several sailing sites, with one of the largest at **Kitty Hawk Watersports Center** near Windmill Point Restaurant at MP 16 on U.S. 158. Here, lessons are offered at a variety of levels and sailboats can be leased by the hour or day, 441-2756. **The Waterworks** also offers sailing instruction and sailboat rentals from its Whalebone Junction site on U.S. 158, MP 16½, 441-8875.

On Hatteras Island, **Hatteras Watersports** on the soundside in Salvo offers sailing cruises, rentals and lessons. Two-hour trips aboard a Hobie Cat can accommodate up to three people and cost a total of $69 for the entire party. Sunfish and Hobie Cats rent for up to $29 an hour or $88 a day. Showers for sailors also are provided here, 987-2306. **Avon Watersports** employees give sailing lessons, offer cruises aboard catamarans and day sailers and rent Hobie Cats and Sunfish by the hour or day, 995-4970.

On Ocracoke Island, you can sail in Blackbeard's wake aboard a traditional gaff-rigged schooner called *The Windfall* that seats up to 30 passengers. One-hour cruises depart several times daily from **O'Neal's Dockside Store** and cost $10 per person, 928-7245.

Boating

From small skiffs to luxurious pleasure craft, there is dock space for almost every type of boat on the Outer Banks. Most marinas require advance reservations. And space is extremely limited on summer weekends. Call as soon as you make plans to visit the area. Prices vary greatly, depending on the dock location, amenities and type of vessel you're captaining.

If you're not lucky enough to own your own boat, you can still access the sounds, inlets and ocean around the Outer Banks by renting power boats from area outfitters. Most store owners don't require previous boating experience. If you leave a deposit and driver's license, they'll include a brief boating lesson in the rental price. Whether you're looking to lease a craft to catch this evening's fish dinner — or just want to take the kids on an afternoon cruise — you can find a vessel to suit your needs at a variety of marinas. Prices range from $12 an hour to more than $100 per day, depending on the type of boat. Some places require a two-hour or more minimum. Most accept major credit cards.

Marinas, Dock Space and Public Launch Ramps

Public docking facilities are available at the **Waterfront Marina** in Manteo, 473-3320; power and water are supplied at each slip, and rates are based on a per-foot basis. **Pirate's Cove Marina** on Roanoke Island can accommodate pleasure craft up to 65 feet long and includes power, showers and laundry facilities in the slip rental fees, 473-3906. Pirate's Cove personnel also transport boaters to area attractions on land. **Salty Dawg Marina**, also in Manteo, has 55 slips — all with power, water and an air-conditioned bathhouse, 473-3405. Also on Roanoke Island, **Thicket Lump Marina** in Wanchese rents dock space to pleasure and fishing vessels up to 45-feet long by the day, week or year, 473-4500.

On Hatteras Island, **Scotch Bonnet Marina** in Frisco includes a campground, boat slips, vessel sales, service and parts, 995-4242. In Hatteras Village, there's a variety of inlet-side marina options to choose from: **Hatteras Harbor Marina** can accommodate boats up to 57-feet long for the day, month or year, 986-2166. **Teach's Lair Marina** also has a deep draft for up to 65-foot craft docking for the day, week or year, 986-2460. **Willis Boat Land-**

ing accepts small craft up to 25-feet for short or long-term stays, 986-2208. And **Oden's Dock** has a deeper draft for up to 65-foot vessels by the day, week or year, 986-2555.

O'Neal's Dockside is on Silver Lake at Ocracoke Island and is open year round for sail or power boat docking, 928-1111. The **National Park Service** also operates public boat slips on Silver Lake in Ocracoke, 928-5111. From April through November, dockage here costs 50¢ per foot plus $3 a day for 110-volt electricity hookups or $5 a day for 220-volt connections. During the rest of the year, the cost is 25¢ per foot while the electric hookups stay the same price. There's a two-week limit on summer stays, and dock space is assigned on a first-come, first-served basis. In addition to the marinas, free anchorage is allowed year round in Silver Lake itself.

If you just need a place to put your boat in the water, you'll find free public launch ramps on the soundside end of **Wampum Drive** in Duck; on **Kitty Hawk Bay** in Kitty Hawk; at the end of **Soundside Road**, behind Jockey's Ridge State Park in Nags Head; below the **Washington Baum Bridge** between Nags Head and Manteo; near **Thicket Lump Lane** in Wanchese; at the oceanside end of **Lighthouse Road** in Buxton; and on the sound in **Ocracoke Village**.

Boat Rentals

For folks who don't own power boats but want to explore the vast waters of this region, **Waterworks Too** in Duck rents motor, pontoon and airboats from its site near the Duck Landing Water Tower, 261-7245. **North Duck Watersports** also rents boats, 261-4200.

Farther south, **The Waterworks** rents jet and pontoon boats from its Whalebone Junction site on the soundside of U.S. 158, 441-8875; and from the Nags Head-Manteo Causeway, 441-6822. **Nags Head Watersports**, on the north side of the same causeway, rents 17- to 32-foot fishing boats, aluminum and fiberglass pontoon boats and powerful jet boats, 480-2236. And **Willett's Wetsports** at Caribbean Corners on the causeway rents jet and paddle boats, 441-4112.

At Pirate's Cove Marina in Manteo, **Club Nautico** rents deluxe 20-foot boats powered by Evinrude engines, 473-5633.

Hatteras Jack in Rodanthe rents 14- and 16-foot power skiffs by the hour or day for boating along the shallow sounds. A short instruction course is included in the rental price, 987-2428. **Avon Watersports** also rents motorboats, 995-4970. In Frisco, **Scotch Bonnet Marina** rents and services boats, 995-4242.

And on Ocracoke Island, **Island Rentals** rents 16-foot fiberglass flat-bottom boats (with 25-hp motors) that hold four adults for $55 a half-day, $80 a day or $350 a week, not including fuel, 928-5480.

Personal Watercraft

If you feel a need for speed — and enjoy the idea of riding a motorcycle across the water — more than a dozen Outer Banks outposts rent personal watercraft by the hour. No experience is necessary to navigate these powerful boat-like devices. Even first-time drivers can do donuts, leap waves and reach cruising levels of more than 40 mph after only a few minutes of practice. And unlike landlocked go-carts and other speedy road rides, there aren't any lanes to stick to on the open sound or ocean.

Several styles of personal watercraft have developed over the past decade. Wave Runners allow drivers to maneuver these crafts sitting down and a second passenger to hold on, also sitting, from behind. Jet Skis don't have seats and can accommodate only one person at a time in a standing or kneeling position. Newer

Runabouts, also known as blasters, give riders the choice of standing or sitting. Wave Runners are the easiest style craft to balance and control because you don't have to worry as much about tipping over. But Jet Skis are more prone to tricks — and spills — and better able to leap ocean waves. Almost all of these motorized vessels can cruise for up to two hours on five gallons of fuel.

Personal watercraft are akin to motorboats with inboard motors that power a water pump. There aren't any propellers or outside engine parts. So fingers and toes generally stay safe. Like other motorized boats, however, personal watercraft are loud — and can be dangerous if you don't know what you're doing. Most rental outposts include brief instructions and sometimes even a video on how to handle Wave Runners, Jet Skis and Runabouts.

Practicing on Personal Watercraft

Basic operations of a personal watercraft include an ignition and stall button on the left handle; the throttle on the right. Push the start button on the left to take off. Your right hand can control the speed by turning the throttle forward or back. If you fall off, a wrist lanyard that wraps around your hand automatically snaps away from the handle and shuts off the engine. To get aboard again, climb on from the back. Always steer to the right when approaching another personal watercraft — just like you would on the road.

A quick, easy trick on Jet Skis — and Wave Runners, if you're game — is to throw the throttle open then turn hard. It's like doing a 360-degree donut on the water. As the back of the personal watercraft comes around, the front submerges. Gun the throttle again and you can fly out over your own wake.

While most rental shops are on the sound side of the Outer Banks, where the water's surface is generally slicker and depths are much more shallow, a few personal watercraft outlets will let you take the vessels into the ocean. There, shore break and offshore waves provide great takeoffs and challenges to more experienced Jet Ski drivers. But watch out for surfers, swimmers and other Jet Ski drivers who might not see you coming.

Renting Personal Watercraft

Jet Skis and Wave Runners sell for $5,000 to $10,000 new. Several Outer Banks rental shops also sell used personal watercraft for cheaper prices at the end of the summer season. Remember, you'll probably need a trailer to haul these vessels behind your vehicle.

If you're just here on vacation — or don't think you'd ride one enough for the price to pay off — shops from Corolla through Hatteras Island rent personal watercraft beginning at $30 a half-hour. Some more powerful models cost more, of course. And additional charges sometimes apply for extra riders on the Wave Runners. Personal watercraft also can be rented by the hour, day or even week at some spots.

In Corolla, **Kitty Hawk Water Sports** rents personal watercraft from its TimBuck II Shopping Village location, 453-6900 or (800) 654-0781. **Corolla Outback Adventures** rents Wave Runners from its store at the Winks Shopping Cen-

Insiders' Tips

Corolla Surf Shop also has a museum of antique surfboards, photos and memorabilia dating to the 1930s.

ter, 453-4484. And **Outer Banks Outdoors** rents several styles of personal watercraft from its docks at the Inn at Corolla Light, 453-8602.

North Beach Sailing Center at Barrier Island in Duck rents Wave Runners, 261-7100. **North Duck Watersports**, on N.C. 12 just north of Duck, rents Jet Skis, 261-4200. **Waterworks Too** has Sea-Doos — like Wave Runners but more powerful and able to accommodate one adult and up to two children — and several other sorts of personal watercraft to rent at its Duck Landing Water Tower location, 261-7245.

In Kitty Hawk, **Promenade Watersports** rents Wave Runners at its MP ¼ location near the Outer Banks base of the Wright Memorial Bridge, 261-4400.

Nags Head has several personal watercraft outposts: **The Waterworks**, on the west side of U.S. 158 at MP 16½, 441-8875 and at the Nags Head-Manteo Causeway, 441-6822. **Soundside Watersports** is also at MP 16 on the west side of U.S. 158, 441-4270. **Willett's Wetsports**, on the south side of the Nags Head-Manteo Causeway at Caribbean Corners, rents Jet Skis, Sea Doos and Wave Runners, 441-4112. Also on the causeway, **Nags Head Water Sports** offers early-bird discounts on Wave Runners from 9 to 11 AM and can be reached at 480-2236. **Kitty Hawk Water Sports Center** is on the west side of U.S. 158 at MP 16 near Windmill Point Restaurant, 441-2756.

Sea Breeze Wave Runners rents all sorts of personal watercraft from its Wanchese shop on Hooker Road, 473-5566.

On Hatteras Island, **Rodanthe Watersports** is on N.C. 12, 987-1431. **Hatteras Water Sports** is nearby in Salvo, renting personal watercraft that seat from one to three people, 987-2306. **Avon Watersports** rents Jet Skis and Wave Runners, 995-4970. In Buxton, you can rent personal watercraft at **Fox Watersports**, 995-4102.

Many shops require that personal watercraft operators be age 14 or older. Younger children, however, can ride on two- and three-seat models behind their parents or other responsible adults.

Inside Fishing

The diversity of fish available in the waters surrounding the Outer Banks makes this area a hot spot for anglers from far and wide. Charter boats leave the docks year round for offshore waters teeming with big game fish. The inlets, sounds, rivers and lakes abound with saltwater and freshwater species, and surf-casters and pier anglers have plenty of opportunity to catch a variety of species from the surf. Whether you're a novice or pro angling with heavy or light tackle for food or sport, the Outer Banks is a world-class fishing center.

Most anglers don't need too much coaxing to go fishing. Since you may be new to our area, however, we'll explain why you *must* wet a line in our waters. First, many record-breaking fish have been caught here — both offshore and inshore — including the International Game Fishing Association's all-tackle record for blue marlin (1,142 pounds) in 1974, and the all-tackle world-record bluefish (31 pounds, 12 ounces), caught off Hatteras in 1972. And then there was that world-record red drum caught off Avon, a record-breaking Spanish mackerel caught in Ocracoke Inlet, a lemon shark caught off Buxton and a scalloped hammerhead shark landed off Cape Point. Let's not leave out an oyster toadfish and a myriad of saltwater fly-rod and saltwater-line class world-record catches.

So, you say, "Well, they have water so they have fish." Ah, but it's much more than fish. Physical conditions exist here that you won't find anywhere else. And that ain't no fish story!

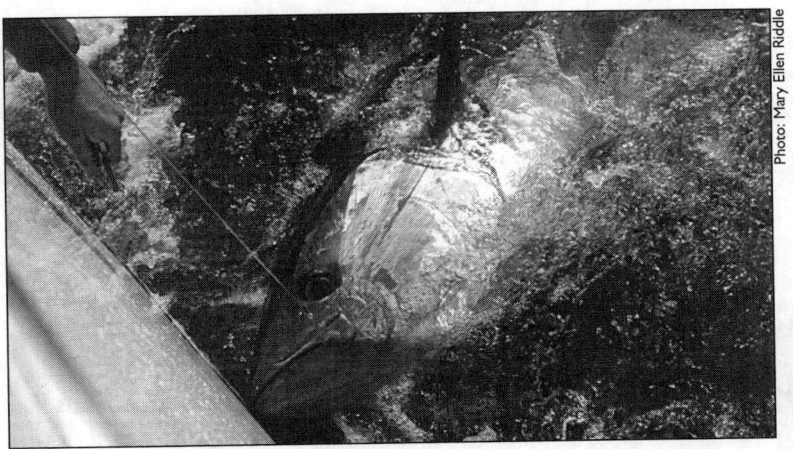

Photo: Mary Ellen Riddle

The wrecks off Hatteras Island draw anglers from the world over every winter to partake in some of the hottest bluefin tuna fishing found anywhere.

The Outer Banks has an experienced charter fleet that takes locals and visitors fishing in inshore and offshore waters every day that the weather permits. When you call to book a boat (see our Marinas listings in this chapter), you may find it hard to know what kind of trip to choose unless you've fished before. While anyone who's dropped a line in the water knows you can't predict catching fish, the experienced charter boat captains know what species should be in the area and will help you make choices the morning of the trip.

In the next sections, we describe offshore and inshore angling. Offshore trips generally leave the docks at 5:30 AM, and inshore trips are half-day excursions that leave twice daily. Intermediate trips can last all day but generally don't travel as far as the Gulf Stream. We feel certain you'll have a pleasant adventure no matter how far out you venture.

Offshore Fishing

Offshore from the Outer Banks is an area called The Point that's rich in tuna, dolphin, wahoo, billfish and shark. This spot has unique characteristics that give it a reputation for attracting and harboring a variety and quantity of fish. Three currents, including the warm Gulf Stream (see our Natural Wonders chapter), move across this spot 37 miles southeast of Oregon Inlet, carving intricate patterns of canyons and crevices on the ocean floor. This ancient topography provides a nutrient-rich environment for fish. Ocean currents flow over the floor and circulate, or well up, as they hit the canyons and crevices. A lot of nutrients on and around the formations attract baitfish. Also because of this upwelling, baitfish are moved around and concentrated in the area, and that's really attractive to big game fish.

What also helps set this spot apart is it's proximity to the edge of the Continental Shelf. Where there's a drop-off, you'll find a concentration of baitfish because of the nutrient-rich waters present and currents playing off the edge to stir things up. Anglers don't have to travel far to get to The Point since the Shelf is particularly narrow off Cape Hatteras. And The Point is the last spot where the Gulf Stream appears near the Shelf before it veers off in an east-northeasterly direction. Weather permitting, there are some days when the Gulf Stream entirely covers The Point. Other days, prevailing winds can push it farther offshore.

At about 50 miles wide and a half-mile deep, the Gulf Stream has temperatures that rarely drop below 65 to 70 degrees, providing a comfortable habitat for a variety of sea life. The Gulf Steam flows at an average rate of 2.5 mph, at times quickening to 5 mph. This steadfast flow carries away millions of tons of water per second, continually pushing along sea life in its path, including fish, microscopic plants and animals (a.k.a. plankton) and gulfweed. Gulfweed lines the edge of the Gulf Stream when the winds are favorable, creating a habitat for baitfish. You can easily pull up a handful of vegetation and find it teeming with minute shrimp and fish. Anglers fish these "grass lines" as well as the warm-water eddies that spin off from the Gulf Stream. These warm pockets, which vary in size from 20 to 100 miles

Insiders' Tips

Frantic bird activity, such as gulls dipping and diving on the water, is a sure sign fish are feeding underneath. The birds are eating the "scraps" leftover by the feeding fish. Cast your bait or lure near the diving birds.

long by a half-mile to a mile wide, are sometimes filled with schools of dolphin (mahi mahi), tuna and mako.

Blue marlin, wahoo and dolphin show up at the Point in April and May. Yellowfin, big-eye and blackfin tuna are the anglers' mainstay year round. A significant population of yellowfin inhabit this area in the winter, providing a tremendous seasonal fishery.

While most anglers are holed up in winter cleaning their rods and reels, with windows shut tight to seal out the cold, visitors to the Outer Banks can cast a line into the Gulf Stream — on some days wearing just short sleeves. You have to be patient to fish in winter, because plenty of bad weather days make traveling offshore a waiting game. But, if you hold out, you can fight a deep-diving tuna.

Deep-swimming reef fish, such as grouper, snapper and tilefish, also inhabit The Point. Because of the strong current, however, you must travel a little bit south of The Point to fish for them effectively.

Fishing Report

For the latest word on what's biting, check with the following sources:

WOBR (95.3 FM):	*473-5665*
Red Drum Tackle Shop	*995-5414*
Oregon Inlet Fishing Center	*441-6301*
Kitty Hawk Fishing Pier	*261-2772*
Nags Head Fishing Pier	*441-5141*
Hatteras Island Fishing Pier	*987-2323*
Frisco Pier	*986-2533*
O'Neal's Dockside	*928-1111*

Also read *The Virginian-Pilot's* daily "North Carolina" section and *The Carolina Coast* for Damon Tatem's report. Check out Joe Malat's informative column and fishing reports in the new *Outer Banks Sentinel*. And look for Ed Wilkerson's fishing and hunting column in the *Sportfishing Report* magazine and *The Coastland Times* newspaper.

Catch-and-release

Catch-and-release fishing for bluefin tuna has anglers from across the globe traveling to Hatteras to partake in a bonanza that has really revived winter offshore charter fishing along the Outer Banks. For three years, captains have been noticing a massive congregation of bluefin tuna inhabiting the wrecks about 20 miles from Hatteras Inlet (see our sidebar in this chapter). We've seen the action firsthand, and the quantity of bluefin that inhabit the Gulf Stream and the frequency with which they bite are phenomenal.

Fish weighing from 200 to more than 700 pounds have been caught. These giants, which U.S. biologists allege comprise an overstressed fishery in most parts of the world, are a federally protected species, so anglers release them. (Just reeling in a bluefin of any magnitude will make the blood of an avid angler run hot!) The bluefin seem to strike with less provocation on the choppy days — plus there aren't tons of boats flooding the area during rougher weather. On days when the fish are spooked by excessive boat traffic or simply aren't bit-

Insiders' Tips

When surf fishing, never lay your rod and reel down in the sand. Sand grains will damage the reel. Experienced surf casters use "sand spikes," pieces of plastic pipe pushed firmly down in the sand, to hold their rods and reels.

Giant Tuna Gather in Gulf Stream

As soon as the herring head hit the sea's surface, the gray-green water beside our boat began to boil.

Around, beneath, on all sides of *The Bullfrog*, giant bluefin tuna lunged from the Atlantic, biting at the bait. Fish as heavy and as long as the burliest Dallas Cowboys lineman surrounded the stern, splashing their powerful tails. A 300-pound tuna grabbed the line less than five seconds after John McGee tossed his first baited line overboard.

The angler was in for a fight.

"Yeeeooowiiieee!" McGee shouted, jamming the graphite rod into his gut. "This girl's a-goin'."

"Stop yakkin'. Start crankin,'" Capt. Bob Eakes bellowed from behind the fisherman's left elbow. "Crank. Crank. Hold her. Don't let that baby get the best of you. Crank. Crank. Crank. Crank. Crank!"

Strapped into a wide, wooden chair bolted to "The Bullfrog's" fiberglass deck, McGee stood up in his seat several times during his struggle to bring in the big bluefin. The fish fought ferociously, darting from one side of the boat to the other. Diving and leaping and — most of all — running from the 35-foot vessel, the tuna took a football field's length of line before it finally began tiring.

McGee's biceps ached by the time the bluefin bounced alongside the boat about 10 minutes after the fight started. In the January sunshine, he stripped off his sweat-soaked jacket and tried to hold his line steady. Suddenly, the fish's round head broke through the ocean's surface — an enormous, unblinking wolflike eye opened wide.

Then Eakes — in a fluid fury — grabbed the monofilament leader in his gloved left hand, swung a home-made tagging stick with his right, and jabbed a slender orange identification tag into the tuna's tough shoulder. The captain dropped the stick, picked up a small gaff and hooked the barb of the circle hook hanging from the corner of the fish's mouth. He yanked the metal hook backward until its eyelet popped through the bluefin's thick skin. Pulling the tuna by the leader, Eakes towed it about 30 feet behind the boat. Then he cut the line.

The giant fish was free.

It was never handled by human hands. It never even left the water. Five minutes after the fisherman had reeled it in, the captain had tagged, unhooked and released the powerful bluefin — which dove deep and swam away.

Anglers from across the country caught and let go more than 250 trophy-size tuna in January off Hatteras Island. Thousands of bluefin weighing between 150 and 600 pounds have been schooling in the Gulf Stream off the southern Outer Banks during cold months. No one knows why they're wintering here. They didn't start showing up until two years ago. But anglers, charter boat captains, Hatteras Island hotel and restaurant owners — even biologists — are ecstatic that the bluefin are around.

"There've been a few fish around here before. But never like this," Charter boat Capt. Walt Spruill said from his Hatteras Island home. "I took out four parties that first winter, in '94. Last year, I got 15 days on the ocean. I went out 12 days during the first part of January.

"Tagged 83 big bluefin in that time. Not all were giants. Lots of fish in the 150 to 250-pound range. They're all awesome. It's the experience of a lifetime.

"Makes me want to go out there and just spank those bad boys."

One of the largest fish in the world, bluefin tuna live throughout the Atlantic. They can grow up to 10 feet long and weigh as much as 1,500 pounds. Traditionally, they've swam along the northeastern coast in the summers, but there's been no winter fishery. New York and New Jersey have had charter boat fleets for the fish since the 1950s.

But for the past few winters, masses of bluefin have congregated between Hatteras and Ocracoke inlets off North Carolina's barrier islands. They seem to enjoy the warm Gulf Stream waters 16 to 22 miles offshore. The fish prefer temperatures of 65 to 85 degrees and swim in depths up to 150 feet. Lately, they've seemed excited about the free food thrown by saltwater anglers who chum for bluefin by tossing boxes of bait overboard each day. One captain in mid-January called over the marine radio that the tremendous tuna were so thick around his boat that he couldn't see the water.

Bluefin around *The Bullfrog* were so hungry they leapt at a chicken bone Eakes tossed into the ocean; a plastic popper strung across a spinning reel; even a paper towel that blew overboard.

"The fish populations — and angling interests — in bluefins have been exploding in the last three or so winters. And it seems to be growing tenfold every year," National Marine Fisheries Service biologist Chuck Manooch said. "There were a remarkable number of hook-ups off Hatteras just in January. Boats are coming from all over the coast to catch and release these big fish. Bluefin hook up real quickly. That makes them ideal for tagging. And we need to get all the information we can about this species."

About 50 recreational boats fished off the Outer Banks in the winter of 1996, coming from as far as New York and South Carolina. For the first winter anyone can remember, the usually sleepy docks at Hatteras Village overflowed with charter vessels. Hotels and restaurants that never opened in January filled with flush-faced anglers. Fishing enthusiasts from Colorado to Florida to Oregon and even Germany booked charter trips. Full-day Gulf Stream excursions cost between $800 and $1,000 for six people.

The giant fish don't taste very good, most seafood lovers say. But they're apparently good raw. Japanese sushi chefs covet the bluefins - which sell for $30,000 to $60,000 each in Tokyo. But the United States has tight restrictions on keeping the fish. Recreational anglers can keep two bluefin per person per day up to 5 feet long; one per boat per day up to 73 inches long; and one per boat per year bigger than that. But they can't sell those tuna.

Commercial restrictions are even tougher.

But the fun of fishing for giant bluefin tuna, sportsmen say, is in the strike, the fight and the satisfaction of releasing the fish alive.

"Fishing isn't always about catching and keeping. It's a lot more exciting and challenging to let 'em go alive than it is to reel 'em in dead," McGee said after releasing his ninth tuna. "I've never had a bad feeling about setting a fish free — whether it weighed a half-pound or 100 pounds more than me."

Scientists aren't sure how many bluefin tuna die after being fought, tagged and released. But they're glad to have tagging information. They're happy anglers aren't killing the fish.

And they all agree that Eakes' innovative methods of using circle hooks and, especially, removing the hooks, greatly increase the fish's chance for survival. On one January trip this year, Eakes tagged and released 27 big bluefin weighing between 150 and 300 pounds. He got the hook out of every fish. As four witnesses watched, each tuna swam away from the boat with a strong splash. Eakes has invented a dual-applicator tagging pole that has greatly improved the chance of tagging the proper area of the tuna.

In 1995, anglers bagged hundreds of bluefin, including at least 13 that had been previously tagged, primarily off the Outer Banks. Spruill caught a 160-pound fish in Jan. 1996 and recovered its tag. The tuna had been previously released off Long Island Aug. 7, 1991.

Eakes alone tagged and released 335 big bluefin tuna in 1995 — more than the total that all other East Coast anglers tagged that year. In January 1996, the International Game Fish Association named him "Captain of the Year for Bluefin." It's no wonder Eakes, who lives in Frisco on Hatteras Island and runs Red Drum Tackle Shop in Buxton, has been asked to speak at sports-fishing conferences from Virginia Beach to Raleigh and has been quoted in international angling magazines about his innovative ideas.

"I've been thinking about it all summer, trying different styles of tagging sticks, hooks and de-hookers," said Eakes, whose curly, snow-white hair falls in bangs just above his Carolina blue eyes. "The quicker you can bring in the fish and the less you have to handle it, the better off the bluefin is. This is the best, biggest catch and release tuna tagging I know of anywhere in the world. And it's right here in Hatteras.

"This is about as good as it gets."

(As appeared in The Virginian-Pilot)

ing for whatever reason, mates will sprinkle the water with chum (cut up fish parts, guts and blood that smells strong and draws fish) to increase the chance of a strike. These giants often jump 4 feet out of the ocean just to bite a bloody bait.

Local anglers troll, chum and use live or dead bait. We've seen great success with 130-pound test line. Some folks like to use lighter tackle for the sport of it, but the heavier the line, the better the condition of the fish when it's released. Circle hooks are also recommended for the fish's comfort — they tend to lodge in the mouth cartilage rather than in the fleshy gullet or gills.

Even though most of the fish are

Headboat fishing can yield a variety of fish and is an enjoyable pastime for both the novice and experienced angler.

caught on heavy tackle, carefully handled and subsequently released, recreational charter boat captains are contemplating a self-imposed quota for catch and release to try to protect the fish even further. When there are large groups of boats present day after day it's likely the same fish will have to do battle over and over.

Fishing parties enjoy feeding the fish and catching them on hook-less lines just to watch the strike. It's like being at a huge aquarium.

You can enjoy most offshore fishing year-round, but with the bluefin fishing off Hatteras, you should book a trip from January through March. Some fish may show up earlier, but your best bet is to stick to these months. You can book charters by calling any of the Outer Banks marinas listed in this chapter. To avoid the crowds, book a weekday trip. Some captains believe excessive fishing and boating activity makes the fish less likely to bite.

Expect to pay from $700 to $900 for six people to charter a boat. (If you have trouble with seasickness, read our sidebar for some tips on easing your discomfort.)

Offshore Headboat Fishing

Headboat fishing can give you an offshore experience without paying the price to charter a boat (see our Inshore Fishing section on headboat fishing). The cutoff age for children's prices varies from boat to boat so inquire ahead. Several large boats take parties — charging "by the head" — offshore all day.

While you won't be targeting tuna here, you still have the chance for plentiful catches of a variety of bottom species — fine-tasting fish in their own right — including black seabass, triggerfish, grey tilefish, amberjack, tautaug, grouper and snapper. The species vary slightly from north to south. Occasionally small shark are hooked over the wrecks and once in a while you'll run into some bigger game fish. But you're generally dropping a line over the side into the reefs or wrecks, not trolling.

The boats are open from the stern to the bow to hold anglers comfortably, and all the gear is supplied. All you have to bring is a cooler with food and drink, sunscreen and a jacket in case the weather changes. Of course, if you're venturing out in winter months, dress in layers. If you're near enough the Gulf Stream and the wind is blowing over it in your direction then you may be able to layer down to a T-shirt. Most of the headboats that go offshore have heat in the salon or an area that can be shut off from the cold air.

Many parents want their children to experience an offshore trip, and that's understandable. You not only fish but often get to see whales, turtles and dolphin. Our advice: Think carefully before you take a real little tyke offshore. The day is long, and the captain doesn't turn around except in an emergency, and that does not include sea sickness. The boat's deck can be slippery, and the water can be choppy. Life vests are available. Captains have their own rules, but generally they discourage bringing youngsters offshore unless they've had some experience. If you have a teen

who wants to go, that's another story. But don't despair. The beauty of our area is the choices it offers anglers of all ages.

The *Country Girl* takes 27 people for an offshore bottom-fishing trip over the wrecks for only $65 per person (see our Marinas section).

Inshore Headboat Fishing

Inshore opportunities abound that will strike the fancy of the novice or expert angler. The offshore gangs don't corner the market on fun here. Inshore generally refers to inlet, sound, lake, river and some close-range ocean fishing on a boat. Several Outer Banks headboats ply the sounds and inlets and occasionally go to the wrecks on calm days.

These excursions provide the perfect chance for your youngster to hold a rod, bait a hook, reel in a fish (we hope) and learn respect for wildlife. The inshore headboats are generally between 60 and 75 feet long and accommodate about 50 people. As with all offshore trips, tackle and bait are provided. We suggest you bring your own food; some headboats sell sodas and snacks, and one Hatteras boat, *Miss Hatteras*, has a full snack bar.

Inshore headboat captains are very accommodating to families, and the mates will give you as much or as little help as you need. They'll tell you if your fish is a "keeper" or needs to be thrown back. If you're squeamish about baiting a hook or handling a fish, a mate will assist you. They seem to have a sense of when to back off and when to lend a helping hand. Half-day bottom fishing trips generally run $20 for kids and $25 for adults.

Expect to catch croaker, trout, spot, flounder, sea mullet, blowtoads and pigfish; these pan-size fish are very tasty. The crew usually can identify your fish if you cannot.

Some of these headboats-by-day offer nonfishing pleasure cruises in the evenings. Many captains enjoy talking with passengers about the area's history. Local boats like the *Miss Oregon Inlet*, *Miss Hatteras*, *Virginia Dare*, *Osprey* and *Crystal Dawn* offer nonfishing excursions. Prices vary but the average is $4 for children and $8 for adults.

A quick tip about kids on boats: Watch them carefully and enforce a no-running code. These boats typically carry a large crowd, and not everyone will have their hooks or rod tips in the right place at the right time.

Remain positive when fishing with kids. Everywhere in the world, there are days when the fish don't bite. If you're having one of those days, let the trip be a lesson in nature, patience and people — and let your imagination roam.

One final word of caution to anglers of any age: Winds can blow a bare hook wayward, so always fasten it to one of the rod's line guides when it's not in the water — or doesn't have a fish on it!

Marinas

The Outer Banks has more than a half-dozen marinas that can help you book a charter for inshore, offshore or headboat fishing. You can call any of these marinas and request a particular captain or boat. If you are new in town, you'll be glad to know that the marinas book reputable captains on a rotating basis.

Insiders' Tips

Dolphin are a type of fish, no kin to the porpoise. They're also known as mahi-mahi.

Challenged Folk Fish Too

Folks dealing with physical challenges can now realize the dream of fighting a big game fish thanks to Capt. Bob Sumners on the *For Play'n*. Sumners, who lost part of his leg in a motorcycle accident, is especially sensitive to the needs of folks with disabilities. He came up with the idea for a spring-loaded gimbal that reverses the usual fishing procedure. This way, a person without legs or the upper-body strength to pull the rod up can push down instead because of the "Geezer Gadget." Sumners and son Scott made a model of the gadget and turned it over to an engineer to perfect.

We know this ingenious idea works because we've seen it in action. More importantly, we've seen the smiles it brings to folks when they catch a big fish. The fish benefit from the "Geezer Gadget" also (it brings in the fish fairly quickly). And some challenged folks now have a marlin or a tuna under their belts because of Capt. Bob Sumners.

Call (800) 633-8998 to outfit your boat with the "Geezer Gadget." Several local charter boats already are equipped with this handy item. And call 261-1320 to reach Sumners and arrange a trip on *For Play'n*.

If you want to insure that you get to go fishing, especially during the busy holiday periods, it's wise to call at least a month in advance to make sure you get on board. The marinas stay open year round, so you can call well in advance of your trip if you know when you'll be vacationing here. Don't be afraid to ask questions — the marina personnel are very helpful — but if you wish to have a lengthy conversation, reservationists have more time to chat in the off-season.

Make-up parties are available for folks who want to hook up with a group to make six. If everything is booked up, ask to be put on a waiting list. The list below represents some of the choices in marinas on the Outer Banks. We list more in our weigh station listing at the end of the chapter.

Hatteras Harbor Marina

N.C. 12 — *986-2166*
Hatteras Village — *(800) 676-4939*

Charter an offshore or inshore excursion here year round. More than 20 vessels depart regularly from this marina. All tackle and bait are supplied, and experienced mates on board will show you the ropes. You don't have to be an expert angler to try tangling with a blue marlin or tuna or live baiting for king mackerel. The marina store carries fishing supplies and gifts. Call for reservations.

Ocracoke Fishing Center

Silver Lake — *928-6661*

Owned by the Anchorage Inn, this fishing center includes five 200-foot piers and a new building where customers can book charter boat trips to the sound, Gulf Stream and inshore areas. Water is at least 6 feet deep along the piers. Docking costs 85¢ per foot per day and includes a pool, telephones and other services. Gas and diesel fuel are available on site. And the boat ramp is free for motel and marina guests. Marine supplies and a small tackle shop are nearby.

Oden's Dock

N.C. 12, Hatteras Village — *986-2555*

This family-owned and operated dock is one of oldest businesses in Hatteras Village. This used to be where Capt. Ernal

Foster would pull up a chair and chat with visitors (see our sidebar on Foster in this chapter). Oden's has a full line of supplies and a repair shop. Also Texaco marine products are available here. For information on getting aboard the *Miss Hatteras* at Oden's, call Capt. Spurgeon Stowe, 986-2365. This state-of-the-art 72-foot-long vessel is equipped with a snack bar, comfortable booths to sit in and an air-conditioned salon. The *Miss Hatteras* offers offshore and inshore bottom fishing excursions, a seafood cruise that's out of this world, bird-watching trips, a history cruise and evening cruises. Capt. Spurgeon is one of the most personable chaps you're going to come across down Hatteras way.

O'Neal's Dockside

Behind the Community Store
Ocracoke *928-1111*

You can charter an offshore or inshore trip here and maybe get to meet Ronnie O'Neal, who runs the *Miss Kathleen*. O'Neal is a native Ocracoker who will treat you like family. His wife, Kathleen — of course — runs an art and original jewelry shop on the island (see our Shopping chapter). The folks at O'Neal's will also help you charter a trip to Portsmouth Island. You can purchase supplies, boating gear and fuel here.

Oregon Inlet Fishing Center

N.C. 12, just north of the
Herbert C. Bonner Bridge *441-6301*

More than 30 well-equipped boats comprise the Oregon Inlet charter fishing fleet. Most captains leave before sunrise and return by 6 PM. Fish cleaners will fillet your day's catch on the docks. A full day of offshore fishing, which includes a two-hour trip to the Gulf Stream, costs $850 per boat; $825 with cash discount. Most boats carry parties of six anglers. Captains supply rods, reels, tackle, bait, ice, coolers and advice. Charter parties can bring their own food and drinks, or box lunches may be ordered 48 hours in advance. Mates working for the charter fleet usually depend heavily on tips for their wages. There are daily limits per person on tuna and dolphin. Most captains require anglers to release marlin and sailfish alive.

Inshore fishing costs $540 for a full day, or $525 with cash discount. Half-day inshore trips are $312; $300 if paid in cash. To make reservations, call the booking desk or contact the charter captains directly. Visa and MasterCard are accepted. Make reservations early. This marina is one of the most popular on the Outer Banks. If you don't have six anglers in your party, marina officials may be able to help you find a "make-up" party — or you can try a headboat for a cheaper day of fishing.

The *Miss Oregon Inlet* is a 65-foot headboat docked at Oregon Inlet that offers half-day fishing for $26 per person, $16 for children younger than 4. Anglers aboard this wide, inshore fishing vessel catch spot, croaker, gray trout, bluefish, mullet and other seasonal species. Bait and tackle are included in the price. In early spring and late fall, the boat makes one trip per day, leaving at 8 AM and returning at 12:30 PM. From Memorial Day through Labor Day there are two trips — 7 to 11:30 AM and noon to 4:30 PM. A non-fishing Twilight Cruise also is offered Tuesday, Thursday, Friday and Saturday at 5:30 PM. Admission is $6 per person, $3 for children younger than 7.

The marina at Oregon Inlet has a bait and tackle shop that opens at 5 AM — just in time to stock up before the boats leave. The tackle shop carries a complete line of surf and deep-sea fishing equipment, drinks and snacks. A taxidermy service also is on the premises for fish you can't bear to leave behind.

Even if you don't want to catch anything, this marina is an educational and exciting experience. Mates usually unload the day's catch on the docks between 4 and 5 PM each day and will proudly pose for photographs with 4-foot tunas or show you how to slice a thick dolphin steak. Check out the World Record Atlantic Blue Marlin as you exit the parking lot. This 1,142-pound fish, which hangs in a glass case near the marina, was caught off the inlet in 1974 by a South Nags Head angler and brought in on Capt. Harry Baum's *Jo-Boy*. Baum still launches his charter boat from these docks along with his brother, Billy, on the *Dream Girl*.

A few of the many other charter boat captains who call Oregon Inlet home are Capt. Omie Tillet, who is called the "Father of the Fleet," on the *Sportsman*; and Tillett's brother, Tony, on the *Carolinian*. And you can't overlook Capt. Buddy Cannady on the *Capt. B.C.* These men grew up on the water, as did their ancestors.

Pirate's Cove Yacht Club

Manteo-Nags Head Cswy. *473-3906*
(800) 367-4728

With 140 wet slips for yachts up to 75 feet long, Pirate's Cove is the Outer Banks' most modern marina. It's surrounded by upscale permanent and rental waterfront homes and has a ship's store that can supply almost every maritime need. Reservations are accepted for dock space. A growing number of charter fishing boats run Gulf Stream trips from Pirate's Cove most of the year. Between 4 and 5 PM each day, visitors can watch captains and crews unload more than a dozen vessels filled with fresh dolphin, tuna and wahoo.

Inshore trip prices vary but average $250 per half day trip. The *Country Girl*, 473-5577, is the only offshore headboat that fishes out of here that will accommodate more than six passengers per trip. For inlet and sound bottom fishing — plus an interesting commentary on the Outer Banks — take a trip on the *Crystal Dawn,* 473-5577, daily except Sundays throughout the year. (The *Crystal Dawn* also offers moonlight cruises along the Manteo waterfront or Wanchese harbor — a nice change of pace.)

Aboard the air-conditioned *Virginia Dare*, passengers can take 1½-hour narrated water tours of the Outer Banks from mid-May through mid-October Mondays through Saturdays. Sight-seeing trips leave Pirate's Cove at 11 AM and 7 PM. At 3 PM, there's a special dolphin-seeking tour. This two-hour trip costs $15 for adults and $8 for children. Other trips cost $10 for adults; $6 for children. And a special moonlight cruise is offered for the same price, Wednesdays through Fridays at 9 PM from mid-June through August.

On all trips anglers just have to furnish food and drink in a small cooler. Coolers for fish can be left in cars back at the dock. All fish is either put on ice in a fish box or on stringers depending on size. Fish-cleaning service is available at the dock. Slip rentals are also available.

If you're interested in learning more about saltwater angling, Pirate's Cove operates a fishing school each March and October.

Besides fishing supplies, the Ship's Store at Pirate's Cove sells sportswear, T-shirts, souvenir hats and drink huggies, groceries and ice. A restaurant above the store includes a raw bar and fresh steamed seafood. Boaters can brown bag liquor at this establishment that sells only beer and wine (see our Restaurants chapter).

Pirate's Cove Marina is scheduled to host the 13th Annual Billfish Tournament in mid-August (see our Annual Events chapter). Other tournaments for kids, small boats and women only are held from June through November. For advance notification, write P.O. Box 1997, Manteo 27954. For more information on Pirate's Cove, see our Attractions chapter.

Salty Dawg Marina

N.C. 64, Manteo *473-3405*

This facility offers more than 50 slips, power, water and bathhouse. It's open year round seven days a week. Call for reservations on holidays. You can also charter offshore fishing trips here. Salty Dawg has a convenient location near accommodations, a grocery store, pharmacy and coin-operated laundry.

Teach's Lair Marina

N.C. 12, Hatteras Village *986-2460*

Joe Morris runs this place — and he does a darn good job of it. You'll enjoy your interaction with this personable individual who coordinates tournaments within the Hatteras community. Offshore and inshore trips depart year round every day from this marina. In the winter of 1996, Teach's was full of bluefin tuna fishermen. Teach's also has a supply store where you can fulfill all your fishing needs, including ice and bait. And don't forget the film! Those bluefin tuna are breathtaking. No one will believe you without picture proof.

Small-boat Fishing

Small boats offer sound, inlet, lake, river and ocean trips that are as varied as the weather. Inshore captains generally book half-day trips but also offer intermediate all-day trips to take you farther out. If you're interested in bluefish, Spanish mackerel, cobia, king mackerel, bonito, trout, flounder, croaker and red drum, virtually any marina will help you book a trip. Half-day trips are a little easier on the pocketbook.

Spanish mackerel are a mainstay of the area. Ocracoke Island captains begin looking for them in late April and typically enjoy catches through late October. Farther north on the Outer Banks, Spanish mackerel usually arrive the first or second week in May, depending on the water temperature. Capt. Ronnie O'Neal (of the *Miss Kathleen*), a native Ocracoker says: "Casting to them is the most sporting way of catching them. Use an eight-pound test on a light spinning rod with a pink StingSilver or a Gold Gotcha plug in close to the beach."

If it's flounder you're after, you can find these flat fish in Oregon Inlet in clear water. Anglers drift bottom rigs on medium-weight spinning tackle. Croakers are found in the sounds around deep holes, oyster rocks and sloughs.

You can dine on almost all inshore species, but one bony fish with little food value that cannot be overlooked is the tarpon. A release category fish, the tarpon is probably one of the strongest fighting fish available inshore. O'Neal has tangled with these beauties in Ocracoke. He recommends fresh-cut bait, such as spot or trout, and very sharp hooks to penetrate the tarpon's hard mouth. Remember, it's one thing to hook up and a whole other to bring a tarpon to the boat. Good luck!

Fishing the Backwaters

Backwater journeys in Dare County take you to a world of great beauty, peace, fish — and the haunts of Capt. V.P. Brinson. If you want the inside scoop on fishing Manns Harbor, Alligator River or East and South Lake, he's the person to go with. No one loves or knows these waters more — even his peers would agree. He even sold his offshore charter boat, after years of traveling to the Gulf Stream, to start an inshore fishing service.

Capt. Brinson has taken the time to learn about the area's waters and can take you to the fish. You can troll, spin- and bait-cast or fly fish year round. You'll find an interesting mix of freshwater and saltwater species in the backwaters. Depending on the season, you can fish for crappie, rockfish (striped bass), largemouth bass, flounder, bream, sheepshead, drum, perch, croaker, spot, catfish and trout. How about that mix?!

The fishing is so laid back, Capt. Brinson occasionally throws in a line himself. In these more protected waters, anglers can fish even when it's blowing offshore. "If a storm comes, you can duck in behind an island. The most you can get is

ON OUR FAST, MODERN CHARTER BOAT FLEET

BEST FISHING ON THE EAST COAST!

VISIT OUR NEWLY REMODELED AND EXPANDED STORE FOR MORE OF EVERYTHING YOU NEED FOR YOUR SPORTFISHING EXPERIENCE AND LEISURE WEAR FOR SPRING AND SUMMER.

TOP NAME BRANDS - SPORTSWEAR - SHOES - T-SHIRTS

SPORTIF - TIMBERLAND - AFTCO BLUEWATER WEAR

TARPONWEAR - SEBAGO - GEAR - AND MORE!

Hatteras Village

986-2166 • 1-800-676-4939

VISA & MASTER CARD ACCEPTED

Home of the Largest Charter Fleet on Hatteras!

And for all Breakfast and Lunch Needs for Your Fishing Trip its...

PRE-ORDERS AVAILABLE

986-2331

Whether you're fishing the bluewater or the backwaters, the Outer Banks is tops when it comes to year-round variety.

wet, and you're usually wading distance from shore," Capt. Brinson said.

Bring your camera. Depending on the time of day and season, you might spot deer, bears and even alligators. It's a nice alternative to ocean fishing and a good choice for families.

You can fish with Capt. Brinson, 473-3059, on the *Phideaux Too*, a 21.5-foot bateau that he constructed himself. If Capt. Brinson's not available, you can always launch your own vessel from any of a number of local ramps (see our Watersports chapter) or contact the nearest marina or tackle shop for more information.

Surf Fishing

Surf fishing has been a popular Outer Banks pastime for years. While there are miles of beach from which to cast a line, experienced local anglers say a surf-caster's success will vary depending on sloughs, temperature, currents and season.

If you're interested in learning some pointers from an angler who has certainly put his time into the sport, pick up a copy of Joe Malat's *Surf Fishing*. This easy-to-read, illustrated book outlines methods of catching species common to our area. Malat shares tips on the lures, rigs, baits and knots favored by local surf anglers. You can also read about catch-and-release techniques and how to locate and land fish. This comprehensive book also includes useful information about tides, currents and wind — and other factors that affect surf fishing.

Malat also leads the Outer Banks Surf Fishing School. This combination classroom and "on the beach" program teaches beginners surf fishing fundamentals. The experienced angler can also pick up tips on how to catch more fish from the beach. One- to three-day schools are usually held during the spring and fall. Call or write Joe Malat for more information: 415 Bridge Lane, Nags Head, North Carolina 27959, 441-4767.

One of the hottest surf-casting spots on the Outer Banks is Cape Point, a sand spit at the tip of Cape Hatteras. Anglers stand waist-deep in the churning waters, dutifully waiting for red drum to strike. You'll also find cobia, tarpon, amberjack, shark, Spanish mackerel and bluefish along with bottom feeders, such as croakers, spot and sea mullet.

Shoaling that takes place off Cape Hatteras makes Cape Point a haven for baitfish, and the influence of the nearby Gulf Stream and its warm-water jetties also contribute to the excellent fishing there. The beach accommodates many four-wheel-drive vehicles and during peak season (spring and fall) is packed with anglers. If you want to try fishing Cape Point, take N.C. 12 to Buxton and turn at the road that leads to the Cape Hatteras Lighthouse; it's well-marked by a sign. Turn right at the "T" in the road by the lighthouse. Then travel straight to the first vehicle access ramp, Ramp 43.

Beat the Seasickness Blues

Almost everyone who has ever been on the water for any length of time has gotten seasick or at least battled that unmistakable queasy feeling. Like many things about the Outer Banks, seasickness is a one-of-a-kind experience. We've spent plenty of time on the water and know what it's like to want to throw yourself overboard.

Here are some dos and don'ts that should help. You'll have to find your own special formula. If you have a tendency or fear of getting seasick and are capable of taking medication:

1. Take an over-the-counter remedy for motion sickness the night before your trip and, again, an hour before departure. This allows time for the medicine to get into your system. Ask your pharmacist about the specifics on these medications. Some will make you more sleepy than others. If you're bringing children along, you'll need to find out whether the medication you are taking is safe for them too.

2. Some folks try a medication patch, which can only be prescribed by a doctor. It fits behind your ear and administers the medication via absorption through the skin.

3. Eat non-greasy food the night before the trip (and no alcohol!) and always eat a non-greasy breakfast. Pancakes and toast are good choices. Regardless of what you may think, a full stomach is much better than an empty one.

4. Carry this notion through by bringing a non-spicy, non-greasy lunch with you. Plus it helps to nibble on saltines or gingersnaps all day. Ginger is an Oriental remedy for motion sickness. Some people actually take ginger capsules, but we like the 'snaps — and the kids do too.

5. Some folks swear that you should drink a lot while offshore. This makes sense when it comes to dehydration, but we've seen plenty of folks get even sicker by downing a soda hoping to ward off the oncoming surge. We refrain from drinking until the latter part of the trip.

6. If you happen to get sick, the worst may be over if you follow this simple rule: Always eat immediately after getting sick (so says Hatteras native Spurgeon Stowe of the *Miss Hatteras*).

7. If your feeling queasy, stay out on deck in the fresh air. Don't hole up in the salon and do not go into the head. *Throw up overboard* if the water is not too rough to keep you away from the edge. And concentrate on the horizon if possible. Orient yourself with a stable point and you should feel better.

8. This may sound bizarre, but another little trick may work. If you're out of shape and have weak stomach muscles, wear something tight across your abdomen. By holding tight to the stomach, the queasy feeling subsides somewhat.

If all else fails, stick to nibbling gingersnaps. We won't leave home without them.

(For more information about driving on the beach, see our Beach Information and Safety chapter.)

A section on surf fishing would not be complete without discussing the bluefish. For years, we've enjoyed the arrival and subsequent blitzes of big bluefish during the Easter season and again around Thanksgiving. During a blitz, big blues chase baitfish up onto to the beach in a feeding frenzy. This puts the blues within striking distance of ready surf-casters. It's a phenomenal sight to watch anglers reel in these fat and ferocious fish one after the other.

Lately, the blues have not blitzed like they use to. As with most species, population figures (or at least landings) tend to rise and fall in cycles; perhaps they're tending toward a low point in the pattern. Maybe the big bluefin tuna, which feed on bluefish, are taking over these days. But blitz or not, you can usually catch some bluefish in the surf or in greater numbers farther offshore.

Fly Fishing

Fly fishing is a sport many Outer Banks anglers swear by. Fly-fishing guide and columnist Brian Horsley is a real Insider when it comes to this style of fishing. Horsley not only guides fishing parties but also fishes almost daily himself and ties and sells his own flies. This Southern Shores angler has the distinction of being the first full-time saltwater fly-fishing guide in North Carolina. He holds a saltwater fly-rod world record in the tippet class for a 16-pound, 9-ounce bluefish he caught off Kitty Hawk Beach on 20-pound test. He dreams about someday catching a white marlin and a big drum on a fly.

Horsley calls the Outer Banks a fly-fishing paradise, calling the fly-fishing opportunities here "unlimited." He takes parties out in his Florida-style skiff, *Flat Out*, and runs nearshore fly-fishing/light tackle charters from the end of April through November. He fishes the Pamlico, Croatan and Roanoke sounds for speckled trout, bluefish, puppy drum, little tunny, flounder and cobia.

To contact Horsley about a fly-fishing excursion, call 261-1541 (evenings); or write him at 227 S. Woodland Drive, Kitty Hawk, North Carolina 27949. A half-day outing for two people costs $180 ($300 for a full day). The cost is $50 for an extra person.

John Dominick's **Outer Banks Fly Angler** at MP 11½ in Pirate's Quay Shopping Center is a must. Dedicated to fly fishing only, John offers fresh or saltwater tackle featuring name brands including Orvis, Sage, Thomas & Thomas, Abel, Islander and others. Fly-tying equipment is available along with a guide service, fly-fishing school and casting instructions. The shop is open year round.

Also ask at other tackle shops for guides and fly-fishing experts.

Pier Fishing

Pier fishing has been delighting anglers on the Outer Banks for more than 50 years. The appeal is obvious: low cost and a chance to fish deeper waters without a boat. The variety of fish available also lures anglers. Depending on the time of year, you can catch croakers, spot, sea mullet, red drum, cobia and occasionally a tarpon, king mackerel, sheepshead or amberjack.

Bait and tackle are sold at each pier, or you can rent whatever gear you need. Avid anglers usually come prepared, but newcomers to the sport are always welcome on the pier, and staff are more than willing to outfit you and offer some fishing tips. Pier fishing is a good way to introduce kids to the sport. Many Outer Banks locals spent their youth on the pier soaking in know-how and area fishing lore. For instance, Garry Oliver, who owns the Outer Banks Pier in South Nags

Head, spent many a summer day at the Nags Head Fishing Pier when he was a lad. Today, Garry is a member of an award-winning surf-casters team.

Kitty Hawk Fishing Pier

Beach Rd., MP 1 *261-2772*

Once you cross the Wright Memorial Bridge and arrive on the Outer Banks, it's a matter of seconds before you get your first glimpse of the ocean at the Kitty Hawk Fishing Pier. Turn left at the fourth traffic light (by Aycock Brown Visitors Center) on U.S. 158 as if you were traveling to Duck. Make an immediate right onto the Beach Road (N.C. 12) and head south. On your left will be a turn onto a short access road that leads to the pier.

The Outer Banks has no oceanfront boardwalks, but the piers more than make up for it. The smell of salt air and tar-treated lumber greets you as you walk the wide plank up to the barn-like structure built in the mid-'50s. The central feature is the breezeway with a bait and tackle shop on the south end of the building and a diner-style restaurant on the north. From the breezeway, the fishing pier itself extends 714 feet over the ocean.

You don't have to fish to appreciate the Kitty Hawk Fishing Pier. For starters, it's an Insider's best kept breakfast secret. Nothing beats the ocean view, the omelets or the pitch and roll of the dining room when the surf's up. Next, pay the $2 to walk out to the end of the pier for an eye-opening experience. Peopled with anglers, this structure has endured many powerful storms, and many citation fish have been caught off its weathered railings.

Kitty Hawk Fishing Pier is open April through Thanksgiving. Parking is ample, and daily admission is $5 for adults and $3 for children. A weekly pass is $25, and season passes are $125. Handicapped persons are admitted free.

Avalon Fishing Pier

Beach Rd., MP 6 *441-7494*

Avalon Pier was built in the mid '50s and is 705 feet long. The pier has lights for night fishing, a snack bar, bait and tackle shop, ice, video games and rental fishing gear. A busy place in-season, the pier is open 24 hours a day. The pier house is open from 5 AM until 2 AM. The pier is closed December through February. Admission prices are $5 for adults and $2.75 for children younger than 12. A weekly pass costs $28. A weekend pass is $13, while a season pass is $100. Wheelchair-bound persons are admitted without charge.

Nags Head Fishing Pier

Beach Rd., MP 12 *441-5141*

This is one of the most popular fishing piers on the Outer Banks. It is 750 feet long and has its own bait and tackle shop. There is night fishing, game tables for the kids and a restaurant. The Pier House Restaurant features fresh seafood and wonderful views of the ocean. The restaurant serves breakfast, lunch and dinner. (See our Restaurants chapter for more information.) The pier is closed December through March and reopens in April. It is open 24 hours during the season. Admission is $5 per day for adults, $12 for a three-day pass and $30 for an eight-day pass. Season rates are $135 for singles and $225 for couples. Kids between the ages

Insiders' Tips

It's at least a two-hour trip by charter boat from Oregon Inlet to the Gulf Stream fishing grounds (1½ hours or less from Hatteras).

of 6 and 12 are always half price. Inquire about cottage rentals near the pier; weekly and nightly rentals are available. These are one- to four-bedroom cottages.

Jennette's Pier

Beach Rd., MP 16½ *441-6116*

Built in 1932, Jennette's is the oldest pier on the Outer Banks, and friends have been gathering here since the last plank was put in place. The current rates are $5 per day, $12.50 for a three-day pass, $25 for a weekly pass, and children 11 and younger gain access for free. Adults can walk out on the pier for $1 per person.

This pier is usually crawling with anglers. (We're told that the activity here has not put a damper on the fish being caught.) It's in the heart of Whalebone Junction — along a hotbed of big catches and tall stories. Rest assured, the pier, busy almost anytime, will be even more so in late spring and summer. The pier opens April 1 and closes November 30. Hours do vary, but the schedule is 6 AM 'til 6 PM April 1 through Memorial Day. The pier is open 24 hours a day, seven days a week from Memorial Day through Labor Day. Snacks are available. Jennette's retail store features items to round out all your fishing and beach needs.

Outer Banks Pier and Fishing Center

Beach Rd., MP 18½ *441-5740*

This 650-foot ocean pier was originally built in 1959 and rebuilt in 1962 after the Ash Wednesday storm. Owner Garry Oliver has all you need in the bait and tackle shop for a day of fishing along this somewhat remote stretch of beach. A 300-foot sound fishing and crabbing pier is also available. The piers are open 24 hours a day from Memorial Day until mid-October and close during the winter. They reopen in late March. Rates are $5 per day, $12.50 for three days, $25 per week, $90 per season for one person and $150 per season for a couple. Drinks and snacks are available.

Hatteras Island Fishing Pier

N.C. 12, Rodanthe *987-2323*

This 35-year-old pier charges only $5 per day to drop a line. You can come with your own gear or buy or rent tackle here. They also sell bait, of course, and drinks and snacks for the hungry angler. The pier is open from Easter until Thanksgiving. It's open 24 hours a day in the summer, other times you can fish from 6 AM 'til 10 PM. The restaurant, Down Under, is located on the premises (see our Restaurants chapter).

Avon Fishing Pier

N.C. 12, Avon *995-5480*

Avon Fishing Pier has a reputation for being a hot spot for red drum. The all-tackle world record red drum, weighing in at 94 pounds 2 ounces, was caught about 200 yards from the pier in 1984. The pier opens at the beginning of April and remains open through Thanksgiving. You can purchase or rent all your fishing supplies here, buy sandwiches and drinks, and also pick up nautical gifts including T-shirts and sand mirrors. Operating hours are 6 AM to 10 PM. After Memorial Day the pier remains open 24 hours a day until it closes for the season. Adults pay $5 to fish all day, and kid's all-day passes are $4.

Cape Hatteras Pier

N.C. 12, Frisco *986-2533*

The Cape Hatteras Pier, locally called the Frisco Pier, is open mid-March through November. The pier is noted for its great king mackerel fishing during the summer and sells or rents everything you'll need for fishing, including live bait for those big kings! Snacks and soft drinks are available. The pier is open from 6 AM 'til 11 PM during the week and 6 AM 'til 1 AM on Friday and Saturday. The Frisco Pier is located on the South Beach, and folks who fish here often boast about the large quantity of fish that frequent the vicinity.

Citation Fish

Citation fish are caught in the waters off the Outer Banks every year. The North Carolina Division of Marine Fisheries manages the N.C. Saltwater Fishing Tournament, which recognizes outstanding angling achievement. The tournament runs yearlong from January 1 through December 31. Except charter boat captains and crew forhire, everyone is eligible for a citation fish award. Eligible waters include North Carolina sounds, surf, estuaries and the ocean. This tournament is for the hook-and-line angler; use of electric or hydraulic equipment is not allowed. There is one award per angler per species, and all fish must be weighed in at an official weigh station. Anglers receive a certificate after the close of the tournament. There is no registration fee. Following is a list of the area's weigh stations, and you can receive rules for the tournament at any of these. We also include a species list. Citations are also awarded for the catch and release of some species.

Official Weigh Stations

DUCK

Bob's Bait & Tackle, Duck Road (N.C. 12), 261-8589

TW's Bait & Tackle Shop, Duck Road (N.C. 12), 261-8300

KITTY HAWK

Kitty Hawk Bait & Tackle, U.S. 158, MP 4½, Kitty Hawk, 261-2955

Kitty Hawk Fishing Pier, Beach Road, MP 1, 261-2772

TW's Bait & Tackle Shop, U.S. 158, MP 4, 261-7848

KILL DEVIL HILLS

Avalon Fishing Pier, Beach Road, MP 6, 441-7494

NAGS HEAD

Tatem's Tackle Box, U.S. 158, MP 13, 441-7346

Jennette's Pier, Beach Road, MP 16½, 441-6116

Nags Head Fishing Pier, Beach Road, MP 12, 441-5141

T.I.'s Bait & Tackle, Beach Road, MP 16½, 441-3166

Whalebone Tackle Shop, Nags Head/ Manteo Causeway, 441-7413

Outer Banks Pier and Fishing Center, Beach Road, MP 18½, 441-5740

MANTEO

Pirate's Cove, Manteo-Nags Head Causeway, 473-3906

Salty Dawg Marina, U.S. 64, 473-3405

OREGON INLET

Oregon Inlet Fishing Center, N.C. 12, 8 miles south of Whalebone Junction, 441-6301

RODANTHE

Hatteras Island Fishing Pier, off N.C. 12, 987-2323

SALVO

The Fishin' Hole, 27202 Sand Street, 987-2351

Insiders' Tips

Use live bait when fishing for big king mackerel.

What to Do When You're Hooked (. . . Not the Fish)

We want you to become hooked on fishing while visiting the Outer Banks and return with a trophy — not an unwanted souvenir in your finger. But it's not unusual to become the bait. Numerous anglers fishing surf, sea or sound are caught with fishhooks daily.

Capt. Allan Foreman, who runs a year-round offshore charter boat here, has a few safety tips to consider when dropping a line into some of the most productive waters in the world: "Be careful to set the pole down in the rod holder so that it's not gonna slide when you bait your hook. If you want to leave the pole for a spell, make sure you wrap the weight around the reel or latch the hook into one of the pole's guides."

Also, Foreman says, a hooked fish can make your pole unwieldy. Before your catch is removed from the hook, once again secure the pole in the holder to avoid a painful snag.

If you do hook yourself, Foreman suggests you leave the hook embedded, pack the wound in ice and bring yourself and another hook just like it to a local medical facility (see our Healthcare chapter).

Dr. Walter Holton of Dare Medical Associates in Manteo, co-author of a first-aid guide, *The Outer Banks Vacationers' First Aid Guide*, that includes safety tips on hooks, says, "Never cut off part of the hook. Leave as much of the hook as possible. It's difficult to remove without the shaft. Trying to push the hook through rarely can be done."

Dr. Holton's book offers helpful diagrams for removing hooks, but if these don't work, or you have concerns about your tetanus booster status or infection, see a physician.

With a little caution, you may be the next angler to reel in a world-record fish — instead of a finger — on the Outer Banks.

Avon

Frank and Fran's Fisherman's Friend, N.C. 12, 995-4171

Avon Fishing Pier, Off N.C. 12, 995-5480

Buxton

Dillon's Corner, N.C. 12, 995-5083

The Red Drum Tackle Shop Inc., N.C. 12, 995-5414

Frisco

Cape Hatteras Fishing Pier Inc., 54221 Cape Hatteras Pier Dr., 986-2533

Frisco Rod & Gun Club, 53610 N.C. 12, 995-5366

Hatteras Village

Hatteras Harbor Marina, N.C. 12, 986-2166

Hatteras Marlin Club, 57174 Saxon Cut Dr., 986-2454

Pelican's Roost, N.C. 12, 986-2213

Teach's Lair Marina, N.C. 12, 986-2460

Village Marina, N.C. 12, 986-2522

Willis Boat Landing, 57209 Willis Ln., 986-2208

OCRACOKE

Tradewinds Tackle Shop, N.C. 12, 928-5491

O'Neal's Dockside, N.C. 12, Silver Lake Harbor, 928-1111

Eligible Species and Minimum Lengths

The following table outlines the North Carolina and federal 1996 minimum length requirements for each species. Fork Length (FL) is measured from lower jaw to middle of fork in tail. Total Length (TL) is measured from tip of snout with mouth closed to tip of compressed tail.

Bag Limits refer to amount of fish you can catch per person per day. Since the amount varies for inshore and offshore fishing and is subject to change, call North Carolina Marine Fisheries, (919) 726-7021 or (800) 682-2632, or National Marine Fisheries, (301) 713-2347 before you cast off. For inland water limits call the Wildlife Resource Commission (919) 733-3633.

- **Amberjack**: 28 in. FL, bag Limit
- **Bass, Black Sea**: 8 in. TL
- **Bluefish**: 12 in. TL, bag limit
- **Cobia**: 33 in. FL, bag limit
- **Croaker**: 3 pounds
- **Dolphin**: no minimum, 60 per charter boat per day.
- **Drum, Red**: 18 in. TL, only one per day larger than 27 in. Inshore bag limit is five per day. Unlawful to catch offshore.
- **Flounder**: Contact DM, limits vary with season
- **Grouper** (any): 20 in. TL, bag limit
- **Mackerel, King**: 20 in. FL, bag limit
- **Mackerel, Spanish**: 12 in. FL, bag limit
- **Marlin, Blue**: 86 FL, bag limit for state regulations but not for federal.
- **Marlin, White**: 62 FL, bag limit same as Blue Marlin
- **Porgy (Silver Snapper)**: 12 in. TL
- **Sailfish**: 67 in. FL, bag limit
- **Shark** (any): No finning, bag limit
- **Snapper, Red**: 20 in. TL, bag limit
- **Tarpon**: No minimum, bag limit
- **Trout, Gray**: 12 in. TL, bag limit
- **Trout, Speckled**: 12 in. TL
- **Tuna, Bigeye**: 22 in. curved FL. Contact NMFS for closure and limits (301) 713-2347.
- **Tuna, Bluefin**: 27 in. curved FL. Contact NMFS for closure and limits (301) 713-2347.
- **Tuna, Yellowfin**: 22 curved FL. Contact NMFS for closure and limits (301) 713-2347.

Bait and Tackle Shops

Terrific tackle shops are scattered from Corolla to Ocracoke. They are good sources not only of rods and reels, bait and other fishing gear but also of tips on what's biting and where. You'll find bait and tackle at all Outer Banks fishing piers and most marinas too, and just about every department store and general store on the islands carries some sort of fishing gear. Many shops also offer tackle rental. Here are other shops to get you headed in the right direction.

Corolla

TACKLE 'N TOURS

Ocean Tr. *453-4266*

Nearly at the northern end of paved

Insiders' Tips

If you want the scoop on viable offshore-fishing days, talk with charter boat captains. They can tell you when it's safe to venture out and when to stay in.

Foster Leaves Sport Fishing Legacy

With his $805 boat, *The Albatross*, and two gamefish reels given as gifts, Capt. Ernal W. Foster hooked the nation on Outer Banks offshore sport fishing in 1939. He started Hatteras Island's first Gulf Stream charter fishing fleet, bringing thousands of visitors to the isolated islands.

Within 20 years, he had single-handedly reeled in the first blue marlin, first white marlin and first sailfish caught from a charter boat off northern North Carolina. In 1958, an angler aboard *The Albatross* released the first blue marlin known to have been deliberately set free. For more than 40 years, this hoary-headed captain carried charter parties to the Gulf Stream almost every day.

Foster died January 8, 1996, of heart failure — a few weeks before his 86th birthday. More than 400 friends, family members and fellow fishermen attended the simple funeral at Hatteras United Methodist Church. Thousands of others across the country continue to mourn the loss of an esteemed angler.

From the stern of his hand-hewn juniper boat, he sought out the secret spots where trophy tuna and big billfish swam. When he was 85, he was known as the only barrier islands captain who could steer a 42-foot boat into a lift slip without bumping a buoy.

"Even the experts touch," said Mike Scott, whose Buxton boatyard has serviced Foster's Albatross fleet for more than 20 years.

"He was amazing. You'd see him coming in the harbor, bringing the boat by himself, wearing that homemade khaki uniform with his name stitched on it, waving at everyone. He and that boat were one. He'd get on board, and 20 years would fall out of his face. I've never seen him without a smile when he was on that boat."

"I think my father would want to be remembered as someone who liked people — and someone who never took more from the sea than he needed," Ernie Foster, 50, said from his office at Manteo High School, where he is a guidance counselor. "He never saw the need to be the captain who threw the most fish on the docks. He used to delight in saying he'd released — instead of caught — the world record sailfish. He knew everything. But he was never a know-it-all.

"A lot of the guys at the docks looked at my father as a tangible contact with a world they'd never experience," said Capt. Foster's only child, who continues to run the family's charter fleet business on weekends and during the summer.

"I'm beginning to accept that he was a character," Ernie Foster said of his father. "His death was truly the end of an era."

The son of an Outer Banks menhaden fisherman, Ernal Foster was born in 1910 in a two-story wooden frame house on the southern tip of Hatteras

Ernal W. Foster

Island. He had three brothers and three sisters. The family spent most of their time working on the water.

Fascinated with fish and the sea — but bored by the confines of a classroom — Ernal Foster dropped out of school in the ninth grade to become a full-time commercial fisherman. He joined the Coast Guard at age 18 and journeyed to Long Island, New York.

If the Great Depression hadn't hit a few years later, he probably would have been a New York plumber instead of the founder of Hatteras Island's first charter fishing fleet.

"He was an apprentice plumber up north after he got out of the Coast Guard. But when times got tight, he refused to stand in bread lines," Ernie Foster said of his father. "He knew he could come home to Hatteras and eat fish he caught for free."

In 1937, Foster commissioned his first boat — *The Albatross* — which still carries charter parties into the Atlantic. By 1952, he owned two other fishing vessels, *Albatross II* and *Albatross III*, all of which still dock at the wooden wharves near his Hatteras Village home. Sharp at the bow and round astern, these flare-bowed boats were built for bad weather, shallow shoals and swollen seas. They're not as quick as modern-day sport-fishing boats. But each one has been to sea thousands of times.

Years ago, charter parties paid $25 for a full day of fishing. Today, anglers pay at least $800 for offshore trips. Many other aspects of sport fishing also have evolved since Capt. Foster first steered away from the Outer Banks shores.

"When he started, everyone commercial fished most of the year and carried charter parties sometimes during the summer," Ernie Foster said. "My father was the first one to devote all his time to charter fishing. At that time, everyone supplied their own tackle. And most everyone already knew how to fish.

"My father carried sportsmen and sportswriters from all over the country out to the Gulf Stream."

Relying on his wits rather than technology, Ernal Foster seldom used a radio, never used charts and could navigate from North Carolina to New York using only a compass. He could find wrecks from memory in a few minutes that other watermen searched weeks for with their electronic navigation devices and fancy fish finders.

During the 1930s, other watermen told tales of strange fish with baseball bats on their noses swimming around Diamond Shoals. But Ernal Foster was the first person to hook and land a big billfish in the area. When he brought the 475-pound blue marlin back to the docks in 1952, more than 300 people from around the Outer Banks came to see the strange sight.

"Ernal Foster probably did more for sports fishing in North Carolina than anyone else you could name," Hatteras Island charter boat captain Steve Coulter said. "He was the most respected and well known of all the old captains. Most anyone who's ever fished out of Hatteras has fished off an Albatross boat at one point. Heck, he carried three generations of anglers off shore."

As he got older, and his heart began to slow, Capt. Foster whittled away his days on the docks — but even that seemingly idle pastime was purposeful. He made perfect, curling shavings of juniper most of the time. But whenever anyone's boat needed a plug, those old, sure fingers could carve a perfect fit within minutes using Foster's famously sharp pocketknife.

"He'd sit out there carving and telling stories that lasted 40 minutes or more," charter boat Capt. Walt Spruill said.

"His mind was just as crisp as the winter's air. He could remember everything. It was always good to listen to him tell about how good life used to be before all us younger fellas came down here and ruined Hatteras for him.

"He was a real inspiration to all us watermen down here," Spruill said seriously. "He surely will be missed."

(As appeared in The Virginian-Pilot.)

highway sits a row of shops and businesses known as Whalehead Landing Station. Tackle 'n Tours offers fishing equipment, rod and reel repairs, rental boats for sound fishing trips and information on offshore charters.

Duck

Bob's Bait & Tackle

Duck Rd. (N.C. 12) *261-8589*

If you're looking for advice on where to catch that "really big one," stop in. The old building is left over from Duck's early days, when a soundside dock out back was the distribution point for shiploads of fresh ocean fish. The shop carries a good supply of reels, rods and bait.

Kitty Hawk

Kitty Hawk Bait & Tackle

U.S. 158, MP 4½ *261-2955*

A great selection of saltwater and freshwater tackle, plus a complete line of fresh bait and live minnows, makes this a good stop for everything you'll need for reelin' in the big ones. You can also rent rods and reels, arrange offshore charters and have your equipment repaired here.

TW's Bait & Tackle

U.S. 158, MP 4 *241-7848*

Just about every store on the Outer Banks carries fishing gear, but you really can't beat TW's Bait & Tackle, next to the 7-Eleven. The gear is topnotch and so is the info on what's biting. Owner Terry "T.W." Stewart has been in business for more than 15 years and can sell you what you need, including ice and live bait. There is another location in Duck, 261-8300.

Whitney's Bait & Tackle

U.S. 158, MP 4½ *261-5551*

Whitney's specializes in custom rods made by Whitney Jones plus offshore and inshore bait and tackle. The shop also offers rod and reel repairs. The walls are lined with Jones' impressive freshwater and saltwater citations and trophies. Call for Whitney's fishing report.

Nags Head

The Fishing Hook

Surfside Plaza, Beach Rd., MP 13½ *441-6661*

Guide service is available here as well as bait, tackle and ice. The shop also carries a full line of camping supplies and offers reel repair.

Tackle Express

U.S. 148, MP 10½ *441-4807*

Tackle Express offers a complete selection of saltwater and freshwater fishing tackle. You can also stock up on cold drinks and beer, grocery items and beach supplies here.

Captain Marty's Fishing and Hunting Tackle Shop

U.S. 158, MP 14 *441-3132*

This new shop opened in the summer of 1996 in Nags Head across from the Outer Banks Mall. It's a good place shop for all kinds of fishing gear and to get fishing charter referrals and lessons.

Tatem's Tackle Box Inc.

U.S. 158, MP 13, Nags Head *441-7346*

This is the original Outer Banks tackle shop, and it's still going strong. The shop sells fresh and frozen bait, tackle, fishing licenses and more and also does reel and rod repairs and makes custom rods. The shop, which is located next to Jockey's Ridge Exxon, is open all year. You can also contact Tatem's by fax, 441-0834.

T.I.'s Bait & Tackle

Beach Rd., MP 16½ *441-3166*

T.I.'s is an official N.C. Weigh Station and member of the N.C. Beach Buggy Association. The shop offers quality tackle and fresh bait and is an authorized Penn parts distributor and repair station. T.I.'s is also a factory-authorized Daiwa service warranty center. The shop is open year-round and can arrange offshore or inshore charter fishing with Capt. Jim Edwards.

Fishing Unlimited

Nags Head/Manteo Causeway *441-5028*

Fishing Unlimited specializes in fresh bait. You can also charter the inshore fishing boat *Fishing Unlimited* and rent 16-foot rowboats here. The shop is open Easter until Thanksgiving.

Salvo

The Fishin' Hole

27202 Sand St. *987-2351*

The Fishin Hole, which in 1996 is marking its 20th year as a general tackle shop, also sells beach supplies. The shop is open from April through mid-December.

Buxton

Dillon's Corner

N.C. 12 *995-5083*

Stop here for an assortment of tackle, including custom rods, and bait. The shop also carries a wide selection of gifts, T-shirts and, in the upstairs shop, fine art (see our Shopping chapter). The shop also offers rod repairs and has gas pumps. Dillon's Corner is open all year, but has shorter hours in winter.

The big bluefish start running in November.

Frank and Fran's Fisherman's Friend

N.C. 12 *995-4171*

A full-service tackle shop, official weigh station and headquarters for the local Red Drum Tournament held every October, Frank and Fran's is an emporium of fishing gear.

Red Drum Tackle Shop

N.C. 12 *995-5414*

Get the latest in fishing information and select gear at Red Drum Tackle Shop. It offers everything you need in the way of custom rods, bait and tackle. A fish-mounting service is also available.

Frisco

Frisco Rod and Gun Club

53610 N.C. 12 *995-5366*

You'll find everything here you need for a hunting or fishing trip on the Outer Banks, including offshore and inshore fishing equipment, fly fishing equipment, guns, ice, bait, tackle and one of the best selections of knives we've seen anywhere. They also carry camping supplies, name-brand outdoor apparel, Sperry Topsiders and T-shirts and offer free air.

Ocracoke

Tradewinds

N.C. 12 *928-5491*

Tradewinds is a one-stop tackle shop that can supply all your fishing needs, including fresh and frozen bait, tackle, clothing items and plenty of good advice about fishing. The shop also offers tackle rentals and rod and reel repair. Tradewinds is open seven days a week from mid-March through mid-December.

Inside **Golf**

Variety is the key to an Outer Banks golf experience — in layouts, club atmosphere and prices. Whether you choose to wander a lush soundside course, practice on a putting green or improve your swing by emptying a bucket of balls, amateurs and pros alike can find something here to satisfy their golfing urges.

Courses are spread from Hatteras Island northward to Corolla and the Currituck County mainland. But it's a good idea to check periodically for any new clubs sprouting up, because golf on the Outer Banks is spreading like wildfire. In the last few years alone, at least three new clubs have opened.

Outer Banks golf has a few natural hazards that may affect your play and — possibly — your score. Something you can't overlook when playing near water — aside from the water itself, of course — is the wind factor, which can turn even the most well-aimed shot wayward.

The good news: While these windswept barrier islands are renowned for kite-flying weather, it is not unusual or uncomfortable to play here year round. Some courses offer more natural shelter than others, so you might want to choose your sites depending on the weather; and you can always shorten your game (that is to say, lay up more often) if necessary. Despite the wind, it's glorious to play golf while breathing salt air under spectacular skyscapes and surrounded by natural vegetation. And nothing beats a summer round followed by a dip in the salty sea.

Check out our course listings; we also include places where you can leisurely empty a bucket or two. All the regulation courses are semiprivate (the general public may pay and play), and all welcome beginners and newcomers as well as seasoned low-handicappers.

Watch for a new golf club opening July 1, 1997. Barnett's Creek, a golfing community and marina featuring 240 homesites, is currently under construction in Grandy. This 18-hole course will include a clubhouse, pro shop and restaurant. It's billed as the first golfing community on the Currituck County mainland.

Regulation and Executive Courses

Currituck Club

N.C. 12 — *453-9400*
Corolla — *(800) 465-3972*
Championship Yardage: 6910
Slope: No rating — *Par: 72*
Men's Yardage: 6537
Slope: No rating — *Par:72*
Ladies Yardage: 4885
Slope: No rating — *Par 72*

Comprising 600 acres of pristine wetlands, the Currituck Club golf and resort community features a links-style course designed by prominent golf architect Rees Jones. Over the years, visitors to this parcel of land have been mostly of the feathered and furred kind. Bearing that in mind, Jones was careful to preserve and protect their habitat while offering golfers a course set amid dunes, wetlands and marsh fringes. Golfers enjoy views of the

Photo: Mary Ellen Riddle

Nags Head Golf Links anchors the Village at Nags Head.

Atlantic Ocean and Currituck Sound. Within the property lies the historic and private Currituck Shooting Club, an outdoor-lovers escape since the mid-1800s.

The 18-hole course is scheduled to open July 1, 1996, offering a limited number of memberships beginning with property owners. The public is invited to play daily; greens fees vary seasonally and daily: July 1 through September 2, $45 to $75 (depending on time of day); September 3 through October 6, $60; October 7 through December 1, $45 (Monday through Thursday) and $50 (Friday through Sunday); December 2 through December 31, $45. Twilight fees (after 4 PM) are $45 from July 1 through October 7 and $40 thereafter until year's end. Rates for 1997 had not been set at press time.

A snack bar and pro shop will be ready by July 1. Coming attractions for 1997: a clubhouse, lockers, a bar and restaurant. Five miles of biking trails, private beach access and the clubhouse will be available to residents. As this area was kept as natural as possible, we think the Currituck Club's course will be one of the most peaceful and pretty golfing spots around.

Duck Woods Country Club

50 Dogwood Tr., Kitty Hawk *261-2609*
Championship Yardage: 6578
Slope: 132 *Par: 72*
Men's Yardage: 6161
Slope: 129 *Par: 72*
Ladies' Yardage: 5407
Slope: 127 *Par: 73*

Golfers speak in hushed tones when you mention this venerable country club. The 18-hole course here is the Outer Banks' oldest — built in 1968. Designed by Ellis Maples, Duck Woods features a traditional layout with tree-lined fairways. Shots must be placed with care, especially on the par 5 14th hole, where water dissects the fairway. Water comes into play on 14 holes.

You might want to warm up before your round; the course begins with a 481-yard par 5 and ends with a 506-yard par 5. The wind is kept at bay at Duck Woods, a more sheltered course than most on the Outer Banks.

While the club accommodates 900 members, it accepts public play year round. Nonmembers can take advantage of the driving range and putting green on the day of play only. Target greens and a practice bunker are available. Duck Woods offers a pro shop and club rentals. Members enjoy clubhouse and locker room privileges and the bar and restaurant. Beer and wine are sold to nonmembers, but no other alcoholic beverages are available, as the club does not hold a liquor license.

Riding is mandatory for nonmembers. Booking is accepted a week in advance for members and two days in advance for nonmembers. Call for more information. The greens fee, including cart, is $63 year round for nonmembers.

Goose Creek Golf and Country Club

U.S. 158 *453-4008*
Grandy *(800) 443-4008*
Championship Yardage: 6191
Slope: 114 *Par: 72*

Men's Yardage: 5943
Slope: 109 *Par: 72*
Ladies' Yardage: 5558
Slope: 116 *Par: 72*

"Public Welcome" is marked in bold lettering in the Goose Creek's print advertising, and after playing this easygoing track, you'll want to return just to be in the Southern-style atmosphere. The greens and fairways on this flat course are blanketed with bermudagrass. Greens are relatively small. Trees line the course, with tighter fairways on the first nine but more undulating and open terrain on the back. Designed and built by Chris Lahr & Associates, with the initial layout done by Jerry Turner, 4-year-old Goose Creek features United States Golf Association-spec bentgrass greens.

It's a player-friendly golf course. Water comes into play on five holes. No. 13 is considered the signature. The hole plays differently according to the wind (it's generally to your back during the summer and in your face in fall and winter).

A driving range and practice green are available. Walking is allowed for members only.

The clubhouse is a former hunting lodge that the owners converted into private locker rooms. Kick back in the pine-paneled lounge for a cool drink or snack. You can nibble on all sorts of sandwiches and treats from buffalo wings to crab cakes.

This is a great course for the entire family, and children are both welcome and encouraged; however, it's recommended that young golfers check in after noon.

Goose Creek is also pocket-friendly. Greens fees range from $28 during late afternoon to $40 for prime morning tee times. A three-day golf pass is offered for $99.

Nags Head Golf Links

Village at Nags Head
5615 S. Seachase Dr.
Off U.S. 158, MP 15 *441-8073*
Nags Head *(800) 851-9404*
Championship Yardage: 6126
Slope: 130 *Par: 71*
Men's Yardage: 5717
Slope: 126 *Par: 71*
Other Yardage: 5354
Slope: 123 *Par: 71*
Ladies' Yardage: 4415
Slope: 117 *Par: 71*

"Love me, love my wind," would be a good slogan for this course. It's a real beach beauty. Architect Bob Moore left most of the natural setting intact here.

Golfers enjoy idyllic views of Roanoke Sound from nearly every hole. With the sound to the west and the ocean to the east, wind plays a constant role here.

If your ball is "blown" off course (or hit off course!), you may need to spend some time searching for it in the dense underbrush that lines the fairways. (We suggest you play a drop and move on.) You really come up against the wind when you reach the 18th hole, which runs very close to the sound. This 583-yard par 5 will test your golfing skills. Think about leaving your woods in the bag and playing only with irons on this course.

It doesn't take but one quick gust of wind to blow your ball off-course on the 221-yard 15th, a lengthy par 3. The green is flanked by a sand trap on the right and fronted by a pond.

Of course, on virtually every barrier island track, you'll have to deal with wetlands. All but four holes are affected by water here.

Golf pro Danny Agapion invites golfers to try this mercurial course, with the wind changing minute by minute. But the environment is so refreshing, we think it's worth a round regardless of what's controlling the shots.

Walking is not allowed. Greens fees average $75. A nine-hole shootout is played every Sunday. Kids play free. Tee times may be booked up to a year in advance.

If you work up an appetite, enjoy good food and excellent views of the Roanoke Sound from the Links Grill — open for lunch only (see our Restaurants chapter for details). Nags Head Golf Links also has a bar, pro shop, driving range, putting green and rental clubs. The course is open every day, except Christmas, from sunrise to sunset. Call for more information.

Ocean Edge Golf Course

Off N.C. 12, Frisco *995-4100*
Blue Yardage: 2948
Slope: No rating *Par: 30*
Red Yardage: 2397
Slope: No rating *Par: 30*
White Yardage: 1400
Slope: No rating *Par: 30*
Yellow Yardage: 1122
Slope: No rating *Par: 30*

The public is welcome at this nine-hole executive course that also permits 18-hole play. Look out for the big pond — the 1st, 2nd, 5th and 8th holes play over the water.

Ocean Edge is open May 1 through October. This Hatteras Island course covers 23 acres of dunes. Tee times are required. Golf carts and club rentals are available. Rates, including cart, are $25 for nine holes and $35 for 18.

The Pointe Golf Club

U.S. 158 E., Powells Point *491-8388*
Championship Yardage: 6320
Slope: 120 *Par: 71*
Men's Yardage: 5911
Slope: 113 *Par: 71*
Other Yardage: 5426
Slope: 109 *Par: 71*
Ladies' Yardage: 4862
Slope: 110 *Par: 71*

Pointe is an 18-hole championship golf course that could be described as "Golfer's Heaven." Both the recreational golfer and the professional will find a challenge on this verdant course created by Russell Breeden. Breeden's unique design

Insiders' Tips

Bring lots of golf balls! Don't waste time searching for a windblown ball on a busy summer day.

Photo: Philip S. Ruckle Jr.

Outer Banks golf courses are challenging and well-maintained.

features soundfront views from wooded and links-style holes with gentle mounds and slopes. This is the first course in the country to feature A1 bentgrass, a new disease-resistant dense grass. But it's no surprise really, because the folks at Pointe are grass experts. Pointe owner Keith Hall is the president of United Turf, and he takes his business seriously (he was responsible for growing the grass that blanketed U.S. soccer fields hosting World Cup play). Expect highly manicured, lush greens and concrete cart paths.

In a rural Carolina setting, Pointe offers a nice respite from the beach scene. The course sports a traditional design, with water hazards coming into play laterally on 15 holes. The signature hole is No. 6, a 457-yard par 4 with a carry over wetlands, a blind shot to the fairway, water, bunkers and slopes to the right.

You can fine-tune your game on the driving range, in the practice bunker or on the full-size putting green. Pointe offers a full-service pro shop headed by resident golf pro David A. Donovan III. Other amenities include a clubhouse, carts, lessons, sales and rentals. Enjoy a cool drink or lunch in the bar and grill.

Walking is allowed after noon for greens fee pass-holders from October 1 through May 24. Greens fees vary, so it's a good idea to call for timely information. In peak season, expect to pay $55; from October 1 through 31, $45; November 1 through January 1, $35; April 1 through 30, $40; May 1 through 24, $45. Call for winter rates. Annual golf packages are available for couples, juniors or individuals through the course; accommodations packages are available through area rental companies.

Pointe Golf Course is 3.5 miles west of the Wright Memorial Bridge. Call for tee times up to a month in advance.

Sea Scape Golf Club

300 Eckner St.
Off U.S. 158 E., MP 2½
Kitty Hawk — *261-2158*
Championship Yardage: 6408
Slope: 127 — *Par: 72*
Men's Yardage: 6052
Slope: 123 — *Par: 72*
Ladies' Yardage: 5536
Slope: 114 — *Par:73*

The second-oldest course on the Outer Banks, Sea Scape is cut into Kitty Hawk's maritime forest. Designed by Art Wall, the course features bermudagrass greens and (fairly wide) fairways.

Opened in 1965, the links-style course was given a recent face-lift, and you can expect partial cart paths on nine holes and restructuring on some of the tees.

Wind is a factor here. And you may find yourself puttering around in sand and brush looking for your ball. Expect a challenge on No. 11. Look to play against the wind on this 410-yard, par 3 hole. You get a real taste of Outer Banks beauty, with water views from almost every hole — especially from the elevated 9th tee. Sea Scape will test your ability and patience, with five par 3s and five par 5s.

The Outer Banks Golf Academy offers golf instruction three days a week for beginning as well as advanced players. Sea Scape offers club fitting, rental clubs, a driving range, bar, restaurant and fully stocked pro shop. Longtime Sea Scape pro Bryan Sullivan is available to discuss your game or the course.

Walking is not allowed. Greens fees range from $40 to $60, including cart. Call ahead for tee times, especially if you plan to play during the summer (there's no established rule, but we were informed that eight months in advance isn't too soon). The course is open every day except Christmas from 7:30 AM until dark.

The Sound Golf Links

101 Clubhouse Dr. *426-5555*
Hertford *(800) 535-0704*
Championship Yardage: 6504
Slope: 124 *Par: 72*
Men's Yardage: 5836
Slope: 119 *Par: 72*
Ladies' Yardage: 4665
Slope: 113 *Par: 72*

The Sound is an 18-hole course within Albemarle Plantation, a world-class golfing and boating community tucked away at the tip of the Albemarle Sound near Hertford. A beautiful new 12,000-square-foot clubhouse overlooks the water. You have to be familiar with the really good golf courses in the Carolinas to know about this Dan Maples original. Owner and designer Maples stamped his signature here. As with all Maples-designed courses, you get a break on the par 4s and 5s, but the par 3s are extremely difficult. It's a target golf course with a few similarities to a links course.

Fairways are wide, and marsh must be carried frequently. It's a fair course overall, but a tough one from the back tees. On the 7th and 13th holes, the landing areas are extremely small. Both are par 4s.

This course is surrounded by undisturbed wetlands and tall pines. Enjoy the ride from the 16th green to the 17th tee over the wetlands. In fact, you'll probably enjoy all of the cart rides over the bridges. The three finishing holes stretch along water and provide breathtaking views.

The clubhouse includes a pro shop and restaurant, The Soundside Grille, which serves lunch and dinner. A driving range and putting green are also available. The marina, available to the public, is the largest in the area.

Greens fees, including cart, range from $30 to $35. Walking is restricted, so call for details. Tee times may be booked up to nine months in advance. The course is approximately an hour's drive from Kitty Hawk.

Practice Ranges

Griggs Driving Range

U.S. 158
Powells Point *491-8277*

Some Insiders empty their first buckets of balls in North Carolina at Griggs Driving Range in Powells Point. This no-frills — balls, clubs, tees and soda ma-

Insiders' Tips

Summer golfers: Schedule a tee time before 9 AM or after 3 PM to miss the crowds.

chine only — practice zone is a strip of land where golfers line up across a fairly wide expanse. There's plenty of elbow room, and golfers are situated just far enough apart to avoid distracting one another. Yardage markers are posted on the range. It's a low-key stop that works for the rank beginner or the more advanced player. Call ahead for operating hours. Times vary with seasons. Fees were not established at press time.

The Promenade

U.S. 158 E., MP ¼, Kitty Hawk 261-4900

Fun for the whole family is a sure bet at The Promenade. On the Currituck Sound at the eastern terminus of the Wright Memorial Bridge, this adventure spot features a 27-hole par 3 putting course on natural grass. Separate putting green and target driving range facilities are available. Minigolf lovers will appreciate the 18-hole themed Waterfall Greens. And youngsters ages 1 through 12 will have a blast at the Smilin' Island playground (see our Recreation Chapter for more information).

Golf Equipment and Supplies

In addition to course pro shops where you can find quality golf supplies, we suggest the following shops for discount equipment. The folks at these places are especially helpful and patient with golfers who are just starting out.

Teed Off

Three Winks Shops
U.S. 158 E., MP 1, Kitty Hawk 261-4653

Just east of the Wright Memorial Bridge, this shop offers top-quality equipment and apparel at discount prices. Custom-built golf clubs are available. This made all the difference to a particular Insider who, at 5'1¾", plays a truly "short" game.

Tennis enthusiasts can stock up on equipment here too.

Smash Hit

Scarborough Faire, N.C. 12
Duck 261-1138

Clothing is the specialty at this golf and tennis shop. You'll find a variety of top fashions here. We like the mail-order policy: Just give a call and describe what you want; Smash Hit will send you samples. Keep what you like and return the rest.

Smash Hit is open year round from 11 AM until 5 PM weekdays; 10 AM until 6 PM on weekends.

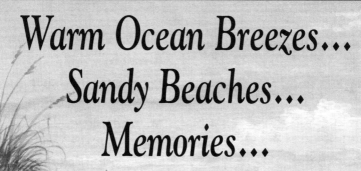

Inside Real Estate

Real estate is a good investment on the Outer Banks despite fluctuations in economy. Prices are still reasonable, but in the emerging market, costs are on the rise. For those who have a dream of owning a place at the beach, there are many different ways to do so.

There is a good deal of new construction here, and it's particularly noticeable in the north beach areas, which are being developed at a breakneck speed. But don't overlook the middle and southern sections of the Outer Banks and Roanoke Island — there are some great lots with views and many older cottages for sale in these areas. While there are homes for sale all over the Outer Banks, there seems to be a particular concentration of them in the central areas, particularly west of the Bypass. The south side of Roanoke Island has handsome lots, some with minimum square footage requirements for houses constructed on them. Many homeowners are renovating older homes and cottages to keep up with the demands of today's rentals.

Whether you're interested in rental income-producing investment properties, second homes or primary residences, there's an avenue for just about everyone to own property on the Outer Banks.

The values of lots and homes have stabilized and more than likely will remain steady. Investor incentives have changed. Realtors suggest that "end users," or those who purchase a property intending to make use of it, will gain the most in this market. Tailor your purchases to your needs. Generally, you can expect to see less erosion of prices with increasing rental incomes for investment properties. Occupancy levels have been increasing about

Photo: Mary Ellen Riddle

There is still land to develop on the Outer Banks, and construction goes on year round.

10 percent every year according to the Chamber of Commerce occupancy tax figures. The increase in renters seems to stay slightly ahead of the increase in new properties.

One thing to keep in mind when deciding to build or buy is the high cost of building on the weather-prone Outer Banks. The harsh environment demands stringent building codes and that shoots the price of your investment up. Local, state and federal agencies and builders are taking a closer look at making structures more storm-resistant. In 1995 on the Outer Banks, an ad hoc committee was formed from representatives of the local building industry, North Carolina insurance companies and the N.C. Building Code Council. The group studied current national trends in building safety and came up with ideas on how to upgrade the building codes while keeping our special environmental conditions in mind. Many of the suggestions that came out of the committee will actually be incorporated in the 1997 state building codes manual. Builders currently adhere to construction standards that must withstand 110 mph winds, and buildings must be designed to resist uplift and increased sheer forces. The movement to make homes safer is a national one, prompted by the destruction caused by hurricanes Hugo and Andrew in Florida and the Gulf Coast.

A voluntary, homegrown project, Blue Sky, cropped up out of similar building-code concerns here in Dare County. The brainchild of Southern Shores town manager Cay Cross, the nationally watched Blue Sky invites builders and homeowners to participate in educating themselves on ways to improve the structure of their standing home or proposed one. The program includes structural design and training and uses an actual building built to Blue Sky specifications (situated next to the Southern Shores Town Hall) as a national training center. Structures within The Currituck Club, a new golfing community on the Currituck Outer Banks, are being built to Blue Sky specifications. The beauty of Blue Sky is that it's a voluntary partnership between government, private industry and the academic community. The goal of Blue Sky is to prevent storm destruction rather than clean up messes after the fact.

Continuing concern for coastal development will partially dictate future building. Water resources and water quality have come under careful scrutiny in recent years. Many of the developers involved with real estate projects on the north beaches make it a point to balance their vision with a great concern for maintaining as much of the integrity of the natural environment as possible. The Currituck Club again offers a good example of this partnership.

If you're looking to buy a timeshare, townhouse, single-family home or lot, select a real estate firm, ask intelligent questions, listen for specific answers and make wise decisions. Some of the questions you should ask include: What type of property do I want? How much is affordable? Will it be rented? Where will the usual services such as water, sewer and electricity come from? What area will offer the highest appreciation, lowest taxes, insurance and the best services? Where are the flood plains? What about fire and rescue services? Is the proximity of schools and churches a consideration? Medical facilities? Business opportunities? What about a nice, quiet get-away-from-it-all fishing retreat versus a luxury mansion? What about a bulkheaded boat dock? Do I want to risk erosion if I buy waterfront property?

Fractional ownership, or co-ownership, is very similar to the concept of time-sharing. With fractional ownership you share the ownership of a building/house with other parties. Most fractional ownership properties are divided into five-week segments for 10 owners, with two weeks reserved for maintenance each year. The weeks of ownership are spread throughout the year with some weeks in prime time, others in the off-season. At some resorts the weeks rotate through the years, which means everyone is assigned the most favorable season at some point. Port Trinitie and Ships Watch in Duck are two fractional-ownership developments.

Make sure you are dealing with a N.C. Buyer Agency. If so, you as a buyer will be represented in the transaction instead of just the seller. North Carolina law requires the seller to disclose the condition of the property. Ask to review this seller disclosure form before making an offer to purchase! Call the **Dare County Board of Realtors**, 441-4036, for more information.

We've provided you with a rundown here of whole ownership and timeshare properties. Included in this chapter are some of the brightest and best developments in the area and a list of notable real estate firms, architects, builders and designers. If you're in pursuit of a home at the beach then this chapter will help get you started.

Residential Resort Communities

We've listed most of the newer and more established oceanside and soundside residential communities to give you an idea of what's here on the Outer Banks. We start as far north as you can go and still be on the Outer Banks and continue south to the southern banks of Hatteras Island and Ocracoke Island. These communities include resorts that offer recreational amenities and easy access to the ocean and sound and those that provide a mixture of seasonal and year-round living and neighborhoods with more of a year-round lifestyle. Most developments have strict architectural guidelines to ensure quality development. It should also be noted that there are many one-road (dead-end streets) subdivisions scattered throughout the Outer Banks. Some of these subdivisions offer private roads and private ocean or sound accesses. These neighborhoods offer great rental opportunities but fewer amenities. Call your local real estate professional for more information about sales or rentals (see the Real Estate Sales section at the end of this chapter).

If you are a potential purchaser, don't forget to inquire about neighborhood homeowner fees. These are costs in addition to your monthly mortgage payments. They can be assessed on a monthly or annual basis.

Carova

North Swan Beach, Swan Beach, Seagull and Penny's Hill Subdivisions

Off the paved road — *453-3111*
north of N.C. 12 — *(800) 654-5224*

Access to these subdivisions is by four-wheel-drive vehicle only. Enter the beach at the ramp in Corolla's Ocean Hill. (Be sure to read the rules of the road.) You'll be in Fruitville Beach Township. Enjoy the 12-mile ride out to the northernmost subdivision, Carova Beach. You'll be

Insiders' Tips

Whether you're interested in rental income-producing investment properties, second homes or primary residences, there's an avenue for just about everyone to own property on the Outer Banks.

riding on some of the widest beaches anywhere, but it's recommended you drive at low tide. It's debatable whether or not there will ever be a paved road through these areas. Most of the time it's just you and nature. (Driving into Virginia is no longer permitted from here, and there's a posted area and gate to prevent crossing the border.) Watch for the herds of wild horses!

Virginia's False Cape State Park borders Carova on the north, and North Swan Beach borders Carova on the south. As you continue southward, you'll come to Swan Beach, Seagull and Penny's Hill subdivisions. Development began in Carova Beach in 1967, followed by development in North Swan Beach and Swan Beach. Carova Beach is the largest subdivision off the paved road. There was a planned road through this area when development began, but the road came up from Duck to Ocean Hill in the south instead.

Carova consists of approximately 2,000 lots. Resales are available in most areas. If you're wondering how many cottages have been built in this 12-mile stretch, there are approximately 400 improved lots from Ocean Hill to the Virginia line and 2,500 property owners. There are 75 registered voters, indicating a small supply of year-round residents. The Seagull and Penny's Hill subdivisions are much smaller.

The Carova subdivision offers lots fronting the canals, sandy trails and open water between Currituck Sound and the Atlantic Ocean. Swan Beach and North Swan Beach offer ocean-to-sound lots. Ocean Beach and Penny Hill do not include sound frontage. Basic amenities are offered, including electricity, telephone and water/sewer by individual well and septic. Cable television is not offered in this area, but we've been told that television reception from Hampton Roads' networks is excellent. Carova's volunteer fire department has just been enlarged. Riggs Realty knows this area better than most, and employees there are the most active as far as off-road beach sales go.

Corolla

The Villages at Ocean Hill

N.C. 12 *261-8311*

On the northern end of the Outer Banks in the village of Corolla, Ocean Hill lies at the northern end of the paved road. This unique resort community covers 153 acres, including lakefront, oceanfront and soundfront lots. There are 300 single-family homesites. This second-home neighborhood-type project is still very much available to the buying public. There are no year-round residents at this time, but many of the owners plan to retire here. Amenities include oceanfront and lakefront pools, tennis courts and a freshwater lake. Wide, white, sandy beaches are also part of the package. There are strict architectural guidelines to ensure quality development. Call Twiddy & Company for sales information and your local Duck or Corolla Realtor for rental information.

Corolla Light Resort Village

N.C. 12 *453-3000*

More than 200 acres comprise this northern Outer Banks resort. Construction began in 1985, and some very large luxury homes were built here as well as elegant three-bedroom condos and four-bedroom villas. Home sizes range from 1,300 square feet to 3,600 square feet. When it all began, Corolla Village was a sleepy, well-hidden oceanside community with a lighthouse, post office and a small general store. The developer, Richard A. Brindley, and the marketing and sales team at Brindley & Brindley Realty, have created a beautiful ocean-to-sound resort that boasts two oceanfront pool complexes, tennis courts scattered throughout the resort, a soundside pool, a watersports center and, most recently, an indoor sports center that houses a competition-size indoor pool, tennis courts, racquetball courts and exercise rooms. Two miniature golf courses complete the recreational amenities. The resort has its own water-treatment facility, and there are strict architectural guidelines to ensure quality development. Corolla Light Village Shops are in the heart of this development. Contact Brindley & Brindley for sales information and your local Corolla Realtor for rental information.

Monteray Shores

N.C. 12 *453-3600, 473-1030*

Monteray Shores, on the soundside of this northern Outer Banks area, features magnificent homes with a unique Caribbean style. The red tile roofs, arched verandas, spacious decks and an abundance of windows make these homes a popular contrast to the wooden structures found in most Outer Banks residential communities. But if you prefer Outer Banks-style homes, they also are available here. This community features single-family residences and offers sound or ocean views from every homesite. While there are no oceanfront lots, the full gymnasium, soundside clubhouse, junior Olympic swimming pool, hot tub, four tennis courts, jogging trails, stocked fishing ponds, boat ramps and other recreational amenities provide a dash of sophistication and luxury to this area of the northern Outer Banks. The nearby Monteray Shores Shopping Plaza includes a four-screen movie theater, a Food Lion grocery store, specialty shops and eateries. These services provide a tremendous convenience for visitors and residents of the northern Outer Banks. Contact Bob DeGabrielle & Associates, 453-3600, for sales information; they have an exclusive listing in this resort. For rental information, contact R & R Realty, 821 Ocean Trail, Suite 4, Corolla 27927, 453-3001.

Buck Island

N.C. 12 *453-6661*

In a small section of the northern Outer Banks lies the exclusive community of Buck Island. This development is across from the TimBuck II Shopping Village on Ocean Trail. It is an oceanfront and oceanside development. There are 78 single-family homesites and 41 townhome sites. A limited number of choice homesites are still available to the prospective buyers. Buck Island is reminiscent of the nautical seaside villages of Kiawah and Nantucket and boasts timeless Charleston-style architecture along a promenade of hardwood trees and turn-of-the-century street lights. A guarded entrance, pristine ocean beach, beach cabana, pool and tennis courts complement the commitment to full service and excellence that has become the hallmark of developer Buck Thornton. Homesites, custom homes and Charleston-style townhomes offer a variety of opportunities if you wish to own a retreat on the northern Outer Banks.

TimBuck II Shopping Center includes over 60 shops and six restaurants. The shopping center features ground-level covered parking, public restrooms and the signature seaside village architecture found throughout Buck Island resort. You can call or write for more information: P.O. Box 4502, Corolla 27927. 790 Ocean Trail.

Spindrift

Ocean Tr., Corolla *261-3566*
near the Currituck Club *(800) 334-6315*

Spindrift has 40,000-square-foot lots, large in comparison to neighboring developments. The single-family residential development offers no amenities but the privacy here can't be beat. You can build a dream home and be assured that you will not be within an arm's length of your neighbor. Call Britt Real Estate at the numbers above for more information.

Crown Point

N.C. 12 *453-2105*

Crown Point is 1 mile north of Ocean Sands and 10 miles north of Duck. This is a single-family subdivision with oceanfront and oceanside properties. It is completely separate from the Ocean Sands subdivision. There are approximately 90 homes here with a third of the project remaining for single-family development. Crown Point is a very popular resort for weekly rentals. Amenities include a swimming pool, tennis courts and private beach access. Contact Coastland Realty for sales information and your local Duck or Corolla Realtor for rentals.

Ocean Sands

N.C. 12 *453-2105*

Ocean Sands is an oceanside and oceanfront planned unit development, or PUD, considered to be a model of coastal development by land use planners, government officials and environmentalists alike. The Ocean Sands concept is centered around clusters of homes that form small colonies buffered by open space. This design eliminates through traffic while increasing privacy and open vistas. Clusters are devoted to single-family dwellings, multifamily dwellings and appropriate commercial usage. Many of the approximately 600 residences at Ocean Sands are placed in rental programs. Amenities include tennis courts, an Olympic-size swimming pool, nature trails and a fishing lake stocked with bass. The development has private roads guarded by a security force. Ocean Sands is a family-oriented community buffered on the east by the Atlantic Ocean and on the west by the exclusive Currituck Club Golfing Community. A section consisting of 166 lots is now offered for sale. Contact Coastland Realty for sales information and your local Duck or Corolla Realtor for rentals.

Pine Island

N.C. 12 *453-4216, 473-6511*

Pine Island resort is on 385 acres, with 300 single-family homesites and 3 miles of oceanfront. This planned oceanfront and oceanside community is bordered on the west by 5,000 acres of perpetually preserved marsh, islands and uplands that comprise the National Audubon Society Pine Island Sanctuary. Homesites are generous, and there are strict architectural guidelines. Central water and sewer and underground utilities are available. Owners have access to a tennis court and swimming pool. As development continues there will be additional tennis courts, swimming pools, a bathhouse, jogging paths and more. Property owners also have access to a private landing strip. The existing Pine Island homesites are but a portion of the Pine Island design, which also includes the Pine Island Racquet Club and the Pine Island Hotel, Villa and Beach Club. For those of you who are familiar with Sanderling, Pine Island will function much like that resort except on a larger scale, and everything will be private. Contact Bob DeGabrielle & Associates, 453-3600, for sales information; they have an exclusive listing in this resort. Contact any Duck or Corolla real estate professional for rental information.

Duck

Sea Ridge and Osprey

Duck Rd. (N.C. 12) *261-3566*

This area, 1½ miles north of the village of Duck, claims to have the best views on the Outer Banks and has lots and homes available. No matter how tall you are, you can stand from your lot and see a complete 360° panoramic view of the ocean and sound. Natural beauty is this development's calling card! Call Britt Real Estate for more information.

Sanderling

Duck Rd. (N.C. 12) *Sales 261-2181*
Rentals 261-3211

This ocean-to-sound community just north of Duck consists of nearly 300 homes and lots and is one of the most desirable residential communities on the Outer Banks. The heavy vegetation, winding lanes and abundant wildlife offer the most seclusion of any resort community on the beach. The developers have taken care to leave as much natural growth as possible, and there are strict building requirements to ensure privacy and value. The Sanderling Inn Resort is just north of the residential area. Homeowners have their own recreational amenities including miles of nature trails, the Soundside Raquet and Swimming Club and sailing and canoeing opportunities. Real Escapes is the primary handler of this community. Call 261-2181 for sales and rental information.

Port Trinitie

Duck Rd. (N.C. 12)
2 mi. north of Duck Village *261-3922*

Port Trinitie, situated on 23 acres of oceanfront/oceanside property, stretches across Duck Road and offers some gorgeous soundfront views. Amenities include two swimming pools, two tennis courts, a soundside pier and gazebo and an oceanfront gazebo. This development began with condominiums, which are co-ownership properties, but Port Trinitie now offers an even mixture of whole ownership single-family dwellings (cottages and townhomes) and co-owned condos. This family-oriented resort is primarily built out, but resales are available through your local Realtor. You can contact the homeowners association for rental information.

NorthPoint

Duck Rd. (N.C. 12) *480-2700*

Fractional ownership is popular here at NorthPoint, though some lots remain for individual ownership and development. There is an enclosed swimming pool, tennis and basketball courts and a long soundfront pier for fishing, crabbing and small boat dockage. One of the first fractional ownership developments on the northern Outer Banks, NorthPoint has enjoyed good values on resales.

Ships Watch

1251 Duck Rd. (N.C. 12) *261-2231*
(800) 261-7924

Mid-Atlantic Country magazine portrayed this community as "the Palm Beach of the Outer Banks." Ships Watch is a community of luxurious seaside homes in the village of Duck. Pampered vacationers, complete service and maintenance and attention to details are characteristics of this resort. Carefully placed on high rolling dunes, the homes offer spectacular views of either the ocean, the Currituck Sound or both. An Olympic-size pool, tennis courts, jogging trail, soundside pier and boat ramp, golf privileges and weekly socials offer entertainment options for the whole family. This resort provides rentals, fractional and whole ownership. Parlayed as a high-end property, developer Buck Thornton and his associates have experienced great success with this resort. Contact Ships Watch for sales and rental information.

Schooner Ridge Beach Club

Duck Rd. (N.C. 12) *261-6771*

Schooner Ridge is in the heart of Duck Village, but its oceanfront/oceanside homes are well hidden from the hustle and bustle. The high, sandy hills fronting the Atlantic Ocean are perfect for these large single-family homes with ample windows and decks. All lots are sold, but Britt Real Estate handles many of the resales for Schooner Ridge. The community offers indoor and outdoor recreational amenities. Bike paths wind through the area, and all the shops in the village are within walking distance.

Insiders' Tips

Carefully check neighborhood restrictive covenants before you buy. Many have minimum square footage requirements for new homes.

Nantucket Village

Duck Rd. (N.C. 12) *261-2224*

This private resort consists of 36 townhouse units developed on Currituck Sound just south of Duck. This is a year-round development offering an indoor pool and an outdoor tennis court. The sandy, soundside beach is free of marsh grasses and is an ideal place for wading and enjoying watercraft. Most units are available as rentals. For 1996, Nantucket Village will be adding 12 more units. Call Jim Breit at Ducks Real Estate for more information on the new units.

Ocean Crest

Duck Rd. (N.C. 12)
Near Nantucket Village *261-2000*

This is an ocean-to-sound resort consisting of 54 lots that hit the market in August 1992. Lots are 15,000 square feet or larger and are zoned for single-family dwellings. This is an upscale neighborhood with very strict architectural guidelines. Homes must be 2,000 square feet or larger. Amenities include a swimming pool, tennis courts, private ocean access and good water views. Contact Southern Shores Realty for sales information; they have an exclusive listing in this subdivision.

Southern Shores

Southern Shores is a unique 2,600-acre incorporated town with its own government and police force. Although there is a shopping center on its western boundary, commercial zoning/development is not allowed elsewhere. This town has dense maritime forests along the soundside fringe, wide open sandhills in the middle and beachfront property. The substantial year-round population attests to the popularity of Southern Shores. Development has been carefully paced through the years, and there are still many lots that remain undeveloped. It is considered one of the most desirable places to live on the Outer Banks. Southern Shores Realty on N.C. 12 in Southern Shores, 261-2000, is a good place to get started when looking for rentals or sales in this area, although many real estate companies represent this area.

Kitty Hawk

Martin's Point

U.S. 158, MP 0 *261-3892*
(800) 404-3892

Martin's Point is an exclusive waterfront community of magnificent custom homes and homesites. There are stringent building requirements, a guarded entry and some of the most beautiful maritime forests found anywhere. Homes range from 1,200 square feet to 13,000 square feet. This is primarily a year-round neighborhood. Rentals are available on a very limited basis. Owners here have easy access to an elementary school, shopping and golf.

When you arrive on the Outer Banks at the eastern terminus of the Wright Memorial Bridge, the entrance to Martin's Point is on your immediate left. The community is closed to drive-through inspections, but if you're considering a permanent move to the Outer Banks, it's an upscale area you'll want to look at. Stop in at Sun Realty adjacent to the Martin's Point gate or call the numbers above for more information.

Kitty Hawk Landing

W. Kitty Hawk Rd. *No central phone*

This is a residential community of mostly year-round residents. It's on the far western edges of Kitty Hawk. To get there, turn west off U.S. 158 at milepost 4 onto West Kitty Hawk Road and just keep driving until you see the signs. The community borders Currituck Sound. It has deep canals, tall pines and gorgeous sunsets. Contact your local Realtor for more information.

Sandpiper Cay Condominiums

Sand Dune Dr. *261-2188*

This resort community consists of 280 condominium units and is near Sea Scape Golf Course. One hundred fifty-five of the units are second homes, and 40 percent of the units are either long-term rentals or primary residences, making this a year-round resort. Less than 3 percent of the units are available for short-term or weekly leases. All of the original inventory has been sold, though some resales are available. All units are priced less than $100,000, including two-story townhouses and single-story garden units. Amenities include a large outdoor pool, clubhouse and tennis court. Homeowners fees apply. Contact Sandpiper Cay for more information.

Kill Devil Hills

First Flight Village

First St. *No central phone*

This is one of the Outer Banks' most popular year-round neighborhoods in the central area of the beach. Generally, there aren't many truly year-round areas available on the Outer Banks, making First Flight especially attractive to many families. The entrance to First Flight Village is on the west side of U.S. 158 at milepost 7½. This is a family-oriented neighborhood, so if you're considering a permanent move to the Outer Banks, you should check out this community. There are quite a few long-term rentals available in this area as well. First Flight Village real estate is considered moderately priced. Contact your local beach real estate professional for sales and rental information.

Colington Island

Colington Harbour

Colington Rd. *441-5886*

Development began more than 20 years ago on this big island. To get to there, turn off U.S. 158 at the Wright Brothers Memorial onto Ocean Bay Boulevard, which eventually turns into Colington Road. Colington Harbour is about 4 miles down the winding road. This community has some 12 miles of bulkheaded deep-water canals and soundfront lots. Access to Albemarle Sound and the Atlantic Ocean is through Oregon Inlet, which is approximately 25 miles by boat south of Colington Island. The area has a large number of luxury homes complete with boat docks, but there are also many average-size homes. This community combines a year-round population of more than 2,000 with seasonal and weekly renters. The picnic area, playground, sandy beach on Kitty Hawk Bay, boat ramp, boat slips for rent and fuel dock are available to all residents, including year-round renters. Clubhouse activities, the Olympic-size swimming pool, children's pool and tennis court are available to club members. What makes Colington Harbour popular is its remoteness, private entry and the many canals that offer waterfront living to most residents.

Colington Heights

Colington Harbour *261-3815*

This is the last developable subdivision within Colington Harbour. There are 23 lots on approximately 35 acres. The inventory includes wooded interior lots, waterview lots and waterfront properties. Essentially, this is a maritime forest development. Large lot sizes contribute to the privacy of the area. Roads are private, and there is private beach access on Albemarle Sound. Architectural controls are in effect, and the developer has paid all of the water-impact fees, making the real estate even more attractive. Contact Beach Realty for more information.

Cliffs of Colington

Schoolhouse Rd. *261-8686*

Cliffs of Colington features 29 large wooded lots from ¾-acre to 125,000 square feet. With private road access, these homesites, some of which are soundfront, are on 52 acres of unique forest. The development has underground utilities, good restrictive covenants and architectural controls. Included is private a soundside park and sandy beach, county water and individual septic (soundfront lots have central septic). Tennis courts are planned. The location is a plus — a nice combination of privacy yet near schools and shopping centers. Numerous lots are available, and some homes are also for sale here. Contact Debbie Lawson at Resort Realty for more information.

Nags Head

South Ridge

U.S. 158, MP 13 441-2800, 441-2450

This subdivision is on the hill behind the Nags Head Post Office. Ultimately, there will be 150 homes in this neighborhood consisting of second homes, investment properties and year-round residences. Owners and renters can enjoy the ocean and sound views. Contact RE/MAX Ocean Realty for additional information; they have an exclusive sales listing in this development.

The Village at Nags Head

U.S. 158, MP 15 (800) 548-9688
Sales 441-8533, Rentals 480-2224

Development began about eight years ago at the Village, and this community has become one of the bestsellers on the Outer Banks. The golf course, with a beautiful clubhouse and popular restaurant, and the oceanfront recreational complex with tennis courts and a pool, make this attractive residential community most desirable. Single-family homes and townhomes provide something for everyone. The Ammons Corporation developed this large community that spans from the ocean to the sound. The oceanfront homes are some of the largest and most luxurious anywhere. There's plenty to do whether you live or vacation here. It's an excellent choice for beach living, vacation rentals or investment.

Roanoke Island

Pirate's Cove

Manteo/Nags Head Cswy. (800) 762-0245
Sales 473-1451, Rentals 473-6800

Pirate's Cove is a distinctive residential-marina-resort community. Hundreds of acres of protected wildlife marshlands border Pirate's Cove on one side, while the peaceful waters of Roanoke Sound are on the other. Deep-water canals provide each owner with a dock at the door, and the centrally located marina is home to many large yachts and fishing boats. Pirate's Cove offers homesites, homes, condominiums and even dockominiums fronting deep-water canals. There's always activity here. Fishing tournaments seem as important as sleeping to many of the residents, and locals and visitors can get in on the fun. Other recreational amenities include lighted tennis courts, swimming pools, a Jacuzzi, a sauna, a restaurant and a beautifully appointed clubhouse. Scheduled recreational activities for all ages are available, as are watersports including Waverunner and boat rentals. One of the prettiest settings on the Outer Banks enhances the Victorian-nautical design of these homes.

Heritage Point

Pearce Rd. 473-1450

This year-round resort community is subdivided into 111 lots off U.S. 64/264 W. next to Fort Raleigh National Historic Site. Site improvements and restrictive covenants are in place. Interior, soundview and soundfront lots overlooking the Croatan and Albemarle sounds are available. Lot sizes range from just less than an acre to more than 3 acres. The community sports two tennis courts, and so far, 14 slips of the proposed 111-slip boat basin are completed. A parking area and common beach is provided for homeowners. Homeowner association fees apply. Contact Heritage Realty for more information; they have an exclusive sales listing in this development.

Rodanthe

Resort Rodanthe

N.C. 12 (800) 334-4745

This resort consists of 20 condominium units diagonally facing the oceanfront. All units have ocean and sound views. The condos are for sale, but owners also rent them. Amenities include a swimming pool and private ocean access. Couples or small families would be happy here, as only one- and two-bedroom units are available.

Mirlo Beach

N.C. 12 987-2350

This sound-to-oceanfront resort community is 12 miles south of the Oregon Inlet Bridge, adjacent to Pea Island National Wildlife Refuge. There are approximately 10 large oceanfront cottages in Mirlo Beach, each sleeping an average of 12 people comfortably. Amenities include tennis courts and private beach and sound accesses. This resort has a solid rental history. Contact Midgett Realty for sales and rental information.

Waves

St. Waves

N.C. 12 995-4600

This subdivision, developed during the 1980s, consists of approximately 55 lots and 20 houses. Homes and homesites are available for sale. These properties offer ocean, sound and lake views. The homes are upscale, and architectural controls are in effect. Amenities include a swimming pool, tennis court and a centrally located lake. St. Waves maintains an excellent rental history. Contact Hatteras Realty for more information.

Avon

Kinnakeet Shores

N.C. 12 *995-5821*

Once a desolate stretch of narrow land between the Atlantic Ocean and Pamlico Sound, Kinnakeet Shores is a residential community that is being carefully developed. It consists of 500 acres next to beautiful marshlands and one of the best windsurfing areas in the world. Recreational amenities include swimming pools and tennis courts. This is the largest development on Hatteras Island, and the homes tend to be big, reminding us of the ones on the northern beaches. This is primarily a second-home development, offering one of the most popular rental programs on the island. A small shopping plaza with a Food Lion grocery store is in Avon, as are a handful of restaurants. The village of Buxton is only 5 miles away. Contact Sun Realty for additional sales and rental information.

Buxton

Hatteras Pines

N.C. 12 *995-4600*

This 150-acre subdivision is nestled in a maritime forest in the heart of Buxton. Consisting of 114 lots rolling along the dunes and ridges, it may be one of the safest places on the island to build a year-round home because of the shelter of the woods. The roads for this development are intact, along with protective covenants. A pool and tennis court are planned. Contact Hatteras Realty for more information.

Photo: Mary Ellen Riddle

Many artists call the Outer Banks home.

Hatteras Village Area

Hatteras By The Sea

N.C. 12 *986-2570*

This rather small community of 36 lots on 25 acres is one of the last oceanfront areas available for residential living. There's not much land on the southern end of the Outer Banks, and a good portion is preserved by the National Seashore designation. A large pool and some carefully designed nature paths are included. Sunrise and sunset views are unobstructed here.

Timesharing

Timesharing is a deeded transaction under the jurisdiction of the North Carolina Real Estate Commission. A deeded share is one-52nd of the unit property being purchased. This deed grants the right to use the property in perpetuity. Always ask if the property you're inspecting is deeded timeshare because there is such a thing as undeeded timeshare, which is the right to use a property, but the property reverts to the developer in the end. What you are buying is the right to use a specific piece of real estate for a week per share. The weeks are either fixed at the time of sale, or they rotate yearly.

Some disadvantages of being locked into a time and place have been partly removed by RCI (Resort Condominiums Inc.), a timeshare bank. There are other similar operations. Members trade their weeks to get different time slots at a variety of locations around the world. Qualifying for the purchase of a timeshare unit can be no more difficult than qualifying for a credit card, but be aware of financing charges that are higher than regular mortgages.

Most timeshare resorts on the Outer Banks are multifamily constructions, with recreational amenities that vary from minimal to luxurious and sometimes include the services of a recreational director. Timeshare units usually come furnished and carry a monthly maintenance fee. Tax advantages for ownership and financing are not available to the purchaser of a timeshare, so investigate this angle.

Many offer "free weekends" — you agree to a sales pitch and tour of the facilities in exchange for accommodations. Listen, ask questions and stay in control of your money and your particular situation. If you get swept away, you'll only have five days to change your mind, if you so desire, according to North Carolina Time Share Act that governs the sale of timeshares. If you can afford the relatively small amount of money to cover your vacation lodgings for years to come, along with the option of trading for another location, timesharing is a rather hassle-free and attractive option for many people.

It is best to keep the purchase of timeshares in proper perspective; your deeded share only enables you to vacation in that property during a designated time period each year for as long as you own that share. This makes timeshare very different from other potential investments. All real estate investment decisions require thorough research and planning, and timeshare is no exception. The rental of timeshare units should not really be of any special concern to you because a rental in any case is a onetime deal — just like renting a motel room or a cottage for a week — and you're not being asked to buy anything.

Timeshare salespeople are licensed — to everyone's advantage — and they earn commissions. Some great arrangements are out there, some not so good. Check thoroughly before you buy.

Several Outer Banks companies specialize in timesharing. The following list includes some of the reputable businesses to contact.

Barrier Island Ocean Pines

N.C. 12, Duck *261-3525*

Ocean Pines offers timesharing opportunities featuring oceanfront one- and two-bedroom condominiums. Amenities include an indoor pool, tennis courts, Jacuzzis and, of course, the beach.

Barrier Island Station

N.C. 12, Duck *261-3525*

Barrier Island, one of the largest timeshare resorts on the Outer Banks, is on a high dune area of ocean to sound property. These are multifamily units of wood construction. There is an attractive, full-service restaurant

Insiders' Tips

Watch out for unexpected fees when building. Water tap fees can vary by as much as $1,000.

and bar with a soundside sailing center, in addition to the beach. A full-time recreation director is on board here for a variety of planned activities and events. Indoor swimming, tennis courts and other recreational facilities round out a full amenities package. This is a popular resort in a just as popular seaside village.

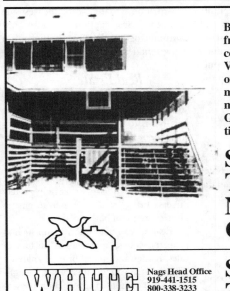

Barrier Island Station at Kitty Hawk

1 Cypress Knee Tr.
Kitty Hawk *261-4610*

Barrier Island Station at Kitty Hawk is a brand-new multi-family vacation ownership resort. The setting in a maritime forest is incredible. The 100 acres of private land sports a million-dollar sports complex featuring an indoor pool, Jacuzzi, aerobic and nautilus workout facilities. You can also shoot some pool or play Ping Pong in the game room. Condominiums are one, two or three bedrooms. The privacy can't be beat. The community is also near two shopping centers.

Bodie Island Realty

Beach Rd., MP 17
Nags Head *441-9110, 441-0452*

This company manages timeshares in the Bodie Island Beach Club in Nags Head. The Beach Club features two pools, an oceanfront sundeck, a gameroom, miniature golf and a playground. The company also handles resales of timeshare units in complexes up and down the Outer Banks.

Dunes South Beach and Racquet Club

Beach Rd., MP 18
Nags Head *441-4090*

Townhome timesharing at this resort

features two- and three-bedroom units with fireplaces, washers and dryers and Jacuzzis. There are 20 units and most are oceanfront. The remainder of the units are oceanside. A pool, tennis court, putting green and playground make up the recreational amenities.

Outer Banks Beach Club

Beach Rd., MP 9
Kill Devil Hills *441-7036*

The round, wooden buildings of the Outer Banks Beach Club were the first timesharing opportunities built and sold on the Outer Banks. The 160 units include oceanfront, oceanside and clubhouse units across the street, near the clubhouse with an indoor pool. There are also two outdoor pools in great oceanfront locations. One-, two- and three-bedroom units also have access to whirlpools, tennis courts and a playground. There is a full-time recreation director offering a variety of activities and games.

Outer Banks Resort Rentals

Pirates Quay Shopping Center
U.S. 158, MP 11, Nags Head *441-2134*

This company deals exclusively with timeshares, handling rentals and resales at all of the timeshare complexes on the Outer Banks. All of the units this company represents are furnished and self contained, and all have swimming pools.

Sea Scape Beach and Golf Villas

U.S. 158, MP 2½, Kitty Hawk *261-3837*

There's plenty of recreation here. Tennis courts, two swimming pools, an indoor recreation facility, weight room and game room. The Villas are next to a golf course. The multifamily units are of wood construction, and they are on the west side of U.S. 158. Sea Scape offers a unique opportunity for timeshare ownership and an active rental program.

Real Estate Sales

Visitors to the Outer Banks may stumble upon their dream home, but your best bet is to contact local Realtors. Remember, real estate agents and brokers are not necessarily Realtors. Brokers and their agents must join the Board of Realtors to become members, but Realtors subscribe to a strict code of ethics that help protect buyers and sellers. They help to ensure fair treatment for both parties.

Realtors can offer information such as property values, appreciation, history of sales, resales and neighborhood analyses. They can tell you whether or not a neighborhood is composed of year-round or seasonal residents, and they can render an opinion as to whether or not you'll be satisfied with the area you are considering.

Boards of Realtors are your best resource for answers about major developments and fair market prices. They supervise the Multiple Listing Service. Only brokers and their agents who are Realtors have access to MLS information. For your real estate-related questions, we've listed the addresses and telephone numbers for the state and county Board of Realtors.

North Carolina Association of Realtors (NCAR), 2901 Seawell Road, P.O. Box 7918, Greensboro 27417, (910) 294-1415.

Dare County Board of Realtors Inc., P.O. Drawer G, 110 W. Oregon Avenue, Kill Devil Hills 27948, (919) 441-4036.

Insiders' Tips

When purchasing a lot, make sure the sale is contingent on a health department evaluation for a septic system.

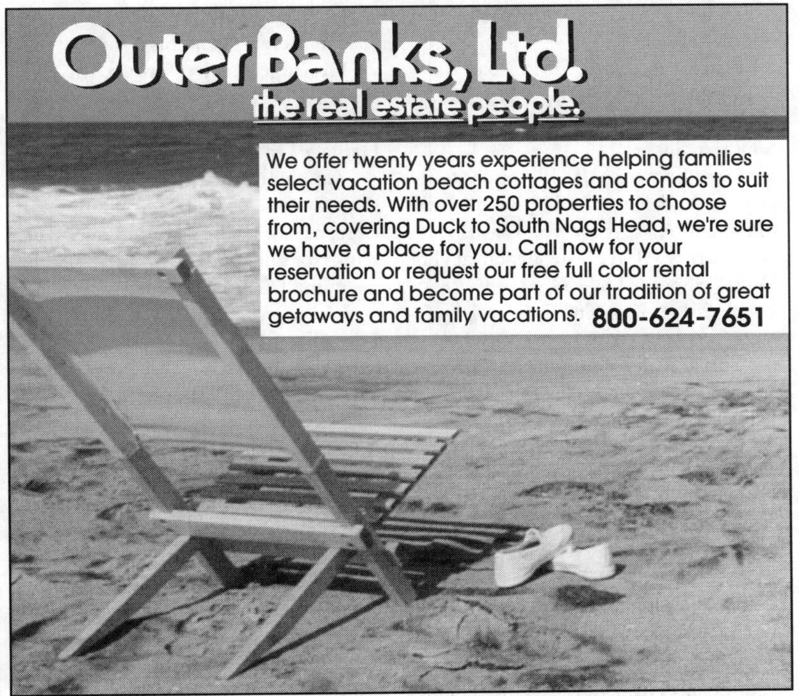

Following are some Outer Banks real estate sales companies, their locations and contact information. While this list is not inclusive, it is representative of reputable real estate sales companies on the Outer Banks. Most, if not all, of these companies are members of the Board of Realtors. Call the Dare County Board of Realtors to be sure.

20/20 Realty Ltd., 516 U.S. 64, Manteo, 473-2020, represents Roanoke Island and the Outer Banks.

Atlantic Realty, U.S. 158, MP 2, Kitty Hawk, 261-2154 or (800) 334-8401, represents Corolla to South Nags Head. A second location is in Corolla at TimBuck II Shopping Village, 453-4110, (800) 669-9245.

BC Construction Builders Inc., U.S. 158, MP 2½, Kitty Hawk, 261-5050, represents Carova to Hatteras and Roanoke Island. It offers construction, a full turnkey (ready to move in) service.

Beach Realty & Construction/Kitty Hawk Rentals, U.S. 158, MP 2, Kitty Hawk, 261-3815, handles real estate sales, rentals and construction. A second location is in Duck on Duck Road (N.C. 12) near Sanderling; call 261-6600 or (800) 849-3825. A third location is in Kill Devil Hills on U.S. 158, MP 6, 441-1106 or (800) 635-1559. This company represents Ocean Hill to Nags Head.

Bodie Island Realty, U.S. 158, MP 6, Kill Devil Hills, 441-9443; and Old Oregon Inlet Road, MP 17, Nags Head, 441-9110. Bodie Island Realty offers general real estate, timeshare and timeshare resales. It covers Corolla to north Hatteras.

Brindley & Brindley Realty & Development Inc., 1023 Ocean Trail (N.C. 12) in the Brindley Building at Corolla Light,

453-3000, represents Carova Beach to Southern Shores.

Britt Real Estate, Duck Road (N.C. 12) north of Duck Village, 261-3566 or (800) 334-6315, represents Corolla to Southern Shores.

Cape Escape, N.C. 12, (opposite the post office) Salvo, 987-2336, handles sales in Rodanthe, Waves and Salvo.

Century 21 At The Beach at The Dunes Shops, U.S. 158, MP 3½, Kitty Hawk, 261-2855 or (800) 245-0021, represents Carova Beach to South Nags Head.

Christi Real Estate and Construction, 4628 U.S. 158, Kitty Hawk, 261-6400 or (800) 282-6401, handles sales and construction from Corolla to Nags Head.

Coastland Realty, Ocean Trail (N.C. 12) in Corolla, 453-2105, offers real estate sales only and represents the northern Outer Banks and specifically Ocean Sands and Crown Point.

Cove Realty, between the Beach Road and U.S. 158, MP 14, 441-6391 or (800) 635-7007, represents Nags Head and South Nags Head and specializes in Old Nags Head Cove.

The D.A.R.E. Company, 106 E. Third Street, Kill Devil Hills, 441-1521, represents Dare and Currituck counties.

Dolphin Realty, N.C. 12 in Hatteras Village, 986-2241 or (800) 338-4775, represents properties on Hatteras Island.

Duck's Real Estate, Duck Road (N.C. 12), 261-2224 or (800) 992-2976, represents Carova to South Nags Head.

Gardner Realty, Beach Road, MP 16, Nags Head, 441-8985 or (800) 468-4066, represents the areas of Kitty Hawk, Kill Devil Hills and Nags Head but specializes in the area of South Nags Head.

Hatteras Realty, N.C. 12, Avon, 995-4600, represents Hatteras Island.

Heritage Realty Group Inc., 405 Queen Elizabeth Street, Manteo, 473-1707, represents Roanoke Island and the Heritage Point development.

Karichele Realty, 66 Sunset Boulevard, Corolla, 453-2377, or TimBuck II, Corolla, 453-4400, covers the entire Outer Banks for sales and the northern beaches including Duck and Corolla for rentals.

Kitty Dunes Realty, U.S. 158, MP 4½ in Kitty Hawk, 261-2173, and 1180 Ocean Trail (N.C. 12) in Corolla at the Corolla Light Village Shops, 453-DUNE, represents Carova to Oregon Inlet. This company also has Colington Realty, 2141 Colington Road, 441-3863. Residents of Canada should contact the Canadian representative (514) 376-4382.

Joe Lamb Jr. & Associates, Realtors, U.S. 158, MP 2, Kitty Hawk, 261-4444, (800) 552-6257, represents Kitty Hawk, Kill Devil Hills, Nags Head and some northern Outer Banks areas.

Lawson Realty, N.C. 12, Frisco, 995-5847, covers sales on Hatteras Island.

Frank Mangum Realty Inc., U.S. 158, MP 10½, Nags Head, 441-3600 or (800) 279-5552, handles sales covering the entire Outer Banks. Visit the company's Internet site at http://www.mangumrealty.com.

Midgett Realty represents the southern end of the Outer Banks and has three locations on Hatteras Island. Call 986-2841 or (800) 527-2903 for the Hatteras Village location, 995-5333 for the Avon location and 987-2350 for the office in Rodanthe.

Sharon Miller Realty on Ocracoke Is-

Insiders' Tips

Local columnist Chris Kidder writes a thought-provoking and humanized real estate column for *The Virginian-Pilot's* weekend tabloid *Carolina Coast*.

land, 928-5711 or 928-5731, represents Ocracoke Island properties.

Nags Head Realty, U.S. 158, MP 10½, Nags Head, 441-4311 or (800) 222-1531, represents Carova to Oregon Inlet.

Ocean Country Realty, N.C. 12, Avon, 995-6700, represents Hatteras Island properties.

Ocracoke Island Realty Inc., 928-6261 or 928-7411, represents Ocracoke Island properties.

Outer Banks, Ltd., U.S. 158, MP 10½, Nags Head, 441-7156, represents Corolla to Nags Head and Roanoke Island.

Outer Banks Resort Rentals, Pirate's Quay, U.S. 158, MP 11, Nags Head, 441-2134. Marvin Beard represents the sales and rentals of timeshares only from Duck to South Nags as well as a few in Hatteras.

Outer Beaches Realty, N.C. 12 in both Avon and Waves, represents Hatteras Island. Call 995-4477 in Avon and 987-2771 in Waves.

Jim Perry & Company in the Jim Perry Building on U.S. 158, MP 5½, Kill Devil Hills, 441-3051 and (800) 222-6135, represents all areas of the Outer Banks.

Pirate's Cove on the Manteo/Nags Head Causeway, 473-1451 and (800) 762-0245, represents properties in Pirate's Cove.

Real Escapes Properties, Duck Road in Duck Village, 261-2181, represents Sanderling.

RE/MAX Ocean Realty, U.S. 158, MP 6½, Kill Devil Hills, 441-2450, represents Corolla to Hatteras Village.

Resort Realty in the Resort Realty Building on U.S. 158, MP 4½, Kitty Hawk, 261-8282, represents the entire Outer Banks. The company has a Duck location on Duck Road, 261-8686; and a

Corolla location in the TimBuck II Shopping Center, 453-3700.

Riggs Realty in the Austin Building at 1152 Ocean Trail (N.C. 12) in Corolla, 453-3111, specializes in the northern beaches. This company is involved with sales only (no rentals).

Salvo Real Estate, 26204 Monitor Lane, Salvo, 987-2343, covers sales on the entire Outer Banks.

Sea Oats Realty, U.S. 158, MP 11½, Pirate's Quay, Nags Head, 480-2325, handles real estate sales from Duck to South Nags Head.

Seaside Realty, U.S. 158, MP 3, Kitty Hawk, 261-5500 and (800) 395-2525, represents Corolla to South Nags Head.

Southern Shores Realty, N.C. 12, Southern Shores, 261-2000 and (800) 334-1000, represents Corolla to Nags Head.

Sun Realty, U.S. 158, MP 9, Kill Devil Hills, 441-8011, represents the entire Outer Banks and has locations from Corolla to Avon. Call 453-8811 in Corolla; 261-4183 in Duck; 261-3892 in Kitty Hawk; 967-2755 in Salvo; and 995-5821 in Avon.

Surf or Sound Realty, N.C. 12, Avon, 995-6052, represents Hatteras Island.

Mercedes Tabano, N.C. 12, Rodanthe, 987-2711, represents Hatteras Island.

Twiddy & Company Realty, 1181 Duck Road, 261-8311, in Duck, represents Corolla through Southern Shores. A Corolla office is at the corner of Ocean Trail and Second Street, 453-3325.

The Villages at Ocean Hill is on N.C. 12 just before the end of the paved road, 261-8311, and represents Carova Beach to Southern Shores.

Village Realty at the Village at Nags Head, U.S. 158, MP 15, Nags Head, 441-8533, represents the Village at Nags Head.

Water Side Realty Inc., N.C. 12, Buxton, 995-6001 and (800) 530-0022, represents Avon to Hatteras.

Stan White Realty & Construction Inc., U.S. 158, MP 10½, Nags Head, 441-1515 and (800) 338-3233, represents Duck to Hatteras Village.

Woodard Realty & Construction Inc. in the Village Plaza at 947-D W. Kitty Hawk Road, 261-1962 and (800) 782-2118, represents the Outer Banks and Currituck for construction and Corolla to South Nags Head for sales.

Residential Construction

There is a growing trend of people building year-round homes on the Outer Banks. Building a custom home has its perks — you can build the home of your dreams and choose the location. Many folks dream about owning oceanfront property, and for some, it's the perfect choice. But you may want to consider your year-round needs before you go bananas over the view. You can get away from beach crowds and ever-changing tenants by purchasing a lot in a neighborhood. Also, many already-built homes were designed for vacationers and do not have much storage or closet space.

Obviously, when you design your own home you can include closets galore. While some new construction costs more initially than purchasing an existing home, your costs may be less in the long run when you consider repairs and energy efficiency. New building codes require more insulation which lowers your cooling and heating costs.

Some tips to keep in mind if you plan to build: Visit homes similar to the one you want. A walk-through can be a real wake-up call and dismiss any fantasy you may have about what the space is going to feel like. Find a builder that understands your needs and will build what you want rather than their own idea of a dream home. Some builders only work from a few plans. When shopping for contractors, don't just compare prices. Make sure you are comparing the product and aim for the highest quality.

If you're building to rent, make sure

you get your brochure printed before the fall rental season begins. Delays can really affect your success in renting. You may want to choose a company to handle your property that is not already overwhelmed with rentals. This way there is less competition to rent within the company and they can give you more attention. You want your property to stand out.

North Carolina law requires that building contractors have a license, helping to assure that you maintain a secure state of mind. Some still get around the laws, so check qualifications and reputation before signing on the dotted line. Contact the **Outer Banks Homebuilders Association,** P.O. Box 398, Kitty Hawk 27949, 255-1733, for information about local builders and building services. Members subscribe to a code of ethics that help protect your interests. Get in touch with owners of local homes to query them about their experiences with builders. Ask lenders. If you're itching to buy a lot or home, going to the real estate company first is fine, but you can reverse the situation and go to a lender first instead. They'll also know the reputable sales and construction companies all over the Outer Banks.

Building a home in a coastal environment exposes you to more than a trifling of codes and restrictions. Regulations set by the North Carolina Coastal Management Authority (CAMA) are in place to protect the environment. Use them to protect yourself as well. CAMA will become a familiar acronym to you here as you go through the building process.

Local building codes and restrictions vary in each area of the beach. Try to meet with local planning boards. Although the builder obtains permits, it's always good for you to know how it's done and what's required.

Do your homework before you buy or build. The best real estate agents have plenty of general information; some have specific information, which is what you need. Get educated with specific, printed information. The best builders know the ropes too. Questions that come up after the fact can drive you up a wall if you live out of town and the builder is out on the construction site driving nails and not in the office answering the phone.

A road tour of the Banks will reveal a wide variety of homes. It can get tough to choose what you want. And what about furnishings? Does that wall space allow for a proper-size bed or sofa? What can be used on the windows?

We've listed designers, architects, builders and interior decorators to help you get started. This list is nowhere near inclusive, but these are folks whose good reputations have withstood the test of time.

General Contractors

B.C. Construction Inc., Kitty Hawk, 261-5050

Beach Realty and Construction, Kitty Hawk, 261-3815

Brumfield Realty and Construction Inc., Kill Devil Hills, 441-2130

Carolina Beach Builders, Kill Devil Hills, 441-5598

Cartwright Builder & General Contractor, Kill Devil Hills, 441-6341

Christi Real Estate & Construction, Kitty Hawk, 261-6400

Creef Construction Company, Southern Shores, 491-2300

Dixon & Meekins, General Contractors, Kill Devil Hills, 441-2100

Olin Finch & Co., Duck, 261-8710

Fulcher Homes, Kitty Hawk, 261-3316

Gardner Realty, Nags Head, 441-8985 or (800) 468-4066

Hoffman Builders Inc., Nags Head, 441-5331

Homeport Realty and Construction, Ocracoke, 928-6141

Allen Huddleston, Southern Shores, 261-2134

Mancuso Development, Corolla, 453-8921

Midgett Realty, Hatteras Village, 986-2841

Newcomb Builders Inc., Kitty Hawk, 441-1803

Newman Homes Construction Inc., Kitty Hawk, 261-3844

Outer Banks Homes, Kill Devil Hills, 441-8254

Real Escapes Ltd., Duck Village, 261-2181

Sandalwood Construction Company Inc., Kitty Hawk, 261-3258

The Shotton Company, Port Trinitie, 261-5555

Snearer Construction Co. Inc., Kitty Hawk, 261-2228

Stormont & Company, Kitty Hawk, 261-8724

Bo Taylor Fine Homes Inc., Nags Head, 441-8544

Thornton Construction Ltd., Corolla, 491-8711

Lee Tugwell, General Contractors Inc., Manteo, 473-3620

Waldt Construction Company, Duck, 473-1334

Stan White Realty and Construction Inc., Nags Head, 441-1515

Woodard Realty & Construction Co. Inc., Kitty Hawk, 261-1962

Carl Worsley Co. General Contractor, Nags Head, 441-2327

Designers and Architects

Benjamin Cahoon Architect, Nags Head, 441-0271

Carolina Beach Builders, Kill Devil Hills, 441-5598

Dare Designs, Kill Devil Hills, 441-5704

Design Associates II, Southern Shores, 261-8498

Dixon Design Associates Inc., Corolla, 453-4279

Alex Engart, AIA, Duck, 261-4473

Greg Frucci AIA, Nags Head, 441-5136

Mike Florez & Associates, Kitty Hawk, 261-7127

Magnacorp Design, Duck, 261-4447

Lester Powell Building Designs, Nags Head, 480-3888, 473-5529

Real Escapes Ltd., Duck Village, 261-2181

Sandcastle Design Group, Southern Shores, 261-2766

Thornton Construction, Ltd., Corolla, 473-6500, 491-8711

John F. Wilson, IV, Manteo, 473-3282

Interior Design/Decorating

A&B Carpets, Manteo, 473-3219; Kitty Hawk, 261-8106; Hatteras area, 995-6030

Ambrose Furniture, Kitty Hawk, 261-4836

Decor by the Shore, Kitty Hawk, 261-6222

Interiors, Kitty Hawk, 261-4105

Island Design, Southern Shores, 261-7822

Joan's, Corolla, TimBuck II, 453-8844

Manteo Furniture, Manteo, 473-2131

Sally Newell Interiors, Ocracoke, 928-6141

Outer Banks Textiles, Kill Devil Hills, 441-7563

Phelps Drapery & Interiors Ltd., Kitty Hawk, 261-6644

Village Home Furnishings, Nags Head, 441-6868

Viking Furniture, Kill Devil Hills, 441-6444

Inside Healthcare

The multitude of folks who visit the Outer Banks annually far out number our year-round residents so rescue, ambulance and medical agencies are fully prepared to assist visitors who come to our paradise. Unfortunately in a real life paradise, accidents happen and illnesses crop up when you least expect them. Professionals here can help you with anything from a scraped knee to a major medical challenge. A growing number of alternative medical services are also available. Massage, chiropractic and acupressure therapies, nutritional counseling, stress management and fitness training are now common on the Outer Banks. Our medical community expands every year, so here's some updated information that we hope will make your stay on the Outer Banks a safe and smooth one. And remember, whether you vacation on our barrier islands or in New York City, some common sense in dealing with emergencies always helps, especially in the case of water safety. Read on for some tips that could be literal life savers.

Emergency Numbers

Dial 911 for all emergency services in Dare and Currituck counties, including ocean rescue.

The emergency-only numbers for the U.S. Coast Guard are 995-6410 in Dare and Currituck counties and 938-3711 on Ocracoke Island.

Medical Centers and Clinics

Chesapeake Medical Specialists

U.S. 158, in The Marketplace
Southern Shores *261-5800*

Fourteen specialists form the framework for this affiliate of Virginia's Chesapeake General Hospital. Available services here include urology; obstetrics and gynecology; orthopedics; audiology; pediatrics; rheumatology; dermatology; ear, nose and throat; and allergy care. Minor office surgery is performed on the premises and surgeons specializing in colon/rectal, plastic, vascular and general surgery work through this complex. This is not an emergency-care facility. No referrals are necessary. Call for insurance information. The facility serves patients by appointment Monday through Friday from 9 AM to 5 PM.

Beach Medical Care

U.S. 158, Southern Shores *261-4187*

Beach Medical Care is a family and urgent-care practice. Psychological counseling (261-5190), audiology services, and speech, language, occupational and physical therapy (261-9049) are all close at hand for those on the northern Outer Banks. Call for more information and appointments.

Regional Medical Center

U.S. 158, MP 1½
Kitty Hawk *261-9000*

The communities of the Outer Banks rely on this medical center for convenient and competent healthcare. The facility offers the widest range of services on the Outer Banks and strives to provide quick and easy access to the appropriate diagnostic and healthcare departments for those in need. In addition, preventive and educational programs are also offered here. This medical complex consists of:

Urgent Care/Family Medicine *261-4187*

Physicians from Beach Medical Care staff this center that provides urgent care and family medicine for scheduled and walk-in patients seven days a week. Off-season hours are 9 AM to 9 PM. Summer season extended hours are 8 AM to 9 PM.

RMS Surgery & Procedure Center *261-9009*

This is an outpatient surgery center. Procedures such as breast biopsy, hernia repair, laparoscopy, D and C, tonsillectomy, adenoidectomy, oral surgery, cosmetic plastic surgery and tendon repair are performed here.

Medical Specialists *261-9000*

Staffed with approximately 30 medical specialists in rotation, the group provides care for a wide range of needs. A directory of physicians and specialties can be obtained by calling the above number. Lab Corp Laboratories is located here, and blood tests are handled quickly for in-house diagnosis.

Radiology and Imaging *261-4311*

Outer Banks Radiology provides routine as well as diagnostic services such as mammograms, ultrasounds and fluoroscopy.

Coastal Women's Clinic, Ltd. *338-2151*

This full-service clinic provides outpatient services for all types of medical needs for women, including routine gynecological examinations.

First Flight Family Practice

2518 S. Croatan Hwy. (U.S. 158, MP 10½)
Nags Head *441-3177*

Dr. Charles Davidson provides general medical care from Monday through Thursday. X-ray services are available. Appointments can be made during office hours, from 8 AM to 6 PM.

Virginia Dare Women's Center

U.S. 158, MP 10½
Nags Head *441-2144*

Appointments are available for women-centered medical care. Patty Johnson is the center's certified nurse-midwife and family nurse practitioner. Maternity care, baby and youth care and pap smears are offered along with generalized care. The center is open Monday, Tuesday and Thursday from 9 AM to 1 PM and 2 PM to 5 PM.

Outer Banks Medical and Emergency Care

W. Barnes St., at U.S. 158, MP 11
Nags Head *441-7111*

This is the only 24-hour medical facility on the beach. Walk-ins are welcome, and there is an X-ray laboratory on the premises. Appointments for family medical care are accepted.

MacDowell Family Health Center

U.S. 64, Manteo *473-2500*

Dr. Brian MacDowell provides com-

Insiders' Tips

Read our tips in the Fishing chapter to avoid getting stuck with a hook. If it happens, don't panic. Outer Banks medical folk have plenty of experience in getting them out.

plete family medical care at this office. Dr. MacDowell has an excellent bedside manner. X-ray services are available, and some lab work is done on the premises. Psychological counseling services are provided by Debra MacDowell, MA, NCC. Individual, marriage and family counseling is provided. Call for an appointment. The center's general hours are 8:30 AM to 5 PM Monday, Wednesday and Friday. Tuesday and Thursday hours are 8:30 AM to 12:30 PM.

Dare Medical Associates

U.S. 64, Manteo *473-3478*

Dr. Walter Holton provides family service and acute care from this office. X-ray services are available. Hours are 8 AM to 5 PM Monday through Friday.

Hatteras Island Medical Center

N.C. 12, Buxton *986-2756*

Dr. Seaborn Blair III, Dr. J. Al Hodges Jr. and Katie Williams, a family nurse practitioner (FNP), help staff this board-certified family practice on the lower end of Hatteras Island. X-ray services are available. The facility maintains 24-hour emergency call coverage and office hours on weekdays from 8:30 AM to 5 PM. Saturday hours are 9 AM to 1 PM.

Buxton Medical Care

N.C. 12, Buxton *995-4455*

Dr. J. Al Hodges and Katie Williams, FNP, offer comprehensive family medical care and operate a 24-hour emergency referral service. Their hours are Monday, Wednesday and Friday from 1:30 PM to 5:30 PM.

Ocracoke Health Center

N.C. 12 (Past the fire house)
Ocracoke *928-1511*

Kenneth De Barth, PAC, provides general medical care for all ages in this small island clinic. Off-season hours are Monday, Tuesday, Wednesday and Friday from 8:30 AM to noon and 1 PM to 5 PM. Call for summer hours. For emergencies call the rescue squad at 911.

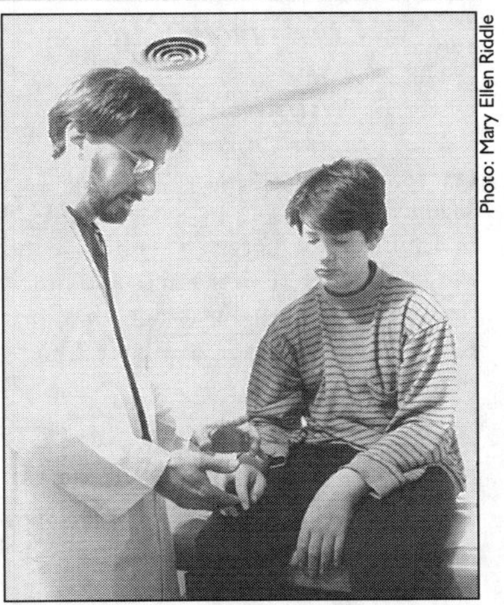

Photo: Mary Ellen Riddle

Competent healthcare providers are available on the Outer Banks, and the range of services offered is growing every year.

Dentists

Though not a complete list of the dentists located on the Outer Banks, the following includes those who have indicated they're available for emergency care.

Budde & Bueker, DDS, U.S. 158, MP 5½ (In Executive Center), Kill Devil Hills, 441-5811

Frank Ausband, DDS, U.S. 158, MP 11, Nags Head, 441-0437

Jeffrey Jacobson, DDS, Colington Road, Colington, 441-8882

Latta, J. Randall, DDS, The Waterfront, Manteo, 473-5774

Michael Morgan, DDS, Juniper Trail, Southern Shores, 261-2358

Chiropractic Care

Wellness Center of the Outer Banks

U.S. 158, in The Marketplace
Southern Shores 261-5424

Daniel Goldberg, DC, offers a full range of chiropractic services and nutrition management. Massage therapist Kim Conners also is available by appointment.

Dare Chiropractic

U.S. 158, MP 5
Kitty Hawk 261-8885

Burt Rubin, DC; Allan Kroland, DC; and B.L. Ackley, DC; have the largest full-service chiropractic clinic on the beach. Nutritional counseling and stress management support are available. Call for an appointment.

Outer Banks Chiropractic Clinic

U.S. 158, MP 10
Nags Head 441-1585

Craig Gibson, DC, has office hours by appointment.

Related Services

Ask-A-Nurse

(800) 832-8836

Call Ask-A-Nurse while visiting the Outer Banks for this free service from Albemarle Hospital. This number gives you access to 24-hour phone consultations with specially trained nurses. A comforting and knowledgeable staff helps direct callers to the appropriate facility or agency that may best serve their needs.

Dare Vision Center

U.S. 158 at MP 9
Kill Devil Hills 441-4872
U.S. 64, Manteo 473-2155

Dare Vision Center offers primary, full scope optometric care, treatment of eye diseases and eye emergencies. The Vision Center also offers eye glasses and contact lenses.

Professional Opticians

U.S. 158 at MP 14, Outer Banks Mall
Nags Head 441-6353
MP 1, The Marketplace
Southern Shores 261-8777

Expect professional care here and good prices for eyeglasses and contact lens fitting. Professional Opticians offers a children's department and name brand sunglasses. Senior citizens discounts are available. Lab on the premises. It's open 10 AM until 6 PM, Monday through Friday, and 10 AM until 5 PM on Saturday.

Outer Banks Hotline

U.S. 64, Manteo 473-3366

Hotline is a 24-hour crisis counseling service that also provides shelter to victims of abuse. This agency operates thrift shops on U.S. 64 in Manteo and at MP 8 on U.S. 158 in Kill Devil Hills, conducts regular public-awareness seminars and trainings.

Children and Family Counseling Services

2600 N. Croatan Hwy. (U.S. 158) 441-5040

Kathy S. Burrus, MSW, CCSW, offers individual and family counseling to visitors and year-round residents.

Insiders' Tips

Take a taxi if you're out drinking. Police protection is prevalent in Kill Devil Hills. The maximum legal blood alcohol content (BAC) in North Carolina is .08.

Ellen McCreery, MS, LPC, CRC-SAC, CSAC

U.S. 64, Manteo *473-4801*

Ellen McCreery provides substance abuse counseling and works with both the individual and family. DWI assessments and court-ordered treatments are also offered. Call for an appointment.

Melinda Mogowski, MS,NCC,CCSW

Nags Head *441-3536*

Melinda Mogowski provides individual and family counseling. Call for an appointment.

Jean Toner, MSW, CCSW

Buxton *995-4455*

Jean Toner offers substance abuse counseling and adolescent and adult psychotherapy through Buxton Medical Care. For private counseling call 995-4828.

Albemarle Mental Health

Sun Professional building, Avon *995-4951*

Alcoholics Anonymous

261-1681, 441-6020, 473-5389, 995-4240 or 995-4283

Al-Anon

(800) 344-2666

Call this number for referrals in the Outer Banks area.

Inside Services and Information Directory

Although the Outer Banks are primarily a summer resort destination, most services anyone would need are available here year round.

For information on lifeguard services, see our chapter on Beach Information and Safety, and for information on medical facilities see our Healthcare chapter. For services on the Outer Banks not listed in this directory, pick up either the Beach Book or Sprint/Carolina telephone book; *The Carolina Coast* free weekly tabloid; or call the Outer Banks Chamber of Commerce at 441-8144.

We begin with contacts you may need to reach in an emergency.

Police, Fire and Rescue

Police Departments

Emergencies	*911*
Hatteras Village	*995-6111, 995-4412*
Kill Devil Hills	*480-4020*
Kitty Hawk	*261-3895, 473-3444*
Manteo	*473-2069*
Nags Head	*441-6386*
Southern Shores	*261-3331*

If there is no listing for a particular community, call the nearest sheriff's department.

County Sheriff Departments

Emergencies	*911*
Duck (Dare)	*261-3185*
Hatteras Island (Dare)	*986-2146*
North of Oregon Inlet (Dare)	*473-3481*
Northern Outer Banks (Currituck)	*232-2216*
Ocracoke Is. (Hyde)	*928-7301, (800) 347-3171*

N. C. Highway Patrol

Emergencies	*911*
Headquarters	*(800) 441-6127*
Duck	*261-3185*
Hatteras	*995-4412*
Kill Devil Hills	*480-4036*
Kitty Hawk	*261-3895*
Manteo	*473-2069*
Nags Head	*441-6386*
Southern Shores	*261-3331*

If there is no listing for a particular community, call the nearest sheriff's department.

Fire Departments

Emergencies	*911*
Avon (unmanned)	*995-5021*
Buxton (unmanned)	*995-5241*
Carova Beach	*453-8690*
Chicamacomico	*987-2347*
Colington	*441-6234*
Corolla	*453-3242*
Duck	*261-3929*
Frisco (unmanned)	*995-5522*
Hatteras Inlet	*986-2175*
Kill Devil Hills	*480-4060*
Kitty Hawk	*261-2666*
Roanoke Island	*473-2300*
Nags Head	*441-5909*
Ocracoke	*928-4831*
Salvo (unmanned)	*987-2411*
Southern Shores	*261-2272*
Stumpy Point	*473-1124*
Wanchese	*473-5454, 473-2300*

Burn permits are required on the Outer Banks for outdoor fires of any kind and are available at area fire departments. Bonfires are permitted on certain areas of the beach with a permit from the town or National Park Service. Call the town offices for the area you're interested in or the Park Service at the numbers listed below.

If you need a fire extinguisher, they are available at the Outer Banks Kmart and Wal-Mart. If you need your extinguisher serviced, call the Fire Defense Center, 261-1314 or 491-2478. They will pick up and deliver refills and new extinguishers.

U.S. Coast Guard

Buxton — *995-6413*
Hatteras — *986-2175*
N. of Oregon Inlet — *441-1685*
Ocracoke — *928-3711, 995-6452**
24-Hour Search and Rescue — *995-6411*
**Call goes through Hatteras and is more reliable according to Coast Guard.*

National Park Service

North of Oregon Inlet — *473-2111, 441-6644*
South of Oregon Inlet — *995-4474*
Ocracoke Island — *928-4531*

Crisis Hotlines

Dare County Crimeline

473-3111

Call this number to report information you may have about a crime in Dare County.

National Response Center

(800) 424-8802

Report hazardous chemical or oil spills to this center.

Outer Banks Hotline

U.S. 64, Manteo — *473-3366*

Outer Banks Hotline offers confidential counseling and information for any crisis. This nonprofit organization also operates a shelter for battered women and their children.

Poison Control Center

Duke University — *(800) 672-1697*

This is a 24-hour emergency hotline.

Animal Services

Kitty Hawk, Nags Head, Manteo and Hatteras Island all have established veterinary clinics. Most of the vets rotate an around-the-clock emergency service. Some also care for horses, exotic pets, sea mammals, wild birds and farm animals.

Animal Shelters

Dare County Animal Shelter

1029 Driftwood Dr.
Manteo — *473-1101, Ext. 250*
Kill Devil Hills — *480-4047*

On Roanoke Island, the Dare County Animal Shelter offers an adoption program for stray and abandoned animals and serves as a pound for animals picked up off the streets. Dog catchers in all areas of Dare County except for Kill Devil Hills bring confiscated pets here. The Kill Devil Hills animal control officer can be reached at 480-4020.

The nonprofit Outer Banks Spay-Neuter Fund offers financial assistance for people who can't afford to keep their pets from reproducing and operates a cat shelter for stray, abandoned or injured cats. Call 441-7918 for more information.

Kennels, Home Services and Rescue Services

A few rental cottages and only a couple of hotels accept pets. If you need to board yours, try one of these local services.

Animal Hospital of Nags Head, 441-8611

Animal Rescue and Spaying Assistance, Southern Shores, 261-6869

Coastal Animal Hospital, Kitty Hawk, 261-3960

Martin's Point Veterinary Hospital, U.S. 158, MP 0, Kitty Hawk, 261-2250

Outer Banks Animal Hospital, Outer Banks Mall, Nags Head, MP 14, 441-2776 or, for nighttime emergencies, 441-6066

Outer Banks SPCA, Manteo, 473-1101, Ext. 272

Roanoke Island Animal Hospital, Manteo, 473-3117

Salty Dog Grooming & Boarding, Colington, 441-6501

Site Sitters, Inc., Nags Head, 441-5030

Wags and Purrs, Kill Devil Hills, 441-7918. These folks offer short-term in-home pet sitting year round.

Automotive Services

The Outer Banks automotive services and parts stores are extremely busy in summer months, so try to get your car or truck tuned up before taking a vacation. If you do need automotive assistance on the barrier islands, however, here's a handy listing of some businesses we recommend:

A B & H Automotive Inc., Pond Rd., Wanchese, 473-5845

Accurate Auto Service, U.S. 158, Kill Devil Hills, 480-3544

A-OK Mobile Mechanic, Salvo, 987-1155

Autotech, U.S. 158, MP 10¼, Nags Head, 441-5293

Ballance Gulf & Oil Company, N.C. 12, Hatteras Village, 986-2424

Colony Tire Corp., U.S. 64 and Budleigh Street, Manteo, 473-6155

D & J Auto Service, U.S. 64, Manteo, 473-2163

Farrow Brothers Automotive, N.C. 12, Avon, 995-5944

Golden Gears Auto Service, 2004 S. Croatan Highway, Kill Devil Hills, 480-4653

Kill Devil Hills Amoco Auto Repair, U.S. 158, MP 6, Kill Devil Hills, 441-7283, 441-3069

Kitty Hawk Exxon, Beach Road, MP 1, Kitty Hawk, 261-2720

Manteo Wrecker Service (AAA), 137 Jovers Lane, Wanchese, 473-5654

Mobile Services, Kitty Hawk, 261-5089

Outer Banks Chrysler/Plymouth/Dodge/Jeep, U.S. 158, MP 6, Kill Devil Hills, 441-1146

Pugh's Car Care Center, U.S. 158, MP 10¼, Nags Head, 441-1931

Red Drum Texaco, N.C. 12, Buxton, 995-5645

R.D. Sawyer Ford, U.S. 64, south of Manteo, 473-2141

Seto's Texaco (AAA), U.S. 158, MP 5, Kitty Hawk, 261-3138

Child Care

If you are looking for reputable child care providers, a good place to start is the **Dare County Department of Social Services**, 473-1471. The staff can supply you with a list of individuals who offer in home day care and are registered with the state.

At Your Service

Kitty Hawk *261-5286*

The Outer Banks' oldest babysitting service, At Your Service offers painstakingly screened sitters who are well-trained, bonded and insured. During the summer months, most sitters are college students, but the staff also includes recent college graduates, graduate students, teachers, local mothers and grandmothers.

AuPairCare

Dare County *(800) 4AUPAIR*

AuPairCare connects Outer Banks families with live-in European au pairs on yearly cultural visas who provide affordable, long-term, live-in child care. Host families choose from well-qualified, English-speaking applicants between the ages of 18 and 25. Unlike employees, au pairs function much like family members, sharing meals, social occasions and the family home. Local community counselors are close at hand to provide guidance and support. This is a great way to share the world with your children.

Better Beginnings

Kitty Hawk *261-2833*

This owner-operated year-round service provides day care for families on the Outer Banks. The state-licensed service accepts children ages 6 weeks to 12 years and provides lunch and two snacks daily.

Sunsational Sitters

441-TOTS (8687)

Sunsational Sitters sends mature, trained child care personnel directly to your hotel, motel or cottage, allowing you some free time while on vacation. Sitters are bonded and insured, trained in CPR and first aid and have passed extensive reference, background and police checks. Service is available 24 hours a day, seven days a week. Early reservations are recommended.

Civic Services

Boards of Commissioners

Dare County *473-1101*
Currituck County *232-2075*
Hyde County *(800) 842-0820*

Town Halls

Kill Devil Hills *480-4000*
Kitty Hawk *261-3552*
Southern Shores *261-2394*
Manteo *473-2133*
Nags Head *441-5508*

Voter Registration

Dare County
Board of Elections *473-1101, Ext. 319*

Libraries

The main **Dare County Public Library**, 473-2372, is on U.S. 64 in Manteo across from Manteo Elementary School.

The **Kill Devil Hills** branch library, 441-4331, is off U.S. 158 between the Baum Center and the water treatment plant near Colington Road.

The **Hatteras Village** branch of the Dare County Library, 986-2385, is in the county recreation building across from Burrus' Red & White store.

The **Ocracoke Library** is behind the fire hall.

Dare County also offers outreach library services for shut-ins, call any branch for more information. Fax machines and Internet computer connections are available at each branch library.

Outer Banks History Center, 473-2655, on Ice Plant Island, Manteo, has reference materials available to the public.

Liquor Sales

Most restaurants in Duck, Kitty Hawk, Kill Devil Hills and Nags Head serve mixed drinks. Areas where you are allowed to "brown-bag" your own liquor are found in Corolla, Manteo, Wanchese and the beaches south of Oregon Inlet.

Some restaurants serve only beer and wine, which also can be purchased at most convenience and grocery stores. Liquor by the bottle is available only in Alcohol Beverage Control stores, as follows:

ABC Stores

Ocean Tr., Corolla *453-2895*
Duck Rd., in Wee Winks Sq., Duck *261-6981*
U.S. 158, MP 1, Kitty Hawk *261-2477*
U.S. 158, MP 10, Nags Head *441-5121*
U.S. 64/264, Roanoke Island *473-3557*
N.C. 12, Osprey Shopping Center Buxton *995-5532*
N.C. 12, next to Variety Store Ocracoke Island *928-3281*

Insiders' Tip

Corolla and Southern Shores have door-to-door recycling pickups.

ABC Store hours are generally 10 AM to 9 PM Monday through Saturday. Major credit cards are accepted except at the Ocracoke store. Personal checks are not accepted at any liquor store. The maximum purchase per person is 8 liters unless you have a special permit. Legal age for admittance to a store is 21 years.

Media

Newspapers

Although these barrier islands are far from a media mecca, news coverage of the Outer Banks is growing each year. One major daily has had a strong presence here for a decade already. And a handful of small weekly and monthly local publications fill their own niches. Stores throughout the Outer Banks carry a wide range of papers during the week and on Sunday.

Look for copies of *The Washington Post*, *The New York Times*, *The Wall Street Journal*, the *Richmond Times-Dispatch*, the *Raleigh News & Observer* and others at Nags Head News, 480-6397, at the Food Lion Shopping Center, U.S. 158, MP 10. Costs may be inflated for some papers as the Outer Banks is considered a remote distribution area.

The Coastland Times

Manteo 473-2105
Kill Devil Hills 441-2223

The Coastland Times, a local paper, is published on Sundays, Tuesdays and Thursdays. It's available at area newsstands and convenience stores; mail delivery is available.

The Daily Advance

Outer Banks Circulation 426-4625

An Elizabeth City-based daily broadsheet, this newspaper can be found at some newsstands on the beach.

Hatteras Monitor

Frisco 995-5378

The *Hatteras Monitor* is published 11 times a year as a source of news and local feature stories for Hatteras and Ocracoke islands.

Island Breeze

Hatteras Village 986-2421

The *Island Breeze*, a Hatteras and Ocracoke tabloid, comes out monthly except during the winter.

North Beach Sun

Kill Devil Hills *480-2787*

Another newspaper with local appeal is the *North Beach Sun*. Gulfstream Publishing offers this popular tabloid filled with personal and local news from the Northern Outer Banks. It's published quarterly and is distributed to post-office-box holders, convenience stores, real estate offices and other businesses along the beach.

The Outer Banks Sentinel

Nags Head *480-2234*

The Outer Banks Sentinel began publishing in March 1996. This weekly broadsheet paper provides news, features on area personalities, editorials and columns about the Outer Banks. It is published every Thursday and is sold at area newsstands and bookstores. Mail delivery is available.

The Virginian-Pilot

Nags Head Bureau *441-1628*

This Norfolk, Virginia-based daily broadsheet (235,000 circulation) combines "big-city paper" experience with extensive local knowledge to cover regional news from northeastern and coastal North Carolina and beyond. A separate North Carolina section is published daily, with articles and photographs composed by an Outer Banks-based news staff. The newspaper is available at area newsstands, convenience stores and at your doorstep each morning.

The Carolina Coast, a free, weekly entertainment and news publication produced by *The Virginian-Pilot*, is available each weekend at grocery and general stores and other locations throughout the Outer Banks. It features indepth columns on real estate, art, entertainment, fishing and the commentary of Pulitzer Prize-winning editor Ronald L. Speer.

Magazines

Sportfishing Report

Central Square
U.S. 158, MP 11, Nags Head *480-3133*

Sportfishing Report, an informative saltwater fishing magazine, covers North Carolina coastal surf, sound and sea, history and profiles, with a special emphasis on the Outer Banks.

Outer Banks Magazine

P.O. Box 1938, Manteo 27954 *473-3590*

For 14 years, this annual four-color feature magazine has been capturing the culture, history and flavor of life on the Outer Banks. Mail subscriptions are available, and you can buy the publication on newsstands and at gift and specialty shops.

Television

Falcon Cable TV

441-2881

This company supplies cable connection service for most of the Outer Banks, except Ocracoke. Most motels, hotels and cottages have cable connections. Some add special features such as HBO, Showtime, Cinemax, The Movie Channel, Disney Channel and other special offerings. Channel 12, a local access network, features Outer Banks Panorama, an informative program on communities, shopping, res-

Insiders' Tips

Dog licenses must be purchased annually at the Dare County Animal Shelter on Roanoke Island, 473-1101, Ext. 148.

taurants, real estate, recreation and attractions of the barrier islands. Falcon also offers six channels of Pay-Per-View movies, events and concerts. You need a Tocom converter from the cable office to access these. Channel 19, a scroll channel, provides a continuous preview of all programming carried on channels 2 through 61.

Radio Stations

WOBR FM 95.3

Wanchese *473-2444*

The Outer Banks' first native radio station, WOBR plays adult contemporary music and offers local news broadcasts, national satellite shows and up-to-the-minute weather forecasts. The request line is 473-2444. WOBR leases its AM (1530) station to the Outer Banks Worship Center for Christian programming.

WRSF FM 105.7

Nags Head *441-1024, (800) 553-4494*

Dixie 105.7 plays "today's hottest country" and also airs local news and weather broadcasts. The contest line number is (800) 422-3494.

WVOD FM 99.1

Manteo *473-1993*

"The Sound" broadcasts from a studio on the Manteo waterfront. This locally owned station began broadcasting in the spring of 1986. Disc jockeys play a varied format centering around adult contemporary and classic rock 'n' roll. Sunday morning listeners can tune in to Sunday Classics, featuring classical music; a beach music show airs on Sunday afternoons. A community-minded station, WVOD also offers air space for public service announcements and personnel for charitable causes. This station is a great source for information on local school closings, road conditions and other regional and local news. Requests and contest entries should be called in to 473-9863.

WNHW FM 92

Kill Devil Hills *480-1500*

Carolina 92 plays a variety of country music, including contemporary, crossover, traditional, folk and rockabilly. The station also airs music features, including a weekly countdown on Sunday afternoons. CNN news and sports — including the popular Winston Cup Today racing update daily at 5:30 PM — local news and weather, fishing and beach reports also are available on this Kill Devil Hills radio station. WNHW's Ken Mann is an Outer Banks native and has long been associated with quality broadcasting in Dare County. The news department can be reached at 480-1130, and the request line is 441-9292.

WCXL 104.1 FM

Dare County Office *480-0440*

This 100,000-watt station based in Elizabeth City covers the Outer Banks with an adult contemporary and beach music mix. There's also a local business office in Dare County.

WERX 102.5 FM

482-2130

WERX is a 50,000-watt station with a progressive format — rock, alternative, jazz and other forms of contemporary music — playing 24 hours a day for the Outer Banks, Edenton, Elizabeth City and Greenville.

Package Shipment

Outer Banks Transit

U.S. 158, MP 9, Kill Devil Hills *441-7090*

Outer Banks Transit makes it an easy matter to ship and pick up packages via the U.S. Postal Service, UPS, Airbourne Express and Federal Express. This postal outpost sells packaging materials, and employees offer help and advice to accommodate every shipping need. Courier service to the Norfolk, Virginia, area is available daily for almost any item. Outer Banks Transit also has photocopy machines, fax services and money orders.

United Parcel Service

Etheridge Rd., Roanoke Island *(800) 742-5877*

UPS has a separate service center on Roanoke Island and several drop boxes throughout the Outer Banks. Packages can be shipped weekdays from 3:30 PM to 5:45 PM from the Manteo offices. Some size limitations apply. Overnight shipping is available to many destinations in the United States.

Island Pharmacy, at Chesley Mall, U.S. 64, Manteo, offers UPS shipping services.

Federal Express

(800) 463-3339

Federal Express has drop boxes all around the Outer Banks — and door pickup in most areas. Large self-service boxes can are near Surfside Books at the Seagate North Shopping Center in Kill Devil Hills, in Manteo at Chesley Mall and in front of Manteo Booksellers. Call the toll-free number above for information or to get a package picked up. If you're in a rental cottage, make sure you know the house number and street and can give the courier exact directions.

Provisions for the Disabled

North Carolina businesses are required to provide at least one handicapped parking space nearest buildings and entryways. Please reserve these spaces, marked with wheelchair signs, for those licensed to use them. Violators are subject to fines.

Outer Bankers are becoming more aware of the needs of those with disabilities. Some very special services are available, such as a modern wooden ramp that extends into Jockey's Ridge State Park. Available with it are tapes for the visually impaired, made and donated by the Girl Scouts. Ocean Atlantic Rentals now

has a special wheelchair with huge sand tires for getting down to the water. There are also unique accommodations for handicapped anglers (see our Fishing chapter). Visit a local library to see a copy of *Access North Carolina*, a detailed guide to the state's handicapped-accessible vacation spots, including many on the Outer Banks. This guide tells about parking, ramps, restrooms, campgrounds and programs. To obtain a free copy in advance of your vacation, call (800) VISIT NC.

Recycling

With trash being trucked up to three hours off the Outer Banks, to the mainland, most locals know the need to recycle on this fragile fringe of barrier islands. Only Corolla and Southern Shores offer door-to-door pickup. But visitors and residents alike are urged to go to the extra effort of rinsing, sorting and transporting as much of their garbage as possible to area recycling centers. Many of the beach accesses now have bins near the parking areas throughout the summer for cans, bottles and other recyclable waste. Please carry all of your trash off the beach with you. Fixed and moving recycling bins also can be found throughout the Outer Banks, with schedules varying from town to town and during different times of the year.

Most frequently used items are accepted at area recycling centers. But some types of plastic can't be used here. And lids and labels have to be removed. One bad can spoil the whole load. Recyclable materials include: colored or office paper, newspaper, magazines, corrugated cardboard, aluminum cans, steel cans, green, brown and clear glass, milk and water jugs, plastic #1 and #2 items with

Photo: Mary Ellen Riddle

Whether you worship at Mount Olivet United Methodist church or not, stop by for a look at the beautiful stained-glass windows.

a recycle logo on the bottom. Newspapers need to be tied with string or stacked in paper bags because the wind blows them around so badly on the beach.

Here's a north-to-south geographical list of recycling centers. Some are manned. Some move around. Check with local town offices for current schedules. Or call the Dare County Recycling Center for more information, 473-1101, ext. 156.

• **Carova Beach** — A permanent bin is north of Swan Beach subdivision.

• **Corolla** — Door-to-door collection.

• **Duck** — Duck Fire Station, 8 AM to noon Fridays and Saturdays in winter and 8 AM to 5 PM daily in summer.

• **Southern Shores** — Behind the fire station on Dogwood Trail across from Kitty Hawk Elementary School. Open Tuesday and Saturday from 9 AM until noon. Curbside pickup every Saturday in special town-provided bins.

• **Kitty Hawk** — Please use the Dare County drop-off site in Kill Devil Hills.

• **Kill Devil Hills**, 480-4044 — Dare County Public Works Complex off W. Ocean Bay Boulevard (Colington Road) behind the Wright Memorial grounds. Hours are Monday through Friday 8 AM to 4 PM and Saturday 8 AM to 2 PM.

• **Nags Head**, 441-1122 — At the Public Works building on Lark Street, behind the Food Lion, 7 AM to 3:30 PM Monday through Friday. Town Hall has a permanent, covered bin. Meekins Avenue behind Village Furniture, 10 AM to sunset on Tuesdays. Nags Head Cove at the clubhouse, 10 AM to sunset on Fridays. North Ridge behind the Mormon Church from 10 AM to sunset on Thursdays. Baltic Street between N.C. 12 and Memorial Avenue, Mondays from 10 AM to sunset. Outer Banks Mall, Wednesdays from 10 AM to sunset. In South Nags Head behind the old fire station full-time.

• **Manteo**, 473-1583 — Behind the Duke of Dare Motel on Fernando Street, Tuesday and Saturday from 8 AM to noon.

• **Dare County-Manteo**, 473-1101, Ext. 156 — At the Manteo Transfer Station, Bowsertown Road. Monday through Saturday, 8 AM to 5 PM.

• **Rodanthe/Waves/Salvo** — At Chicamacomico Volunteer Fire Station, daylight hours daily.

• **Buxton** — Behind Centura Bank, Monday through Saturday, 10 AM to 4:30 PM.

• **Ocracoke** — Hyde County Jail has a permanent recycling bin.

Rental Services

From baby strollers to video cameras to off-road vehicles, you can rent almost anything you want on the Outer Banks. Please refer to our Weekly and Long-term Cottage Rentals chapter. Or call the Chamber of Commerce for advice, 441-8144.

Telegraph Service

Western Union

(800) 325-6000

You can send and pick up cables,

telegrams and money from three Outer Banks locations or get information by calling the toll-free number above. Western Union locations include Island Pharmacy, Chesley Mall, U.S. 64, Manteo, 473-5801; Beach Pharmacy II, N.C. 12, Buxton, 995-4450; and Beach Pharmacy, N.C. 12, Hatteras Village, 986-2400.

Tourist Information

Outer Banks Chamber of Commerce
Ocean Bay Blvd., Kill Devil Hills *441-8144*

Dare County Tourist Bureau
U.S. 64, Manteo *473-2138*

Aycock Brown Visitor Center
Off U.S. 158, MP 1½, Kitty Hawk *261-4644*

Whalebone Junction Visitor Kiosk
N.C. 13, at the north entrance of Cape Hatteras National Seashore *No phone*

Roanoke Island Visitor Kiosk
U.S. 64, at the north end of Roanoke Island *No phone*

Beach Access Bulletin Board Service
Modem Information *480-4636*
Voice line *441-1521*

Using this local computer bulletin board service, you can obtain beach information — including a local calendar of events — access local and international e-mail, chat with locals and view beach and historic photography. The Internet address is: http://www.outer-banks.nc.us/beachaccess.

Utility Information

North Carolina Power

Emergency	*473-6780, (800) 945-0633*
Non-emergency:	
Residential	*473-6790, (800) 944-8538*
Commercial	*473-6799, (800) 723-9942*
Energy efficiency	*(800) 772-4338*
Before You Dig	*(800) 632-4949*

Carolina Telephone

Repair	*(919) 977-7100*
Multiline key and data	*(800) 842-5400*

Cable TV

Outer Banks, Roanoke Island and Manns Harbor	*441-2881*
Hatteras Island	*995-5370*

Weather Report

Call 473-5665 to hear a recording of the latest weather report, provided by WOBR-FM 95.3. Or call the National Weather Service's 24-hour recorded message at Buxton, 995-5610.

Worship Centers

A comprehensive list of worship services is published in the Sunday edition of *The Coastland Times*.

Index of Advertisers

Index

Symbols

A

B

D

J

K

L

T

Y

Z

ORDER FORM

Fast and Simple!

Mail to:
Insiders Guides Inc.
P.O. Drawer 2057
Manteo, NC 27954

Or:
for VISA or
MasterCard orders call
(800) 765-BOOK

Name ____________________

Address ____________________

City/State/Zip ____________________

Qty.	Title/Price	Shipping	Amount
	Insiders' Guide to Richmond/$14.95	$4.00	
	Insiders' Guide to Williamsburg/$14.95	$4.00	
	Insiders' Guide to Virginia's Blue Ridge/$17.95	$4.00	
	Insiders' Guide to Virginia's Chesapeake Bay/$14.95	$4.00	
	Insiders' Guide to Washington, DC/$14.95	$4.00	
	Insiders' Guide to North Carolina's Outer Banks/$17.95	$4.00	
	Insiders' Guide to Wilmington, NC/$14.95	$4.00	
	Insiders' Guide to North Carolina's Central Coast/$14.95	$4.00	
	Insiders' Guide to North Carolina's Mountains/$17.95	$4.00	
	Insiders' Guide to Myrtle Beach/$14.95	$4.00	
	Insiders' Guide to Atlanta/$14.95	$4.00	
	Insiders' Guide to Boca Raton & the Palm Beaches/$14.95	$4.00	
	Insiders' Guide to Sarasota/Bradenton/$14.95	$4.00	
	Insiders' Guide to Northwest Florida/$14.95	$4.00	
	Insiders' Guide to Tampa Bay/$14.95	$4.00	
	Insiders' Guide to Mississippi/$14.95	$4.00	
	Insiders' Guide to Lexington, KY/$14.95	$4.00	
	Insiders' Guide to Louisville/$14.95	$4.00	
	Insiders' Guide to Cincinnati/$14.95	$4.00	
	Insiders' Guide to the Twin Cities/$14.95	$4.00	
	Insiders' Guide to Boulder/$14.95	$4.00	
	Insiders' Guide to Denver/$14.95	$4.00	
	Insiders' Guide to Branson/$14.95	$4.00	
	Insiders' Guide to Civil War in the Eastern Theater/$14.95	$4.00	
	Insiders' Guide to Cape Cod/$14.95	$4.00	
	Insiders' Guide to Greater Charleston/$17.95	$4.00	

Payment in full (check or money order) must accompany this order form.
Please allow 2 weeks for delivery.

N.C. residents add 6% sales tax ____________

Total ____________

Who you are and what you think are important to us.

Fill out the coupon and we'll give you an Insiders' Guide® for half price ($7.48 off)

Which book(s) did you buy? ____________________

Where do you live? ____________________

In what city did you buy your book? ____________________

Where did you buy your book? ❑ catalog ❑ bookstore ❑ newspaper ad ❑ retail shop ❑ other ____________________

How often do you travel? ❑ yearly ❑ bi-annually ❑ quarterly ❑ more than quarterly

Did you buy your book because you were ❑ moving ❑ vacationing ❑ wanted to know more about your home town ❑ other ____________________

Will the book be used by ❑ family ❑ couple ❑ individual ❑ group

What is you annual household income? ❑ under $25,000 ❑ $25,000-$35,000 ❑ $35,000-$50,000 ❑ $50,000-$75,000 ❑ over $75,000

How old are you? ❑ under 25 ❑ 25-35 ❑ 36-50 ❑ 51-65 ❑ over 65

Did you use the book before you left for your destination? ❑ yes ❑ no

Did you use the book while at your destination? ❑ yes ❑ no

On average per month, how many times do you refer to your book? ❑ 1-3 ❑ 4-7 ❑ 8-11 ❑ 12-15 ❑ 16 and up

On average, how many other people use your book? ❑ no others ❑ 1 ❑ 2 ❑ 3 ❑ 4 or more

Is there anything you would like to tell us about Insiders' Guides? ____________________

Name ____________________ Address ____________________

City ____________________ State _____ Zip ____________________

We'll send you a voucher for $7.48 off any Insiders' Guide© and a list of available titles as soon as we get this card from you. Thanks for being an Insider!

BUSINESS REPLY MAIL

FIRST-CLASS MAIL PERMIT NO. 20 MANTEO, NC

POSTAGE WILL BE PAID BY ADDRESSEE

THE INSIDERS' GUIDES INC.
PO BOX 2057
MANTEO NC 27954-9906